W9-DCM-584

INRI

When Christians gather to worship, we recall and celebrate the timeless stories of our faith through word and song. With this in mind, artist Yolanda Durán adorned the letters of the word "Gather" with the stories of our faith. From left to right, the first panels depict Adam and Eve's fall from grace; the miraculous encounters of Noah and Moses with water, the sign of our baptism; and John the Baptist in the desert, dressed in clothing made of camel's hair, foretelling the coming of the promised Messiah. The next panel portrays the peaceful night and new dawn of the joyous Nativity. The panels go on to illustrate the Last Supper, the crucifixion, the empty tomb, and finally, the second coming of Christ, all echoing the words we sing each time we proclaim the mystery of faith: "Christ has died, Christ is risen, Christ will come again."

The spine of the hymnal is crowned with a dove, the symbol of the Holy Spirit. The back cover is framed with the symbols of the four evangelists: Matthew, the divine man, symbol of Christ's incarnation; Mark, the winged lion, symbol of the royalty of Christ; Luke, the winged ox, symbol of Christ's priestly office; and John, the rising eagle, symbol of the grace of the Holy Spirit.

GATHER
COMPREHENSIVE

SECOND
EDITION

CHOIR
EDITION

GIA PUBLICATIONS, INC.
CHICAGO

G-6200C

Cover design by Yolanda Durán.

Book design based upon *Worship—Third Edition* by Michael Tapia.

Published with the approval of the Committee on the Liturgy, United States Conference of Catholic Bishops.

ISBN 1-57999-253-6

1 2 3 4 5 6 7 8 9 10 11 12 13 14 15 16 17 18 19 20

PREFACE

The publication of *Gather Comprehensive—Second Edition* marks the release of GIA's tenth hymnal and service book for Roman Catholic parishes in the United States since the Second Vatican Council. Each of these volumes has had a unique character, and while several have been widely adopted by American parishes, the precursor to this edition, published in 1994, has risen above all the others.

The decision to revise a hymnal is essentially dictated by the church community itself. Increasing inquiries about the possibility of a revision along with a significant drop in adoptions readily signal the time to address the matter. To begin this particular project we incorporated a tool that we hadn't used in a number of years.

A large representative number of parishes who had used *Gather Comprehensive* for an extended period were randomly chosen to receive a detailed and extensive survey. For each item in the original edition, we asked if they had used the item; if not, did they feel that they would use it in the future, and if they felt it should be included in a new edition. The results of this survey became a major factor in choosing the contents for this second edition.

In *Gather Comprehensive—Second Edition* the ritual and service music offerings have been considerably expanded making it even more comprehensive than the original. The established mass settings have been retained, several exciting new settings have been added, and the rites of Christian Initiation, Baptism, Funeral, etc. have been added with appropriate service music. The section of psalms near the beginning of the hymnal retains the most widely sung settings, and in keeping with the spirit of the revised *General Instruction of the Roman Missal* and the document *Liturgiam Authenticam,* all of the lectionary psalm refrains for Sundays and solemnities set by Michel Guimont are now included near the back of the volume.

Like its precursor, this edition includes both contemporary and traditional, or folk-style and classical, or piano/guitar-based and organ-based music—depending on how one chooses to identify musical styles—with the mix leaning toward the former in each case. The accompaniments for many items in the first category are clearly pianistic and cannot effectively be played on the organ without adaptation. To maintain the integrity of performance practice, it is our strong recommendation that these pieces be played on the piano as intended. Other accompaniments, of course, can effectively be played on either organ or piano.

It must be remembered that a hymnal is inherently a book for the gathered assembly. While expanded octavo versions for choir and various instruments exist for many of the titles in this hymnal, hymnal items have been edited to be accessible for the most commonly found resources of assembly with cantor and accompanist.

The introductions to the rites and seasons are by Gabe Huck, taken from *Worship—Third Edition.* Further acknowledgment is hereby given to Jeffry Mickus for project direction, editing, engraving, and book layout; and to Philip Roberts, engraver; Victoria Krstansky and Clarence Reiels, proofreaders; Ronald F. Krisman, Spanish editor; Sarah Parker, survey coordinator; Timothy Redmon, permissions editor; and to all who responded to our survey or supplied detailed recommendations.

Soli Deo gloria.

Alexander Harris
Publisher
Robert J. Batastini
Senior Editor
Kathryn R. Cuddy
Michael A. Cymbala
Kelly Dobbs Mickus
Stephen Petrunak
Editors

Contents

Hymns and Songs

Indexes

Morning Praise

The Church's sense for how to pray in the morning comes from our Jewish heritage. Whatever the day, whatever the difficulties, the tradition has been to begin the day with praise for the creator. The sign of the cross, first traced on the Christian at baptism, is again made to begin the new day and its prayer. In the hymn and the psalms, in the scripture and intercessions, each one who prays and the community together finds what it is to stand at the beginning of a new day as a Christian. The morning's prayer gives the day its meaning when, through the years, these prayers become one's own.

OPENING DIALOG 1

Stand

Freely
Presider:
Ho - ly God! Fill us this day with new
Assembly:
breath! And we shall be liv - ing words of
praise!
♩ = ca.116
To Morning Hymn

Text: J. Tasch Jordan, adapt.
Music: David Haas

2 MORNING HYMN

1. Sing your joy, pro - claim God's glo - ry!
2. All the earth is filled with re - joic - ing,
3. May we learn to be - come your King - dom.
4. Light our way, O God of the liv - ing,
Rise and sing, the morn - ing has come!
Light and life the won - der of God!
May we be your kind - ness and truth!
May we learn to see with new eyes!
Bless our God and praise all cre - a - tion;
Christ has tri - umphed! Ris - en for ev - er!
Love is our call - ing, gift of your pres - ence;
Je - sus the Lord, our pow - er and prom - ise;
Song of the earth, and light from heav - en:
Joy of our hearts, and hope of our dream - ing:
Chil - dren of God, and spir - it of Je - sus:
light for the blind, and food for the hun - gry:
God is a - live! Al - le - lu -
God is a - live! Al - le - lu -
God is a - live! Al - le - lu -
God is a - live! Al - le - lu -
1.- 3.
D.C.
4.
ia!
ia!
ia!
ia!

Text: David Haas
Music: SUMMIT HILL, Irregular; David Haas

PSALMODY

The singing of one or more psalms is a central part of Morning Praise. Psalm 63, given below, is one of the premier morning psalms. Psalm 51 is commonly substituted for Psalm 63 on Wednesday and Friday, as well as during Lent. Other appropriate psalms for morning are Psalms 5, 8, 33, 42, 47, 66, 72, 80, 85, 93, 95, 98, 100, 118, 148, 149, and 150.

PSALM 63 3

Sit

Refrain
Slow and lyrical
As morn-ing breaks I look to you; I look to
you, O Lord, to be my strength this day, as morn-ing
breaks, as morn - ing breaks.
Verse 1
1. O God, you are my God, for you I long; for
you my soul is thirst - ing. My bod - y pines for you
like a dry, wea - ry land with - out wa - ter. So I
gaze on you in your ho-ly place to see your strength and your glo-ry.
D.C.

Verse 2
2. For your love is bet - ter than life, my lips will
speak your praise. So I will bless you all my life,
in your name I will lift up my hands. My soul shall be
D.C.
filled as with a ban-quet, my mouth shall praise you with joy.
Verse 3
3. On my bed I re - mem - ber you. On you I
muse through the night for you have been my help;
in the shad - ow of your wings I re - joice. My
rit.
D.C.
soul clings to you; your right hand holds me fast.

Text: Psalm 63:2-3, 4-6, 7-9; © 1963, 1986, The Grail, GIA Publications, Inc., agent; refrain trans. © 1974, ICEL
Music: Michael Joncas, © 1985, OCP Publications

PSALM PRAYER

Stand

All respond: **Amen.**

WORD OF GOD 4

Sit

Reader concludes: The word of the Lord.

Assembly: **Thanks be to God.**

GOSPEL CANTICLE 5

Stand. All make the sign of the cross as the canticle begins.

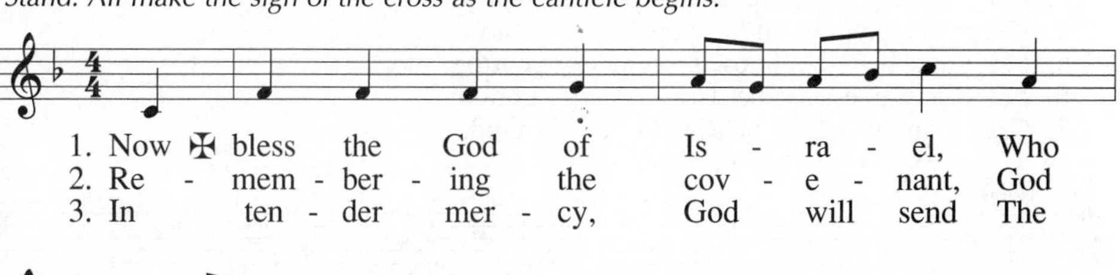
1. Now ✠ bless the God of Is - ra - el, Who
2. Re - mem - ber - ing the cov - e - nant, God
3. In ten - der mer - cy, God will send The

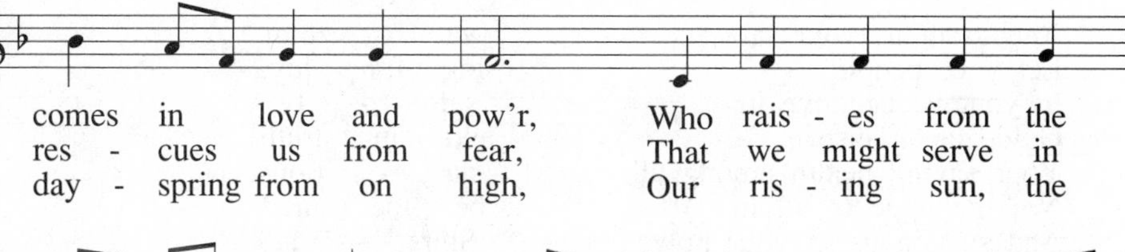
comes in love and pow'r, Who rais - es from the
res - cues us from fear, That we might serve in
day - spring from on high, Our ris - ing sun, the

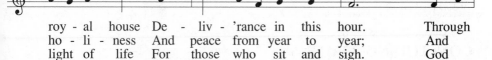

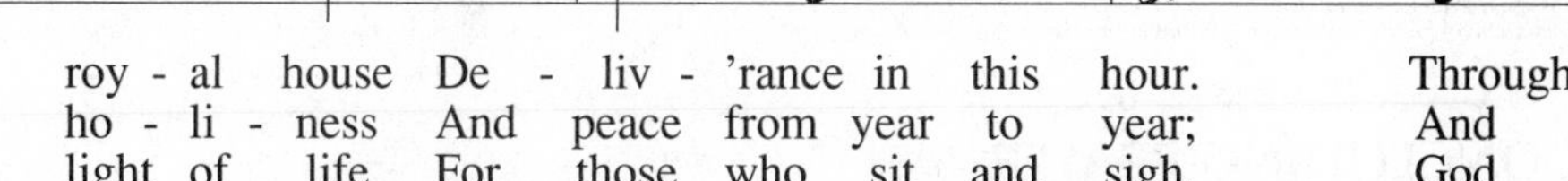
roy - al house De - liv - 'rance in this hour. Through
ho - li - ness And peace from year to year; And
light of life For those who sit and sigh. God

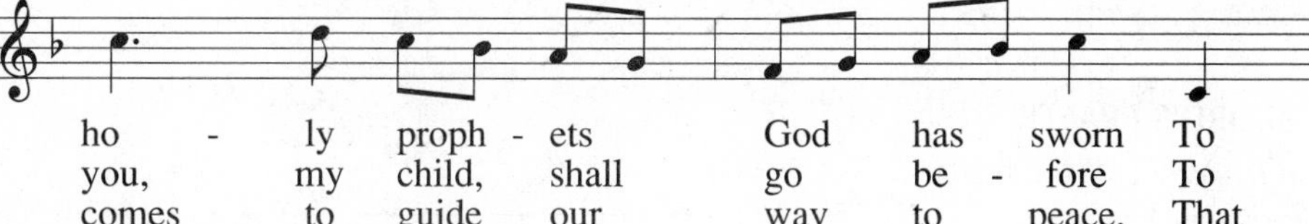
ho - ly proph - ets God has sworn To
you, my child, shall go be - fore To
comes to guide our way to peace, That

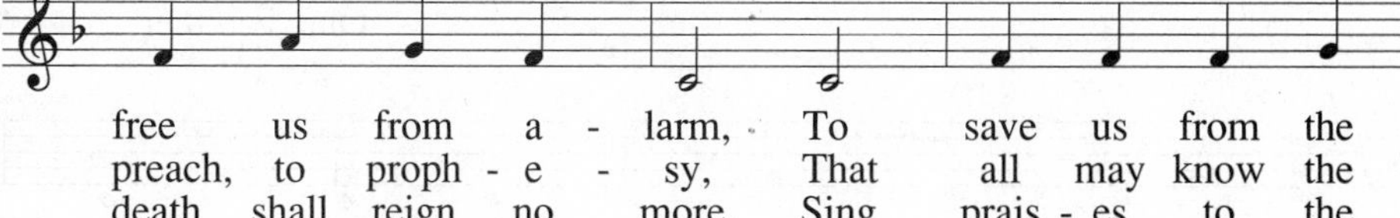
free us from a - larm, To save us from the
preach, to proph - e - sy, That all may know the
death shall reign no more. Sing prais - es to the

heav - y hand Of all who wish us harm.
ten - der love, The grace of God most high.
Ho - ly One! O wor - ship and a - dore!

Text: *Benedictus,* Luke 1:68-79; Ruth Duck, © 1992, GIA Publications, Inc.

Music: FOREST GREEN, CMD; English; harm. by Michael Joncas, © 1987, GIA Publications, Inc.

6 MORNING PRAYERS

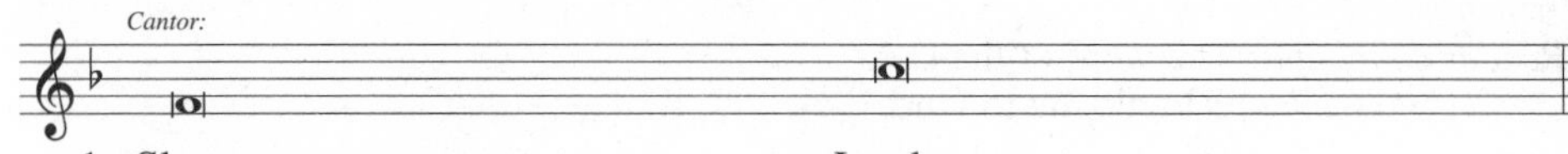
Cantor:

1. Show us your mercy Lord;
2. Clothe your ministers with righteousness;
3. Give peace, O Lord, in all the world;
4. Keep this nation under your care;
5. Let your way be known upon earth;
6. Let not the needy be for - gotten;
7. Create in us clean hearts, O God;

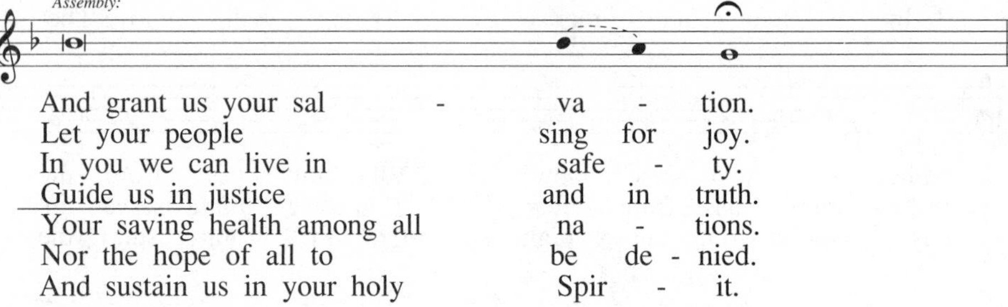
Assembly:
And grant us your sal - va - tion.
Let your people sing for joy.
In you we can live in safe - ty.
Guide us in justice and in truth.
Your saving health among all na - tions.
Nor the hope of all to be de - nied.
And sustain us in your holy Spir - it.

Text: *The Book of Common Prayer*
Music: David Haas, © 1986, GIA Publications, Inc.

CONCLUDING PRAYER

All respond: **Amen.**

7 LORD'S PRAYER

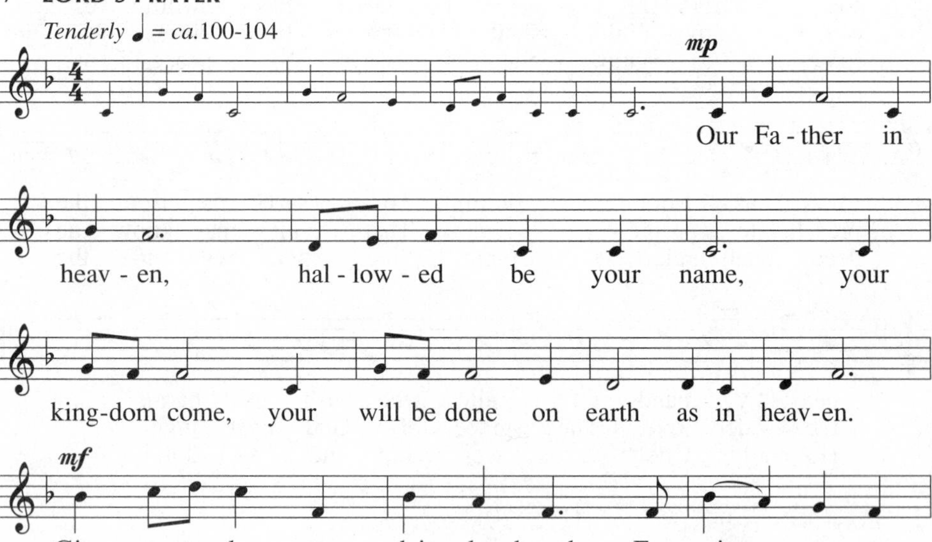
Tenderly ♩ = ca.100-104
mp
Our Fa - ther in
heav - en, hal - low - ed be your name, your
king-dom come, your will be done on earth as in heav-en.
mf
Give us to-day our dai - ly bread. For - give us our

sins as we for-give those who sin a - gainst us.
f
Save us from the time of trial and de - liv - er us from
rit.
broaden
e - vil, for the king - dom, the pow'r and the
rit.
mf
glo - ry are yours, now and for ev - er.

Music: David Haas, © 1986, GIA Publications, Inc.

FINAL BLESSING

8

mf
Presider:
Let us bless the Lord.
Assembly:
And give God thanks.
Presider:
May the Lord al-might-y bless our days and our deeds with
In tempo
peace.
All:
rit.
f
A - men.

Text: David Haas
Music: David Haas

Evensong

The Church gathers in the evening to give thanks for the day that is ending. In the earliest tradition, this began with the lighting of the lamps as darkness fell and the hymn of praise of Christ who is "radiant Light . . . of God the Father's deathless face." The evening psalms and the Magnificat bring the day just past to focus for the Christian: "God has cast down the mighty from their thrones, and has lifted up the lowly"; "God has remembered the promise of mercy, the promise made to our ancestors." Prayers of intercession are almost always part of the church's liturgy, but those which conclude evening prayer are especially important. As day ends, the church again and again lifts up to God the needs and sorrows and failures of all the world. Such intercession is the daily task and joy of the baptized.

9 LIGHT PROCLAMATION

Stand

Presiding minister or assistant:
Light and peace in Je - sus Christ our Lord.
Assembly:
Thanks be to God.

10 EVENING HYMN

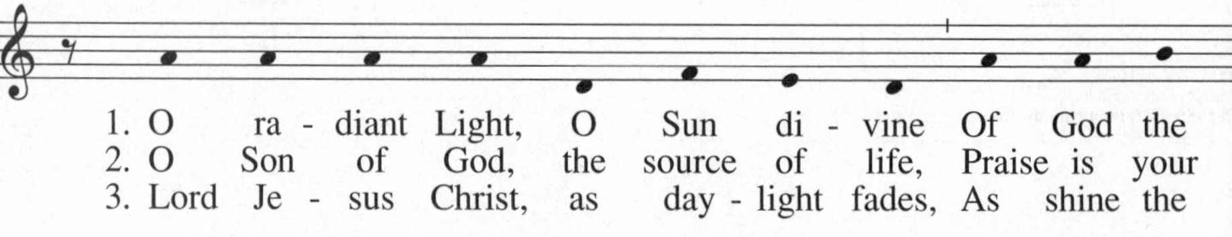

1. O ra - diant Light, O Sun di - vine Of God the
2. O Son of God, the source of life, Praise is your
3. Lord Je - sus Christ, as day - light fades, As shine the

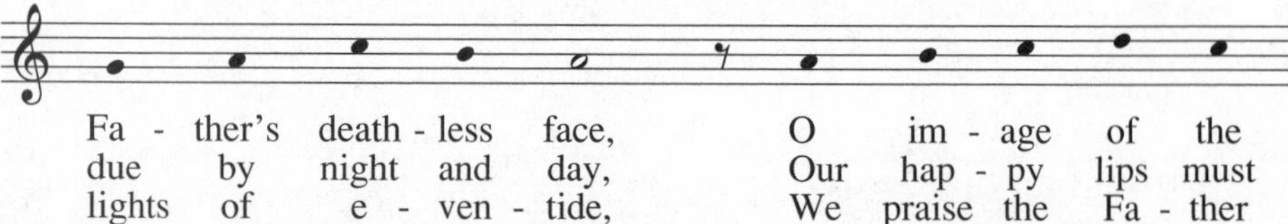

Fa - ther's death - less face, O im - age of the
due by night and day, Our hap - py lips must
lights of e - ven - tide, We praise the Fa - ther

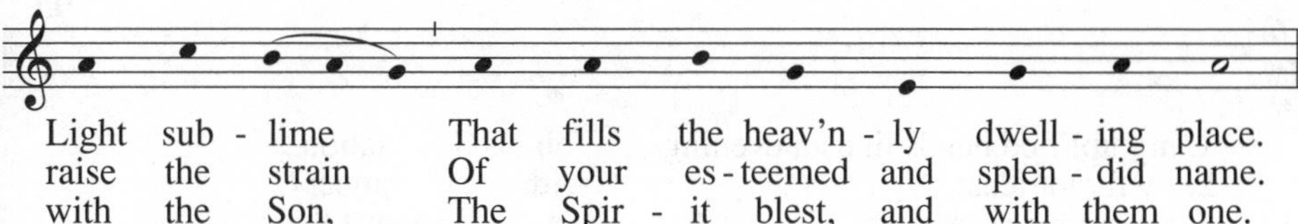
Light sub - lime That fills the heav'n - ly dwell - ing place.
raise the strain Of your es - teemed and splen - did name.
with the Son, The Spir - it blest, and with them one.

Text: *Phos Hilaron,* Greek, c.200; tr. by William G. Storey, ©
Music: JESU DULCIS MEMORIA, LM; Mode I; acc. by Richard Proulx, © 1975, GIA Publications, Inc.

PSALMODY

The singing of one or more psalms is a central part of Evensong. Psalm 141, given below, is one of the premier evening psalms. It is customary to use incense as it is sung. Other appropriate psalms for evening are Psalms 4, 19, 23, 27, 84, 91, 104, 110, 111, 112, 114, 115, 117, 118, 121, 122, 130, 136, 139, and 145.

PSALM 141 / INCENSE PSALM 11

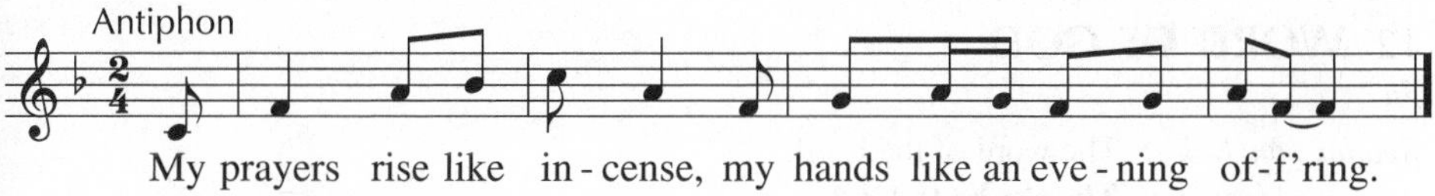

Antiphon

My prayers rise like in - cense, my hands like an eve - ning of - f'ring.

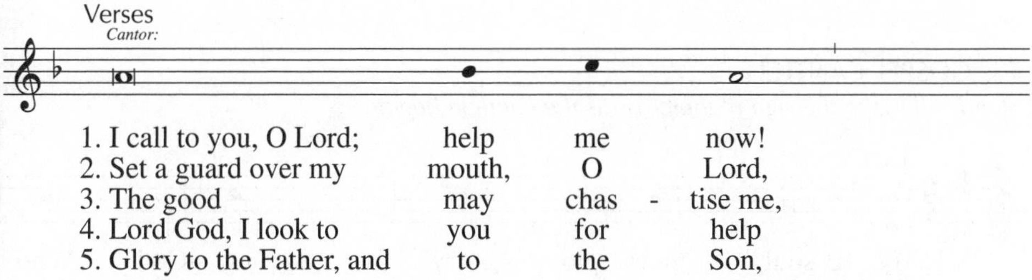

Verses

Cantor:

1. I call to you, O Lord; help me now!
2. Set a guard over my mouth, O Lord,
3. The good may chas - tise me,
4. Lord God, I look to you for help
5. Glory to the Father, and to the Son,

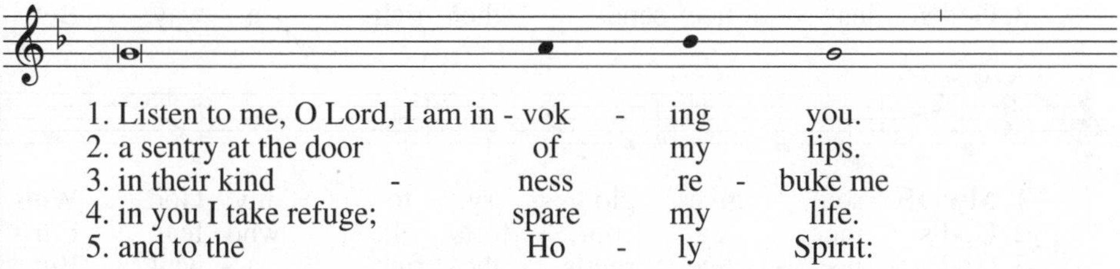

1. Listen to me, O Lord, I am in - vok - ing you.
2. a sentry at the door of my lips.
3. in their kind - ness re - buke me
4. in you I take refuge; spare my life.
5. and to the Ho - ly Spirit:

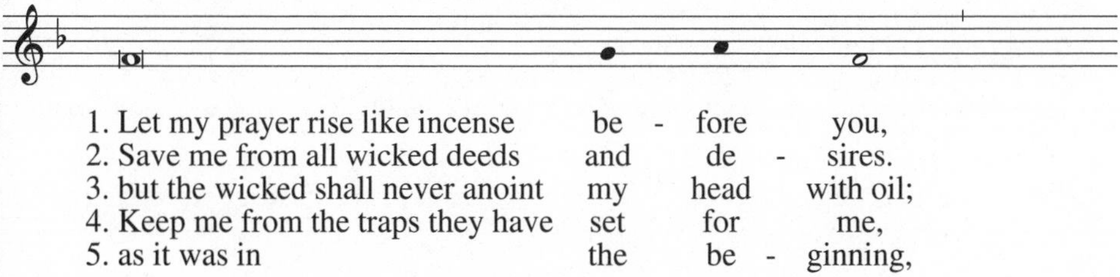

1. Let my prayer rise like incense be - fore you,
2. Save me from all wicked deeds and de - sires.
3. but the wicked shall never anoint my head with oil;
4. Keep me from the traps they have set for me,
5. as it was in the be - ginning,

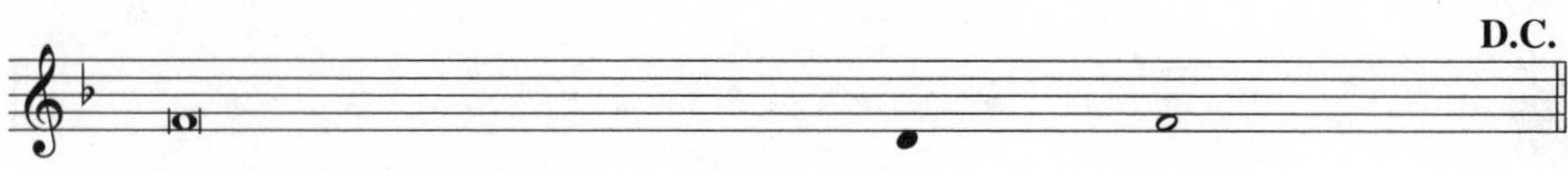
D.C.
1. my uplifted hands like an evening ob - lation.
2. I will not feast with sinners.
3. my prayer rises ever a - gainst them.
4. save me from the snares of those who do evil.
5. is now, and will be for ever. A - men.

Text: Psalm 141; Howard Hughes, SM
Music: Howard Hughes, SM

PSALM PRAYER

Stand

All respond: **Amen.**

12 WORD OF GOD

Sit

Reader concludes: The word of the Lord.
Assembly: **Thanks be to God.**

13 GOSPEL CANTICLE

Stand. All make the sign of the cross as the canticle begins.

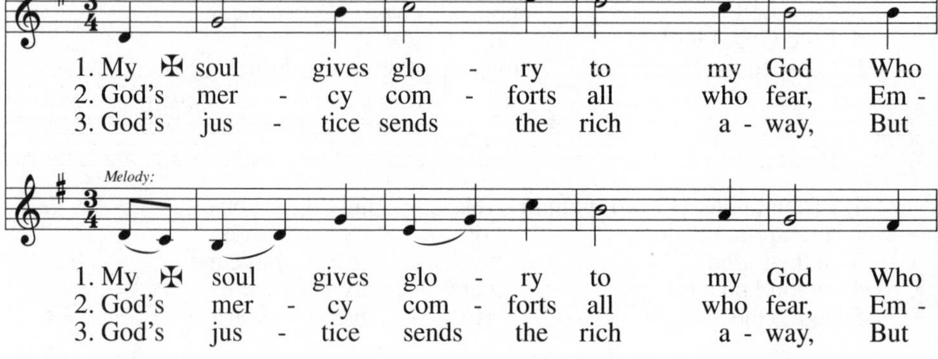
Descant:
1. My ✠ soul gives glo - ry to my God Who
2. God's mer - cy com - forts all who fear, Em -
3. God's jus - tice sends the rich a - way, But
Melody:
1. My ✠ soul gives glo - ry to my God Who
2. God's mer - cy com - forts all who fear, Em -
3. God's jus - tice sends the rich a - way, But

reach - es down with lov - ing grace To lift me
brac - ing with a stead - fast arm That casts the
feeds the poor with lav - ish things. Each hun - gry
reach - es down with lov - ing grace To lift me
brac - ing with a stead - fast arm That casts the
feeds the poor with lav - ish things. Each hun - gry
from my low es - tate And set me in the
might - y from their thrones, But keeps the hum - ble
soul now fills with joy And joins the song that
from my low es - tate And set me in the
might - y from their thrones, But keeps the hum - ble
soul now fills with joy And joins the song that
high - est place. Mag - ni - fi - cat, mag - ni - fi -
safe from harm. Mag - ni - fi - cat, mag - ni - fi -
Mar - y sings: Mag - ni - fi - cat, mag - ni - fi -
high - est place. Mag - ni - fi - cat, mag - ni - fi -
safe from harm. Mag - ni - fi - cat, mag - ni - fi -
Mar - y sings: Mag - ni - fi - cat, mag - ni - fi -

cat! With all my heart, I an - swer
cat! The weak find strength; the wea - ry,
cat! To God, Cre - a - tor, Christ, the
cat! With all my heart, I an - swer
cat! The weak find strength; the wea - ry,
cat! To God, Cre - a - tor, Christ, the
Yes When God an - noun - ces won - drous news. And
rest. God's prom - ise sounds from age to age: The
Son; And Ho - ly Spir - it— tri - une God: All
Yes When God an - noun - ces won - drous news. And
rest. God's prom - ise sounds from age to age: The
Son; And Ho - ly Spir - it— tri - une God: All
ev - 'ry age shall call me blest.
need - y of the world are blest.
prais - es to the Three - in - One.
ev - 'ry age shall call me blest.
need - y of the world are blest.
prais - es to the Three - in - One.

Text: Mary Louise Bringle, © 2004, GIA Publications, Inc.
Music: MAGNIFICAT, LMD; Michael Joncas, © 1979, 1988, GIA Publications, Inc.

GENERAL INTERCESSIONS 14

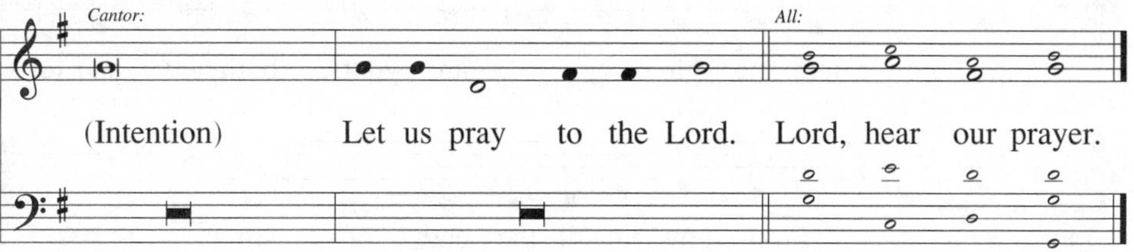
Cantor:
All:
(Intention) Let us pray to the Lord. Lord, hear our prayer.

Music: Byzantine chant; harm. by Robert J. Batastini, © 1986, GIA Publications, Inc.

LORD'S PRAYER 15

Our Fa - ther, who art in heav - en,

hal - low - ed be thy name. Thy king - dom come,

thy will be done on earth as it is in

heav - en. Give us this day our dai - ly bread;

and for - give us our tres - pass - es as we for -

give those who tres - pass a - gainst us; and

lead us not in - to temp - ta - tion, but de -

liv - er us from e - vil. For the king - dom,

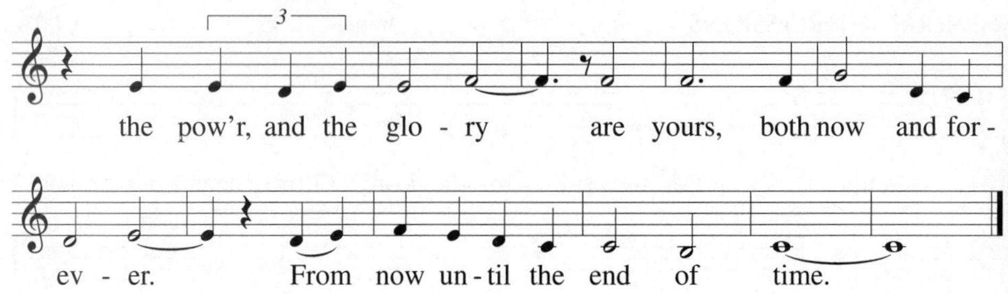
3
the pow'r, and the glo - ry are yours, both now and for -
ev - er. From now un - til the end of time.

Music: Steven C. Warner; acc. by Karen Schneider Kirner, © 1980, 1993, World Library Publications

16 FINAL BLESSING

mf
Presider:
Let us bless the Lord.
Assembly:
And give God thanks.
Presider:
May the Lord al-might-y bless our days and our deeds with

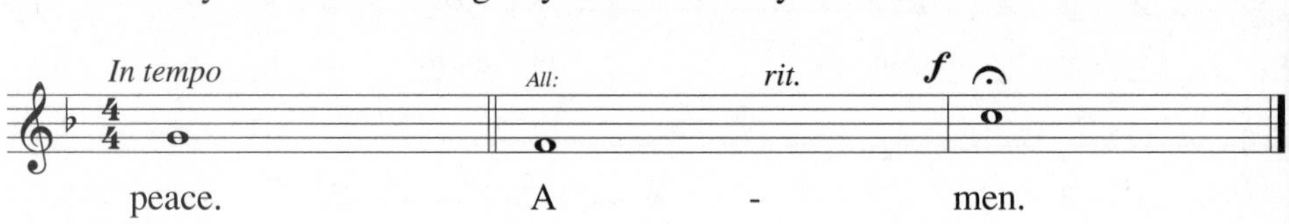
In tempo
All:
rit.
f
peace. A - men.

Text: David Haas
Music: David Haas

Psalm 15: They Who Do Justice 17

Refrain

Melody:
They who do jus - tice will live in the pres - ence of
Harmony:
They who do jus - tice will live in the pres - ence of
God! They who do jus - tice will
God! They who do jus - tice will
1., 5.
Last time to coda
live in the pres - ence of God!
live in the pres - ence of God!

Verses
2.-4.
Cantor:
1. Those who walk blame-less-ly and live their lives do-ing jus-tice,
2. Who harm not an-oth-er, nor take up re-proach to their neigh-bor,
3. Who show no con-di-tion in shar-ing the gifts of their treas-ure,
Melody:
pres-ence of God!
who keep the truth in their heart, and slan-der not with their tongue!
who hate the sight of the wick-ed, but hon-or the peo-ple of God!
who live not off the poor: They will stand firm for ev-er!
D.C.
Coda

Text: Psalm 15:2-5; David Haas, © 1989, GIA Publications, Inc.; refrain trans. © 1969, ICEL
Music: David Haas, © 1989, GIA Publications, Inc.

Psalm 16: Keep Me Safe, O God 18

Refrain
mf
a tempo
Keep me safe, O God: you are my hope;
you are my hope, O God.
1. rit.
2. Last time
Verses*
1. I say to God, "you are my on - ly God,
2. I find in God al - ways my cup of joy;
3. I bless my God: God who has coun - seled me.
4. I keep my God al - ways be - fore my eyes;
5. And so my heart al - ways is glad in God;
6. For you will not ev - er a - ban - don me,
7. The path of life you have re - vealed to me,
I have no good ex - cept in you."
and God will keep my life se - cure.
At night my heart gives coun - sel too.
with God be - side me I'm se - cure.
my bod - y too shall dwell se - cure.
or let your ser - vant lose the path.
and in your pres - ence is my joy.
rit.
D.C.

** Verses may be selected according to liturgical need.*

Text: Psalm 16; John Foley, SJ, © 1993, GIA Publications, Inc.; refrain trans., © 1969, ICEL
Music: John Foley, SJ, © 1993, GIA Publications, Inc.

19 Psalm 16: You Will Show Me the Path of Life

Refrain I

You will show me the path of life, you, my hope and my shel-ter;

To verses
In your pres-ence is end-less joy, at your side is my home for - ev-er.

Refrain II

To verses
Keep me safe, O God, I take ref - uge in you.

Refrain III

To verses
You are my in - her - i - tance, O Lord.

Verses

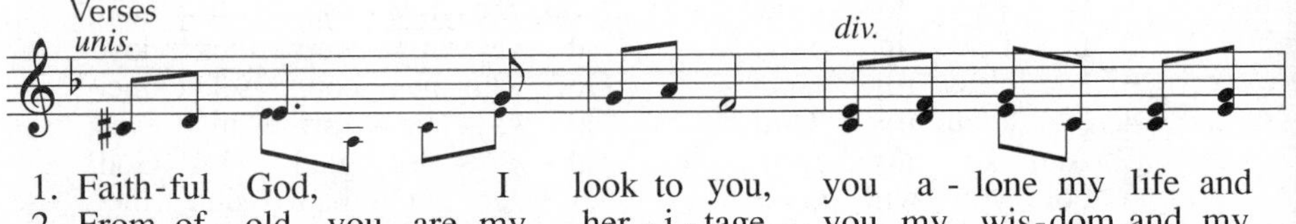
unis.
div.
1. Faith-ful God, I look to you, you a - lone my life and
2. From of old you are my her - i - tage, you my wis-dom and my
3. So my heart shall sing for joy, in your arms I rest se -

for - tune, nev - er shall I look to oth - er gods,
safe - ty, through the night you speak with - in my heart,
cure - ly, you will not a - ban - don me to death,

poco. rit.
To refrain
you shall be my one hope.
si - lent - ly you teach me.
you shall not de - sert me.

Psalm 19: Lord, You Have the Words 20

Refrain
To verses
Final ending
Lord, you have the words of ev-er-last-ing life.
Verse 1
1. The law of the Lord is per-fect, re-fresh-ing the soul; the
Lord's rule is to be trust-ed, the sim-ple find wis-dom.
D.C.
Verse 2
2. The fear of the Lord is ho-ly, a-bid-ing for ev-er; the de-
crees of the Lord are true, all of them just.
D.C.
Verse 3
3. The pre-cepts of the Lord are right, they glad-den the heart, the com-
mand of the Lord is clear, giv-ing light to the eye.
D.C.
Verse 4
4. They are worth more than gold, than the fin - est gold,
sweet-er than hon-ey, than hon-ey from the comb.
D.C.

Text: Psalm 19:8, 9, 10, 11; David Haas, © 1983, GIA Publications, Inc.; refrain trans., © 1969, ICEL
Music: David Haas, © 1983, GIA Publications, Inc.

21 Psalm 19: Words of Everlasting Life / Palabras de Vida Eterna

Bilingual Refrain
Lord, you have the words of ev-er-last-ing life. Tú tie-nes, Se-ñor, pa-la-bras de vi-da e-ter-na. ter-na.
To repeat
To verses
Last time
Verses in English
Verse 1
1. The law of the Lord is per-fect, re-fresh-ing the soul; The rule of the Lord is to be trust-ed, giv-ing wis-dom to the sim-ple.
D.C.
Verse 2
2. The pre-cepts of the Lord are right, de-light-ing the heart; the com-mand of the Lord is clear, en-light-en-ing the eye.
D.C.

Verse 3
3. The fear of the Lord is ho - ly, en - dur - ing for - ev - er. The de - crees of the Lord are true, all of them just.
D.C.
Verse 4
4. They are more pre - cious than gold, than the pur - est of gold; and sweet - er are they than syr - up, or hon - ey from the comb.
D.C.
Verses in Spanish
Verse 1
1. La ley del Se - ñor es per - fec - ta y es des - can - so del al - ma; fie - les las pa - la - bras del Se - ñor, in - stru - yen al ig - no - ran - te.
D.C.

Verse 2
2. Los man - da - tos del Se - ñor son rec - tos y‿a -
le - gran el co - ra - zón; Son luz los pre - cep - tos del Se -
D.C.
ñor a - lum - bran - do‿el ca - mi - no.
Verse 3
3. La vo - lun - tad de Dios es san - ta y pa - ra
siem - pre es - ta - ble; los man - da - tos del Se - ñor son ver - da -
D.C.
de - ros y‿en - te - ra - men - te jus - tos.
Verse 4
4. Más pre - cio - sos que‿el o - ro y las
pie - dras más fi - nas; y más dul - ces que la
D.C.
miel de‿un pa - nal que go - te - a.

Psalm 22: My God, My God 22

Refrain ♩ = 76
mf a tempo
Last time rit. and
My God, my God, O why have you a - ban - doned me?
mf
Verse 1
1. All who see me laugh at me, they mock me and they shake their
heads: "He re - lied on the Lord, let the Lord be his ref-uge."
poco rit.
D.C.
Verse 2
2. As dogs a - round me, they cir - cle me a - bout.
Wound - ed me and pierced me, I can num - ber all my bones.
poco rit.
D.C.
Verses 3, 4
3. My cloth - ing they di - vid - ed, for my
4. I will praise you to my peo - ple, and pro -
gar - ments cast - ing lots, O Lord, do not de -
claim you in their midst, O fear the Lord, my
sert me, but hast - en to my aid.
peo - ple, give glo - ry to God's name.
poco rit.
D.C.

23 Psalm 23: Shepherd Me, O God

Refrain
mp
Shep-herd me, O God, be - yond my wants, be -
mp
Shep-herd me, be - yond my wants, be -

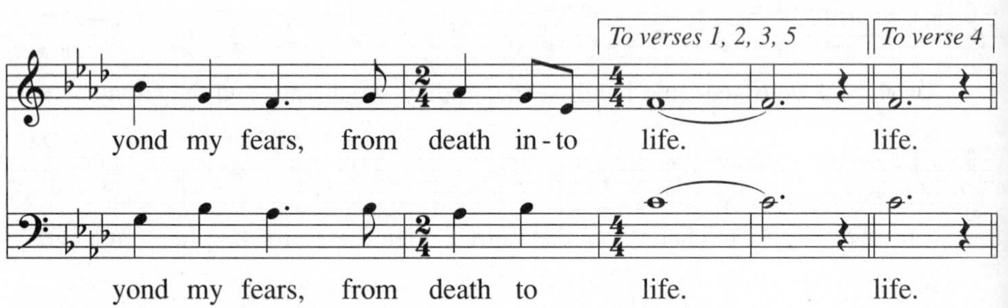
To verses 1, 2, 3, 5
To verse 4
yond my fears, from death in-to life. life.
yond my fears, from death to life. life.

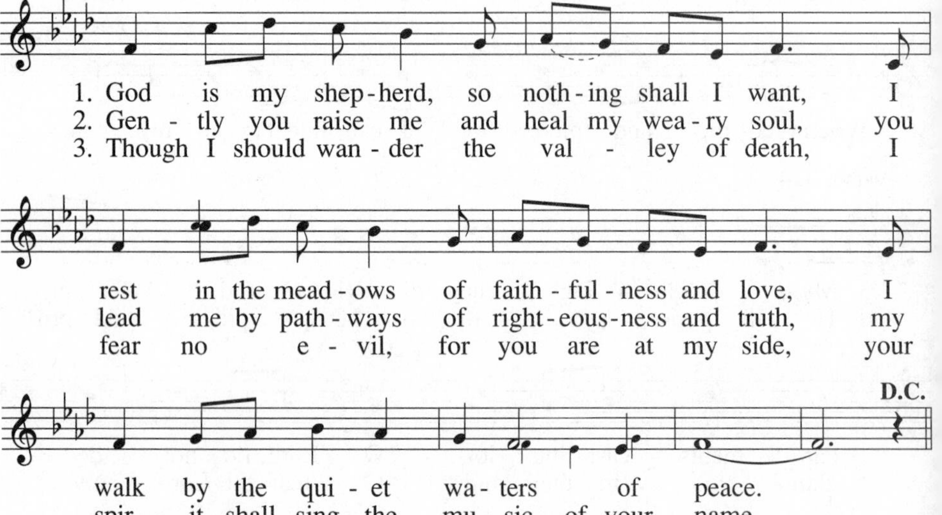
Verses 1, 2, 3
1. God is my shep-herd, so noth-ing shall I want, I
2. Gen - tly you raise me and heal my wea-ry soul, you
3. Though I should wan - der the val - ley of death, I
rest in the mead-ows of faith - ful - ness and love, I
lead me by path-ways of right-eous-ness and truth, my
fear no e - vil, for you are at my side, your
D.C.
walk by the qui - et wa - ters of peace.
spir - it shall sing the mu - sic of your name.
rod and your staff, my com- fort and my hope.

Verse 4
f
4. You have set me a ban-quet of love
in the face of ha-tred,
pp unis.
crown-ing me with
love be-yond my pow'r to hold.
rit.
D.C.
Verse 5
p
5. Sure-ly your kind-ness and mer-cy fol-low me
all the days of my life; I will dwell in the
poco rit.
a tempo
house of my God for ev-er-more.
Final Refrain
p a bit slower
Shep-herd me, O God, be-yond my wants, be-
yond my fears, from death in-to life.

Text: Psalm 23; Marty Haugen
Music: Marty Haugen

24 Psalm 23: My Shepherd Is the Lord

Antiphon I

My shep-herd is the Lord, noth-ing in-deed shall I want.

Text: Psalm 23; The Grail
Music: Joseph Gelineau, SJ

Antiphon II

The Lord is my shep-herd, noth-ing shall I want: he
leads me by safe paths, noth-ing shall I fear.

Text: Psalm 23; The Grail
Music: A. Gregory Murray, OSB

Psalm Tone

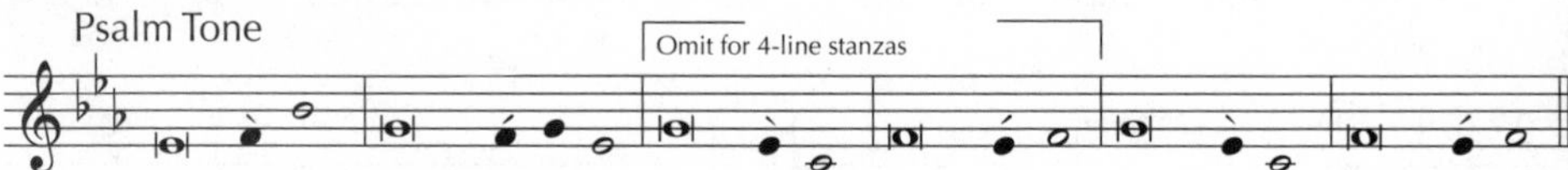
Omit for 4-line stanzas

Music: Richard Proulx,

Gelineau Tone

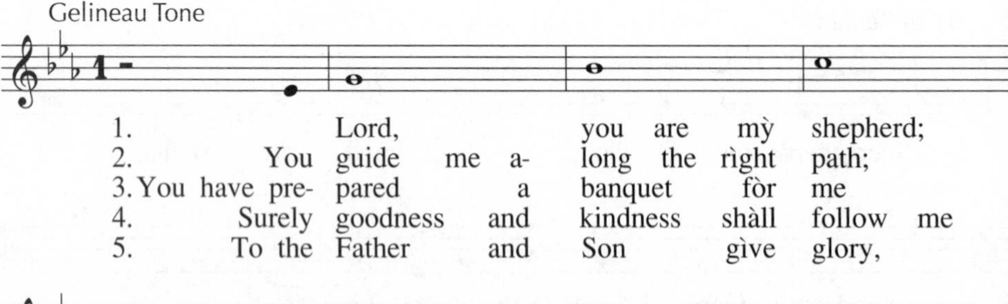
1. Lord, you are mỳ shepherd;
2. You guide me a- long the rìght path;
3. You have pre- pared a banquet fòr me
4. Surely goodness and kindness shàll follow me
5. To the Father and Son gìve glory,

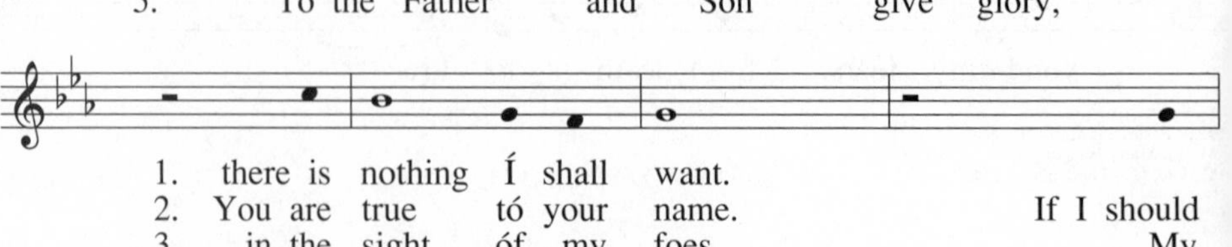
1. there is nothing Í shall want.
2. You are true tó your name. If I should
3. in the sight óf my foes. My
4. all the days óf my life. In the
5. give glory tó the Spirit. To God who

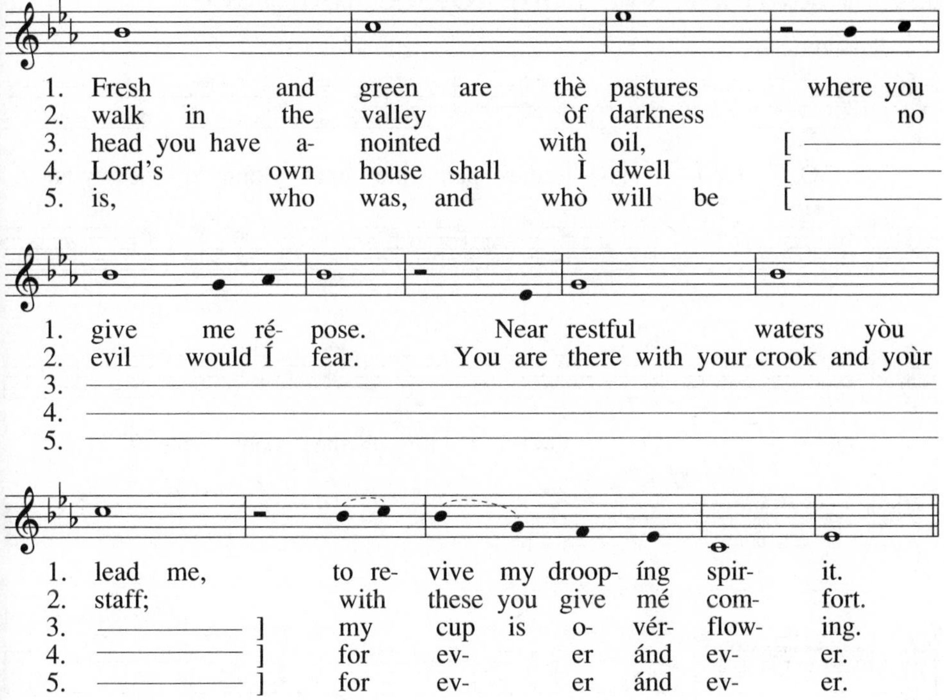
1. Fresh and green are thè pastures where you
2. walk in the valley òf darkness no
3. head you have a- nointed wìth oil, [
4. Lord's own house shall Ì dwell [
5. is, who was, and whò will be [
1. give me ré- pose. Near restful waters yòu
2. evil would Í fear. You are there with your crook and yòur
3.
4.
5.
1. lead me, to re- vive my droop- íng spir- it.
2. staff; with these you give mé com- fort.
3.] my cup is o- vér- flow- ing.
4.] for ev- er ánd ev- er.
5.] for ev- er ánd ev- er.

Text: Psalm 23; The Grail
Music: Joseph Gelineau, SJ

25 Psalm 24: We Long to See Your Face

Refrain I
mp
O God, this is the peo - ple that longs to see your
face. O God, this is the peo - ple that
mf
longs to see your face.
div.
To verses
Final ending
Refrain II
O-pen wide your gates; Let the King of Glo - ry in! O-pen wide your
gates; Let the King of Glo - ry in!

Verses
mp
1. All the earth is yours, O God, the world and those who dwell on it.
2. Who can as - cend your moun - tain, God? Or who may stand in this ho - ly place?
3. They shall re - ceive your bless - ing, God, their Sav - ior shall re - ward them.
You have found - ed it up - on the seas and es - tab - lished it up - on the riv - ers.
Those whose hands are sin - less, hearts are clean, and de - sire not the van - i - ty of earth.
Such is the face that seeks for you, that seeks your face, O God of Ja - cob.
To refrain

Text: Psalm 24; Kevin Keil, © 1993, GIA Publications, Inc.; refrain I trans. © 1969, ICEL
Music: Kevin Keil, © 1993, GIA Publications, Inc.

26 Psalm 25: To You, O Lord

Refrain
mf
To you, O Lord, I lift my soul,
mf
to you, I lift my soul.
Last time
Last time
Verse 1
1. Lord, make me know your ways,
teach me your paths and keep me in the way of your
truth, for you are God, my Sav - ior.
poco rit.
D.C.
Verse 2
mp
2. For the Lord is good and right - eous, re -
veal - ing the way to those who wan - der,
gen - tly lead - ing the poor and the hum - ble.
rit.
D.C.

Verse 3
f
3. To the ones who seek the Lord, who look to God's
mf
word, who live God's love, God will al - ways be
mp
poco rit.
D.C.
near, and will show them mer - cy.

Text: Psalm 25:4-5, 8-9, 12-14; Marty Haugen, © 1982, GIA Publications, Inc.; refrain trans. © 1969, ICEL
Music: Marty Haugen, © 1982, GIA Publications, Inc.

27 Psalm 25: Remember Your Mercies

Refrain I
f
To verses
Re - mem - ber your mer - cies, O Lord.
f
Refrain II
f
To verses
Teach me your ways, O Lord.
f
Verses
piu mosso
1. Your ways, O Lord, make known to me, teach me your paths. Guide me, teach me, for you are my Sav - ior.
2. Re - mem - ber your com - pas - sion, Lord, and your kind - ness of old. Re - mem - ber this, and not my sins, in your good-ness, O Lord.
3. Good and just is the Lord, the sin - ners know the way. God guides the meek to jus - tice, and teach - es the hum - ble.
To refrain

Text: Psalm 25:4-5, 6-7, 8-9; David Haas, © 1985, GIA Publications, Inc.; refrain trans. © 1969, ICEL
Music: David Haas, © 1985, GIA Publications, Inc.

Psalm 25: To You, O Lord 28

Refrain
To you, O Lord, I lift up my soul. To you, O Lord, I lift up my soul.
To verse 1 and Final ending
To verses 2., 3.
Final ending
Verse 1
1. Lord, make me know your ways. Lord, teach me your paths.
Make me walk in your truth, for you are God my Sav-ior.
D.C.
Verse 2
2. The Lord is good and up-right. He shows the path to those who stray. God guides the hum-ble in the right path. He teach-es his way to the poor.
D.C.

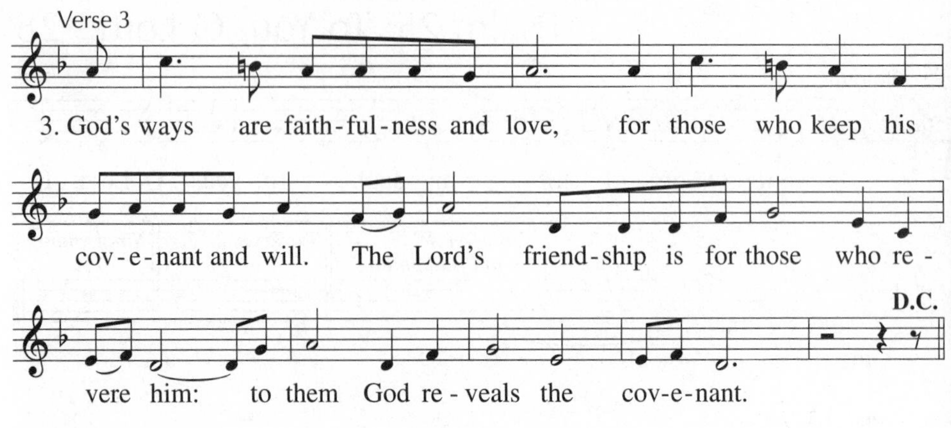
Verse 3
3. God's ways are faith-ful-ness and love, for those who keep his
cov-e-nant and will. The Lord's friend-ship is for those who re -
D.C.
vere him: to them God re - veals the cov-e-nant.

Text: Psalm 25:4-5, 8-9, 10, 14; Stephen Pishner, © 2000, GIA Publications, Inc.; refrain trans. © 1969, ICEL
Music: Based on VENI EMMANUEL; Stephen Pishner, © 2000, GIA Publications, Inc.

29 Psalm 27: The Lord Is My Light

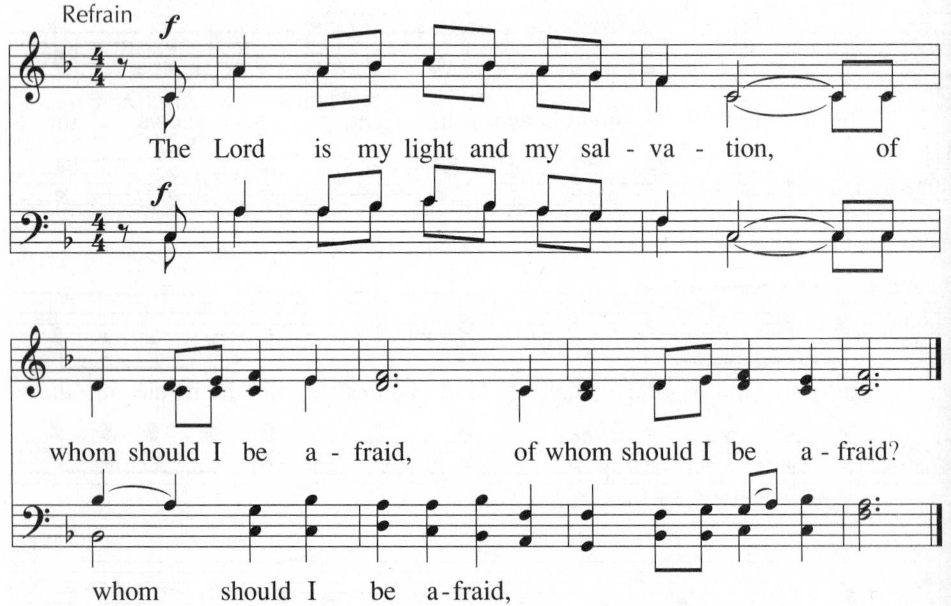
Refrain
f
The Lord is my light and my sal - va - tion, of
f
whom should I be a - fraid, of whom should I be a - fraid?
whom should I be a-fraid,

Verse 1
mf
1. The Lord is my light and my help; whom should I fear? The
poco rit.
D.C.
Lord is the strong-hold of my life; be-fore whom should I shrink?
Verse 2
mf
2. There is one thing I ask of the Lord; for this I long: to
poco rit.
D.C.
live in the house of the Lord all the days of my life.
Verse 3
mf
3. I be - lieve I shall see the good-ness of the Lord
in the land of the liv - ing; hope in
rit.
f
D.C.
God, and take heart. Hope in the Lord!

Text: Psalm 27:1-2, 4, 13-14; David Haas
Music: David Haas

30 Psalm 30: I Will Praise You, Lord

Refrain
mf
I will praise you, Lord, you have res - cued me,
I will praise you, Lord, for your mer-cy. I will praise you, Lord,
Last time
you have res - cued me: I will praise you, Lord.
Verse 1
mp
1. I will praise you, Lord, you have res - cued me and have
not let my en - e - mies re - joice o - ver me. O
f
dim.
Lord, you have raised my soul from the dead, re -
D.C.
stored me to life from those who sink in - to the grave.
Verse 2
mp
2. Sing psalms to the Lord, you who love him,
give thanks to his ho - ly name. His

f
dim.
an - ger lasts but a mo - ment; his fa - vor through life. At
D.C.
night there are tears, but joy comes with dawn.
Verse 3
mp
3. The Lord lis - tened and had pit - y.
The Lord came to my help. For
f
dim.
me you have changed my mourn - ing in - to danc - ing; O
D.C.
Lord my God, I will thank you for ev - er.

31 Psalm 31: I Put My Life in Your Hands / Pongo Mi Vida

Refrain
mp
Ab - ba, Ab - ba, I put my life in your
Ab - ba, Ab - ba, pon - go mi vi - da en tus
Descant: Ab - ba,
Melody: Ab - ba,
hands. Ab - ba, Ab - ba, I put my
ma - nos. Ab - ba, Ab - ba, pon - go mi
To verses
Last time
life in your hands.
vi - da en tus ma - nos.
Verses 1, 2
mf
1. In you, O Lord, I take ref - uge; let me
1. En ti bus - co pro - tec - ción. No que - de
mf
2. For all my foes re - proach me; all my
2. En ti pon - go to - da mi fe, hab - la -
nev - er be put to shame. In your jus - tice res - cue
yo nun - ca de - frau - da - do. Pon-me a sal - vo, pues tú e - res
friends are now put to flight. I am for - got - ten, like the
ré de tu bon - dad. Por fa - vor es - tás siem-pre con -

rit.
D.C.
me, in your hands I com - mend my spir - it.
jus - to. A tus ma - nos en - co - mien - do mi es - pí - ri - tu.
rit.
D.C.
dead, like a dish that now is bro - ken.
mi - go. Tú ha - ces la luz del ca - os.
Verse 3
3. I place my trust in you; in your
3. Tú e - res mi es - pe - ran - za; só - lo
hands is my des - ti - ny. Let your face shine up - on your
tú mi sal - va - ción. Con tu mi - se - ri - cor - dia,
ser - vant, in your hands I will place my life.
ven. Es - cu - cha mi o - ra - ción.
rit.
D.C.

Text: Psalm 31:2, 6, 12-13, 15-17 (English); 2, 6, 7-8, 15, 17, 23 (Spanish); David Haas; Spanish trans. by Jeffrey Judge
Music: David Haas

32 Psalm 33: Let Your Mercy Be on Us

Refrain
Let your mer - cy be on us, O God,
Let your mer - cy be on us,
Last time
as we place our trust in you.
Last time
Verse 1
1. Your words, O God, are truth in - deed, and all your works are
ev - er faith - ful; you love jus - tice and right, your com -
pas - sion fills all cre - a - tion.
D.C.
Verse 2
2. See how the eye of God is watch - ing, ev - er guard - ing all who
wait in hope, to de - liv - er them from death and sus -

D.C.
tain them in time of fam - ine.
Verse 3
3. Ex - ult, you just, in the Lord, for
praise is the song of the right - eous! How
hap - py the peo - ple of God, the ones whom
poco rit.
D.C.
God has cho - sen!
Verse 4
4. Our soul is wait - ing for God, for
God is our help and our shield. May your
kind - ness, O God, be up - on us who
poco rit.
D.C.
place our hope in you.

Text: Psalm 33:1, 4-5, 12, 18-19, 20, 22; Marty Haugen, © 1987, GIA Publications, Inc.; refrain trans. © 1969, ICEL
Music: Marty Haugen, © 1987, GIA Publications, Inc.

33 Psalm 34: The Cry of the Poor

Refrain ♩ = 66
Descant:
mp
The Lord hears the cry of the poor. Bless - ed be the Lord.
Melody:
The Lord hears the cry of the poor. Bless - ed be the Lord.
Verses
mf ♩ = 76
1. I will bless the Lord at all times, with praise ev - er in my mouth. Let my soul glo - ry in the Lord, who will
2. Let the low - ly hear and be glad: the Lord lis - tens to their pleas; and to hearts bro - ken God is near, who will
3. Ev - 'ry spir - it crushed God will save; will be ran - som for their lives; will be safe shel - ter for their fears, and will
4. We pro - claim your great - ness, O God, your praise ev - er in our mouth; ev - 'ry face bright - ened in your light, for you
hear the cry of the poor.
rit.
D.C.

Text: Psalm 34:2-3, 6-7, 18-19, 23; John Foley, SJ
Music: John Foley, SJ

Psalm 34: Taste and See 34

Refrain
mf
Taste and see the good-ness of the
mf
good - ness of the
Lord, the good - ness of the
good - ness of the
To verses
Last time
Lord.
Verse 1
1. I will bless the Lord at all times, God's praise
ev - er in my mouth. Glo - ry in the Lord for
poco rit.
D.C.
ev - er, and the low - ly will hear and be glad.

Verse 2
f
2. Glo - ry in the Lord with me, let us to -
geth - er ex - tol God's name.
I sought the Lord, who an - swered me and de -
poco rit.
D.C.
liv - ered me from all my fears.
Verse 3
f
3. Look to God that you might be ra - diant with
mf
joy, and your fac - es free from all shame.
The Lord hears the suf - fer - ing
mp
poco rit.
D.C.
souls, and saves them from all dis - tress.

Text: Psalm 34:2-3, 4-5, 6-7; Marty Haugen, © 1980, GIA Publications, Inc.; refrain trans. © 1969, ICEL
Music: Marty Haugen, © 1980, GIA Publications, Inc.

Psalm 40: Here I Am 35

Refrain
Here I am, Lord, here I am.
Here I am, here I am, here I am.
Here I am, Lord, here I am, here I am.
Here I am, Lord, here I am.
I come to do your will.
Last time
Verses
1. Long was I wait - ing for God, and then he heard my cry.
2. You asked me not for sac - ri - fice, for slaugh-tered goats or lambs.
3. You wrote it in the scrolls of law what you would have me do.
4. I spoke be - fore your ho - ly peo - ple, the good news that you save.

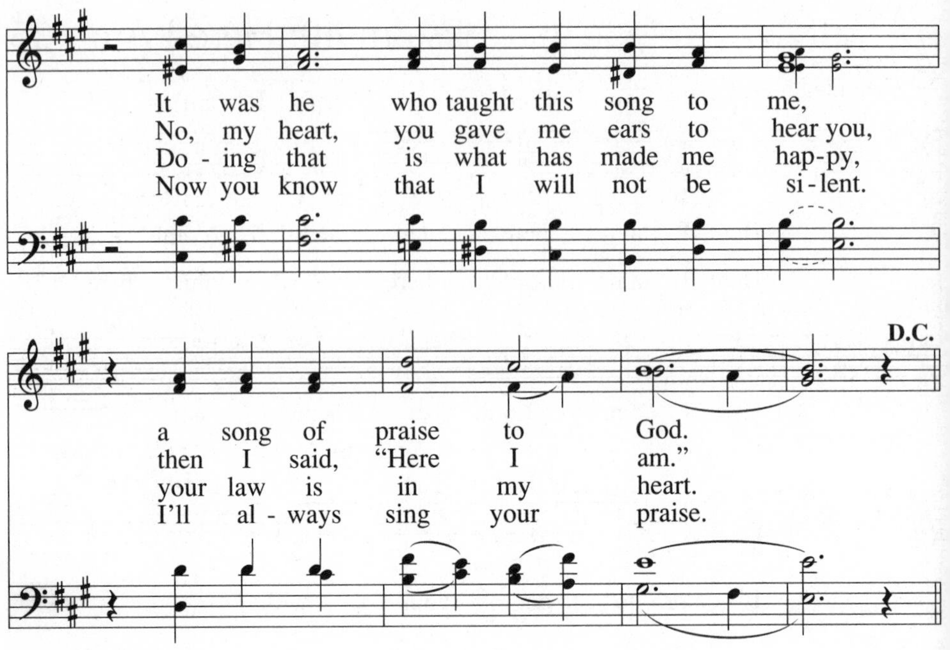
It was he who taught this song to me,
No, my heart, you gave me ears to hear you,
Do - ing that is what has made me hap-py,
Now you know that I will not be si-lent.
D.C.
a song of praise to God.
then I said, "Here I am."
your law is in my heart.
I'll al - ways sing your praise.

Text: Psalm 40; Rory Cooney, © 1971, 1991, North American Liturgy Resources; refrain trans. © 1969, ICEL
Music: Rory Cooney, © 1971, 1991, North American Liturgy Resources
Published by OCP Publications

36 Psalm 47: God Mounts His Throne

Ostinato Refrain*

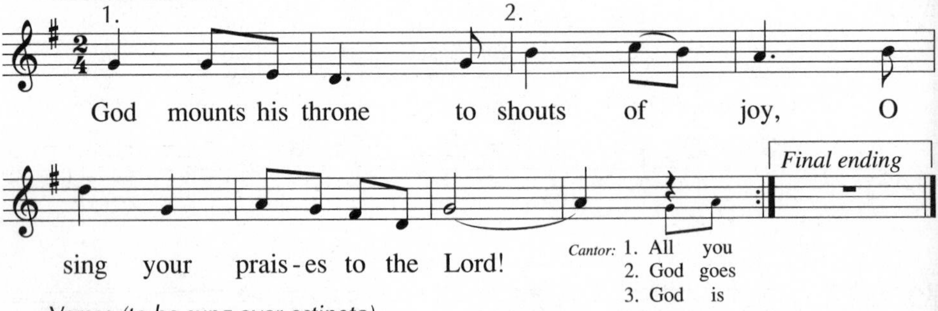

1. God mounts his throne 2. to shouts of joy, O sing your prais-es to the Lord!

Cantor: 1. All you
2. God goes
3. God is

Final ending

Verses *(to be sung over ostinato)*

Verse 1

1. All you peo-ples, clap your hands, shout to God in glad-ness, the Lord we must fear, king of all the earth.

To refrain

**May be sung in canon.*

Verse 2
2. God goes up to shouts of joy, sound the trum-pet
blast. Sing praise to our God, praise un-to our king!
To refrain
Verse 3
3. God is king of all the earth, sing with all your
skill to the king of all na-tions, God en-throned on high!
To refrain

Text: Psalm 47:2-3, 6-7, 8-9; Marty Haugen
Music: Marty Haugen

Psalm 51: Create in Me 37

Refrains
I Cre-ate in me a clean heart, O God. God.
II I will a-rise and go to my God. God.
Verses
1. Have mer-cy on me, O God. In the great-ness of your
2. Stay close to me, O God. In your pres-ence keep me
3. Your sal-va-tion is joy to me. In your wis-dom show the
love, cleanse me from my sin. Wash me.
safe. Fill me with your spir-it. Re-new me.
way. Lead me back to you. Teach me.
rit.
D.C.

Text: Psalm 51:3-4, 12-13, 14-15; David Haas, © 1987, GIA Publications, Inc.; refrain I trans. © 1969, ICEL
Music: David Haas, © 1987, GIA Publications, Inc.

38 Psalm 51: Create in Me / Crea en Mí

*Ostinato Refrains
Last time
Cre - ate in me a clean heart, Oh God. Cre -
Last time
Oh Dios, cre - a en mí un co - ra - zón pu - ro.
Verses in English (Superimposed on Ostinato Refrains)
1. A pure heart cre - ate for me, God. Stead - y my
wea - ry spir - it. Do not cast me a - way from your
pres - ence, nor take your spir - it from me.
2. Save me and bring back my joy. Sup - port me and
strength - en my will. Then I will teach trans -
gres - sors your ways and sin - ners will re - turn to you.
3. In sac - ri - fice you take no de - light. Burnt of - f'rings
you would re - fuse. My sac - ri - fice, a con - trite
spir - it, a changed heart you would not re - fuse.

*The English and Spanish refrains may be sung separately or together.

Verses in Spanish (Superimposed on Ostinato Refrains)
1. Cre-a en mí un co-ra-zón pu-ro, re-nué-va-me con es-
pí-ri-tu fir-me; no me a-rro-jes le-jos de tu
ros-tro, no me qui-tes tu es-pí-ri-tu san-to.
2. De-vuél-ve-me la a-le-grí-a de tu sal-va-
ción, a-fián-za-me con es-pí-ri-tu ge-ne-ro-so:
en-se-ña-ré a los mal-va-dos tus ca-mi-nos,
los pe-ca-do-res vol-ve-rán a ti.
3. Los sa-cri-fi-cios no te sa-tis-fa-cen: un ho-lo-caus-to,
no lo que-rrí-as. Mi sa-cri-fi-cio un es-pí-ri-tu que-bran-
ta-do; no lo des-pre-cias un co-ra-zón cam-bia-do.

39 Psalm 51: Be Merciful, O Lord

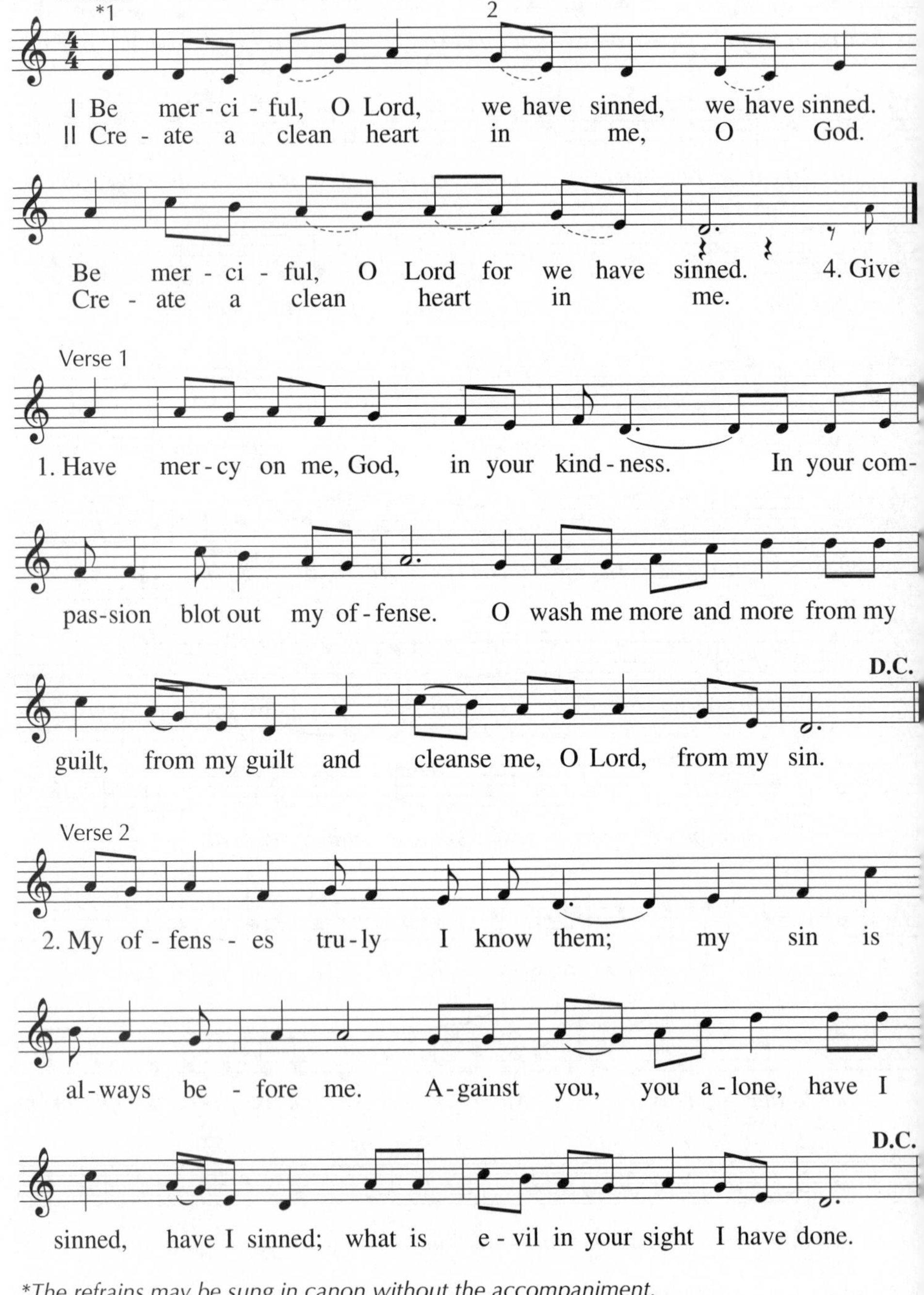
Refrains
*1
2
I Be mer - ci - ful, O Lord, we have sinned, we have sinned.
II Cre - ate a clean heart in me, O God.
Be mer - ci - ful, O Lord for we have sinned. 4. Give
Cre - ate a clean heart in me.
Verse 1
1. Have mer - cy on me, God, in your kind - ness. In your com-
pas-sion blot out my of - fense. O wash me more and more from my
D.C.
guilt, from my guilt and cleanse me, O Lord, from my sin.
Verse 2
2. My of - fens - es tru - ly I know them; my sin is
al-ways be - fore me. A-gainst you, you a - lone, have I
D.C.
sinned, have I sinned; what is e - vil in your sight I have done.

*The refrains may be sung in canon without the accompaniment.

Verse 3
3. A pure heart cre - ate for me, O God, put a
stead - fast spir-it with - in me. Do not cast me a - way from your
D.C.
pres - ence, O Lord, nor de - prive me of your ho - ly spir - it.
Verse 4
(4.) me a - gain the joy of your help, Lord; with a
3
spir - it of fer - vor sus - tain me. O Lord, o - pen my lips, O
D.C.
Lord, o - pen my lips and my mouth shall de - clare your praise.

Text: Psalm 51:3-4, 5-6, 12-13, 14, 17; © 1963, 1993, The Grail, GIA Publications, Inc., agent; refrain trans. © 1969, ICEL
Music: Based on WONDROUS LOVE, Stephen Pishner, © 1998, GIA Publications, Inc.

40 Psalm 51: Have Mercy, Lord

Antiphon

Have mer - cy, Lord, cleanse me from all my sins.

Text: Psalm 51; The Grail
Music: Joseph Gelineau, SJ

Psalm Tone

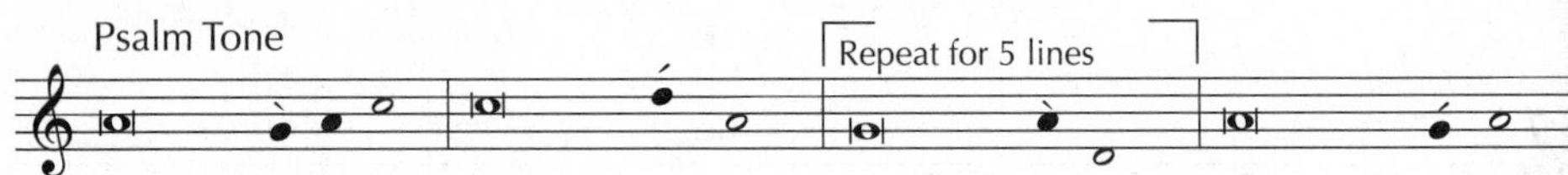
Repeat for 5 lines

Music: Chrysogonus Waddell, OCSO, © Gethsemani Abbey

Gelineau Tone

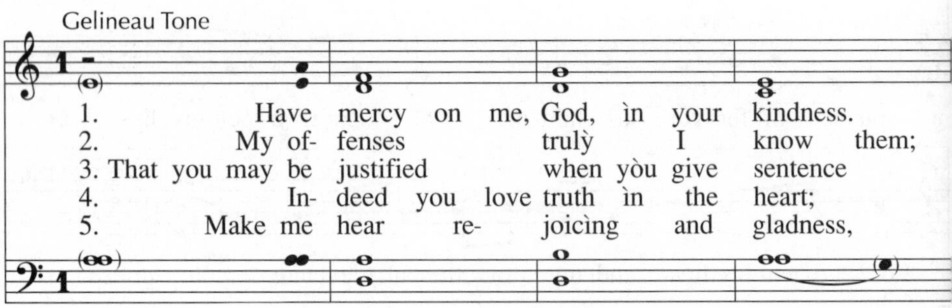
1. Have mercy on me, God, ìn your kindness.
2. My of- fenses trulỳ I know them;
3. That you may be justified when yòu give sentence
4. In- deed you love truth ìn the heart;
5. Make me hear re- joicìng and gladness,

1. In your com- passion blot out my óf- fense.
2. my sin is always bé- fore me.
3. and be with- out re- proach when yóu judge,
4. then in the secret of my heart teach mé wisdom.
5. that the bones you have crushed may ré- vive.

1. O wash me more and more from mỳ guilt
2. Against you, you a- lone, have Ì sinned;
3. O see, in guilt I wàs born,
4. O purify me, then I shall bè clean;
5. From my sins turn a- way yòur face

1. and cleanse me from mý sin.
2. what is evil in your sight I háve done.
3. a sinner was I cón- ceived.
4. O wash me, I shall be whiter thán snow.
5. and blot out all mý guilt.

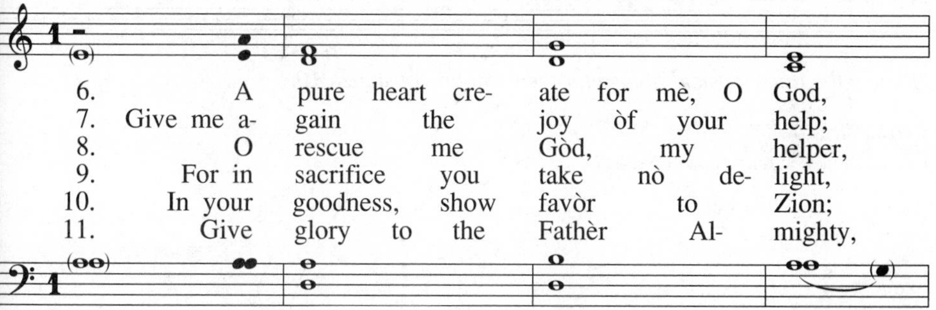
6. A pure heart cre- ate for mè, O God,
7. Give me a- gain the joy òf your help;
8. O rescue me Gòd, my helper,
9. For in sacrifice you take nò de- light,
10. In your goodness, show favòr to Zion;
11. Give glory to the Fathèr Al- mighty,

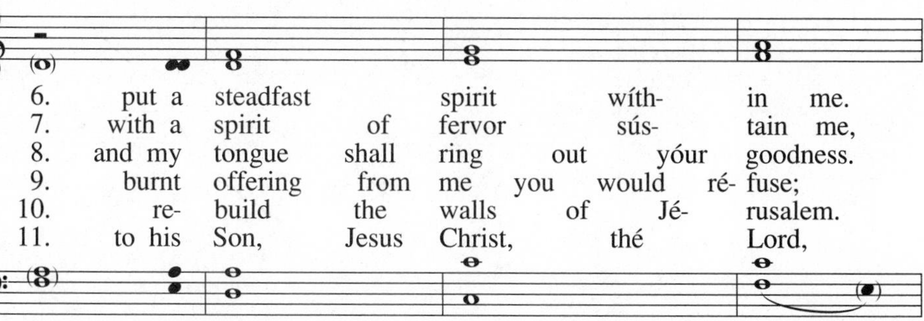
6. put a steadfast spirit wíth- in me.
7. with a spirit of fervor sús- tain me,
8. and my tongue shall ring out yóur goodness.
9. burnt offering from me you would ré- fuse;
10. re- build the walls of Jé- rusalem.
11. to his Son, Jesus Christ, thé Lord,

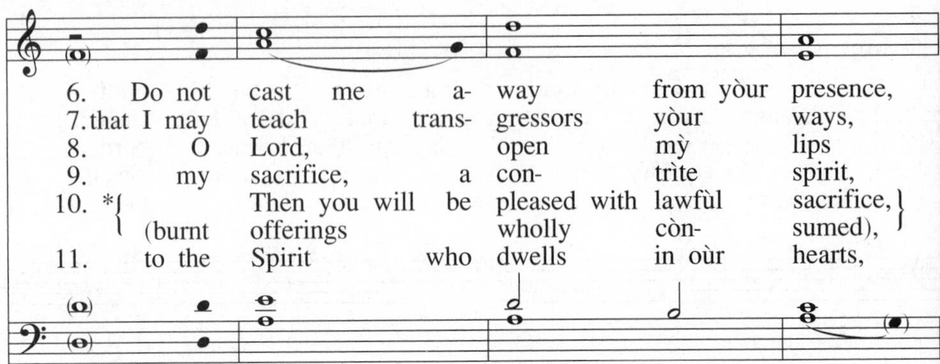
6. Do not cast me a- way from yòur presence,
7. that I may teach trans- gressors yòur ways,
8. O Lord, open mỳ lips
9. my sacrifice, a con- trìte spirit,
10. *{ Then you will be pleased with lawfùl sacrifice, }
(burnt offerings wholly còn- sumed),
11. to the Spirit who dwells in oùr hearts,

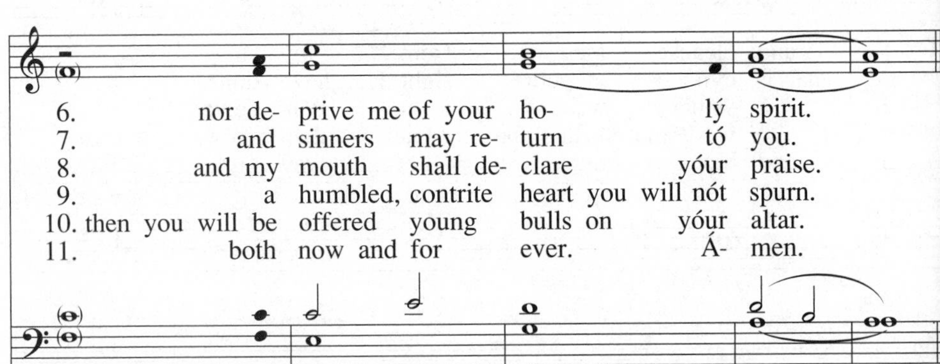
6. nor de- prive me of your ho- lý spirit.
7. and sinners may re- turn tó you.
8. and my mouth shall de- clare yóur praise.
9. a humbled, contrite heart you will nót spurn.
10. then you will be offered young bulls on yóur altar.
11. both now and for ever. Á- men.

**Repeat the third musical phrase for the extra line of stanza 10.*

Text: Psalm 51; The Grail
Music: Joseph Gelineau, SJ

Psalm 51: Be Merciful, O Lord 41

Refrain
Be mer-ci-ful, O Lord, for we have sinned; be
mp
Be mer-ci-ful, O Lord, we have sinned; be
mp
Be mer-ci-ful, O Lord, for we have sinned; be
mer-ci-ful, O Lord, for we have sinned.
Last time
mer-ci-ful, O Lord, we have sinned.
Last time
mer-ci-ful, O Lord, we have sinned.
Verse 1
1. Have mer - cy on me, God, in your kind - ness,
in your com - pas-sion, blot out my of - fense.
O wash me more and more from my guilt and my
sor-row, and cleanse me from all of my sin.
D.C.
Verse 2
2. My of - fens-es, tru - ly I know them, and my sins are

al - ways be - fore me; a-gainst you a - lone have I
D.C.
sinned, O Lord, what is e-vil in your sight I have done.
Verse 3
3. Cre - ate in me a clean heart, O God,
put your stead - fast spir - it in my soul.
Cast me not a - way from your pres-ence, O
D.C.
Lord, and take not your spir - it from me.
Verse 4
4. Give back to me the joy of your sal - va - tion,
let your will - ing spir - it bear me up
and I shall teach your way to the ones who have
D.C.
wan - dered, and bring them all home to your side.

Text: Psalm 51:3-4, 5-6, 12-13, 14-15; Marty Haugen, © 1983, GIA Publications, Inc.; refrain trans. © 1969, ICEL
Music: Marty Haugen, © 1983, GIA Publications, Inc.

Psalm 63: Your Love Is Finer than Life 42

Refrain
Descant:
O God, I seek you, my soul thirsts for
Melody:
O God, I seek you, my soul thirsts for
you, your love is fin - er than life.
Last time
div.
you, your love is fin - er than life.
Last time
Verses
1. As a dry and wea - ry des - ert land, so my soul is thirst - ing for my God, and my flesh is faint for the God I seek, for your love is more to me than life.
2. I think of you when at night I rest, I re - flect up - on your stead - fast love, I will cling to you, O Lord my God, in the shad - ow of your wings I sing.
3. I will bless your name all the days I live, I will raise my hands and call on you, my joy - ful lips shall sing your praise, you a - lone have filled my hun - gry soul.
D.C.

Text: Psalm 63; Marty Haugen
Music: Marty Haugen

43 Psalm 63: My Soul Is Thirsting

With longing
Refrain
My soul is thirst-ing, my soul is thirst-ing,
To verses
Last time
my soul is thirst-ing for you, O Lord my God. God.
Verse 1
1. O God, you are my God whom I seek; O God, you are my
God whom I seek; for you my flesh pines, my soul
D.S.
thirsts like the earth, parched, life-less, with-out wa-ter.
Verse 2
2. Thus have I gazed toward you in your ho-ly place to see your
pow-er and your glo-ry. Your kind-ness is a great-er
D.S.
good than life it-self; my lips will glo-ri-fy you.

Verse 3
3. Thus will I bless you while I live; Lift-ing up my hands I will
call up-on your name. As with a ban-quet shall my soul be sat-is-
fied; with ex - ul - tant lips my mouth shall praise you.
D.S.
Verse 4
4. For you have been my help, you have been my help; in the
shad-ow of your wings I shout for joy. My soul clings
fast to you; your right hand holds me firm; in the
shad - ow of your wings I sing for joy.
D.S.

Text: Psalm 63:2, 3-4, 5-6, 8-9; verses adapt. © 1970, Confraternity of Christian Doctrine, Washington, D.C.; refrain by Michael Joncas, © 1987, GIA Publications, Inc.
Music: Michael Joncas, © 1987, GIA Publications, Inc.

44 Psalm 63: My Soul Is Thirsting

Antiphon I

My soul is thirst - ing for you, O
Lord, thirst - ing for you my God.

Text: *Lectionary for Mass,* © 1969, 1981, ICEL
Music: Richard Proulx, © 1975, GIA Publications, Inc.

Antiphon II

In the morn - ing I will sing, will
sing glad songs of praise to you.

Text: *Praise God in Song*
Music: David Clark Isele
© 1979, GIA Publications, Inc.

Psalm Tone

Music: Richard Proulx, © 1986, GIA Publications, Inc.

Gelineau Tone

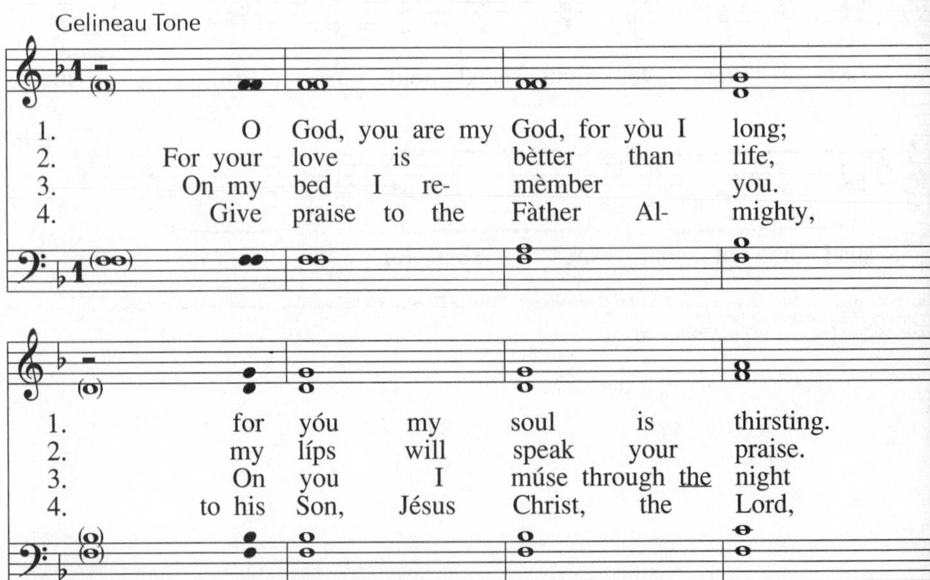
1. O God, you are my God, for yòu I long;
2. For your love is bètter than life,
3. On my bed I re- mèmber you.
4. Give praise to the Fàther Al- mighty,
1. for yóu my soul is thirsting.
2. my líps will speak your praise.
3. On you I múse through the night
4. to his Son, Jésus Christ, the Lord,

1. My body pìnes for you
2. So I will bless you àll my life,
3. for you have bèen my help;
4. [
1. like a dry, weary lánd without water.
2. in your name I will líft up my hands.
3. in the shadow of your wíngs I re- joice.
4.]
1. So I gaze on you in the sànctuary
2. My soul shall be filled as wìth a banquet,
3. My soul clìngs to you;
4. to the Spirit who dwèlls in our hearts,
1. to see your stréngth and your glory.
2. my mouth shall práise you with joy.
3. your ríght hand holds me fast.
4. both now and for éver. A- men.

Text: Psalm 63:2-9; The Grail
Music: Joseph Gelineau, SJ

45 Psalm 66: Let All the Earth

Refrain
Melody:
Let all the earth cry out in joy to the Lord;
Tenor:
Alto:
Cry out in joy un - to the Lord,
Let all the earth cry out in joy to the
Al - le - lu - ia;
Cry out in joy un - to the
Al - le - lu - ia;
1.-3.
To verses
Last time
rit.
Lord!
Lord! to the Lord!
Lord!
Lord! to the Lord!
Verses
1. Cry out in joy to the Lord, all peo - ples on
2. Lead - ing your peo - ple safe through fire and
3. Heark - en to me as I sing my love of the
earth, sing to the praise of God's name,
wa - ter, bring - ing their souls to life,
Lord, who an - swers the prayer of my heart.

pro - claim - ing for ev - er,
we sing of your glo - ry,
God leads me in safe - ty,

D.C.

"tre - men - dous your deeds for us." Oh
your love is e - ter - nal. Oh
from death un - to life. Oh

Text: Psalm 66:1-3, 12, 16; Marty Haugen
Music: Marty Haugen

46 Psalm 72: Every Nation on Earth

Refrain I
♪ = 184
Ev - 'ry na - tion on earth will a - dore you, Lord;
ev - 'ry na - tion on earth will a - dore you, Lord.
To verses
Last time
Refrain II
♪ = 184
In his days jus - tice will flou - rish;
in his days full - ness of peace for - ev - er - more.
To verses
Last time

Verse 1
1. O God, with your judg - ment en - dow the king; with your
jus - tice en - dow the king's son. With
jus - tice he will gov - ern your peo - ple, your af -
To refrain
flict - ed ones with right judg - ment.
Verse 2
2. Jus - tice shall flow'r in his days, last - ing
peace 'til the moon be no more.
May he rule from sea to sea, from the
To refrain
riv - er to the ends of the earth.
Verse 3
3. The kings of Tar-shish and the Isles of - fer gifts, those from
Se - ba and A - ra - bia bring trib - ute.

All kings shall pay him their hom - age,

To refrain

all na - tions shall serve him.

Verse 4

4. He res - cues the poor when they cry out, the af -

flict - ed with no one to help. The

low - ly and poor he shall pit - y, the

To refrain

lives of the poor he will save.

Text: Psalm 72:1-2, 7-8, 10-11, 12-13; Michael Joncas
Music: Michael Joncas
© 1987, 1994, GIA Publications, Inc.

47 Psalm 80/85/Luke 1: Lord, Make Us Turn to You

Refrain
♩ = 88
Lord, make us turn to you, show us your face, and

♩ = 72 *rit.* *To verses* | *Final ending*

we shall be saved.

Verses
a tempo

1. Shep - herd of Is - ra - el, heark - en from your
Ps. 80 2. We are your cho - sen vine, on - ly by your
3. If you will dwell with us, we shall live a -
4. Lord, we are pres - ent here, show us your
Ps. 85 5. Lord, let sal - va - tion rain, show - er down your
6. See, Lord, we look to you, you a - lone can
7. You have done won - drous things, ho - ly is your
Lk. 1 8. You are my joy and song, I would have my
9. You fill all hun - gry hearts, send - ing the

throne and shine forth, O rouse your pow - er,
care do we live, reach out your hand, O
new in your love, O shine up - on us,
kind - ness and love, O speak your word of
jus - tice and peace, the earth shall bring forth
bring us to life, O walk be - fore us
name for all time, your mer - cy and your
life speak your praise, on me your love has
rich emp - ty forth, and hold - ing up in

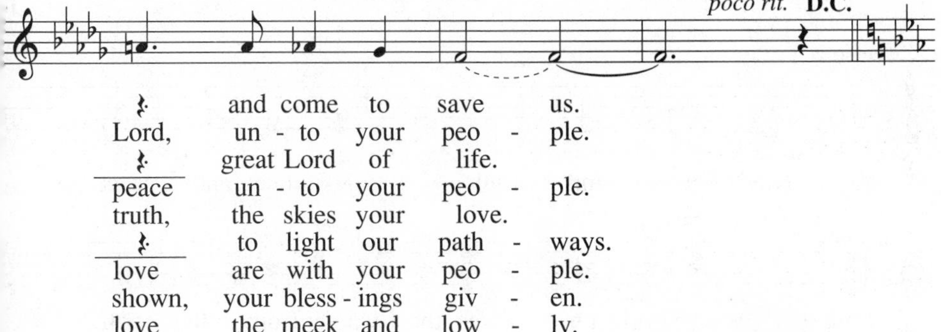
poco rit. **D.C.**
and come to save us.
Lord, un - to your peo - ple.
great Lord of life.
peace un - to your peo - ple.
truth, the skies your love.
to light our path - ways.
love are with your peo - ple.
shown, your bless - ings giv - en.
love the meek and low - ly.

Text: Psalm 80:2-3, 15-16, 18-20; Psalm 85:9-14; Luke 1:46-55; Marty Haugen
Music: Marty Haugen

48 Psalm 85: Lord, Let Us See Your Kindness

Refrain
Lord, let us see your kind - ness;
Last time
Lord, let us see your kind - ness.
Last time
Verse 1
molto rit.
1. Let us hear what our God pro - claims:
Peace to the peo - ple of God, sal - va - tion is
D.C.
near to the ones who fear God.
Verse 2
2. Kind - ness and truth, jus - tice and peace;
truth shall spring up as the wa - ter from the earth,

rit.
D.C.
jus - tice shall rain from the heav - ens.
Verse 3
3. The Lord will come and you shall know his love,
jus - tice shall walk in his path - ways, sal -
rit.
D.C.
va - tion the gift that he brings.

Text: Psalm 85:9-10, 11-12, 13-14; Marty Haugen, © 1983, GIA Publications, Inc.; refrain trans. © 1969, ICEL
Music: Marty Haugen, © 1983, GIA Publications, Inc.

49 Psalm 89: For Ever I Will Sing

Refrain
For ev - er I will sing the
For ev - er sing the
For ev - er I will sing the
good - ness of the Lord, the good - ness of the
good - ness, the good - ness of the Lord, of the
good - ness of the Lord, the good - ness of the
1.- 3.
To verses
4.
Lord.
Lord.
Verse 1
1. "With my cho - sen one I have made a cov - e - nant; I have
sworn to Da - vid my ser - vant: I will es - tab - lish your dy - nas - ty for -

slowing
a tempo
D.C.
ev - er and set up your throne through all a - ges."
Verse 2
2. Hap - py the peo - ple who ac - claim such a God, who
walk, O Lord, in the light of your face, who find their joy ev - 'ry
slowing
a tempo
D.C.
day in your name, who make your jus - tice the source of their bliss.
Verse 3
3. He will say to me: "You are my fa - ther, my
God, the rock who saves me!" I will keep my love for him
slowing
a tempo
D.C.
al - ways; with him my cov - e - nant shall last.
Alternate Verses
Verse 1
1. I have found Da - vid my ser - vant, with my
ho - ly oil I have a - noint - ed him, that my

poco rit.
D.C.
hand may ev - er be with him and my arm make him strong.
poco rit.
Verse 2
2. My faith - ful - ness and love shall be with you, in my
2. My faith - ful - ness and love will be
poco rit.
D.C.
Name your name will be ex - alt - ed.
poco rit.
yours, and you will be ex - alt - ed.
Verse 3
3. He shall cry to me, "My rock of sal -
3. He shall cry to me, "My God, my rock of sal -
poco rit.
D.C.
va - tion, my sal - va - tion."
poco rit.
va - tion, my sal - va - tion."

Text: Psalm 89:4-5, 16-17, 27-29; © 1963, 1993, The Grail, GIA Publications, Inc., agent, alt. verses 21-22, 25, 27, Marty Haugen, © 1988, 1994, GIA Publications, Inc.; refrain trans. © 1969, ICEL
Music: Marty Haugen, © 1988, 1994, GIA Publications, Inc.

Psalm 91: Be with Me 50

Refrain
mf
Be with me, Lord, when I am in trou-ble, be
with me, Lord, I pray.
To verses
Last time
pray.
Verse 1
mf
1. You who dwell in the shel-ter of the Lord, Most High, who a-
bide in the shad-ow of our God,
f
say to the
Lord: "My ref-uge and for-tress, the God in whom I trust."
D.C.
Verse 2
p div.
2. No e-vil shall be-fall you, no pain come
near, for the an-gels stand close by your side,

mp
guard - ing you al - ways and bear - ing you
gen - tly, watch - ing o - ver your life.
D.C.
Verse 3
mp
3. Those who cling to the Lord live se - cure in God's
love, lift - ed high, those who trust in God's name,
div.
f
call on the Lord who will nev - er for - sake you. God will
f
bring you sal - va - tion and joy.
D.C.

Text: Psalm 91:1-2, 10-11, 14-15; Marty Haugen
Music: Marty Haugen

Psalm 95: If Today You Hear God's Voice 51

Refrain
mp
If to - day you hear God's voice, hard - en not your
mp
hearts.
mf
If to - day you hear God's
mf
voice, hard - en not your hearts.
To verses
Final ending
Verse 1
mf
1. Come, ring out our joy to the Lord, hail the
rock who saves us, let us come now be - fore our
f
God, with songs let us hail the Lord.
mf
mp
rit.
D.C.

Verse 2

mf

2. Come, let us bow and bend low, let us kneel be-fore God who made us, *f* for here is our God; we the peo-ple, *mf* the flock that is led by God's *mp* *rit.* hand. **D.C.**

Verse 3

mf

3. O that to-day you would hear God's voice, "Hard-en not your hearts, *f* as on that day in the des-ert, *mf* when your par-ents put me to the *mp* *rit.* test." **D.C.**

Text: Psalm 95:1-2, 6-7, 8-9; David Haas
Music: David Haas

52 Psalm 96: Today Is Born Our Savior

Refrain ♩. = 60
To-day is born our Sav-ior, Christ the Lord. To-day is born our Sav-ior, Christ the Lord.
Verse 1
1. Sing to the Lord a new song; sing to the Lord, all you

D.C.
lands. Sing to the Lord; bless his name.
Verse 2
2. An-nounce his sal - va-tion, day af-ter day. Tell his glo-ry a -
D.C.
mong the na-tions; A - mong all peo-ples, his won-drous deeds.
Verse 3
3. Let the heav - ens be glad and the earth re -
joice; let the sea and what fills it re-sound;
let the plains be joy-ful and all that is in them!
D.C.
Then shall all the trees of the for-est ex - ult.
Verse 4
4. They shall ex-ult be - fore the Lord, for he comes; for he
comes to rule the earth. He shall rule the world with
D.C.
jus-tice and the peo - ples with his con-stan-cy.

Text: Psalm 96; verses trans. © 1970, Confraternity of Christian Doctrine, Washington, D.C.; refrain trans. © 1969, ICEL
Music: Howard Hughes, SM, © 1976, GIA Publications, Inc.

53 Psalm 96: Sing a Song to the Lord's Holy Name

Refrain
Sing a song to the Lord's ho - ly name. May the
Ho - ly name. May the
won - ders of God be pro - claimed. Sing a
won - ders of God be pro - claimed.
song to the Lord, now ac - claim. Al - le - lu - ia, al - le -
Now ac - claim. Al - le - lu - ia, al - le -
lu - ia!
lu - ia! Ho - ly is God's name!

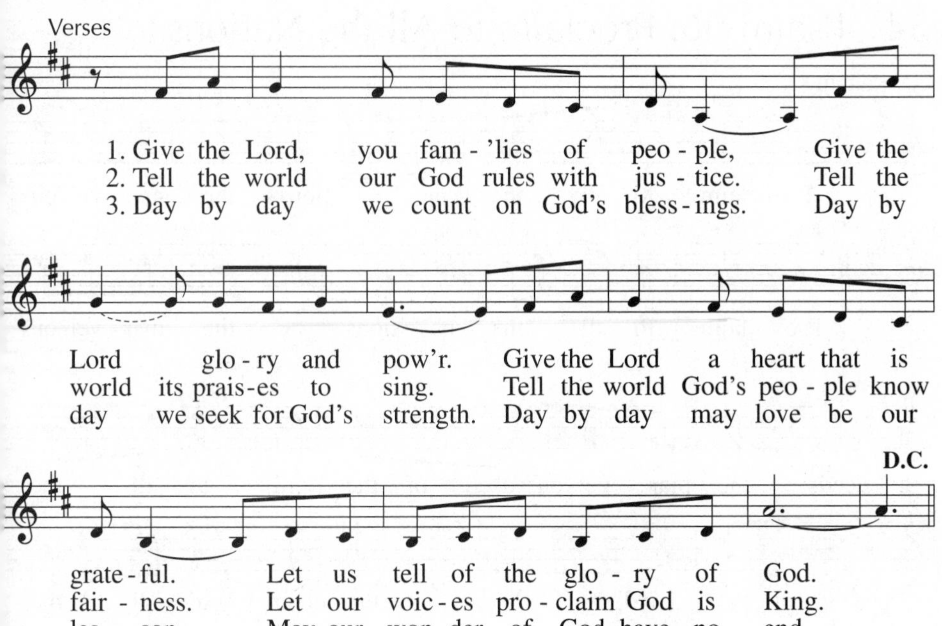
Verses
1. Give the Lord, you fam - 'lies of peo - ple, Give the
2. Tell the world our God rules with jus - tice. Tell the
3. Day by day we count on God's bless - ings. Day by
Lord glo - ry and pow'r. Give the Lord a heart that is
world its prais - es to sing. Tell the world God's peo - ple know
day we seek for God's strength. Day by day may love be our
D.C.
grate - ful. Let us tell of the glo - ry of God.
fair - ness. Let our voic - es pro - claim God is King.
les - son. May our won - der of God have no end.

Text: Psalm 96; Liam Lawton
Music: Liam Lawton; arr. by John McCann

54 Psalm 96: Proclaim to All the Nations

Refrain I
Descant:
Pro-claim to all the na - tions the mar-vel-ous
Melody:
Pro-claim to all the na-tions the mar-vel-ous
deeds, the mar - vel-ous deeds of the Lord, to all the
deeds of the Lord! Pro-claim to all the
To verses
na-tions the mar - vel-ous deeds of the Lord!
na-tions the mar - vel-ous deeds of the Lord!
Refrain II
Descant:
Give the Lord glo - ry and hon - or.
Melody:
Give the Lord glo - ry and hon-or.
To verses
Give the Lord glo - ry and hon - or.
Give the Lord glo - ry and hon - or.

Verses 1, 3, 4
ALL 1. Sing to the Lord a new song. Sing to the Lord all you lands!
MEN 3. Give to the Lord, you na - tions, praise to the Lord of all! Sing glo - ry and praise and sing to the name, a - bove all names!
ALL 4. Wor - ship the Lord, and trem - ble, pro - claim the one who reigns!
Sing to the Lord with all your heart, and bless God's name!
Say to the na - tions: "The Lord is King;" who rules with jus - tice!
To refrain
Verse 2
WOMEN 2. An - nounce sal - va - tion day by day, God's glo - ry through - out the earth! A - mong all the peo - ple in ev - 'ry land, God's won - drous deeds!
To refrain

Text: Psalm 96:1-2, 3, 7-8, 9; David Haas, © 1989, GIA Publications, Inc.; refrains trans. © 1969, ICEL
Music: Marty Haugen; refrain I, David Haas; refrain II adapt. by Diana Kodner; © 1989, 1994, GIA Publications, Inc.

55 Psalm 98: All the Ends of the Earth

Refrain I
unis.
All the ends of the earth have seen the pow-er of God;
div.
To verses
all the ends of the earth have seen the pow-er of God.
div.
Refrain II
unis.
Sing to the Lord a new song, for God has done won-der-ful
div.
deeds. Sing to the Lord a new song, for
div.
To verses
God has done won - der - ful deeds.
Refrain III
unis.
The Lord comes to the earth to

div.
rule the earth with jus - tice. The Lord comes to the
div.
To verses
earth to rule the earth with jus - tice.
Verse 1
1. Sing to the Lord a new song, for God has done won - drous
deeds; whose right hand has won the vic - t'ry for
To refrain
us, God's ho - ly arm.
Verse 2
2. The Lord has made sal - va - tion known, and jus - tice re -
vealed to all, re - mem - ber - ing kind - ness and faith - ful -
To refrain
ness to Is - ra - el.

Verse 3

3. All of the ends of earth have seen sal - va - tion by our God. Joy-ful - ly sing out all you lands, break forth in song.

To refrain

Verse 4

4. Sing to the Lord with harp and song, with trum - pet and with horn. Sing in your joy be-fore the king, the king, our Lord.

To refrain

Text: Psalm 98:1, 2-3, 3-4, 5-6; David Haas, Marty Haugen
Music: David Haas, Marty Haugen; refrain II, III adapt. by Diana Kodner

56 Psalm 100: We Are God's People

Ostinato Refrain

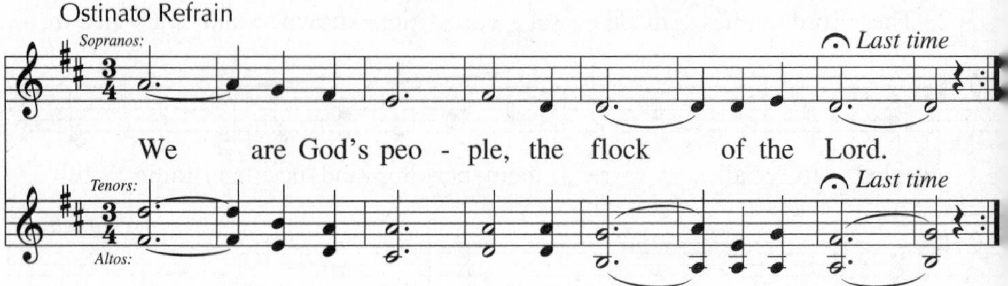
Sopranos:
Last time
We are God's peo - ple, the flock of the Lord.
Tenors:
Last time
Altos:

Verses 1, 3
1. Cry out with joy to the Lord, all you lands, all you lands. Serve the Lord now with glad-ness, come be-fore God sing-ing for joy!
3. Go, now with-in the gates giv-ing thanks, giv-ing thanks. En-ter the courts sing-ing praise, give thanks and bless God's name!
To refrain
Verse 2
2. Know that the Lord is God! Know that the Lord is God, who made us, to God we be-long, God's peo-ple, the sheep of the flock!
To refrain
Verse 4
4. In-deed, how good is the Lord, whose mer-cy en-dures for ev-er, for the Lord, is faith-ful, is faith-ful from age to age!
To refrain

57 Psalm 103: My Soul, Give Thanks to the Lord

Antiphon

My soul, give thanks to the
Lord, and bless God's Ho - ly Name.

Text: Psalm 103:1; © 1963, 1993, The Grail, GIA Publications, Inc., agent
Music: Richard Proulx, © 1986, GIA Publications, Inc.

Psalm Tone

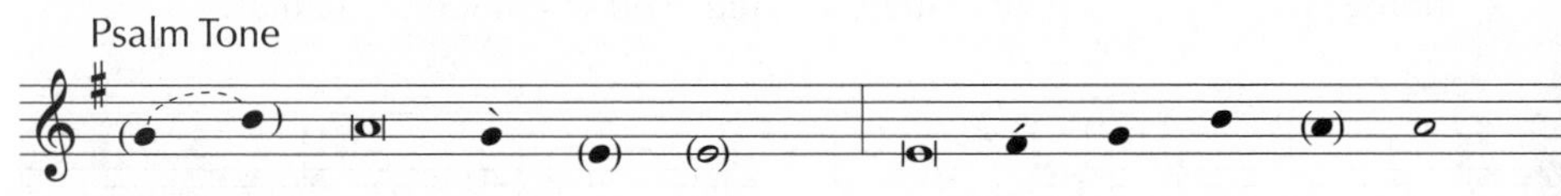

Music: Richard Proulx, © 1986, GIA Publications, Inc.

Gelineau Tone

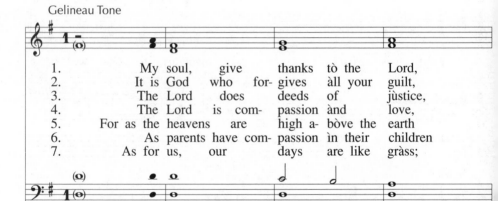

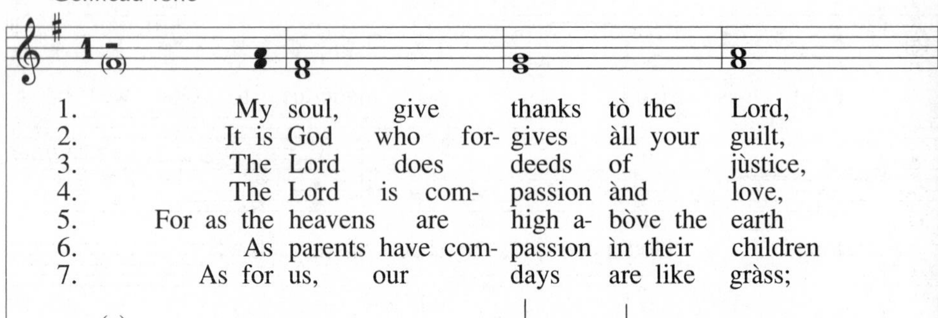
1. My soul, give thanks tò the Lord,
2. It is God who for- gives àll your guilt,
3. The Lord does deeds of jùstice,
4. The Lord is com- passion ànd love,
5. For as the heavens are high a- bòve the earth
6. As parents have com- passion ìn their children
7. As for us, our days are like gràss;

1. all my be- ing bléss God's ho- ly name.
2. who heals every óne of your ills,
3. gives judge- ment for áll who are op- pressed.
4. slow to anger and rích in mercy.
5. so strong is God's love fór the God-fearing;
6. the Lord has pity on those whó are God-fearing;
7. we flower like the flówer of the field;

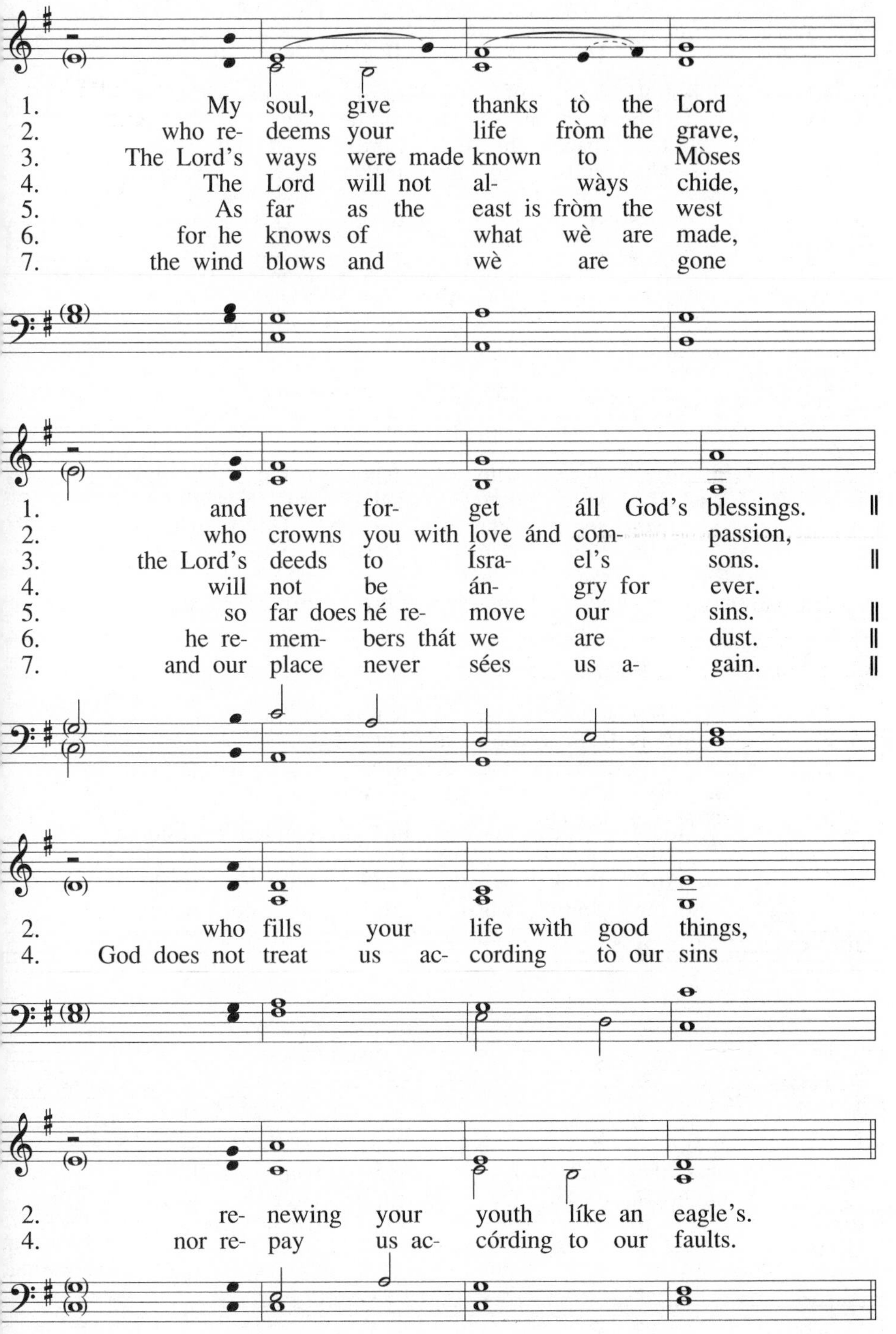
1. My soul, give thanks tò the Lord
2. who re- deems your life fròm the grave,
3. The Lord's ways were made known to Mòses
4. The Lord will not al- wàys chide,
5. As far as the east is fròm the west
6. for he knows of what wè are made,
7. the wind blows and wè are gone
(8)
1. and never for- get áll God's blessings.
2. who crowns you with love ánd com- passion,
3. the Lord's deeds to Ísra- el's sons.
4. will not be án- gry for ever.
5. so far does hé re- move our sins.
6. he re- mem- bers thát we are dust.
7. and our place never sées us a- gain.
2. who fills your life wìth good things,
4. God does not treat us ac- cording tò our sins
(8)
2. re- newing your youth líke an eagle's.
4. nor re- pay us ac- córding to our faults.

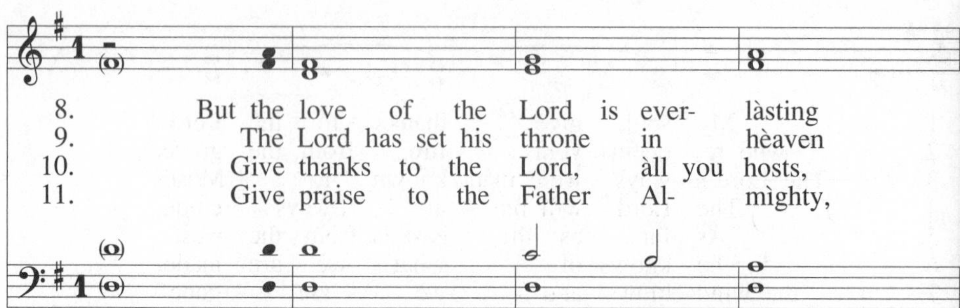
8. But the love of the Lord is ever- làsting
9. The Lord has set his throne in hèaven
10. Give thanks to the Lord, àll you hosts,
11. Give praise to the Father Al- mìghty,

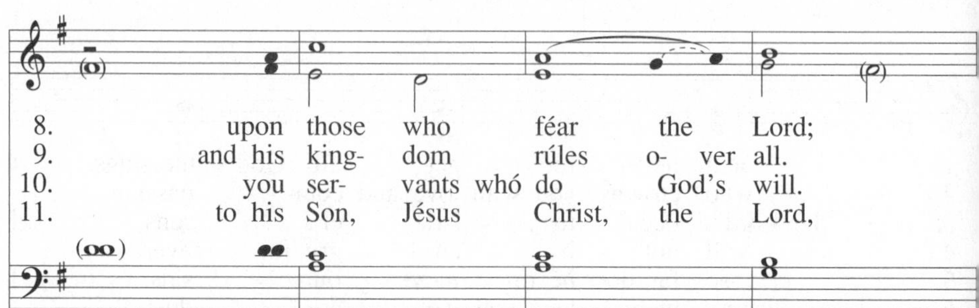
8. upon those who féar the Lord;
9. and his king- dom rúles o- ver all.
10. you ser- vants whó do God's will.
11. to his Son, Jésus Christ, the Lord,

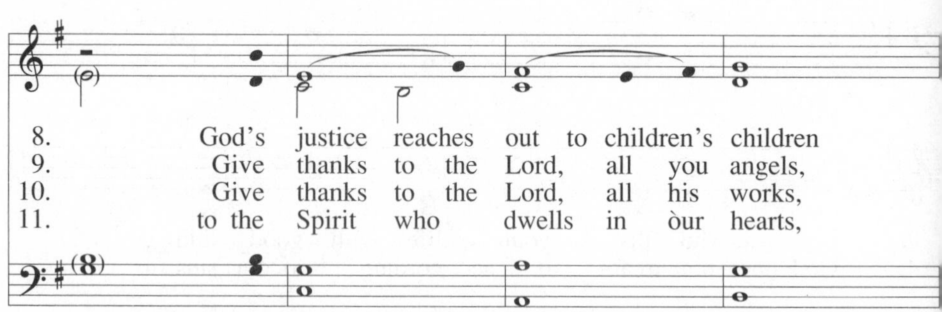
8. God's justice reaches out to children's children
9. Give thanks to the Lord, all you angels,
10. Give thanks to the Lord, all his works,
11. to the Spirit who dwells in òur hearts,

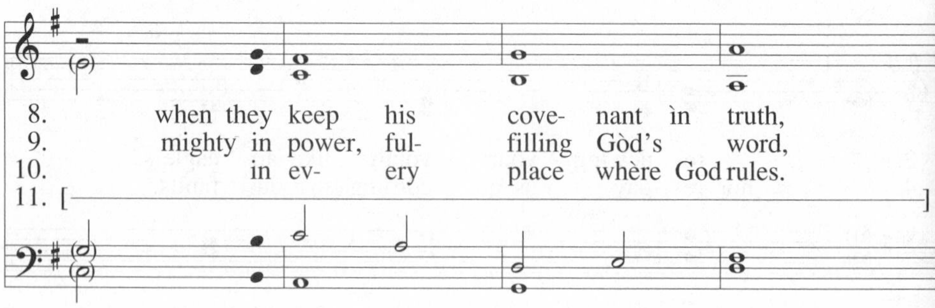
8. when they keep his cove- nant ìn truth,
9. mighty in power, ful- filling Gòd's word,
10. in ev- ery place whère God rules.
11. [ ]

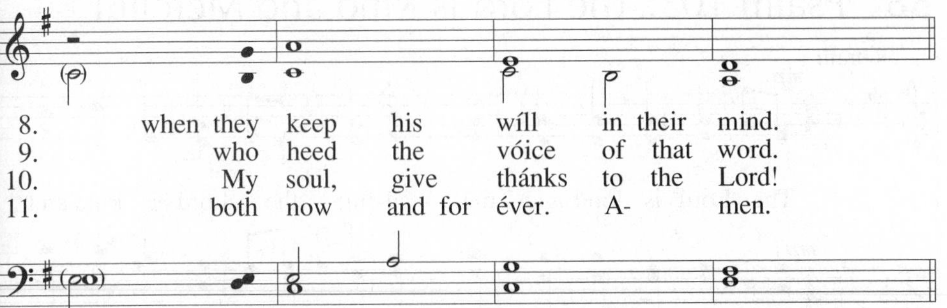
8. when they keep his wíll in their mind.
9. who heed the vóice of that word.
10. My soul, give thánks to the Lord!
11. both now and for éver. A- men.

Text: Psalm 103; The Grail
Music: Joseph Gelineau, SJ

58 Psalm 103: The Lord Is Kind and Merciful

Refrain
mp
The Lord is kind and mer - ci-ful; the Lord is kind and
mer - ci - ful. Slow to an - ger, rich in
kind - ness, the Lord is kind and mer-ci-ful.
1.- 3.
To verses
4.
Verse 1
1. Bless the Lord, O my soul; all my be - ing
bless God's name. Bless the Lord, O my soul; for -
get not all God's bless - ings.
D.C.

Verse 2
mp
2. The Lord is gra - cious and mer - ci - ful, slow to an - ger,
div.
p
full of kind - ness. God is good to all cre - a - tion,
unis.
D.C.
full of com - pas - sion.
Verse 3
mp
3. The good - ness of God is from age to age, bless - ing those who
div.
p
choose to love. And jus - tice toward God's chil - dren; on
unis.
D.C.
all who keep the cov - e - nant.

Text: Psalm 103; Jeanne Cotter
Music: Jeanne Cotter

59 Psalm 103: The Lord Is Kind and Merciful

Refrain
The Lord is kind and mer-ci-ful, the Lord is kind and mer-ci-ful.
Last time
Last time
Verse 1
mf
1. Bless the Lord, O my soul, and all my be-ing bless God's name; bless the Lord, and for-get not God's ben-e-fits.
D.C.
Verse 2
mp
2. God par-dons all your in-iq-ui-ties, and com-forts your sor-rows, re-deems your life from de-struc-tion and crowns you with kind-ness.
D.C.
Verse 3
mf
3. Mer-ci-ful, mer-ci-ful, and gra-cious is our God;

D.C.
slow to an - ger, a - bound - ing in kind - ness.

Text: Psalm 103:1-2, 3-4, 8; para. by Marty Haugen, © 1983, GIA Publications, Inc.; refrain trans. © 1969, ICEL
Music: Marty Haugen, © 1983, GIA Publications, Inc.

Psalm 104: Lord, Send Out Your Spirit 60

Refrain

*1. Lord, send out your 2. Spir - it, and re - 3. new the face of the 4. earth! earth!

Verses

1. Bless the Lord, O my soul, O Lord, my God, you are great in - deed! How man - i - fold are your works, O Lord! The earth is full of your crea - tures!
2. If you take a - way their breath, they die and they re - turn to their dust. When you send forth your Spir - it of life, they are cre - at - ed in your sight!
3. May his glo - ry last for all time; may the Lord be glad in his works. Pleas - ing to him will be my theme; I will be glad in the Lord!

D.C.

May be sung as a canon.

Text: Psalm 104:1, 24, 29-30, 31, 34; Paul Lisicky, © 1985, GIA Publications, Inc.; refrain trans. © 1969, ICEL
Music: Paul Lisicky, © 1985, GIA Publications, Inc.

61 Psalm 116: Our Blessing-Cup / El Cáliz que Bendecimos

Bilingual Refrain
Our bless-ing - cup is a com-mun - ion with the
Our bless-ing - cup is a com - mun - ion with the
Blood of Christ the Lord. El cá-liz que ben-de -
Blood of Christ the Lord. El cá-liz que ben-de -
ci-mos es la co-mu-nión de la san - gre de Cris-to.
Last time
ci - mos co-mu-nión de la san - gre de Cris-to.
Last time
Verses in English
Verse 1
1. How can I re - pay the Lord the good - ness God has
shown to me? The cup of bless - ing I raise; I
call up - on God's name.
D.C.

Verse 2
2. Pain-ful to the eyes of God, the death of faith-ful
ser-vants. I am your ser - vant, your child; you
res - cued me from death.
D.C.
Verse 3
3. Thanks and praise I will of-fer God, and call up - on your
name, Lord. I will ful - fill my vows to the Lord in the
pres - ence of God's peo - ple.
D.C.
Verses in Spanish
Verse 1
1. ¿Có-mo le pa-ga-ré al Se - ñor, mi Dios, to-do el
bien que me ha he-cho? Al-za-ré la co-pa de la sal-va -
ción, e in-vo-ca - ré el nom-bre del Se - ñor.
D.C.

Verse 2

2. Al Se-ñor, que pe-no-sa es la muer-te de sus fie-les.

Soy tu sir-vien-te, tu hi-jo: rom-pi-ste mis ca-de-nas.

D.C.

Verse 3

3. Te o-fre-ce-ré mis gra-cias, Dios, in-vo-can-do tu nom-bre. Cum-pli-ré mis pro-me-sas al Se-ñor en pre-sen-cia de to-do su pue-blo.

D.C.

Text: Psalm 116:12-13, 15-16bc, 17-18; Tony E. Alonso, © 2003, GIA Publications, Inc.; Spanish refrain trans. © 1970, Conferencia Episcopal Española
Music: Tony E. Alonso, © 2003, GIA Publications, Inc.

62 Psalm 116: The Name of God

Refrain I
Descant:
I will take the cup of life, God's name all my days.
Melody:
I will take the cup of life, I will call God's name all my days.
To verses
Last time

Refrain II
Our bless - ing cup is a com - mun - ion with the blood of Christ.
To verses
Last time
Refrain III
In the land of the liv - ing, I will walk with God all my days.
To verses
Last time
Verse 1
1. How can I make a re - turn for the good - ness of God? This sav - ing cup I will bless and sing, and call the name of God!
To refrain
Verse 2
2. The dy - ing of those who keep faith is pre - cious to our God. I am your ser - vant called from your hands, you have set me free!
To refrain
Verse 3
3. To you I will of - fer my thanks and call up - on your name. You are my prom - ise for all to see. I love your name, O God!
To refrain

Text: Psalm 116; David Haas, © 1987, GIA Publications, Inc.; refrain II trans. © 1969, ICEL
Music: David Haas, © 1987, GIA Publications, Inc.

63 Psalm 116: Our Blessing-Cup

Refrain ♩ = 72-76
mp
Our bless - ing - cup is a com - mun - ion with the
blood of the Lord.
To verses
Final ending
Verses ♩ = 76-80
Descant:
Melody:
1. How can I make a re - turn to the Lord for all God has done for me?
2. Pre - cious, in - deed, in the sight of the Lord is the death of the faith - ful ones;
3. Un - to your name I will of - fer my thanks for the debt that I owe to you.

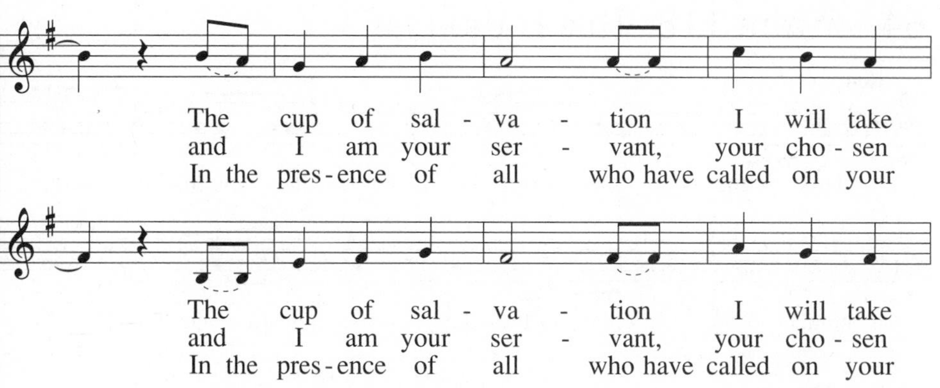
The cup of sal - va - tion I will take
and I am your ser - vant, your cho - sen
In the pres - ence of all who have called on your
The cup of sal - va - tion I will take
and I am your ser - vant, your cho - sen
In the pres - ence of all who have called on your

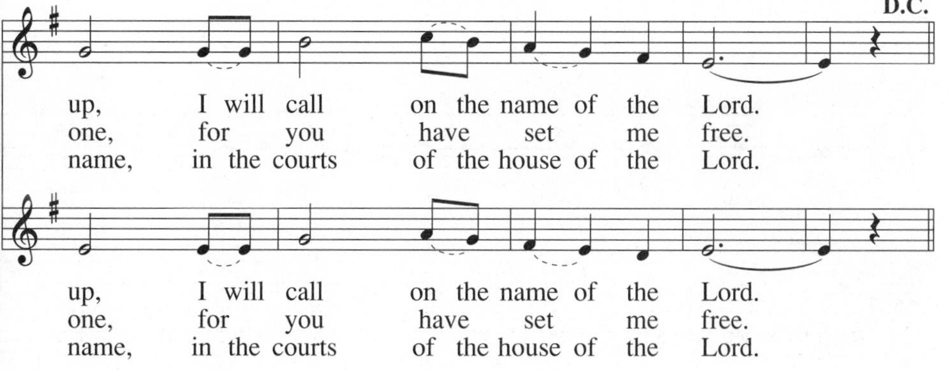
D.C.
up, I will call on the name of the Lord.
one, for you have set me free.
name, in the courts of the house of the Lord.
up, I will call on the name of the Lord.
one, for you have set me free.
name, in the courts of the house of the Lord.

Text: Psalm 116:12-13, 15-16, 17-19; Marty Haugen
Music: Marty Haugen

64 Psalm 118: This Is the Day

Refrain
This is the day the Lord has made; let us re-joice and be glad. This is the day the Lord has made; let us re-joice and be glad.
To verses
Last time
Verse 1
1. Give thanks to the Lord for he is good, his mer-cy en-dures for-ev-er; let the house of Is-ra-el say: "His mer-cy en-dures for-ev-er."
D.C.
Verse 2
2. The Lord's right hand has struck with pow'r, the Lord's right hand is ex-alt-ed; I shall not die, but live and de-clare the works of the Lord.
D.C.

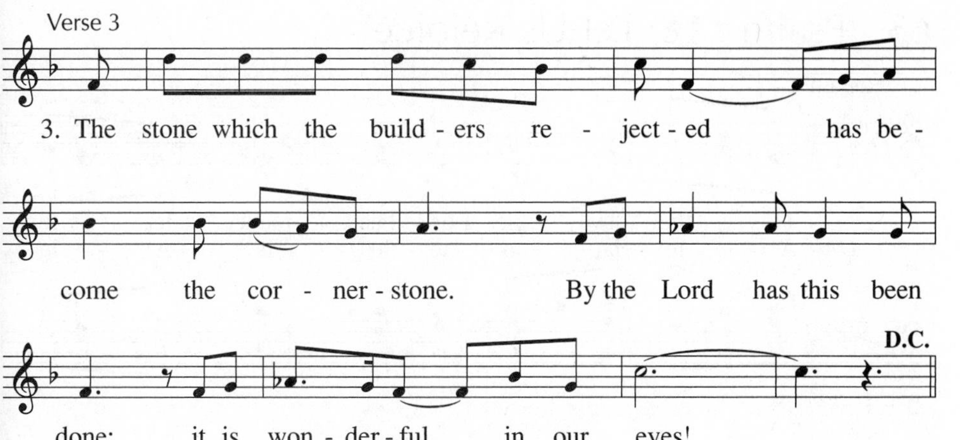
Verse 3
3. The stone which the build - ers re - ject - ed has be -
come the cor - ner - stone. By the Lord has this been
done; it is won - der - ful in our eyes!
D.C.

65 Psalm 118: Let Us Rejoice

Refrain
f
This is the day the Lord has made, let us re - joice and be glad; this is the day the Lord has made, let us re - joice and be glad!
Or: Al - le - lu - ia, al - le - lu - ia! Al - le - lu - ia! Al - le - lu - ia, al - le - lu - ia! Al - le - lu - ia!
Verses 1, 2
Cantors:
mp
1. Give thanks to the Lord, for God is good; God's
2. The hand of the Lord has struck with pow'r, God's
Choir:
mf

Cantors:
Choir:
D.C.
Verse 3
mer - cy en - dures for ev - er; Let the house of
right hand is ex - alt - ed, I shall not die, but
Is - rael say: "God's mer - cy en - dures for ev - er."
live a - new, de - clar - ing the works of the Lord.
3. The stone which the build-ers re - ject - ed has be -
has be - come the
cor - ner - stone,
come the cor - ner - stone, the Lord of love and mer - cy
cor - ner - stone,
has brought won - der to our eyes!

Text: Psalm 118:1-2, 16-17, 22-23; Marty Haugen, © 1983, GIA Publications, Inc.; refrain trans. © 1969, ICEL
Music: Marty Haugen, © 1983, GIA Publications, Inc.

66 Psalm 121: Our Help Comes from the Lord

Refrain
Our help comes from the Lord, the
mak - er of heav - en and earth.
Verse 1
1. I lift up my eyes to the moun - tains: from
where shall come my help? My help shall come from the
D.C.
Lord who made heav - en and earth.
Verse 2
2. May God nev - er al - low you to stum - ble! Let God
3
sleep not, your guard. Nei - ther sleep - ing nor
D.C.
slum - b'ring, God, Is - ra - el's guard.

Verse 3
3. The Lord is your guard and your shade:
and at your right side stands, By day the sun shall not
smite you nor the moon in the night.
D.C.
Verse 4
4. The Lord will guard you from e - vil:
God will guard your soul. The Lord will guard your
go - ing and com - ing both now and for ev - er.
D.C.
Verse 5
5. Glo - ry to the Fa - ther, and to the
Son, and to the Ho - ly Spir - it: as it was in the be -
gin - ning, is now, and will be for ev - er. A - men.
D.C.

67 Psalm 121: Our Help Is from the Lord

Refrain
Our help is from the Lord, the mak-er of heav-en, the mak-er of heav-en and earth.
Last time
Last time
Verse 1
1. I lift my eyes to the moun-tains, from where shall come my help? My help shall come from the Lord, the mak-er of heav-en and earth.
D.C.
Verse 2
2. May our God, ev-er wake-ful, not al-low you to fall. No, he sleeps not nor slum-bers; for Is-ra-el God is at guard.
D.C.

Verse 3
3. God is your guard and pro - tec-tion; by your side God shall
stand. By day the sun shall not harm you, nor the
D.C.
moon in the night.
Verse 4
4. The Lord will shel-ter you from e - vil; God will guard your
soul, will guard your com - ing and your go - ing both
D.C.
now and for - ev - er more.

Text: Psalm 121; Francis Patrick O'Brien
Music: Francis Patrick O'Brien

68 Psalm 122: Let Us Go Rejoicing

Refrain
Let us go re - joic - ing to the house of the Lord;
Let us go to the house of the Lord;
Let us go, O let us go to the house of the Lord;
Let us go, re - joic - ing to the house of the Lord.
Let us go, O let us go to the house of the Lord.
Let us go to the house of the Lord.
Verse 1
1. I re - joiced when I heard them say: "Let us go to the house of the Lord," and now our feet are stand - ing with-in your gates, O Je-ru - sa - lem.
D.C.
Verse 2
2. Je - ru - sa - lem is a cit - y built with u - ni - ty and strength. It is there, it is there that the tribes go up, the tribes of the Lord.
D.C.

Verse 3
3. For Is - ra - el's law is to praise God's name and
there to give God thanks. There are set the
judg - ment thrones for all of Da - vid's house.
D.C.
Verse 4
4. Pray for the peace of Je - ru - sa - lem! "May
those who love you pros - per; May peace ev - er reign with -
in your walls, and wealth with - in your build - ings!"
D.C.
Verse 5
5. For love of my fam - 'ly and love of my friends, I
pray that peace be yours. For love of the house of the
Lord our God I pray for your good.
D.C.

69 Psalm 126: God Has Done Great Things for Us

Refrain
God has done great things for us, filled us with
laugh - ter and mu - sic; God has done great things for
us, filled us with laugh-ter and mu - sic.
Last time
Last time
Verses
Melody:
1. When our God led us back to
2. We pro - claimed to the na - tions what
3. Come re - store our for - tune, re -
Harmony:

free - dom, like dream - ers we be -
you had done for us; your might - y deeds of
new us in your love, as riv - ers through the
held the prom - ised land a - gain;
love, re - stor - ing us to life,
sand, as springs with - in the des - ert;
poco rit.
our mouths were filled with laugh - ter and re -
you lead your peo - ple home to you re -
those who sow in tears shall reap re -
a tempo
poco rit.
D.C.
joic - ing.
joic - ing.
joic - ing.

Text: Psalm 126:1-6; Marty Haugen
Music: Marty Haugen

70 Psalm 128: Blest Are Those Who Love You

Refrain I
Blest are those who love you, hap-py those who
fol - low you, blest are those who seek you, O God.
To verses
Last time
Refrain II
May the Lord bless us, May the Lord pro -
tect us, all the days, all the days of our life.
To verses

Last time
Verse 1
1. Hap - py all those who fear the Lord, and
walk in God's path - way; you will find what you
To refrain
long for: the rich - es of our God.
Verse 2
2. Your spouse shall be like a fruit - ful vine in the
midst of your home, your chil - dren flour - ish like
To refrain
ol - ive plants re - joic - ing at your ta - ble.
Verse 3
3. May the bless - ings of God be yours all the
days of your life, may the peace and the
To refrain
love of God live al - ways in your heart.

Text: Psalm 128:1-2, 3, 5; Marty Haugen
Music: Marty Haugen; refrain II adapt. by Diana Kodner

71 Psalm 130: With the Lord There Is Mercy

Refrain
mp
With the Lord there is mer - cy, and
full - ness of re - demp - tion.
To verses
After final refrain
Verse 1
1. From out of the depths, I cry un - to you, Lord,
hear my voice, come hear my prayer; O let your ear be
o - pen to my plead - ing.
D.C.
Verse 2
2. If you, O Lord, should mark our guilt, then
who could stand with - in your sight? But in
you is found for - give - ness for our fail - ings.
D.C.

Verse 3
3. Just as those who wait for the morn-ing light, e - ven
more I long for the Lord, my God, whose word to me shall
ev - er be my com - fort.
D.C.

Text: Psalm 130:1-2, 3-4, 5-6; Marty Haugen, © 1983, GIA Publications, Inc.; refrain trans. © 1969, ICEL
Music: Marty Haugen, © 1983, GIA Publications, Inc.

72 Psalm 131: My Soul Is Still

Refrain
In you, O Lord, I have found my peace, I have found my peace.
Verse 1
1. My heart is not proud, my eyes not a-bove you; You fill my soul. I am not filled with great things, nor with thoughts be - yond me.
D.C.
Verse 2
2. My soul is still, my soul stays qui-et, long-ing for you like a weaned child in its moth-er's arms; so is my soul a child with you.
D.C.

Psalm 136: Love Is Never Ending 73

Cantor:
1. We give thanks un - to you, O God of might:
2. In your wis - dom and love you shaped the skies:
3. You have filled all the skies with glo - ry and light:
4. From of old you have led your peo - ple in faith:
5. You de - liv - ered the ones who called un - to you:
6. You have o - pened the sea and brought your peo - ple through:
7. You re - mem - ber your prom - ise age to age:
8. You give food and life to all liv - ing things:
mp
(Hum or Ooh)
All: f
for your love is nev - er end - ing,
f
for your love is nev - er end - ing,

Cantor:
We give thanks un - to you, the God of gods:
You spread out the earth up - on the sea:
The sun for the day and moon for night:
You have shown your com - pas - sion, strength and love.
From bond - age to free - dom, you brought them forth:
Brought them in - to a land that flows with life:
You show mer - cy on those of low de - gree:
We give thanks un - to you, the God of all:
mp
(Hum or Ooh)
All: f
for your love is nev - er end - ing.
f
for your love is nev - er end - ing.

Text: Psalm 136; Marty Haugen
Music: Marty Haugen

Psalm 138: The Fragrance of Christ 74

Refrains I-III
mf
I Lord, may our prayer rise like in - cense in your
II In the pres - ence of the an - gels, O
III Lord, on the day that I cried out for
mf
rise in your
of the an - gels,
that I cried for
sight, may this place be filled with the fra-grance of
Lord, may we praise your name, may we praise your
help, you an - swered me, you an - swered
Christ.
name.
me.
1.- 3. To verses
Last time
Verses
mf Melody:
1. I will thank you, Lord, with all of my
2. I will thank you, Lord, for your faith - ful-ness and
3. All who live on earth shall give you
mf Harmony:

heart, you have heard the words of my mouth.
love, be - yond all my hopes and dreams.
thanks when they hear the words of your voice.
f
In the pres - ence of the an - gels I will
On the day that I called you
And all shall sing of your
f
bless you, I will a - dore be -
an - swered; you gave life to the
ways: "How great is the
D.C.
fore your ho - ly tem - ple.
strength of my soul.
glo - ry of God!"
D.C.

Text: Psalm 138:1-5; David Haas
Music: David Haas

Psalm 141: Let My Prayer Rise Up 75

Refrain
All:
Let my prayer rise up like in-cense be - fore you, the
lift-ing up of my hands as an of-fer-ing to you.
Verse 1
Leader or group 1:
1. O God, I call to you, come to me now; O
All or group 2:
1. O God, I call to you,
hear my voice when I cry to you.
come to me now; O hear my voice when I cry to
Refrain
Let my prayer rise up like in-cense be - fore you, the
you. Let my prayer rise up like in-cense be -
lift-ing up of my hands as an of - fer-ing to
fore you, the lift-ing up of my hands as an

Verse 2
you. 2. Keep watch with - in me, God;
of - fer - ing to you. 2. Keep
deep in my heart may the light of your love be
watch with - in me, God; deep in my heart may the
Refrain
burn - ing bright. Let my prayer rise
light of your love be burn - ing bright.
up like in - cense be - fore you, the lift - ing up of my
Let my prayer rise up like in - cense be - fore you, the
hands as an of - fer - ing to you.
lift - ing up of my hands as an of - fer - ing to you.

Verse 3
3. All praise to the God of all– Cre - a - tor of life; all
3. All praise to the God of all– Cre-
praise be to Christ and the Spir - it of love.
a - tor of life; all praise be to Christ and the
Refrain
Let my prayer rise up like in-cense be -
Spir-it of love.
Let my prayer rise up like
fore you, the lift-ing up of my hands as an
in - cense be - fore you, the lift-ing up of my
of-fer-ing to you.
hands as an of-fer-ing to you.

Text: Psalm 141; Marty Haugen
Music: *Holden Evening Prayer,* Marty Haugen

76 Psalm 145: I Will Praise Your Name

Refrain
Assembly:
I will praise your name, my King and my God. I will praise your name, my King and my God.
To verses
Last time
Verse 1
1. I will give you glo - ry, my God a - bove, and
I will bless your name for ev - er. Ev-'ry day

D.C.
I will bless and praise your name for ev - er.
Verse 2
2. The Lord is full of grace and mer - cy,
who is kind and slow to an-ger. God is good in
D.C.
ev-'ry way, and full of com - pas - sion.
Verse 3
3. Let all your works give you thanks, O Lord, and
let all the faith-ful bless you. Let them speak of your
D.C.
might, O Lord, the glo - ry of your king - dom.
Verse 4
4. The Lord is faith - ful in word and deed, and
al-ways near, his name is ho - ly. Lift-ing up all
D.C.
those who fall, God rais - es up the low - ly.

Text: Psalm 145:1-2, 8-9, 10-11, 13b-14; David Haas
Music: David Haas

77 Psalm 147: Bless the Lord, My Soul

Refrain
Bless the Lord, my soul, who
O bless the Lord, my
Bless the Lord, my soul, who
heals the bro - ken - heart - ed.
Last time
soul, who heals the bro - ken - heart - ed.
Last time
heals the bro - ken - heart - ed.
Last time
Verses
1. Praise the Lord, O Je - ru - sa - lem, chant
2. All praise to you, O gra-cious God, your
3. You heal the hurt and bro - ken heart, you
4. The peace of God shall be your hope, God's
prais - es to your God. The strength of God is your
good - ness fills the earth. You raise a - new Je -
bind up ev - 'ry wound, you num - ber all the
fin - est wheat, your food, the word of God fills
D.C.
for - tress sure, and bless - ed are your chil - dren.
ru - sa - lem, and gath - er all your lost ones.
stars of night and call each one by name.
all the earth, as rap - id as the whirl - wind.

Text: Psalm 147:12-13, 1-2, 3-4, 14-15; Marty Haugen
Music: Marty Haugen

Psalm 150: Praise God in This Holy Dwelling 78

Al-le - lu - ia! Al - le - lu - ia! Al-le - lu - ia!
1. Praise God in this ho - ly dwell - ing;
2. Praise God with the blast of trum - pet;
3. Praise God with re - sound - ing cym - bals;
4. Praise God, the al - might - y Fa - ther;
Praise God on the might - y throne;
Bring praise now with lyre and harp;
With cym - bals that crash, give praise;
Praise Christ, the be - lov - ed Son;
Prais - ing for all won - der - ful deeds;
Prais - ing with the tim - brel and dance;
O let ev - 'ry - thing that has breath,
Give praise to the Spir - it of love;

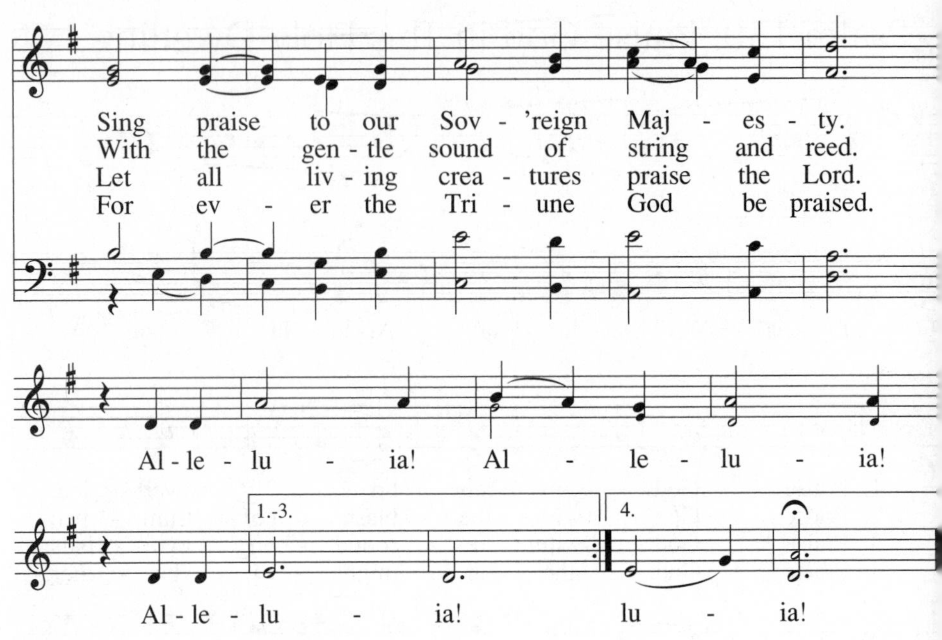
Sing praise to our Sov - 'reign Maj - es - ty.
With the gen - tle sound of string and reed.
Let all liv - ing crea - tures praise the Lord.
For ev - er the Tri - une God be praised.
Al - le - lu - ia! Al - le - lu - ia!
1.-3.
4.
Al - le - lu - ia! lu - ia!

Text: Psalm 150:1-2, 3-4, 5-6; adapt. by Omer Westendorf
Music: Jan M. Vermulst, arr. by Charles G. Frischmann

79 Exodus 15: Song of Moses

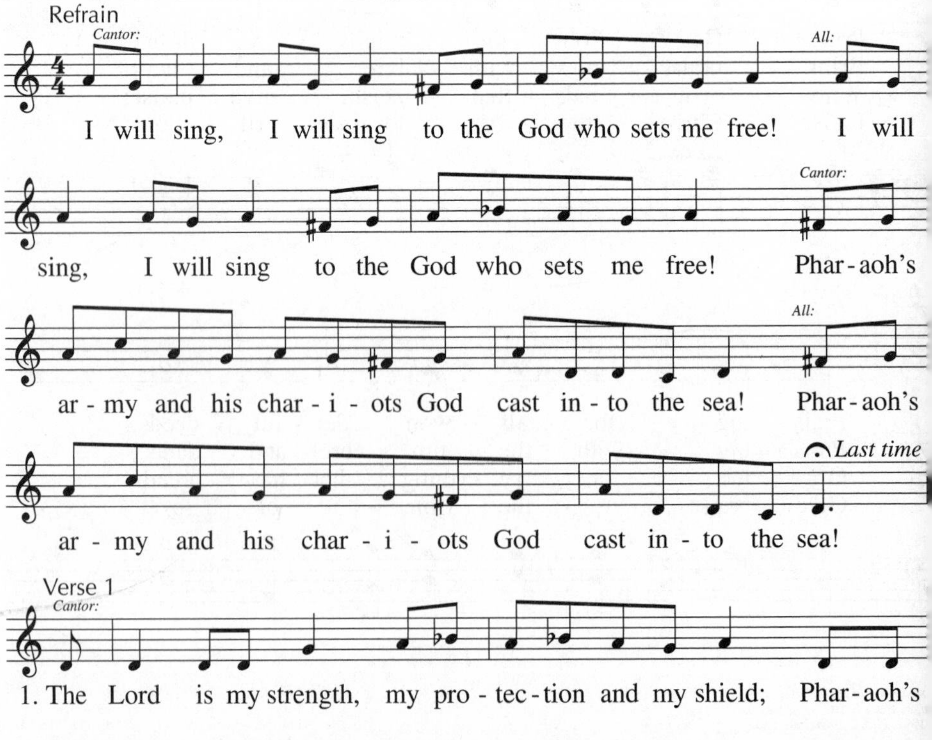

Refrain

Cantor: I will sing, I will sing to the God who sets me free! *All:* I will sing, I will sing to the God who sets me free! *Cantor:* Phar - aoh's ar - my and his char - i - ots God cast in - to the sea! *All:* Phar - aoh's ar - my and his char - i - ots God cast in - to the sea! *Last time*

Verse 1

Cantor: 1. The Lord is my strength, my pro - tec - tion and my shield; Phar - aoh's

ar - my and his char - i - ots God cast in - to the sea. Our
God is a war - ri - or whose name is "the Lord," God of
D.C.
might, God of vic - to - ry!
Verse 2
2. The brave and the might - y, the pride of Phar - aoh's ar - my, God
plunged them to the bot - tom of the sea like a stone. The
hand of the Lord is mag - nif - i - cent in pow - er; the
D.C.
Lord has crushed our foes!
Verse 3
3. O God who re - deems, who de - liv - ers us from slav - 'ry, you
set us on the moun - tain of your ho - ly place. Your
throne and your tem - ple shall en - dure for all time; your
D.C.
reign shall nev - er end!

xt: Exodus 15; Scott Soper
usic: Scott Soper

80 Exodus 15: Song at the Sea

Refrain
Melody:
Let us sing to the Lord who is
Harmony:
Let us sing, sing to the Lord,
Last time
cov - ered in won - drous glo - ry.
Last time
Verse 1
1. I will sing to the Lord, in glo - ry tri -
um - phant; horse and rid - er are thrown to
the sea. God of strength, of song, of sal -
va - tion, God of mine, hear these prais - es.
D.C
Verse 2
2. My God is a war - rior whose name is "The

Lord." Phar-oah's ar-my is thrown to the
sea. Your right hand is mag-nif-i-cent in pow'r, your right
hand has crushed the en-e-my.
D.C.
Verse 3
3. In your mer-cy you led the peo-ple you redeemed. You brought them to your
sa-cred home. There you will
plant them on the moun-tain that is yours. The
shall reign
Lord shall reign for-ev-er!
D.C.

ext: Exodus 15; Niamh O'Kelly-Fischer
lusic: Niamh O'Kelly-Fischer

81 Isaiah 12: With Joy You Shall Draw Water

Refrain I
With joy you shall draw wa - ter from the
springs of end - less life; With joy you shall draw
springs of end - less, end - less life; With joy you shall draw
life;
springs of end - less, end - less life; joy you shall draw
wa - ter from the
Last time
To verses
wa - ter from the liv - ing well of God.
Last time
Last time
Refrain II
Cry out with joy and glad - ness, for the

Lord is in your midst, the ho - ly one of
Lord is in, is in your midst, the ho - ly one of
Lord is in your midst,
Lord is in, is in your midst, ho - ly one of
Is - ra - el, cry out, cry out with joy.
Last time
To verses
Is - ra - el, cry out, cry out with joy.
Last time
Last time
Verses
Melody:
1. God in - deed is my Sav - ior, I will
2. Give thanks and praise the name of God, sing
3. Shout with joy, O Zi - on, for
Harmony:
nev - er be a - fraid, my strength and cour - age
out to all the earth the won - drous deeds that
dwell - ing in your midst is the Ho - ly One of
To refrain
is the Lord, my Sav - ior and my song.
God has done, our Sav - ior and our song.
Is - ra - el, your Sav - ior and your song.

Text: Isaiah 12:2-3, 4, 6; Marty Haugen
Music: Marty Haugen; refrain II adapt. by Diana Kodner

82 Daniel 3:52-90: Canticle of Daniel

Refrain
Last time
God is praised and ex - alt - ed a-bove all for - ev - er.
Last time
Verse 1
Assembly (response for every verse):
Bless the Lord!
1. An - gels of the Lord, you
Bless the Lord!
heav - ens, all wa - ters a-bove the
Bless the Lord!
heav - ens, all you hosts of the
D.C.
Lord, sun and moon, stars of heav - en, bless the Lord!
Verse 2
Bless the Lord!
2. Ev - 'ry show - er and dew, all
Bless the Lord!
wind and heat, cold and chill, dew and
Bless the Lord!
rain, ice and snow, nights and

D.C.
days, lights and dark - ness and clouds, bless the Lord!
Verse 3
Bless the Lord!
3. Moun - tains and hills, ev-'ry-thing
Bless the Lord!
grow-ing from the earth, springs, seas and
Bless the Lord!
riv-ers, all wa-ter crea-tures, all you
D.C.
birds, all you beasts, sons of man, bless the Lord!
Verse 4
Bless the Lord!
4. O Is - ra - el, priests and ser-vants of the
Bless the Lord
3
Lord, spir-its and souls of the just,
Bless the Lord!
3
ho-ly men, hum-ble of heart, Ha-nan-iah, Az-a -
D.C.
ri - ah, Mish - a - el, bless the Lord!

Text: Daniel 3:52-90; adapt. from the *New American Bible,* © 1970, Confraternity of Christian Doctrine, Inc.
Music: John Angotti; arr. by Paul A. Tate, © 2002, World Library Publications

83 Luke 1:46-55: Holy Is Your Name

Verses
1. My soul is filled with joy as I sing to God my sav-ior: you have looked up-on your ser-vant, you have vis-it-ed your peo-ple.
2. I am low-ly as a child, but I know from this day for-ward that my name will be re-mem-bered, for all will call me bless-ed.
3. I pro-claim the pow'r of God, you do mar-vels for your ser-vants; though you scat-ter the proud heart-ed and de-stroy the might of princ-es.
4. To the hun-gry you give food, send the rich a-way emp-ty. In your mer-cy you are mind-ful of the peo-ple you have cho-sen.
5. In your love you now ful-fill what you prom-ised to your peo-ple. I will praise you, Lord, my sav-ior, ev-er-last-ing is your mer-cy.
Refrain
And ho-ly is your name through all gen-er-a-tions! Ev-er-last-ing is your mer-cy to the peo-ple you have cho-sen, and ho-ly is your name.
Final ending

Text: Luke 1:46-55, David Haas
Music: WILD MOUNTAIN THYME, Irregular; Irish traditional; arr. by David Haas

Luke 1:46-55: Magnificat 84

Refrain
Descant:
Pro - claim the great-ness of God; re - joice in God. Re - joice in God, my Sav-ior!
Melody:
Pro - claim the great-ness of God; re - joice in God, my Sav-ior! Re - joice in God, my Sav - ior!
Verses
unis.
1. For he has fa - vored his low - ly one, and all shall call me bless - ed. The al - might - y has done great things for me, and ho - ly is his name.
2. He fa - vors those who fear his name, in ev - 'ry gen - er - a - tion. He has shown the might and strength of his arm, and scat-tered the proud of heart.
3. He has cast the might - y from their thrones, and lift - ed up the low - ly. He has filled the hun - gry with all good gifts, and sent the rich a - way.
4. He has helped his ser - vant Is - ra - el, re - mem - ber - ing his mer - cy. He prom - ised his mer - cy to A - bra - ham and his chil - dren for ev - er - more.
div.
Melody:
D.C.

Text: Luke 1:46-55; James J. Chepponis
Music: James J. Chepponis

85 Luke 2: Nunc Dimittis

Descant:
3. Sign of won - der, man - y rise and fall. In the si - lence break our walls. O Lord, O Lord, now our
Melody:
1. Now, O Lord, dis-miss your ser-vants With your word; give us re-lease. For our eyes have seen sal-va - tion, Prom-ised ev - er to in-crease. Lord, dis-miss us, Lord, dis - miss us; Now let us de -
2. Light, en-light - 'ning ev - 'ry peo-ple, Glo - ry of your Is - ra - el. Seen in vi - sions of the sag - es, Heard in what the proph-ets tell. Lord, dis-miss us, Lord, dis - miss us; Now in ev - 'ry
3. Child of Mar - y, sing of won-der, By you, man - y rise and fall. In the speak - ing and the si - lence, Pierce our hearts and break our walls. Lord, dis-miss us, Lord, dis - miss us; Now, our God, our

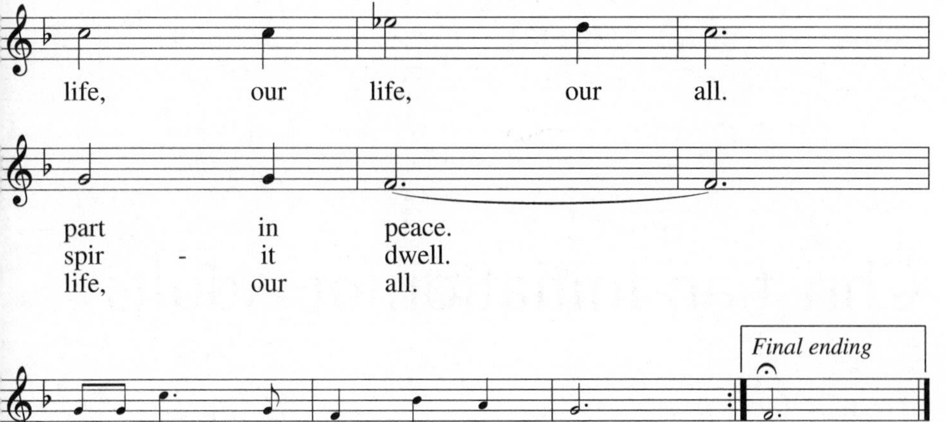
life, our life, our all.
part in peace.
spir - it dwell.
life, our all.
Final ending

Text: *Nunc Dimittis,* Sylvia Dunstan, © 1995, GIA Publications, Inc.
Music: PEACETIME, 8 7 8 7 8 7; David Haas, © 2003, GIA Publications, Inc.

Christian Initiation of Adults

86
The passage of an adult into the Christian community takes place over an extended period of time. The members of the local church, the catechists and sponsors, the clergy and the diocesan bishop take part in the journey from inquiry through the catechumenate to baptism, confirmation and eucharist. The candidates are invited by example to pray, reflect on the scriptures, to fast and to join in the community's practice of charity. They are to learn the way of Jesus from the members of the church.

This journey of the candidates and community is marked by liturgical rites; thus the community publicly acknowledges, encourages and strengthens the candidates. The first of these is the rite of becoming catechumens. It concludes the sometimes lengthy period during which those who have come to ask about the way of the church and the life of a Christian have heard the gospel proclaimed and seen it practiced. Those who then feel called to walk in this way of Christ's church ask to begin the journey toward baptism. If the church judges the inquirers ready, they are accepted into the order of catechumens.

Those who have entered the catechumenate are already part of the household of Christ. During this time the catechumens are to hear and reflect on God's word, to learn the teachings and practices of the church, to become gradually accustomed to the ways of prayer and discipline in the church, to observe and to join in the good works of Christians. Ordinarily the catechumens are present on Sunday for the liturgy of the word and may be dismissed after the homily—to continue prayer and study with their catechists—since they cannot join in the eucharist.

Rites of exorcism and blessing may be celebrated during the catechumenate. Through such rites the church prays that the catechumens will be purified, strengthened against all evil and thus eagerly grow in faith and good works. The very presence of the catechumens—at the Sunday liturgy, in these special rites and in everyday life—is itself a source of strength and blessing to the faithful.

Each year as Lent begins, the bishop, with the help of the local pastor and others involved with the catechumens, is to call those catechumens who are judged ready to prepare themselves for baptism at the Easter Vigil. Thus the catechumens become the "elect", the chosen, and for the forty days of Lent they make preparations: praying, fasting, doing good works. All the faithful join them in this. On several Sundays in Lent the rites of scrutiny take place when the assembled church prays over the elect. During Lent also the catechumens may publicly receive the words of the church's creed and of the Lord's Prayer.

Good Friday and Holy Saturday are days of prayer, fasting and preparation for the rites of the Easter Vigil. On the night between Saturday and Sunday, the church assembles to keep vigil and listen to many readings from scripture. Then the catechumens are called forward for baptism and confirmation. These rites are found in the Easter Vigil.

The newly baptized, now called neophytes, take a special place in the Sunday eucharist throughout the fifty days of Eastertime. This is a time for their full incorporation into the local community.

All of these stages of initiation take place in the midst of the community. In various rites, the faithful show the Christian life to the inquirers and catechumens. In turn, the faithful are strengthened and challenged in their faith by the presence of the catechumens.

Those who seek to belong to the Roman Catholic church and who are already baptized may take some part in the catechumenate but they are not baptized again. Rather, they are received into the full communion of the Roman Catholic Church.

ACCEPTANCE INTO THE ORDER OF CATECHUMENS 87

INTRODUCTORY RITES

The presider greets the assembly: candidates, sponsors, members of the parish. The candidates are asked what it is that they seek and each replies. After each candidate has responded, the following may be sung:

88

rit.
We stand with you, we pray for you, O ho-ly child of God!

Text: David Haas
Music: David Haas

89

We praise you, Lord, we praise you, Lord,
we praise you, Lord, and we bless you.

Music: Marty Haugen,

CANDIDATES' FIRST ACCEPTANCE OF THE GOSPEL

The presider solemnly asks if the candidates are ready to begin walking this way of the gospel. The sponsors and all present are asked if they stand ready to assist the candidates as they strive to know and follow Christ. All respond: **We are.**

SIGNING OF THE CANDIDATES WITH THE CROSS

The sign of the cross marks the candidates for their new way of life. The presider signs each on the forehead saying:

N., receive the cross on your forehead.
It is Christ himself who now strengthens you
with this sign of his love.
Learn now to know him and follow him.

Sponsors and others also sign the candidates. Ears and eyes and other senses may also be signed. The presider prays that the catechumens may share in the saving power of the cross.

One of the following musical settings with assembly acclamations may be used:

90

mp
Priest: Receive the sign of the cross....
All:
Christ will be your strength! Learn to know and fol - low him.

Music: David Haas, © 1988, GIA Publications, Inc.

91

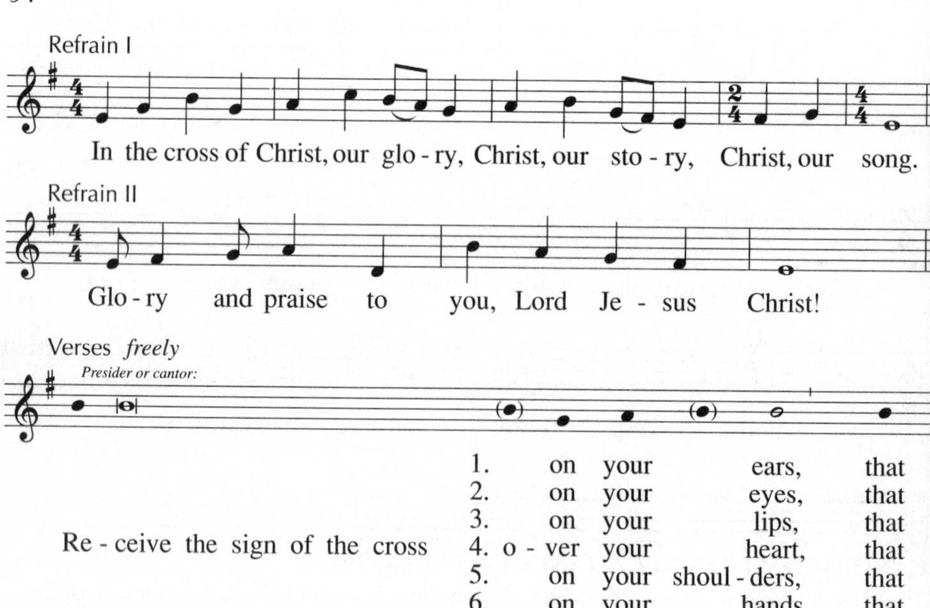
Refrain I
In the cross of Christ, our glo - ry, Christ, our sto - ry, Christ, our song.
Refrain II
Glo - ry and praise to you, Lord Je - sus Christ!
Verses freely
Presider or cantor:
Re - ceive the sign of the cross
1. on your ears, that
2. on your eyes, that
3. on your lips, that
4. o - ver your heart, that
5. on your shoul - ders, that
6. on your hands, that
7. on your feet, that

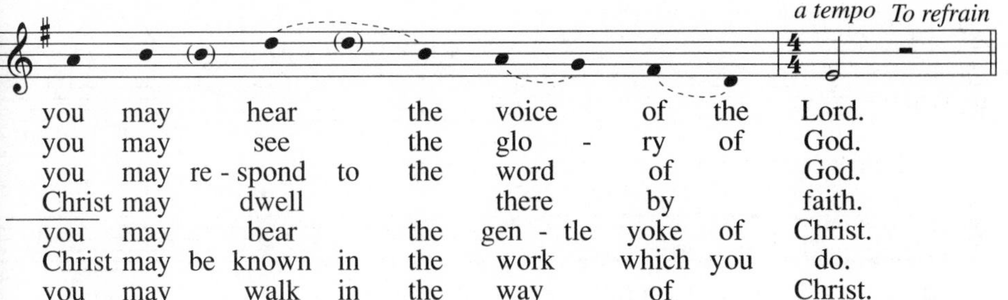
a tempo
To refrain
you may hear the voice of the Lord.
you may see the glo - ry of God.
you may re - spond to the word of God.
Christ may dwell there by faith.
you may bear the gen - tle yoke of Christ.
Christ may be known in the work which you do.
you may walk in the way of Christ.

Text: Adapt. by Marty Haugen
Music: Marty Haugen

INVITATION TO THE CELEBRATION OF THE WORD OF GOD 92

The assembly may go into the church for the liturgy of the word singing the following psalm:

Refrain

Descant:

Come, my chil - dren, come to me, and

Melody:

Come, my chil - dren, come to me, and

1. *To verses*

you will know the fear of the Lord.

you will know the fear of the Lord.

Last time

Lord.

Lord.

Verses

2.- 4. *Descant:* *Melody:*

Lord.

Cantor:

1. I will bless the Lord at all times, God's song is al - ways on my lips. In the Lord my soul shall make its boast, the hum - ble will hear and be glad.
2. Glo - ry in the Lord with me, May God's name al - ways be our joy. God an - swered me when I cried, and freed me from my fear.
3. Look to God and shine with joy! May God free your fac - es from all shame! God hears the cry of all the poor, and saves all who live in their fear.

D.C.

Text: Psalm 34; adapt. by David Haas
Music: David Haas

93 LITURGY OF THE WORD

There may be one or more readings from scripture, together with a responsorial psalm. After the homily, a book containing the scriptures may be given to the new catechumens for their study and prayer throughout the time of the catechumenate.

INTERCESSIONS

All join in prayer for the new catechumens.

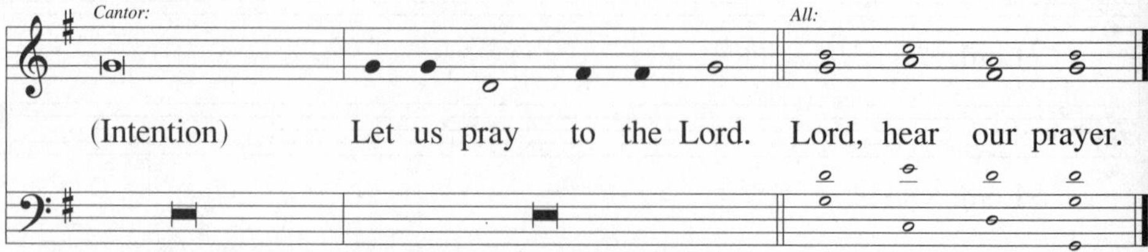
Cantor:
(Intention)
Let us pray to the Lord.
All:
Lord, hear our prayer.

Music: Byzantine chant; harm. by Robert J. Batastini,

RITES OF THE CATECHUMENATE 94

DISMISSAL OF THE CATECHUMENS

When the catechumens are present at Mass, they are usually dismissed after the homily. Only when they have been baptized are they able to join the faithful in the reception of the eucharist. After their dismissal, the catechumens remain together and are joined by their catechists or others to pray and reflect on the scripture.

The following may be sung to accompany the dismissal: 95

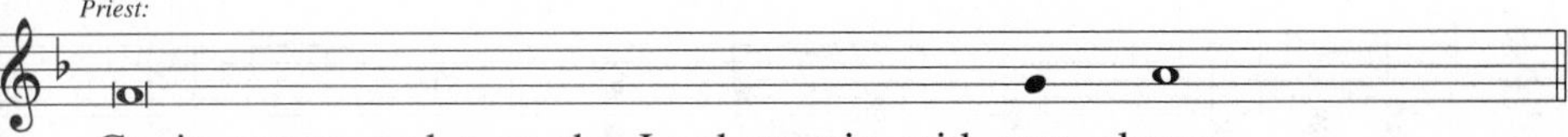
Priest:
Go in peace, and may the Lord remain with you always.

All:
Go now in peace, go now in peace,
Christ will be your way, your truth, your life.

Text: *Rite of Christian Initiation of Adults*, © 1985, ICEL
Music: Lynn Trapp, © 1991, Morning Star Music Publishers

96

Repeat as needed
Go in peace, the peace of Christ, and learn the ways of God.

Text: Marty Haugen
Music: Marty Haugen
© 1997, GIA Publications, Inc.

97

May the Word be a lamp for our feet,
and a light to guide our path!

Text: David Haas
Music: David Haas

CELEBRATIONS OF THE WORD OF GOD

On Sundays, after the catechetical sessions, before the liturgical seasons and at other times the catechumens and others may join for liturgy: song, reading of scripture, psalmody, prayer and silence are normally part of such a service.

MINOR EXORCISMS

At appropriate times during the catechumenate, the catechists or other ministers may lead the community in prayers of exorcism over the catechumens. These prayers acknowledge the struggle against evil and ask that God strengthen the catechumens.

BLESSINGS OF THE CATECHUMENS

Prayers of blessing and the laying on of hands may take place whenever the catechumens gather for instruction of other purposes. Catechists or other ministers ask these blessings over the catechumens.

ANOINTINGS AND PRESENTATIONS

During the catechumenate or during Lent, the candidates may be anointed with the oil of catechumens as a sign of strength given for their struggle to live the gospel. At some point in this time they are publicly presented with the church's treasury of prayer and faith, the Our Father and the Creed.

RITE OF ELECTION OR ENROLLMENT OF NAMES

At the beginning of Lent, it is the responsibility of the bishop to call those who are judged ready to prepare for the sacraments of initiation at Easter. The bishop is to consult first with the pastors, catechists and others. The rite may take place at the cathedral. If the rite takes place in the parish church, the bishop may designate the pastor to act in his place.

This rite is also called the "Enrollment of Names." Each candidate now gives his/her name, or writes it down. When all have been enrolled, the bishop says: "You have been chosen to be initiated into the sacred mysteries at the Easter Vigil." He then speaks to them and to their sponsors about their lenten preparation for baptism.

While or immediately after the candidates have signed their names, a hymn or acclamation (e.g., no. 794) may be sung.

SCRUTINIES 98

The scrutinies occur on the Third, Fourth and Fifth Sundays of Lent. The elect are called before the community for exorcism and prayer. This rite may conclude with the following song, sung prior to dismissal of the elect:

Refrain
First Scrutiny: God of all pow-er, foun-tain of grace: O liv-ing wa - ter, show your face! God of all pow-er, foun-tain of grace: O liv-ing wa - ter, show your face!
Second Scrutiny: God of all mer-cy, re - store our sight: Lead us from dark-ness in - to light! God of all mer-cy, re - store our sight: Lead us from dark - ness in - to light!
Third Scrutiny: God of the liv-ing, not of the dead: Raise us to life be-yond our death! God of the liv-ing, not of the dead: Raise us to life be - yond our death!
rit.
Last time
Verses
Freely
First Scrutiny: 1. Come to us, O liv - ing wa - ter, Lord, we thirst for
2. Come to us, God of for - give - ness, foun - tain of our
3. Come to us, God of com - pas - sion, com - fort in our
Second Scrutiny: 1. Come to us, Lord Je - sus, O king - dom of all
2. Come to us, light in our dark - ness, help us all to
3. Come to us, O sav - ing light, burn with - in our
Third Scrutiny: 1. Come to us, O ris - en Christ, prom - ise of new
2. Come to us, O ho - ly one, vic - t'ry from the
3. Come to us, Great God of pow - er, sign to all the

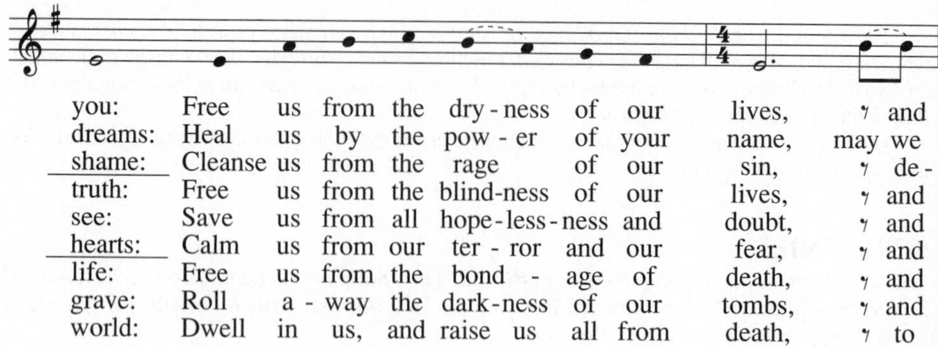
4/4
you: Free us from the dry - ness of our lives, and
dreams: Heal us by the pow - er of your name, may we
shame: Cleanse us from the rage of our sin, de -
truth: Free us from the blind-ness of our lives, and
see: Save us from all hope-less-ness and doubt, and
hearts: Calm us from our ter - ror and our fear, and
life: Free us from the bond - age of death, and
grave: Roll a - way the dark-ness of our tombs, and
world: Dwell in us, and raise us all from death, to

D.C.
3/4
pur - i - fy our hearts to hear your word!
drink of you and nev - er thirst a - gain!
liv - er us, and keep us in your peace!
lead us to the vi - sion of your light!
o - pen up our eyes to fol - low you!
show to us the free - dom of your way!
share with us the hope of your glo - ry!
breathe in us the won - der of new life!
live, to pray, to heal, and to for - give!

Text: David Haas
Music: David Haas

PREPARATORY RITES

Various preparation rites take place during the day on Holy Saturday. These include prayer, recitation of the Creed, and the rite of Ephphetha (opening of ears and mouth).

SACRAMENTS OF INITIATION

The sacraments of initiation take place at the Easter Vigil.

PERIOD OF MYSTAGOGIA

"Mystagogia" refers to the fifty-day period of postbaptismal celebration when the newly baptized are gradually drawn by the community into the fullness of Christian life and prayer. The newly baptized retain a special place in the assembly and are mentioned in the prayers of intercession. A special celebration, on Pentecost or just before, may mark the conclusion of the whole period of initiation.

The Baptism of Children

99

Children are baptized in the faith of the church: of parents, godparents, the local parish, the church throughout the world, the saints. Bringing their children for baptism, the parents profess their commitment to make a home where the gospel is lived. And the godparents and all members of the community promise to support the parents in this. Thus the children enter the waters of baptism and so are joined to this people, all baptized into the death and resurrection of Christ.

Baptism is celebrated above all at the Easter Vigil, but also on other Sundays, for Sunday is the Lord's day, the day when the church gathers to proclaim the paschal mystery. Although baptism may take place at the Sunday Mass, it is always to be celebrated in an assembly of members of the church.

RECEPTION OF THE CHILDREN 100

The parents and godparents are welcomed by all. The priest/deacon asks the names of the children and questions the parents about their own expectations and willingness to take on the responsibilities this baptism brings. The godparents are asked if they are ready to assist the parents to become Christian mothers and fathers.

With joy, then, the priest/deacon, the parents and godparents make the sign of the cross on the child's forehead: "I claim you for Christ our Savior by the sign of his cross."

All then go in procession to the place where the scriptures will be read. The following antiphon, or a hymn, may be sung during this procession:

The assembly repeats each phrase after the cantor.

Cantor:
There is one God and

Fa - ther of all,
He is
Assembly:
There is one God and Fa-ther of all,
o - ver all and through all,
He lives in all of us;
He is o-ver all and through all,
He
All of us are one,
u -
lives in all of us;
All of us are one,
nit - ed in Christ Je - sus.
u - nit - ed in Christ
repeat ad lib.
Je - sus.

Text: ICEL, © 1969
Music: Marty Haugen, © 1995, GIA Publications, Inc.

LITURGY OF THE WORD

101

FIRST READINGS

One or more passages from scripture are read. At the conclusion of each:

Reader: The word of the Lord.
Assembly: **Thanks be to God.**

RESPONSORIAL PSALM

The following psalm may follow the first reading:

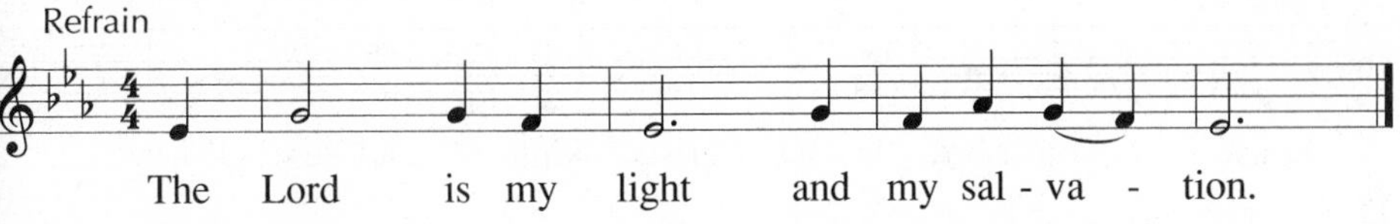
Refrain
The Lord is my light and my sal - va - tion.

Text: *Lectionary for Mass,* © 1969, ICEL
Music: Anthony E. Jackson, © 1984

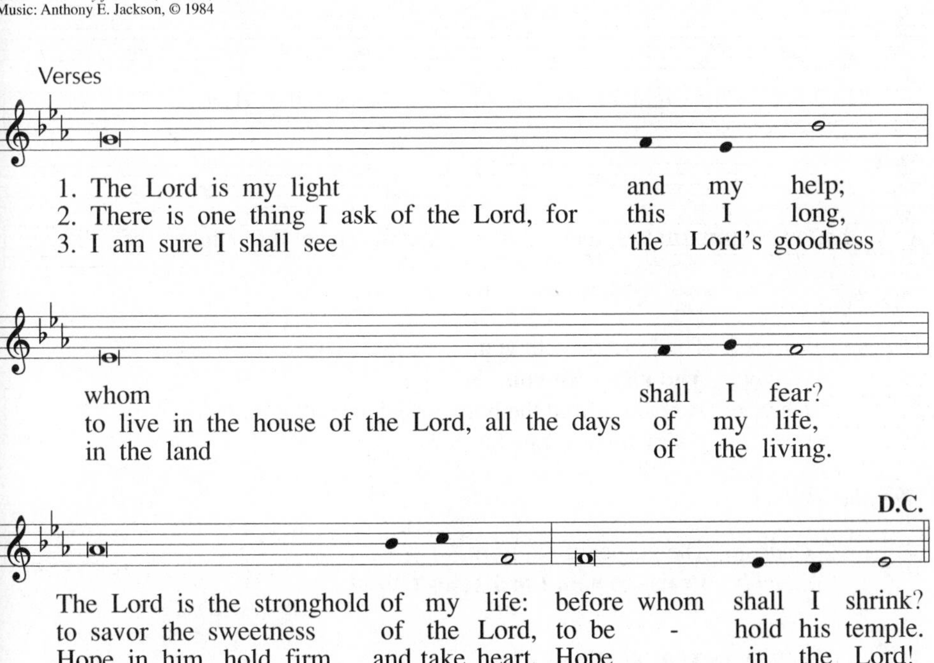
Verses
1. The Lord is my light and my help;
2. There is one thing I ask of the Lord, for this I long,
3. I am sure I shall see the Lord's goodness
whom shall I fear?
to live in the house of the Lord, all the days of my life,
in the land of the living.
D.C.
The Lord is the stronghold of my life: before whom shall I shrink?
to savor the sweetness of the Lord, to be - hold his temple.
Hope in him, hold firm and take heart. Hope in the Lord!

Text: Psalm 27:1, 4, 13-14, © 1963, The Grail, GIA Publications, Inc., agent
Music: Cyril Baker, © The Antilles Episcopal Conference

102 GOSPEL

Before the gospel reading, this acclamation is sung:

Cantor, then all:
Al-le-lu-ia, al - le-lu - ia, al - le - lu - ia.

During Lent:

Cantor, then all:
Praise to you, Lord Je - sus Christ, king of end-less glo - ry!

Cantor:
I am the light of the world, says the Lord;

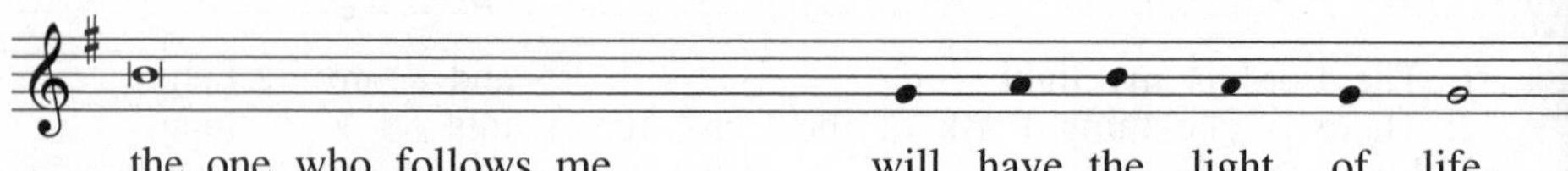
the one who follows me will have the light of life.

Deacon (or priest): The Lord be with you.
Assembly: **And also with you.**
Deacon: A reading from the holy gospel according to N.
Assembly: **Glory to you, Lord.**

After the reading:

Deacon: The gospel of the Lord.
Assembly: **Praise to you, Lord Jesus Christ.**

103 GENERAL INTERCESSIONS

All join in prayer for the church, the needs of the world, the poor, the children to be baptized and their parents.

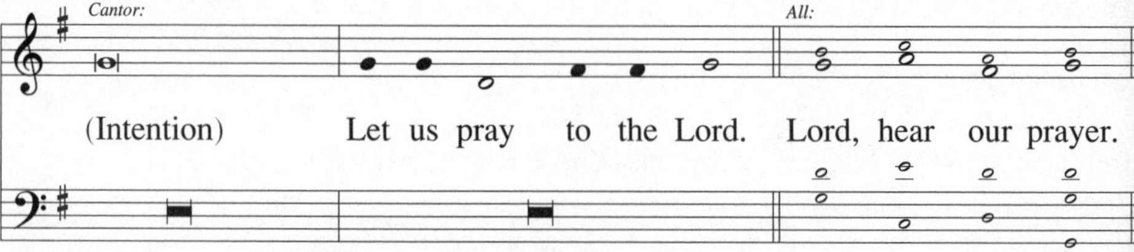
Cantor:
All:
(Intention) Let us pray to the Lord. Lord, hear our prayer.

This prayer concludes with the litany of the saints which may include the patron saints of the children and of the local church.

104

Cantor: *All:*

1. Holy Mary, Mother of God, pray for us.
2. Saint John the Bap - tist, pray for us.
3. Saint Jo - seph, pray for us.
4. Saint Peter and Saint Paul, pray for us.

The names of other saints may be added here. The litany concludes:

5. All you saints of God, pray for us.

PRAYER OF EXORCISM AND ANOINTING 105

The priest/deacon stands before the parents with their infants and prays that God deliver these children from the power of evil. The children may be anointed with the oil of catechumens, an anointing which makes them strong for their struggle against evil in their lives or the priest/deacon may lay hands on each child. The priest/deacon lays hands on each child to show the love and concern the Church has for them. If there is a procession to the baptistry, the following may be sung:

Cantor, then all:
We come to you, Lord Je - sus, fill us with your
1. life. We
2. life. Make us
Cantor:
chil - dren of the
Fa - ther and one in
1. you. Make us
All:
2. you.

Text: ICEL, © 1969
Music: Ronald Arnatt, © 1984, GIA Publications, Inc.

SACRAMENT OF BAPTISM 106

BLESSING AND INVOCATION OF GOD OVER BAPTISMAL WATER

When all are gathered at the font, the priest/deacon leads a blessing of the water, unless the baptismal water has already been blessed.

RENUNCIATION OF SIN AND PROFESSION OF FAITH

The priest/deacon then questions the parents and godparents, and they make a renunciation of sin and evil and profess their faith. The assembly listens to their responses. The priest/deacon then invites all to give their assent to this profession of faith:

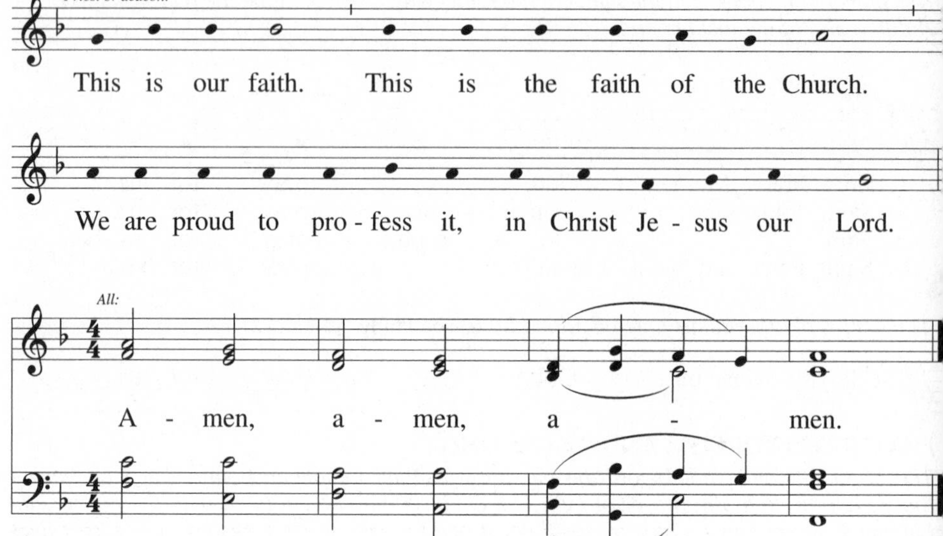
Priest or deacon:
This is our faith. This is the faith of the Church.
We are proud to pro - fess it, in Christ Je - sus our Lord.
All:
A - men, a - men, a - men.

Text: ICEL, © 1969
Music: Danish Amen

107 BAPTISM

One by one, the infants are brought to the font by their parents. There the parents express their desire to have their child baptized in the faith of the church which they have professed. The infant is then immersed in the water three times (or water is poured over the infant's head three times) as the priest/deacon says: "N., I baptize you in the name of the Father, and of the Son, and of the Holy Spirit." All may respond to each baptism with an acclamation.

f
p Cantor:
You have put on Christ, in him you have been bap - tized.
Al - le - lu - ia, al - le - lu - ia.
mf *1. 2.
All:
You have put on Christ, in him you have been bap - tized.

*May be sung in canon.

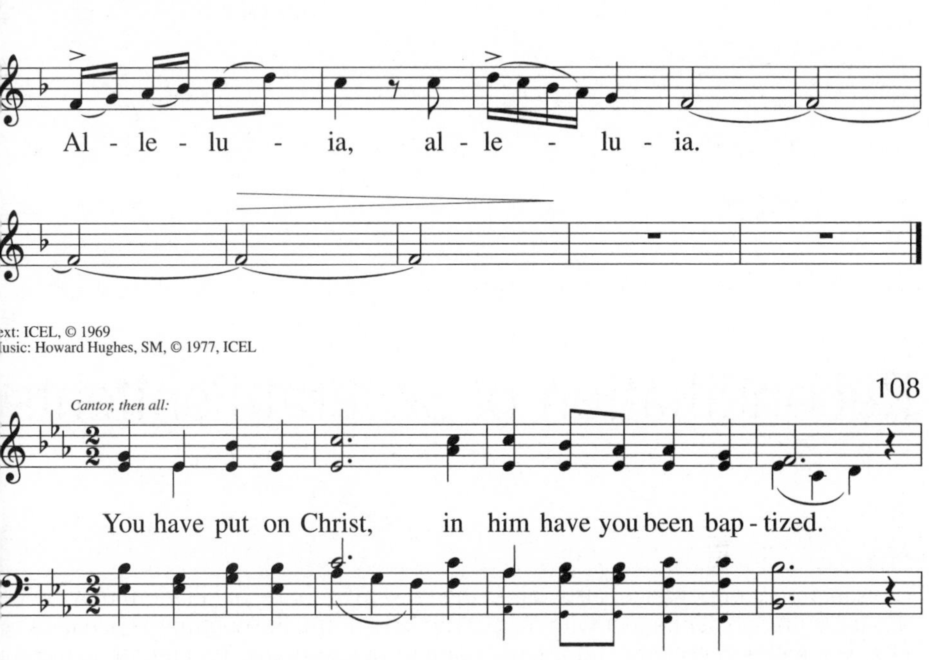
Al - le - lu - ia, al - le - lu - ia.
Cantor, then all:
You have put on Christ, in him have you been bap - tized.

ext: ICEL, © 1969
usic: Howard Hughes, SM, © 1977, ICEL

108

Al - le - lu - ia, al - le - lu - ia, al - le - lu - ia.

ext: ICEL, © 1969
usic: J. William Greene, © 1998, GIA Publications, Inc.

ANOINTING WITH CHRISM 109

The priest/deacon anoints each child on the crown of the head with holy chrism, a mixture of oil and perfume. The word "Christ" means "anointed." The baptized child has been "Christ-ed" and the sweet smell of the anointing reminds all of this.

CLOTHING WITH THE BAPTISMAL GARMENT AND GIVING OF THE CANDLE

The infants are then clothed in baptismal garments and a candle for each of the newly baptized is lighted from the paschal candle.

Optional *The priest/deacon may touch the ears and mouth of each child: "May Jesus soon touch your ears to receive his word, and your mouth to proclaim his faith."*

CONCLUSION AND BLESSING

If baptism is celebrated at Mass, the liturgy continues with the eucharist. Otherwise, all process to the altar, carrying lighted candles. The above acclamation may be sung again during this procession. All then pray the Lord's Prayer, the parents are blessed and the liturgy concludes with a hymn of praise and thanksgiving.

Reconciliation of Several Penitents

110

The sacrament of penance, also called the sacrament of reconciliation, may be cel
ebrated with one penitent or with many. The latter form, the communal penance ser
vice, is a gathering of a few or a large number of Christians. Together they listen t
the scriptures, sing psalms and hymns, pray, individually confess their sins an
receive absolution, then praise God whose mercy and love are greater than our evil
In the rite of penance, the members of the church confront the struggle that wa
entered at baptism. There has been failure, evil done and good undone, but the pen
itent church comes again and again to name and renounce its sins and to return t
the way of the Lord.

111 INTRODUCTORY RITES

An appropriate hymn or psalm may be sung.

GREETING

The priest and people greet each other in these or other words:

Priest: Grace, mercy, and peace be with you
from God the Father and Christ Jesus our Savior.

Assembly: **And also with you.**

OPENING PRAYER

After silent prayer, the priest concludes the gathering rite with a solemn prayer.

112 CELEBRATION OF THE WORD OF GOD

FIRST READINGS

One or more passages from scripture are read. At the conclusion of each:

Reader: The word of the Lord.

Assembly: **Thanks be to God.**

RESPONSORIAL PSALM

The following psalm may follow the first reading:

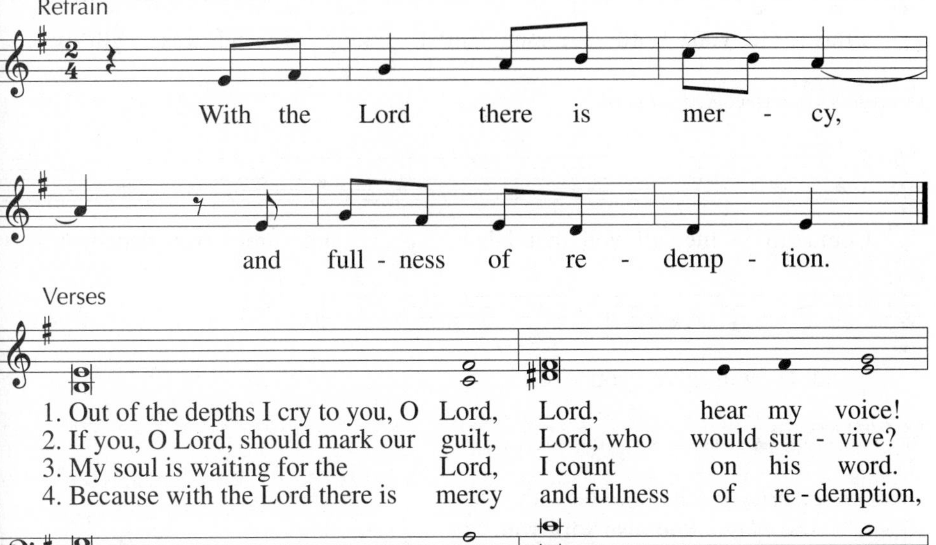
Refrain
With the Lord there is mer - cy,
and full - ness of re - demp - tion.
Verses
1. Out of the depths I cry to you, O Lord, Lord, hear my voice!
2. If you, O Lord, should mark our guilt, Lord, who would sur - vive?
3. My soul is waiting for the Lord, I count on his word.
4. Because with the Lord there is mercy and fullness of re - demption,

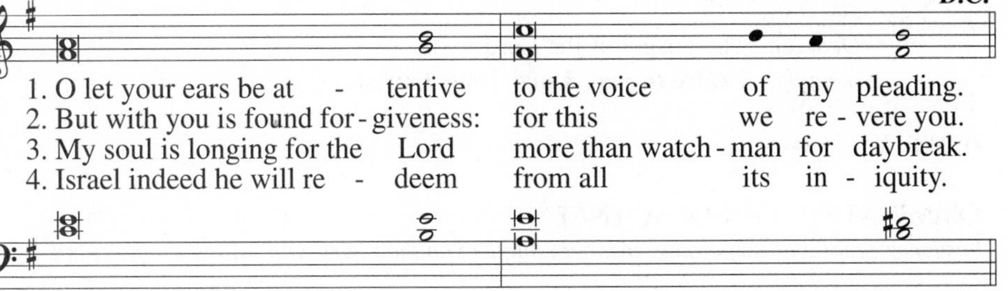
D.C.
1. O let your ears be at - tentive to the voice of my pleading.
2. But with you is found for - giveness: for this we re - vere you.
3. My soul is longing for the Lord more than watch - man for daybreak.
4. Israel indeed he will re - deem from all its in - iquity.

Text: Psalm 130:1-2, 3-4, 5-6, 7-8; © 1963, The Grail, GIA Publications, Inc., agent; refrain trans. © 1969, ICEL
Music: Michel Guimont, © 1995, GIA Publications, Inc.

GOSPEL

113

Before the gospel reading, this acclamation is sung:

Cantor, then all:
Al - le - lu - ia, al - le - lu - ia, al - le - lu - ia.

Music: Chant Mode VI; acc. by Richard Proulx, © 1985, GIA Publications, Inc.

During Lent:

Cantor, then all:
Praise to you, Lord Je-sus Christ, king of end-less glo-ry!

Text: ICEL, © 1969
Music: Frank Schoen, © 1970, GIA Publications, Inc.

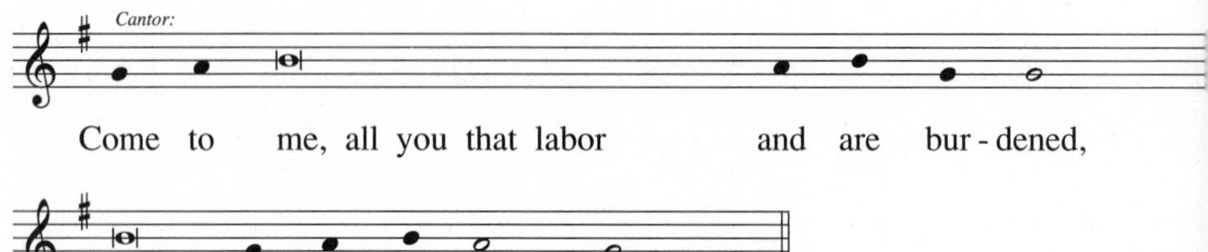
Cantor:
Come to me, all you that labor and are bur-dened,
and I will give you rest.

Text: © 1969, ICEL
Music: Tone 6F; acc. by Robert J. Batastini, © 1986, GIA Publications, Inc.

Deacon (or priest): The Lord be with you.
Assembly: **And also with you.**
Deacon: A reading from the holy gospel according to N.
Assembly: **Glory to you, Lord.**

After the reading:

Deacon: The gospel of the Lord.
Assembly: **Praise to you, Lord Jesus Christ.**

HOMILY

EXAMINATION OF CONSCIENCE

In silence or through some other manner all reflect on their lives with sorrow for their sins.

114 SACRAMENT OF PENANCE

GENERAL CONFESSION OF SINS

Kneeling (or with another posture that expresses sorrow,) all join in confession.
This form may be used:

I confess to almighty God,
and to you, my brothers and sisters,
that I have sinned through my own fault
in my thoughts and in my words,
in what I have done,
and in what I have failed to do;
and I ask blessed Mary, ever virgin,
all the angels and saints,
and you, my brothers and sisters,
to pray for me to the Lord our God.

115

Standing, all join in a litany using one of the following responses, or a song asking God's mercy. The Lord's Prayer is then recited or sung (see no. 150 and 164).

A **We pray you, hear us.**

B **Lord, be merciful to me, a sinner.**

C **Lord, have mercy.**

INDIVIDUAL CONFESSION AND ABSOLUTION 116

One by one the penitents approach the priest confessors. All confess their sins, accept some fitting act of satisfaction and the counsel of the confessor. Then the priest extends his hands over the penitent's head and speaks the prayer of absolution, concluding: "Through the ministry of the church may God give you pardon and peace, and I absolve you from your sins in the name of the Father, and of the Son, and of the Holy Spirit." The penitent responds, "Amen." (Note: On those occasions when general absolution is permitted, the rest of the rite remains the same.)

PROCLAMATION OF PRAISE FOR GOD'S MERCY

The priest invites all to give thanks and to show by their lives—and in the life of the whole community—the grace of repentance. A psalm, canticle or hymn may be sung to proclaim God's mercy.

CONCLUDING PRAYER OF THANKSGIVING

This prayer is spoken by the priest.

BLESSING AND DISMISSAL

The priest blesses all present and the deacon or other minister dismisses the assembly.

All respond: **Thanks be to God.**

Funeral Mass

117
The rites which surround the death of a Christian extend from the Viaticum (last communion) and final prayers before death through the wake service and funeral Mass to the burial of the body or ashes. In all of this the community affirms its faith in the communion of saints and the resurrection of the dead. The family and friends are helped in their time of sorrow with prayer and song. Thus they express present grief even as they hold to the church's lasting hope. Following is the rite of the funeral Mass.

INTRODUCTORY RITES

118 GREETING

The priest greets the assembly at the door, using these or similar words.

Priest: The grace and peace of God our Father and the Lord Jesus Christ be with you.
Assembly: **And also with you.**

The body is sprinkled with holy water.

SONG

As the procession enters the church, an appropriate song is sung.

The Mass continues as usual with the Opening Prayer, no. 139.

119 FINAL COMMENDATION

Following the prayer after Communion, the commendation begins with an invitation to silent prayer.

120 SONG OF FAREWELL

The following or another appropriate responsory or song may be sung.

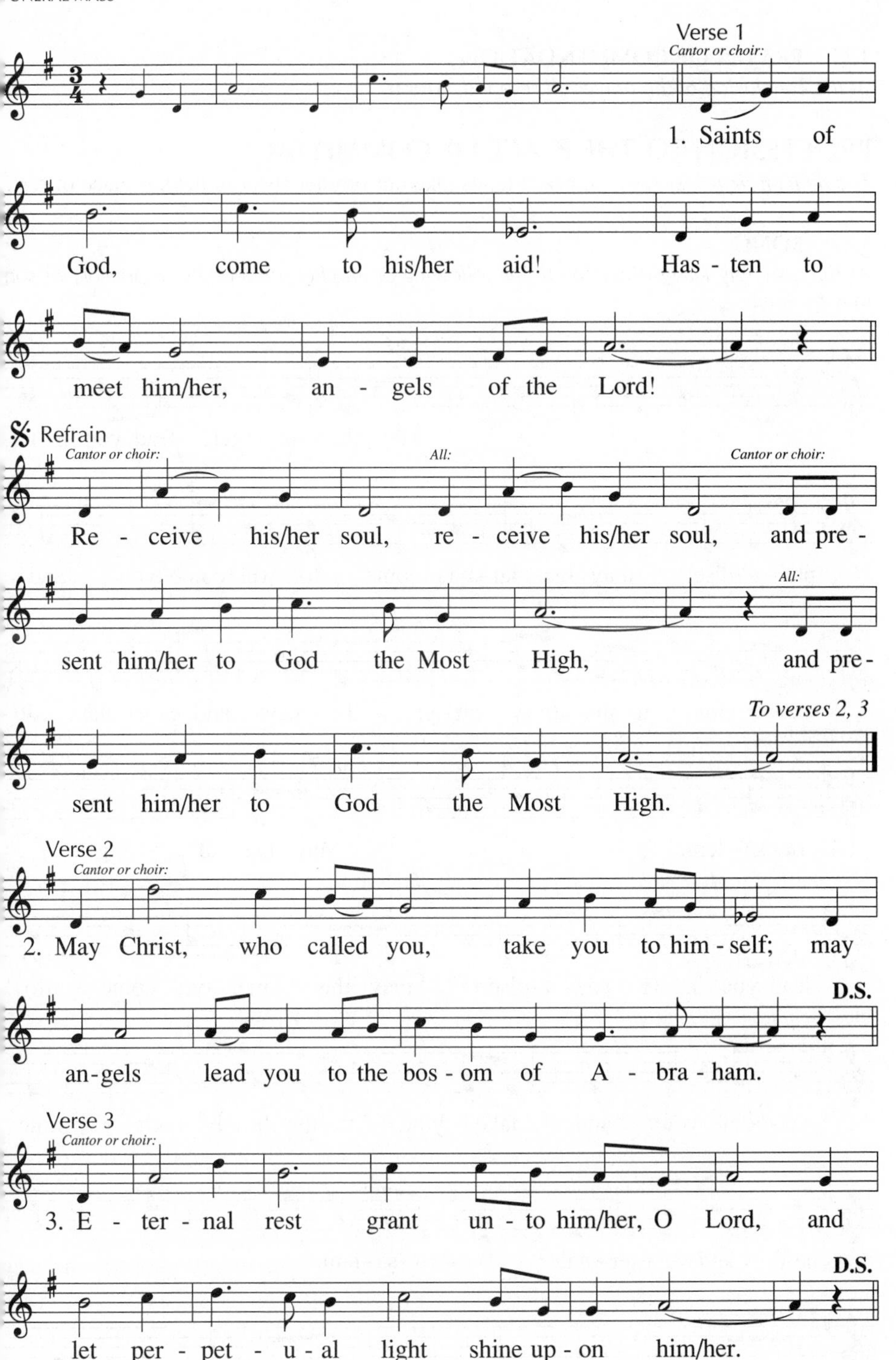
Verse 1
Cantor or choir:
1. Saints of God, come to his/her aid! Has - ten to meet him/her, an - gels of the Lord!
Refrain
Cantor or choir:
Re - ceive his/her soul,
All:
re - ceive his/her soul,
Cantor or choir:
and pre - sent him/her to God the Most High,
All:
and pre - sent him/her to God the Most High.
To verses 2, 3
Verse 2
Cantor or choir:
2. May Christ, who called you, take you to him - self; may an - gels lead you to the bos - om of A - bra - ham.
D.S.
Verse 3
Cantor or choir:
3. E - ter - nal rest grant un - to him/her, O Lord, and let per - pet - u - al light shine up - on him/her.
D.S.

Text: *Order of Christian Funerals,* © 1985, ICEL
Music: Steven R. Janco, © 1990, GIA Publications, Inc.

121 **PRAYER OF COMMENDATION**

At the conclusion of the prayer all respond: **Amen.**

PROCESSION TO THE PLACE OF COMMITTAL

The deacon or priest says: In peace let us take our brother/sister to his/her place of rest.

122 **SONG**

As the assembly leaves the church, the following or another appropriate responsory or son may be sung.

Cantor or choir: mf
May the an - gels lead you in - to par - a - dise; may the mar - tyrs come to wel - come you and take you to the ho - ly cit - y, the new and e - ter - nal Je - ru - sa - lem.
All: f
May the an - gels lead you in - to par - a - dise; may the mar - tyrs come to wel - come you and take you to the ho - ly cit - y, the new and e - ter - nal Je - ru - sa - lem.
mp Cantor or choir:
May the choirs of an - gels wel - come you and

lead you to the bos-om of A-bra-ham; and where Laz-a-rus is
poor no long-er, may you have e-ter-nal rest.
mf
p
All: f
May the an-gels lead you in-to
Optional descant: mf
In pa-ra-di-sum
par-a-dise; may the mar-tyrs come to wel-come you and
de-du-cant te an-ge-
take you to the ho-ly cit-y, the new and e-ter-nal Je-
li.
ru-sa-lem.

Text: *Order of Christian Funerals,* © 1985, ICEL
Music: Steven R. Janco, © 1990, GIA Publications, Inc.

Holy Communion Outside Mass

123
When for good reason communion cannot be received at Mass, the faithful may share in the paschal mystery through the liturgy of the word and the reception of holy communion.

INTRODUCTORY RITES

An appropriate hymn or psalm may be sung.

124 GREETING

If the minister is a priest or deacon, the usual form of greeting is used:

Assembly: **And also with you.**

If the minister is not a priest or deacon, another form of greeting may be used:

Assembly: **Blessed be God forever.**

PENITENTIAL RITE

The minister invites silent reflection and repentance. After some silence:

Assembly: **I confess to almighty God,**
and to you, my brothers and sisters,
that I have sinned through my own fault
in my thoughts and in my words,
in what I have done,
and in what I have failed to do;
and I ask blessed Mary, ever virgin,
all the angels and saints,
and you, my brothers and sisters,
to pray for me to the Lord our God.

The forms found at no. 136 may also be used.

CELEBRATION OF THE WORD OF GOD 125

FIRST READINGS

One or more passages from scripture are read. At the conclusion of each:

Reader: The word of the Lord.
Assembly: **Thanks be to God.**

RESPONSORIAL PSALM

An appropriate psalm may follow the first reading.

GOSPEL 126

Before the gospel reading, the alleluia or Lenten acclamation is sung.

[*Deacon (or priest):* The Lord be with you.
Assembly: **And also with you.**]
Reader: A reading from the holy gospel according to N.
Assembly: **Glory to you, Lord.**

After the reading:

Reader: The gospel of the Lord.
Assembly: **Praise to you, Lord Jesus Christ.**

GENERAL INTERCESSIONS 127

The assembly joins in prayer for the needs of the world, of the poor, and of the church.

HOLY COMMUNION 128

The minister invites all to join in the Lord's Prayer, then to exchange a sign of peace. The minister then raises the eucharistic bread and all respond to the invitation.

Assembly: **Lord, I am not worthy to receive you,
but only say the word and I shall be healed.**

A psalm or hymn may be sung during communion. Afterwards, there may be a period of silence or the singing of a psalm or hymn. The minister then recites a concluding prayer.

CONCLUDING RITE

All are blessed and dismissed.

Presiding minister: Go in the peace of Christ.
Assembly: **Thanks be to God.**

Eucharistic Exposition and Benediction

129
"Exposition of the holy eucharist . . . is intended to acknowledge Christ's marvelou presence in the sacrament. Exposition invites us to the spiritual union with him tha culminates in sacramental communion. Thus it fosters very well the worship whic is due to Christ in spirit and in truth.

This kind of exposition must clearly express the cult of the blessed sacrament i its relationship to the Mass. The plan of the exposition should carefully avoid any thing which might somehow obscure the principal desire of Christ in instituting th eucharist, namely, to be with us as food, medicine, and comfort" (Holy Communio and Worship of the Eucharist outside of Mass, #82).

130 EXPOSITION

As the priest or deacon prepares the holy eucharist for adoration, the following or anothe suitable song is sung:

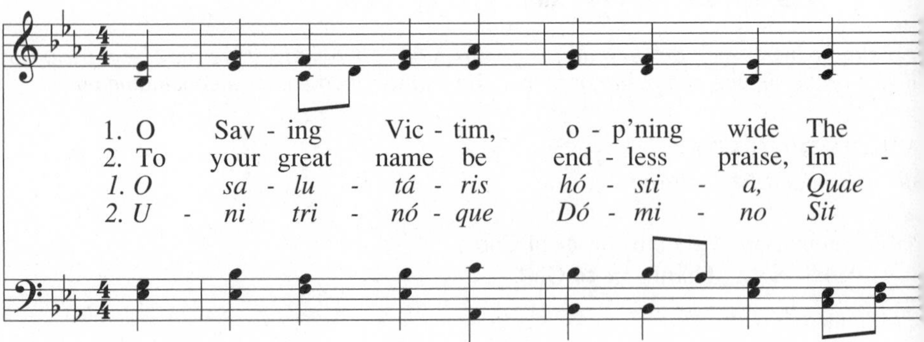
1. O Sav - ing Vic - tim, o - p'ning wide The
2. To your great name be end - less praise, Im -
1. O sa - lu - tá - ris hó - sti - a, Quae
2. U - ni tri - nó - que Dó - mi - no Sit

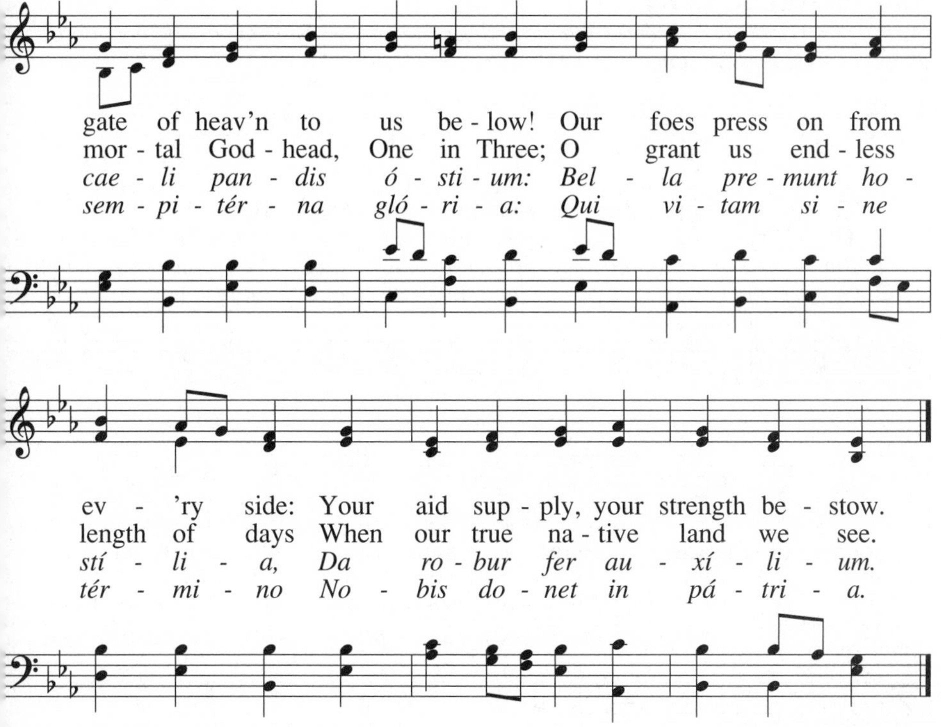
gate of heav'n to us be - low! Our foes press on from
mor - tal God - head, One in Three; O grant us end - less
cae - li pan - dis ó - sti - um: Bel - la pre - munt ho -
sem - pi - tér - na gló - ri - a: Qui vi - tam si - ne
ev - 'ry side: Your aid sup - ply, your strength be - stow.
length of days When our true na - tive land we see.
stí - li - a, Da ro - bur fer au - xí - li - um.
tér - mi - no No - bis do - net in pá - tri - a.

Text: Thomas Aquinas, 1227-1275; tr. by Edward Caswall, 1814-1878, alt.
Music: DUGUET, LM; Dieu donne Duguet, d.1767

ADORATION 131

During the adoration there are prayers, songs, Scripture readings, and possibly a homily to develop a better understanding of the eucharistic mystery. Silent prayer is also encouraged. If time allows, the Liturgy of the Hours may be celebrated here.

132 BENEDICTION

As the priest or deacon incenses the Blessed Sacrament, the following or another appropriate hymn or song may be sung:

1. Come a - dore this won - drous pres - ence, Bow to Christ the source of grace. Here is kept the an - cient prom - ise Of God's earth - ly dwell - ing - place. Sight is blind be - fore God's glo - ry, Faith a - lone may see his face.
2. Glo - ry be to God the Fa - ther, Praise to his co - e - qual Son, Ad - o - ra - tion to the Spir - it, Bond of love, in God - head one. Blest be God by all cre - a - tion Joy - ous - ly while a - ges run.
1. Tan - tum er - go Sa - cra - mén - tum Ve - ne - ré - mur cér - nu - i: Et an - tí - quum do - cu - mén - tum No - vo ce - dat rí - tu - i: Prae - stet fi - des sup - ple - mén - tum Sén - su - um de - fé - ctu - i.
2. Ge - ni - tó - ri, Ge - ni - tó - que Laus et ju - bi - lá - ti - o, Sa - lus, ho - nor, vir - tus quo - que Sit et be - ne - dí - cti - o: Pro - ce - dén - ti ab u - tró - que Com - par sit lau - dá - ti - o.

Text: Thomas Aquinas, 1227-1274; tr. by James Quinn, SJ, © 1969. Used by permission of Selah Publishing Co., Inc.
Music: ST. THOMAS, 8 7 8 7 8 7; John F. Wade, 1711-1786

After a prayer, the priest or deacon blesses the assembly with the Blessed Sacrament.

REPOSITION 133

As the priest or deacon replaces the Sacrament in the tabernacle, the assembly sings or says the following acclamations:

Blessed be God.
Blessed be his holy name.
Blessed be Jesus Christ, true God and true man.
Blessed be the name of Jesus.
Blessed be his most sacred heart.
Blessed be his most precious blood.
Blessed be Jesus in the most holy sacrament of the altar.
Blessed be the Holy Spirit, Consoler.
Blessed be the great Mother of God, Mary most holy.
Blessed be her holy and immaculate conception.
Blessed be her glorious assumption.
Blessed be the name of Mary, virgin and mother.
Blessed be Saint Joseph, her most chaste spouse.
Blessed be God in his angels and in his saints.

The Order of Mass

134
Each church gathers on the Lord's Day to listen to the Scriptures, to offer prayers, to give thanks and praise to God while recalling God's gifts in creation and saving deeds in Jesus, and to share in holy communion.

In these rites of word and eucharist, the Church keeps Sunday as the Lord's Day, the day of creation and resurrection, the "eighth day" when the fullness of God's kingdom is anticipated. The Mass or eucharistic celebration of the Christian community has rites of gathering, of word, of eucharist, of dismissal. All those who gather constitute the assembly. One member of this assembly who has been ordained to the presbyterate or episcopate, the priesthood, leads the opening and closing prayers and the eucharistic prayer, and presides over the whole assembly. A member ordained to the diaconate may assist, read the gospel, and preach. Other members of the assembly are chosen and trained for various ministries: These are the readers, servers, ushers, musicians, communion ministers. All of these assist the assembly. It is the assembly itself, all those present, that does the liturgy.

The Order of Mass which follows is familiar to all who regularly join in this assembly. It is learned through repetition. This Order of Mass leaves many decisions to the local community and others are determined by the various seasons of the liturgical year.

INTRODUCTORY RITES

The rites which precede the liturgy of the word assist the assembly to gather as a community. They prepare that community to listen to the Scriptures and to celebrate the eucharist together. The procession and entrance song are ways of expressing the unity and spirit of the assembly.

GREETING

All make the sign of the cross.

Priest: In the name of the Father, and of the Son, and of the Holy Spirit.
Assembly: **Amen.**

After the sign of the cross one of the greetings is given.

A

Priest: The grace of our Lord Jesus Christ and the love of God and the fellowship of the Holy Spirit be with you all.

Assembly: **And also with you.**

B

Priest: The grace and peace of God our Father and the Lord Jesus Christ be with you.

Assembly: **Blessed be God, the Father of our Lord Jesus Christ.** *or:* **And also with you.**

C

Priest: The Lord be with you. (*Bishop:* Peace be with you.)

Assembly: **And also with you.**

BLESSING AND SPRINKLING OF HOLY WATER 135

On Sundays, especially during the season of Easter, instead of the penitential rite below, the blessing and sprinkling of holy water may be done. The following or another appropriate song is sung as the water is sprinkled.

Refrain
mf Descant:
If we have died to our - selves in Je - sus, then
f Melody:
If we have died to our - selves in Je - sus, then

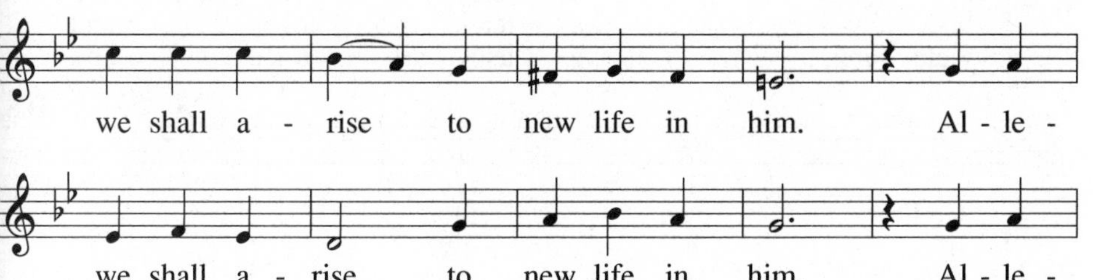

we shall a - rise to new life in him. Al - le -
we shall a - rise to new life in him. Al - le -

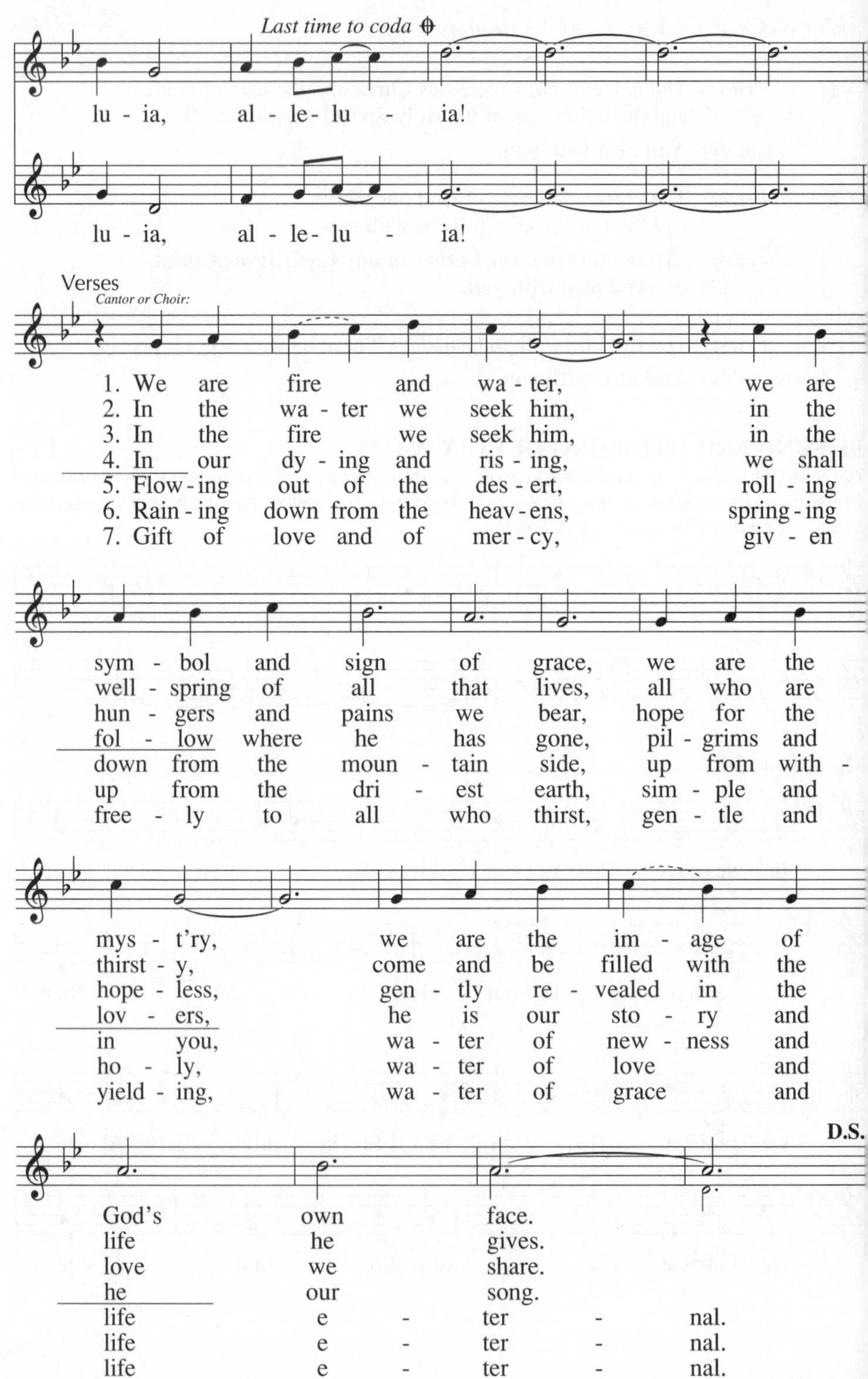
Last time to coda
lu - ia, al - le - lu - ia!
lu - ia, al - le - lu - ia!
Verses
Cantor or Choir:
1. We are fire and wa - ter, we are
2. In the wa - ter we seek him, in the
3. In the fire we seek him, in the
4. In our dy - ing and ris - ing, we shall
5. Flow - ing out of the des - ert, roll - ing
6. Rain - ing down from the heav - ens, spring - ing
7. Gift of love and of mer - cy, giv - en
sym - bol and sign of grace, we are the
well - spring of all that lives, all who are
hun - gers and pains we bear, hope for the
fol - low where he has gone, pil - grims and
down from the moun - tain side, up from with -
up from the dri - est earth, sim - ple and
free - ly to all who thirst, gen - tle and
mys - t'ry, we are the im - age of
thirst - y, come and be filled with the
hope - less, gen - tly re - vealed in the
lov - ers, he is our sto - ry and
in you, wa - ter of new - ness and
ho - ly, wa - ter of love and
yield - ing, wa - ter of grace and
D.S.
God's own face.
life he gives.
love we share.
he our song.
life e - ter - nal.
life e - ter - nal.
life e - ter - nal.

Coda
ia!
Al - le - lu - ia!
ia!
Al - le - lu - ia!
no rit.
Al - le - lu - ia!
no rit.
Al - le - lu - ia!

Text: *Mass of Creation,* Marty Haugen
Music: *Mass of Creation,* Marty Haugen

PENITENTIAL RITE

136

The priest invites all to be mindful of their sins and of the great mercy of God. After a time of silence, one of the following forms is used.

A

Assembly: **I confess to almighty God,**
and to you, my brothers and sisters,
that I have sinned through my own fault
in my thoughts and in my words,
in what I have done,
and in what I have failed to do;
and I ask blessed Mary, ever virgin,
all the angels and saints,
and you, my brothers and sisters,
to pray for me to the Lord our God.

B

Priest: Lord, we have sinned against you: Lord, have mercy.
Assembly: **Lord, have mercy.**
Priest: Lord, show us your mercy and love.
Assembly: **And grant us your salvation.**

C *The priest or another minister makes a series of invocations according to the following pattern.*

Priest: (Invocation)
Lord, have mercy.

Assembly: **Lord, have mercy.**

Priest: (Invocation)
Christ, have mercy.

Assembly: **Christ, have mercy.**

Priest: (Invocation)
Lord, have mercy.

Assembly: **Lord, have mercy.**

The penitential rite always concludes:

Priest: May almighty God have mercy on us, forgive us our sins,
and bring us to everlasting life.

Assembly: **Amen.**

137 KYRIE

Unless form C of the penitential rite has been used, the Kyrie follows.

Melody:
Lord, have mer - cy. Christ, have mer - cy.
Harmony:
Ky-ri - e e - le - i - son. Chri - ste e - le - i - son.
Lord, have mer - cy.
Last time rit. and
Ky-ri - e e - le - i - son. Ky-ri - e. Chri - ste.

Optional Verses*

Cantor or priest:

1. God of all cre - a - tion, earth and sea and sky,
2. God of ev - 'ry na - tion, God of all who live,
3. God of our sal - va - tion, God of grace and peace,

May be sung over ostinato Kyrie, or in alternation with the Kyrie using the same accompaniment.

Last time rit. and
God of all e - ter - ni - ty: hear us, hear us.
God of meek and low - ly ones: hear us, hear us.
God of wis - dom and of love: hear us, hear us.

Text: *Mass of Creation,* Marty Haugen
Music: *Mass of Creation,* Marty Haugen

GLORIA 138

The Gloria is omitted during Advent, Lent, and most weekdays.

Refrain

f

and

Glo - ry to God in the high - est, and

f

Glo - ry to

mf peace to his peo - ple on earth.

peace to his peo - ple on earth.

mf

God and peace to peo - ple on earth.

Verse 1

mf *Cantor or choir:*

Lord God, heav - en - ly King, al - might - y

God and Fa - ther, we wor - ship you, we

poco rit. **D.S.**

give you thanks, we praise you for your glo - ry.

Verse 2
Cantor or choir:
Lord Je - sus Christ, on - ly Son of the Fa - ther, Lord
God, Lamb of God, you take a - way the sin of the
world: have mer - cy on us; you are seat - ed at the
cresc.
right hand of the Fa - ther: re - ceive our prayer.
mf
poco rit.
f
D.S.
Verse 3
mf
Cantor or choir:
For you a - lone are the Ho - ly One, you a - lone are the
Lord, you a - lone are the Most High,
div.
f
ff
Je - sus Christ, with the Ho - ly
Spir - it, in the glo - ry of God, the
in the glo - ry of the

poco rit.
to Final refrain
A - men! A - men!
Fa - ther.
A - men! A - men!
A - men! A - men!
Final refrain
a tempo
ff
All:
Glo - ry to God, and peace
Glo-ry to God in the high-est,
and peace
Glo-ry to God,
to his peo - ple on earth.
fff
no rit.
to his peo - ple on earth.
no rit.
peace to peo - ple on earth.

sic: *Mass of Creation,* Marty Haugen, © 1984, GIA Publications, Inc.

)PENING PRAYER 139

\fter the invitation from the priest, all pray for a while. The introductory rites conclude with he proper opening prayer and the Amen of the assembly.

.ITURGY OF THE WORD 140

Vhen the Church assembles, the book containing the Scriptures (Lectionary) is pened and all listen as the readers and deacon (or priest) read from the places ssigned. The first reading is normally from the Hebrew Scriptures (Old Testament), he second from the letters of the New Testament, and the third from the Book of Gospels. Over a three-year cycle, the Church reads through the letters and gospels nd a portion of the Hebrew Scriptures. During the Sundays of Ordinary Time, the etters and gospels are read in order, each Sunday continuing near the place where he previous Sunday's readings ended. During Advent/Christmas and Lent/Easter, he readings are those which are traditional and appropriate to these seasons.

The Church listens to and—through the weeks and years—is shaped by th Scriptures. Those who have gathered for the Sunday liturgy are to give their fu attention to the words of the reader. A time of silence and reflection follows each c the two readings. After the first reading, this reflection continues in the singing of th psalm. A homily, bringing together the Scriptures and the life of the community, fo lows the gospel. The liturgy of the word concludes with the creed, the dismissal c the catechumens and the prayers of intercession. In the latter, the assembly contir ues its constant work of recalling and praying for the universal Church and all thos in need.

This reading and hearing of the word—simple things that they are—are th foundation of the liturgical celebration. The public reading of the Scriptures and th rituals which surround this—silence and psalm and acclamation, posture and ges ture, preaching and litany of intercession—gather the Church generation after ger eration. They gather and sustain and gradually make of us the image of Christ.

READING I

In conclusion:

Reader: The word of the Lord.
Assembly: **Thanks be to God.**

After a period of silence, the responsorial psalm is sung.

READING II

In conclusion:

Reader: The word of the Lord.
Assembly: **Thanks be to God.**

A time of silence follows the reading.

141 GOSPEL

Before the gospel, an acclamation is sung.

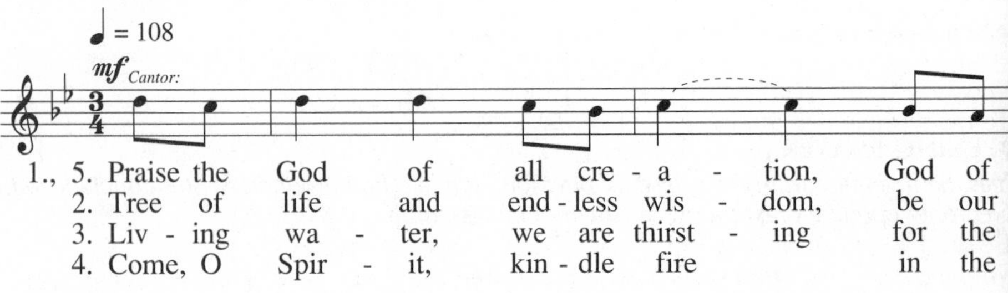
♩ = 108
mf Cantor:
1., 5. Praise the God of all cre - a - tion, God of
2. Tree of life and end - less wis - dom, be our
3. Liv - ing wa - ter, we are thirst - ing for the
4. Come, O Spir - it, kin - dle fire in the

All:
mer - cy and com - pas - sion:
root, our growth and glo - ry:
life that you have prom - ised:
hearts of all your peo - ple:
Al - le - lu - ia! Al - le -
Al - le - lu - ia! Al - le -
Last time rit.
1.-4.
Last time
lu - ia! Praise the Word of truth and life! life!
lu - ia! Praise the Word of truth and life! life!

Alternate Verses

Speak, O Lord, your servant listens, yours the word of life eternal:
To the humble and the lowly you reveal the Kingdom's myst'ry:
Praise the Word who lived among us, made us children of the Kingdom:
You are light, Lord, for our darkness, break upon our waiting spirits:
Gentle shepherd, you who know us, call us all into your presence:
Be our way, Lord, be our truth, Lord, be our hope of life eternal:
We who love you, seek your truth, Lord, come and make your home within us:
We shall watch, Lord, we shall pray, Lord, for we know not when you cometh:

Text: *Mass of Creation,* Marty Haugen
Music: *Mass of Creation,* Marty Haugen

During Lent one of the following acclamations replaces the alleluia.

A
= 76
Refrain
Descant:
f – ff
Praise to you, Lord
Praise to you, Lord
Je - sus Christ, king of end - less glo - ry!
Je - sus Christ, king of end - less glo - ry!
Verses
Cantor or choir: mp
1st Sun. We do not live on bread a - lone, but we live on ev - 'ry word from our God.
2nd Sun. From the shin - ing cloud a voice is heard— "This is my be - lov - ed Son, hear his words."
3rd Sun. "Come, take the wa - ter that I give, if you drink you will nev - er thirst a - gain."
4th Sun. "I am the Light of all the world, all who fol - low me will have the light of life."
5th Sun. "I am the Res - ur - rec - tion, I am life to all who trust in my name."
6th Sun. Christ was o - be - dient un - to death, e - ven death on the wood of the cross.
General Turn to the Lord with all your heart, for the time of sal - va - tion is here.
D.S.

Text: ICEL, © 1969
Music: *Mass of Creation,* Marty Haugen, © 1984, GIA Publications, Inc.

Or:

B **Praise and honor to you, Lord Jesus Christ!**

C **Glory and praise to you, Lord Jesus Christ!**

D **Glory to you, Word of God, Lord Jesus Christ!**

Deacon (or priest): The Lord be with you.
Assembly: **And also with you.**
Deacon: A reading from the holy gospel according to N.
Assembly: **Glory to you, Lord.**

After the reading:

Deacon: The gospel of the Lord.
Assembly: **Praise to you, Lord Jesus Christ.**

HOMILY

PROFESSION OF FAITH 142

We believe in one God,
the Father, the Almighty,
maker of heaven and earth,
of all that is seen and unseen.

We believe in one Lord, Jesus Christ,
the only Son of God,
eternally begotten of the Father,
God from God, Light from Light,
true God from true God,
begotten, not made, one in Being with the Father.
Through him all things were made.
For us men and for our salvation he came down from heaven:

All bow at the following words up to: and became man.

by the power of the Holy Spirit
he was born of the Virgin Mary, and became man.
For our sake he was crucified under Pontius Pilate;
he suffered, died, and was buried.
On the third day he rose again
in fulfillment of the Scriptures;
he ascended into heaven
and is seated at the right hand of the Father.
He will come again in glory to judge the living and the dead,
and his kingdom will have no end.

We believe in the Holy Spirit, the Lord, the giver of life,
who proceeds from the Father and the Son.
With the Father and the Son he is worshiped and glorified.
He has spoken through the Prophets.
We believe in one holy catholic and apostolic Church.
We acknowledge one baptism for the forgiveness of sins.
We look for the resurrection of the dead,
and the life of the world to come. Amen.

143 *At Masses with children, the Apostles' Creed may be used:*

We believe in God, the Father almighty,
creator of heaven and earth.

We believe in Jesus Christ, his only Son, our Lord.
He was conceived by the power of the Holy Spirit
and born of the Virgin Mary.
He suffered under Pontius Pilate,
was crucified, died, and was buried.
He descended to the dead.
On the third day he arose again.
He ascended into heaven,
and is seated at the right hand of the Father.
He will come again to judge the living and the dead.

We believe in the Holy Spirit,
the holy catholic Church,
the communion of saints,
the forgiveness of sins,
the resurrection of the body,
and the life everlasting. Amen.

144 GENERAL INTERCESSIONS

The people respond to each petition as follows, or according to local practice.

To repeat
Last time
Cantor:
For (intention) let us pray to the Lord.
Assembly:
Lord, hear our prayer. prayer.

Music: *Mass of Creation,* Marty Haugen, © 1984, GIA Publications, Inc.

LITURGY OF THE EUCHARIST 145

To celebrate the eucharist means to give God thanks and praise. When the table has been prepared with the bread and wine, the assembly joins the priest in remembering the gracious gifts of God in creation and God's saving deeds. The center of this is the paschal mystery, the death of our Lord Jesus Christ which destroyed the power of death and his rising which brings us life. That mystery into which we were baptized we proclaim each Sunday at the eucharist. It is the very shape of Christian life. We find this in the simple bread and wine which stir our remembering and draw forth our prayer of thanksgiving. "Fruit of the earth and work of human hands," the bread and wine become our holy communion in the body and blood of the Lord. We eat and drink and so proclaim that we belong to one another and to the Lord.

The members of the assembly quietly prepare themselves even as the table is prepared. The priest then invites all to lift up their hearts and join in the eucharistic prayer. All do this by giving their full attention and by singing the acclamations from the "Holy, holy" to the great "Amen." Then the assembly joins in the Lord's Prayer, the sign of peace and the "Lamb of God" litany which accompanies the breaking of bread. Ministers of communion assist the assembly to share the body and blood of Christ. A time of silence and prayer concludes the liturgy of the eucharist.

PREPARATION OF THE ALTAR AND THE GIFTS

Bread and wine are brought to the table and the deacon or priest prepares these gifts. If there is no music, the prayers may be said aloud, and all may respond: **"Blessed be God for ever."** *The priest then invites all to pray.*

Assembly: **May the Lord accept the sacrifice at your hands**
for the praise and glory of his name,
for our good, and the good of all his Church.

The priest says the prayer over the gifts and all respond: **Amen.**

EUCHARISTIC PRAYER 146

The central prayer of the Mass begins with this greeting and invitation between priest and assembly.

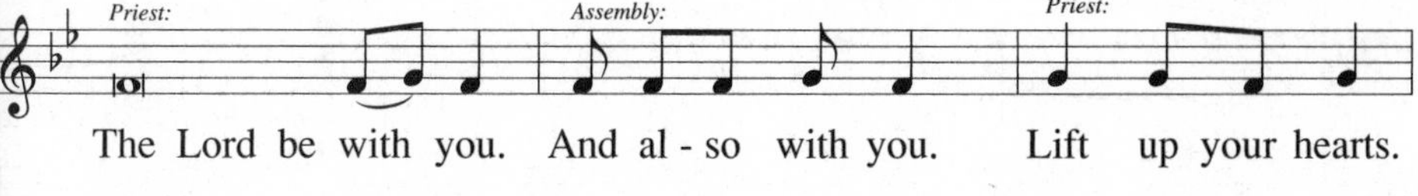
Priest:
Assembly:
Priest:
The Lord be with you. And al - so with you. Lift up your hearts.

Assembly: *Priest:*

We lift them up to the Lord. Let us give thanks to the Lord, our God.

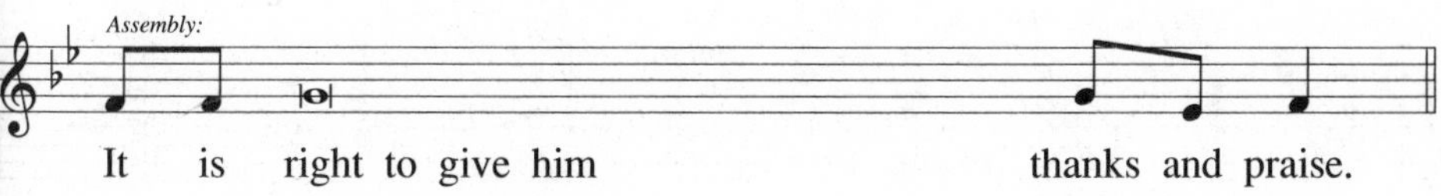
Assembly:
It is right to give him thanks and praise.

Music: *Mass of Creation,* Marty Haugen, © 1984, GIA Publications, Inc.

147 *The Sanctus acclamation is sung to conclude the introduction to the eucharistic prayer.*

f
Ho-ly, ho-ly,
ho - ly Lord, God of pow-er, God of might,
heav - en and earth are full of your glo - ry.
div. ff
Ho - san - na in the high - est.
mf unis.
Bless - ed is he who comes in the name of the
Lord. Ho - san - na in the high - est,
fff rit.
molto rit.
ho - san - na in the high - est.

Music: *Mass of Creation,* Marty Haugen, © 1984, GIA Publications, Inc.

One of the following acclamations follows the priest's invitation: "Let us proclaim the mystery of faith."

148-A

♩ = 84-86
Priest:
Let us pro-claim the mys-ter-y of faith:
All:
Christ has died, Christ is ris-en, Christ will come a-gain.
Christ has died, Christ is ris-en, Christ will come a-gain!
rit.

Text: ICEL, © 1973
Music: *Mass of Creation,* Marty Haugen, © 1984, GIA Publications, Inc.

148-B

Cantor:
Dy-ing you de-stroyed our
Priest:
Let us pro-claim the mys-ter-y of faith:
death, ris-ing you re-stored our life.
Assembly:
Dy-ing you de-stroyed our death, ris-ing you re-

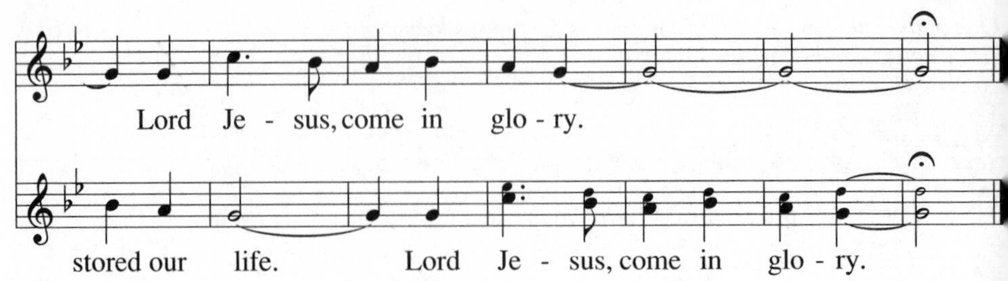
Lord Je - sus, come in glo - ry.
stored our life. Lord Je - sus, come in glo - ry.

Text: ICEL, © 1973
Music: *Mass of Creation,* Marty Haugen, © 1990, GIA Publications, Inc.

148-C

Freely

Priest:

Let us pro-claim the mys-ter - y of faith:

All:

When we eat this bread, when we drink this cup,

When we eat and drink this cup,
When we eat this bread, when we drink this cup, we pro-

When we eat and drink this cup,

claim your death, Lord Je - sus, un -

til you come in glo - ry.

Text: ICEL, © 1973
Music: *Mass of Creation,* Marty Haugen, © 1993, GIA Publications, Inc.

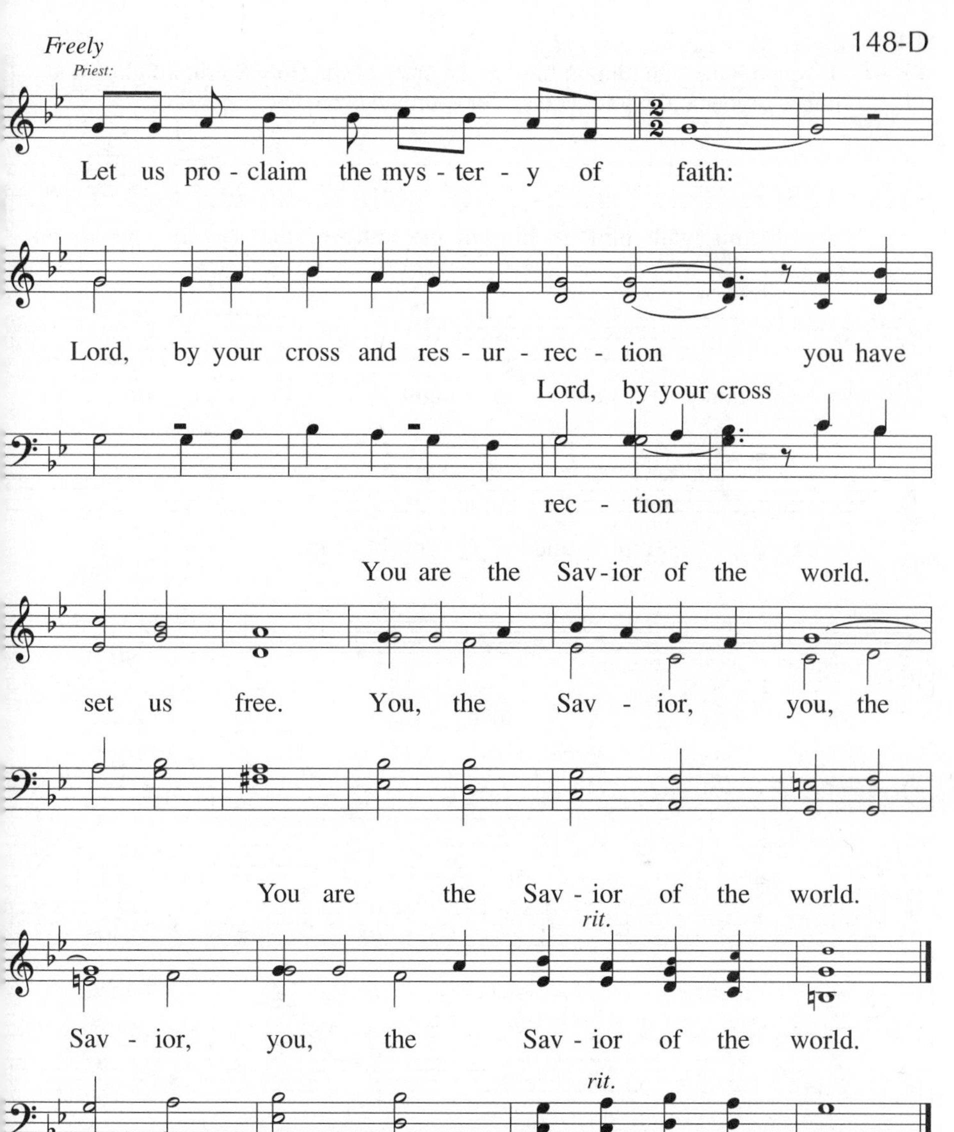
148-D
Freely
Priest:
Let us pro - claim the mys - ter - y of faith:
Lord, by your cross and res - ur - rec - tion you have
Lord, by your cross
rec - tion
You are the Sav - ior of the world.
set us free. You, the Sav - ior, you, the
You are the Sav - ior of the world.
rit.
Sav - ior, you, the Sav - ior of the world.
rit.

Text: ICEL, © 1973
Music: *Mass of Creation*, Marty Haugen, © 1993, GIA Publications, Inc.

149 *The eucharistic prayer concludes:*

Priest: Through him, with him, in him, in the unity of the Holy Spirit, all glory and honor is yours, almighty Father, for ever and ever.

Priest:
Through him, with him, in him, in the unity of the Ho - ly Spir - it, all
glory and honor is yours, al - might - y Fa - ther, for
ev - er and ev - er.
Melody:
A - men, a - men, a - men!
A - men, a - men, a - men!
rit.
rit.

COMMUNION RITE

150

The priest invites all to join in the Lord's Prayer.

Gently ♩ = 80-84
mf
Our Fa - ther, who art in
div.
unis.
heav-en, hal - low-ed be thy name; thy king-dom come; thy
div.
unis.
div.
will be done on earth as it is in heav-en.
div.
f
unis.
mf
Give us this day our dai-ly bread; and for-give us our tres-pass-es
f
unis.
mf
poco rit.
mp
mf
as we for-give those who tres - pass a-gainst us; and
poco rit.
mp
mf

a tempo
div.
mp
lead us not in-to temp-ta-tion, but de-liv-er us from e-vil.
as necessary
Deliver us, Lord...
poco rit.
...for the coming of our Savior, Jesus Christ.
All:
f a tempo
For the king-dom, the pow-er, and the glo-ry are yours,
rit.
now and for ev - er - more. A - men.

Music: *Mass of Creation,* Marty Haugen, © 1984, GIA Publications, Inc.

151 *Following the prayer "Lord, Jesus Christ," the priest invites all to exchange the sign of peace.*

Priest: The peace of the Lord be with you always.
Assembly: **And also with you.**

All exchange a sign of peace.

Then the eucharistic bread is solemnly broken and the consecrated bread and wine are prepared for holy communion. The litany "Lamb of God" is sung during the breaking of the bread. 152

mp
poco rit.
Cantor or choir:
a tempo
poco rit.
All:
a tempo
1. Je - sus, Lamb of God,
2. Je - sus, Bread of Life,
3. Je - sus, Prince of Peace,
Last time: Je - sus, Lamb of God,
you take a-way the sins of the
1.-3.
poco rit.
world: have mer - cy on us.
4.
rit.
world: grant us your peace.

Additional Invocations:

Jesus, Word of God,…
Jesus, Tree of Life,…
Jesus, Lord of Lords,…
Jesus, King of Kings,…
Jesus, Fire of Love,…
Jesus, Bread of Peace,…
Jesus, Hope for all,…

153 *The priest then invites all to share in holy communion.*

Priest: This is the Lamb of God...his supper.
Assembly: **Lord, I am not worthy to receive you,**
but only say the word and I shall be healed.

Minister of communion: The body (blood) of Christ.
Communicant: **Amen.**

A song or psalm is ordinarily sung during communion. After communion, a time of silence is observed or a song of thanksgiving is sung. The rite concludes with the prayer after communion to which all respond: **Amen.**

154 CONCLUDING RITE

The liturgy of word and eucharist ends very simply. There may be announcements of events and concerns for the community, then the priest gives a blessing and the assembly is dismissed.

GREETING AND BLESSING

Priest: The Lord be with you.
Assembly: **And also with you.**

Optional

When the bishop blesses the people he adds the following:

Bishop: Blessed be the name of the Lord.
Assembly: **Now and for ever.**

Bishop: Our help is in the name of the Lord.
Assembly: **Who made heaven and earth.**

The blessing may be in a simple or solemn form. All respond to the blessing or to each part of the blessing: **Amen.**

DISMISSAL

The deacon or priest then dismisses the assembly:

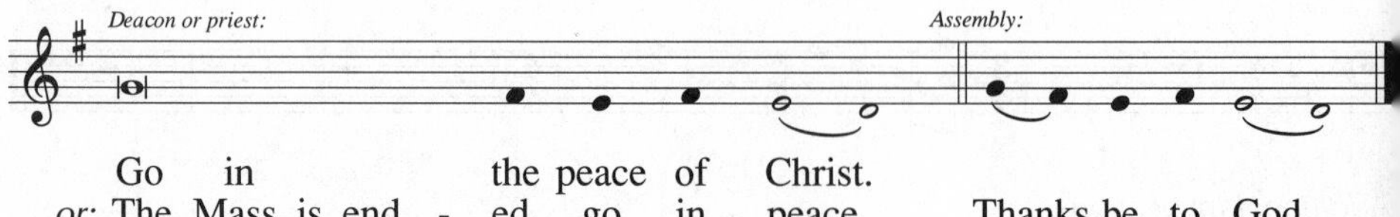
Deacon or priest:
Assembly:

Go in the peace of Christ.
or: The Mass is end - ed, go in peace. Thanks be to God.
or: Go in peace to love and serve the Lord.

EASTER DISMISSAL

The deacon or priest then dismisses the assembly:

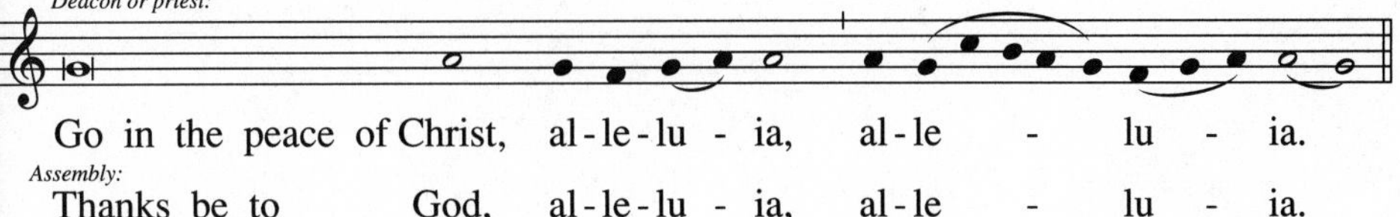
Deacon or priest:
Go in the peace of Christ, al-le-lu - ia, al-le - lu - ia.
Assembly:
Thanks be to God, al-le-lu - ia, al-le - lu - ia.

Composite Setting

155 **SPRINGS OF WATER**

Moving
Refrain
Descant:
Springs of wa - ter, O bless the Lord!
Springs of wa - ter, bless the Lord! Give him
Praise for ev - er! ev - er!
To verses
Last time
glo - ry and praise for ev - er! ev - er!
Verses
Cantor:
1. O - ceans of earth, sing glo - ry to God!
2. Riv - ers and lakes, sing glo - ry to God!
3. Brooks of the hills, sing glo - ry to God!
4. Show - ers and springs, sing glo - ry to God!

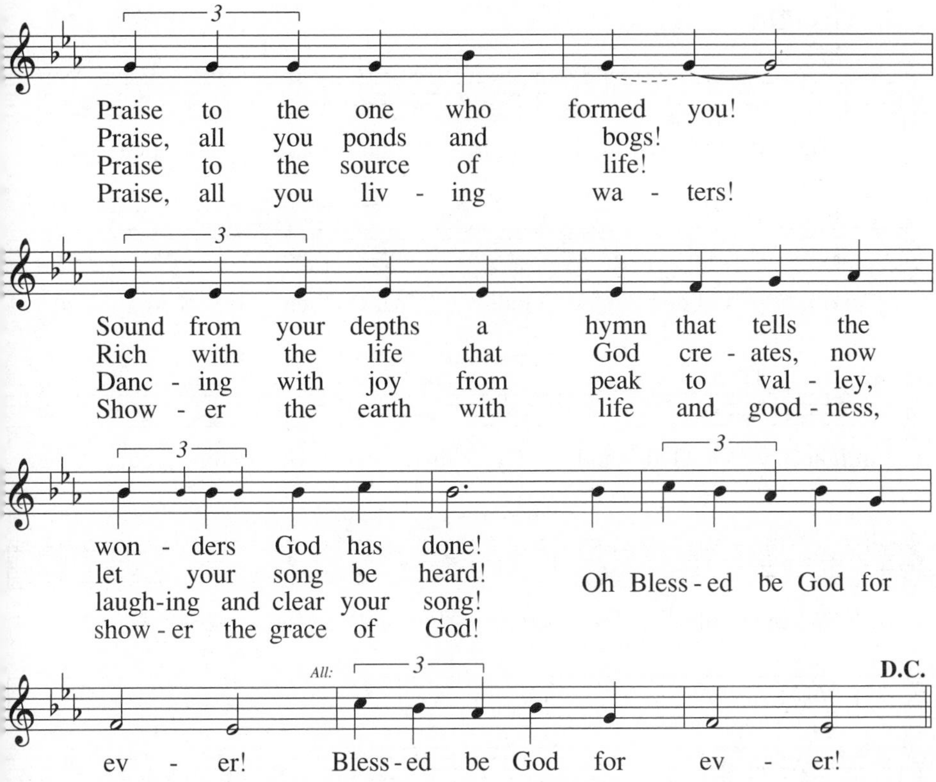

Praise to the one who formed you!
Praise, all you ponds and bogs!
Praise to the source of life!
Praise, all you liv - ing wa - ters!

Sound from your depths a hymn that tells the
Rich with the life that God cre - ates, now
Danc - ing with joy from peak to val - ley,
Show - er the earth with life and good - ness,

won - ders God has done!
let your song be heard!
laugh-ing and clear your song!
show - er the grace of God!
Oh Bless - ed be God for

ev - er! *All:* Bless - ed be God for ev - er! **D.C.**

Text: Refrain trans. © 1973, ICEL; additional text by Marty Haugen, © 1994, GIA Publications, Inc.
Music: Marty Haugen, © 1994, GIA Publications, Inc.

KYRIE ELEISON

156

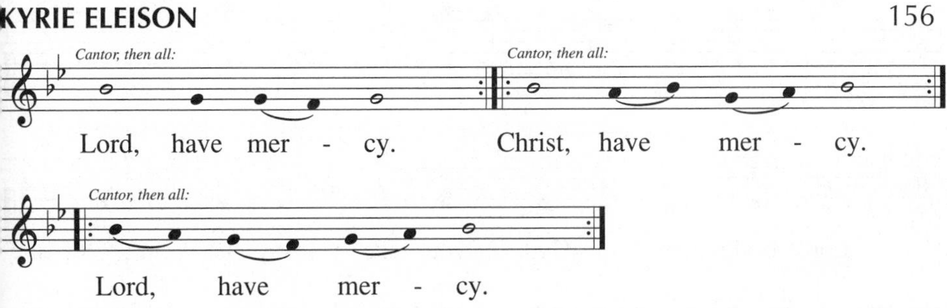
Cantor, then all:
Lord, have mer - cy.
Cantor, then all:
Christ, have mer - cy.
Cantor, then all:
Lord, have mer - cy.

Music: *Litany of the Saints;* adapt. by Richard Proulx, © 1971, GIA Publications, Inc.

Or:

Cantor, then all:
Ky - ri - e e - le - i - son.
Cantor, then all:
Chri - ste e - le - i - son.
Cantor, then all:
Ky - ri - e e - le - i - son.

Music: *Litany of the Saints;* adapt. by Richard Proulx, © 1971, GIA Publications, Inc.

157 **GLORIA**

mf
Glo - ry to God in the high - est, and peace to his peo - ple on
earth. Lord God, heav - en - ly King, al -
f
might - y God and Fa - ther, we wor - ship you, we
give you thanks, we praise you for your glo - ry.
f
Slighty slower
mf
Choir (Congr. ad lib):
Lord Je - sus Christ, on - ly Son of the Fa - ther,
mf
Lord God, Lamb of God, you take a - way the sin of the
world: have mer - cy on us; you are

seat - ed at the right hand of the Fa - ther:
re - ceive our prayer.
re - ceive, re - ceive our prayer.
re - ceive our prayer.
All:
Tempo primo
For you a - lone are the Ho - ly One, you a - lone are the
Lord, you a - lone are the Most High,
Je - sus Christ, with the Ho - ly Spir - it, in the glo - ry of
God the Fa - ther. A - men.
rit.

Music: *A New Mass for Congregations,* Carroll T. Andrews, © 1970, GIA Publications, Inc.

158 GOSPEL ACCLAMATION

Cantor, then all:
Al - le - lu - ia, al - le - lu - ia, al - le - lu - ia.

Music: Chant Mode VI; acc. by Richard Proulx, © 1985, GIA Publications, Inc.

Lenten Acclamation

Cantor, then all:
Praise to you, Lord Je - sus Christ, king of end - less glo - ry!

Text: ICEL, © 1969
Music: Frank Schoen, © 1970, GIA Publications, Inc.

Tone for verses

Cantor:
D.C.

Music: Tone 6F

159 GENERAL INTERCESSIONS

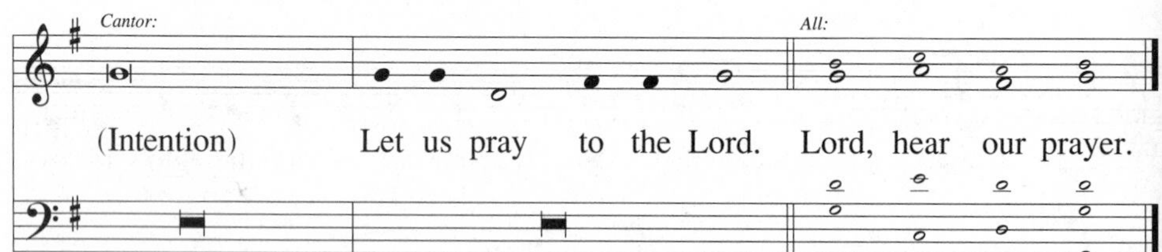
Cantor:
All:
(Intention) Let us pray to the Lord. Lord, hear our prayer.

Music: Byzantine chant; harm. by Robert J. Batastini, © 1986, GIA Publications, Inc.

160 PREFACE DIALOG

Priest:
Assembly:
The Lord be with you. And al - so with you.
Priest:
Assembly:
Lift up your hearts. We lift them up to the Lord.

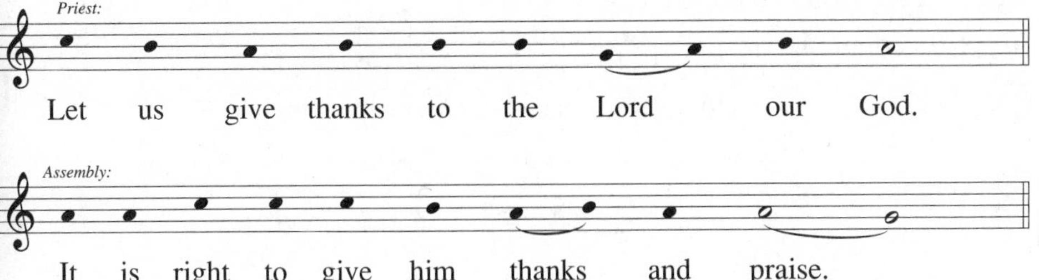
Priest:
Let us give thanks to the Lord our God.
Assembly:
It is right to give him thanks and praise.

Music: Sacramentary, 1974

SANCTUS 161

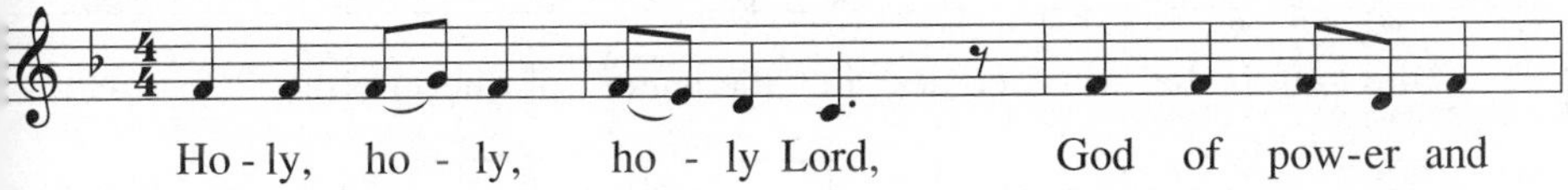

Ho - ly, ho - ly, ho - ly Lord, God of pow-er and

Ho - ly, ho - ly, ho - ly Lord, God of pow-er and

might, heav - en and earth are full of your glo -

might, heav - en and earth are full of your glo -

ry. Ho - san - na in the high - est.
ry. Ho - san - na in the high - est.
Bless-ed is he who comes in the name of the Lord. Ho -
Bless-ed is he who comes in the name of the Lord. Ho -
san - na in the high - est.
san - na in the high - est.

Music: *People's Mass,* Jan Vermulst, 1925-1994, acc. by Richard Proulx,

MEMORIAL ACCLAMATION 162

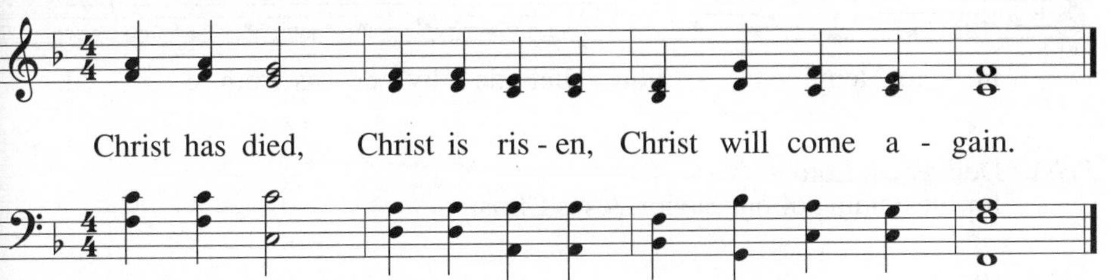
Christ has died, Christ is ris - en, Christ will come a - gain.

Text: ICEL, © 1973
Music: *Danish Amen Mass,* David Kraehenbuehl; © 1970, World Library Publications

AMEN 163

A - men, a - men, a - men.

Music: Danish Amen

COMMUNION RITE 164

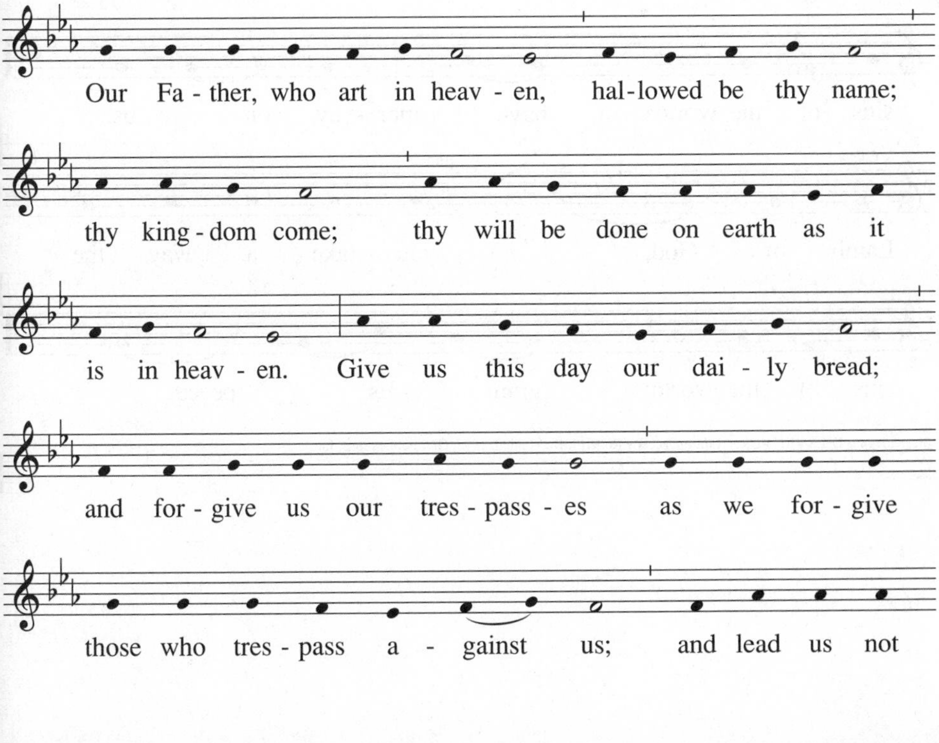

Our Fa - ther, who art in heav - en, hal-lowed be thy name;

thy king - dom come; thy will be done on earth as it

is in heav - en. Give us this day our dai - ly bread;

and for - give us our tres - pass - es as we for - give

those who tres - pass a - gainst us; and lead us not

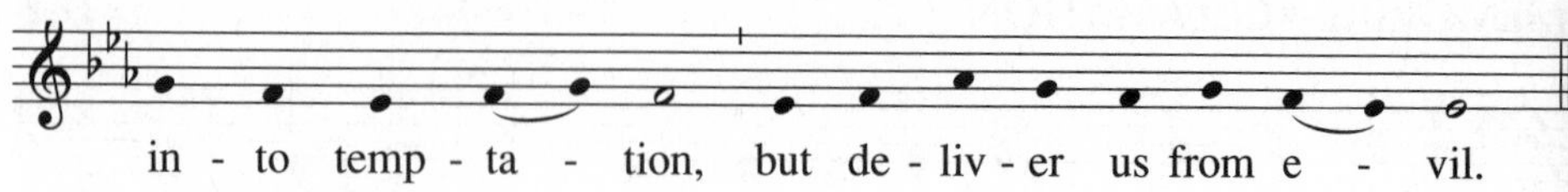
in - to temp - ta - tion, but de - liv - er us from e - vil.

Priest: Deliver us, Lord…
for the coming of our Savior, Jesus Christ.

All:
For the king - dom, the pow'r, and the
glo - ry are yours, now and for ev - er.

Music: Traditional chant, adapt. by Robert Snow, 1964; acc. by Robert J. Batastini, © 1975, 1993, GIA Publications, Inc.

165 AGNUS DEI

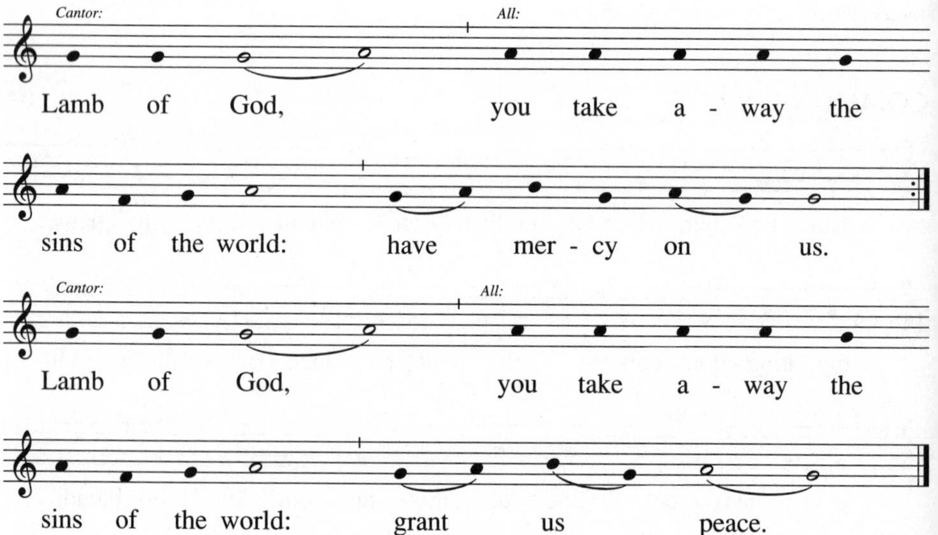
Cantor:
Lamb of God,
All:
you take a - way the
sins of the world: have mer - cy on us.
Cantor:
Lamb of God,
All:
you take a - way the
sins of the world: grant us peace.

Music: Agnus Dei XVIII, Vatican Edition; acc. by Robert J. Batastini, © 1993, GIA Publications, Inc.

DISMISSAL

166-A

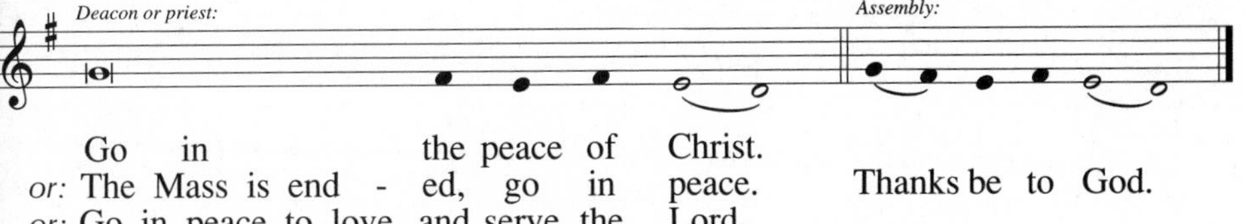
Deacon or priest:
Assembly:
Go in the peace of Christ.
or: The Mass is end - ed, go in peace.
or: Go in peace to love and serve the Lord.
Thanks be to God.

EASTER DISMISSAL

166-B

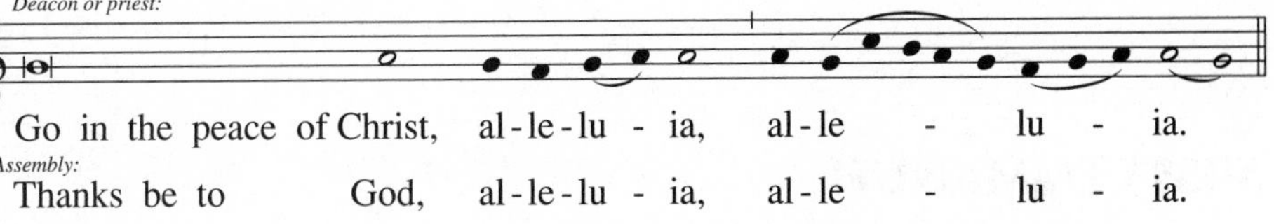
Deacon or priest:
Go in the peace of Christ, al - le - lu - ia, al - le - lu - ia.
Assembly:
Thanks be to God, al - le - lu - ia, al - le - lu - ia.

Setting One

MISSA EMMANUEL

167 SANCTUS

Cantor:
Ho-ly, ho-ly, ho - ly Lord, God of pow'r and God of might.
All:
Ho-ly, ho-ly, ho - ly Lord, God of pow'r and God of might.
Cantor:
Heav - en and earth are full of your glo - ry.
Ho-san - na in the high - est, ho-san-na in the high - est.
All:
Ho-san - na in the high - est, ho-san-na in the high - est.
Cantor:
Bless - ed is he who comes in the name of the Lord
Ho-san - na in the high - est, ho-san-na in the high - est.

All:
Ho-san - na in the high - est, ho-san-na in the high - est.

Music: *Missa Emmanuel,* Richard Proulx, © 1991, 2002, GIA Publications, Inc.

MEMORIAL ACCLAMATION 168

Cantor, then all:
Christ has died, Christ is ris - en, Christ will come a - gain.

Text: ICEL, © 1973
Music: *Missa Emmanuel,* Richard Proulx, © 1991, 2002, GIA Publications, Inc.

AMEN 169

Cantor, then all:
A - men, a - men, a - men, a - men.

Music: *Missa Emmanuel,* Richard Proulx, © 1991, 2002, GIA Publications, Inc.

AGNUS DEI 170

Cantor:

1. Je - sus, wis - dom and might - y Lord,
2. Je - sus, true branch of Jes - se's tree,
3. Key of Da - vid and Day - spring from on high,
4. De - sire of na - tions, our Em - man - u - el,
you take a - way the

1.-3.
Assembly:
Repeat as needed
sins of the world: have mer - cy on us. Have mer - cy on us.

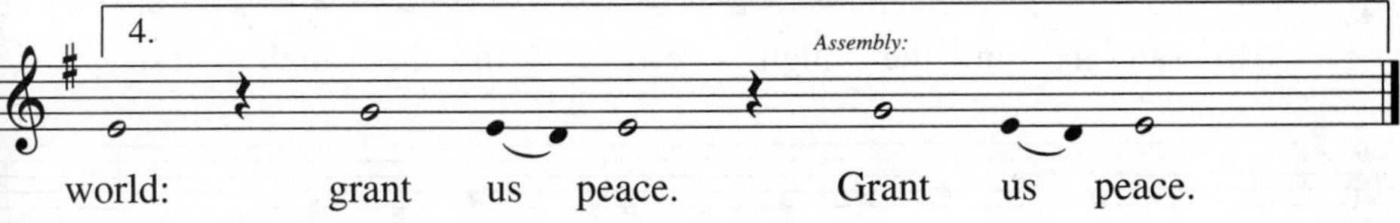
4.
Assembly:
world: grant us peace. Grant us peace.

Music: *Missa Emmanuel,* Richard Proulx, © 1991, 2002, GIA Publications, Inc.

Setting Two

CORPUS CHRISTI MASS

171 SANCTUS

Cantor, then all:
Ho - ly, ho - ly, ho - ly Lord, God of pow'r and might.
Cantor:
Heav'n and earth are full of your glo - ry.
Ho - san - na in the high - est, in the high - est.
All:
Ho - san - na in the high - est, in the high - est.
Cantor:
Blest is he who comes in the name of the Lord.
Ho - san - na in the high - est, in the high - est.
All:
Ho - san - na in the high - est, in the high - est.

Music: *Corpus Christi Mass, Adoro te devote*, setting by Richard Proulx, © 1992, 2002, GIA Publications, Inc.

MEMORIAL ACCLAMATION 172

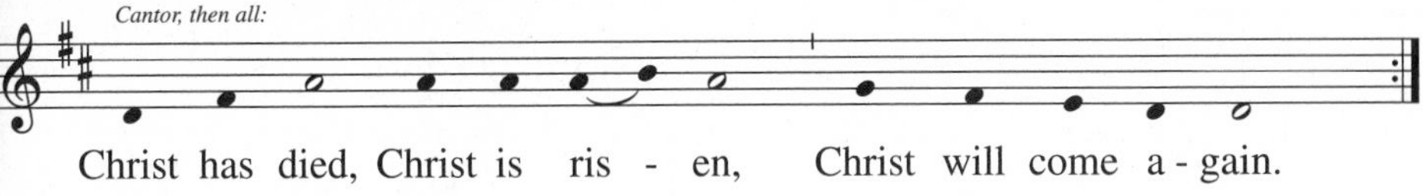
Cantor, then all:
Christ has died, Christ is ris - en, Christ will come a - gain.

Text: ICEL, © 1973
Music: *Corpus Christi Mass, Adoro te devote*, setting by Richard Proulx, © 1992, 2002, GIA Publications, Inc.

AMEN 173

Cantor, then all:
A - men, a - men, a - men.

Music: *Corpus Christi Mass, Adoro te devote,* setting by Richard Proulx, © 1992, 2002, GIA Publications, Inc.

AGNUS DEI 174

Cantor:
1. Je - sus, Lamb of God, Bear - er of our sins,
2. Je - sus, Lamb of God, Sav - ior of the world,
3. Je - sus, Lamb of God, Bread come down from heav'n,
4. Je - sus, Lamb of God, Shep - herd of our souls,

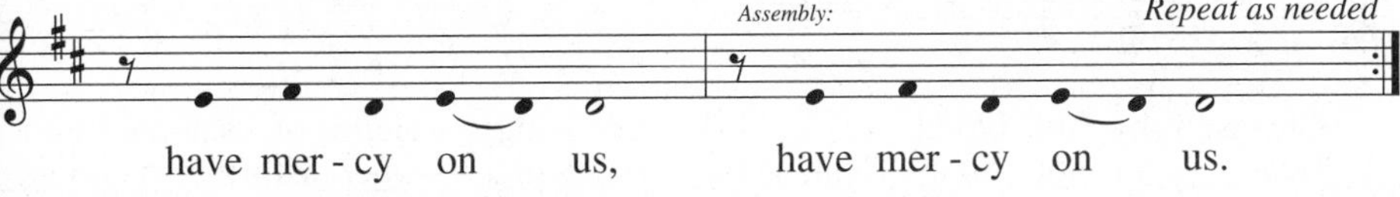
Assembly:
Repeat as needed
have mer - cy on us, have mer - cy on us.

Cantor:
5. Je - sus, Lamb of God, gen - tle Prince of peace,

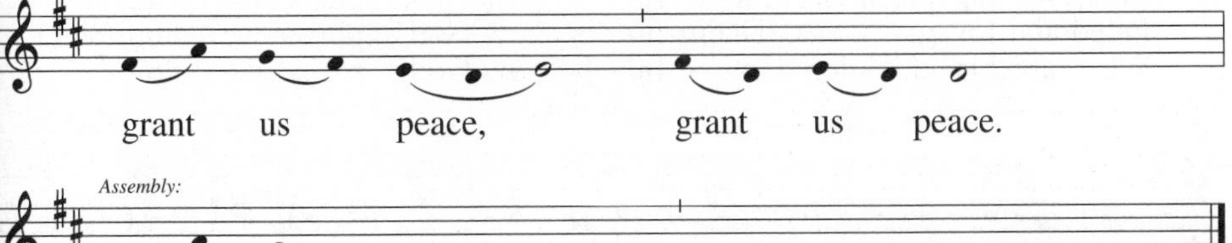
grant us peace, grant us peace.
Assembly:
Grant us peace, grant us peace.

Music: *Corpus Christi Mass, Adoro te devote*, setting by Richard Proulx, © 1992, 2002, GIA Publications, Inc.

Setting Three

MASS OF THE ANGELS AND SAINTS

175 SPRINKLING RITE

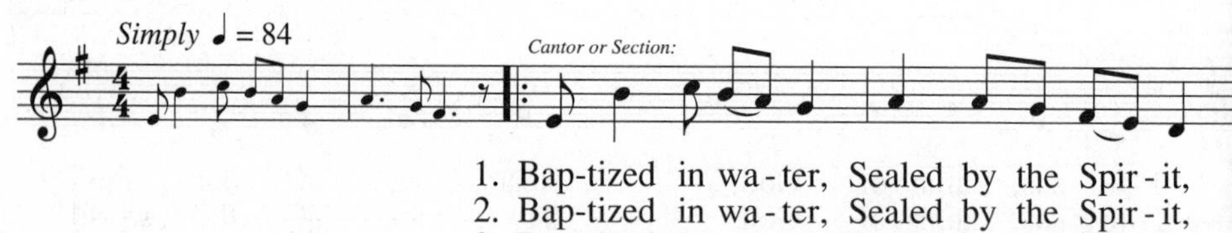
Simply ♩ = 84
Cantor or Section:

1. Bap-tized in wa - ter, Sealed by the Spir - it,
2. Bap-tized in wa - ter, Sealed by the Spir - it,
3. Bap-tized in wa - ter, Sealed by the Spir - it,

Cleansed by the blood of Christ our King: Heirs of sal - va - tion,
Dead in the tomb with Christ our King: One with his ris - ing,
Marked with the sign of Christ our King: Born of one Fa - ther,

3

Trust - ing his prom - ise; Faith - ful - ly now God's praise we sing.
Freed and for - giv - en, Thank-ful - ly now God's praise we sing.
We are his chil - dren, Joy - ful - ly now God's praise we sing.

All:
3
1., 2.
3.

Faith - ful-ly now God's praise we sing.
Thank-ful-ly now God's praise we sing.
Joy - ful-ly now God's praise we sing.

KYRIE ELEISON

176

Gently ♩ = 76
Cantor:
mp
Lord Je - sus, man-na from on high, food for pil-grims and bread of life: Lord, have mer - cy.
Christ Je - sus, wine of joy, blood poured out for sin-ners, and cup of sal-va-tion: Christ, have mer - cy.
All:
mf
Descant:
Lord, have mer - cy.
Christ, have mer - cy.
Cantor:
mf
Lord Je - sus, Lamb of God sac-ri-fice of praise, and guest of the sin-ner: Lord, have mer - cy.
All:
mf
Lord, have mer - cy.

Music: *Mass of the Angels and Saints*, Steven R. Janco, © 1996, GIA Publications, Inc

177 GLORIA

Refrain Intonation
Cantor (or Section):
With drive ♩. = 60-63
mf
Glo - ry to God in the
high - est, and peace to his peo - ple on earth.
God's
Refrain
All:
Glo-ry to God in the high - est, and peace to his peo-ple on
earth.
Verse 1
mf Cantor (or Section):
1. Lord God, heav - en - ly King, al -
might-y God and Fa - ther, we wor-ship you, we
give you thanks, we praise you for your glo - ry.
Refrain
All:
Glo-ry to God in the high - est, and peace to his peo-ple on earth.
mf
Glo-ry to God in the high - est, and peace to his peo-ple on earth.
mf
Glo - ry to God, and peace on earth.

Verse 2
Choir, Sopranos (Cantor: Soprano line)
mp
2. Lord Je - sus Christ, on - ly Son of the Fa - ther,
Altos: mp
2. Lord Je - sus Christ, on - ly Son of the
mf
Lord God, Lamb of God, you take a-way the sin of the world: have
Fa - ther, Lord God, Lamb of God: have mer - cy, have
Men: mf
Lord God, Lamb of God, you take a-way the sin of the world: have
f
mer - cy on us; you are seat - ed at the right hand of the
mer - cy on us; you are seat - ed at the right hand of the
mer - cy on us; you are seat - ed at the right hand of the

ff
non rit.
re - ceive our prayer.
Fa - ther: re - ceive our prayer.
ff
non rit.
re - ceive our prayer.
Refrain
All:
Glo-ry to God in the high - est, and peace to his peo-ple on
f
Glo-ry to God in the high - est, and peace to his peo-ple on
f
Glo - ry to God, and peace on
Verse 3
earth.
Choir:
mf
earth. 3. For you a - lone are the Ho - ly One,
mf
earth.
f you a - lone are the
you a - lone are the Lord, you a - lone are the
f

mf
Most High, Je - sus Christ, with the Ho - ly
mf
cresc.
Fa - ther.
Spir - it, in the glo - ry of God the Fa - ther.
cresc.
Refrain
All:
Glo - ry to God in the high - est, and peace to his peo - ple on earth.
f
Glo - ry to God in the high - est, and peace to his peo - ple on earth.
f
Glo - ry to God, and peace on earth.
Cantor (or Section):
Descant:
rit.
f
Melody:
A - men. A - men.
Choir: f rit.
A - men.
f rit.

Music: *Mass of the Angels and Saints*, Steven R. Janco, © 1996, GIA Publications, Inc.

178 ALLELUIA

With drive ♩. = 60-63
Refrain Intonation
Cantor or Section:
Al - le - lu - ia, al - le - lu - ia, al - le - lu - ia!
Al - le - lu - ia, al - le - lu - ia, al - le - lu - ia!
Refrain
All:
mf/f
Al - le - lu - ia, al - le - lu - ia, al - le - lu - ia.
mf/f
al - le - lu - ia,
Last time rit.
To verse
Final ending
Al - le - lu - ia, al - le - lu - ia, al - le - lu - ia. ia.
al - le - lu - ia,
Cantor:
Speak, O Lord, your servant is list-'ning;
All:
Al - le - lu - ia.
Cantor:
you have the words of ev - er - last - ing life.
All:
D.S.
Al - le - lu - ia.

Music: *Mass of the Angels and Saints*, Steven R. Janco, © 1996, GIA Publications, Inc.

LENTEN GOSPEL ACCLAMATION 179

Sturdily ♩. = 60-63

Refrain Intonation

mf Cantor (or Section):

Glo-ry, praise and hon-or to you, Lord Je - sus Christ.

𝄋 Refrain

Last time rit.

Descant: *mf/f*

Lord Je - sus Christ.

𝄋 *All:* *mf/f*

Last time rit.

Glo-ry, praise and hon-or to you, Lord Je - sus Christ.

mf/f

Lord Je-sus Christ.

Verse*

Cantor: *freely*

a tempo **D.S.**

*The verse of the day should be taken from the Lectionary.

Music: *Mass of the Angels and Saints*, Steven R. Janco, © 1996, GIA Publications, Inc.

GENERAL INTERCESSIONS 180

♩ = 88
Cantor:
a tempo
For… that… We
Last time
Fine
All:
Descant:
pray to the Lord: Lord, hear our prayer.

180-A

Alternate Responses

Cantor:
All:
...we pray to the Lord: Lord, have mer - cy.

180-B

Cantor:
All:
...we pray to the Lord: Gra-cious-ly hear us.

Music: *Mass of the Angels and Saints*, Steven R. Janco, © 1996, GIA Publications, Inc.

181 PREFACE DIALOG

♩. = 60-63
Priest:
Assembly:
The Lord be with you. And
al - so with you.
Priest:
Assembly:
Lift up your hearts. We
lift them up to the Lord.
Priest:
Let us give thanks to the
Lord our God.
Assembly:
It is right to give him thanks and praise.

Music: *Mass of the Angels and Saints*, Steven R. Janco, © 1996, GIA Publications, Inc.

SANCTUS

182

With bounce ♩. = 60-63
All:
mf
Ho - ly, ho - ly, ho - ly Lord,
God of pow-er and might, heav'n and earth are full of your glo -
ry.
Ho - san - na, ho - san - na, ho -
div. f
f Ho - san - na, ho - san - na, ho -
san - na in the high - est. Ho - san - na, ho -
san - na, ho - san - na, ho - san - na, ho -
san - na, ho - san - na in the high - est.
san - na, ho - san - na in the high - est.

mf unis.
Bless - ed is he who comes in the name of the
Ho - san - na, ho - san - na, ho -
f div.
Lord. Ho - san - na, ho - san - na, ho -
f
Descant: f
Ho - san - na, ho -
san - na in the high - est. Ho - san - na, ho -
san - na, ho - san - na, ho - san - na, ho -
rit.
san - na, ho - san - na in the high - est.
san - na, ho - san - na in the high - est.
rit.
san - na, ho - san - na in the high - est.*

**The congregation's final note is the alto "E".*

MEMORIAL ACCLAMATION A 183

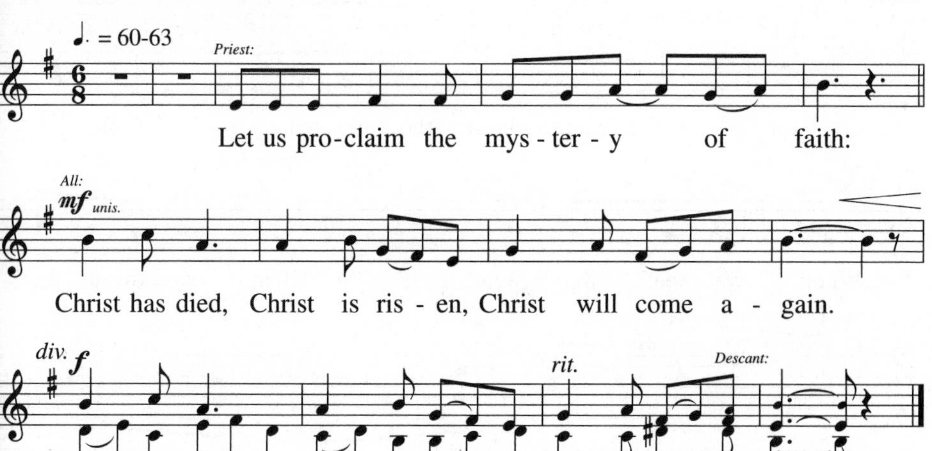
♩. = 60-63
Priest:
Let us pro-claim the mys - ter - y of faith:
All:
mf unis.
Christ has died, Christ is ris - en, Christ will come a - gain.
div. f
rit.
Descant:
Christ has died, Christ is ris - en, Christ will come a - gain.
f
rit.

MEMORIAL ACCLAMATION B 184

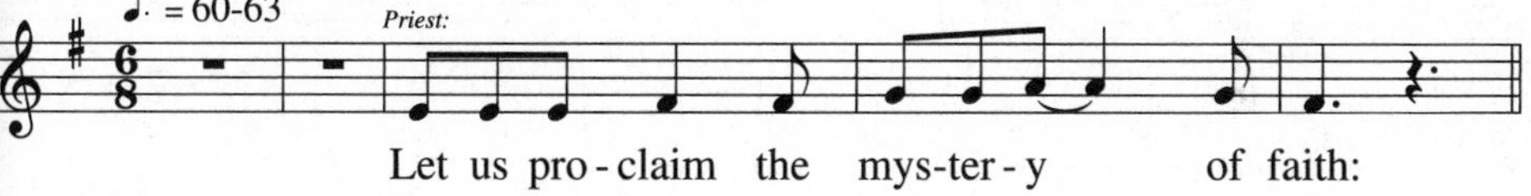
♩. = 60-63
Priest:
Let us pro-claim the mys-ter-y of faith:

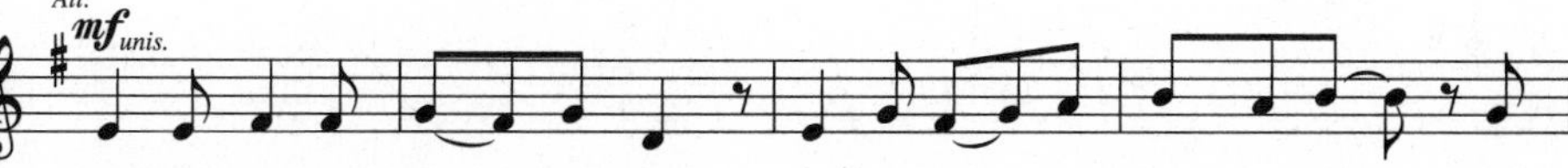
All:
mf unis.
Dy-ing you de - stroyed our death, ris-ing you re-stored our life. Lord

div.
f
rit.
Je - sus, come in glo - ry. Lord Je - sus, come in glo - ry.
f
rit.

185 MEMORIAL ACCLAMATION C

♩. = 60-63

Priest:

Let us pro-claim the mys-ter - y of faith:

All: ***mf*** *unis.*

When we eat this bread, when we drink this cup, we pro - claim your death, Lord Je - sus, un - til you come in glo - ry.

div. ***f*** *rit.*

Text: ICEL, © 1973
Music: *Mass of the Angels and Saints*, Steven R. Janco, © 1996, GIA Publications, Inc.

186 MEMORIAL ACCLAMATION D

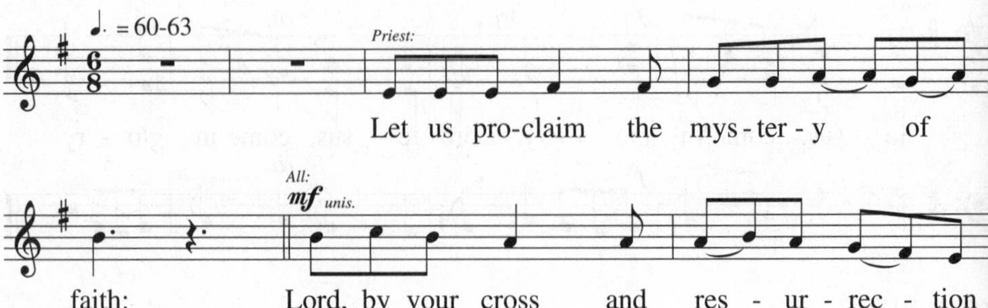

♩. = 60-63
Priest:
Let us pro-claim the mys-ter - y of
faith:
All:
mf unis.
Lord, by your cross and res - ur - rec - tion

div.
f
you have set us free. You are the Sav - ior
You are the Sav - ior
rit.
Descant:
of the world, the Sav - ior of the world.
rit.
of the world,

Text: ICEL, © 1973
Music: *Mass of the Angels and Saints*, Steven R. Janco, © 1996, GIA Publications, Inc.

AMEN

187

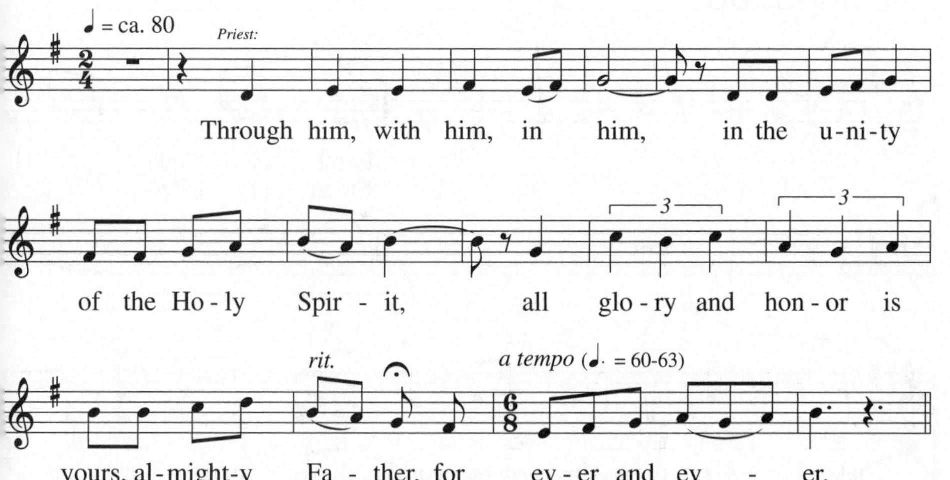
♩ = ca. 80
Priest:
Through him, with him, in him, in the u-ni-ty
of the Ho-ly Spir - it, all glo-ry and hon-or is
rit.
a tempo (♩. = 60-63)
yours, al-might-y Fa - ther, for ev-er and ev - er.

All: *f*

A - men.

A - men, A - men, A - men, A - men.

rit. *ff*

Descant:

Melody:

A - men.

rit. *ff*

A - men, A - men, A - men.

rit. *ff*

Music: *Mass of the Angels and Saints*, Steven R. Janco, © 1996, GIA Publications, Inc.

188 AGNUS DEI

Gently ♩ = ca. 84
Cantor or choir:
mp
Lamb of God, you
Bread of Life,
take a-way the sins of the world: have mer - cy on

+Assembly:
us. Have mer - cy on us.
mf
unis.
div.
Lamb of God, you take a-way the sins of the world:
mf
Descant: rit.
mf Grant us peace.
mp
+Assembly:
grant us peace. Grant us peace.
mp
mf rit.

Music: *Mass of the Angels and Saints*, Steven R. Janco, © 1996, GIA Publications, Inc.

Additional Tropes

Advent
Promise of God
Long-awaited Savior
Rod of Jesse
Key of David

Christmas
Prince of peace
Word made flesh
Son of God
Light of the world

Lent
Mercy of God
Healer of souls
Refuge of sinners
Tree of life

Easter
Risen Lord
Paschal Lamb
Shepherd of all
Dawn from on high

Ordinary Time
Saving cup
Hope of the poor
Justiceof God
Bread of pilgrims
Lord of love
King of kings

Setting Four

BENEATH THE TREE OF LIFE

189 SPRINKLING RITE

Refrain* ♩. = 56-58
Descant:
Springs of wa - ter,
Springs of wa - ter, bless the Lord. Sing your glo - ry and
Sing your glo - ry and praise for - ev - er! Al - le - lu - ia!
praise for - ev - er. Al - le - lu - ia! Sing your
To verses
Final ending
Glo - ry and praise!
glo - ry and praise!

*Refrain may be sung continously under verses.

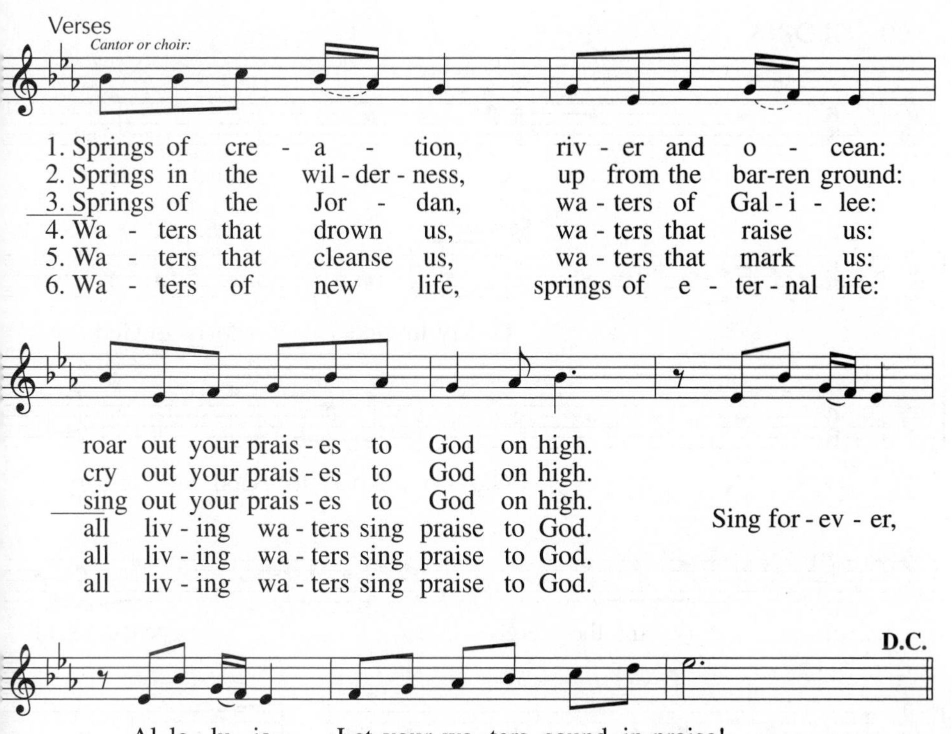
Verses
Cantor or choir:
1. Springs of cre - a - tion, riv - er and o - cean: roar out your prais - es to God on high.
2. Springs in the wil - der - ness, up from the bar-ren ground: cry out your prais - es to God on high.
3. Springs of the Jor - dan, wa - ters of Gal - i - lee: sing out your prais - es to God on high.
4. Wa - ters that drown us, wa - ters that raise us: all liv - ing wa - ters sing praise to God.
5. Wa - ters that cleanse us, wa - ters that mark us: all liv - ing wa - ters sing praise to God.
6. Wa - ters of new life, springs of e - ter - nal life: all liv - ing wa - ters sing praise to God.
Sing for - ev - er, Al-le - lu - ia. Let your wa - ters sound in praise!
D.C.

190 GLORIA

♩. = 56-58
Refrain
Descant: (after vs. 2)
Glo - ry, glo - ry,
Melody:
Glo-ry to God, glo-ry to God,
Optional harmony:
Glo - ry, glo-ry to God, glo-ry to
glo - ry in the high - est, peace to his
glo - ry to God in the high - est, and peace to his peo - ple,
God, to God in the high - est, and peace to his peo - ple,
1., 2. To verses 1 and 2
peo-ple, peace to his peo - ple, his
1., 2. To verses 1 and 2
peace to his peo-ple, peace to his peo-ple on earth.
peace to his peo-ple, peace to his peo-ple, his peo-ple on earth.

3.
To verse 3
4.
peo - ple on earth.
peo - ple on earth.
3.
To verse 3
4.
earth.
earth.
peo - ple on earth.
peo - ple on earth.
Verse 1
1. Lord God, heav - en - ly King, al - might - y
God and Fa - ther, we wor - ship you, we
D.S.
give you thanks, we praise you for your glo - ry.
Verse 2
2. Lord Je - sus Christ, on - ly Son of the Fa - ther,
2. Lord Je - sus, Lord Je - sus Christ, Son of the Fa - ther,
Lord God, Lamb of God, you take a - way the sin of the
on us; you are seat - ed at the
world: have mer - cy, have mer - cy on us; seat - ed at the

D.S.
right hand of the Fa - ther: re - ceive our prayer.
Verse 3
T, B unis.
div.
you a-lone are the
3. For you a-lone are the Ho - ly One, you a - lone, a -
Lord,
lone are the Lord, you a-lone are the Most High,
in the
Je - sus Christ, with the Ho - ly Spir - it, in the
Fa - ther.
D.S.
glo - ry of God, the glo - ry of God.
Fa - ther.
glo - ry of God, the glo - ry of God.

ALLELUIA

191

♩. = 56-58
Refrain
Descant:
Al - le - lu - ia,
Al-le-lu-ia, Al-le-lu-ia,
Al - le, Al-le-lu - ia, Al-le-lu -
Al - le-lu - ia, Al - le-lu - ia,
Al - le-lu - ia, Al-le-lu - ia, Al-le-lu -
Al - le-lu - ia.
Al - le-lu - ia, Al-le-lu-ia, Al - le-lu-ia,
ia, Al - le, Al-le-lu-ia, Al - le-lu-ia,
Al - le-lu - ia, Al - le-lu, Al-le,
Last time
ia, Al-le-lu - ia, Al-le-lu - ia.
Al - le-lu - ia.
Last time
Al - le-lu-ia, Al - le-lu - ia, Al-le-lu-ia.
Last time
Al - le-lu-ia, Al - le-lu - ia.

Verses
D.S.

Music: *Beneath the Tree of Life*, Marty Haugen, © 2000, 2001, GIA Publications, Inc.

192 SANCTUS

♩ = 92

All:

Ho-ly, ho-ly, ho-ly Lord,

Descant:

God of pow-er and might.

God of pow-er and might, heav-en and earth are

Ho - san - na,

full of your glo - ry. Ho - san - na, ho -

Ho- san - na,

div.

full of your glo - ry. Ho - san - na, ho -

ho - san - na, san - na in the high - est.

san - na, ho - san - na

ho - san - na, san - na in the high - est.

san - na, ho - san - na in the high - est.

Bless-ed is he, bless-ed is he who comes in the name of the
Lord.
unis.
Ho - san - na, ho - san - na,
Ho - san - na, ho - san - na, ho -
Ho - san - na, ho - san - na, ho -
san-na in the high - est, ho-san-na in the high - est!
san-na
in the high - est, ho - san - na in the high - est!
san-na
san-na

Music: *Beneath the Tree of Life*, Marty Haugen, © 2000, 2001, GIA Publications, Inc.

193 MEMORIAL ACCLAMATION

All:

Christ has died. Christ is ris - en.

Descant:

Christ will come a - gain. Christ has

Christ will come a - gain. Christ has died.

died, and ris - en. Christ will come, will come a-gain.

Christ is ris - en. Christ will come a - gain.
Christ will come, will come a-gain.

Christ is ris - en. Christ will come a - gain.

Text: ICEL, © 1973
Music: *Beneath the Tree of Life*, Marty Haugen, © 2000, 2001, GIA Publications, Inc.

194 AMEN

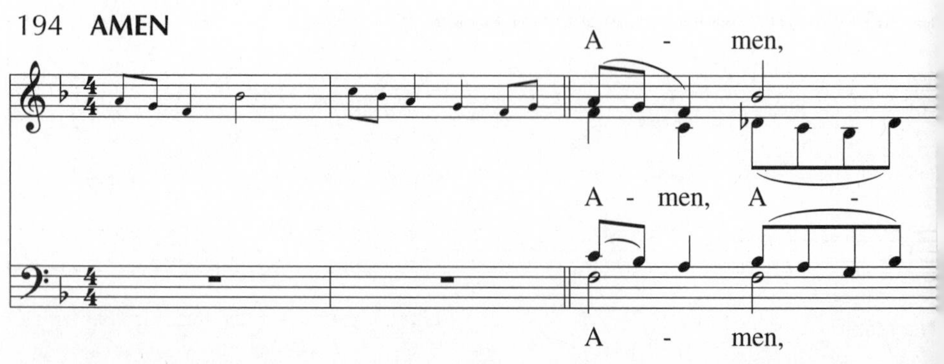
A - men,
A - men, A -
A - men,

A - men, A - men!
men, A - men, A - men, A - men!
A - men, A - men!

Music: *Beneath the Tree of Life*, Marty Haugen, © 2000, 2001, GIA Publications, Inc.

AGNUS DEI

195

Last time to coda ⊕

Cantor:

Lamb of God, you take a - way the sins of the world:
Bread of Life, you give your - self as food for the world:
Cup of Life, poured out as God's com - pas - sion and love:
Prince of Peace, you heal the wounds of ha - tred and strife:
*Lamb of God, you take a - way the sins of the

Last time to coda ⊕

Keyboard or Choir: hum or oo

To repeat

All:

Repeat as needed

have mer - cy on us. Have mer - cy on us.

hum or oo Have mer - cy on us.

Have mer - cy on us.

*Last time

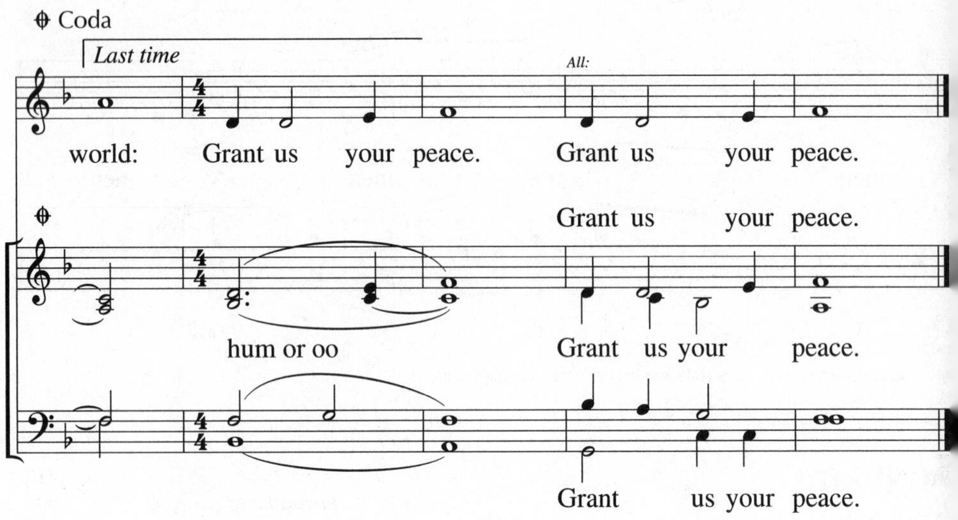
Coda
Last time
All:
world: Grant us your peace. Grant us your peace.
Grant us your peace.
hum or oo
Grant us your peace.
Grant us your peace.

Music: *Beneath the Tree of Life*, Marty Haugen, © 2000, 2001, GIA Publications, Inc.

Setting Five

DO THIS IN MEMORY OF ME

GLORIA

196

In one 𝅗𝅥. = 54-60
Refrain
Descant:
Glo - ry to God! Glo - ry!
Glo-ry, glo - ry to God! Glo-ry in the
Glo - ry! Peace, peace to his peo - ple!
high - est! Peace, peace to his peo - ple on
1.-3. To verses
4.
Glo - ry, Glo - ry to God! Glo-ry to God!
earth! 3. For

Verse 1
1. Lord God, heav - en - ly King, al - might - y
God and Fa - ther, we wor - ship you, we
D.C.
give you thanks, we praise you for your glo - ry.
Verse 2
2. Lord Je - sus Christ, on - ly Son of the Fa -
ther, Lord God, Lamb of God, you take a -
way the sin of the world: have mer - cy on us;
you are seat - ed at the right hand of the Fa -
D.C.
ther: re - ceive our prayer.
Verse 3
(3.) you a - lone are the Ho - ly One, you a - lone are the
Lord, you a - lone are the Most

div.
High, Je - sus Christ, with the Ho - ly
div.
High, Je - sus Christ, with the Ho - ly

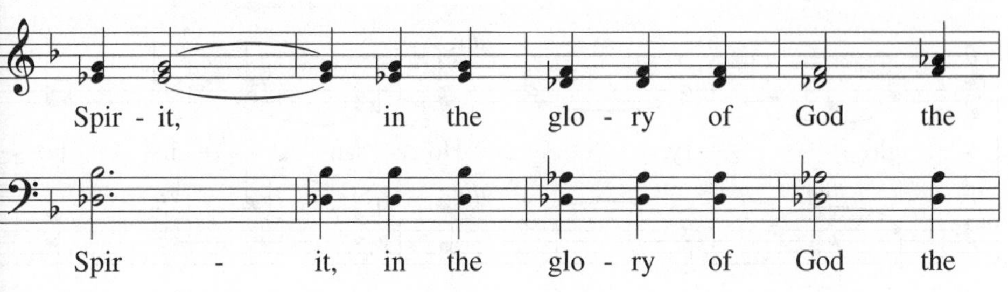
Spir - it, in the glo - ry of God the
Spir - it, in the glo - ry of God the

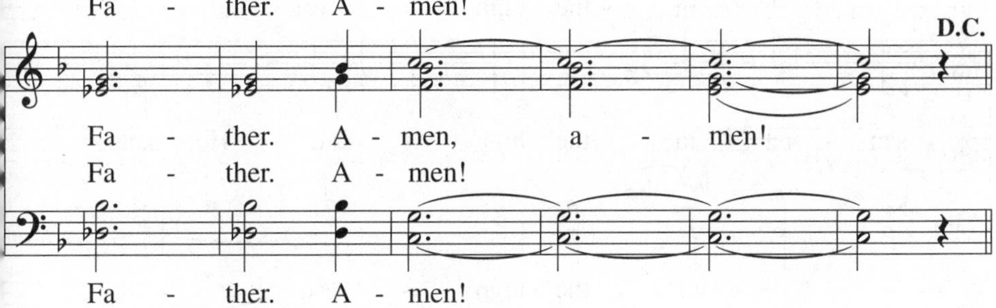
Fa - ther. A - men!
D.C.
Fa - ther. A - men, a - men!
Fa - ther. A - men!
Fa - ther. A - men!

ALLELUIA 197

In one = 54-60
Al-le - lu - ia, al - le - lu - ia!
Al-le - lu - ia! Al-le - lu - ia!
Verse
D.C.

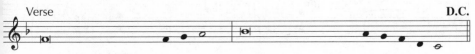

198 SANCTUS

In one 𝅗𝅥. = 54-60
Ho - ly, ho - ly, ho - ly, Lord, God of
pow - er and might, heav - en and earth are full of your
div.
glo - ry. Ho - san - na, ho -
div.
in the high - est.
san - na in the high - est. Ho - san -
in the high - est.
unis.
na. Bless - ed is he who comes in the name of the
unis.
div.
Lord. Ho - san - na, ho - san - na
div.

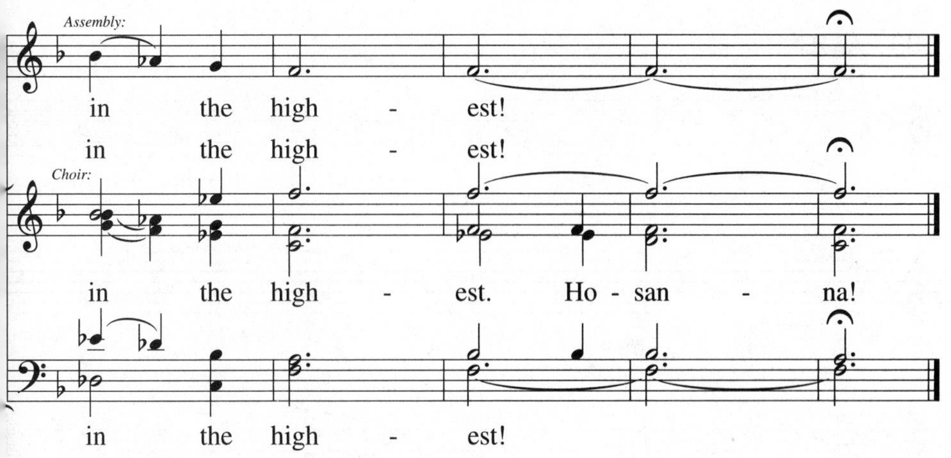
Assembly:
in the high - est!
in the high - est!
Choir:
in the high - est. Ho - san - na!
in the high - est!

Music: *Do This in Memory of Me*, David Haas, © 2003, GIA Publications, Inc.

MEMORIAL ACCLAMATION 199

Christ has died. Christ is ris - en.

Assembly:
Christ will come, Christ will come a -

Choir:
Christ will come, Christ will come a -

div.

Christ will come a -

gain.

gain.

rit.

gain. Christ will come.

gain.

Text: ICEL, © 1973
Music: *Do This in Memory of Me*, David Haas, © 2003, GIA Publications, Inc.

200 AMEN

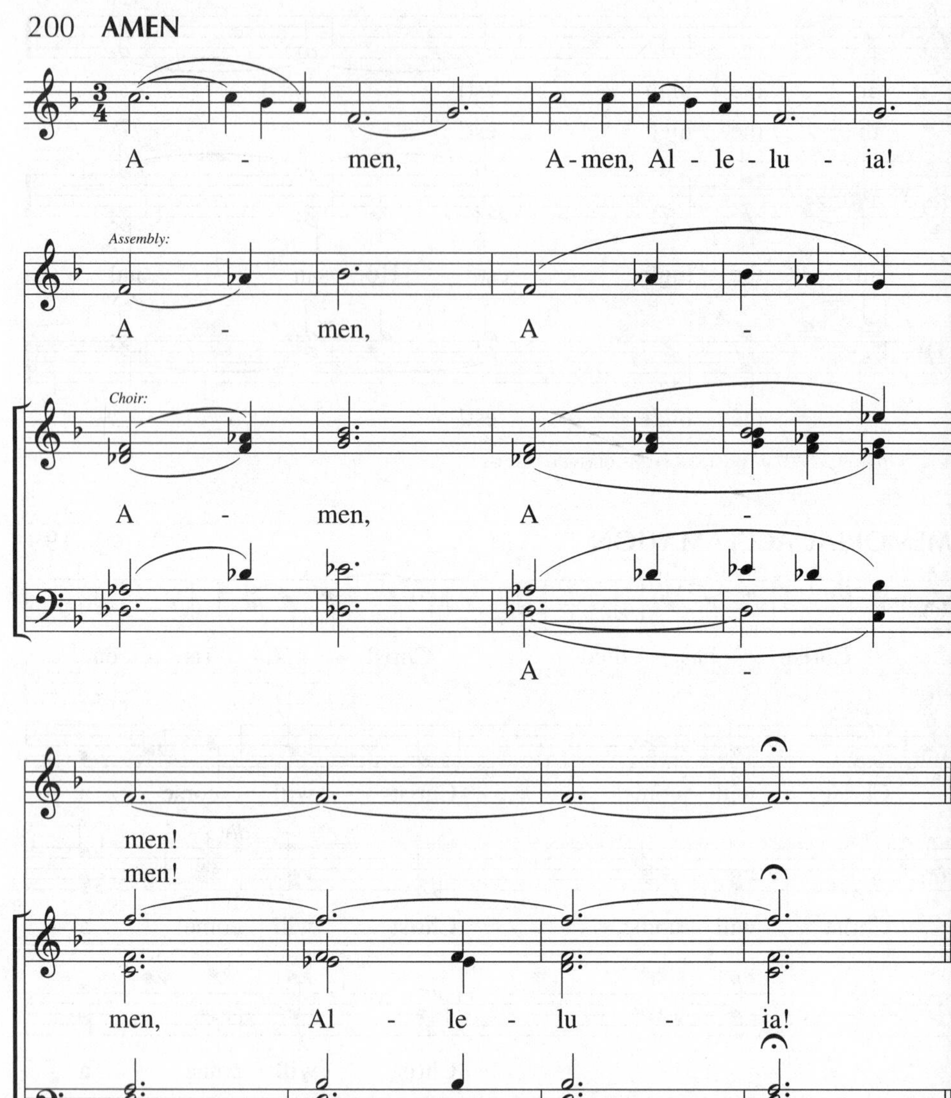
A - men, A-men, Al - le - lu - ia!
Assembly:
A - men, A -
Choir:
A - men, A -
A -
men!
men!
men, Al - le - lu - ia!
men!

Music: *Do This in Memory of Me*, David Haas, © 2003, GIA Publications, Inc.

AGNUS DEI

201

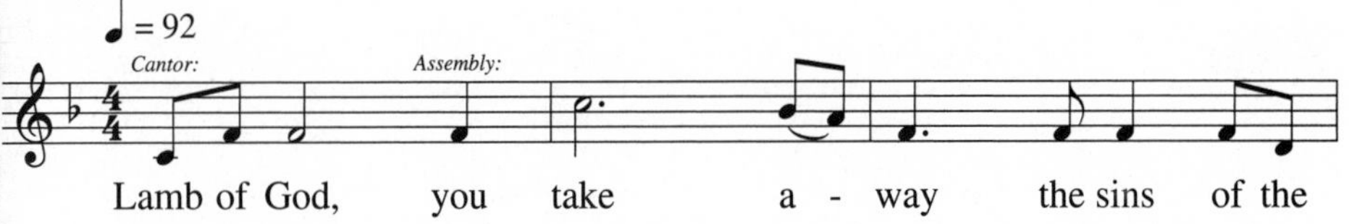
♩ = 92
Cantor:
Assembly:
Lamb of God, you take a - way the sins of the

1., 2.
div.
world: have mer - cy on us.
div.

3.
world: grant us your peace, grant us your peace.

Music: *Do This in Memory of Me*, David Haas, © 2003, GIA Publications, Inc.

Setting Six

A COMMUNITY MASS

202 **KYRIE**

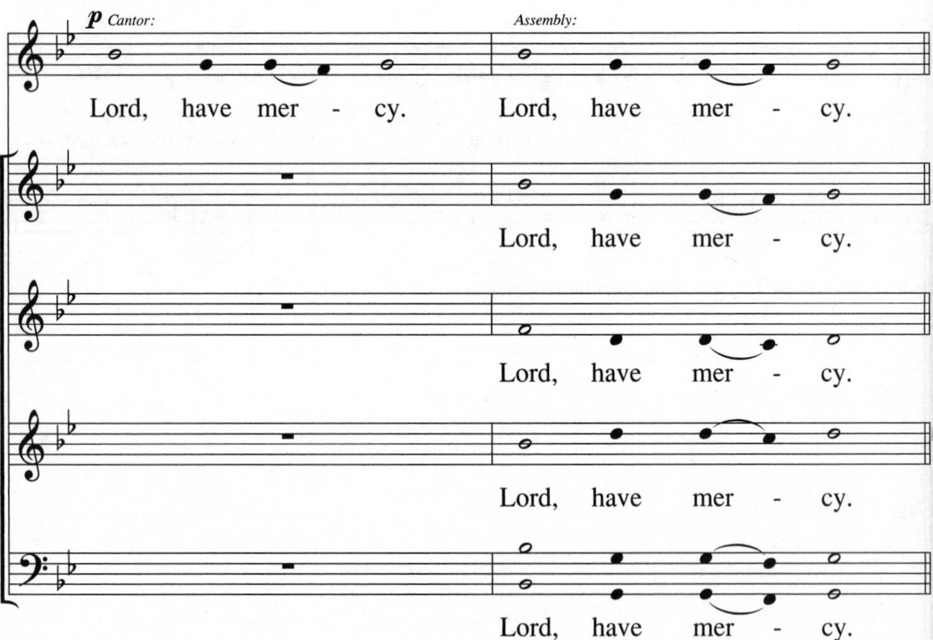

p Cantor:
Lord, have mer - cy.
Assembly:
Lord, have mer - cy.
Lord, have mer - cy.
Lord, have mer - cy.
Lord, have mer - cy.
Lord, have mer - cy.

mp Cantor:
Assembly:
Christ, have mer - cy. Christ, have mer - cy.
Christ, have mer - cy.
Christ, have mer - cy.
Christ, have mer - cy.
Christ, have mer - cy.
mf Cantor:
Assembly:
Lord, have mer - cy. Lord, have mer - cy.
dim.
Lord, have mer - cy.
dim.
Lord, have mer - cy.
dim.
Lord, have mer - cy.
Lord, have mer - cy.
dim.
Lord, Lord.

Music: *A Community Mass,* Richard Proulx, © 1971, 1977, GIA Publications, Inc.

203 GLORIA

Glo - ry to God in the
high - est, and peace to his peo-ple on earth. Lord God, heav-en-ly
King, al - might - y God and Fa-ther, We wor - ship you, we
give you thanks, we praise you for your glo - ry.
Mixed voices:
Soprano:
Lord, Je - sus Christ, on - ly
Alto:
Lord Je - sus Christ, on - ly
Tenor:
Lord, Je - sus Christ, on - ly
Bass:
Lord, on - ly
Unison voices:
Lord, Je - sus Christ, on - ly

Son of the Fa - ther, Lord, God,
Son of the Fa - ther, Lord, God,
Son of the Fa - ther, Lord, God,
Son of the Fa - ther, Lord,
Son of the Fa - ther, Lord, God,
Lamb of God, you take a - way the sin of the
Lamb of God, you take a - way the sin of the
Lamb of God, you take a - way the sin of the
you take a - way the sin of the
Lamb of God, you take a - way the sin of the

world: have mer - cy on us; you
world: have mer - cy on us;
world: have mer - cy on us;
world: have mer - cy on us;
world: have mer - cy on us;
are seat - ed at the right hand of the
you are seat - ed at the right hand of the
you are seat - ed at the right hand of the
you at the right hand of the
you are seat - ed at the right hand of the

Fa - ther: re - ceive our pray'r, re -
Fa - ther: re - ceive our pray'r, re -
Fa - ther: re - ceive,
Fa - ther: re - ceive, re -
Fa - ther: re - ceive our pray'r, re -
rall.
ceive, re - ceive our pray'r.
rall.
ceive re - ceive our pray'r.
rall.
re - ceive our pray'r.
rall.
ceive, re - ceive our pray'r.
rall.
ceive, re - ceive our pray'r.

f All:

For you a-lone are the Ho-ly One, you a-lone are the Lord, you a-lone are the Most High, Je-sus Christ with the Ho-ly Spir-it in the glo-ry of God the Fa-ther. A-men.

Sop. Descant

A-men.

Music: *A Community Mass,* Richard Proulx, © 1971, 1977, GIA Publications, Inc.

204 SANCTUS

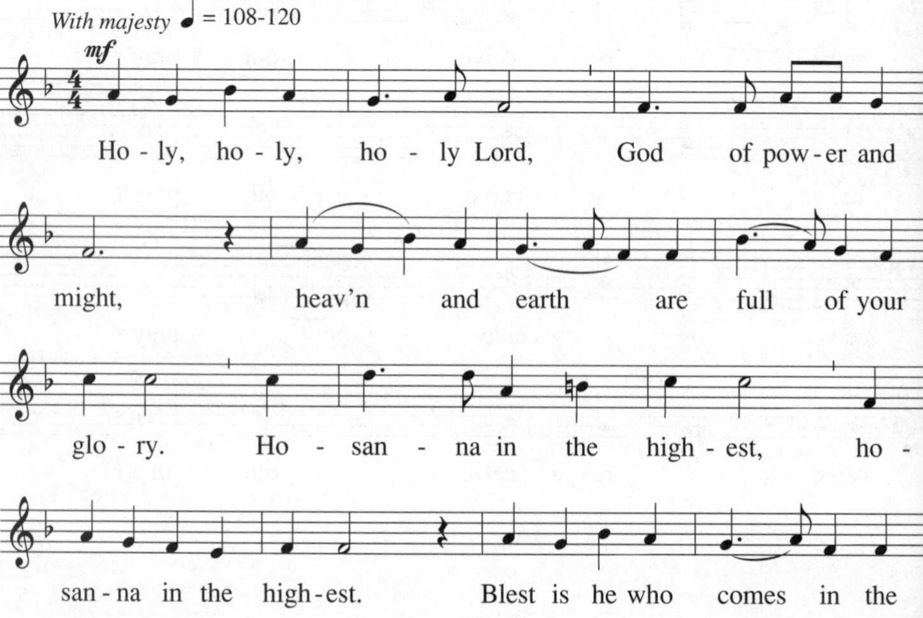
With majesty ♩ = 108-120
mf
Ho-ly, ho-ly, ho-ly Lord, God of pow-er and might,
heav'n and earth are full of your glo-ry.
Ho-san-na in the high-est, ho-san-na in the high-est.
Blest is he who comes in the

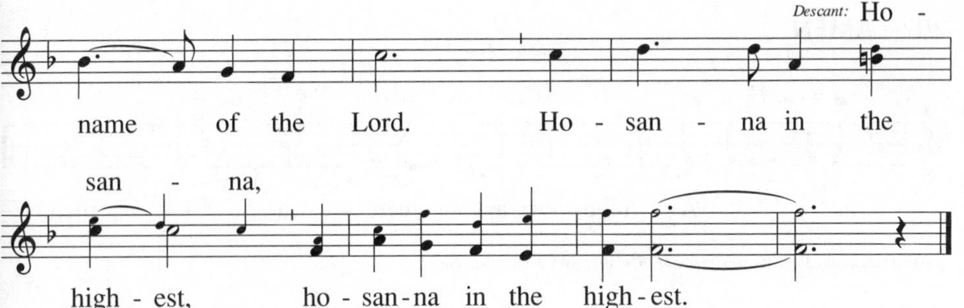
Descant: Ho -
name of the Lord. Ho - san - na in the
san - na,
high - est, ho - san - na in the high - est.

Music: *A Community Mass*, Richard Proulx, © 1971, 1977, GIA Publications, Inc.

MEMORIAL ACCLAMATION A 205

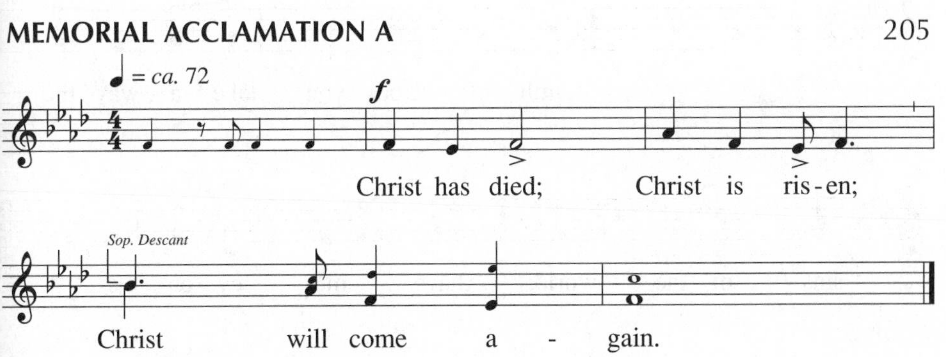
♩ = ca. 72
f
Christ has died; Christ is ris - en;
Sop. Descant
Christ will come a - gain.

Text: ICEL, © 1973
Music: *A Community Mass,* Richard Proulx, © 1971, 1977, GIA Publications, Inc.

MEMORIAL ACCLAMATION C 206

♩ = 108-120
When we eat this bread and drink this cup, we pro -
claim your death, Lord Je - sus, un - til you come in glo - ry.

Text: ICEL, © 1973
Music: *A Community Mass*, Richard Proulx, © 1988, GIA Publications, Inc.

207 AMEN

= ca. 72
f
Sop. Descant
A - men, a - men, a - men.

Music: *A Community Mass,* Richard Proulx, © 1971, 1977, GIA Publications, Inc.

208 AGNUS DEI

Gently

mp

Lamb of God, you take a - way the sins of the world: have mer - cy on us.

mf Sop. Descant

Lamb of God, you take a - way the sins of the world: grant us peace.

rall.

grant us peace.

Music: *A Community Mass,* Richard Proulx, © 1971, 1977, GIA Publications, Inc.

Setting Seven

MASS OF REMEMBRANCE

KYRIE

209

♩ = 72-76
Refrain
All: mp
Ky-ri - e e - le - i-son, Chri - ste e - le - i - son,
Descant: pp
Lord, have mer - cy, Christ, have mer - cy,
To verses
Ky - ri - e e - le - i - son.
Lord, have mer - cy.

Last time
son.
cy.
Verses 1, 2
Priest, deacon, or cantor:
1. Lord Je - sus, you came to gath - er the na - tions
2. You come in word and sac - ra - ment to
rit.
D.S.
in - to the peace of God's King - dom.
strength - en us in ho - li - ness.
Verse 3
Priest, deacon, or cantor:
3. You will come in glo - ry with sal -
rit.
D.S.
va - tion for your peo - ple.

Music: *Mass of Remembrance,* Marty Haugen, © 1987, GIA Publications, Inc.

GLORIA

210

♩ = 112-120

f Priest or cantor:
Glo - ry to God in the high-est, and peace to his peo-ple on earth.

All:
Glo - ry to God in the high-est, and peace to his peo-ple on earth.

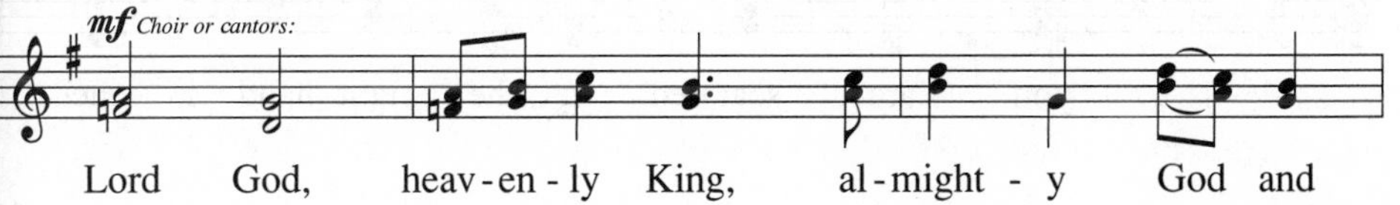
mf Choir or cantors:
Lord God, heav - en - ly King, al - might - y God and

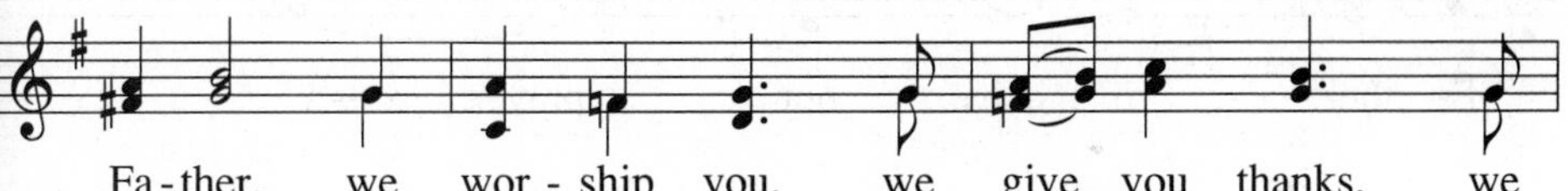
Fa - ther, we wor - ship you, we give you thanks, we

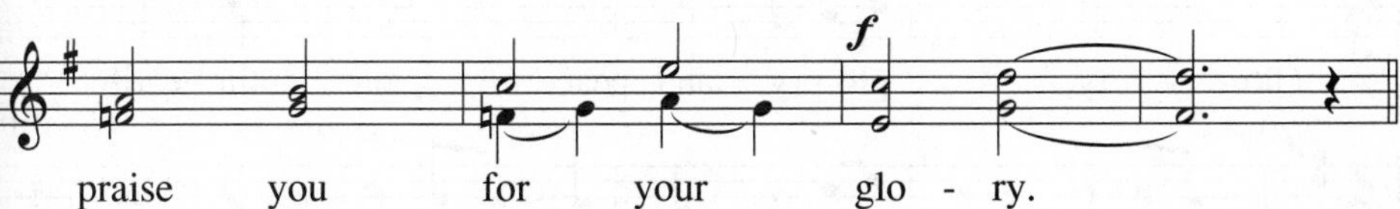
praise you for your glo - ry.
f

All: f
Glo - ry to God in the high-est, and peace to his peo-ple on earth.

Glo - ry to God in the high-est, and peace to his peo-ple on earth.

p Choir or cantors:
Lord Je - sus Christ, on - ly Son of the Fa-ther,
Lord God, Lamb of God, you take a - way the
sin of the world: have mer - cy on us;
you are seat - ed at the right hand of the
Fa - ther: re - ceive our prayer.
f Descant:
Glo - ry, glo - ry, and peace on the earth.
f All:
Glo - ry to God in the high-est, and peace to his peo-ple on earth.
Glo - ry, glo - ry and peace on the earth.
Glo - ry to God in the high-est, and peace to his peo-ple on earth.

Choir or cantors:
For you a - lone are the Ho-ly One, you a-lone are the
Lord, you a - lone are the Most High,
cresc.
Je - sus Christ, with the Ho - ly Spir - it, in the
glo - ry of God the Fa-ther. A - men, a - men.
A - men. A -
Descant:
Glo - ry, glo - ry, and
men! A -
All: Glo - ry to God in the high - est, and
peace on the earth. Glo - ry,
men! A - men!
peace to his peo-ple on earth. Glo - ry to God in the
rit.
glo - ry and peace on the earth!
A - men! A - men!
high - est, and peace to his peo-ple on earth!

Music: *Mass of Remembrance*, Marty Haugen, © 1987, GIA Publications, Inc.

211 ALLELUIA

♩ = 108-116
f 1. Cantor, then all:
2.
3.
To repeat
Al - le - lu - ia, al - le - lu - ia, al - le - lu - ia!
Descant:
Al - le - lu - ia, al - le - lu - ia!
To verses
Last time (repeat as needed to finish canon)
ff
ia! ia! Al - le - lu - ia!
ia! ia! Al - le - lu - ia!
Verse 1
mf Cantor or schola:
1. Speak, O Lord, your ser - vant is lis - t'ning,
D.S.
you have the words of ev - er - last - ing life.
Verse 2
mf Cantor or schola:
2. "I am the Light of the world," says the Lord,
D.S.
"All who fol - low me shall have the light of life."

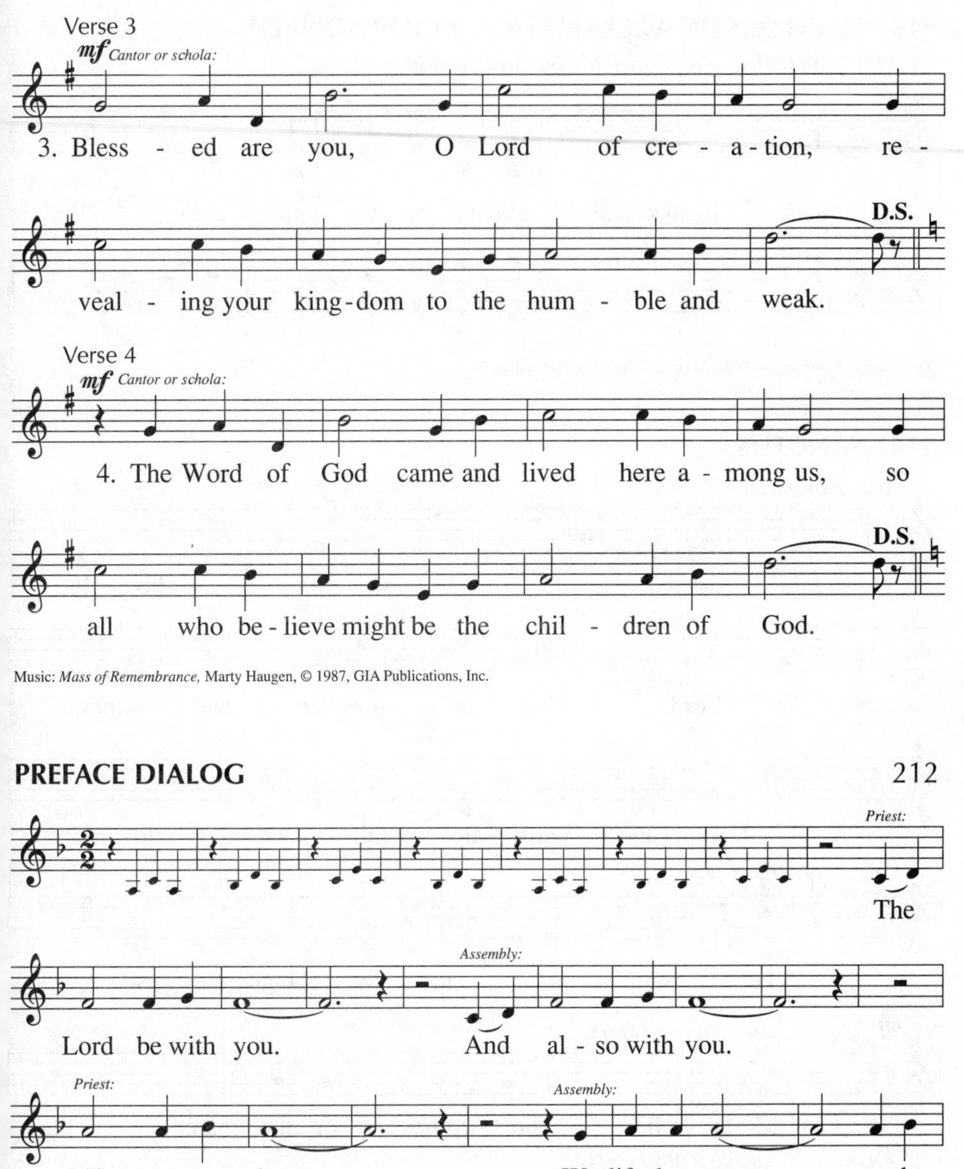
Verse 3
mf Cantor or schola:
3. Bless - ed are you, O Lord of cre - a - tion, re - veal - ing your king - dom to the hum - ble and weak.
D.S.
Verse 4
mf Cantor or schola:
4. The Word of God came and lived here a - mong us, so all who be - lieve might be the chil - dren of God.
D.S.

Music: *Mass of Remembrance,* Marty Haugen, © 1987, GIA Publications, Inc.

PREFACE DIALOG 212

Priest:
The Lord be with you.
Assembly:
And al - so with you.
Priest:
Lift up your hearts.
Assembly:
We lift them up to the Lord.
Priest:
Let us give thanks to the Lord our God.
Assembly:
It is right to give him thanks and praise.
poco rit.

Music: *Mass of Remembrance,* Marty Haugen, © 1987, GIA Publications, Inc.

213 EUCHARISTIC ACCLAMATION IA (OPTIONAL)*

**As in the Eucharistic Prayers for Masses with Children.*

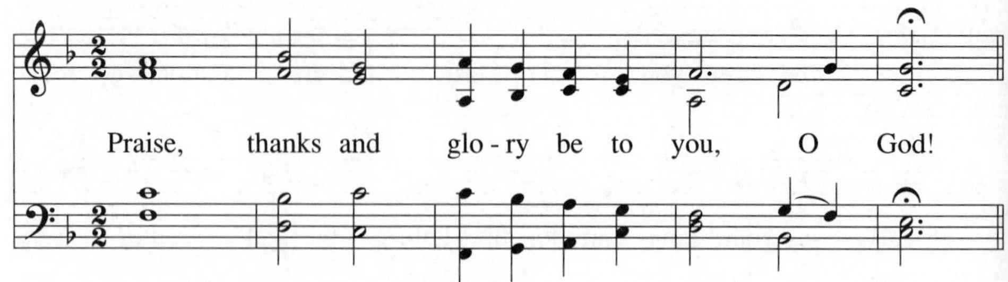
Praise, thanks and glo - ry be to you, O God!

Music: *Mass of Remembrance*, Marty Haugen, © 1987, GIA Publications, Inc.

214 SANCTUS

With movement 𝅗𝅥 = 72

f

Ho - ly, ho - ly,

ho - ly Lord, God of pow - er and might,

heav'n and earth are full of your glo - ry.

ff *Melody:* *Harmony:* *dim.*

Ho - san - na in the high - est.

mp *Melody:* *poco a poco cresc.*

Bless - ed is he who comes in the name of the

mp *Harmony:* *poco a poco cresc.*

Bless - ed is he who comes in the

f

Lord. Ho - san - na in the high -

name of the Lord.

f

Ho - san - na

ff
rit.
est. Ho - san - na in the high - est!
rit.
in the high - est, the high - est!

Music: *Mass of Remembrance,* Marty Haugen, © 1987, GIA Publications, Inc.

EUCHARISTIC ACCLAMATION IB (OPTIONAL) 215

Praise, thanks and glo - ry be to you, O Christ!

Music: *Mass of Remembrance*, Marty Haugen, © 1987, GIA Publications, Inc.

MEMORIAL ACCLAMATION 216

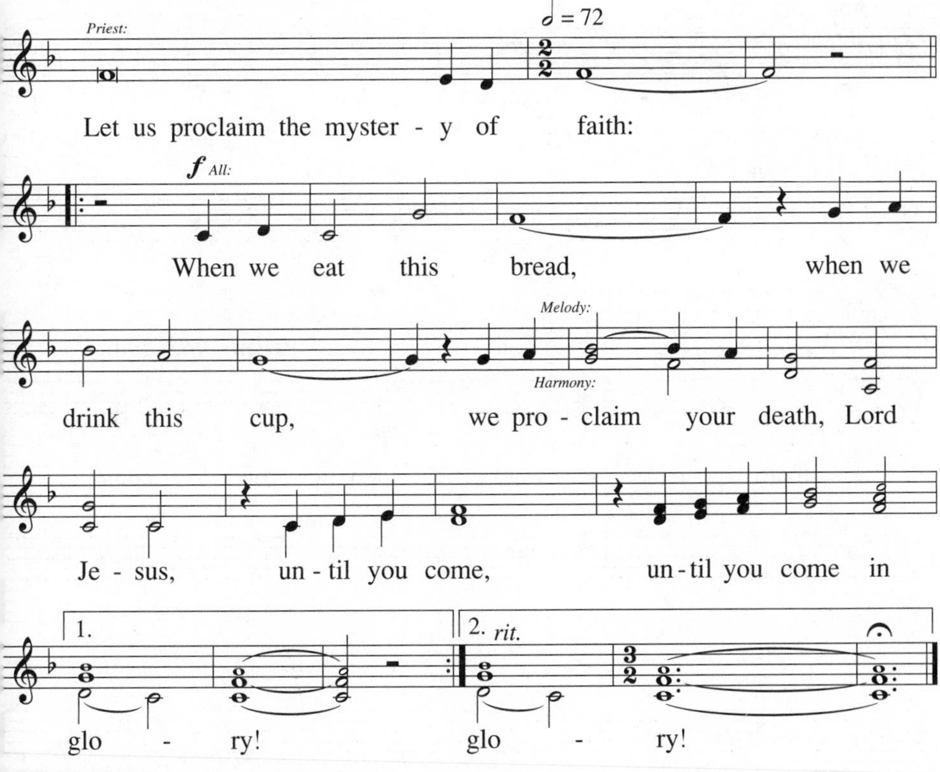

Priest: ♩ = 72

Let us proclaim the myster - y of faith:

f All:

When we eat this bread, when we drink this cup, we pro - claim your death, Lord Je - sus, un - til you come, un - til you come in

Melody: *Harmony:*

1. glo - ry! 2. *rit.* glo - ry!

Text: ICEL, © 1973
Music: *Mass of Remembrance*, Marty Haugen, © 1987, GIA Publications, Inc.

217 EUCHARISTIC ACCLAMATION II (OPTIONAL)

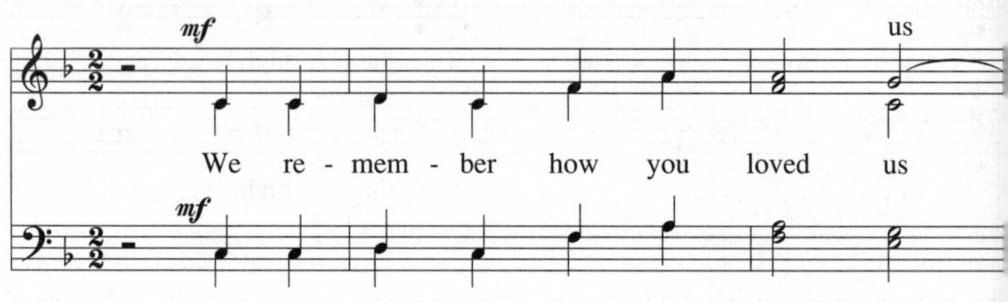
mf
us
We re - mem - ber how you loved us
mf

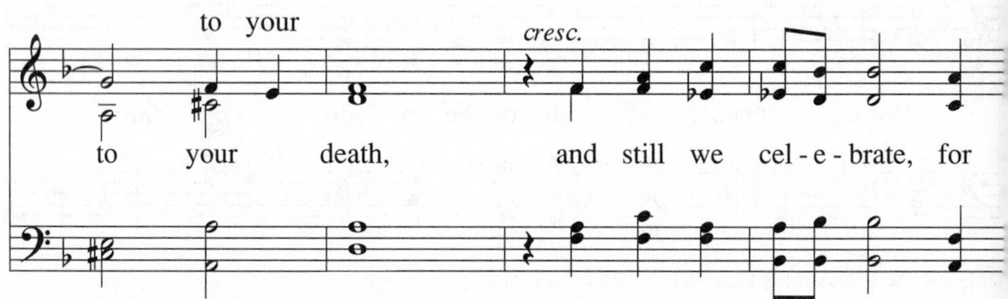
to your
cresc.
to your death, and still we cel - e - brate, for

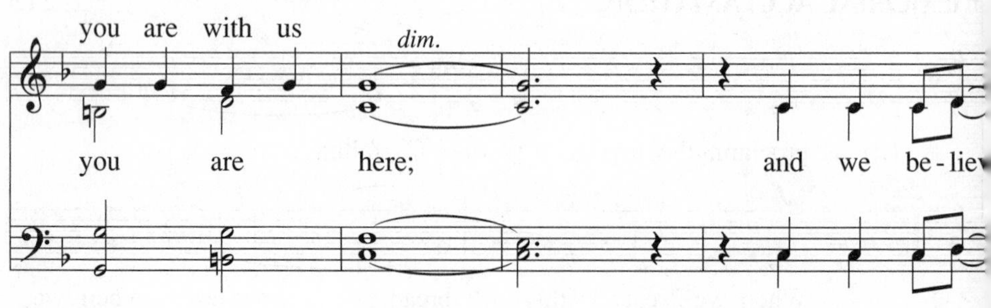
you are with us
dim.
you are here; and we be - lie

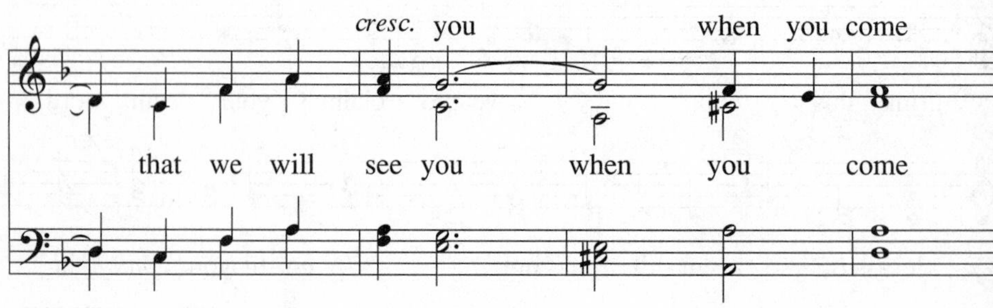
cresc. you
when you come
that we will see you when you come

cresc.
ff
in your glo - ry, Lord. We re -
ff

dim.
mf
rit.
mp
mem - ber, we cel - e - brate, we be -
mf
mp

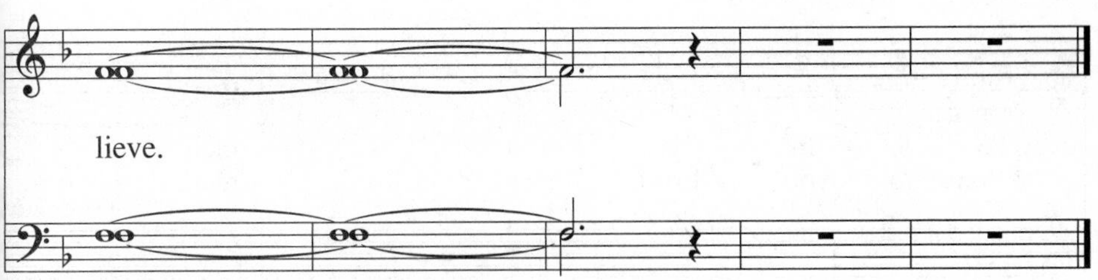
lieve.

Music: *Mass of Remembrance*, Marty Haugen, © 1987, GIA Publications, Inc.

EUCHARISTIC ACCLAMATION III (OPTIONAL) 218

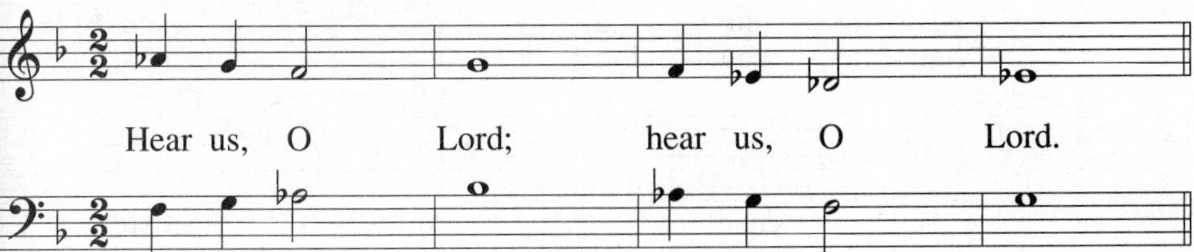
Hear us, O Lord; hear us, O Lord.

Music: *Mass of Remembrance*, Marty Haugen, © 1987, GIA Publications, Inc.

219 AMEN

𝅗𝅥 = 72
mf Priest:
cresc. poco a poco
Through him, with him, in him, in the
u - ni - ty of the Ho - ly Spir - it, all
glo - ry and hon - or is yours, al - might - y Fa - ther,
f
for ev - er and ev - er.
f All:
Harmony:
Al - le - lu - ia, a - men!
*Praise to you, Lord, a - men!
Descant: f
Al - le - lu - ia,
*Praise to you, Lord,
rit.
ff
Al - le - lu - ia, a - men!
Praise to you, Lord, a - men!
a - men! A - men!
a - men! A - men!

*During Lent

Music: *Mass of Remembrance*, Marty Haugen, © 1987, GIA Publications, Inc.

AGNUS DEI

220

♩ = 80
mp Cantor(s):
mf All:
1. *Lamb of God,
2. Prince of Peace, you take a - way the sins of the
3. Bread of Life,
mp Schola:
mf
1. *Lamb of God,
2. Prince of Peace, you take a - way the sins of the
3. Bread of Life,
To repeat
world: have mer - cy on us.
world: have mer - cy on us.
Last time
slowing p
rit. pp
world: grant us peace, grant us peace.
slowing p
rit. pp
world: grant us peace, grant us peace.

* *"Lamb of God" is sung the first and last times. Alternate intervening invocations include: Ancient Cup, Bread of Peace, Wine of Hope, Lord of Lords.*

Setting Eight

MASS OF LIGHT

221 **KYRIE**

♩ = 88-92
Cantor:
Assembly:
Ky - ri - e e - le - i - son. Ky - ri - e e - le - i - son.
Cantor:
Assembly:
Chri - ste e - le - i - son. Chri - ste e - le - i - son.
Cantor:
Assembly:
Ky - ri - e e - le - i - son. Ky - ri - e e - le - i - son.

GLORIA 222

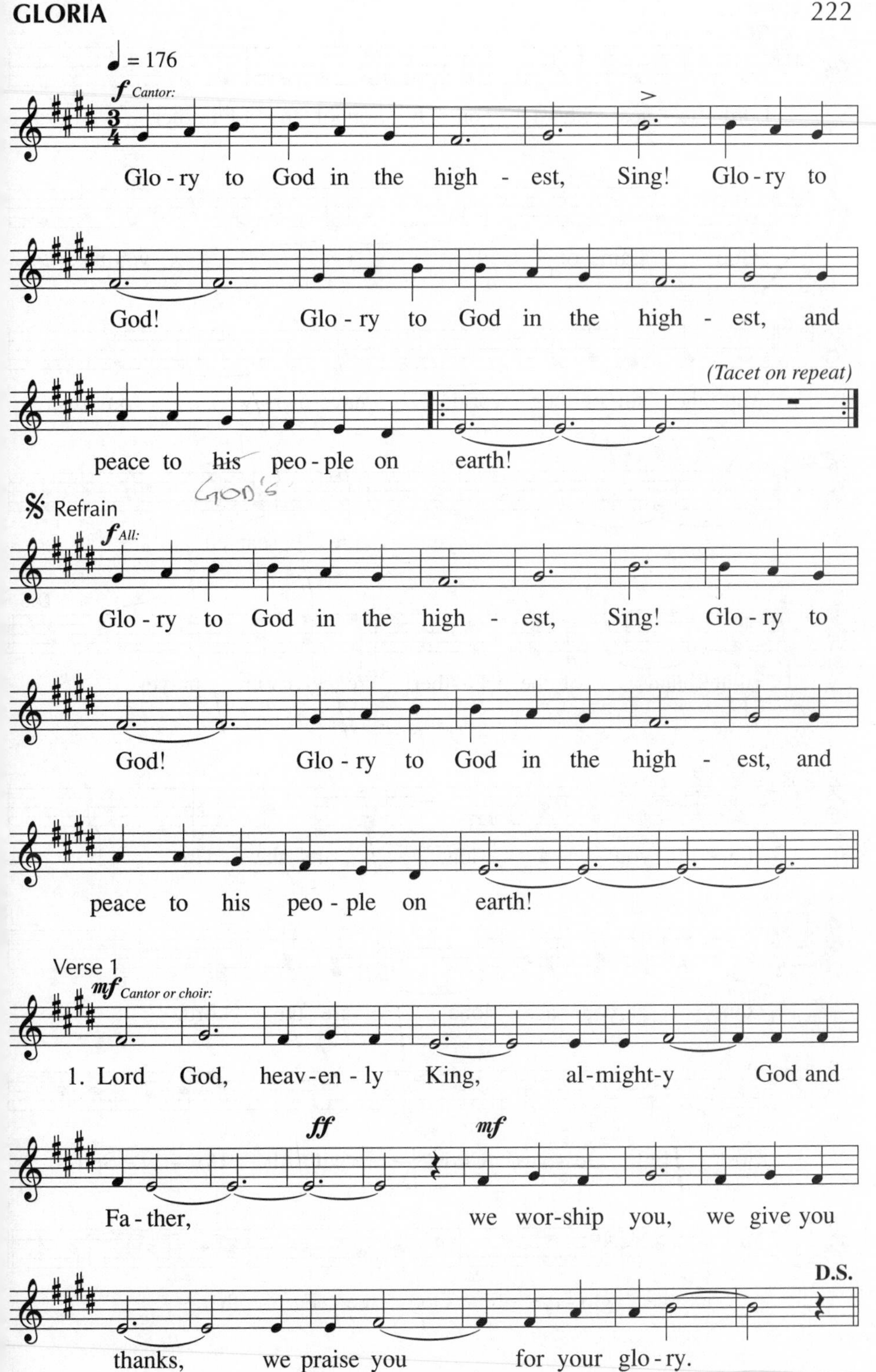
♩ = 176
f Cantor:
Glo-ry to God in the high-est, Sing! Glo-ry to God! Glo-ry to God in the high-est, and peace to his peo-ple on earth!
(Tacet on repeat)
Refrain
f All:
Glo-ry to God in the high-est, Sing! Glo-ry to God! Glo-ry to God in the high-est, and peace to his peo-ple on earth!
Verse 1
mf Cantor or choir:
1. Lord God, heav-en-ly King, al-might-y God and Fa-ther,
ff
mf
we wor-ship you, we give you thanks, we praise you for your glo-ry.
D.S.

Verse 2
mf Cantor or choir:
2. Lord Je - sus Christ, on - ly Son of the Fa - ther, Lord
f
mf
God, Lamb of God, you take a -
way the sin of the world: have mer-cy on us;
f
Harmony:
Melody:
you are seat-ed at the
D.S.
right hand of the Fa-ther: re-ceive our prayer.
Verse 3
mp legato
Women:
3. For you a - lone are the Ho - ly
One, you a - lone are the Lord, the
All: f
Most High, Je - sus Christ, with the Ho - ly Spir-it,
in the glo - ry of God the Fa - ther.

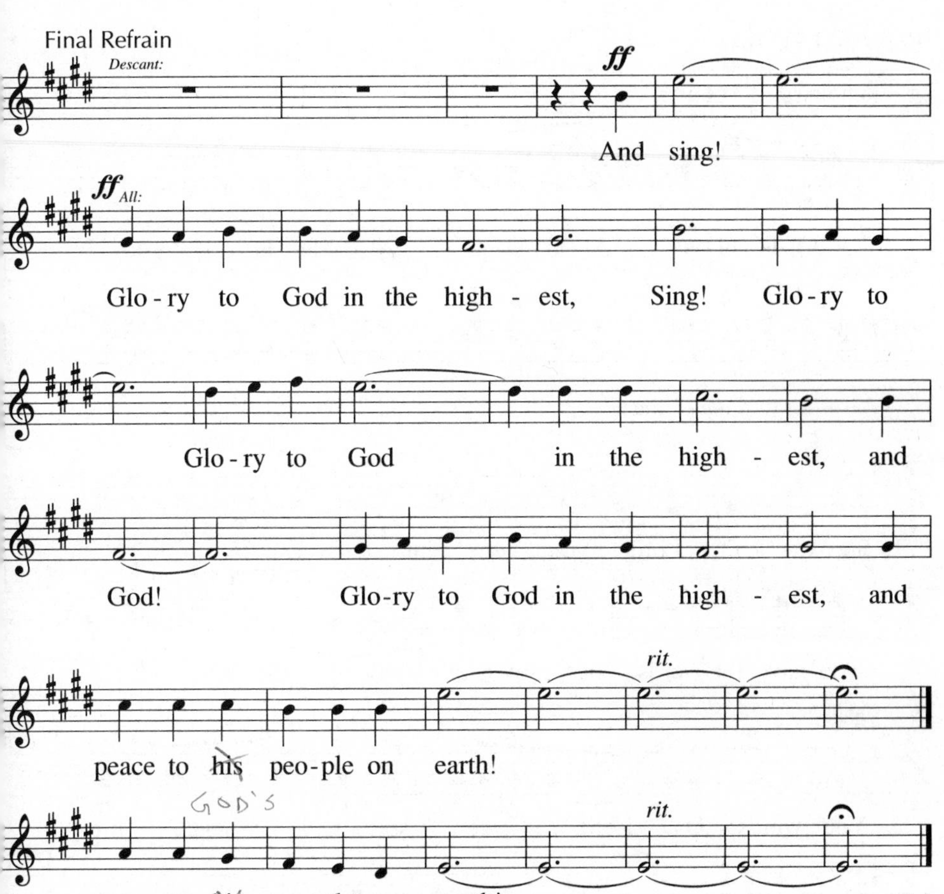
Final Refrain
Descant:
ff
And sing!
ff All:
Glo - ry to God in the high - est, Sing! Glo - ry to
Glo - ry to God in the high - est, and
God! Glo-ry to God in the high - est, and
rit.
peace to his peo-ple on earth!
GOD'S
rit.
peace to his peo-ple on earth!

Music: *Mass of Light,* David Haas, © 1988, GIA Publications, Inc.

223 ALLELUIA

Refrain ♩. = 54-60
Cantor or choir, then all:
Al - le - lu - ia! Al - le - lu - ia! Al - le - lu - ia!
Verses for Ordinary Time
Verse 1
Cantor:
1. Speak, O Lord, your ser - vant is lis - t'ning:
D.C.
you have the words of ev - er - last - ing life!
Verse 2
2. Your words, O Lord, are spir - it and life,
D.C.
you have the words of ev - er - last - ing life!
Verse 3
3. I am the way, the truth, and the life.
D.C.
No one comes to God, ex - cept through me!

Additional verses may be found in the original published edition of "Mass of Light."

Music: *Mass of Light,* David Haas, © 1988, GIA Publications, Inc.

LENTEN GOSPEL ACCLAMATION 224

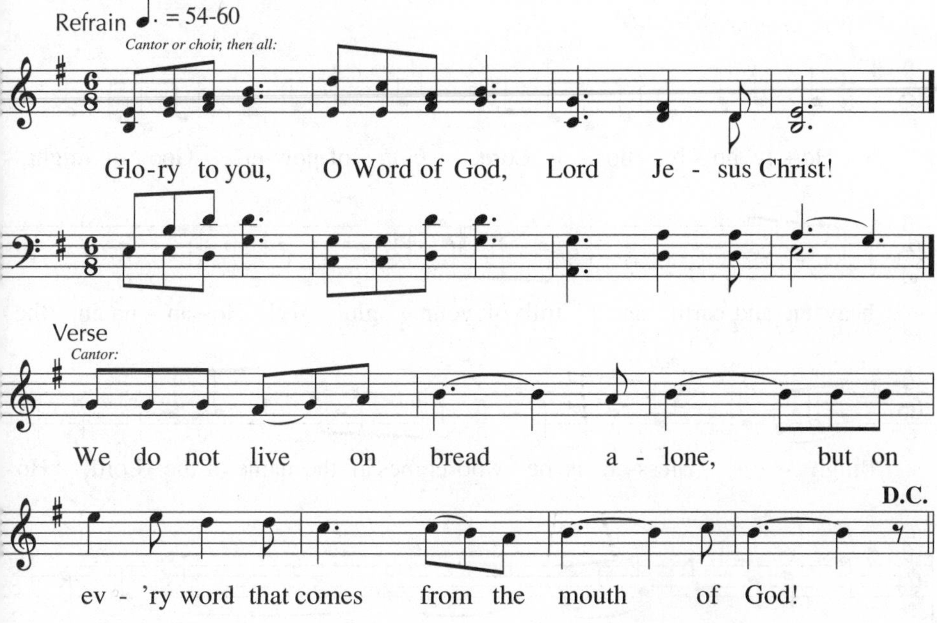
Refrain ♩. = 54-60
Cantor or choir, then all:
Glo-ry to you, O Word of God, Lord Je - sus Christ!
Verse
Cantor:
We do not live on bread a - lone, but on
ev - 'ry word that comes from the mouth of God!
D.C.

Additional verses may be found in "Who Calls You by Name", a collection of music for the RCIA, and in the original published edition of "Mass of Light."

Text: ICEL, © 1969
Music: *Mass of Light,* David Haas, © 1988, GIA Publications, Inc.

PREFACE DIALOG 225

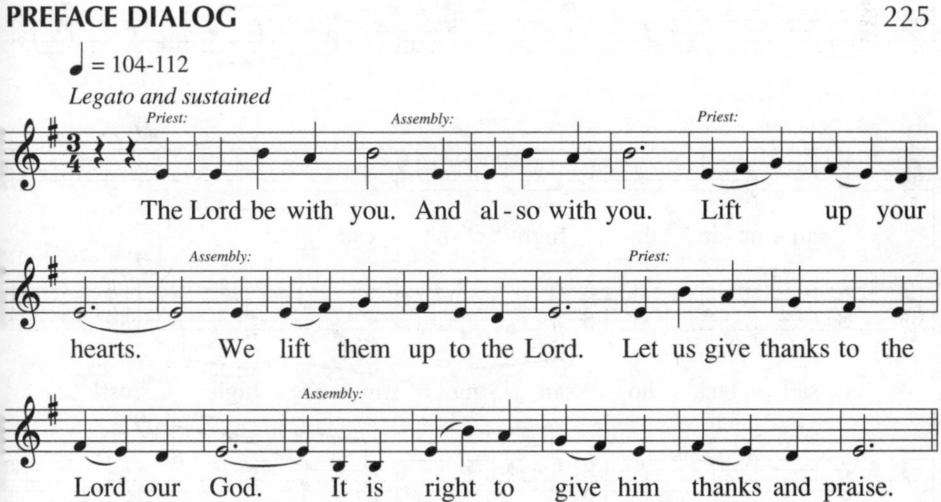
♩ = 104-112
Legato and sustained
Priest:
Assembly:
Priest:
The Lord be with you. And al - so with you. Lift up your
Assembly:
Priest:
hearts. We lift them up to the Lord. Let us give thanks to the
Assembly:
Lord our God. It is right to give him thanks and praise.

Music: *Mass of Light,* David Haas, © 1988, GIA Publications, Inc.

226 SANCTUS

With strength ♩. = 54-60
f All:
Ho - ly, ho - ly, ho - ly Lord, God of pow-er, God of might,
heav-en and earth are full of your glo - ry! Ho-san - na in the
mp
high - est! Bless-ed is he who comes in the name of the Lord! Ho-
f
san - na in the high - est! Ho -
f
Ho-san - na in the high - est! Ho -
f
ff
san - na in the high - est!
ff
san - na, ho - san - na in the high - est!
ff

Music: *Mass of Light,* David Haas, © 1988, GIA Publications, Inc.

EUCHARISTIC ACCLAMATION I (OPTIONAL)* 227

*As in the Eucharistic Prayers for Masses with Children.

f
Ho - san - na in the high - est!

Music: *Mass of Light,* David Haas, © 1988, GIA Publications, Inc.

MEMORIAL ACCLAMATION 228

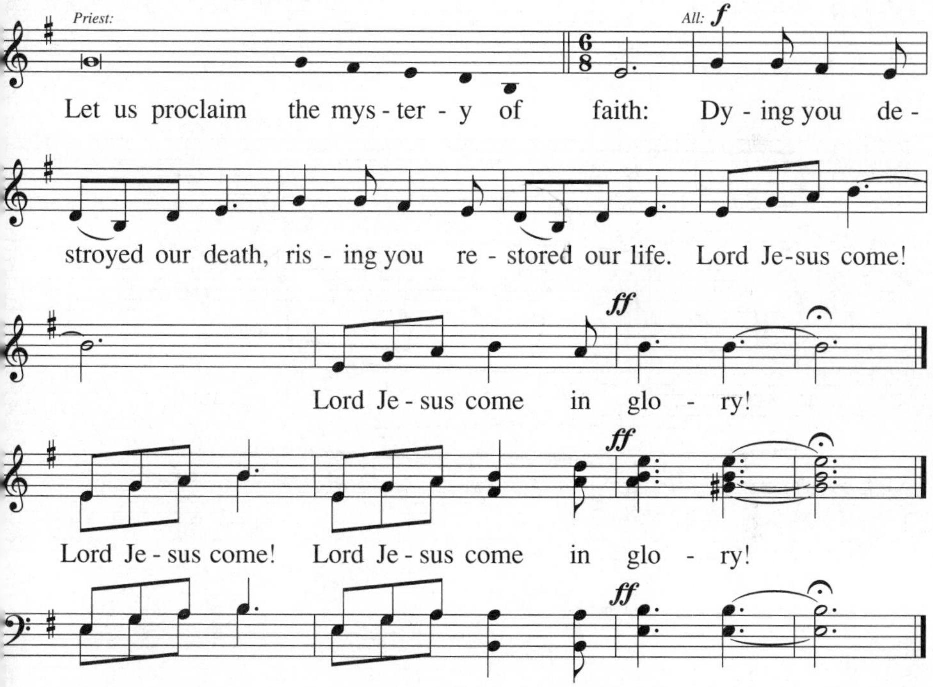

Priest: Let us proclaim the mys - ter - y of faith:

All: f Dy - ing you de - stroyed our death, ris - ing you re - stored our life. Lord Je - sus come! Lord Je - sus come in glo - ry!

ff Lord Je - sus come! Lord Je - sus come in glo - ry!

Text: ICEL, © 1973
Music: *Mass of Light,* David Haas, © 1988, GIA Publications, Inc.

EUCHARISTIC ACCLAMATION II (OPTIONAL) 229

Hear us, hear us. Hear us, hear us.

This refrain is repeated continually under the spoken prayer of the priest.

Music: *Mass of Light,* David Haas, © 1988, GIA Publications, Inc.

230 AMEN

With strength
A - men, a - men! A - men,
A - men, a - men! A - men,
a - men!
a - men!

Music: *Mass of Light,* David Haas, © 1988, GIA Publications, Inc.

AGNUS DEI

231

♩ = 88-92
mp Cantor:
All:
*Lamb of God,
Bread of Life, you take a - way the
Son of God,
To repeat
sins of the world: have mer -
cy on us.
mp Schola:
Have mer - cy on us.
Last time
world: grant us your peace.
p
Grant us your peace.

*"Lamb of God" is sung the first and last times. Alternate intervening invocations include: "Saving Cup," "Hope for all," "Prince of Peace," "Wine of Peace," etc.

Setting Nine

JUBILATION MASS

232 **KYRIE**

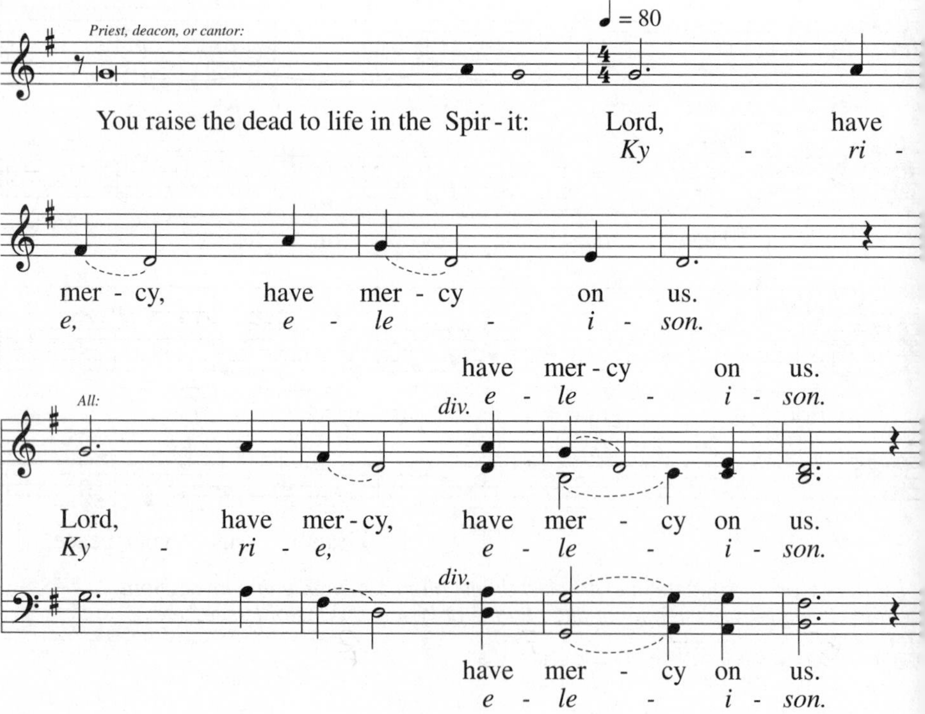
♩ = 80
Priest, deacon, or cantor:
You raise the dead to life in the Spir - it: Lord, have mer - cy, have mer - cy on us.
Ky - ri - e, e - le - i - son.
All:
Lord, have mer - cy, have mer - cy on us.
Ky - ri - e, e - le - i - son.
div.
have mer - cy on us.
e - le - i - son.

Priest, deacon, or cantor:
You bring pardon and peace to the sin-ner: Christ, have mer-cy, have mer-cy on us.
Chri - ste, e - le - i - son.
All:
Christ, have mer-cy, have mer - cy on us.
Chri - ste, e - le - i - son.
div.
Priest, deacon, or cantor:
You bring light to those in dark-ness: Lord, have mer-cy, have mer-cy on us.
Ky - ri - e, e - le - i - son.
All:
Lord, have mer - cy, have mer - cy on us, on us.
Ky - ri - e, e - le - i - son, Ky - ri - e.

Music: *Jubilation Mass*, James J. Chepponis, © 1999, GIA Publications, Inc.

233 GLORIA

Refrain ♩. = 63
Cantor, then all:
mf/f
Glo-ri-a! Glo-ri-a! Glo-ry to God in the high-est! Glo-ri-a! Glo-ri-a! And peace to his peo-ple on earth! earth!
1. 2.
Verse 1
mf Cantor:
1. Lord God, heav-en-ly King, al-might-y God and Fa-ther,
Choir:
mf
we wor-ship you, we give you thanks, we praise you for your glo-ry.
div.
we wor-ship you, we give you praise for your glo-ry.
praise your glo-ry.
Refrain
unis. f All:
Glo-ri-a!
unis. f
Glo-ri-a!

Glo - ry to God in the high - est!
div.
Glo - ri - a! Glo - ry to God!
div.
Glo - ri - a! Glo - ry to God!
And peace to his peo - ple on earth!
unis.
div.
Glo - ri - a! Glo - ri - a! And peace on earth!
unis.
div.
Glo - ri - a! Glo - ri - a! Peace on earth!
Verse 2
Cantor:
2. Lord Je - sus Christ, on - ly Son of the Fa - ther,
Lord God, Lamb of God,
Choir:
unis.
you take a-way the
unis.

div.
sin of the world: have mer - cy on us;
div.
Cantor:
you are seat - ed at the right hand of the Fa - ther:
Choir:
re - ceive our prayer, re - ceive our prayer.
Refrain
unis.
Glo - ry to God in the high - est!
f All:
div.
2
Glo - ri - a! Glo - ri - a! Glo - ry to God!
f unis.
div.
Glo - ri - a! Glo - ri - a! Glo - ry to God!
Cantor:
mf
3. For
And peace to his peo - ple on earth!
unis.
div.
Glo - ri - a! Glo - ri - a! And peace on earth!
unis.
div.
Glo - ri - a! Glo - ri - a! Peace on earth!

Verse 3
you a-lone are the Ho-ly One, you a-lone are the Lord,
Choir: mf
Glo-ri-a! Glo-ri-a!
mf
Cantor:
you a-lone are the Most High, Je - sus Christ,
Choir:
unis.
with the Ho - ly Spir-it, in the glo-ry of
unis.
with the Ho - ly Spir-it,
div.
God the Fa - ther, of God the Fa - ther.
div.
in the glo-ry of God, of God the Fa - ther.

Final Refrain
ff Descant:
Glo - ri - a! Glo - ri - a!
Glo-ry to God in the high-est!
All:
ff unis.
div.
Glo-ri-a! Glo-ri-a! Glo - ry to God!
ff unis.
div.
Glo-ri-a! Glo-ri-a! Glo - ry to God!
Glo - ri - a! Peace on earth!
And peace to his peo-ple on earth!
unis.
div.
Glo-ri-a! Glo-ri-a! And peace on earth!
unis.
div.
Glo-ri-a! Glo-ri-a! Peace on earth!
Choir:
rit.
A - men, A - men!
rit.
A - men, A - men!

Music: *Jubilation Mass,* James J. Chepponis, © 1999, GIA Publications, Inc.

GOSPEL ACCLAMATION 234-A

♩. = 63
Refrain
Cantor, then all:
Al - le - lu - ia, al - le - lu - ia, al - le - lu - ia!
Al - le - lu - ia, al - le - lu - ia, al - le - lu - ia!
al - le - lu - ia. Al - le - lu - ia, al - le - lu - ia!
div.
To verse
Last time
ia!
rit.
ia! Al - le-lu - ia!
Verse
Cantor:
Speak, O Lord, your ser - vant is lis - ten-ing;
you have the words of ev - er-last - ing life.
D.S.

*Choose either part.

Additional verses may be found in the original published edition of "Jubilation Mass." The notes given here can also be modified to fit the verse of the day from the Lectionary.

234-B LENTEN GOSPEL ACCLAMATION

♩. = 63
Refrain
Cantor, then all:
Glo - ry to you, Word of God, Lord Je - sus Christ.
Glo - ry to you, Word of God, Lord Je - sus Christ!
div.
Glo - ry to you,
To verse
Last time
Christ!
rit.
Christ! Glo - ry to you!
Verse
Cantor:
Speak, O Lord, your ser - vant is lis - ten-ing;
you have the words of ev - er-last - ing life.
D.S.

*Choose either part.

Text: ICEL, © 1969
Music: *Jubilation Mass,* James J. Chepponis, © 1999, GIA Publications, Inc.

Additional verses may be found in the original published edition of "Jubilation Mass." The notes given here can also be modified to fit the verse of the day from the Lectionary.

SANCTUS

235

♩ = 104

f

Ho - ly, ho - ly, ho - ly Lord,

f

God of pow-er and might, heav-en and earth are

div. Ho - san - na, ho -

full of your glo - ry. Ho - san - na, ho -

div.

Ho - san - na,

san - na, ho - san - na in the high - est.

san - na in the high - est.

ho - san - na in the high - est.

Ho -

unis. *div.*

Bless-ed is he who comes in the name of the Lord. Ho -

unis.

san - na, ho - san - na, ho - san - na in the
san - na, ho - san - na in the
div.
Ho - san - na, ho - san - na in the
Assembly:
ff
high - est. Ho - san - na, ho - san - na, ho -
Choir: high - est.
ff
high - est. Ho - san - na, ho - san - na
ff unis.
high - est. Ho - san - na, ho - san - na, ho -
rit.
san - na in the high - est!
rit.
in the high - est!
div. rit.
san - na in the high - est!

MEMORIAL ACCLAMATION A 236

♩= 100
Descant: f
Christ has died, Christ is ris - en,
f
Christ has died, Christ is ris - en,
f
Christ will come a - gain. ff Christ has died,
ff div.
Christ will come a - gain. Christ has died,
ff div.
rit.
Christ is ris - en, Christ will come a - gain!
rit.
Christ is ris - en, Christ will come a - gain!
rit.

237 MEMORIAL ACCLAMATION B

♩ = 100
f
Dy - ing you de - stroyed our death,
f
ris - ing you re - stored our life.
div.
Lord
glo - ry,
Lord
Je - sus, come in glo - ry, Lord
div.
Lord Je - sus, come, Lord
Assembly:
rit.
Je - sus, come in glo - ry!
Je - sus, come in glo - ry!
Choir:
rit.
Je - sus, come in glo - ry!
rit.
Je - sus, come in glo - ry!

MEMORIAL ACCLAMATION C

♩= 100
f
When we eat this bread and
f
drink this cup, we pro-claim your death, Lord Je - sus, un -
div.
glo - ry, un -
til you come in glo - ry, un -
div.
un - til you come, un -
Assembly:
til you come in glo - ry!
rit.
til you come in glo - ry!
Choir:
rit.
til you come in glo - ry!
rit.
til you come in glo - ry!

xt: ICEL, © 1973
ısic: *Jubilation Mass,* James J. Chepponis, © 1999, GIA Publications, Inc.

239 MEMORIAL ACCLAMATION D

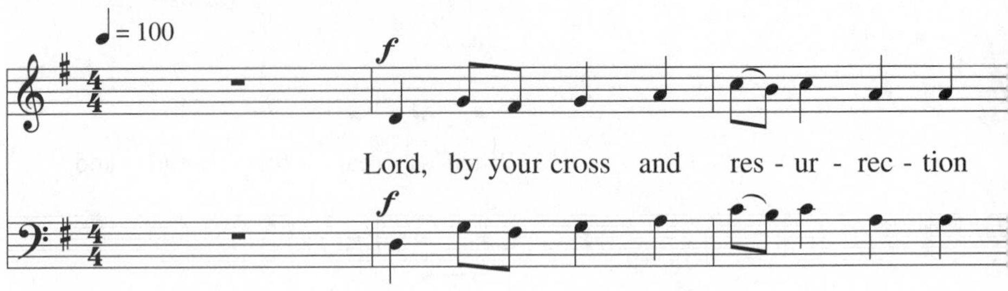
♩ = 100
f
Lord, by your cross and res - ur - rec - tion
f

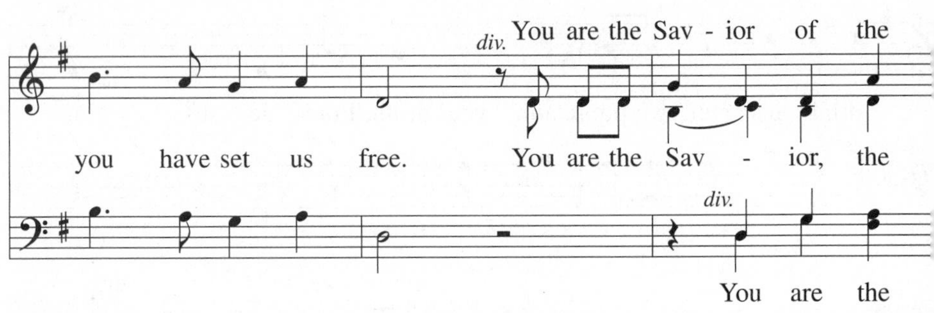
div.
You are the Sav - ior of the
you have set us free.
You are the Sav - ior, the
div.
You are the

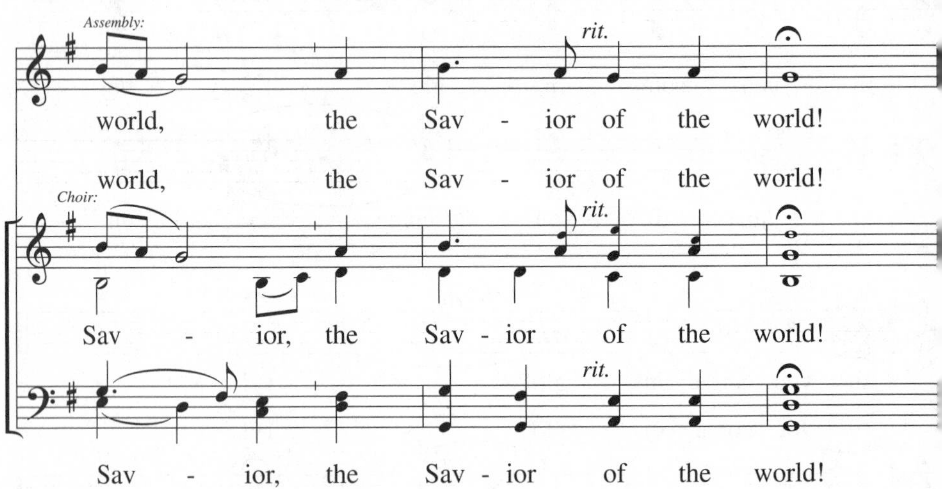
Assembly:
rit.
world, the Sav - ior of the world!
world, the Sav - ior of the world!
Choir:
rit.
Sav - ior, the Sav - ior of the world!
rit.
Sav - ior, the Sav - ior of the world!

AMEN

240

♩ = 100
Descant:
A - men, A - men, A - men. A - men, A - men, A - men!
A - men, A - men, A - men. A - men, A - men, A - men!
div.
rit.

Music: *Jubilation Mass,* James J. Chepponis, © 1999, GIA Publications, Inc.

241 AGNUS DEI

♩ = 80
Cantor:
All:
Last time to coda
Lamb of God,* you take a-way the sins of the

have mer - cy on us.
div.
world, have mer - cy on us.
div.

Coda
div.
peace.
world, grant us peace, grant us peace.
div.

** First and last invocation is always "Lamb of God." Additional invocations may be chosen from the following:*

ADVENT
Lord of light
Promised Savior
Son of Mary
King of glory
Root of Jesse

CHRISTMAS
Prince of peace
King of kings
Lord of lords
Christ the Lord
Light eternal

LENT
Source of mercy
Hope of sinners
Living water
Light in darkness
Life eternal

EASTER
Risen Lord
Paschal Lamb
King exalted
Gentle shepherd
Mighty victor

ORDINARY TIME
Bread of life
Saving cup
Word of God
Gift of love
Source of blessing
Mighty healer
Patient teacher
Firm foundation
Fruitful vine
Meek of heart

Setting Ten

BLACK MOUNTAIN LITURGY

KYRIE

242

♩. = 60
Optional Invocation*
Cantor, then all:
Lord, have mer - cy.
Cantor, then all:
Christ, have mer - cy.
Cantor:
Lord, have mer - cy.
All:
Lord, have mer - cy.

Invocations may be spoken or improvised over these 2 measures, which are then inserted before each response.

243 GLORIA

♩. = 60-70
Refrain
Glo-ry to God in the high - est, and peace to his peo-ple on
earth. (3. For)
Verse 1
1. Lord God, heav-en - ly King, al -
might - y God and Fa - ther, we wor-ship you,
we give you thanks, we praise you for your glo - ry.
*opt. D.C.
Verse 2
2. Lord Je-sus Christ, on - ly Son of the Fa - ther, Lord God, Lamb of
God, you take a - way the sin of the world: have
mer - cy on us; you are seat-ed at the right hand
of the Fa - ther: re - ceive our prayer. (3. For)
opt. D.C.
Verse 3
you a-lone are the Ho-ly One, you a-lone are the Lord,

*May be sung with or without refrains.

you a-lone are the Most High, Je - sus Christ, with the Ho - ly

Spir-it, in the glo-ry of God the Fa - ther. A -

If Final Refrain is used Final Refrain

men. Glo-ry to God in the high - est, and

If Final Refrain is not used

peace to his peo-ple on earth. men.

Music: *Black Mountain Liturgy,* Sally Ann Morris, © 2003, GIA Publications, Inc.

GOSPEL ACCLAMATION 244

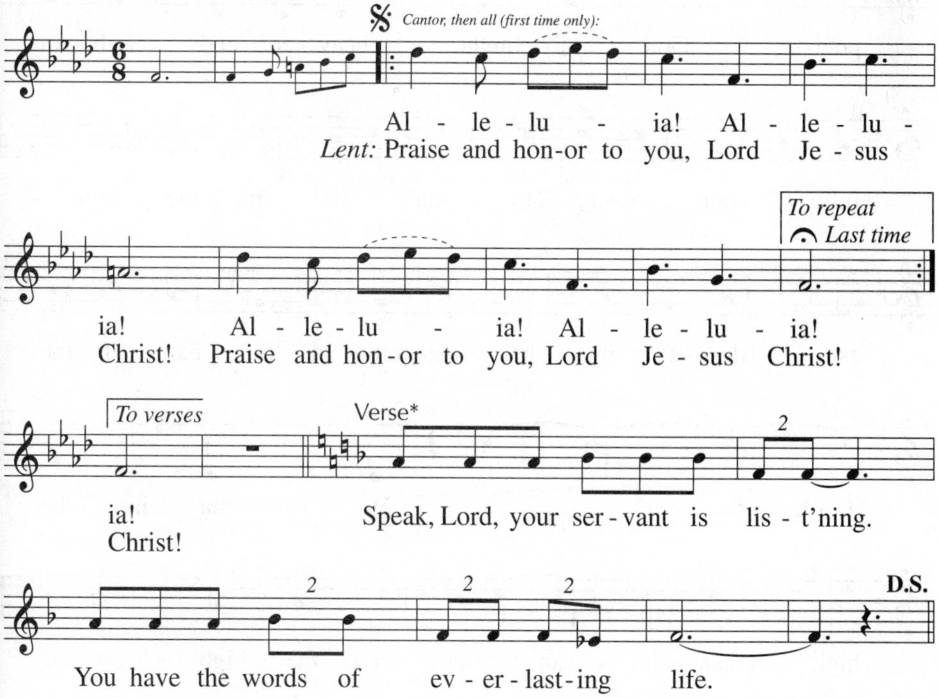

Cantor, then all (first time only):

Al - le - lu - ia! Al - le - lu -
Lent: Praise and hon-or to you, Lord Je - sus

To repeat
Last time

ia! Al - le - lu - ia! Al - le - lu - ia!
Christ! Praise and hon-or to you, Lord Je - sus Christ!

To verses

Verse*

ia! Speak, Lord, your ser - vant is lis - t'ning.
Christ!

D.S.

You have the words of ev - er - last-ing life.

*Other verses can be fitted to this melody.

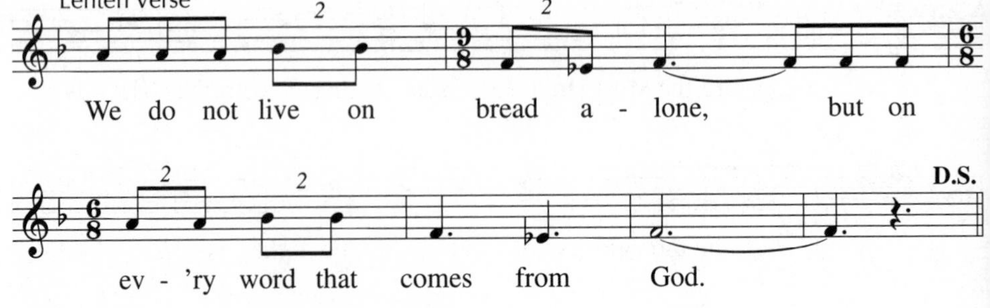
Lenten Verse*
We do not live on bread a - lone, but on
ev - 'ry word that comes from God.
D.S.

*Other verses can be fitted to this melody.

Text: ICEL, © 1969
Music: *Black Mountain Liturgy,* Sally Ann Morris, © 2003, GIA Publications, Inc.

245 SANCTUS

♩. = 65

Ho - ly, ho - ly, ho - ly Lord, God of
pow - er, God of might, heav - en and earth are
full of your glo - ry. Ho - san - na in the high -
est. Bless - ed is he who comes in the name of the
Lord. Ho - san - na in the
high - est, ho - san - na in the high - est.

Music: *Black Mountain Liturgy,* Sally Ann Morris, © 2003, GIA Publications, Inc.

MEMORIAL ACCLAMATION 246

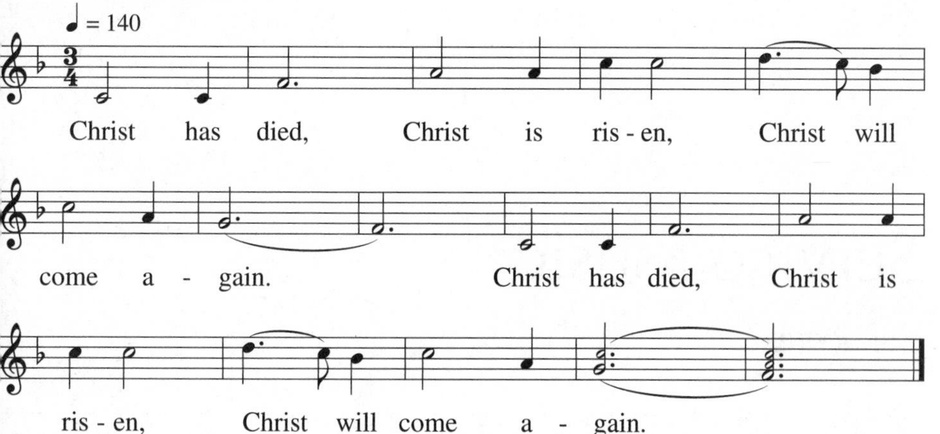
♩ = 140
Christ has died, Christ is ris - en, Christ will
come a - gain. Christ has died, Christ is
ris - en, Christ will come a - gain.

Text: ICEL, © 1973
Music: *Black Mountain Liturgy,* Sally Ann Morris, © 2003, GIA Publications, Inc.

AMEN 247

♩ = 120

A - men, a - men. A - men, a - men.

Music: *Black Mountain Liturgy,* Sally Ann Morris, © 2003, GIA Publications, Inc.

AGNUS DEI 248

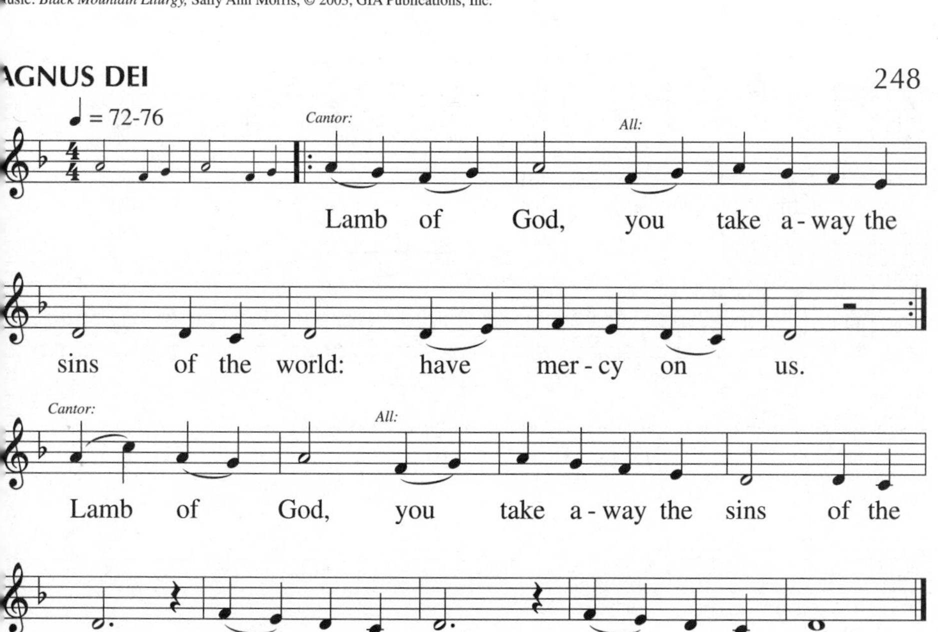
♩ = 72-76
Cantor:
All:
Lamb of God, you take a - way the
sins of the world: have mer - cy on us.
Cantor:
All:
Lamb of God, you take a - way the sins of the
world: grant us peace. Grant us peace.

Music: *Black Mountain Liturgy,* Sally Ann Morris, © 2003, GIA Publications, Inc.

Service Music

249 KYRIE

Ky - ri - e e - lei - son. Ky - ri - e e - lei - son.
Chri - ste e - lei - son. Chri - ste e - lei - son.
Ky - ri - e e - lei - son. Ky - ri - e e - lei - son.

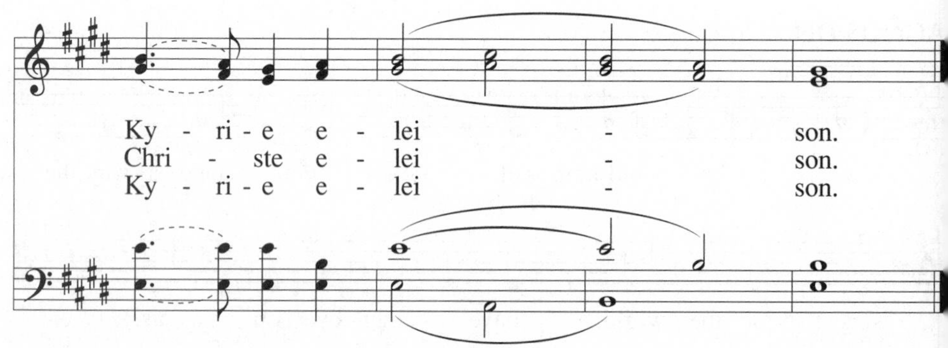
Ky - ri - e e - lei - son.
Chri - ste e - lei - son.
Ky - ri - e e - lei - son.

Music: Russian Orthodox; arr. by John L. Bell, © 1990, Iona Community, GIA Publications, Inc., agent

GLORIA

♩ = 120
Glo - ry to God in the high-est and
peace to his peo - ple on earth. Lord God, heav - en - ly
King, al - might - y God and Fa - ther, we wor-ship you, we
give you thanks, we praise you for your glo - ry.
Lord Je-sus Christ, on - ly Son of the Fa - ther, Lord God, Lamb of
God, you take a - way the sin of the world: have

you are seat - ed at the right hand
mer - cy on us; you are seat - ed at the right hand
of the Fa - ther:
of the Fa - ther: re - ceive our prayer.
For you a - lone are the Ho - ly One, you a - lone are the Lord,
you a - lone are the Most High, Je - sus Christ,
with the Ho - ly Spir - it, in the glo - ry of God the Fa - ther.
A - men, a - men, a - men.

GLORIA

251

I (Cantor/choir)
Glo-ry to God in the high - est, and peace to his peo-ple on earth.
II (Assembly)
Lord God, heav'n-ly King, al-might-y God and Fa - ther.
I
We wor-ship you, we give you thanks, we praise you for your glo - ry.
II
Lord Je - sus Christ, on - ly Son of the Fa - ther,
Lord God, Lamb of God,
I
you take a - way the sin of the world:
have mer - cy on us;
II
you are seat - ed at the right hand of the
Fa - ther: re - ceive our prayer.
I
For you a - lone are the
Ho - ly One, you a - lone are the Lord, you a -
lone are the Most High, Je - sus Christ,
II
with the Ho - ly Spir - it,
in the glo - ry of God the Fa - ther.
Slower
A - men.

Music: *Congregational Mass;* John Lee, © 1970, GIA Publications, Inc.

252 GLORIA

Exuberantly ♩ = 176
Refrain
f Descant:
Glo - ry, glo - ry,
f Melody:
Give glo - ry to God in the high - est, and
Al - le - lu - ia.
peace to his peo - ple on earth.
Verse 1
mp
1. Lord God, heav-en - ly King, al-might - y
f
God and Fa - ther, we wor - ship you, we
subito mp
f
D.C.
give you thanks, we praise you for your glo - ry.
Verse 2
mp
2. Lord Je - sus Christ, on - ly
Son of the Fa - ther, Lord God,

f
Lamb of God, you take a - way the
mp
sin of the world: have mer - cy up - on us;
f
you are seat - ed at the right hand of the
ff
subito mp
rit. D.C.
Fa - ther: re - ceive our prayer.
Verse 3
Calmly ♩ = 160
rit.
p cresc.
3. You a - lone are the
mf
Ho - ly One, you a - lone are the Lord,
mf cresc.
f
you a - lone are the Most High,
mf
f
f
ff
Je - sus Christ, with the Ho - ly
rit.
D.C.
Spir - it, in the glo - ry of God the Fa - ther.

Music: John B. Foley, SJ, © 1978, John B. Foley and OCP Publications

253 GLORIA

Refrain/Canon—*4 voices**
1.
2.
Glo - ri - a, glo - ri - a, in ex - cel - sis De - o!
3.
4.
Glo - ri - a, glo - ri - a, al - le - lu - ia, al - le - lu - ia!
Verse 1
Cantor or choir:
1. Glo - ry to God in the high - est, and
peace to his peo - ple on earth.
Lord God, heav - en - ly King, al - might - y God and
Fa - ther, we wor - ship you, we give you
Refrain ad lib.
thanks, we praise you for your glo - ry.
Verse 2
2. Lord Je - sus Christ, on - ly Son of the Fa - ther,
Lord God, Lamb of God, you take a - way the

**The refrain may be sung as an ostinato throughout all or part of the text, or it may be sung as a response at the beginning and after each section of the text.*

sin of the world: have mer - cy on us;
you are seat - ed at the right hand
Refrain ad lib.
of the Fa - ther: re - ceive our prayer.
Verse 3
3. For you a - lone are the Ho - ly One,
you a - lone are the Lord, you a - lone are the
Most High, Je - sus Christ, with the Ho - ly
Spir - it, in the glo - ry of God the Fa - ther.
To refrain
A - men, a - men, a - men, a - men!

254 GLORIA

All:
Glo-ry to God in the high-est, and peace to his peo-ple on
earth. Glo-ry to God in the high-est, and
peace to his peo-ple on earth.
Cantor or T. B.:
Lord God,
heav-en-ly King, al-might-y God and Fa-ther.
All:
Glo-ry to God in the high-est, and peace to his peo-ple on
earth.
Cantor or S. A.:
We wor-ship you, we give you thanks,
we praise you for your glo-ry.
All:
Glo-ry to God in the
high-est, and peace to his peo-ple on earth.
Cantor or T. B.:
Lord Je-sus

Christ, on - ly Son of the Fa - ther.
All:
Glo - ry to God in the high - est, and peace to his peo - ple on earth.
T. B.:
Lord God, Lamb of God, you take a - way the
sin of the world; have mer - cy on us;
S. A.:
you are
seat - ed at the right hand of the Fa - ther:
T. B.:
re - ceive our prayer
All:
Glo - ry to God in the
high - est, and peace to his peo - ple on earth.
Glo - ry to God in the high - est, and peace to his peo - ple on

Cantor or T. B.:
earth. For you a - lone are the Ho - ly One,
All or S. A.:
(Glo - ry to God!)
Cantor or T. B.:
you a - lone are the Lord,
All or S. A.:
(Glo - ry to God!)
Cantor or T. B.:
you a - lone are the Most High,
All or S. A.:
(Glo - ry to God!)
Cantor or T. B.:
Je - sus Christ,
All or S. A.:
(Glo - ry to God!)
Choir:
All:
with the Ho - ly Spir - it, (Glo - ry to God!)
with the Ho - ly Spir - it, (Glo - ry to God!)

Choir:
in the glo - ry of God, the Fa - ther.
in the glo - ry of God, the Fa - ther.
Broader
rit.
All:
Glo -
Glo - ry to God in the
Glo -
Glo - ry to God in the
ry! Glo - ry! Glo - ry!
high - est, and peace to his peo - ple on earth.
ry! Glo - ry! Glo - ry!
high - est, and peace to his peo - ple on earth.

Glo - ry! Glo - ry!
Glo-ry to God in the high-est, and peace to his peo-ple on
Glo - ry! Glo - ry!
Glo-ry to God in the high-est, and peace to his peo-ple on
Glo - ry!
earth. A - men. A - men. A -
Glo - ry! A - men. A - men. A -
earth. A - men. A - men. A -
still broader
A men.
men. A - men, A - men.
men. A - men.
men. A - men, A - men.

Music: *Mass of the Bells;* Alexander Peloquin, © 1972, 1973, GIA Publications, Inc.

GLORIA

255

Gló-ri-a in ex-cél-sis De-o. Et in ter-ra pax ho-mí-ni-bus
bo-nae vo-lun-tá-tis. Lau-dá-mus te.
Be-ne-dí-ci-mus te. A-do-rá-mus te.
Glo-ri-fi-cá-mus te. Grá-ti-as á-gi-mus ti-bi
pro-pter ma-gnam gló-ri-am tu-am. Dó-mi-ne De-us, Rex cae-
lé-stis, De-us Pa-ter om-ní-po-tens.
Dó-mi-ne Fi-li u-ni-gé-ni-te, Je-su Chri-ste.
Dó-mi-ne De-us, A-gnus De-i, Fí-li-us Pa-tris.
Qui tol-lis pec-cá-ta mun-di, mi-se-ré-re no-bis.
Qui tol-lis pec-cá-ta mun-di, sú-sci-pe de-pre-ca-ti-ó-
nem no-stram. Qui se-des ad déx-te-ram Pa-tris,

mi-se-ré-re no - bis. Quó-ni-am tu so-lus San-ctus.
Tu so-lus Dó - mi - nus. Tu so-lus Al - tís - si-mus,
Je - su Chri - ste. Cum San - cto Spí - ri - tu,
in gló-ri - a De - i Pa - tris. A - men.

256 GLORIA

Joyfully ♩ = 100

Refrain *Last time to Coda*

Glo - ry to God in the high-est, and peace to his peo-ple on earth.

Verse 1 **D.C.**

1. Lord God, heav-en-ly King, al - might-y God and Fa-ther.

Verse 2

2. We wor - ship you, we give you thanks, we

D.C.

praise you, we praise you for your glo - ry.

Verse 3 ♩ = 88

expressively, slower

3. Lord Je - sus Christ, on - ly Son of the

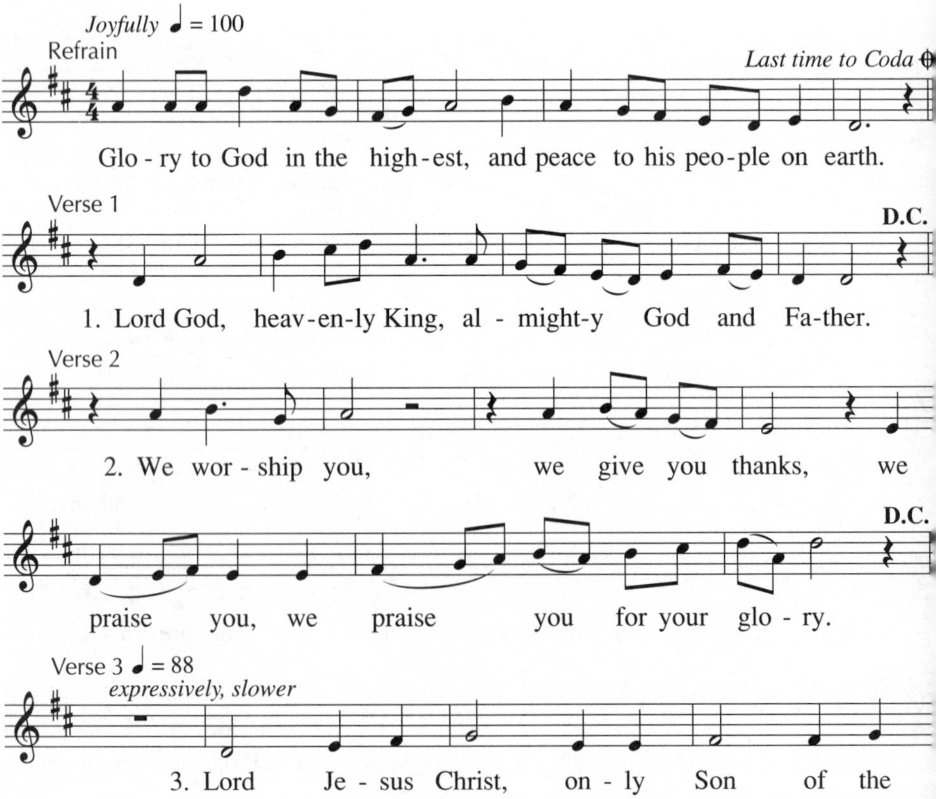

Fa-ther, Lord God, Lamb of God, you take a-way the
sin of the world: have mer - cy on us; you are
rit.
a tempo
seat - ed at the right hand of the Fa - ther: re -
accel.
♩ = 100
D.C.
ceive, re - ceive our prayer.
Verse 4
4. For you a-lone are the Ho-ly One, you a - lone are the
Lord, you a - lone are the Most High,
Je - sus Christ, with the Ho - ly Spir-it in the
D.C.
glo - ry of God the Fa - ther.
Coda
Descant:
Glo-ry to God, A - men. A - men!
Glo-ry to God in the high-est, and peace to his peo-ple on earth.

Music: *Melodic Gloria*, James J. Chepponis, © 1986, GIA Publications, Inc.

257 GLORIA

Refrain ♩. = 60
Descant:
Glo-ry to God, glo-ry to God,
glo - ry! Glo-ry to God, glo - ry,
peace to his peo-ple on earth.
Melody:
Glo-ry to God, glo-ry to God, glo-ry to God in the
high - est heav - en. Glo-ry to God, glo-ry to God,
peace to his peo-ple, his peo-ple on earth.
Harmony:
peace to his peo-ple on earth.

Verse 1
1. Lord God, heav-en-ly King, al - might-y God and
Fa - ther, we wor-ship you, we give you thanks, we
praise you for your glo - ry.
D.C.
Verse 2
2. Lord Je - sus Christ, on - ly Son of the Fa - ther,
Lord God, Lamb of God, you take a-way the
sin of the world: have mer - cy on us;
you are seat-ed at the right hand of the
re - ceive our prayer.
D.C.
Fa-ther: re-ceive our prayer.

Verse 3

3. For you a-lone are the Ho-ly One, you a-lone are the Most High,
Lord, you a-lone are the Most High,
Je - sus Christ,
Je - sus Christ, with the Ho - ly Spir-it, in the glo - ry, the glo - ry, the glo-ry of God the Fa - ther.

D.C.

Music: *Mass of the Celtic Saints*, Liam Lawton; arr. by John McCann, © 1998, GIA Publications, Inc.

258 CHILDREN'S DISMISSAL FOR LITURGY OF THE WORD

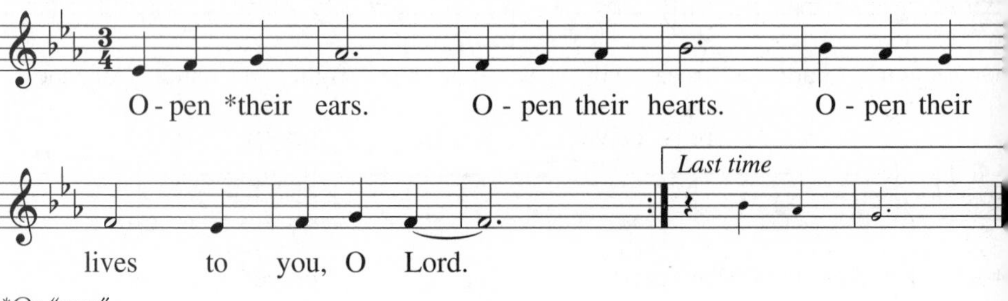
O-pen *their ears. O-pen their hearts. O-pen their
lives to you, O Lord.
Last time

*Or "our"

Text: Francis Patrick O'Brien
Music: Francis Patrick O'Brien
© 2003, GIA Publications, Inc.

CHILDREN'S DISMISSAL FOR LITURGY OF THE WORD 259

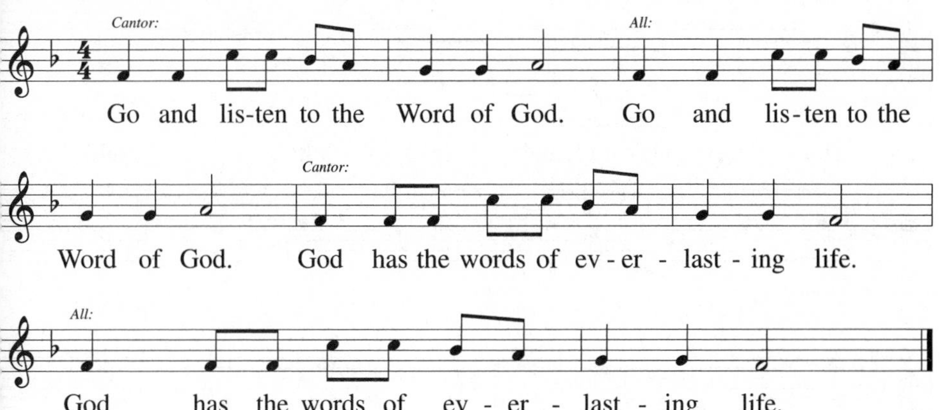
Cantor:
All:
Go and lis-ten to the Word of God. Go and lis-ten to the
Word of God.
Cantor:
God has the words of ev - er - last - ing life.
All:
God has the words of ev - er - last - ing life.

Text: Robert J. Batastini
Music: Robert J. Batastini

ALLELUIA 260

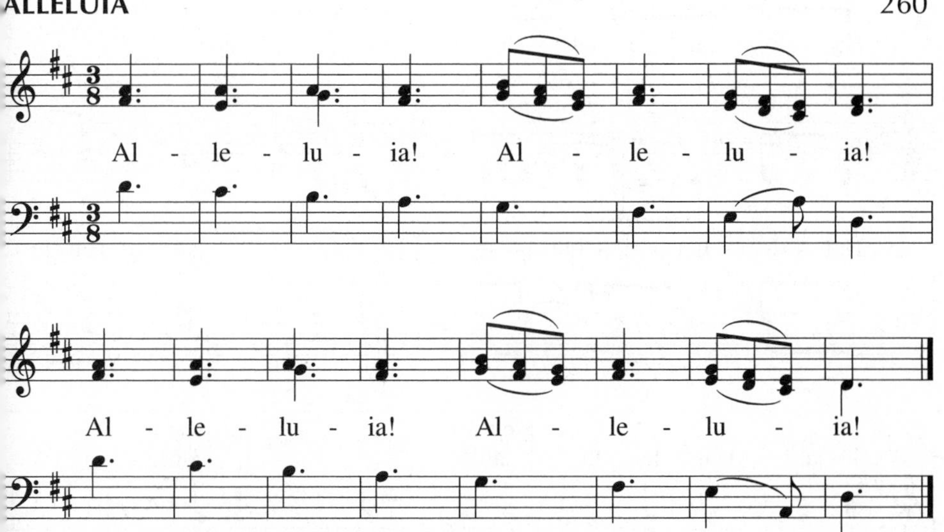
Al - le - lu - ia! Al - le - lu - ia!
Al - le - lu - ia! Al - le - lu - ia!

Music: Norah Duncan IV,

Tone

Music: Robert J. Batastini,

261 HALLE, HALLE, HALLE

Hal - le, hal - le, hal - le - lu - jah!
lu - jah!
Hal - le, hal - le, hal - le - lu, Hal - le - lu - jah!
Hal - le, hal - le, hal - le - lu - jah!
Hal - le, hal - le, hal - le - lu - jah! Hal - le -
To repeat
Last time
lu - jah! Hal - le - lu - jah! jah!
lu - jah! Hal - le - lu, hal le - lu - jah! jah!
lu - jah! Hal - le - lu - jah! jah!

Gospel Verse*

Ordinary time verses:
1. Oh God to whom shall we go? You a-lone have the words of life. Let your words be our prayer and the song we sing: Hal-le-lu-jah, hal-le-lu-jah.
2. My sheep hear my voice, says the Lord. When I call them, they fol-low me. I will lead them to rest by the rest-ful streams: Hal-le-lu-jah, hal-le-lu-jah.
3. I am the light of the world says the Lord. Walk in the light of life. All who fol-low my words shall have life in-deed: Hal-le-lu-jah, hal-le-lu-jah.
Easter verse:
4. Now Christ is raised up from death, he will nev-er die a-gain. All who fol-low his way shall have life in him: Hal-le-lu-jah, hal-le-lu-jah.

*Verse is sung over the instrumental refrain, with optional humming.

262 ALLELUIA

Refrain
Cantor:
Al - le - lu - ia! Al-le-lu - ia!
All:
Al - le - lu - ia! Al-le-lu - ia!
Cantor:
Al - le - lu - ia! Al-le-lu - ia!
All:
Al - le - lu - ia! Al-le-lu - ia!
To verse
Final ending
ia!
Verses
Cantor:
Ordinary time: 1. Speak, O Lord, your ser - vant is lis - t'ning; you have the words, you have the words of ev - er - last - ing life!
2. Your words, O Lord, are Spir - it and life; you have the words, you have the words of ev - er - last - ing life!
D.C.
Advent: 3. Pre - pare the way, a straight path for God; and all will see, all will see the sal -
Christmas: 4. Good news! Great joy to the world! To - day is born, to - day is born our

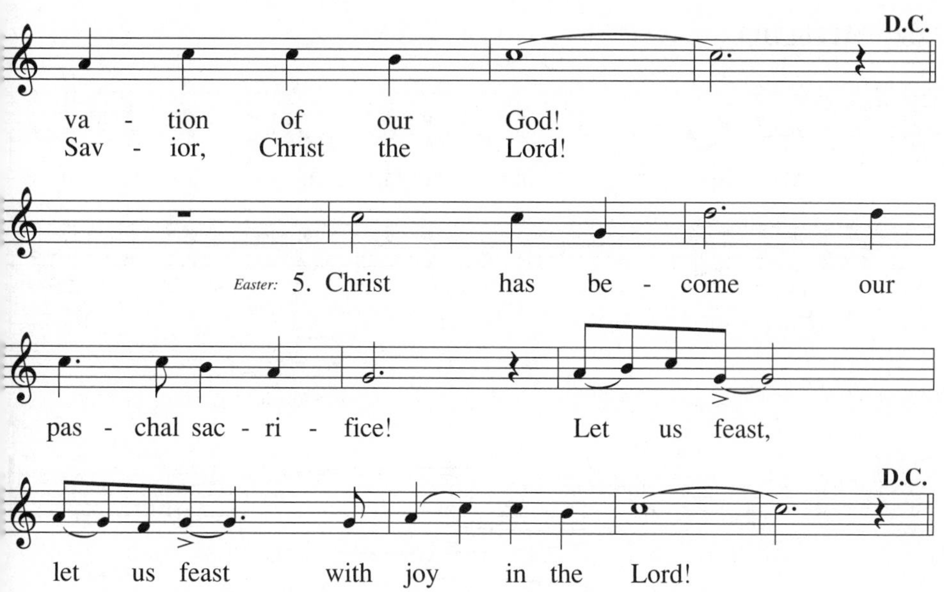
D.C.
va - tion of our God!
Sav - ior, Christ the Lord!
Easter: 5. Christ has be - come our
pas - chal sac - ri - fice! Let us feast,
D.C.
let us feast with joy in the Lord!

ALLELUIA

263

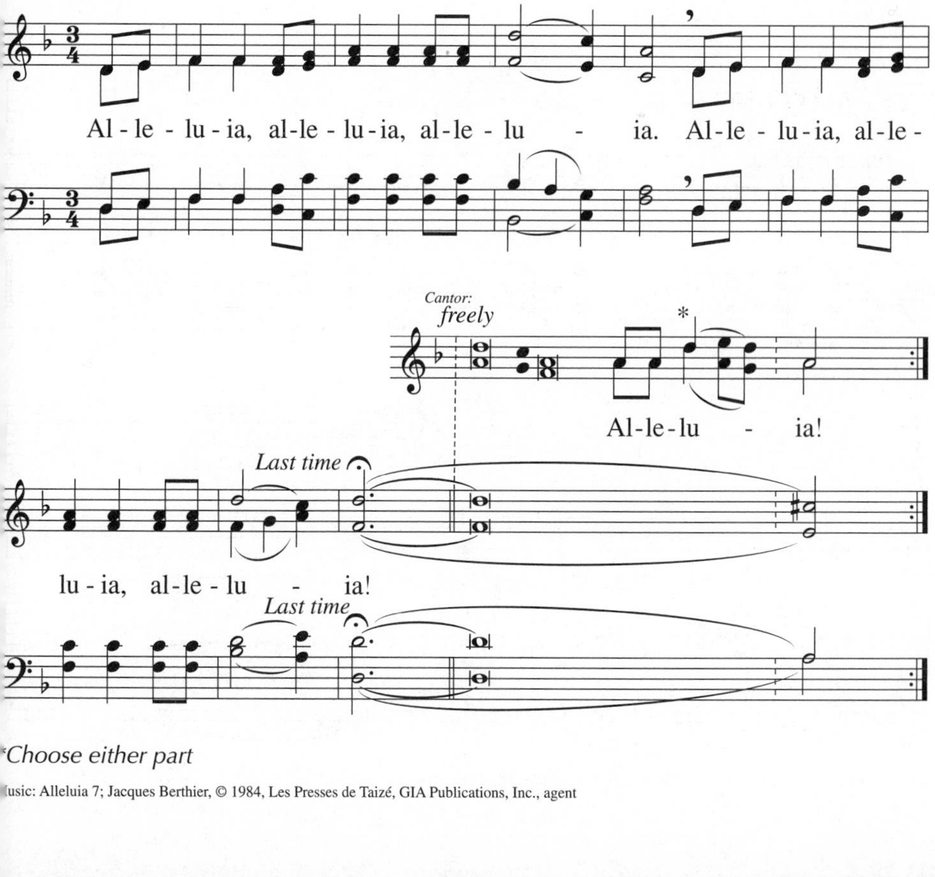

Al - le - lu - ia, al - le - lu - ia, al - le - lu - ia. Al - le - lu - ia, al - le -

Cantor: *freely*

Al - le - lu - ia!

lu - ia, al - le - lu - ia!

Last time

Last time

*Choose either part

264 ALLELUIA

Al-le-lu - ia, al-le - lu-ia, al - le - lu - ia, al-le -
Al-le-lu - ia.
lu - ia!

Music: Alleluia 17; Jacques Berthier, © 1998, Les Presses de Taizé, GIA Publications, Inc., agent

265 ALLELUIA

Al - le - lu - i - a, al - le - lu - i - a,
Al-le-lu-i - a.
al - le - lu - i - a!

Music: Alleluia 18; Jacques Berthier, © 1998, Les Presses de Taizé, GIA Publications, Inc., agent

CELTIC ALLELUIA 266

Refrain
Descant:
Al - le - lu - ia, al - le - lu - ia!
Melody:
Al - le - lu - ia, al - le - lu - ia!
Verses
1. The Word of the Lord lasts for ev - er.
2. God brings the world to him - self
3. The Word of the Lord is a - live, the
4. Fa - ther of all you are bless-ed, cre -
5. "I call you friends," says the Lord,
6. "The sheep of my flock," says the Lord,
7. "E - ven if you have to die,
8. Stay a - wake, pray at all times,
What is the Word that is liv - ing? It is
now through his Christ re - con - cil - ing; he has
Word of God is ac - tive— it can
a - tor of earth and heav - en, for the
"you who are my dis - ci - ples. I make
"hear - ing my voice, they will lis - ten; they will
close to my Word keep faith - ful; for your
pray - ing that you may be strength-ened, that with

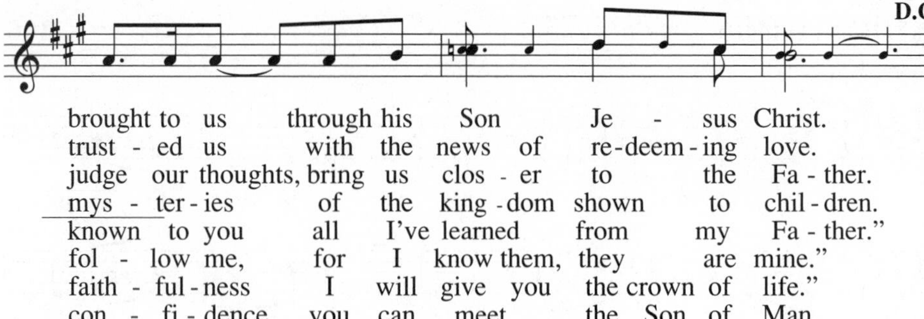
D.C.
brought to us through his Son Je - sus Christ.
trust - ed us with the news of re-deem-ing love.
judge our thoughts, bring us clos - er to the Fa - ther.
mys - ter-ies of the king-dom shown to chil-dren.
known to you all I've learned from my Fa - ther."
fol - low me, for I know them, they are mine."
faith - ful-ness I will give you the crown of life."
con - fi-dence you can meet the Son of Man.

Text: Fintan O'Carroll and Christopher Walker
Music: Fintan O'Carroll and Christopher Walker

GOSPEL ACCLAMATION VERSES FOR ORDINARY TIME

Consult the table at the end of these verses to determine the appropriate verse for each Sunday.

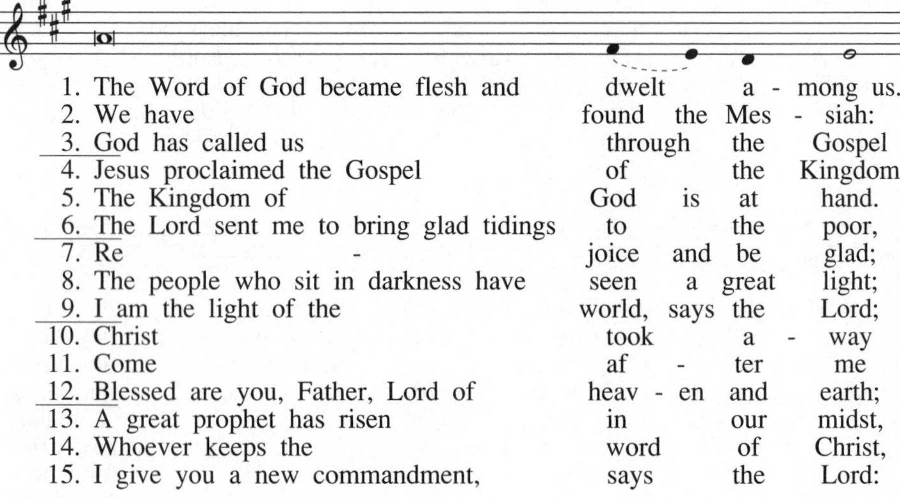
1. The Word of God became flesh and dwelt a - mong us.
2. We have found the Mes - siah:
3. God has called us through the Gospel
4. Jesus proclaimed the Gospel of the Kingdom
5. The Kingdom of God is at hand.
6. The Lord sent me to bring glad tidings to the poor,
7. Re - joice and be glad;
8. The people who sit in darkness have seen a great light;
9. I am the light of the world, says the Lord;
10. Christ took a - way
11. Come af - ter me
12. Blessed are you, Father, Lord of heav - en and earth;
13. A great prophet has risen in our midst,
14. Whoever keeps the word of Christ,
15. I give you a new commandment, says the Lord:

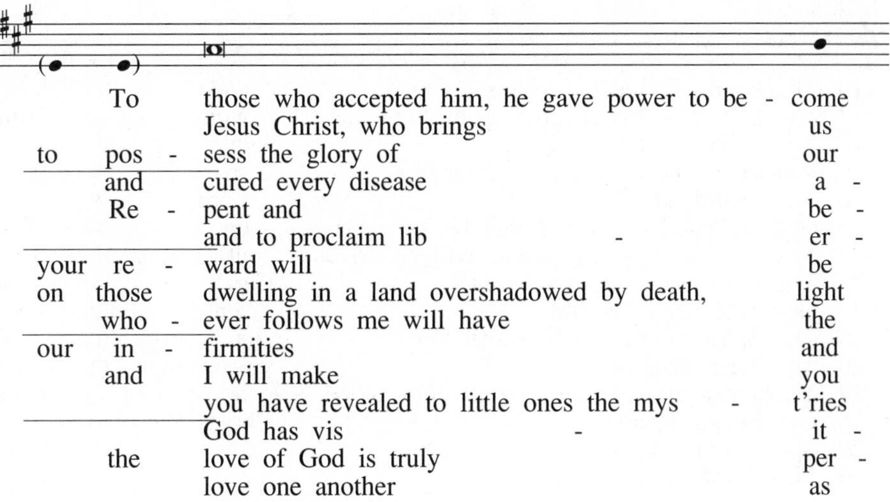
To those who accepted him, he gave power to be - come
Jesus Christ, who brings us
to pos - sess the glory of our
and cured every disease a -
Re - pent and be -
and to proclaim lib - er -
your re - ward will be
on those dwelling in a land overshadowed by death, light
who - ever follows me will have the
our in - firmities and
and I will make you
you have revealed to little ones the mys - t'ries
God has vis - it -
the love of God is truly per -
love one another as

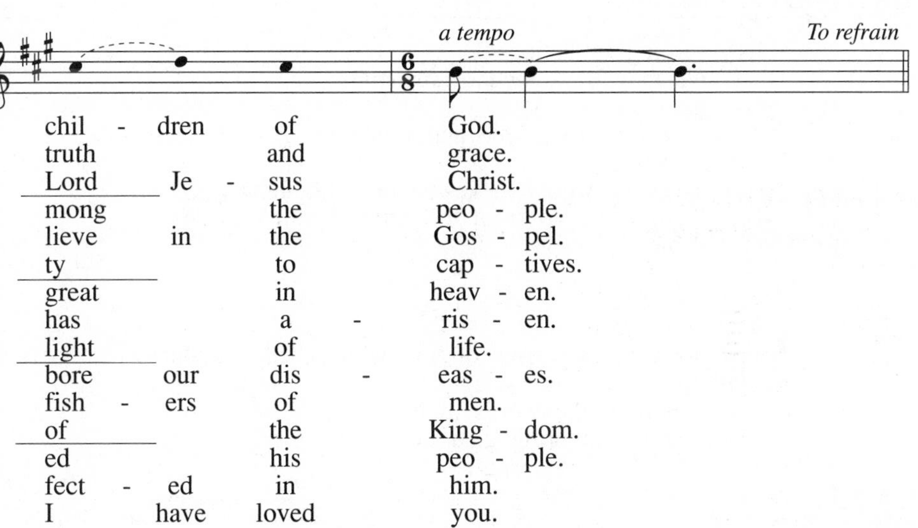
a tempo
To refrain
chil - dren of God.
truth and grace.
Lord Je - sus Christ.
mong the peo - ple.
lieve in the Gos - pel.
ty to cap - tives.
great in heav - en.
has a - ris - en.
light of life.
bore our dis - eas - es.
fish - ers of men.
of the King - dom.
ed his peo - ple.
fect - ed in him.
I have loved you.

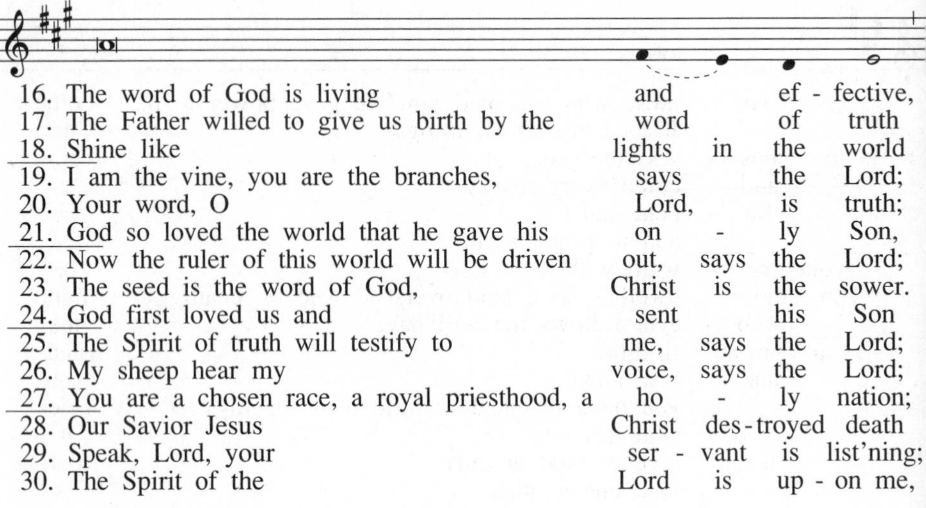

a tempo *To refrain*

16. The word of God is living and effective, discerning reflections and thoughts of the heart.
17. The Father willed to give us birth by the word of truth that we may be a kind of firstfruits of his creatures.
18. Shine like lights in the world as you hold on to the word of life.
19. I am the vine, you are the branches, says the Lord; whoever remains in me and I in him will bear much fruit.
20. Your word, O Lord, is truth; consecrate us in the truth.
21. God so loved the world that he gave his only Son, so that everyone who believes in him might have eternal life.
22. Now the ruler of this world will be driven out, says the Lord; and when I am lifted up from the earth, I will draw ev'ry one to myself.
23. The seed is the word of God, Christ is the sower. All who come to him will live for ever.
24. God first loved us and sent his Son as expiation for our sins.
25. The Spirit of truth will testify to me, says the Lord; and you also will testify.
26. My sheep hear my voice, says the Lord; I know them, and they follow me.
27. You are a chosen race, a royal priesthood, a holy nation; announce the praises of him who called you out of darkness into his wonderful light.
28. Our Savior Jesus Christ destroyed death and brought life to light through the Gospel.
29. Speak, Lord, your servant is list'ning; you have the words of everlasting life.
30. The Spirit of the Lord is upon me, for he sent me to bring glad tidings to the poor.

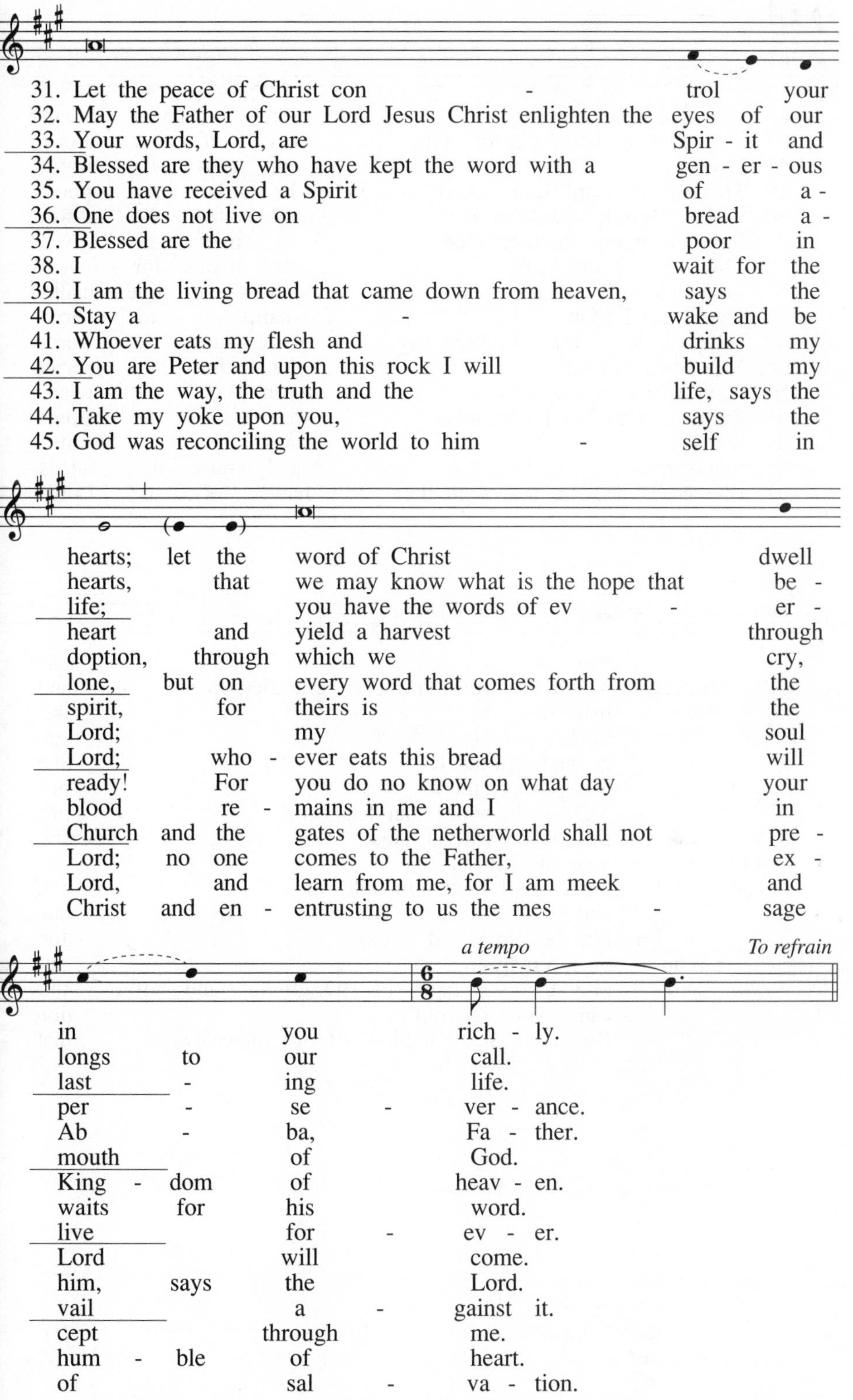
31. Let the peace of Christ con - trol your
32. May the Father of our Lord Jesus Christ enlighten the eyes of our
33. Your words, Lord, are Spir - it and
34. Blessed are they who have kept the word with a gen - er - ous
35. You have received a Spirit of a -
36. One does not live on bread a -
37. Blessed are the poor in
38. I wait for the
39. I am the living bread that came down from heaven, says the
40. Stay a - wake and be
41. Whoever eats my flesh and drinks my
42. You are Peter and upon this rock I will build my
43. I am the way, the truth and the life, says the
44. Take my yoke upon you, says the
45. God was reconciling the world to him - self in
hearts; let the word of Christ dwell
hearts, that we may know what is the hope that be -
life; you have the words of ev - er -
heart and yield a harvest through
doption, through which we cry,
lone, but on every word that comes forth from the
spirit, for theirs is the
Lord; my soul
Lord; who - ever eats this bread will
ready! For you do no know on what day your
blood re - mains in me and I in
Church and the gates of the netherworld shall not pre -
Lord; no one comes to the Father, ex -
Lord, and learn from me, for I am meek and
Christ and en - entrusting to us the mes - sage
a tempo
To refrain
in you rich - ly.
longs to our call.
last - ing life.
per - se - ver - ance.
Ab - ba, Fa - ther.
mouth of God.
King - dom of heav - en.
waits for his word.
live for - ev - er.
Lord will come.
him, says the Lord.
vail a - gainst it.
cept through me.
hum - ble of heart.
of sal - va - tion.

46. Let your face shine up -	on		your	servant;
47. May I never boast except in the	cross	of	our	Lord
48. Open	our	hearts,	O	Lord,
49. Though our Lord Jesus Christ was rich,	he	be -	came	poor,
50. I have chosen you from the	world,	says	the	Lord,
51. If we love one another, God	re -	mains	in	us
52. The word of the Lord	re -	mains	for -	ever.
53. In all circum -	stanc -	es,	give	thanks,
54. The Son of Man	came		to	serve
55. Whoever loves me will keep my	word,	says	the	Lord;
56. You have but one	Fa -	ther	in	heaven
57. Jesus Christ is the first	born	of	the	dead;
58. Remain in me as I remain in	you,	says	the	Lord.
59. Be vigi -	lant	at	all	times
60. Stand erect	and	raise	your	heads
61. Blessed is he who comes in the	name	of	the	Lord!

		and	teach
	through	which the world has been crucified to me	and
	to	listen to	the
so	that	by his poverty	you
	to	go and bear fruit	that
and	his	love is brought to	per -
		This is the word that has been	pro -
	for	this is the will of God	for
and	to	give his life as	a
and	my	Father will love him and we	will
		and	one
	to	him be glory and power,	for -
	Who -	ever remains	in
	and	pray that you have the strength to stand before	the
	be -	cause your redemp -	tion
		Blessed is the Kingdom of our father David	that

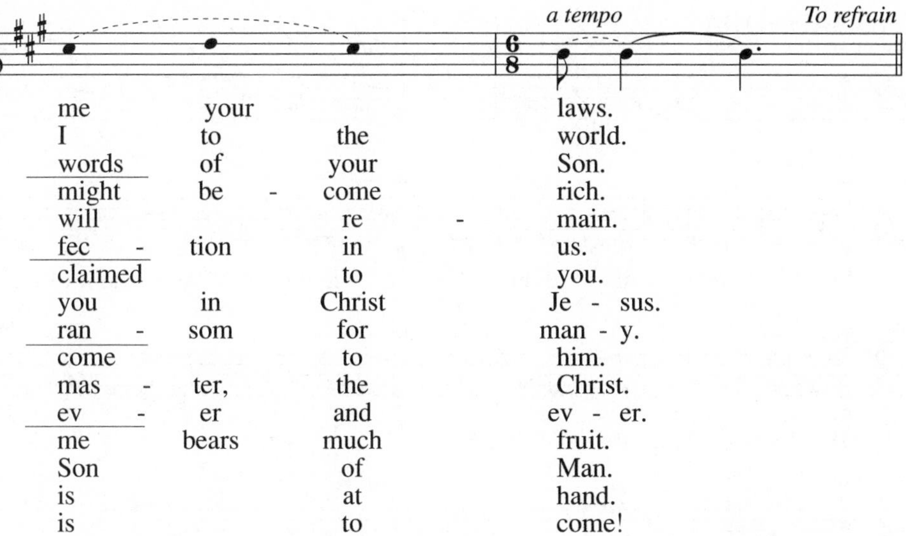
a tempo
To refrain
me your laws.
I to the world.
words of your Son.
might be - come rich.
will re - main.
fec - tion in us.
claimed to you.
you in Christ Je - sus.
ran - som for man - y.
come to him.
mas - ter, the Christ.
ev - er and ev - er.
me bears much fruit.
Son of Man.
is at hand.
is to come!

Sunday in Ordinary Time	Year A	Year B	Year C
2	1	2	3
3	4	5	6
4	7	8	6
5	9	10	11
6	12	13	7
7	14	6	15
8	16	17	18
9	19	20	21
10	6	22	13
11	5	23	24
12	25	13	26
13	27	28	29
14	12	30	31
15	23	32	33
16	12	26	34
17	12	13	35
18	36	36	37

Sunday in Ordinary Time	Year A	Year B	Year C
19	38	39	40
20	4	41	26
21	42	33	43
22	32	17	44
23	45	4	46
24	15	47	45
25	48	3	49
26	26	20	49
27	50	51	52
28	32	37	53
29	18	54	16
30	55	28	45
31	56	55	21
32	40	37	57
33	58	59	60
34	61	61	61

267 ALLELUIA

Cantor: Al - le-lu - ia, al - le-lu - ia! *Assembly:* Al - le-lu - ia, al - le-lu - ia!

Cantor: Al - le-lu - ia, al - le-lu - ia! *Assembly:* Al - le-lu - ia, al - le-lu - ia!

Cantor: Al - le-lu - ia, al - le-lu - ia! *Assembly:* Al - le-lu - ia, al - le-lu - ia!

Cantor: Al - le-lu - ia, al - le-lu - ia! *Assembly:* Al - le-lu - ia, al - le-lu - ia!

Music: *Joyful Alleluia;* Howard Hughes, SM, © 1973, 1979, GIA Publications, Inc.

Tone for verses
D.C.

Music: *Lutheran Book of Worship*, © 1978, Augsburg Fortress

ALLELUIA

268

Refrain

Cantor, then all:

Al-le-lu-ia, al-le- lu - ia. Al-le-lu-ia, al-le- lu -

1. ia. 2. ia.

Verse

Final Refrain

T.B. and Assembly:

Al - le - lu - ia, al - le - lu -

Al - le - lu - ia, al - le - lu - ia.

ia. Al - le - lu - ia, al - le - lu - ia.

**Optional harmonies in cue notes.*
This gospel acclamation may be used with #28.

269 ALLELUIA

mf Cantor:
f Assembly:
mf Cantor:
Al - le - lu - ia. Al - le - lu - ia. Al - le - lu - ia.

f Assembly:
mf Cantor:
f Assembly:
Al - le - lu - ia. Al - le - lu - ia. Al - le - lu - ia.

Tone for verses

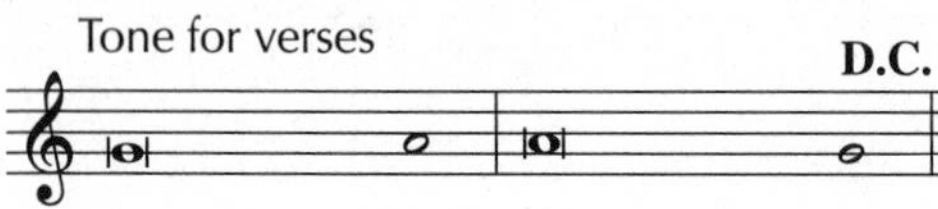
D.C.

Music: *Alleluia in C,* Howard Hughes, SM, © 1973, 1982, GIA Publications, Inc.

270 ALLELUIA

Al - le - lu - ia, al - le - lu - ia, al - le - lu - ia.

Music: A. Gregory Murray, OSB, © 1958, The Grail, GIA Publications, Inc., agent

Tone for verses

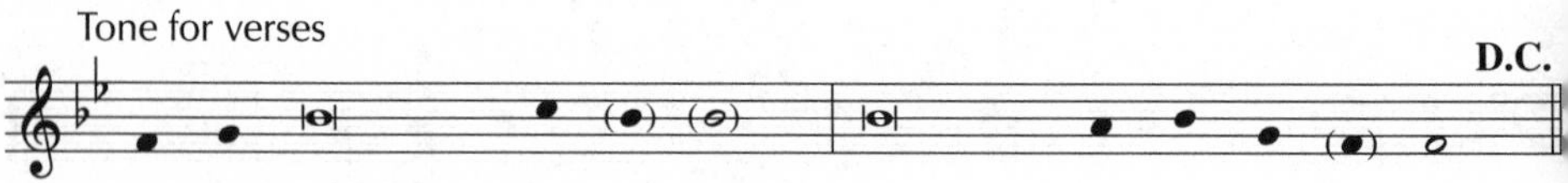
D.C.

Music: tone VIII-g; acc. by Richard Proulx, © 1975, GIA Publications, Inc.

HONDURAS ALLELUIA

271

Cantor:
¡A-le - lu-ya, a-le-lu - ya! ¡A-le - lu-ya, a - le-lu - ya! ¡A-le-
lu - ya, a - le - lu - ya! ¡El Se - ñor re - su - ci - tó!
All:
¡A - le-
lu - ya, a - le - lu - ya! ¡A - le - lu - ya, a - le - lu - ya! ¡A - le-
Last time
lu - ya, a - le - lu - ya! ¡El Se - ñor re - su - ci - tó! ¡A - le -
Last time

Music: *The Honduras Alleluia*, Rob Glover, © 1997, GIA Publications, Inc.

272 ALLELUIA / ALELUYA

With joy ♩ = 139-144
Refrain
f Cantor, then all:
Al - le - lu - ia, al - le - lu - ia, al - le - lu - ia!
Al - le - lu - ia, al - le - lu - ia, al - le - lu - ia!
Al - le - lu - ia! Al - le - lu - ia! Al - le - lu - ia!
¡A - le - lu - ya! ¡A - le - lu - ya! ¡A - le - lu - ya!
Verse
1. Speak Lord, your ser - vant is lis - t'ning: You have the
1. Cris - to, yo soy tu sir-vien-te: ¡En ti es -

D.C.
words of ev - er - last - ing life!
tán la paz y la ver - dad!

Additional Verses

Ordinary Time
2. The Word of God lives with us!
3. Your words, O God, are spir - it and life,
4. I am the way, the truth, and the life,
5. I call you friends, says the Lord,
6. O - pen our hearts, O Lord, to
7. Be faith - ful 'til death, says the Lord,

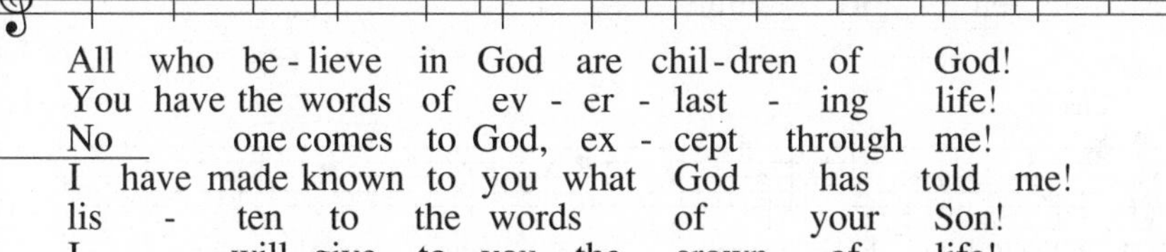
D.C.
All who be - lieve in God are chil - dren of God!
You have the words of ev - er - last - ing life!
No one comes to God, ex - cept through me!
I have made known to you what God has told me!
lis - ten to the words of your Son!
I will give to you the crown of life!

Advent

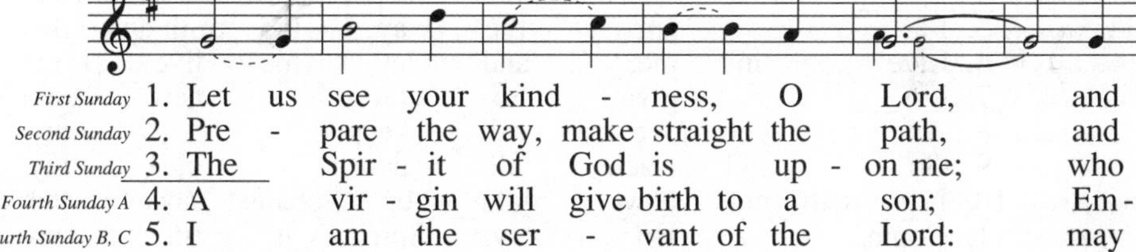
First Sunday 1. Let us see your kind - ness, O Lord, and
Second Sunday 2. Pre - pare the way, make straight the path, and
Third Sunday 3. The Spir - it of God is up - on me; who
Fourth Sunday A 4. A vir - gin will give birth to a son; Em -
Fourth Sunday B, C 5. I am the ser - vant of the Lord: may

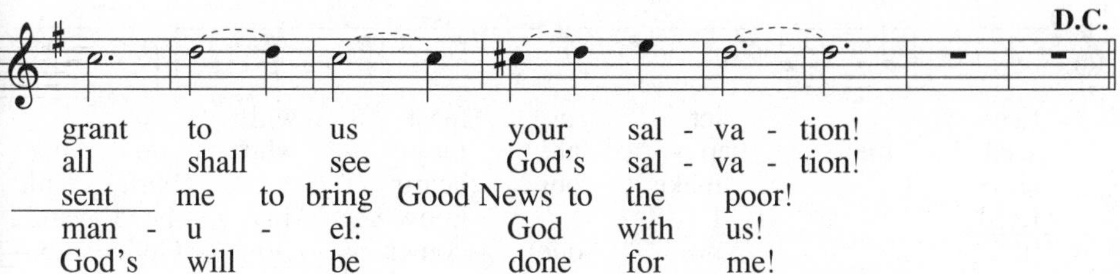
D.C.
grant to us your sal - va - tion!
all shall see God's sal - va - tion!
sent me to bring Good News to the poor!
man - u - el: God with us!
God's will be done for me!

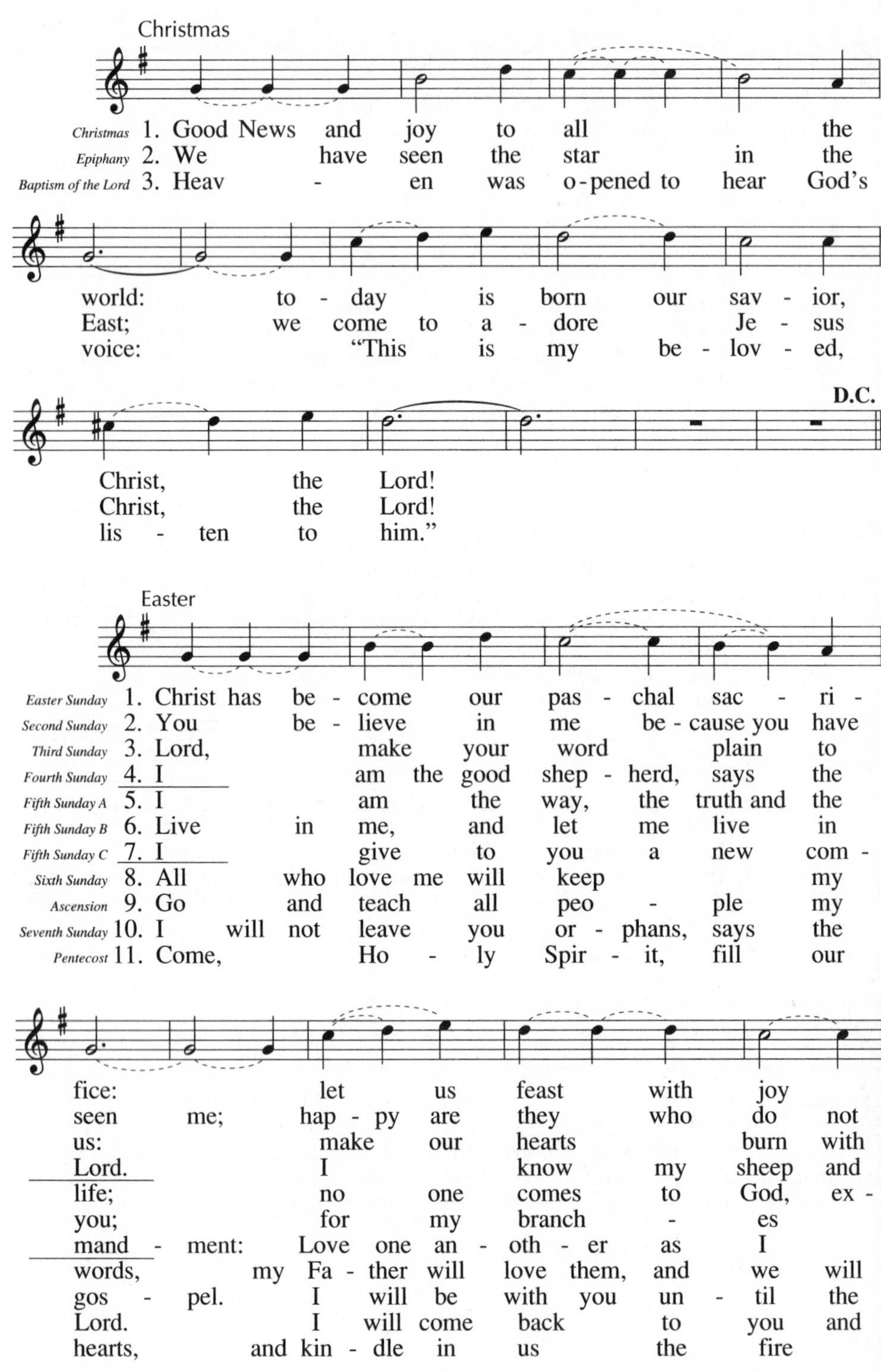
Christmas
Christmas 1. Good News and joy to all the world: to - day is born our sav - ior, Christ, the Lord!
Epiphany 2. We have seen the star in the East; we come to a - dore Je - sus Christ, the Lord!
Baptism of the Lord 3. Heav - en was o-pened to hear God's voice: "This is my be - lov - ed, lis - ten to him."
D.C.
Easter
Easter Sunday 1. Christ has be - come our pas - chal sac - ri - fice: let us feast with joy
Second Sunday 2. You be - lieve in me be - cause you have seen me; hap - py are they who do not
Third Sunday 3. Lord, make your word plain to us: make our hearts burn with
Fourth Sunday 4. I am the good shep - herd, says the Lord. I know my sheep and
Fifth Sunday A 5. I am the way, the truth and the life; no one comes to God, ex -
Fifth Sunday B 6. Live in me, and let me live in you; for my branch - es
Fifth Sunday C 7. I give to you a new com - mand - ment: Love one an - oth - er as I
Sixth Sunday 8. All who love me will keep my words, my Fa - ther will love them, and we will
Ascension 9. Go and teach all peo - ple my gos - pel. I will be with you un - til the
Seventh Sunday 10. I will not leave you or - phans, says the Lord. I will come back to you and
Pentecost 11. Come, Ho - ly Spir - it, fill our hearts, and kin - dle in us the fire

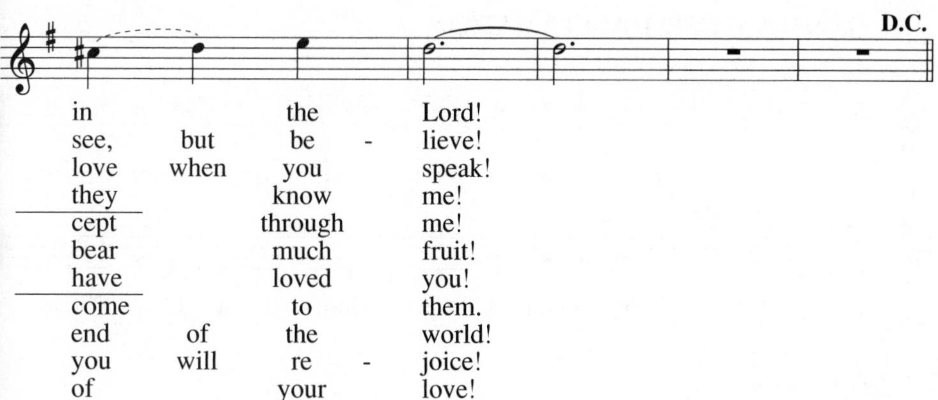
D.C.
in the Lord!
see, but be - lieve!
love when you speak!
they know me!
cept through me!
bear much fruit!
have loved you!
come to them.
end of the world!
you will re - joice!
of your love!

Music: *Mass for the Life of the World,* David Haas, arr. by Rob Glover, © 1993, GIA Publications, Inc.

ALLELUIA

273

Al - le, Al - le-lu, Al - le-lu - ia! Al - le,
Al - le-lu, Al - le-lu - ia! Al - le, Al - le-lu,
Al - le-lu - ia! Al - le, Al - le-lu, Al - le-lu - ia!

Music: Liam Lawton, © 1995, Veritas Publications/Liam Lawton, GIA Publications, Inc., agent

Tone

Music: Robert J. Batastini, © 2004, GIA Publications, Inc.

274 LENTEN GOSPEL ACCLAMATION

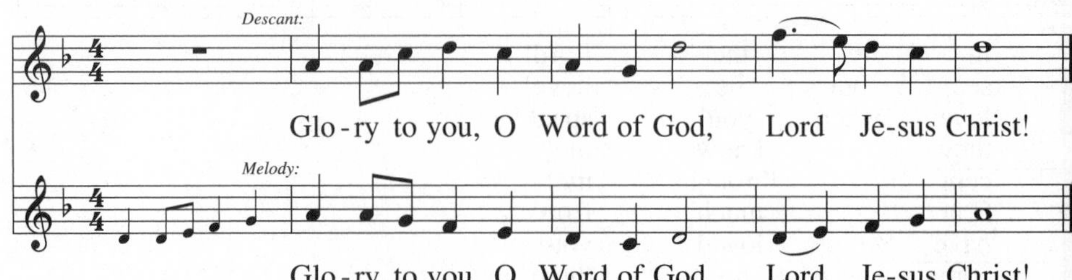
Descant:
Glo-ry to you, O Word of God, Lord Je-sus Christ!
Melody:
Glo-ry to you, O Word of God, Lord Je-sus Christ!

Tone for verses

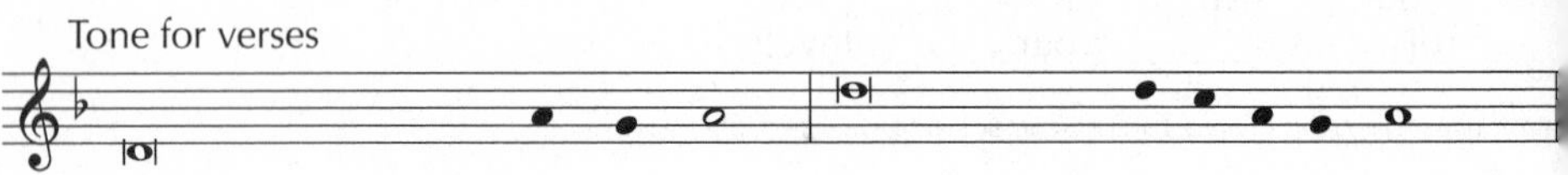

275 LENTEN GOSPEL ACCLAMATION

Refrain

Cantor, then all:

Praise and hon - or to you, O Lord, O Lord.

Praise and hon - or to you, Lord Je - sus Christ.

Verse

Final Refrain

Assembly:

Praise and hon - or to you, O Lord, O Lord.

Choir:

Praise to you, O Lord, O Lord.

Praise and hon - or to you, O Lord, O Lord.

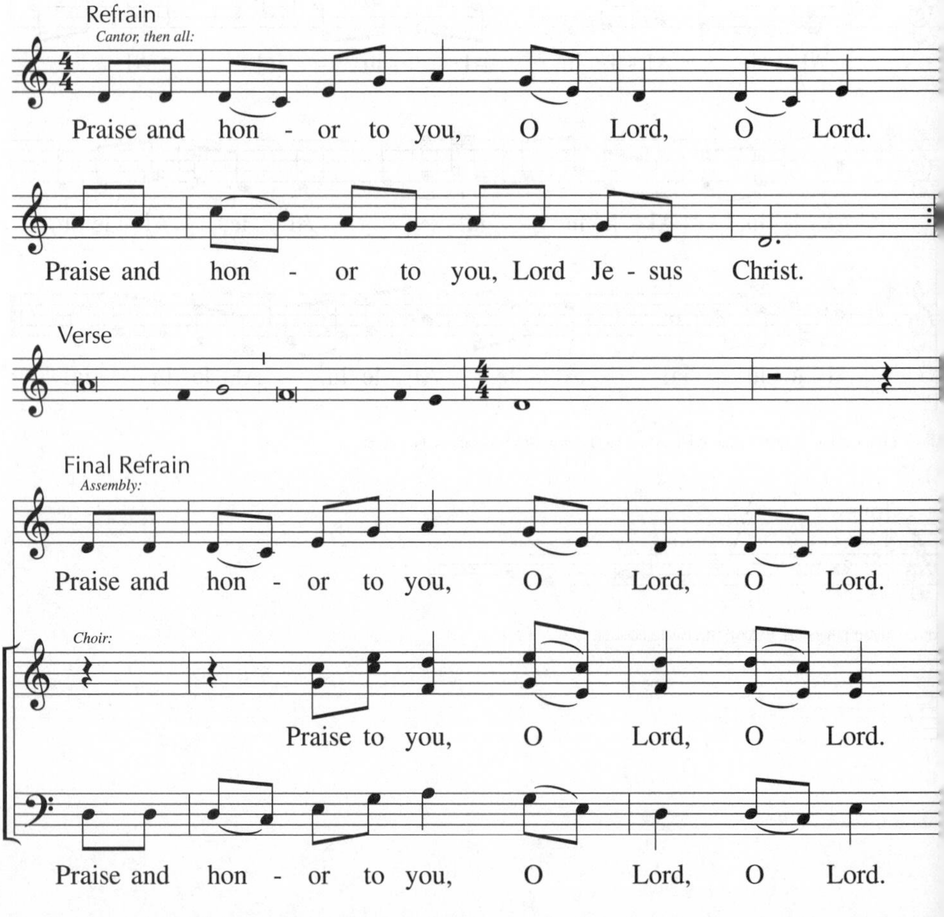

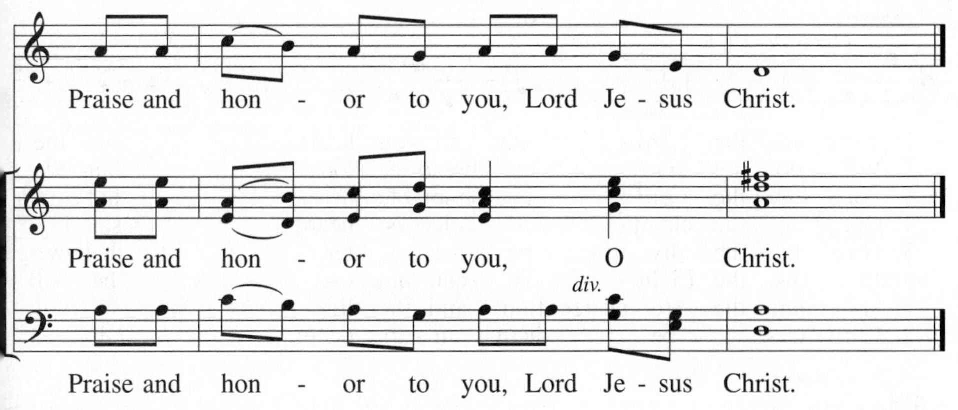
Praise and hon - or to you, Lord Je - sus Christ.
Praise and hon - or to you, O Christ.
div.
Praise and hon - or to you, Lord Je - sus Christ.

This gospel acclamation may be used with #39.

Text: ICEL, © 1969
Music: Based on WONDROUS LOVE, Stephen Pishner, © 1998, GIA Publications, Inc.

LENTEN GOSPEL ACCLAMATION 276

Refrain

Praise to you, Lord Je - sus, king of end - less glo - ry,

1.- 7. To verses accel. 8.

Sav - ior of the world, Sav - ior of the world. world.

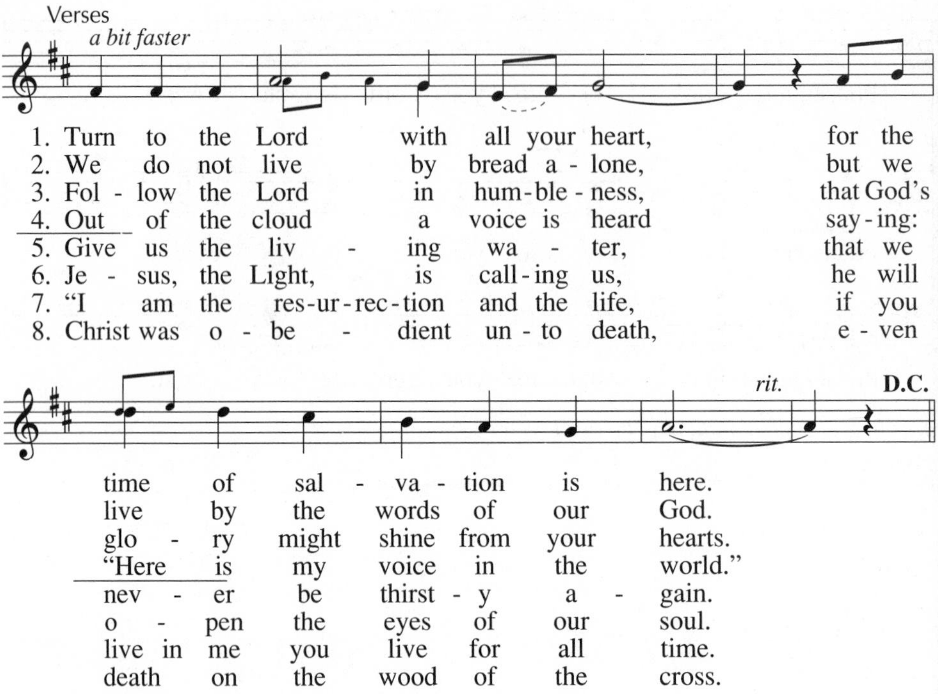

Verses
a bit faster

1. Turn to the Lord with all your heart, for the
2. We do not live by bread a - lone, but we
3. Fol - low the Lord in hum-ble - ness, that God's
4. Out of the cloud a voice is heard say - ing:
5. Give us the liv - ing wa - ter, that we
6. Je - sus, the Light, is call - ing us, he will
7. "I am the res-ur-rec-tion and the life, if you
8. Christ was o - be - dient un - to death, e - ven

rit. **D.C.**

time of sal - va - tion is here.
live by the words of our God.
glo - ry might shine from your hearts.
"Here is my voice in the world."
nev - er be thirst - y a - gain.
o - pen the eyes of our soul.
live in me you live for all time.
death on the wood of the cross.

Text: Marty Haugen
Music: Marty Haugen

277 GENERAL INTERCESSIONS

Refrain
mp
God ev - er - faith - ful, God ev - er - mer - ci - ful,
God of your peo - ple, hear our prayer.

Verses

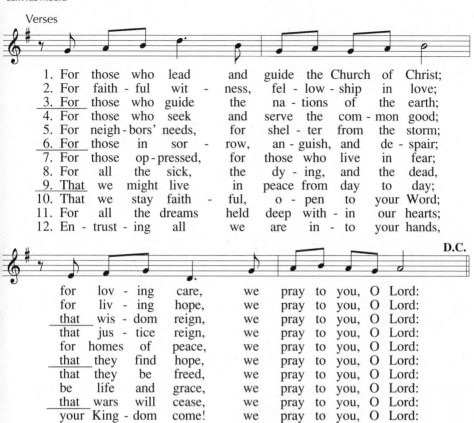

1. For those who lead and guide the Church of Christ; for lov - ing care, we pray to you, O Lord:
2. For faith - ful wit - ness, fel - low - ship in love; for liv - ing hope, we pray to you, O Lord:
3. For those who guide the na - tions of the earth; that wis - dom reign, we pray to you, O Lord:
4. For those who seek and serve the com - mon good; that jus - tice reign, we pray to you, O Lord:
5. For neigh - bors' needs, for shel - ter from the storm; for homes of peace, we pray to you, O Lord:
6. For those in sor - row, an - guish, and de - spair; that they find hope, we pray to you, O Lord:
7. For those op - pressed, for those who live in fear; that they be freed, we pray to you, O Lord:
8. For all the sick, the dy - ing, and the dead, be life and grace, we pray to you, O Lord:
9. That we might live in peace from day to day; that wars will cease, we pray to you, O Lord:
10. That we stay faith - ful, o - pen to your Word; your King - dom come! we pray to you, O Lord:
11. For all the dreams held deep with - in our hearts; for all our needs, we pray to you, O Lord:
12. En - trust - ing all we are in - to your hands, we call your name, and pray to you, O Lord:

D.C.

Text: Michael Joncas
Music: Michael Joncas

GENERAL INTERCESSIONS

278

Fine
D.C.
Ky - ri - e, Ky - ri - e, e - le - i - son. (hum)

*Descant ad lib. 2nd time only

Music: Jacques Berthier, © 1980, Les Presses de Taizé, GIA Publications, Inc., agent

279 GENERAL INTERCESSIONS

Ky - ri - e e - le - i - son,
Ky - ri - e e - le - i - son.

Music: Jacques Berthier, © 1998, Les Presses de Taizé, GIA Publications, Inc., agent

280 GENERAL INTERCESSIONS

Ky - ri - e, Ky - ri - e, Ky - ri - e e -
1.
2.
lei - son. lei - son.

Music: Jacques Berthier, © 1998, Les Presses de Taizé, GIA Publications, Inc., agent

GENERAL INTERCESSIONS 281

Response
Cantor:
O, Lord, hear our prayer. Lord, hear us. O, Lord, hear our prayer.
All:
Last time
O, Lord, hear our prayer. Lord, hear us. O, Lord, hear our prayer.
Last time
Petitions*
Choir:
Oo
All:
O, Lord, hear our prayer.
Choir:
Oo
All:
D.S.
O, Lord, hear our prayer.

*Petitions are spoken over the choir Oo's.

282 GENERAL INTERCESSIONS

Gra-cious Lord, hear us we pray.

Music: Ronald F. Krisman, © 1977, GIA Publications, Inc.

283-A GENERAL INTERCESSIONS–ADVENT

Cantor: Come quick - ly, Lord, in mer - cy come. *All:* Come quick - ly, Lord, in mer - cy come.

Intercessions | *To repeat* | *After each Intercession* *Cantor:* Lift up, O Church, this world to God: *All:* Come quick - ly, Lord, in mer - cy come. *To Intercessions*

Text: Gabe Huck, © 2004
Music: Based on CONDITOR ALME SIDERUM; adapt. and arr. by Tony Alonso, © 2004, GIA Publications, Inc.

GENERAL INTERCESSIONS–CHRISTMAS 283-B

mp Cantor:
Child of Mar - y, hear our prayer.
mf All:
Child of Mar - y, hear our prayer.
Intercessions
After each Intercession
f Cantor:
All cre - a - tion raise your voic - es:
All:
To Intercessions
Child of Mar - y, hear our prayer.

Text: Gabe Huck, © 2004
Music: Based on DIVINUM MYSTERIUM; adapt. and arr. by Tony E. Alonso, © 2004, GIA Publications, Inc.

GENERAL INTERCESSIONS–LENT 283-C

Cantor:
Hear, O Lord, en - fold us in your mer - cy.
All:
Hear, O Lord, en - fold us in your mer - cy.
Intercessions
After each Intercession
Cantor:
All:
To Intercessions
Cry out for God's mer-cy: Hear, O Lord, en - fold us in your mer-cy.

Text: Gabe Huck, © 2004
Music: Based on PARCE DOMINE; adapt. and arr. by Tony Alonso, © 2004, GIA Publications, Inc.

283-D GENERAL INTERCESSIONS–EASTER

f *Cantor or choir:*

Hear us, Sav - ior, hear our prayer.

All:

Hear us, Sav - ior, hear our prayer.

Intercessions

Ooo

D.C.

Text: Gabe Huck, © 2004
Music: Tony Alonso, © 2004, GIA Publications, Inc.

284 GENERAL INTERCESSIONS

Hear our prayer.
Ó - ye - nos.
Hear our prayer, Lord. Hear our prayer, hear our
Se - ñor, ó - ye-nos. Ó - ye - nos, ó - ye -
Hear our prayer, Lord.
Se - ñor, Ó - ye -

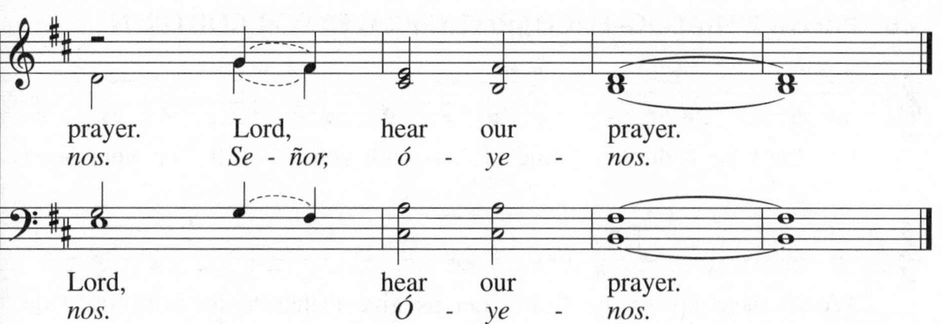
prayer. Lord, hear our prayer.
nos. Se - ñor, ó - ye - nos.
Lord, hear our prayer.
nos. Ó - ye - nos.

Music: Tony E. Alonso, © 2001, GIA Publications, Inc.

GENERAL INTERCESSIONS 285

Refrain

Lord, hear our prayer; De-us, ex-au - di

nos; Se-ñor, es-cú - cha - nos.

Last time

Last time

Verses

Cantor:

D.C.

Music: Michael Hay, © 1994, World Library Publications

286 PREFACE DIALOG–EUCHARISTIC PRAYER FOR CHILDREN

Priest:
Assembly:
Priest:
The Lord be with you. And al - so with you. Lift up your hearts.

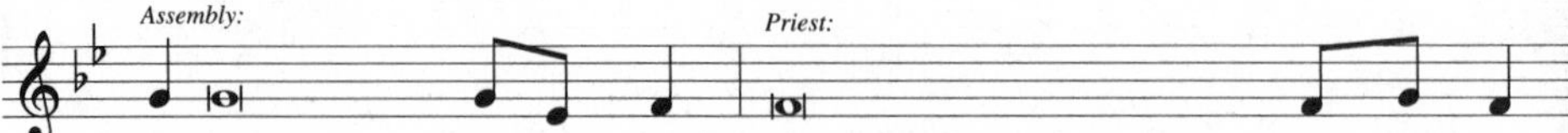
Assembly:
Priest:
We lift them up to the Lord. Let us give thanks to the Lord, our God.

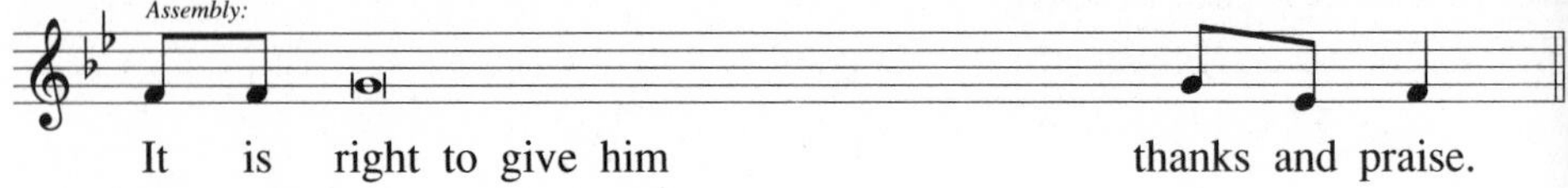
Assembly:
It is right to give him thanks and praise.

Music: *Mass of Creation,* Marty Haugen, © 1984, GIA Publications, Inc.

287 CHILDREN'S ACCLAMATION 1

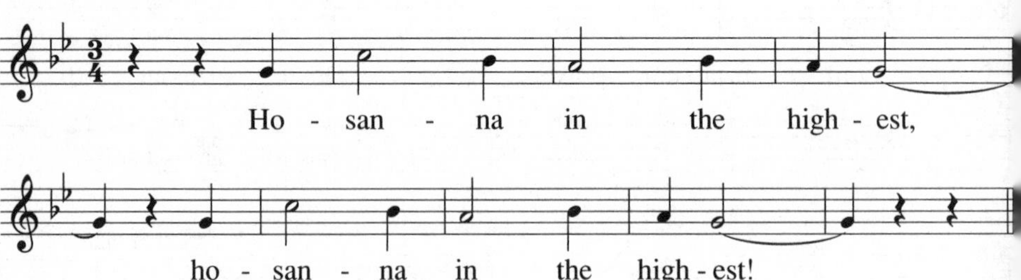
Ho - san - na in the high - est,
ho - san - na in the high - est!

Music: Eucharistic Prayer for Children, *Mass of Creation,* Marty Haugen, adapt by Rob Glover, © 1989, GIA Publications, Inc.

288 SANCTUS

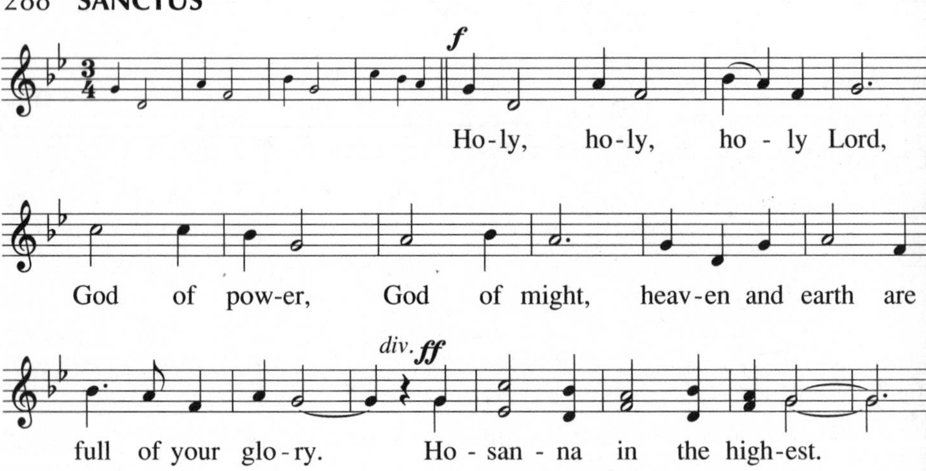
f
Ho - ly, ho - ly, ho - ly Lord,
God of pow - er, God of might, heav - en and earth are
div. ff
full of your glo - ry. Ho - san - na in the high - est.

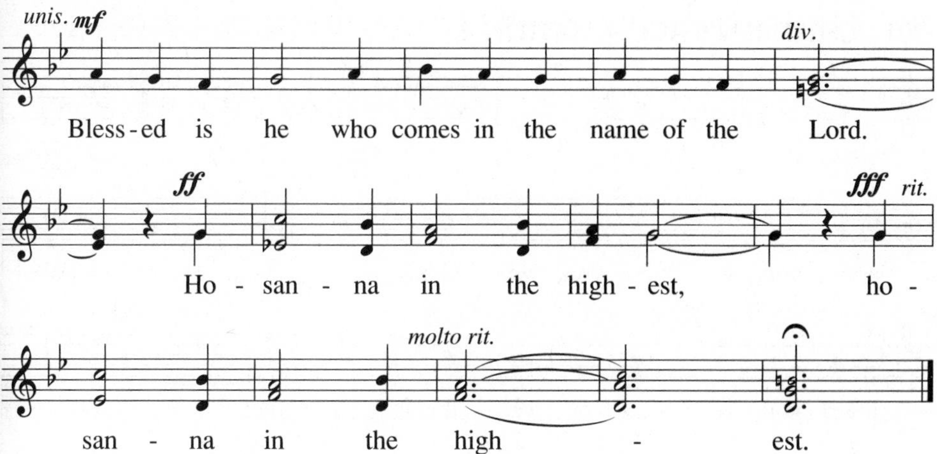
unis. mf
div.
Bless-ed is he who comes in the name of the Lord.
ff
fff rit.
Ho - san - na in the high - est, ho -
molto rit.
san - na in the high - est.

Music: *Mass of Creation,* Marty Haugen, © 1984, GIA Publications, Inc.

An SATB version appears at number 147.

CHILDREN'S ACCLAMATION 2 289

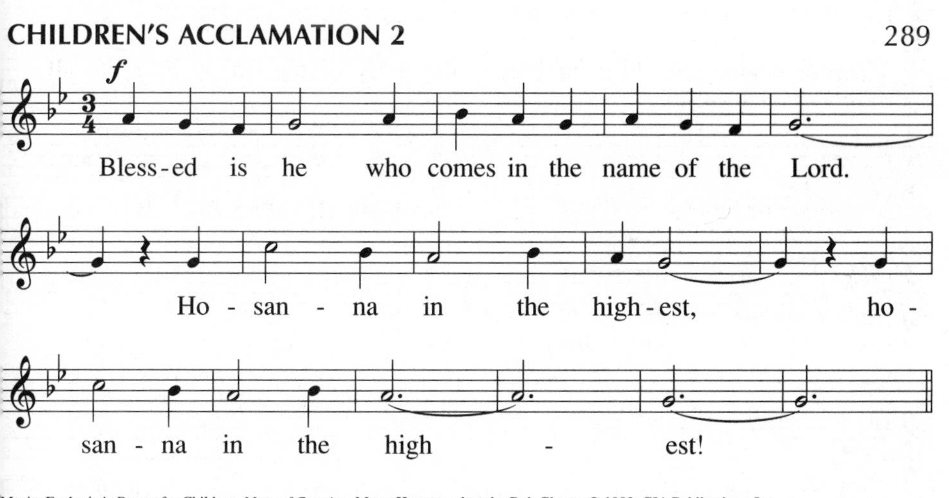
f
Bless-ed is he who comes in the name of the Lord.
Ho - san - na in the high-est, ho -
san - na in the high - est!

Music: Eucharistic Prayer for Children, *Mass of Creation,* Marty Haugen, adapt. by Rob Glover, © 1989, GIA Publications, Inc.

CHILDREN'S ACCLAMATION 3 290

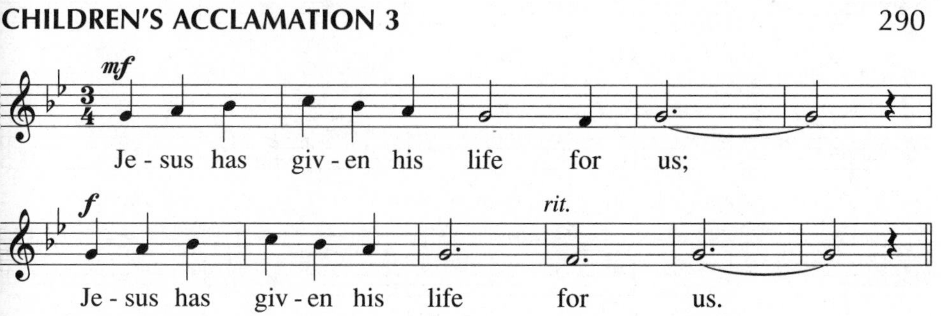
mf
Je - sus has giv - en his life for us;
f
rit.
Je - sus has giv - en his life for us.

Text: ICEL, © 1975
Music: Eucharistic Prayer for Children, *Mass of Creation,* Marty Haugen, adapt. by Rob Glover, © 1989, GIA Publications, Inc.

291 CHILDREN'S ACCLAMATION 4

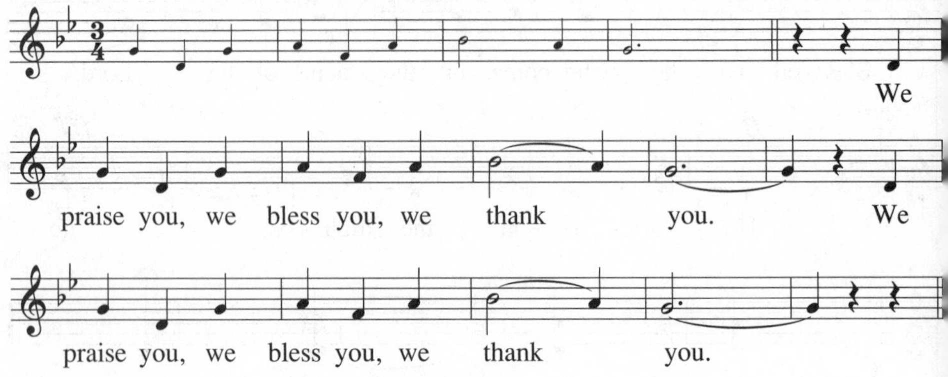
We
praise you, we bless you, we thank you. We
praise you, we bless you, we thank you.

Text: ICEL, © 1975
Music: Eucharistic Prayer for Children, *Mass of Creation,* Marty Haugen, adapt. by Rob Glover, © 1989, GIA Publications, Inc.

292 DOXOLOGY AND GREAT AMEN

Priest:

Through him, with him, in him, in the unity of the Ho - ly Spir - it, all

glory and honor is yours, al - might - y Fa - ther, for

ev - er and ev - er.

All:

Descant:

A - men, a - men, a - men!

Melody:

A - men, a - men, a - men!

rit.

A - men, a - men, a - men!

rit.

A - men, a - men, a - men!

Music: *Mass of Creation,* Marty Haugen, © 1984, GIA Publications, Inc.

SANCTUS–LAND OF REST 293

Ho - ly, ho - ly, ho - ly Lord, God of pow-er and
might, heav-en and earth are full of your glo - ry. Ho -
div.
san - na in the high - est. Bless - ed is he who comes
unis.
in the name of the Lord. Ho - san - na in the
high - est, ho - san - na in the high - est.

Music: *Land of Rest*, adapt. by Marcia Pruner, © 1980, Church Pension Fund; acc. by Richard Proulx, © 1986, GIA Publications, Inc.
choral arr. Kelly Dobbs Mickus, © 2004, GIA Publications, Inc.

294 MEMORIAL ACCLAMATION

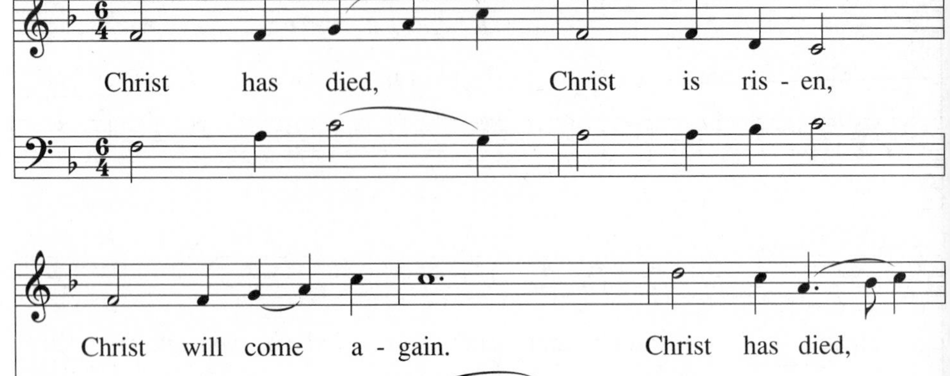
*
Christ has died, Christ is ris - en,

Christ will come a - gain. Christ has died,

div.
Christ is ris - en, Christ will come a - gain.
div.

Text: ICEL, © 1973
Music: *Land of Rest,* adapt. by Richard Proulx, © 1986, GIA Publications, Inc.; choral arr. by Kelly Dobbs Mickus, © 2004, GIA Publications, Inc.

**For a shorter version of this acclamation, sing the first two measures and the last two measures.*

295 AMEN

A - men, a - men, a - men.

Music: *Land of Rest,* adapt. by Richard Proulx, © 1986, GIA Publications, Inc.; choral arr. by Kelly Dobbs Mickus, © 2004, GIA Publications, Inc.

SANCTUS–MASS FOR BENILDE-ST. MARGARET

♩ = 108
Ho - ly, ho - ly, ho - ly Lord, God of pow'r and might,
heav'n and earth are full of your glo - ry. Ho -
san - na, ho - san - na,
Ho - san - na,
ho - san - na in the high - est! Ho -
san - na, ho - san - na,
Ho - san - na,
ho - san - na in the high - est.

Bless - ed, bless-ed is he who comes in the name of the
Lord.
Ho - san - na, ho - san - na,
Ho - san - na,
Ho - san - na, ho - san - na, ho -
Ho - san - na,
nan - na in the high - est!
Ho - san - na, ho -
Ho -
Ho - san - na, ho -
Ho -
san - na,
san - na,
san - na, ho - san - na in the high - est!
san - na,

Music: *Mass for Benilde–St. Margaret*, Michael Mahler, © 2004, GIA Publications, Inc.

MEMORIAL ACCLAMATION 297

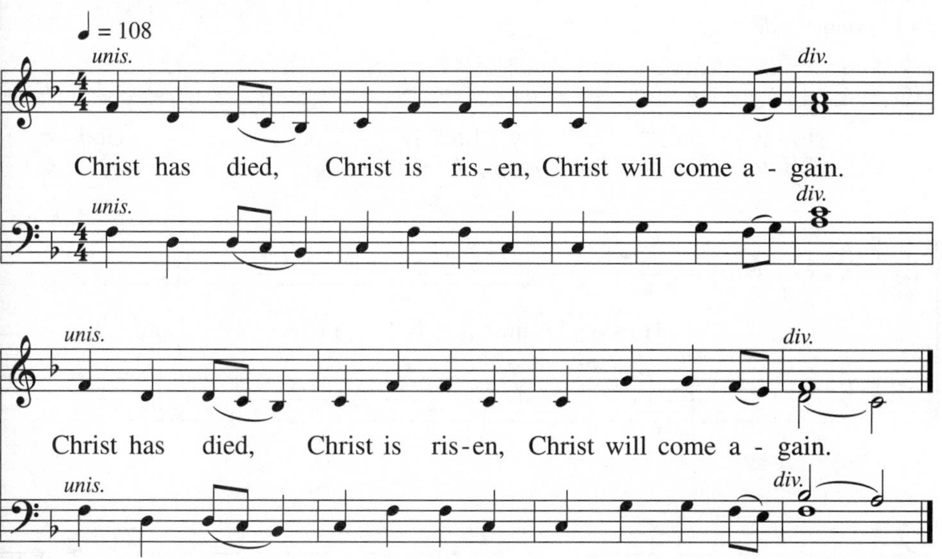
♩ = 108
unis.
div.
Christ has died, Christ is ris - en, Christ will come a - gain.
unis.
div.
unis.
div.
Christ has died, Christ is ris-en, Christ will come a - gain.
unis.
div.

Text: ICEL, © 1973
Music: *Mass for Benilde–St. Margaret,* Michael Mahler, © 2004, GIA Publications, Inc.

AMEN 298

♩ = 108

A - men, a - men,
A - men, a - men,
A - men, a - men, a - men, a - men.
A - men, a - men,

A - men, a - men,
A-men, a - men,
A - men, a - men, a - men, a - men.
A-men, a - men,

Music: *Mass for Benilde–St. Margaret,* Michael Mahler, © 2004, GIA Publications, Inc.

299 SANCTUS–MASS FOR THE LIFE OF THE WORLD

Gospel style
Melody:
Ho - ly, ho - ly, ho - ly Lord, God of
San - to, San - to, San - to es el Se - ñor,
Harmony:
Ho - ly, ho - ly, ho - ly Lord.
pow'r God of might, heav - en and
Dios del U - ni - ver - so. Lle - nos es - tán el
Pow - er, God of might.
f
earth are full of your glo - ry, Ho -
cie - lo y la tie - rra de tu glo - ria. ¡Ho -
f
Full of glo - ry, Ho -

san - na in the high - est! Blest is
san - na en el cie - lo! Ben -
san - na in the high - est! Blest is
he who comes in the
di - to el que vie - ne en
Blest is he,
he is he, he who comes,
Bless - ed,
name of the Lord. Ho -
nom - bre del Se - ñor. ¡Ho -
name of the Lord.

san - na! Ho -
san - na! ¡Ho -
Ho - san - na! Ho -

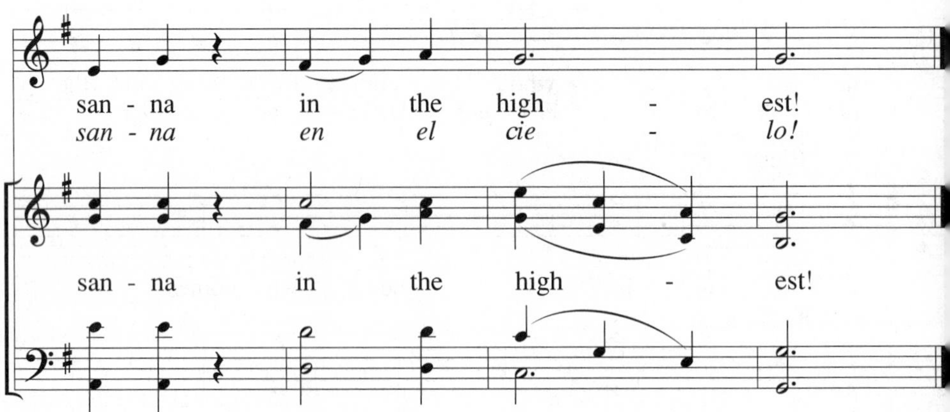
san - na in the high - est!
san - na en el cie - lo!
san - na in the high - est!

Text: Spanish adapt. by Ronald F. Krisman, © 2004, GIA Publications, Inc.
Music: *Mass for the Life of the World,* David Haas, arr. by Rob Glover, © 1993, GIA Publications, Inc.

300 MEMORIAL ACCLAMATION

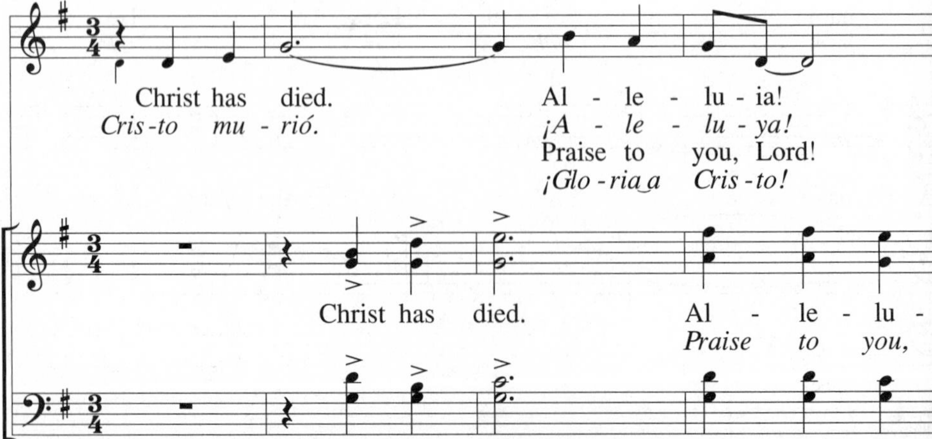
Christ has died. Al - le - lu - ia!
Cris-to mu - rió. ¡A - le - lu - ya!
Praise to you, Lord!
¡Glo - ria a Cris - to!
Christ has died. Al - le - lu -
Praise to you,

Christ is ris - en. Al - le - lu - ia!
Re - su - ci - tó! ¡A - le - lu - ya!
Praise to you, Lord!
¡Glo - ria al Se - ñor!
ia! Ris - en. Al - le - lu -
Lord! Praise to you,
f
Christ will come a - gain.
Cris - to de nue - vo ven - drá.
f
ia! Come a - gain.
Lord!
Al - le - lu - ia! Al - le - lu - ia!
¡A - le - lu - ya! ¡A - le - lu - ya!
Praise to you, Lord! Praise to you, Lord!
¡Glo - ria a Cris - to! ¡Glo - ria al Se - ñor!
Al - le - lu - ia! Al - le - lu - ia!
Praise to you, Lord! Praise to you, Lord!

301 AMEN

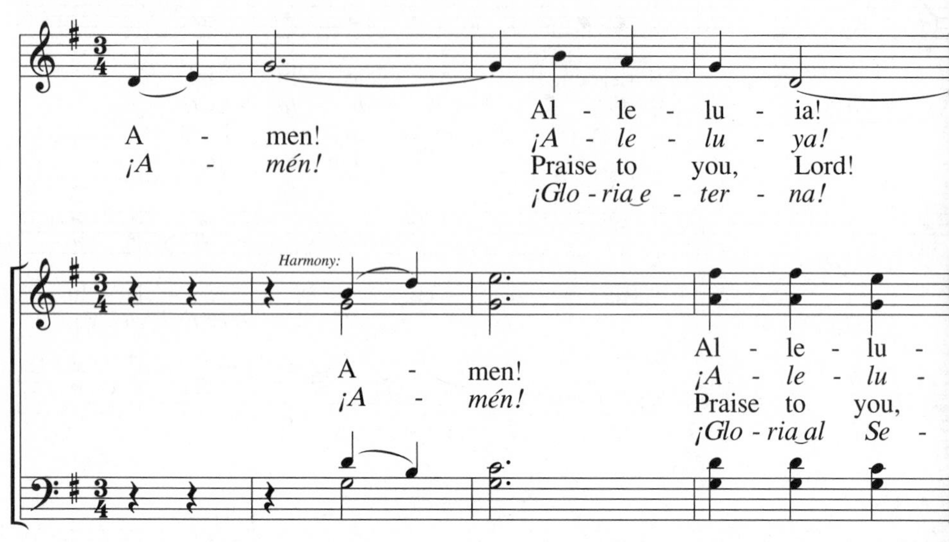
Harmony:
A - men!
¡A - mén!
Al - le - lu - ia!
¡A - le - lu - ya!
Praise to you, Lord!
¡Glo - ria e - ter - na!
A - men!
¡A - mén!
Al - le - lu -
¡A - le - lu -
Praise to you,
¡Glo - ria al Se -

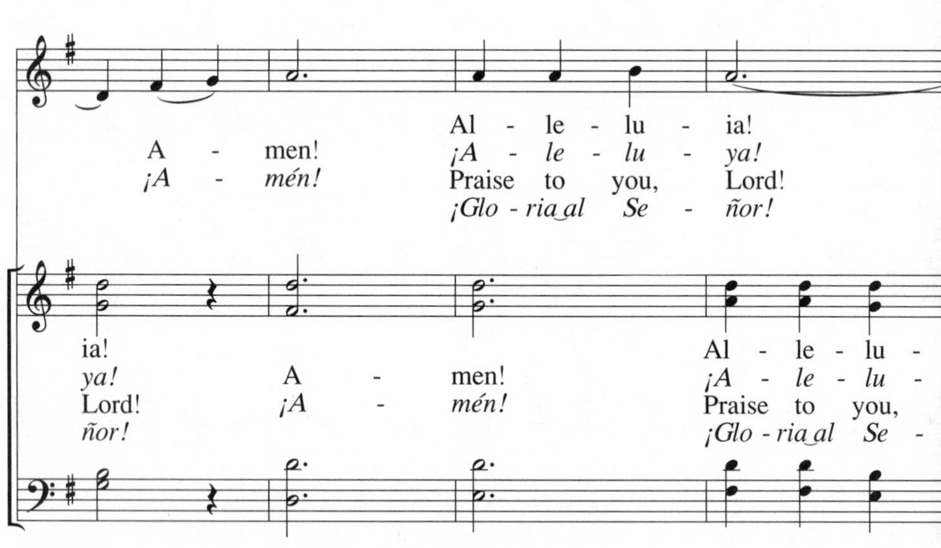
A - men!
¡A - mén!
Al - le - lu - ia!
¡A - le - lu - ya!
Praise to you, Lord!
¡Glo - ria al Se - ñor!
ia!
ya!
Lord!
ñor!
A - men!
¡A - mén!
Al - le - lu -
¡A - le - lu -
Praise to you,
¡Glo - ria al Se -

A - men! A - men!
¡A - mén! ¡A - mén!
ia!
ya! A - men!
Lord! ¡A - mén!
ñor!
Al - le - lu - ia!
¡A - le - lu - ya! A - men!
Praise to you, Lord! ¡A - men!
¡Glo - ria e - ter - na!
Al - le - lu - ia!
¡A - le - lu - ya! A - men!
Praise to you, Lord! ¡A - men!
¡Glo - ria e - ter - na!

Text: Spanish adapt. by Ronald F. Krisman, © 2004, GIA Publications, Inc.
Music: *Mass for the Life of the World,* David Haas, arr. by Rob Glover, © 1993, GIA Publications, Inc.

302 AGNUS DEI

Flowing
mp
Cantor:
*Lamb of
Cor - de - ro de
All:
mf
God, you take a - way the sins of the world: have
Dios, que qui - tas el pe - ca - do del mun - do,
mp
mf
you take a - way the sins of the world: have
que qui - tas el pe - ca - do del mun - do,
mp
mf
mp
rit.
mer - cy on us.
ten pie - dad de no - so - tros.
mp
rit.
mer - cy on us.
ten pie - dad de no - so - tros.
mp
rit.

*Other invocations may be used: King of kings, Prince of Peace, Bread of Life, Ancient Cup, Pan de Vida (Bread of Life), Copa de Promesa (Cup of Promise), Sangre de la Cruz, (Blood of the Cross), Mi Redentor (My Redeemer), etc.

Last time:
Cantor:
mp
All:
Lamb of God, you take a - way the sins of the
Cor - de - ro de Dios, que qui - tas el pe - ca - do del
mp
you take a - way the sins of the
que qui - tas el pe - ca - do del
mp
mf
molto rit.
f
world: grant us your peace.
mun - do, da - nos la paz.
mf
molto rit.
f
world: grant us your peace.
mun - do, da - nos la paz.
mf
f

Music: *Mass for the Life of the World,* David Haas, © 1987, 1993, GIA Publications, Inc.

303 SANCTUS–MASS OF PLENTY

Ho - ly,
O ho - ly,
ho - ly, ho - ly Lord, God of
O ho - ly,
pow-er and might, heav - en and earth,
Heav - en and
heav - en and earth are full of your glo - ry.
earth

Ho - san - na in the
Ho - san - na in the
high - est, ho - san - na in the
high - est, ho - san - na in the
high - est. Bless - ed is he,
high - est. Bless - ed is
bless-ed is he who comes in the name of the Lord.
he

Ho - san - na in the
Ho - san - na in the
high - est, ho - san - na in the
high - est, ho - san - na in the
*
high - est. Ho - san - na in the
high - est. Ho - san - na in the
**
high - est, ho - san - na in the high - est.
high - est, ho - san - na in the high - est.

*This section may be used as an additional acclamation with the Children's Eucharistic Prayer.
**Melody in alto.

MEMORIAL ACCLAMATION 304

S, A unis.
Christ has died, Christ is ris - en,
T, B unis.

div.
Christ will come a - gain. Christ has died,
div.
has died,

*
rit.
Christ is ris - en, Christ will come a - gain.
is ris-en, Christ will come a - gain.

*Melody in alto.

Text: ICEL, © 1973
Music: *Mass of Plenty,* Rob Glover, © 2000, GIA Publications, Inc.

305 **AMEN**

Priest:
Through him, with him, and in him, in the
u-ni-ty of the Ho-ly Spir-it, all glo-ry and hon-or is
yours, al-might-y Fa-ther, for ev-er and ev - er.
All:
A - men, al - le - lu - ia, a -
men, al - le - lu - ia! A - men, al - le-
div.
al - le -
lu - ia, a - men, al - le - lu - ia!
al - le - lu - ia!

*Melody in alto.

Music: *Mass of Plenty*, Rob Glover, © 2000, GIA Publications, Inc.

SANCTUS–DEUTSCHE MESSE

Slowly ♩ = ca. 72
mp
Ho - ly, ho - ly, ho - ly Lord, God of pow'r and
might. Ho - ly, ho - ly, ho - ly Lord,
God of pow'r and might.
f
Heav - en and earth are
full, full of your glo - ry.
mf
Ho - san - na in the high - est, ho - san - na in the

f

high - est. Bless - ed is he who comes

f

mp

in the name of the Lord. Ho - san - na in the

mp

dim.

high - est, ho - san - na in the high - est.

dim.

Music: *Deutsche Messe,* Franz Schubert, 1797-1828; adapt. by Richard Proulx, © 1985, 1989, GIA Publications, Inc.

307 MEMORIAL ACCLAMATION

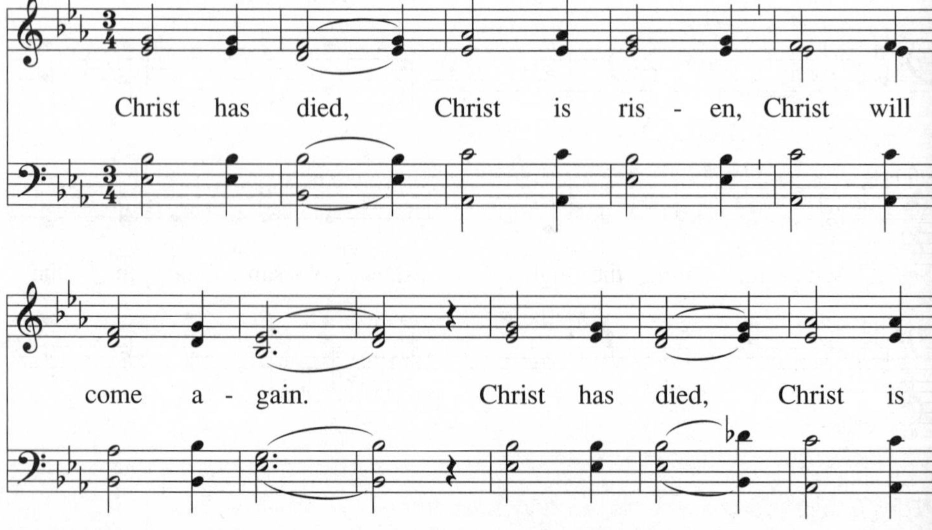
3/4
Christ has died, Christ is ris - en, Christ will
come a - gain. Christ has died, Christ is

ris - en, Christ will come a - gain.

Text: ICEL, © 1973
Music: *Deutsche Messe,* Franz Schubert, 1797-1828; adapt. by Richard Proulx, © 1985, 1995, GIA Publications, Inc.

AMEN 308

♩ = *ca.* 88
mp
A - men, A - men, A - men, A - men, A - men.
mp

Music: *Deutsche Messe,* Franz Schubert, 1797-1828, adapt. by Richard Proulx, © 1985, 1989, GIA Publications, Inc.

SANCTUS–SANTO 309

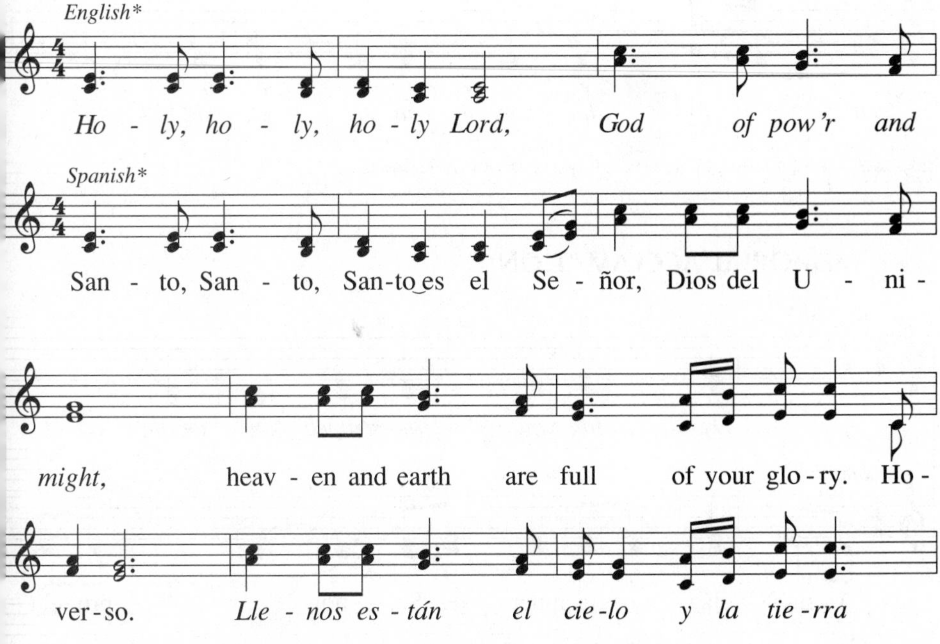

*English**

Ho - ly, ho - ly, ho - ly Lord, God of pow'r and

*Spanish**

San - to, San - to, San-to‿es el Se - ñor, Dios del U - ni -

might, heav - en and earth are full of your glo - ry. Ho -

ver - so. *Lle - nos es - tán el cie - lo y la tie - rra*

**For a bilingual version, sing the words in italics.*

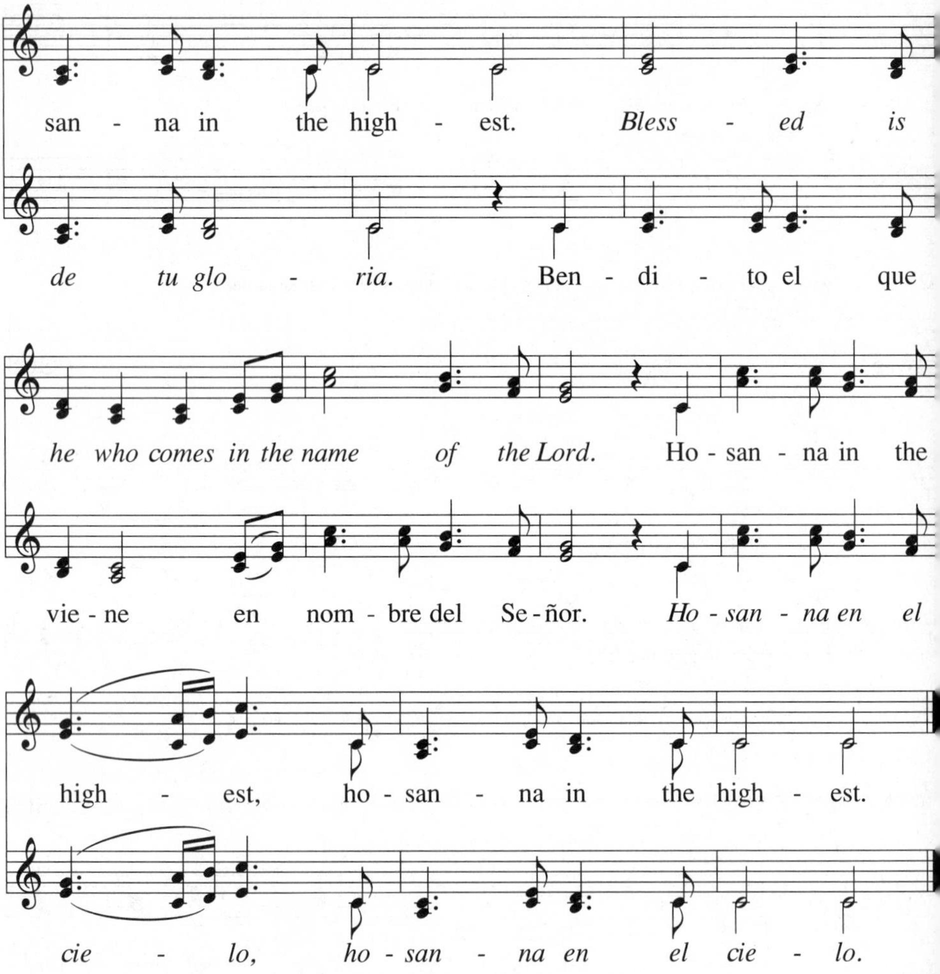

san - na in the high - est. *Bless - ed is*

de tu glo - ria. Ben - di - to el que

he who comes in the name of the Lord. Ho - san - na in the

vie - ne en nom - bre del Se - ñor. *Ho - san - na en el*

high - est, ho - san - na in the high - est.

cie - lo, ho - san - na en el cie - lo.

Music: *Santo*; Argentine folk melody; adapt. by Marty Haugen,

310 MEMORIAL ACCLAMATION

English*
Dy - ing you de - stroyed our death,
Spanish*
A - nun - cia - mos tu muer - te, Se - ñor, pro - cla -

*For a bilingual version, sing the words in italics.

ris - ing you re - stored our life. Lord Je - sus, come in
ma - mos tu re - su-rrec-ción. *!Ven, ven, Se -*
glo - ry, Lord Je - sus, come in glo - ry.
ñor Je - sús! !Ven, Se - ñor Je - sus!

English Text: ICEL, © 1973
Music: *Santo*; Argentine folk melody; adapt. by Marty Haugen, © 2001, GIA Publications, Inc.

AMEN 311

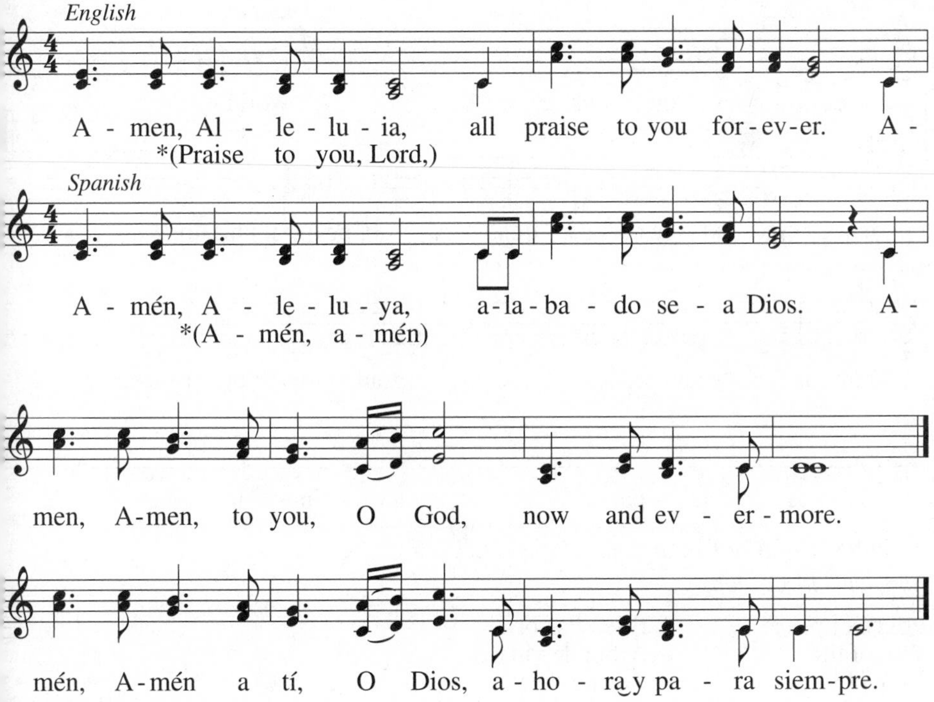

English

A - men, Al - le - lu - ia, all praise to you for-ev-er. A -
*(Praise to you, Lord,)

Spanish

A - mén, A - le - lu - ya, a-la-ba - do se - a Dios. A -
*(A - mén, a - mén)

men, A-men, to you, O God, now and ev - er - more.

mén, A-mén a tí, O Dios, a - ho - ra y pa - ra siem-pre.

*During Lent/En Cuaresma

Music: *Santo*; Argentine folk melody; adapt. by Marty Haugen, © 2001, GIA Publications, Inc.

312 AGNUS DEI

Cantor:
*Lamb of God,
Bread of Life, you take a - way the
Sav - ing Cup,
Cantor:
*Cor - de - ro de Dios,
Pan de Vi - da, que qui - tas el pe -
San - ta Co - pa,
To repeat
All:
sin of the world: have mer - cy on us, have
All:
ca - do del mun - do, ten pie - dad de no - so - tros,
mer - cy on us.
Last time
world:
ten pie - dad de no - so - tros.
Cantor:
(Cor-) mun - do,
All:
grant us your peace, grant us your peace.
da - nos la paz, da - nos la paz.

*"Lamb of God/Cordero de Dios" first and last times.

Additional Invocations

Prince of peace…	Buen Pastor…
Tree of life…	Árbol de vida…
King of kings…	Rey de reyes…
Son of God…	Hijo de Dios…

Music: *Santo;* Argentine folk melody; adapt. by Marty Haugen, © 2001, GIA Publications, Inc.

SANCTUS–ST. LOUIS JESUITS MASS 313

Ho - ly, ho - ly, ho - ly Lord, God of pow'r and
might, heav - en and earth are full of your glo -
ry. Ho - san - na, ho - san - na on high.
Descant:
Bless - ed is he who comes in the name of the Lord.
Melody:
Bless - ed is he who comes in the name of the Lord. Ho -
Ho - san - na, ho - san - na, ho -
san - na in the high - est, ho - san - na in the high - est, ho -
div.
san - na, ho - san - na on high.
san - na, ho - san - na on high.

Music: *St. Louis Jesuits Mass;* Robert J. Duffordt, SJ and Daniel L. Schutte, © 1973, Robert J. Duffordt, SJ and Daniel L. Schutte; acc. by Diana Kodner
Published by OCP Publications

314 MEMORIAL ACCLAMATION

Priest:
Let us pro - claim the mys - ter - y of faith:
All:
When we eat this bread of life, when we drink of this
ho - ly cup, we pro - claim your death, O Lord,
1.
till you come a - gain.
2.
till you come a - gain!

Text: ICEL, © 1973
Music: *St. Louis Jesuits Mass;* Robert J. Dufford, SJ and Daniel L. Schutte, © 1973, Robert J. Dufford, SJ and Daniel L. Schutte
Published by OCP Publications

AMEN 315

Freely
Priest:
Through him, with him, and in him, in the u-ni-ty
of the Ho-ly Spir-it, all glo-ry and hon-or is yours,
al-might-y Fa-ther, for ev-er and ev-er.
All:
Descant:
A-men, al-le-lu-ia.
Melody:
A-men, al-le-lu-ia, for
A-men, a-men. Al-le-lu-ia, for
ev-er and ev-er, for ev-er, al-le-lu-ia, for
ev-er and ev-er. A-men.
ev-er and ev-er. A-men.

Music: *St. Louis Jesuits Mass;* Robert J. Dufford, SJ and Daniel L. Schutte, © 1973, Robert J. Dufford, SJ and Daniel L. Schutte
Published by OCP Publications

316 SANCTUS

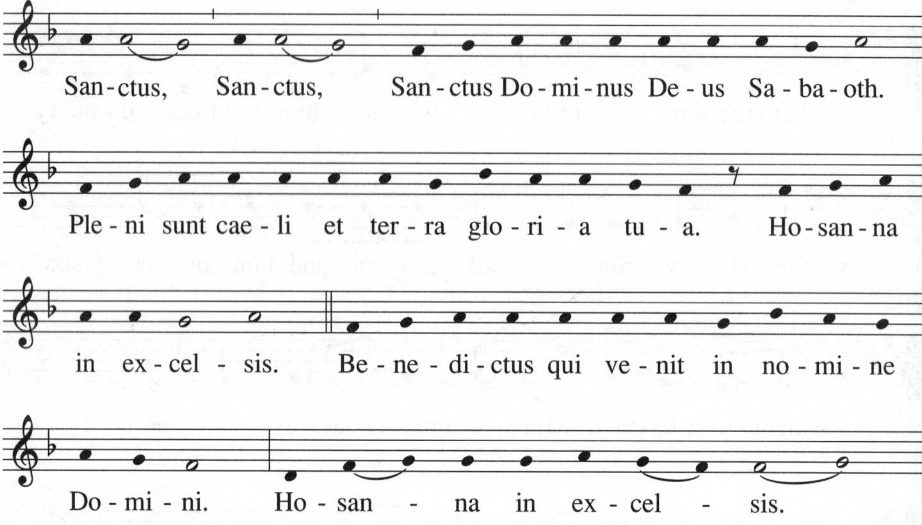
San-ctus, San-ctus, San-ctus Do-mi-nus De-us Sa-ba-oth.
Ple-ni sunt cae-li et ter-ra glo-ri-a tu-a. Ho-san-na
in ex-cel-sis. Be-ne-di-ctus qui ve-nit in no-mi-ne
Do-mi-ni. Ho-san-na in ex-cel-sis.

Music: *Sanctus XVIII, Vatican Edition;* acc. by Gerard Farrell, OSB, © 1986, GIA Publications, Inc.

316-A MEMORIAL ACCLAMATION

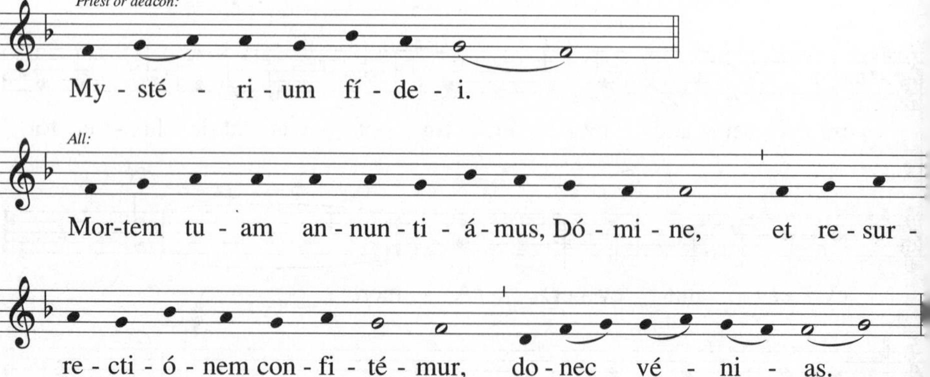
Priest or deacon:
My-sté-ri-um fí-de-i.
All:
Mor-tem tu-am an-nun-ti-á-mus, Dó-mi-ne, et re-sur-
re-cti-ó-nem con-fi-té-mur, do-nec vé-ni-as.

Music: Vatican Edition; acc. by Richard Proulx, © 1995, GIA Publications, Inc.

AMEN 316-B

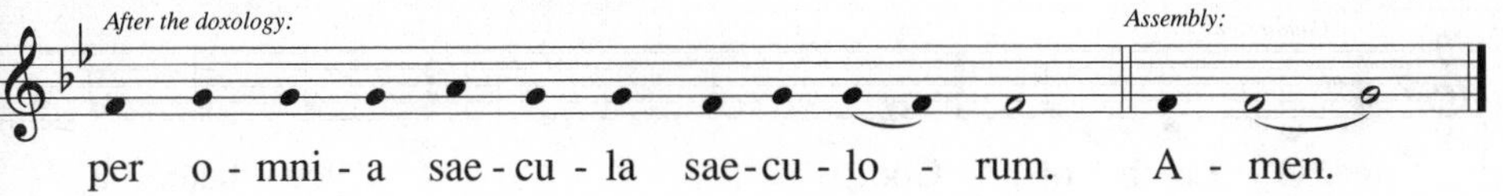
After the doxology:
Assembly:
per o - mni - a sae - cu - la sae-cu - lo - rum. A - men.

AGNUS DEI 317

Cantor or Choir:

*Lamb

All:

of God, you take a - way the sins of the world,

To repeat

have mer - cy on us.

Last time

grant us peace.

Alternates: 1. Emmanuel, 2. Prince of peace, 3. Son of God, 4. Word made flesh, 5. Paschal Lamb, 6. Bread of Life, 7. Lord Jesus Christ, 8. Lord of Love, 9. Christ the Lord, 10. King of kings.

318 AGNUS DEI

Cantor:
*O Lamb of God, you take a - way the sins of the world: have mer - cy on us. O Lamb of God, you take a - way
All:
*O Lamb of God, you take a - way the sins of the world: have mer - cy on us. O Lamb of God, you take a -

*Additional Invocations

Advent
O Morning Star
O Word of God
Emmanuel

Christmas
O Word made flesh
Emmanuel

Lent
O Tree of Life

Easter
O Risen Lord
O Cornerstone
O Spring of Life

General
O Bread of Life
O Cup of Joy
O Prince of Peace

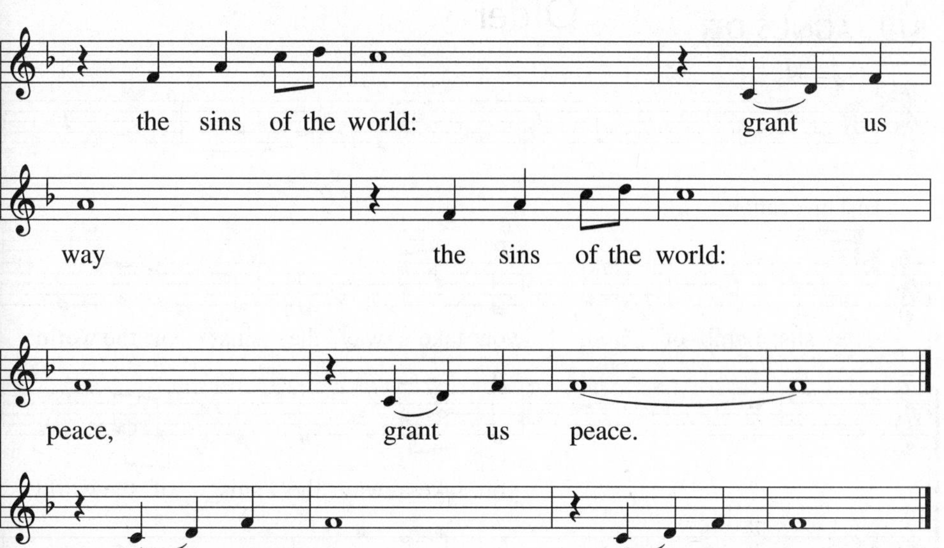
the sins of the world: grant us
way the sins of the world:
peace, grant us peace.
grant us peace, grant us peace.

Music: Ralph R. Stewart, © 1999, GIA Publications, Inc.; acc. by Robert J. Batastini, © 2003, GIA Publications, Inc.

319 AGNUS DEI

𝅗𝅥 = 44
First Invocation
Cantor: mp
All: p
Je - sus, Lamb of God,
you take a-way the sins of the world:
you take a-way the sins of the world:
mp
have mer - cy, have mer - cy on us.
us.
have mer - cy, have mer - cy on us, have mer - cy.
Invocations
Cantor: mp
All: p
1. Bread of life and sav - ing cup,
2. King of kings and Lord of lords,
3. Lov - ing Sav - ior, Prince of peace,
you take a-way the
Ah,
you take a - way the

mp
sins of the world: have mer - cy, have
mp
sins of the world: have mer - cy, have
mer - cy on us.
us.
mer - cy on us, have mer - cy.
Last Invocation
mf Cantor:
mp All:
Je - sus, Lamb of God, you take a - way the
mp
you take a - way the

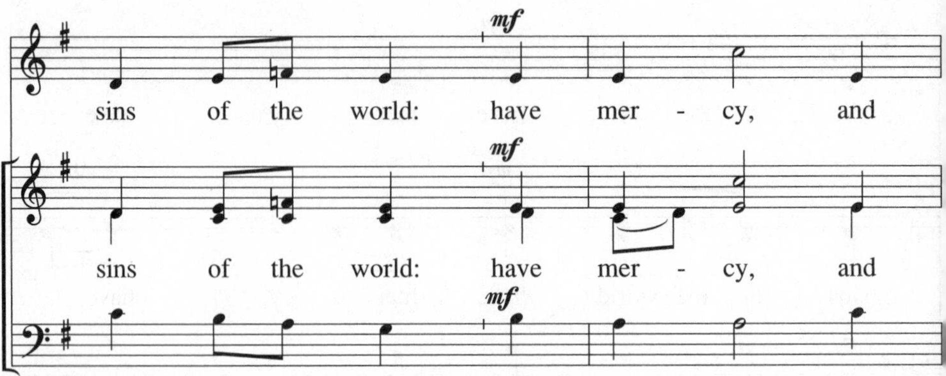
mf
sins of the world: have mer - cy, and
mf
sins of the world: have mer - cy, and
mf

rit.
dim.
p
grant us your peace.
rit.
dim.
p
grant us your peace.
rit.
div.
dim.
p

Alternate Invocations

General II:
1. Jesus, food for hungry hearts,
2. Jesus, God's own Promised One,
3. Jesus, at our kingdom-feast,

General III:
1. Jesus, Way that leads to God,
2. Jesus, Truth that comes from God,
3. Jesus, Life bestowed in God,

Advent:
1. Hope for all of humankind,
2. Dawn in darkness, Morning Star,
3. Key of David, Lord of might,

Christmas:
1. Son of God and Son of Man,
2. King, Messiah, David's Son,
3. Holy Child of Bethlehem,

Lent:
1. Jesus, light for blinded eyes,
2. Jesus, hope for haunted lives,
3. Jesus, servant of our God,

Eastertide:
1. Jesus, risen from the tomb,
2. Jesus, victor over death,
3. Jesus, future of our lives,

AGNUS DEI

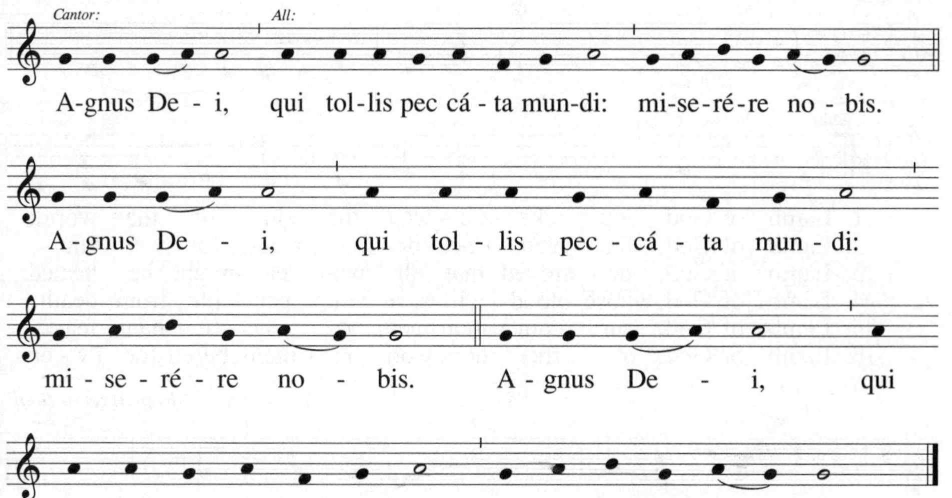
Cantor:
All:
A-gnus De - i, qui tol-lis pec cá - ta mun-di: mi-se-ré-re no - bis.
A-gnus De - i, qui tol - lis pec - cá - ta mun - di:
mi - se - ré - re no - bis. A - gnus De - i, qui
tol - lis pec - cá - ta mun - di: do - na no - bis pa - cem.

Music: *Vatican Edition XVIII;* acc. by Robert J. Batastini,

321 LAMB OF GOD: MAY WE BE ONE

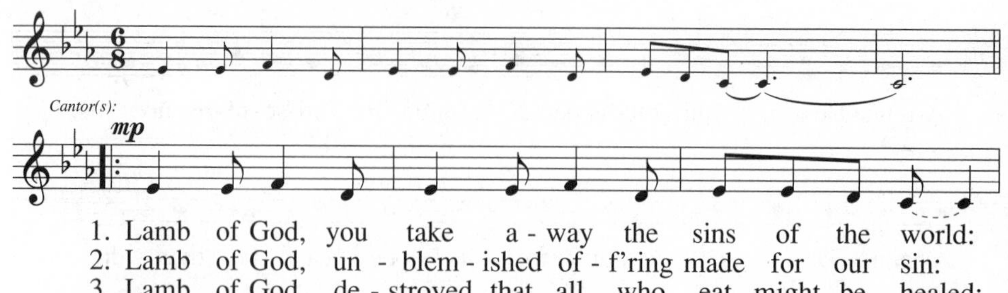
Cantor(s):
mp
1. Lamb of God, you take a - way the sins of the world:
2. Lamb of God, un - blem - ished of - f'ring made for our sin:
3. Lamb of God, de - stroyed that all who eat might be healed:
4. Lamb of God, whose blood will save your peo - ple from death:
5. Lamb of God, our com - mon mem - 'ry, cov - e - nant feast:
6. Lamb of God, our free - dom won, re - mem - bered for ev - er:

All:
mf
Repeat as needed
have mer - cy on us, have mer - cy on us.
Tenor:
Alto:
have mer - cy, have mer - cy on us, have mer - cy on us.

Last time
Cantor(s):
mp
Lamb of God, you take a - way the sins of the world,

All:
mf
mp
rit.
grant us peace, grant us peace.
grant us, grant us peace, grant us peace.

Additional invocations:

Lamb of God, the shepherd of all who hunger and thirst…
Lamb of God, joy of the martyrs, song of the saints…
Lamb of God, all peoples will sing your victory song…
Lamb of God, unconquered light of the city of God…
Lamb of God, how blessed are those who are called to your feast…

Text: *Agnus Dei;* additional text by Rory Cooney
Music: Gary Daigle

MAY WE BE ONE (COMMUNION HYMN) 322

Refrain
When we eat this bread and drink this cup,
we pro-claim your death, Lord Je - sus. So as we
div.
may we be - come
share this feast may we be - come, may we be-come heal-ing and
may we be-come
To verses
Last time
light and peace. May we be one. one.

Verses

Cantor:

1. This is the bread of Is - ra - el's wan - d'ring.
2. This is the bread of rain and of sun - light.
3. This is the bless - ing cup of the Sab - bath.
4. This is the wine of plant - ing and prun - ing.
5. This is a peo - ple home - less and wan - d'ring.
6. This is a bread we pass as for - give - ness.

The bread that strength - ened E -
The bread of earth's fer - tile
The cup of Ca - na's a -
The cup of bur - geon - ing
A peo - ple at home with each
A cup we share as our

All

A - men, a - men.

A - men, a - men, a - men.

A - men, a - men.

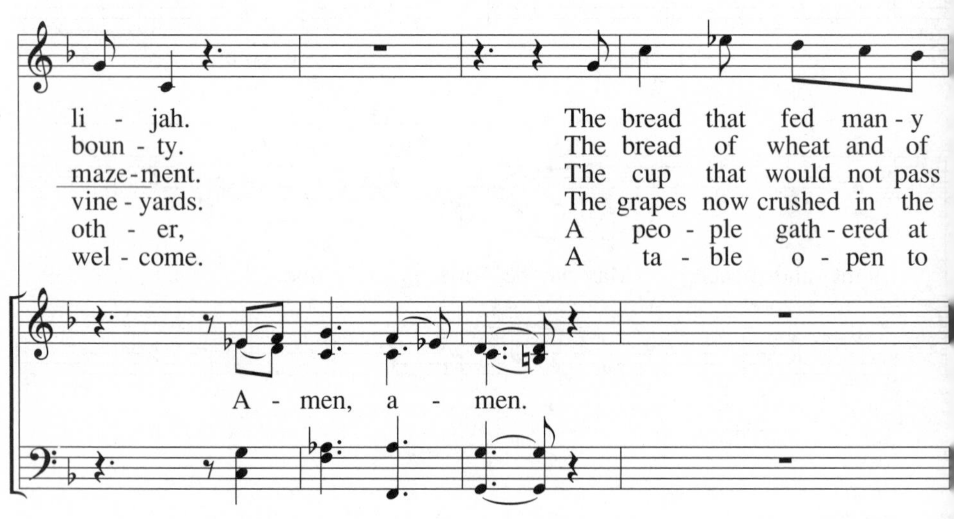
li - jah. The bread that fed man - y
boun - ty. The bread of wheat and of
maze - ment. The cup that would not pass
vine - yards. The grapes now crushed in the
oth - er, A peo - ple gath - ered at
wel - come. A ta - ble o - pen to
A - men, a - men.

thou - sands.
bar - ley.
from you.
wine - press.
ta - ble,
stran - gers.
This is the
This is the
This is the
This is the
This is a
This is a
A - men, a - men.
All:
A - men, a - men, a - men.
A - men, a - men.
bread of Ju - das' be - tray - al.
bread of earth's man - y col - ors.
cup now shared in your mem - 'ry.
wine of wait - ing in dark-ness.
peo - ple grate - ful for bless - ing. And
ban - quet of rest for the wea - ry. And
A - men, a - men.
D.C.
Take and eat; this bread is the life of God.
Take and eat; this bread is the life of God.
Take and drink; this cup is the life of God.
Take and drink; this cup is the life of God.
deep with - in all peo - ple the breath of God.
deep with - in all peo - ple the breath of God.

Text: Rory Cooney, b.1952
Tune: Gary Daigle, b.1957

323 O Come, O Come, Emmanuel

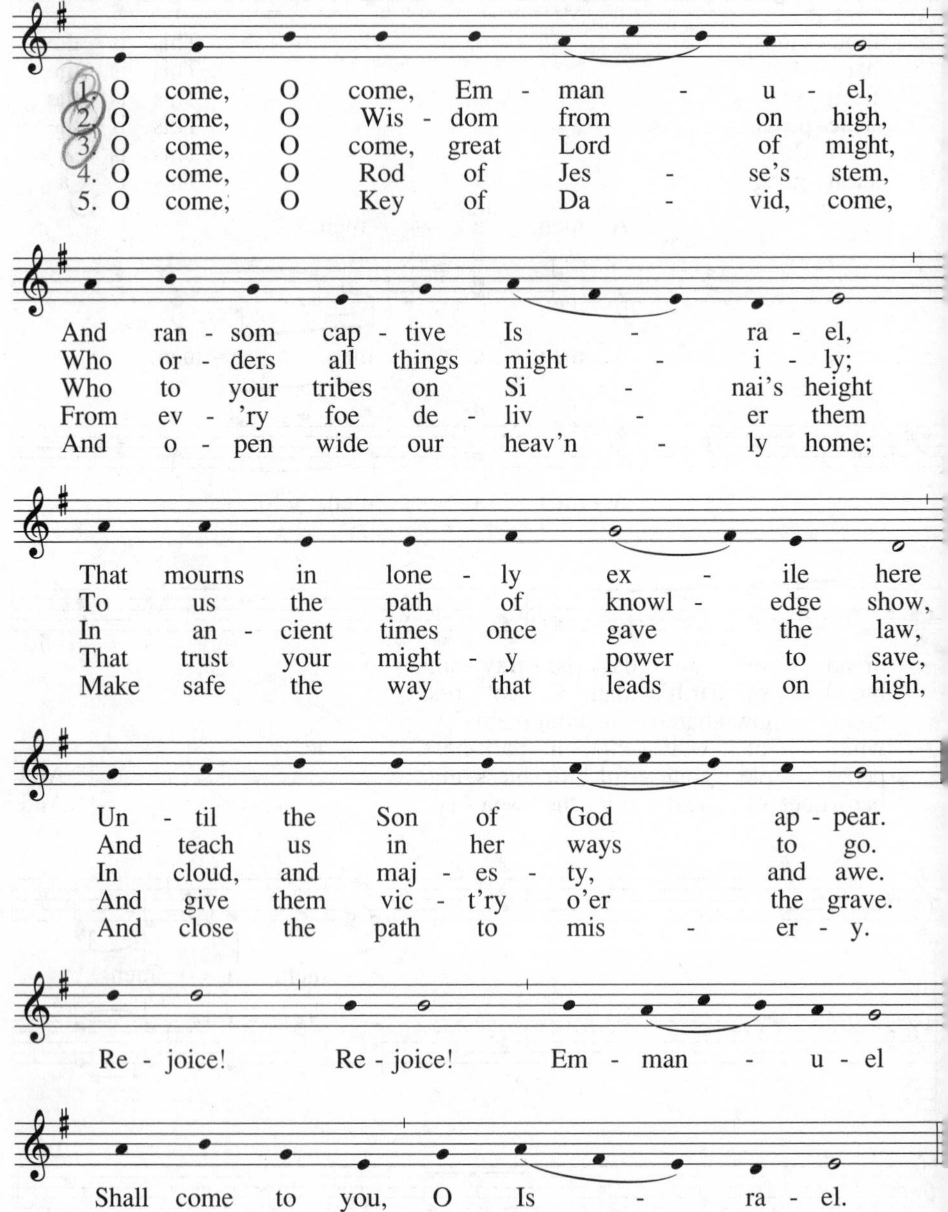
1. O come, O come, Em - man - u - el,
2. O come, O Wis - dom from on high,
3. O come, O come, great Lord of might,
4. O come, O Rod of Jes - se's stem,
5. O come, O Key of Da - vid, come,
And ran - som cap - tive Is - ra - el,
Who or - ders all things might - i - ly;
Who to your tribes on Si - nai's height
From ev - 'ry foe de - liv - er them
And o - pen wide our heav'n - ly home;
That mourns in lone - ly ex - ile here
To us the path of knowl - edge show,
In an - cient times once gave the law,
That trust your might - y power to save,
Make safe the way that leads on high,
Un - til the Son of God ap - pear.
And teach us in her ways to go.
In cloud, and maj - es - ty, and awe.
And give them vic - t'ry o'er the grave.
And close the path to mis - er - y.
Re - joice! Re - joice! Em - man - u - el
Shall come to you, O Is - ra - el.

6. O come, O Dayspring from on high
And cheer us by your drawing nigh;
Disperse the gloomy clouds of night,
And death's dark shadow put to flight.

7. O come, Desire of nations, bind
In one the hearts of humankind;
O bid our sad divisions cease,
And be for us our King of Peace.

Text: *Veni, veni Emmanuel;* Latin 9th C.; tr. by John M. Neale, 1818-1866, alt.
Tune: VENI VENI EMMANUEL, LM with refrain; Mode I; adapt. by Thomas Helmore, 1811-1890; acc. by Richard Proulx, b.1937,

Maranatha, Lord Messiah 324

Verses

Cantor or choir:

1. Gracious God of Wisdom, who hears your people's cry, teach us ways of prudence, O Breath of God Most High.
2. Mighty Voice of Sinai, whom Moses heard in awe, Adonai, now lead us with holy arm and law.
3. Fragrant Bud of Jesse, whose blooming Kings revere, root your words within us, God's words for all to hear.
4. David's Key of Heaven, unlock us from our sins. Freed from error's prison, our life in you begins.
5. Blazing Sun of Justice, the flame of Eastern dawn, scatter clinging shadows, that gloom of death be gone.
6. Sovereign of all Nations, our cornerstone of trust, deliver, in your mercy, your creatures made from dust.
7. Jesus, be God with us, Emmanuel foretold. Feed us like a shepherd, in safely gathered fold.

All:

Refrain

Maranatha, Lord Messiah, long awaited from afar. Come and make your home among us. Let us

Harmony after Verse 3:

Maranatha, Lord Messiah, awaited from afar. Come and make your home among us.

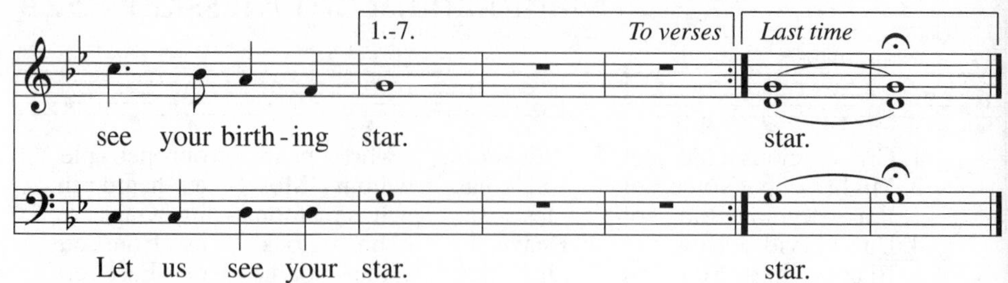
1.-7.
To verses
Last time
see your birth - ing star.
star.
Let us see your star.
star.

Text: Based on the "O" Antiphons; Kathy Powell, b.1942
Tune: Kathy Powell, b.1942

325 Walk in the Reign

Refrain

Close as to - mor - row the sun shall ap - pear.

Free - dom is com - ing and heal - ing is near. And

I shall be with you in laugh - ter and pain to

stand in the wind and walk in the reign, to

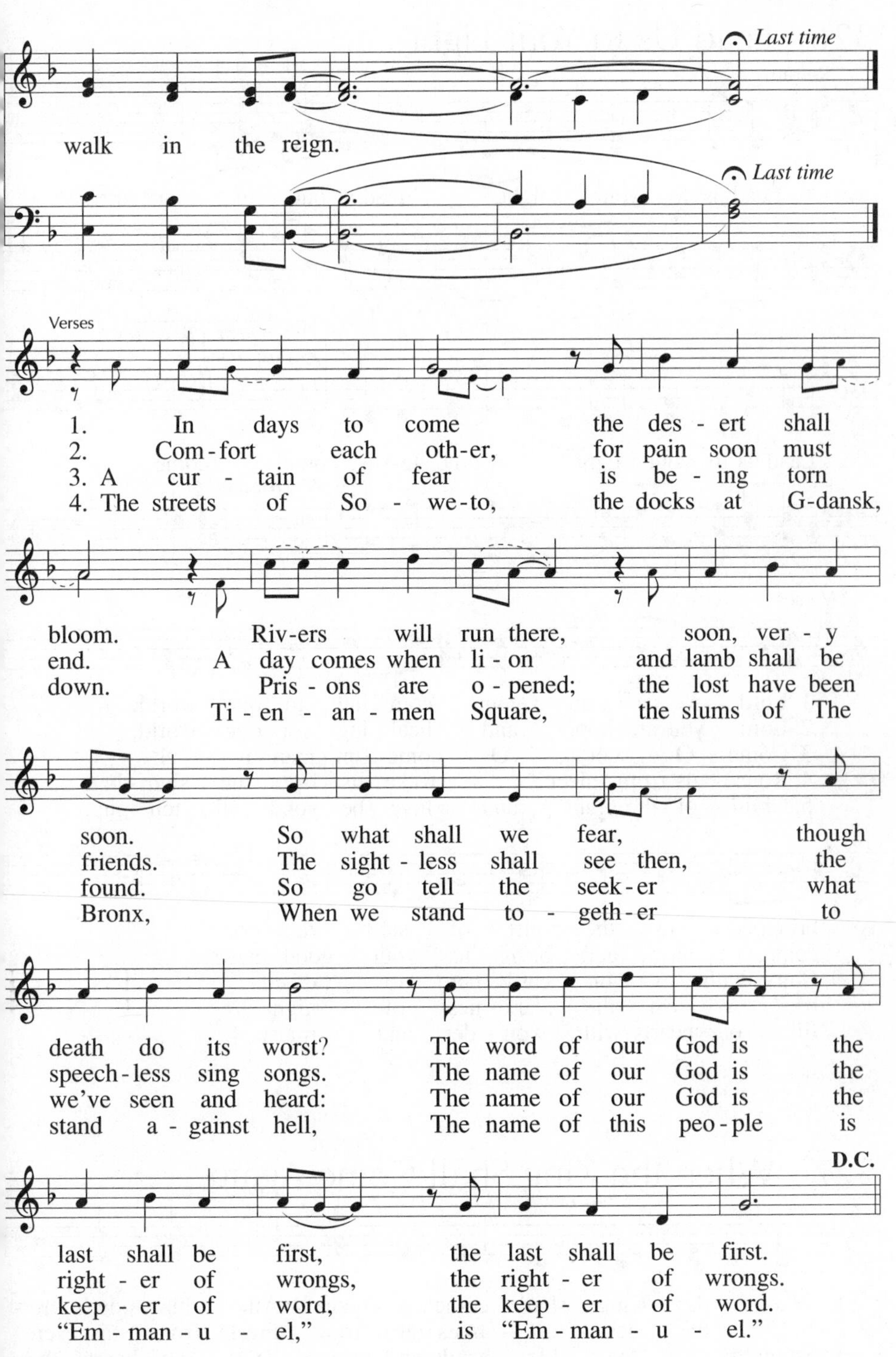
Last time
walk in the reign.
Last time
Verses
1. In days to come the des - ert shall
2. Com - fort each oth - er, for pain soon must
3. A cur - tain of fear is be - ing torn
4. The streets of So - we - to, the docks at G-dansk,
bloom. Riv - ers will run there, soon, ver - y
end. A day comes when li - on and lamb shall be
down. Pris - ons are o - pened; the lost have been
Ti - en - an - men Square, the slums of The
soon. So what shall we fear, though
friends. The sight - less shall see then, the
found. So go tell the seek - er what
Bronx, When we stand to - geth - er to
death do its worst? The word of our God is the
speech - less sing songs. The name of our God is the
we've seen and heard: The name of our God is the
stand a - gainst hell, The name of this peo - ple is
D.C.
last shall be first, the last shall be first.
right - er of wrongs, the right - er of wrongs.
keep - er of word, the keep - er of word.
"Em - man - u - el," is "Em - man - u - el."

Text: Rory Cooney, b.1952
Tune: Rory Cooney, b.1952

326 Lead Us to Your Light

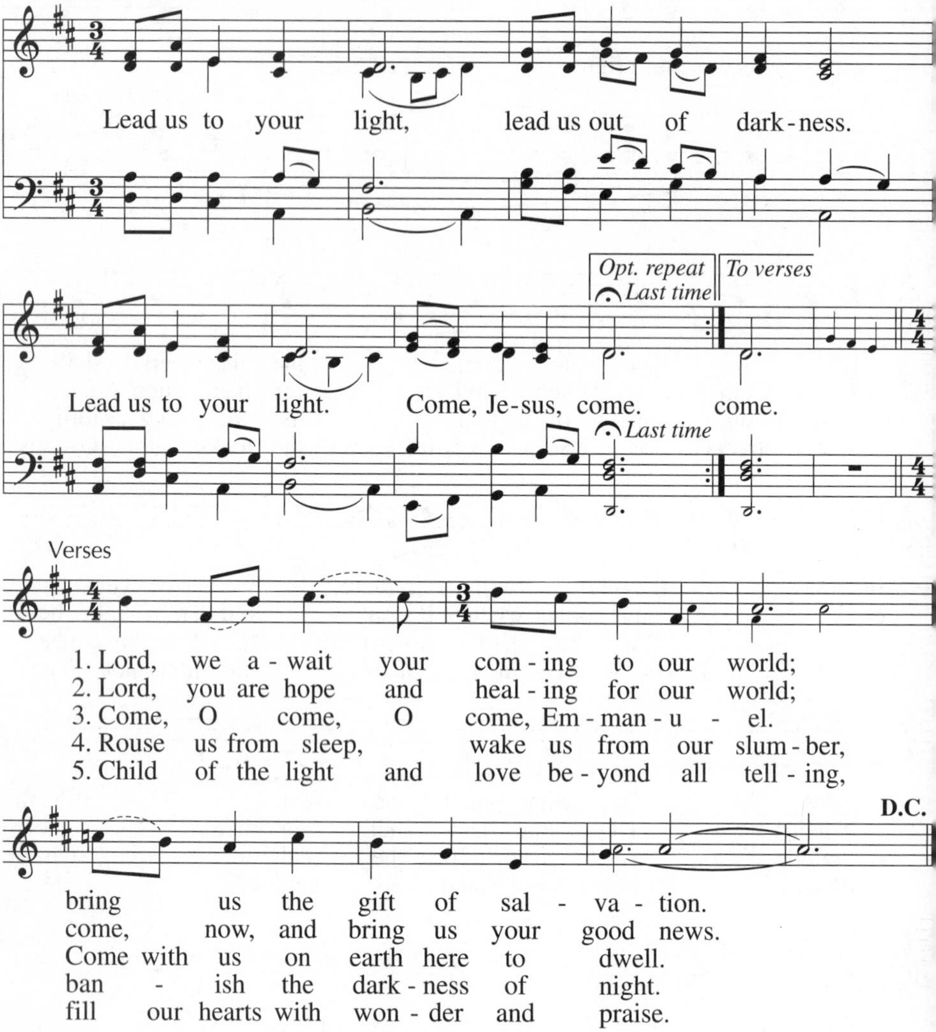

Refrain

Lead us to your light, lead us out of dark-ness.

Opt. repeat *Last time* | *To verses*

Lead us to your light. Come, Je-sus, come. | come.

Verses

1. Lord, we a-wait your com-ing to our world; bring us the gift of sal-va-tion.
2. Lord, you are hope and heal-ing for our world; come, now, and bring us your good news.
3. Come, O come, O come, Em-man-u-el. Come with us on earth here to dwell.
4. Rouse us from sleep, wake us from our slum-ber, ban-ish the dark-ness of night.
5. Child of the light and love be-yond all tell-ing, fill our hearts with won-der and praise.

D.C.

Text: Carol E. Browning, b.1956
Tune: Carol E. Browning, b.1956

327 When the King Shall Come Again

1. When the King shall come a-gain All his pow'r re-
2. In the des-ert trees take root Fresh from his cre-
3. Strength-en fee-ble hands and knees, Faint-ing hearts, be
4. There God's high-way shall be seen Where no roar-ing

veal - ing, Splen - dor shall an - nounce his reign, Life and
a - tion; Plants and flow'rs and sweet - est fruit Join the
cheer - ful! God who comes for such as these Seeks and
li - on, Noth - ing e - vil or un - clean Walks the
joy and heal - ing; Earth no long - er in de - cay,
cel - e - bra - tion; Riv - ers spring up from the earth,
saves the fear - ful; Deaf ears, hear the si - lent tongues
road to Zi - on: Ran - somed peo - ple home - ward bound
Hope no more frus - trat - ed; This is God's re -
Bar - ren lands a - dorn - ing; Val - leys, this is
Sing a - way their weep - ing; Blind eyes, see the
All your prais - es voic - ing, See your Lord with
demp - tion day Long - ing - ly a - wait - ed.
your new birth, Moun - tains, greet the morn - ing!
life - less ones Walk - ing, run - ning, leap - ing.
glo - ry crowned, Share in his re - joic - ing!

Text: Isaiah 35; Christopher Idle, b.1938,
Tune: GAUDEAMUS PARITER, 7 6 7 6 D; Johann Horn, c. 1495-1547

328 Come, Light of the World

1. Come, light of the world,
2. Come, strength of our days,
3. Come, joy for the world,
4. Come, hope of the world,
5. Come, Spir - it of God,
light up our lives, Lord. Come, light of the
strength-en our lives, Lord. Come, strength of our
fill us with glad - ness. Come, joy for the
com - fort your peo - ple. Come, hope of the
be with us now, Lord. Come, Spir - it of
world, light up our hearts. Dis - pel all our
days, strength-en our hearts. Come, fill us with
world, glad - den our hearts. Come, bring us to -
world, com - fort our hearts. Come, heal all our
God, fill us with truth. En - light-en our
dark-ness, re-move all our blind-ness, Come, light of the
cour - age to fol - low you al - ways. Come, strength of our
geth - er with sing - ing and laugh - ter. Come, joy for the
sor - row with love and com-pas - sion. Come, hope of the
lives, Lord, with ra-diance and pow - er. Come, Spir - it of
world, be light for our eyes.
days, be strength for our minds.
world, bring warmth to our lives.
world, bring peace to us all.
God, in - spire all we do.
D.S.
Final ending

Text: Paul Inwood, b.1947
Tune: Paul Inwood, b.1947

Advent Alleluia 329

Cantor:
Hal - le - lu - ia, hal - le - lu - ia,
hal - le - lu - ia, hal - le - lu - ia!
Refrain
All: Hal - le - lu - ia, hal - le - lu - ia,
Hal - le - lu - ia, hal - le - lu - ia,
Hal - le - lu - ia, hal - le - lu - ia,
hal - le - lu - ia, hal - le - lu - ia!
Last time
hal - le - lu - ia!
Last time
hal - le - lu - ia, hal - le - lu - ia!
Verse 1
Cantor:
1. Lord, show us your mer - cy and love, and
grant us your sal - va - tion.
D.S.
Verse 2
Cantor:
2. Pre - pare the way of the Lord, make

straight his paths: all peo-ple shall
see the sal - va - tion of God.
D.S.
Verse 3
Cantor:
3. The Spir - it of the Lord is up - on me, he
sent me to bring good news to the poor.
D.S.
Verse 4
Cantor:
4. A vir - gin will give birth to a Son; a
vir-gin will give birth to a Son; his name will be Em-
man-u - el: God is with us.
D.S.
Verse 5
Cantor:
5. I am the ser - vant of the Lord:
may his will for me be done.
D.S.

Text: *Lectionary for Mass*, © 1969, 1981, ICEL
Tune: Michael Joncas, b.1951, © 1988, GIA Publications, Inc.

Prepare the Way of the Lord 330

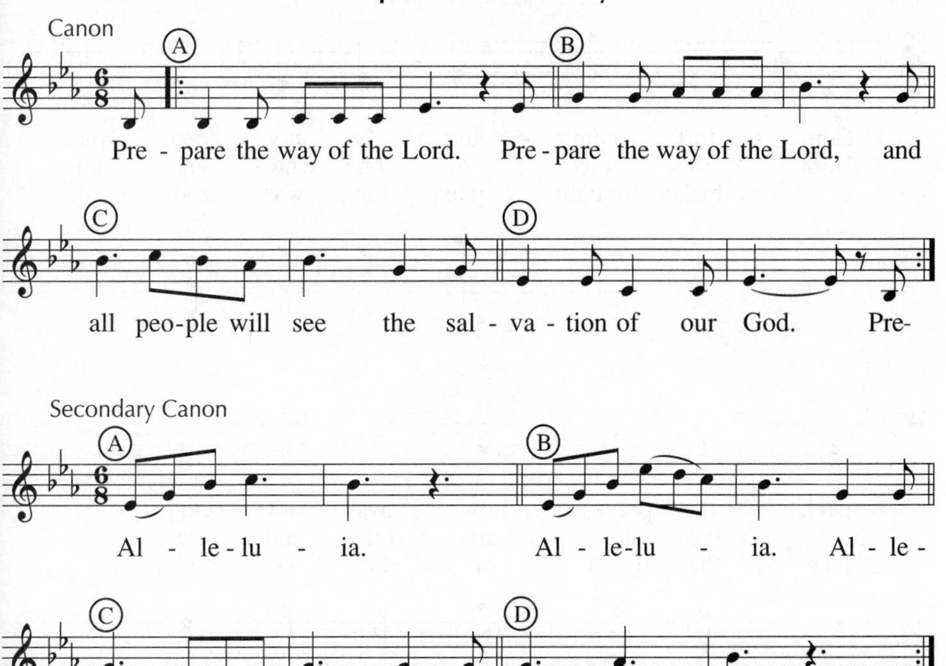
Canon
A
B
Pre - pare the way of the Lord. Pre - pare the way of the Lord, and
C
D
all peo-ple will see the sal - va - tion of our God. Pre-
Secondary Canon
A
B
Al - le-lu - ia. Al - le-lu - ia. Al - le -
C
D
lu - ia. Al - le - lu - ia.

Text: Luke 3:4,6; Taizé Community, 1984
Tune: Jacques Berthier, 1923-1994

331 Comfort, Comfort, O My People

1. Com - fort, com - fort, O my peo - ple,
2. Hark, the voice of one who's cry - ing
3. O make straight what long was crook - ed,
Speak of peace, now says our God;
In the des - ert far and near,
Make the rough - er plac - es plain;
Com - fort those who sit in dark - ness,
Bid - ding all to full re - pent - ance
Let your hearts be true and hum - ble,
Mourn - ing 'neath their sor - row's load.
Since the king - dom now is here.
As be - fits his ho - ly reign.

Speak un - to Je - ru - sa - lem
O that warn - ing cry o - bey!
For the glo - ry of the Lord
Of the peace that waits for them;
Now pre - pare for God a way;
Now o'er earth is shed a - broad;
Tell of all the sins I cov - er,
Let the val - leys rise to meet him
And all flesh shall see the to - ken
And that war - fare now is o - ver.
And the hills bow down to greet him.
That his word is nev - er bro - ken.

Text: Isaiah 40:1-8; *Tröstet, tröstet, meine Lieben;* Johann Olearius, 1611-1684; tr. by Catherine Winkworth, 1827-1878, alt.
Tune: GENEVA 42, 8 7 8 7 77 88; *Genevan Psalter,* 1551; harm. adapt. from Claude Goudimel, 1505-1572

332 Like a Shepherd

Refrain
Descant:
Like a shep - herd he feeds his flock and gath - ers the
Melody:
Like a shep - herd he feeds his flock and gath - ers the
lambs in his arms, hold - ing them care - ful - ly
lambs in his arms, hold - ing them care - ful - ly
close to his heart, lead - ing them home.
close to his heart, lead - ing them home.
Verses 1, 2
1. Say to the cit - ies of Ju - dah: Pre -
2. I my - self will shep - herd them, for
pare the way of the Lord.
oth - ers have led them a - stray. The
Go to the moun - tain top, lift your voice; Je -
lost I will res - cue and heal their wounds and
D.C.
ru - sa - lem, here is your God.
pas - ture them, giv - ing them rest.

Verse 3
3. Come un - to me if you are
heav - i - ly bur - dened, and take my yoke up -
on your shoul - ders, I will give you rest.
D.C.

Text: Isaiah 40:9ff, Ezekiel 34:11, Matthew 11:28ff; Bob Dufford, SJ, b.1943
Tune: Bob Dufford, SJ, b.1943; acc. by Sr. Theophane Hytrek, OSF, 1915-1992, alt.

333 O Come, Divine Messiah

1. O come, Di-vine Mes-si-ah, The world in si-lence waits the day When hope shall sing its tri-umph, And sad-ness flee a-way.
2. O come De-sired of na-tions, Whom priest and proph-et long fore-told, Will break the cap-tive fet-ters, Re-deem the long-lost fold.
3. O come in peace and meek-ness, For low-ly will your cra-dle be: Though clothed in hu-man weak-ness We shall your God-head see.
Dear Sav-ior, haste! Come, come to earth. Dis-pel the night and show your face, And bid us

hail the dawn of grace. O come, Di - vine Mes -
si - ah, The world in si - lence waits the day When
hope shall sing its tri - umph, And sad - ness flee a - way.

ext: *Venez, divin Messie;* Abbé Simon-Joseph Pellegrin, 1663-1745; tr. by S. Mary of St. Philip, 1877
une: VENEZ, DIVIN MESSIE, 7 8 7 6 with refrain; French Noël, 16th C.; harm. by Healey Willan, 1880-1968,

334 Creator of the Stars of Night

Verses
1. Cre - a - tor of the stars of night, Your
2. In sor - row that the an - cient curse Should
3. When this old world drew on toward night, You
4. At your great Name, O Je - sus, now All
5. Come in your ho - ly might, we pray, Re -
6. To God Cre - a - tor, God the Son, And
peo - ple's ev - er - last - ing light, O
doom to death a u - ni - verse, You
came; but not in splen - dor bright, Not
knees must bend, all hearts must bow: All
deem us for e - ter - nal day; De -
God the Spir - it, Three - in - One, Praise,
Christ, Re - deem - er of us all, We
came, O Sav - ior, to set free Your
as a mon - arch, but the child Of
things on earth with one ac - cord, Like
fend us while we dwell be - low From
hon - or, might, and glo - ry be From
pray you hear us when we call.
own in glo - rious lib - er - ty.
Mar - y, blame - less moth - er mild.
those in heav'n, shall call you Lord.
all as - saults of our dread foe.
age to age e - ter - nal - ly.
To next verse*
Last time
To refrain
Refrain
Come, O Lord, and bring your light, O ra-diant

*Hymn may be sung without refrain.

star and heart's de - light. O God-with-us, Em-man-u -
el, with your love, the dark dis - pel.
Last time
Last time

Text: *Conditor alme siderum*, Latin 9th. C.; tr. *The Hymnal 1982*, © 1985, The Church Pension Fund; refrain, Carol E. Browning, b.1956, © 2003, GIA Publications, Inc.
Tune: CONDITOR ALME SIDERUM, LM; Mode IV; acc. and refrain music by Carol E. Browning, b.1956, © 2003, GIA Publications, Inc.

335 Maranatha, Come

Refrain
Melody:
Ma-ra-na - tha, come, come, Lord Je - sus.
Harmony:
Ma-ra-na - tha, come, come, Lord Je - sus.
Ma-ra-na - tha, come, come, O God.
Ma-ra-na - tha, come, come, O God.
To verses
Final ending
Verses
1. Wis - dom of God, guid - ing cre - a - tion,
2. O sa - cred Lord, come in your glo - ry;
3. From Jes - se's stem raise up your peo - ple.
4. O roy - al power, O key of Da - vid,
5. O ra - diant dawn, O sun of jus - tice,
6. Rul - er of all, joy of our long - ing,
7. Sav - ior of all, hope of the na - tions,

D.C.
lead us in ways that are faith - ful to your name.
stretch forth your hand and we shall be free.
Let noth - ing keep you from com - ing to our aid.
o - pen the heav - ens and lead us in - to life.
shine on your peo - ple in dark - ness and in death.
come save the peo - ple you fash - ion from the dust.
bring us to free - dom, E - man - u - el.

Text: Based on the "O" Antiphons; Francis Patrick O'Brien, b.1958
Tune: Francis Patrick O'Brien, b.1958

My Soul in Stillness Waits 336

Refrain

For you, O Lord, my soul in still - ness waits,
truly my hope is in you.

To verses you. *Last time* you.

Verses

1. O Lord of Light, our on - ly hope of glo - ry, your ra - diance shines in all who look to
2. O Spring of Joy, rain down up - on our spir - its, our thirst - y hearts are yearn - ing for your
3. O Root of Life, im - plant your seed with - in us, and in your ad - vent, draw us all to
4. O Key of Knowl - edge, guide us in our pil - grim - age, we ev - er seek, yet un - ful - filled re -
5. Come, let us bow be - fore the God who made us, let ev - 'ry heart be o - pened to the
6. Here we shall meet the Mak - er of the heav - ens, Cre - a - tor of the moun - tains and the

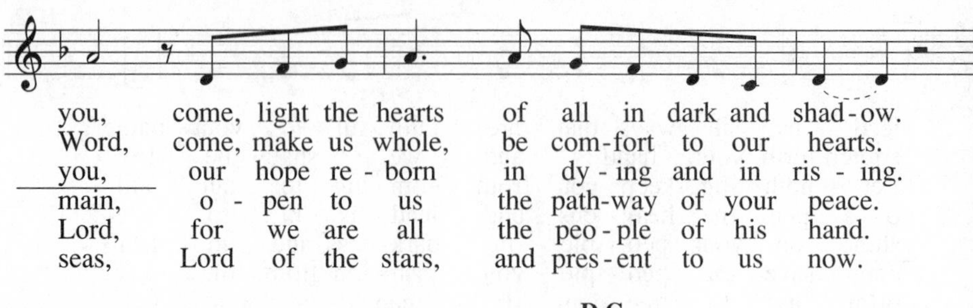
you, come, light the hearts of all in dark and shad-ow.
Word, come, make us whole, be com-fort to our hearts.
you, our hope re - born in dy - ing and in ris - ing.
main, o - pen to us the path-way of your peace.
Lord, for we are all the peo-ple of his hand.
seas, Lord of the stars, and pres-ent to us now.

D.C.

Text: Psalm 95 and "O" Antiphons; Marty Haugen, b.1950
Tune: Marty Haugen, b.1950

337 People, Look East

1. Peo - ple, look East. The time is near Of the
2. Fur - rows, be glad. Though earth is bare. One more
3. Birds, though you long have ceased to build, Guard the
4. Stars, keep the watch. When night is dim One more
5. An - gels an - nounce with shouts of mirth Him who

crown - ing of the year. Make your house fair as you are
seed is plant - ed there: Give up your strength the seed to
nest that must be filled. E - ven the hour when wings are
light the bowl shall brim, Shin - ing be - yond the frost - y
brings new life to earth. Set ev - 'ry peak and val - ley

a - ble, Trim the hearth and set the
nour - ish, That in course the flow'r may
fro - zen He for fledg - ing time has
weath - er, Bright as sun and moon to -
hum - ming With the word, the Lord is
Peo - ple look East and sing to -
ta - ble.
flour - ish.
cho - sen.
geth - er.
com - ing.
Peo - ple look East:
Peo - ple look
day:
Love the Guest is on the way.
Love the Rose is on the way.
Love the Bird is on the way.
Love the Star is on the way.
Love the Lord is on the way.
East:
Love is on the way.

xt: Eleanor Farjeon, 1881-1965, © David Higham Assoc. Ltd.
ne: BESANÇON, 87 98 87; French traditional; harm. by Martin Shaw, 1875-1958, © Oxford University Press

338 Advent Gathering Song

Refrain
on repeat
1.-6. come.
All:
Come, come Em - man - u - el.
Verses
Last time to coda
Cantor:
1. For the Lord of cre - a - tion will
2. Oh the son of Mar - y will
3. See God's mar - vel - ous deeds and
4. For God chose us, and so we will
5. For the an - gel pro - claims he will
6. As the ser - vants of God we
Lord, have mer - cy up - on us and
Christ have mer - cy up - on us and
Lord, have mer - cy up - on us and
Come, Em - man - u - el.
Coda
man - u - el.

Text: James J. Chepponis, b.1956
Tune: James J. Chepponis, b.1956

Warm the Time of Winter 339

Verses
1. When the wind of win-ter blows, bring-ing times of sol-i-tude,
2. When we shiv-er in des-pair, when the chill of death comes near,
3. When in days of fall-en snow, change con-founds or love burns low,
fill the si-lent, ic-y night; be our hearts' com-pas-sion.
hold us, Spir-it, calm our fear, while the eve-ning deep-ens.
from the ash-es may there rise phoe-nix of our grow-ing.
Refrain
Melody:
Ho-ly Light, warm our night; warm the time of
Harmony:
Ho-ly Light, warm our night; warm the time of
win-ter. Ho-ly Light, warm our night; warm the time of
win-ter. Ho-ly Light, warm our night; warm the time of
1., 2.
win - ter.
3.
win - ter.
win - ter.
win - ter.

Text: Ruth Duck, b.1947, © 1992, GIA Publications, Inc.
Tune: Lori True, b.1961, © 2000, GIA Publications, Inc.

340 Wait for the Lord

Ostinato Response
Wait for the Lord, whose day is near.
To verses*
Wait for the Lord: be strong, take heart!
*Verses
Cantor:
1. Pre - pare the way for the
2. The glo - ry of the
3. All the
4. Re - joice in the Lord
5. Seek first the king - dom of
...heart!
Choir or keyboard:
(hum)

*If verses are sung, the response is not repeated as an ostinato, but the response and verses are sung one after the other.

D.C.
Lord. Make a straight path for God.
D.C.
Lord shall be re - vealed.
D.C.
earth will see the Lord.
D.C.
al - ways. God is at hand.
D.C.
God, seek and you shall find.
D.C.

Text: Isaiah 40, Philippians 4, Matthew 6:33, 7:7; Taizé Community, 1984
Tune: Jacques Berthier, 1923-1994

341 Lift Up Your Heads

1. Lift up your heads, e - ter - nal gates, Al - le - lu - ia! See how the King of glo - ry waits, Al - le - lu - ia! The Lord of Hosts is draw - ing near, The Sav - ior of the world is here.
2. But not in arms or bat - tle dress, Al - le - lu - ia! God comes, a child a - midst dis - tress, Al - le - lu - ia! No might - y ar - mies shield the way, On - ly coarse lin - en, wool, and hay.
3. God brings a new face to the brave, Al - le - lu - ia! God re - de - fines who best can save: Al - le - lu - ia! Not those whose pow'r re - lies on threat, Ter - ror or tor - ture, de - struc - tion or debt.
4. God's match - less and ma - jes - tic strength, Al - le - lu - ia! In all its height, depth, breadth, and length, Al - le - lu - ia! Now is re - vealed, its pow'r to prove, By Christ pro - test - ing "God is love!"

Al-le-lu - ia! Al-le-lu - ia! Al - le - lu - ia!
Al - le-lu - ia! Al - le-lu - ia! Al-le-lu - ia!
Al-le-lu - ia! Al-le-lu - ia! Al - le-lu - ia!

ext: George Weissel, 1590-1635; tr. Catherine Winkworth, 1827-1878; adapt. by John L. Bell, b.1949, © 2001, Iona Community, GIA Publications, Inc., agent
une: CH THREE, 8 8 8 8 with alleluias; John L. Bell, b.1949, © 2001, Iona Community, GIA Publications, Inc., agent

Find Us Ready 342

Refrain

Cantor (first time only):

Find us read-y, Lord, not stand - ing still.

Choir:

Find us read-y, Lord, not stand - ing still.

Find us work - ing and lov - ing and do - ing your

Find us work - ing and lov - ing and do - ing your

will. Find us read-y, Lord, faith-ful in love,
will. Find us read-y, Lord, faith-ful in love,
build-ing the king-dom that's here and a-bove,
build-ing the king-dom that's here and a-bove,
build-ing the king-dom of mer-cy and love.
build-ing the king-dom of mer-cy and love.
1.-3. To verses
4.

Verses
Cantor:
1. We must wait for the Lord for we
2. We must make straight the path, God's
3. Lift - ing up those bowed down, we pre -
know not the time.
love re - vealed.
pare for our God.
So here and to - day
With sin cast a - side,
Re - joice in the Lord,
we gath - er and pray, dis - cov - er - ing
God's mer - cy a - live, fear not for
for hope has been born in hearts where our
Refrain
All:
D.S.
love in our midst. Find us
here is your God.
God finds a home.
D.S.
Find us

Text: Tom Booth, b.1961
Tune: Tom Booth, b.1961; acc. by Ed Bolduc

343 A Voice Cries Out

Verse 1
1. Con - sole my peo-ple, the ones dear to me: speak to the
heart of Je - ru - sa - lem: the time of your mourn-ing is
end - ed now, the Lord of life will come.
Refrain
Descant
A voice cries out in the wil - der - ness: Pre - pare a
Melody:
A voice cries out in the wil - der - ness: Pre - pare a
way for the Lord! A voice cries out in the
way for the Lord! A voice cries out in the
Last time
wil - der - ness: Make straight a high-way for God!
Last time
wil - der - ness: Make straight a high-way for God!
Verse 2
2. Ev - 'ry val - ley is made a plain, ev - 'ry

moun-tain is lev - eled the glo - ry of God shall
then be re - vealed, and the na - tions will sing in praise.
D.S.
Verse 3
3. A voice shouts: "Cry!" O what shall I cry? All flesh is like
grass and its flow-ers: the grass may with-er, the flow-er may
fade, but the Word of the Lord is for - ev - er.
D.S.
Verse 4
4. Zi - on, shout from the moun - tain top, lift up your
voice O Je - ru-sa-lem, and say to the peo-ple of
God's own land, "Be - hold, be - hold your God!"
D.S.
Verse 5
5. The Lord will ap - pear as a shep-herd, hold-ing his
lambs in his arms, keep-ing his flock so
close to his heart lead-ing them all, old and young.
D.S.

Text: Isaiah 40:1-11; Michael Joncas, b.1951
Tune: Michael Joncas, b.1951

344 On Jordan's Bank

1. On Jor - dan's bank the Bap - tist's cry An - noun - ces that the Lord is nigh; A - wake and heark - en, for he brings Glad tid - ings of the King of kings.
2. Then cleansed be ev - 'ry heart from sin; Make straight the way of God with - in, And let each heart pre - pare a home Where such a might - y guest may come.
3. For you are our sal - va - tion, Lord, Our ref - uge, and our great re - ward; With - out your grace we waste a - way Like flow'rs that with - er and de - cay.
4. To heal the sick stretch out your hand, And bid the fall - en sin - ner stand; Shine forth, and let your light re - store Earth's own true love - li - ness once more.
5. All praise the Son e - ter - nal - ly, Whose ad - vent sets his peo - ple free; Whom with the Fa - ther we a - dore And Spir - it blest for ev - er - more.

Text: *Jordanis oras praevia;* Charles Coffin, 1676-1749; tr. by John Chandler, 1806-1876
Tune: WINCHESTER NEW, LM; adapt. from *Musikalisches Handbuch*, Hamburg, 1690

Come, O Long Expected Jesus 345

1. Come, O long ex - pect - ed Je - sus,
2. Is - rael's strength and con - so - la - tion,
3. Born your peo - ple to de - liv - er;
4. By your own e - ter - nal Spir - it
Born to set your peo - ple free;
You, the hope of all the earth,
Born a child and yet a king!
Rule in all our hearts a - lone;
From our fears and
Dear de - sire of
Born to reign in
By your all suf -
sins re - lease us;
ev - 'ry na - tion,
us for ev - er,
fi - cient mer - it
Free us from cap - tiv - i - ty.
Come, and save us by your birth.
Now your grac - ious king - dom bring.
Raise us to your glo - rious throne.

t: Haggai 2:7; Charles Wesley, 1707-1788, alt.
ne: STUTTGART, 8 7 8 7; *Psalmodia Sacra,* 1715; adapt. and harm. by William Henry Havergal, 1793-1870, alt.

346 People of the Night

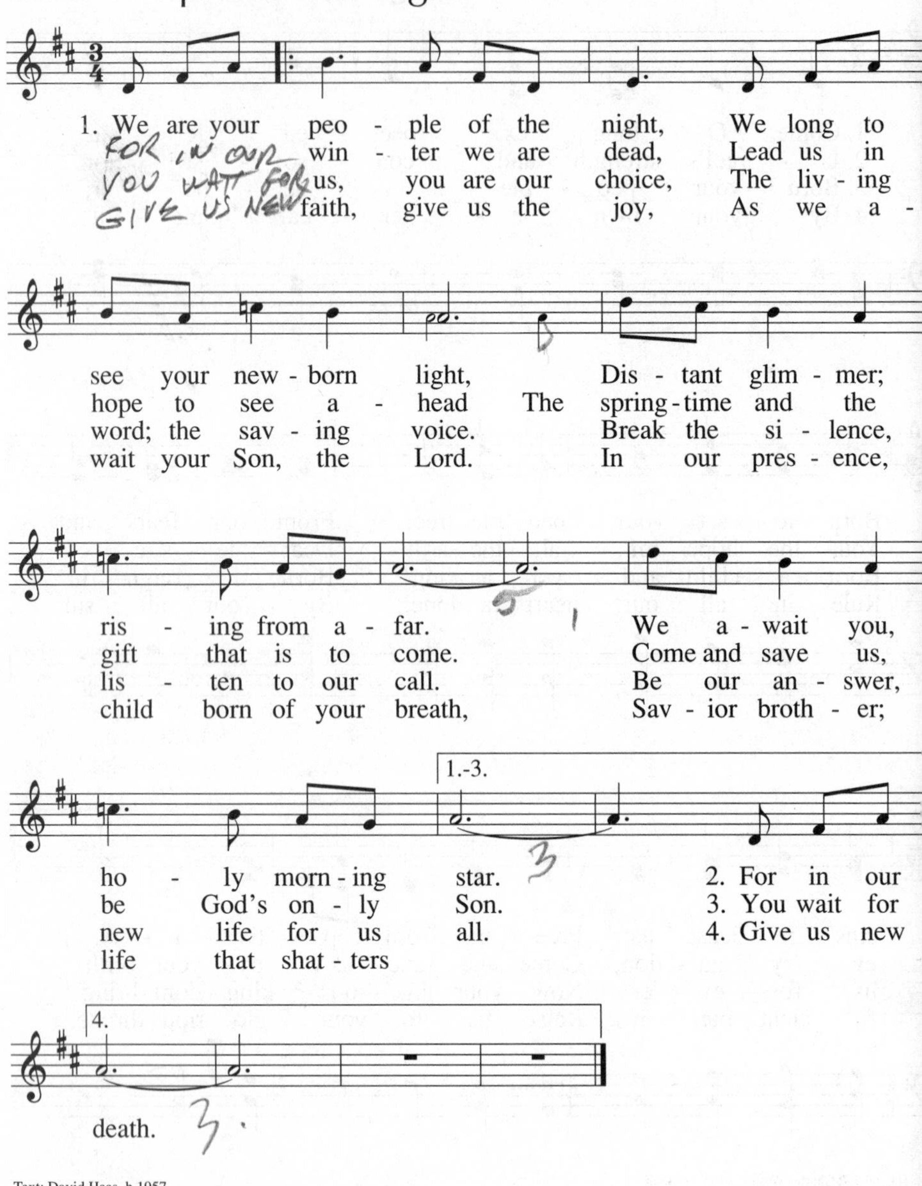
1. We are your peo - ple of the night, We long to see your new - born light, Dis - tant glim - mer; ris - ing from a - far. We a - wait you, ho - ly morn - ing star.
win - ter we are dead, Lead us in hope to see a - head The spring - time and the gift that is to come. Come and save us, be God's on - ly Son.
us, you are our choice, The liv - ing word; the sav - ing voice. Break the si - lence, lis - ten to our call. Be our an - swer, new life for us all.
faith, give us the joy, As we a - wait your Son, the Lord. In our pres - ence, child born of your breath, Sav - ior broth - er; life that shat - ters
1.-3.
2. For in our
3. You wait for
4. Give us new
4.
death.

Text: David Haas, b.1957
Tune: SHEPHERD'S SONG, 88 99; David Haas, b.1957

The King Shall Come When Morning Dawns 347

Descant:
ah
1. The King shall come when morn - ing dawns And
2. Not, as of old, a lit - tle child, To
3. The King shall come when morn - ing dawns And
4. And let the end - less bliss be - gin, By
5. The King shall come when morn - ing dawns And
ah ah
light tri - um - phant breaks. When beau - ty gilds the
suf - fer and to die, But crowned with glo - ry
earth's dark night is past; O haste the ris - ing
wea - ry saints fore - told, When right shall tri - umph
light and beau - ty brings. Hail, Christ, the Lord! Your
(ah) ah
east - ern hills And life to joy a - wakes.
like the sun That lights the morn - ing sky.
of that morn Whose day shall ev - er last.
o - ver wrong, And truth shall be ex - tolled.
peo - ple pray: Come quick - ly, King of kings.

Text: John Brownlie, 1857-1925
Tune: MORNING SONG, CM; John Wyeth, 1770-1858; arr. by Robert J. Batastini, b.1942,

348 Savior of the Nations, Come

1. Savior of the nations, come; Show the glory of the Son! Marvel now, O heav'n and earth, That our Lord chose such a birth.
2. Not by human flesh and blood, By the Spirit of our God Was the word of God made flesh— Woman's offspring, pure and fresh.
3. Wondrous birth! O wondrous child Of the Virgin undefiled! Mighty God and man in one, Eager now his race to run!
4. God Creator is his source, Back to God he runs his course, Down to death and hell descends, God's high throne he reascends.
5. Now your lowly manger bright Hallows night with newborn light; Let no night this light subdue, Let our faith shine ever new.

Text: *Veni, Redemptor gentium;* ascr. to St. Ambrose, 340-397; tr. sts. 1-3a, William Reynolds, 1812-1876; sts. 3b-5, Martin L. Seltz, 1909-1967, alt.
Tune: NUN KOMM DER HEIDEN HEILAND, 77 77; *Geystliche gesangk Buchleyn,* Wittenberg, 1524

God of All People 349

Melody:
1. God of all plac - es: pres - ent, un - seen;
2. God of all dream - ing, near and yet far.
3. God of all peo - ple, dust and the clay.
Harmony:
Voice in our si - lence, song in our midst.
Vi - sion un - heard of, wake us to rest.
Breath of a new wind, fire in our hearts.
We are your peo - ple, know - ing, un - sure.
We are your pres - ence, sent forth a - fraid.
Light born of heav - en, peace on the earth.
1. 2.
Come, Lord Je - sus, come!
Come, Lord Je - sus, come!
Come, Lord Je - sus,
3.
come! Come, Lord Je - sus, come!

Text: David Haas, b.1957
Tune: KINGDOM, 9 9 9 5; David Haas, b.1957

350 Each Winter As the Year Grows Older

1. Each win - ter as the year grows old - er, We
2. When race and class cry out for trea - son, When
3. Yet I be - lieve be - yond be - liev - ing, That
4. So e - ven as the sun is turn - ing, To
5. O Child of ec - sta - sy and sor - rows, O
each grow old - er too. The
si - rens call for war, They
life can spring from death; That
jour - ney to the north, The
Prince of peace and pain, Bright-
chill sets in a lit - tle cold - er; The
o - ver - shout the voice of rea - son, And
growth can flow - er from our griev - ing; That
liv - ing flame, in se - cret burn - ing, Can
en to - day's world by to - mor - row's, Re -
ver - i - ties we knew Seem shak - en and un -
scream till we ig - nore All we held dear be -
we can catch our breath And turn trans - fixed by
kin - dle on the earth, And bring God's love to
new our lives a - gain; Lord Je - sus, come and
1.- 4.
5.
true.
fore.
faith.
birth.
reign!

Text: William Gay, fl. 1969, © 1971, United Church Press
Tune: CAROL OF HOPE, 9 6 9 66; Annabeth Gay, b.1925, © 1971, United Church Press; acc. by Marty Haugen, b.1950, alt.,
© 1987, GIA Publications, Inc.

Awake! Awake, and Greet the New Morn 351

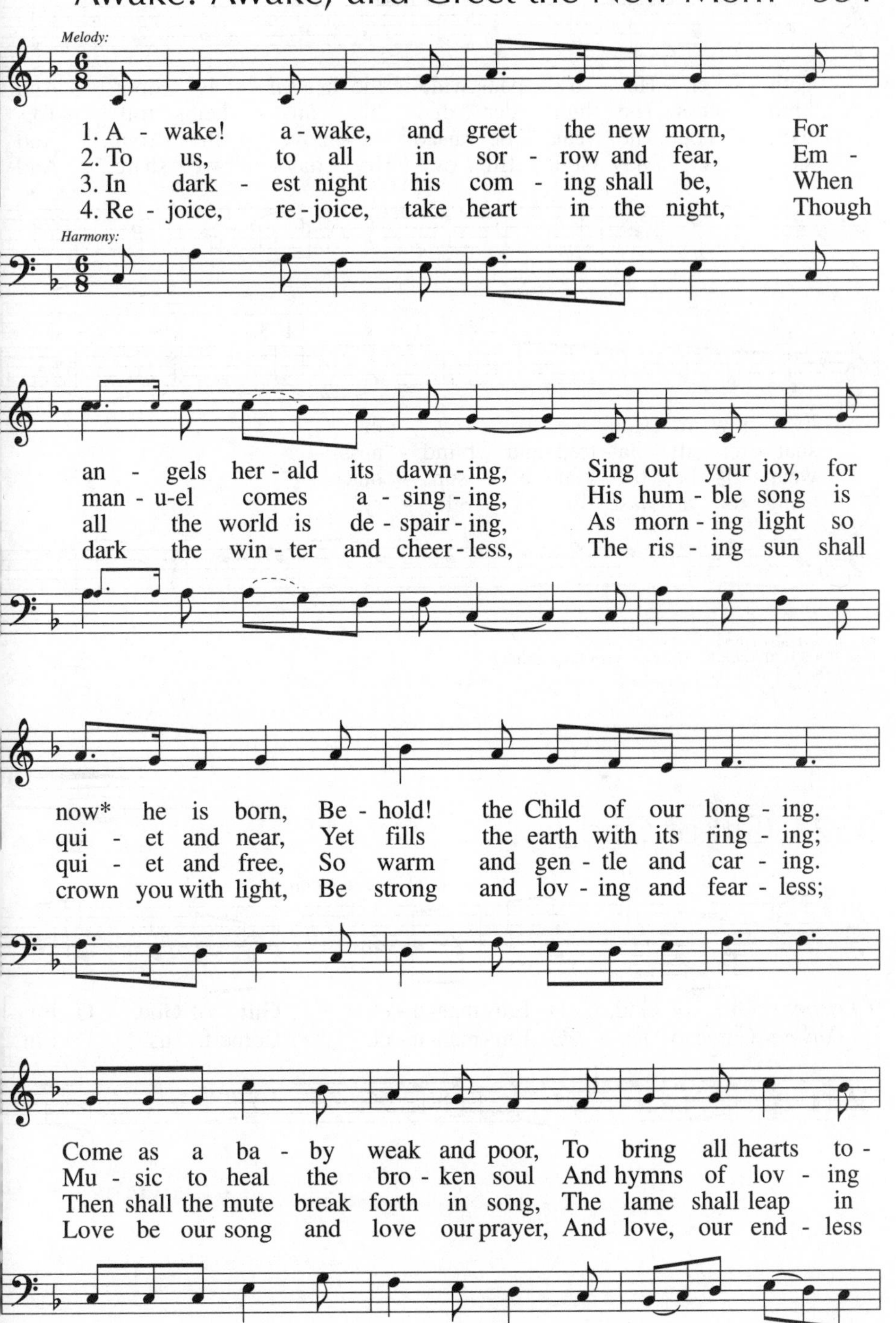
Melody:
1. A - wake! a - wake, and greet the new morn, For
2. To us, to all in sor - row and fear, Em -
3. In dark - est night his com - ing shall be, When
4. Re - joice, re - joice, take heart in the night, Though
Harmony:
an - gels her - ald its dawn - ing, Sing out your joy, for
man - u-el comes a - sing - ing, His hum - ble song is
all the world is de - spair - ing, As morn - ing light so
dark the win - ter and cheer - less, The ris - ing sun shall
now* he is born, Be - hold! the Child of our long - ing.
qui - et and near, Yet fills the earth with its ring - ing;
qui - et and free, So warm and gen - tle and car - ing.
crown you with light, Be strong and lov - ing and fear - less;
Come as a ba - by weak and poor, To bring all hearts to -
Mu - sic to heal the bro - ken soul And hymns of lov - ing
Then shall the mute break forth in song, The lame shall leap in
Love be our song and love our prayer, And love, our end - less

*During Advent: "soon"

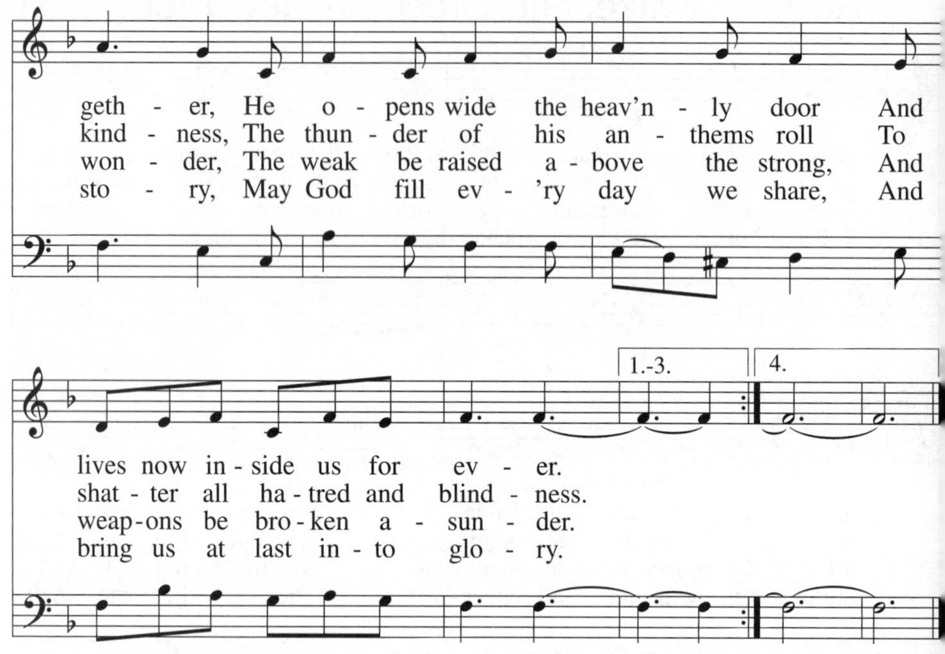
geth - er, He o - pens wide the heav'n - ly door And
kind - ness, The thun - der of his an - thems roll To
won - der, The weak be raised a - bove the strong, And
sto - ry, May God fill ev - 'ry day we share, And
1.-3.
4.
lives now in - side us for ev - er.
shat - ter all ha - tred and blind - ness.
weap - ons be bro - ken a - sun - der.
bring us at last in - to glo - ry.

Text: Marty Haugen, b.1950
Tune: REJOICE, REJOICE, 9 8 9 8 8 7 8 9; Marty Haugen, b.1950

352 Gift of God

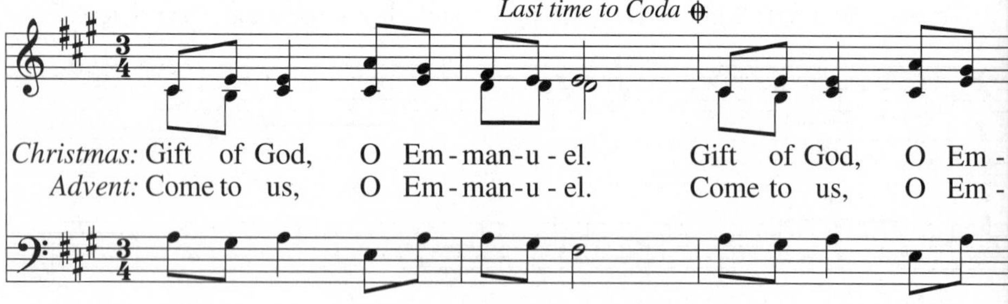
Last time to Coda
Christmas: Gift of God, O Em - man - u - el. Gift of God, O Em -
Advent: Come to us, O Em - man - u - el. Come to us, O Em -

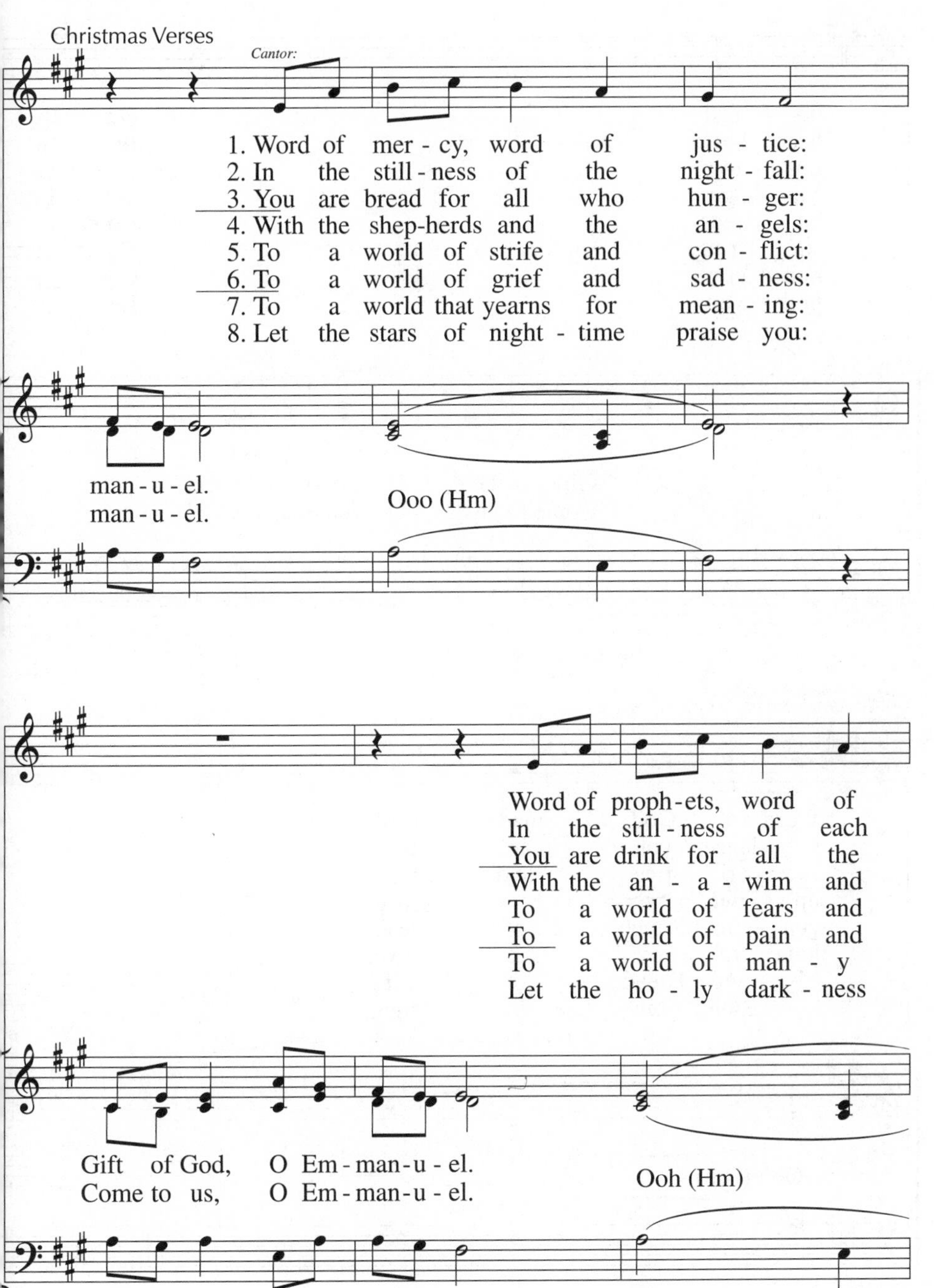
Christmas Verses
Cantor:
1. Word of mer - cy, word of jus - tice:
2. In the still - ness of the night - fall:
3. You are bread for all who hun - ger:
4. With the shep-herds and the an - gels:
5. To a world of strife and con - flict:
6. To a world of grief and sad - ness:
7. To a world that yearns for mean - ing:
8. Let the stars of night - time praise you:
man - u - el.
man - u - el.
Ooo (Hm)
Word of proph - ets, word of
In the still - ness of each
You are drink for all the
With the an - a - wim and
To a world of fears and
To a world of pain and
To a world of man - y
Let the ho - ly dark - ness
Gift of God, O Em - man - u - el.
Come to us, O Em - man - u - el.
Ooh (Hm)

po - ets: Ho - ly
heart - beat: In the
thirst - ing: You are
Ma - gi: We lift
ha - treds: Comes the
suf - f'ring: Comes the
hun - gers: Comes the
praise you: Let cre -
Gift of God, O Em-man-u-el.
Come to us, O Em-man-u-el.
Word of God made flesh.
si - lence, you are here.
sac - ri - fice and feast.
up our prayers to you.
gen - tle Prince of Peace.
hope of joy re - newed.
Liv - ing Bread of Life.
a - tion join in song.
Ooh (Hm)

Coda
Gift of God, O Em - man - u - el.
Come to us, O Em - man - u - el.
Advent Verses
3
1. Come, O Wis - dom, breathe with - in us:
2. Come, O Lord, of an - cient Is - rael:
3. Come, O Root of Jes - se's lin - eage:
4. Come, O Ho - ly Key of Da - vid:
5. Come, O Ra - diant Sun of Jus - tice:
6. Come, O Light of all the na - tions:
7. Come, O Liv - ing Flame of Free - dom:
Come, O might - y ten - der Teach - er:
You who lead us through the des - ert:
Come, O rul - er of all na - tions:
Come, and o - pen hearts to know - ledge:
Come, and shine on those in dark - ness:
Come, bright Morn - ing Star of new hope:
Liv - ing hope of our re - demp - tion:
Come, and show us how to live.
Come, and set your peo - ple free.
Come, and be our Sav - ior sure.
Come, and break the chains of death.
All who dwell in shades of death.
Come, and shine a - mong us here.
Come, and lead us to new life.

Text: Marty Haugen, b.1950
Tune: Marty Haugen, b.1950

353 Joy to the World

[𝄐]
1. Joy to the world! the Lord is come: Let earth re - ceive her King; Let ev - 'ry heart pre - pare him room, And heav'n and na - ture
2. Joy to the world! the Sav - ior reigns: Let us, our songs em - ploy; While fields and floods, rocks, hills, and plains Re - peat the sound - ing
3. No more let sin and sor - rows grow, Nor thorns in - fest the ground; He comes to make his bless - ings flow Far as the curse is
4. He rules the world with truth and grace, And makes the na - tions prove The glo - ries of his right - eous - ness, And won - ders of his
And
Re -
Far
And

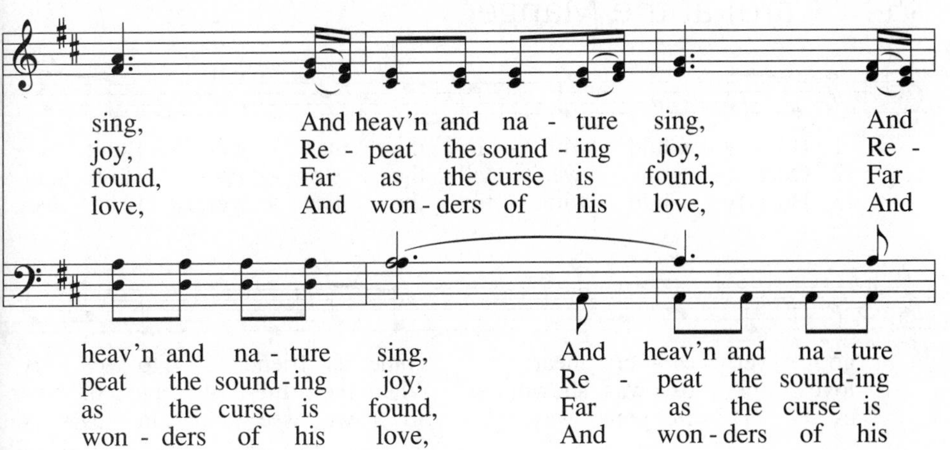
sing, And heav'n and na - ture sing, And
joy, Re - peat the sound - ing joy, Re -
found, Far as the curse is found, Far
love, And won - ders of his love, And
heav'n and na - ture sing, And heav'n and na - ture
peat the sound - ing joy, Re - peat the sound - ing
as the curse is found, Far as the curse is
won - ders of his love, And won - ders of his

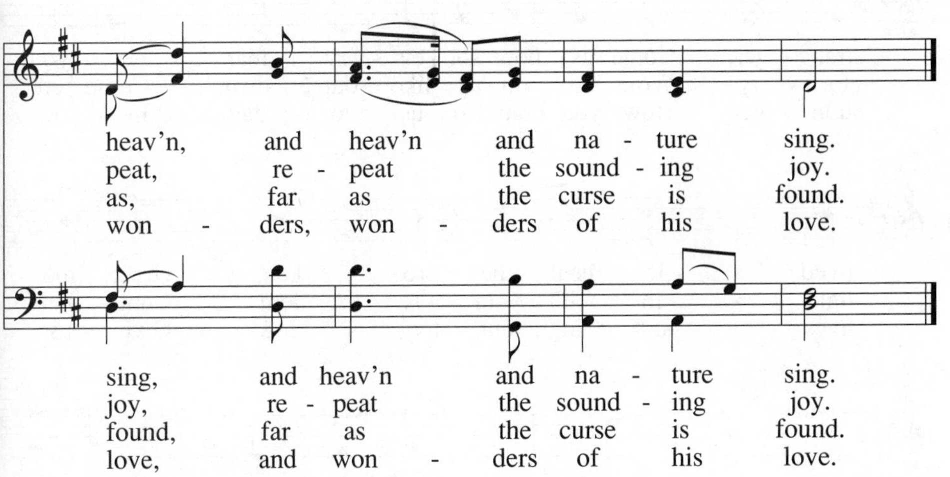
heav'n, and heav'n and na - ture sing.
peat, re - peat the sound - ing joy.
as, far as the curse is found.
won - ders, won - ders of his love.
sing, and heav'n and na - ture sing.
joy, re - peat the sound - ing joy.
found, far as the curse is found.
love, and won - ders of his love.

Text: Psalm 98; Isaac Watts, 1674-1748
Tune: ANTIOCH, CM; arr. from George F. Handel, 1685-1759, in T. Hawkes' *Collection of Tunes*, 1833

354 Carol at the Manger

1. Ho - ly Child with - in the man - ger, Long a -
2. Once a - gain we tell the sto - ry— How your
3. Ho - ly Child with - in the man - ger, Lead us
go yet ev - er near; Come as friend to ev - 'ry
love for us was shown, When the Im - age of your
ev - er in your way, So we see in ev - 'ry
stran - ger, Come as hope for ev - 'ry fear. As you
glo - ry Wore an im - age like our own. Come, en -
stran - ger How you come to us to - day. In our
lived to heal the bro - ken, Greet the
light - en with your wis - dom, Come, and
lives and in our liv - ing Give us
out - cast, free the bound, As you taught us love un -
fill us with your grace, May the fire of your com -
strength to live as you, That our hearts might be for -
spo - ken, Teach us now where you are found.
pas - sion Kin - dle ev - 'ry land and race.
giv - ing And our spir - its strong and true.

Text: Marty Haugen, b.1950
Tune: JOYOUS LIGHT, 8 7 8 7 D; Marty Haugen, b.1950

Star-Child / Niño: Es Astro 355

Last time to Coda
Verses
Descant:
5. Hope - for - peace Child, God's stu - pen - dous sign, Down - to -
5. Es es - pe - ran - za, es Ni - ño del Se - ñor; Ni - ño hu -
Melody:
1. Star - Child, earth - Child, Go - be - tween of God, Love Child,
2. Street child, beat child, No place left to go, Hurt child,
3. Grown child, old child, Mem - 'ry full of years, Sad child,
4. Spared child, spoiled child, Hav - ing, want - ing more, Wise child,
5. Hope - for - peace Child, God's stu - pen - dous sign, Down - to -
1. Ni - ño: es as - tro, Me - dia - dor de Dios; Ni - ño
2. Ni - ño a - bu - sa - do, Po - bre y sin ho - gar; Ni - ño he -
3. Ni - ño: ha cre - ci - do; ¡Cuán - to ha de a - ño - rar! Ni - ño
4. Ni - ño e - xi - gen - te, Tie - ne y quie - re más; Ni - ño
5. Es es - pe - ran - za, es Ni - ño del Se - ñor; Ni - ño hu -

earth Child, Star of stars that shine:
man - no, As - tro de ful - gor.
Christ Child, Heav - en's light-ning rod:
used child No one wants to know:
lost child, Sto - ry told in tears:
faith child Know - ing joy in store:
earth Child, Star of stars that shine:
Cris - to, De los cie - los luz.
ri - do, No le van a a - mar.
tris - te, Llo - ra su pe - sar.
sa - bio, Go - za de la paz.
ma - no, As - tro de ful - gor.
Refrain
Descant:
This year, this year let the day ar -
Oh Dios, da - le en es - ta Na - vi -
Melody:
This year, this year let the day ar -
Oh Dios, da - le en es - ta Na - vi -
rive When Christ - mas comes for ev - 'ry - one,
dad Un dí - a de fe - li - ci - dad
rive When Christ - mas comes for ev - 'ry - one,
dad Un dí - a de fe - li - ci - dad
Coda
ev - 'ry - one a - live.
a la hu-ma - ni - dad.
ev - 'ry - one a - live.
a la hu-ma - ni - dad.

Text: Shirley Erena Murray, b.1931, Spanish tr. by Raquel Gutiérrez-Achón and George Lockwood, © 1994, 1997, Hope Publishing Co.
Tune: NOAH'S SONG, 4 5 4 5 with refrain; Ronald F. Krisman, b.1946, © 2003, GIA Publications, Inc.

Hark! The Herald Angels Sing 356

1. Hark! the her - ald an - gels sing, "Glo - ry to the
2. Christ, by high - est heav'n a - dored, Christ the ev - er-
3. Hail the heav'n - born Prince of Peace! Hail the Sun of

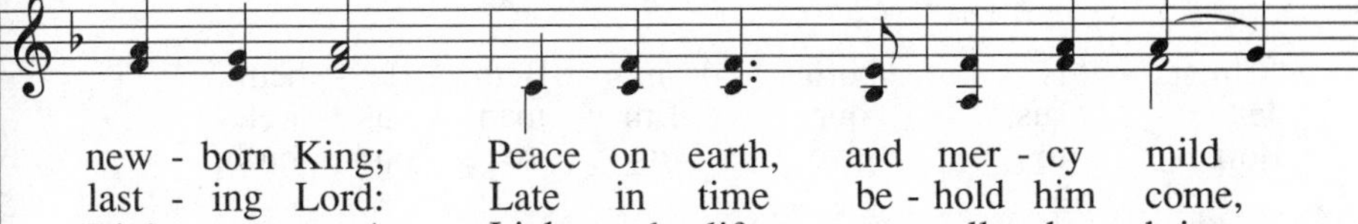

new - born King; Peace on earth, and mer - cy mild
last - ing Lord: Late in time be - hold him come,
Right-eous-ness! Light and life to all he brings,

God and sin - ners rec - on - ciled!" Joy - ful, all you
Off - spring of the Vir - gin's womb. Veiled in flesh the
Ris'n with heal - ing in his wings. Mild he lays his

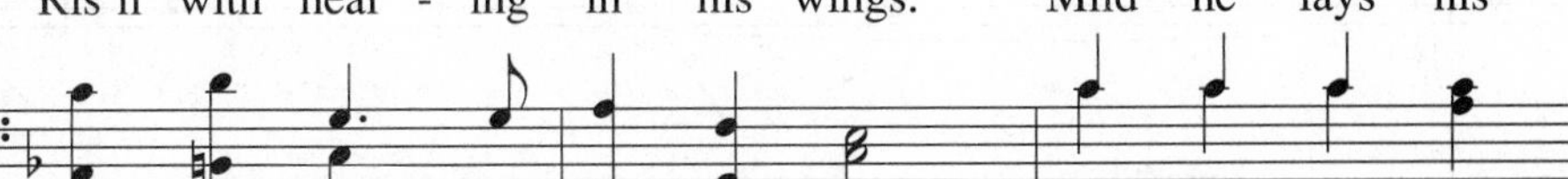

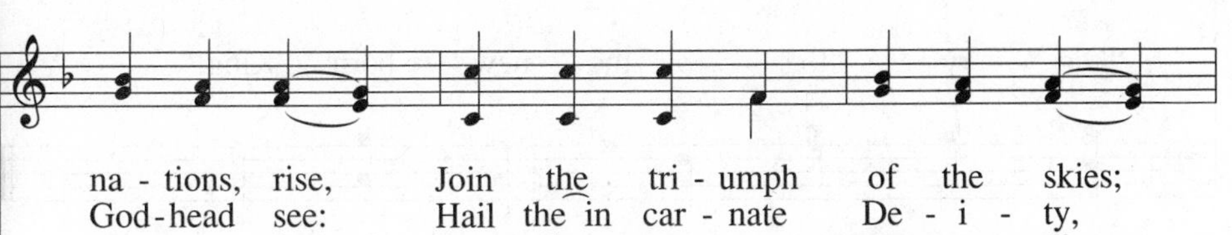

na - tions, rise, Join the tri - umph of the skies;
God-head see: Hail the in car - nate De - i - ty,
glo - ry by, Born that we no more may die,

With the an - gel - ic host pro - claim,
Pleased as man with us to dwell,
Born to raise us from the earth,
"Christ is born in Beth - le - hem!"
Je - sus, our Em - man - u - el.
Born to give us sec - ond birth.
Hark! the her - ald an - gels sing,
Ped.
"Glo - ry to the new - born King!"

Text: Charles Wesley, 1707-1788, alt.
Tune: MENDELSSOHN, 77 77 D with refrain; Felix Mendelssohn, 1809-1847

O Come, All Ye Faithful / Adeste Fideles 357

1. O come, all ye faithful, joyful and triumphant, O
2. God of God, Light of Light,
3. Sing, choirs of angels, sing in exultation,
4. Yea, Lord, we greet thee, born this happy morning,
1. Adéste fidéles, laéti, triumphántes, Ve-
2. Deum de Deo, Lumen de Lúmine
3. Cantet nunc io, chorus angelorum,
4. Ergo qui natus Die hodiérna,
come ye, O come ye to Bethlehem;
Lo! He comes forth from the Virgin's womb.
Sing, all ye citizens of heav'n above!
Jesus, to thee be all glory giv'n;
níte, veníte in Béthlehem.
Gestant puélae víscera.
Cantet nunc aula caeléstium.
Jesu tibi sit glória.
Come and behold him, born the King of angels;
Our very God, begotten not created,
Glory to God, all glory in the highest;
Word of the Father, now in flesh appearing;
Natum vidéte, Regem angelórum.
Deum verum, Génitum, non factum.
Glória, glória, in excélsis Deo.
Patris aeternae verbum caro factum.

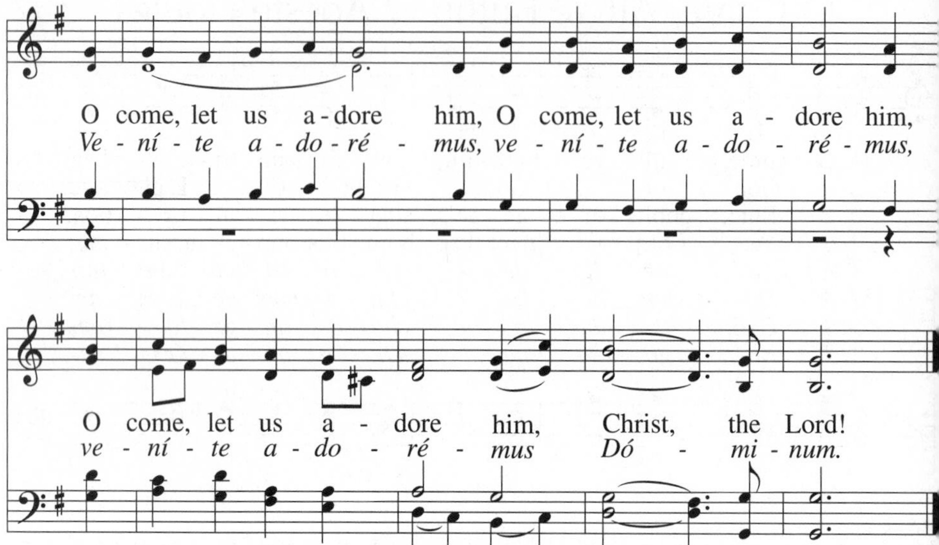
O come, let us a - dore him, O come, let us a - dore him,
Ve - ní - te a - do - ré - mus, ve - ní - te a - do - ré - mus,
O come, let us a - dore him, Christ, the Lord!
ve - ní - te a - do - ré - mus Dó - mi - num.

Text: *Adeste fideles;* John F. Wade, c.1711-1786; tr. by Frederick Oakeley, 1802-1880, alt.
Tune: ADESTE FIDELES, Irregular with refrain; John F. Wade, c.1711-1786

358 Wood of the Cradle

Verses

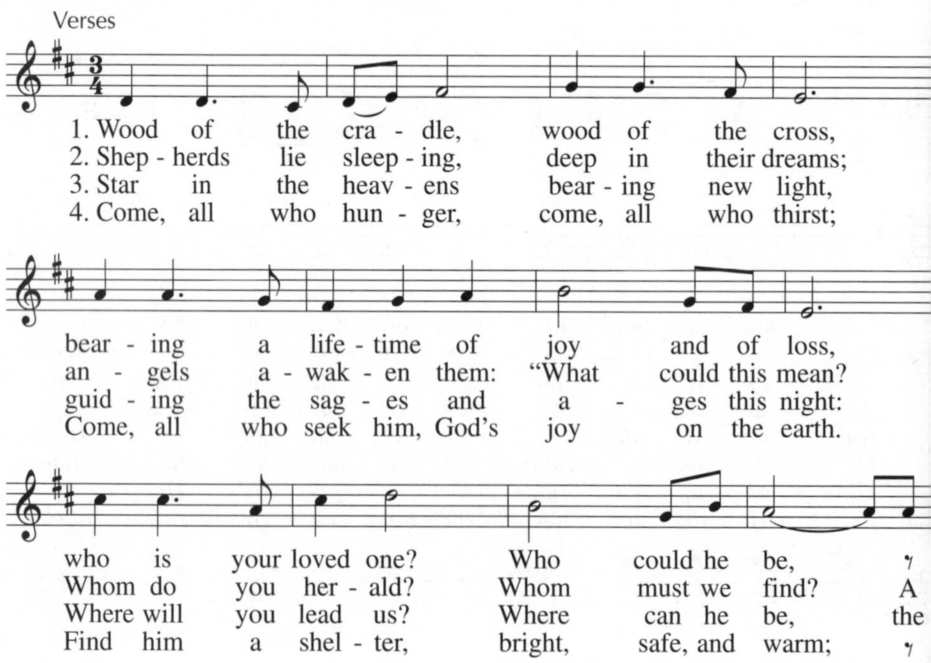
1. Wood of the cra - dle, wood of the cross,
2. Shep - herds lie sleep - ing, deep in their dreams;
3. Star in the heav - ens bear - ing new light,
4. Come, all who hun - ger, come, all who thirst;
bear - ing a life - time of joy and of loss,
an - gels a - wak - en them: "What could this mean?
guid - ing the sag - es and a - ges this night:
Come, all who seek him, God's joy on the earth.
who is your loved one? Who could he be,
Whom do you her - ald? Whom must we find? A
Where will you lead us? Where can he be, the
Find him a shel - ter, bright, safe, and warm;

born in a man - ger to die on a tree?
child in a man - ger? Our God born in time?"
child born of mys - t'ry who died on a tree?
see in all peo - ple his love be - ing born.
Refrain
This, this is Je - sus the Lord, here in the
This, this is Je - sus the, Je - sus the Lord,
come,
bod - y and blood out - poured. Come, come, come
walk in his ways. Kneel at the man - ger and rise
from the grave.
Final ending

Text: Francis Patrick O'Brien, b.1958
Tune: Francis Patrick O'Brien, b.1958

359 O Little Town of Bethlehem

1. O lit - tle town of Beth - le - hem, How
2. For Christ is born of Mar - y, And
3. How si - lent - ly, how si - lent - ly, The
4. O ho - ly Child of Beth - le - hem! De -
still we see thee lie! A - bove thy deep and
gath - ered all a - bove, While mor - tals sleep, the
won - drous gift is giv'n! So God im - parts to
scend to us we pray; Cast out our sin and
dream - less sleep The si - lent stars go by;
an - gels keep Their watch of won - d'ring love.
hu - man hearts The bless - ings of his heav'n.
en - ter in, Be born in us to - day.
Yet in the dark streets shin - eth The
O morn - ing stars, to - geth - er Pro -
No ear may hear his com - ing, But
We hear the Christ - mas an - gels The

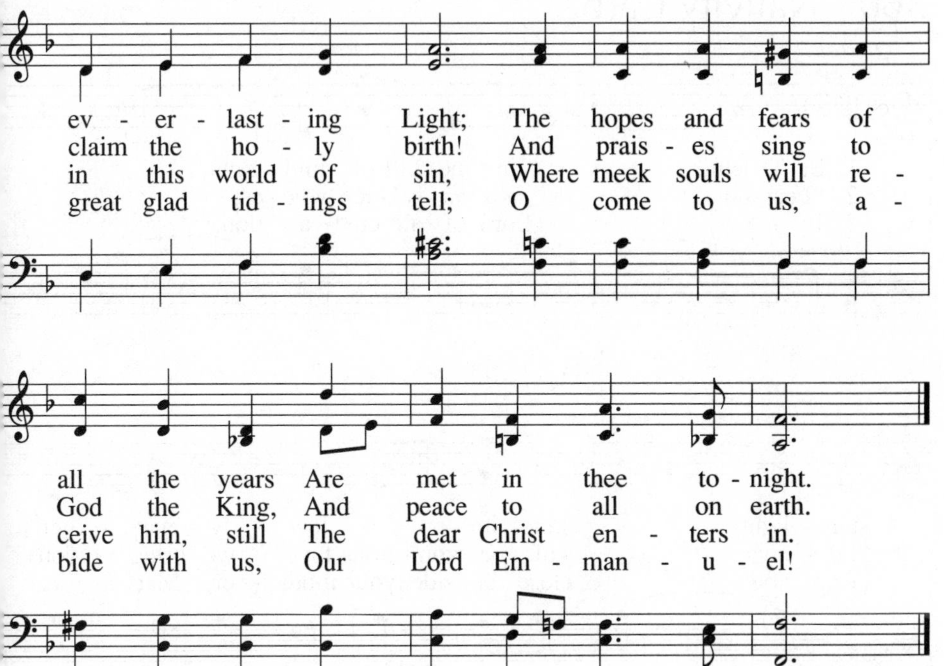
ev - er - last - ing Light; The hopes and fears of
claim the ho - ly birth! And prais - es sing to
in this world of sin, Where meek souls will re -
great glad tid - ings tell; O come to us, a -
all the years Are met in thee to - night.
God the King, And peace to all on earth.
ceive him, still The dear Christ en - ters in.
bide with us, Our Lord Em - man - u - el!

Text: Phillips Brooks, 1835-1893
Tune: ST. LOUIS, 8 6 8 6 7 6 8 6; Lewis H. Redner, 1831-1908

360 Nativity Carol

Verses

Melody:
1. Si - lent, in the chill of mid - night,
2. "Fear not," said an - gel - ic voic - es;
3. Je - sus, Lord of all cre - a - tion,
Harmony:

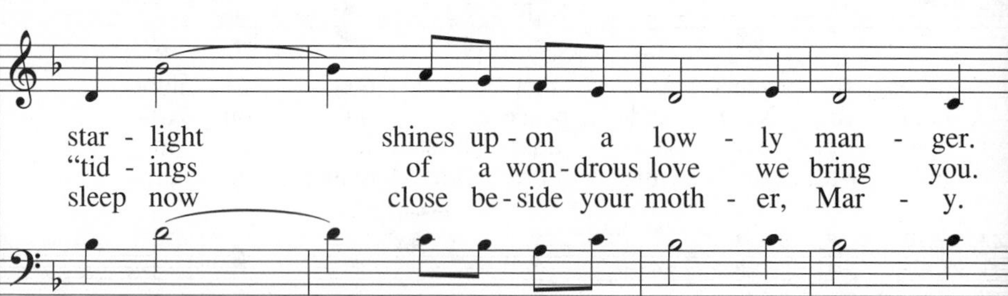
star - light shines up - on a low - ly man - ger.
"tid - ings of a won - drous love we bring you.
sleep now close be - side your moth - er, Mar - y.

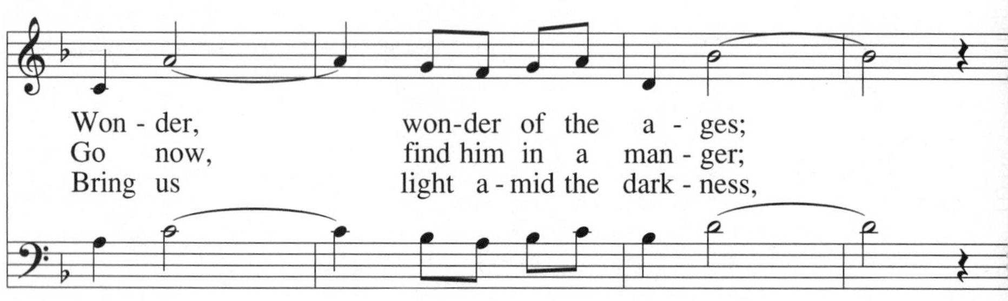
Won - der, won-der of the a - ges;
Go now, find him in a man - ger;
Bring us light a - mid the dark - ness,

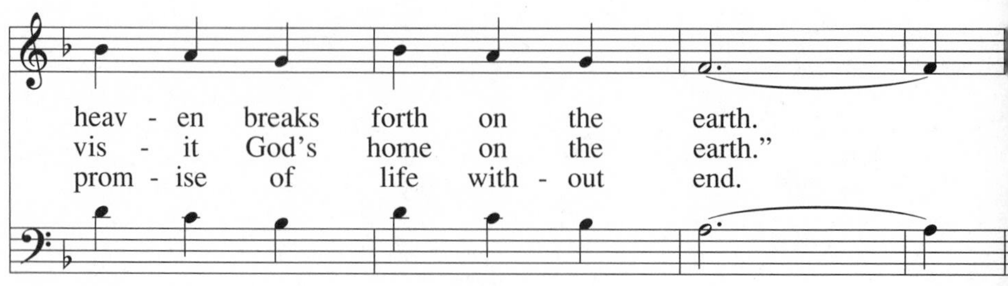
heav - en breaks forth on the earth.
vis - it God's home on the earth."
prom - ise of life with - out end.

Refrain
For a child is born, the world re - joic - es!
Shep - herds and an - gels pro - claim his birth.
This is Je - sus the Lord, our Sav - ior and
broth - er, bear - ing God's peace to the earth.

Text: Francis Patrick O'Brien, b.1958
Tune: Francis Patrick O'Brien, b.1958

361 Angels We Have Heard on High

1. An - gels we have heard on high
2. Shep - herds, why this ju - bi - lee?
3. Come to Beth - le - hem and see
4. See him in a man - ger laid,
Sweet - ly sing - ing o'er the plains,
Why your joy - ous strains pro - long?
Him whose birth the an - gels sing;
Whom the choirs of an - gels praise;
And the moun - tains in re - ply
Say what may the tid - ings be,
Come a - dore, on bend - ed knee,
Mar - y, Jo - seph, lend your aid,
Ech - o back their joy - ous strains.
Which in - spire your heav'n - ly song.
Christ, the Lord, the new - born King.
While our hearts in love we raise.

Glo - - - ri - a
in ex - cel - sis De - o, Glo - -
- - ri - a in ex - cel - sis De - o.

Text: *Les anges dans nos campagnes;* French, c. 18th C.; tr. from *Crown of Jesus Music,* London, 1862
Tune: GLORIA, 7 7 7 7 with refrain; French traditional

362 Sing Alleluia

Verses
Melody:
1. Dark is the night and deep are the shad - ows,
2. Who would be - lieve that here in a man - ger
3. Great is the joy of Mar - y, his moth - er;
4. Hope for the poor, re - lease for the cap - tive,
Harmony:
Qui - et the ba - by bathed in lan - tern light;
God comes a - mong us as a ti - ny child?
Great is the joy of Jo - seph by her side.
Love for the out - cast, light for wea - ry eyes;
Hushed are the sounds of cat - tle and shep - herds;
See in his eyes the glo - ry of heav - en;
Great is the joy of all those in dark - ness,
Word that brings life, em - brac - ing hu - man - i - ty,

Sweet is the mu - sic the an - gels bring this night.
Hear in his laugh - ter the joy of God on high.
Here lies the Sav - ior so soon to die and rise.
Je - sus, com - pan - ion, be born in - to our lives.
Refrain
Sing Al - le - lu - ia, sing Al - le - lu - ia. Wel - come the Sav - ior, the
prom - ise of new life. Sing Al - le - lu - ia, sing Al - le - lu - ia.
All of cre - a - tion sing this night.
D.S.
Final ending

Text: Francis Patrick O'Brien, b.1958
Tune: Francis Patrick O'Brien, b.1958

363 Go Tell It on the Mountain

Refrain
Go tell it on the moun-tain, O-ver the hills and ev - 'ry - where;
Go tell it on the moun - tain That Je - sus Christ is born!
Verses
1. While shep - herds kept their watch - ing O'er si - lent flocks by night, Be - hold through - out the heav - ens There shone a ho - ly light.
2. The shep - herds feared and trem - bled When lo! a - bove the earth Rang out the an - gel cho - rus That hailed our Sav - ior's birth.
3. Down in a low - ly man - ger The hum - ble Christ was born, And God sent us sal - va - tion That bless - ed Christ - mas morn.
D.C.

Text: African-American spiritual; adapt. by John W. Work, Jr., 1871-1925, © Mrs. John W. Work, III
Tune: GO TELL IT ON THE MOUNTAIN, 7 6 7 6 with refrain; African-American spiritual; harm. by Robert J. Batastini, b.1942, © 1995, GIA Publications, Inc.

He Came Down 364

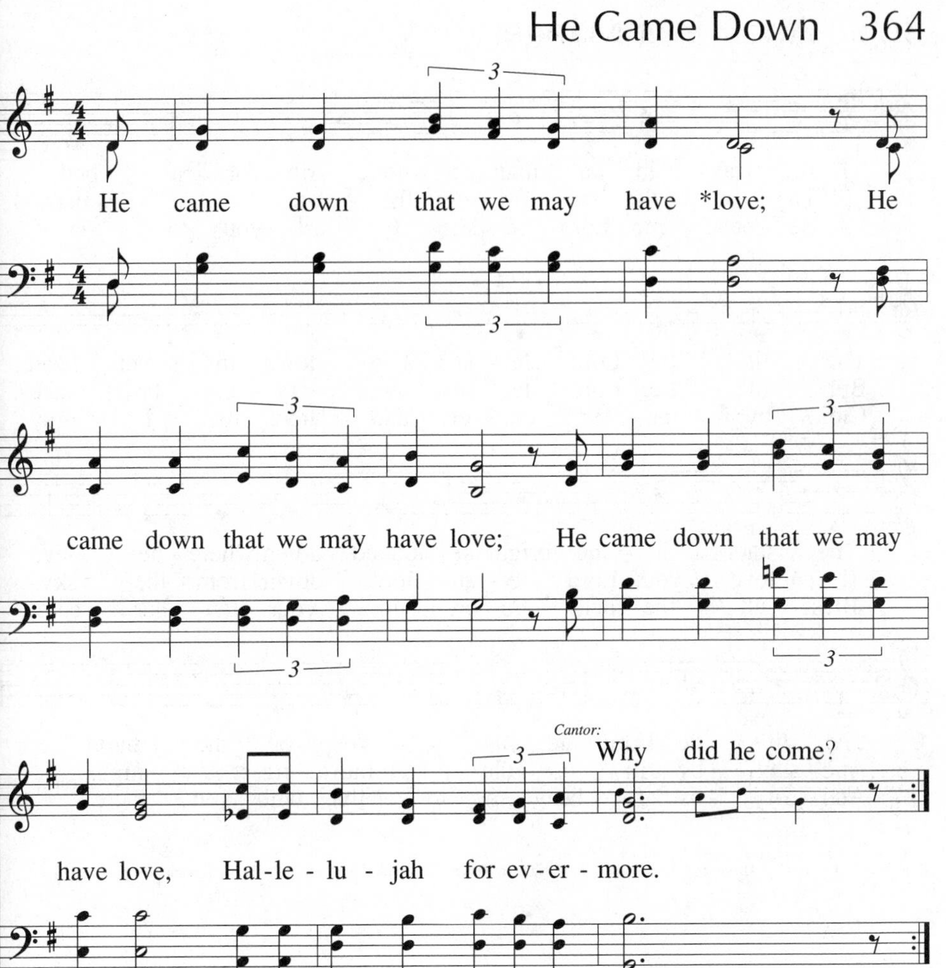
He came down that we may have *love; He came down that we may have love; He came down that we may have love, Hal-le-lu-jah for ev-er-more.
Cantor:
Why did he come?

Substitute peace, joy, hope, life, *etc.*

Text: Cameroon traditional
Tune: Cameroon traditional; transcribed and arr. by John L. Bell, b.1949, © 1990, Iona Community, GIA Publications, Inc., agent

365 Away in a Manger

1. A - way in a man - ger, no crib for a bed,
2. The cat - tle are low - ing; the ba - by a - wakes,
3. Be near me, Lord Je - sus; I ask you to stay

The lit - tle Lord Je - sus laid down his sweet head.
But lit - tle Lord Je - sus, no cry - ing he makes.
Close by me for - ev - er, and love me, I pray.

The stars in the bright sky looked down where he lay,
I love you, Lord Je - sus, look down from the sky,
Bless all the dear chil - dren in your ten - der care,

The lit - tle Lord Je - sus, a - sleep on the hay.
And stay by my cra - dle till morn - ing is nigh.
And fit us for heav - en to live with you there.

Text: St. 1-2, anonymous, st. 3, John T. McFarland, 1851-1913
Tune: MUELLER, 11 11 11 11; James R. Murray, 1841-1905; harm. by Robert J. Batastini, b. 1942, © 1994, GIA Publications, Inc.

366 God Rest You Merry, Gentlemen

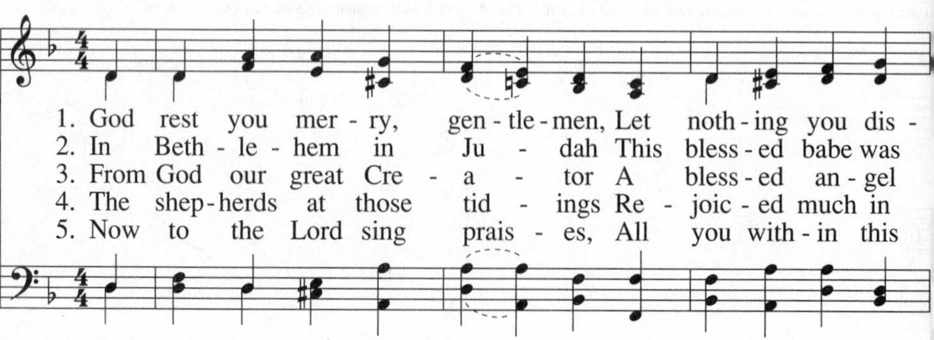
1. God rest you mer - ry, gen - tle - men, Let noth - ing you dis -
2. In Beth - le - hem in Ju - dah This bless - ed babe was
3. From God our great Cre - a - tor A bless - ed an - gel
4. The shep - herds at those tid - ings Re - joic - ed much in
5. Now to the Lord sing prais - es, All you with - in this

may, For Je - sus Christ our Sav - ior Was
born, And laid with - in a man - ger Up -
came, And un - to cer - tain shep - herds Brought
mind, And left their flocks a - feed - ing In
place, And with true love and char - i - ty Each
born up - on this day, To save us all from
on this bless - ed morn: For which his moth - er
tid - ings of the same, How that in Beth - le -
tem - pest, storm, and wind, And went to Beth - le -
oth - er now em - brace; This ho - ly tide of
Sa - tan's pow'r When we were gone a - stray.
Mar - y Did noth - ing take in scorn.
hem was born The Son of God by name.
hem straight - way, The bless - ed babe to find.
Christ - mas All oth - ers shall re - place.
O tid - ings of com - fort and joy, com-fort and
joy; O tid - ings of com - fort and joy!

Text: English carol, 18th C.
Tune: GOD REST YOU MERRY, 8 6 8 6 8 6 with refrain; English 18th C.; harm. by John Stainer, 1840-1901

367 Good Christian Friends, Rejoice

1.-3. Good Chris - tian friends, re - joice With heart and
soul and voice; O give heed to what we say:
soul and voice; Now you hear of end - less bliss:
soul and voice; Now you need not fear the grave:
Je - sus Christ is born to - day! Ox and ass be -
Je - sus Christ was born for this! He has o - pened
Je - sus Christ was born to save! Calls you one and
fore him bow, And he is in the man - ger now.
heav - en's door, And we are blest for ev - er - more.
calls you all To gain his ev - er - last - ing hall.
Christ is born to - day! Christ is born to - day!
Christ was born for this! Christ was born for this!
Christ was born to save! Christ was born to save!

Text: *In dulci jubilo;* Latin and German, 14th C.; tr. by John M. Neale, 1818-1866
Tune: IN DULCI JUBILO, 66 77 78 55; Klug's *Geistliche Lieder,* Wittenberg, 1535; harm. by Robert L. Pearsall, 1795-1856

Child of Mercy 368

Refrain
Descant:
Glo - ri-a
Child of mer-cy, child of peace, Je-sus, Bread of life,
in ex-cel-sis De-o, Glo - -
food to fill our long-ing. Child of jus-tice, child of light,
- ri-a in ex-cel-sis De - o.
Je-sus, sav-ing cup, Em-man-u-el, God with us.
Verses
1. All who walk in dark - ness have seen a great light, to
2. A child is born to us, a son is giv-en us, up-
3. We name him: "Won-der, coun-s'lor, he-ro, might-y God," The
4. We pro-claim good news to you, great tid - ings of joy: To

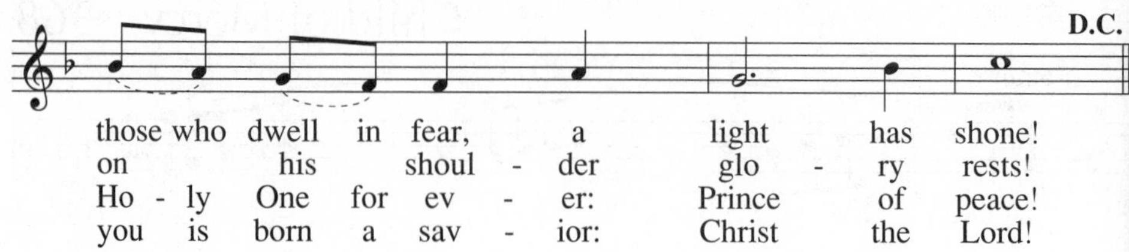
D.C.
those who dwell in fear, a light has shone!
on his shoul - der glo - ry rests!
Ho - ly One for ev - er: Prince of peace!
you is born a sav - ior: Christ the Lord!

Text: Isaiah 9:1, 5; David Haas, b.1957
Tune: David Haas, b.1957

369 Angels, from the Realms of Glory

1. An - gels, from the realms of glo - ry,
2. Shep - herds, in the fields a - bid - ing,
3. Sag - es, leave your con - tem - pla - tions,
4. Though an in - fant now we view him,

Wing your flight o'er all the earth; You who sang cre -
Watch - ing o'er your flocks by night, God on earth is
Bright - er vi - sions beam a - far; Seek the great De -
He shall fill his heav'n - ly throne, Gath - er all the

a - tion's sto - ry, Now pro - claim Mes - si - ah's birth:
now re - sid - ing, Yon - der shines the in - fant light:
sire of na - tions, You have seen his morn - ing star:
na - tions to him; Ev - 'ry knee shall then bow down:

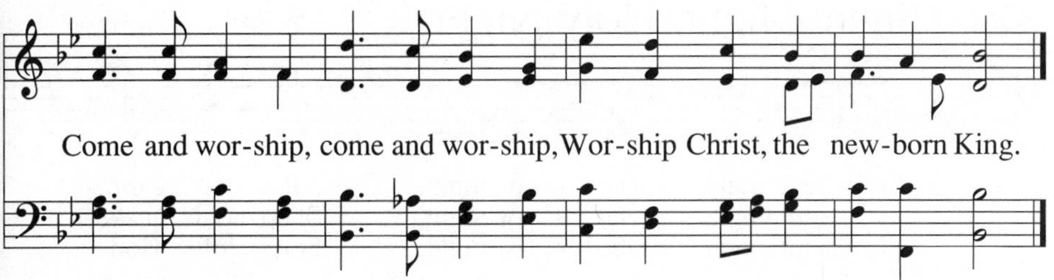
Come and wor-ship, come and wor-ship, Wor-ship Christ, the new-born King.

Text: Sts. 1-3, James Montgomery, 1771-1854; st. 4, *Christmas Box*, 1825
Tune: REGENT SQUARE, 8 7 8 7 8 7; Henry Smart, 1813-1879

Song of the Stable 370

1. Chill of the nightfall,
Lamps in the windows,
Letting their light fall
Clear on the snow;
Bitter December
Bids us remember
Christ in the stable
Long, long ago.

2. Silence of midnight,
Voices of angels,
Singing to bid night
Yield to the dawn;
Darkness is ended,
Sinners befriended,
Where in the stable
Jesus is born.

3. Splendor of starlight
High on the hillside,
Faint is the far light
Burning below;
Kneeling before him
Shepherds adore him,
Christ in the stable
Long, long ago.

4. Glory of daybreak!
Sorrows and shadows,
Suddenly they break
Forth into morn;
Sing out and tell now
All shall be well now;
For in the stable
Jesus is born!

Text: *Chill of the Nightfall,* Timothy Dudley-Smith, b.1926, © 1980, Hope Publishing Co.
Tune: PRIOR LAKE, 5 5 5 4 D; David Haas, b.1957, © 1985, GIA Publications, Inc.

371 Silent Night, Holy Night

1. Si - lent night, ho - ly night, All is calm, all is bright Round yon Vir - gin Moth - er and Child, Ho - ly In - fant so ten - der and mild, Sleep in heav - en - ly peace, Sleep in heav - en - ly peace.
2. Si - lent night, ho - ly night, Shep - herds quake at the sight; Glo - ries stream from heav - en a - far, Heav'n - ly hosts sing al - le - lu - ia; Christ, the Sav - ior, is born! Christ, the Sav - ior, is born!
3. Si - lent night, ho - ly night, Son of God, love's pure light Ra - diant beams from thy ho - ly face, With the dawn of re - deem - ing grace, Je - sus, Lord, at thy birth, Je - sus, Lord, at thy birth.

Text: *Stille Nacht, heilige Nacht;* Joseph Mohr, 1792-1849; tr. John F. Young, 1820-1885
Tune: STILLE NACHT, 66 89 66; Franz X. Gruber, 1787-1863

Night of Silence 372

1. Cold are the peo - ple, win - ter of life, We trem - ble in
2. Voice in the dis - tance, call in the night, On wind you en -
3. Spir - it a - mong us, shine like the star, Your light that guides

shad - ows this cold end - less night, Fro - zen in the snow lie
fold us, you speak of the light, Gen - tle on the ear you
shep - herds and kings from a - far, Shim - mer in the sky so

ros - es sleep - ing, Flow - ers that will ech - o the sun -
whis - per soft - ly, Ru - mors of a dawn so em - brac -
emp - ty, lone - ly, Ris - ing in the warmth of your Son's

rise, Fire of hope is our on - ly warmth,
ing, Breath - less love a - waits dark - ened souls,
love, Star un - know - ing of night and day,

Wea - ry, its flame will be dy - ing soon.
Soon will we know of the morn - ing.
Spir - it we wait for your lov - ing Son.

"Night of Silence" was written to be sung simultaneously with "Silent Night." It is suggested that selected voices hum "Silent Night" while the remaining voices sing the final verse of "Night of Silence". Likewise, the song "Silent Night" may be sung by the choir and congregation as the instruments play "Night of Silence".

Text: Daniel Kantor, b.1960
Tune: Daniel Kantor, b.1960

373 Lo, How a Rose E′er Blooming

1. Lo, how a Rose e'er bloom - ing From
2. I - sa - iah 'twas for - told it, The
3. O Flow'r, whose fra - grance ten - der With
ten - der stem hath sprung! Of Jes - se's lin - eage
Rose I have in mind, With Mar - y we be -
sweet-ness fills the air, Dis - pel in glo - rious
com - ing As seers of old have sung. It
hold it, The Vir - gin Moth - er kind. To
splen - dor The dark-ness ev - 'ry - where; True
came, a blos - som bright, A - mid the cold of
show God's love a - right, She bore to us a
man, yet ver - y God, From sin and death now

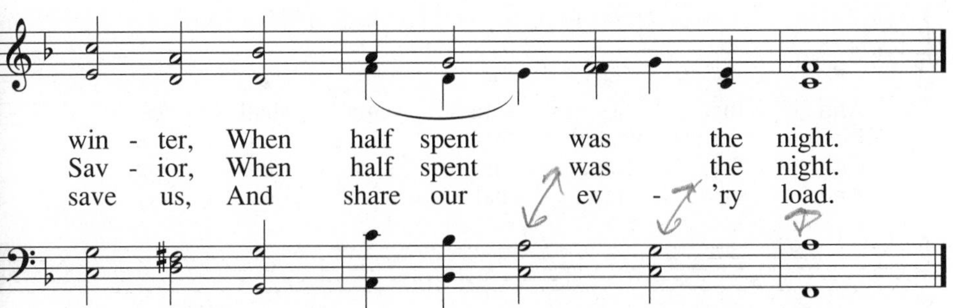
win - ter, When half spent was the night.
Sav - ior, When half spent was the night.
save us, And share our ev - 'ry load.

Text: Isaiah 11:1; *Es ist ein' Ros' entsprungen; Speier Gesangbuch,* 1599; tr. sts. 1-2 by Theodore Baker, 1851-1934; st. 3, *The Hymnal, 1940*
Tune: ES IST EIN' ROS' ENSTSPRUNGEN, 7 6 7 6 6 7 6; *Geistliche Kirchengesang,* Cologne, 1599; harm. by Michael Praetorius, 1571-1621

Of the Father's Love Begotten 374

1. Of the Fa - ther's love be - got - ten,
2. O that birth for ev - er bless - ed,
3. Let the heights of heav'n a - dore him;
4. Christ, to you with God the Fa - ther,

Ere the worlds be - gan to be,
When the Vir - gin, full of grace,
An - gel hosts, his prais - es sing;
Spir - it blest e - ter - nal - ly,

He is Al - pha and O - me - ga,
By the Spir - it blest con - ceiv - ing,
Pow'rs, do - min - ions, bow be - fore him,
Hymn and chant and high thanks - giv - ing,

He the source, the end - ing he,
Bore the Sav - ior of our race;
And ex - tol our God and King;
And un - end - ing prais - es be:

Of the things that are, that have been,
And the Babe, the world's Re - deem - er,
Let no tongue on earth be si - lent,
Hon - or, glo - ry, and do - min - ion,

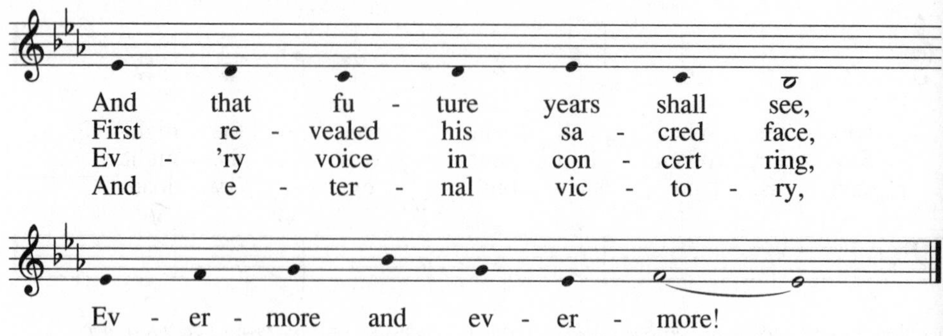
And that fu - ture years shall see,
First re - vealed his sa - cred face,
Ev - 'ry voice in con - cert ring,
And e - ter - nal vic - to - ry,
Ev - er - more and ev - er - more!

Text: *Corde natus ex Parentis;* Aurelius Prudentius, 348-413; tr. by John M. Neale, 1818-1866 and Henry W. Baker, 1821-1877
Tune: DIVINUM MYSTERIUM, 8 7 8 7 8 7 7; 12th C.; Mode V; acc. by Richard Proulx, b.1937, © 1985, GIA Publications, Inc.

375 Rise Up, Shepherd, and Follow

Verses

Leader:
1. There's a star in the East on Christ - mas morn,
2. If you take good heed to the an - gel's words,

All:
Rise up, shep - herd, and fol - low,
Rise up, shep - herd, and fol - low,

Leader:
It will lead to the place where the Christ was born,
You'll for - get your flocks, you'll for - get your herds,

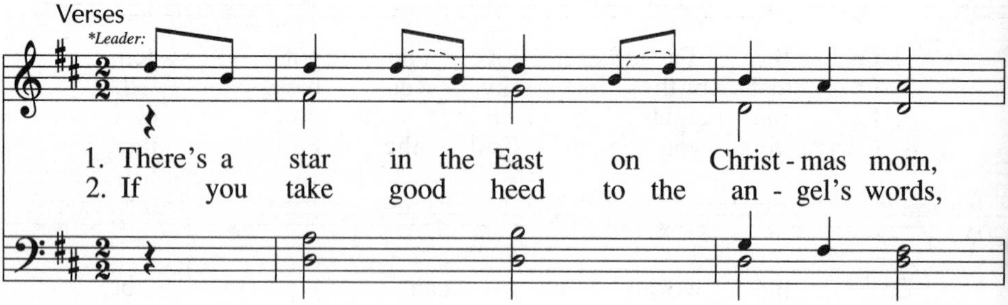

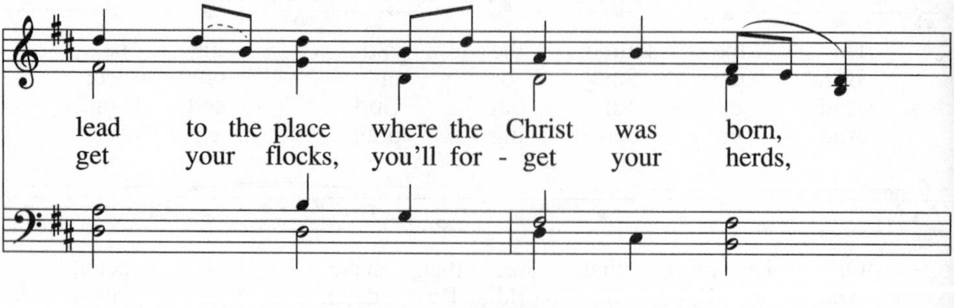

**Choir may hum or sing "oo" or "ah" when leader is singing.*

All:
Rise up, shep - herd, and fol - low.
Refrain
Fol - low, fol - low, Rise up, shep-herd, and
fol - low, Fol - low the Star of Beth - le - hem,
Rise up, shep - herd, and fol - low.

Text: Traditional
Tune: African-American spiritual

376 Where the Promise Shines

Verses
1. When a star is shin - ing o - ver east - ern
2. Where the world is wait - ing for an un - known
3. Lead us on, O Day - star, in the qui - et
hills, When the air is si - lent,
day, Where a voice for - got - ten
night; Guide us through the shad - ow
and the clam - or stills, When the night is
cries, "Pre - pare the way!" Where an earth - ly
with your gen - tle light; Show us in a
wait - ing, and the old hopes rise,
pow - er makes the heart turn cold,
man - ger our re - demp - tion's sign;
Then the time has rip - ened and the heart grows
There the gifts are of - fered— in - cense, myrrh, and
Bring us to a morn - ing where the prom - ise
wise.
gold.
shines.
Refrain
Lead us on, lead us on,
to a morn - ing where the prom - ise shines.

Lead us on, lead us on, to a
Lead us on, lead us to a
lead us to a
morn-ing where the prom - ise shines.
Last time
morn-ing where the prom - ise shines.
Last time
Last time

377 Infant Holy, Infant Lowly

1. In - fant ho - ly, In - fant low - ly, For his bed a
2. Flocks were sleep-ing: Shep-herds keep - ing Vig - il till the
cat - tle stall; Ox - en low - ing, Lit - tle know - ing
morn-ing new. Saw the glo - ry, Heard the sto - ry,
Christ the babe is Lord of all. Swift are wing-ing An - gels sing-ing,
Tid - ings of a gos-pel true. Thus re - joic - ing, Free from sor-row,
No - els ring-ing, Tid - ings bring-ing: Christ the babe is Lord of all.
Prais-es voic-ing Greet the mor-row: Christ the babe was born for you.

Text: Polish carol; para. by Edith M. G. Reed, 1885-1933
Tune: W ZLOBIE LEZY, 44 7 44 7 4444 7; Polish carol; harm. by A. E. Rusbridge, 1917-1969, © Bristol Churches Housing Assoc. Ltd.

The Virgin Mary Had a Baby Boy 378

1. The vir - gin Mar - y had a ba - by boy, the vir - gin Mar - y had a ba - by boy, the vir - gin Mar - y had a ba - by boy, and they say that his name was Je - sus.
2. The an - gels sang when the ba - by born, the an - gels sang when the ba - by born, the an - gels sang when the ba - by born, and they say that his name was Je - sus.
3. The wise men saw where the ba - by born, the wise men saw where the ba - by born, the wise men went where the ba - by born, and they say that his name was Je - sus.
He come from the glo - ry, he come from the glo-rious king-dom.
Oh, yes! be-liev - er! Oh, yes! be-liev - er!
Oh, Oh,
He come from the glo-ry, he come from the glo-rious king-dom.

Text: West Indian carol, © 1945, Boosey and Co., Ltd.
Tune: West Indian carol, © 1945, Boosey and Co., Ltd.; acc. by Robert J. Batastini, b.1942, © 1993, GIA Publications, Inc.

379 It Came upon the Midnight Clear

1. It came up - on the mid - night clear, That
2. Still through the clo - ven skies they come, With
3. Yet with the woes of sin and strife, The
4. For, lo, the days are has - t'ning on, By
glo - rious song of old, From an - gels bend - ing
peace - ful wings un - furled, And still their heav'n - ly
world has suf - fered long; Be - neath the heav'n - ly
proph - ets seen of old, When with the ev - er -
near the earth To touch their harps of gold: "Peace
mu - sic floats O'er all the wea - ry world: A -
hymn have rolled Two thou - sand years of wrong; And
cir - cling years Shall come the time fore - told, When
on the earth, good will to all From
bove its sad and low - ly plains They
war - ring hu - man - kind hears not The
peace shall o - ver all the earth Its

heav'n's all gra - cious King"; The world in sol - emn
bend on hov - 'ring wing, And ev - er o'er its
tid - ings which they bring; O hush the noise and
an - cient splen - dors fling, And all the world give
still - ness lay, To hear the an - gels sing.
Ba - bel sounds The bless - ed an - gels sing.
cease your strife And hear the an - gels sing.
back the song Which now the an - gels sing.

Text: Edmund H. Sears, 1810-1876, alt.
Tune: CAROL, CMD; Richard S. Willis, 1819-1900

380 Once in Royal David's City

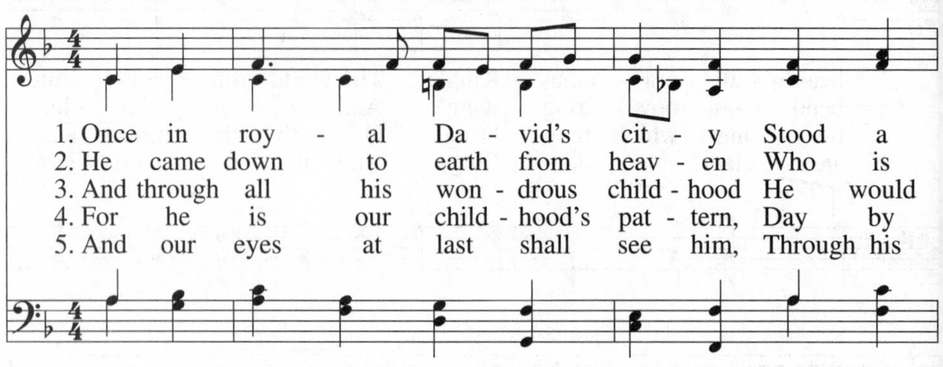
1. Once in roy - al Da - vid's cit - y Stood a
2. He came down to earth from heav - en Who is
3. And through all his won - drous child - hood He would
4. For he is our child - hood's pat - tern, Day by
5. And our eyes at last shall see him, Through his

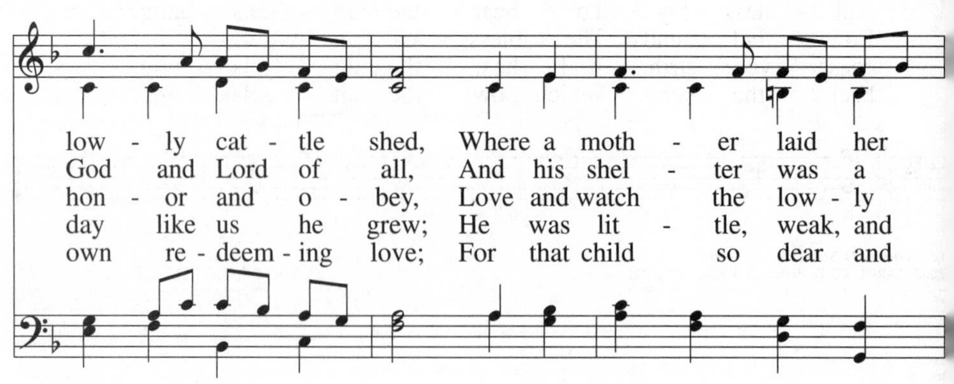
low - ly cat - tle shed, Where a moth - er laid her
God and Lord of all, And his shel - ter was a
hon - or and o - bey, Love and watch the low - ly
day like us he grew; He was lit - tle, weak, and
own re - deem - ing love; For that child so dear and

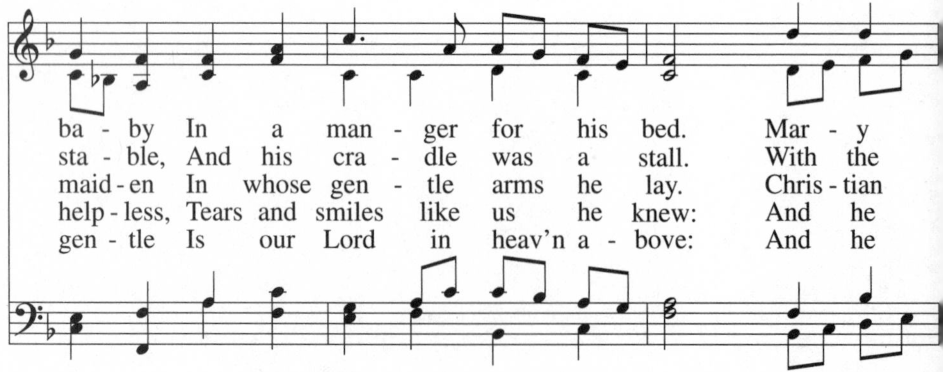
ba - by In a man - ger for his bed. Mar - y
sta - ble, And his cra - dle was a stall. With the
maid - en In whose gen - tle arms he lay. Chris - tian
help - less, Tears and smiles like us he knew: And he
gen - tle Is our Lord in heav'n a - bove: And he

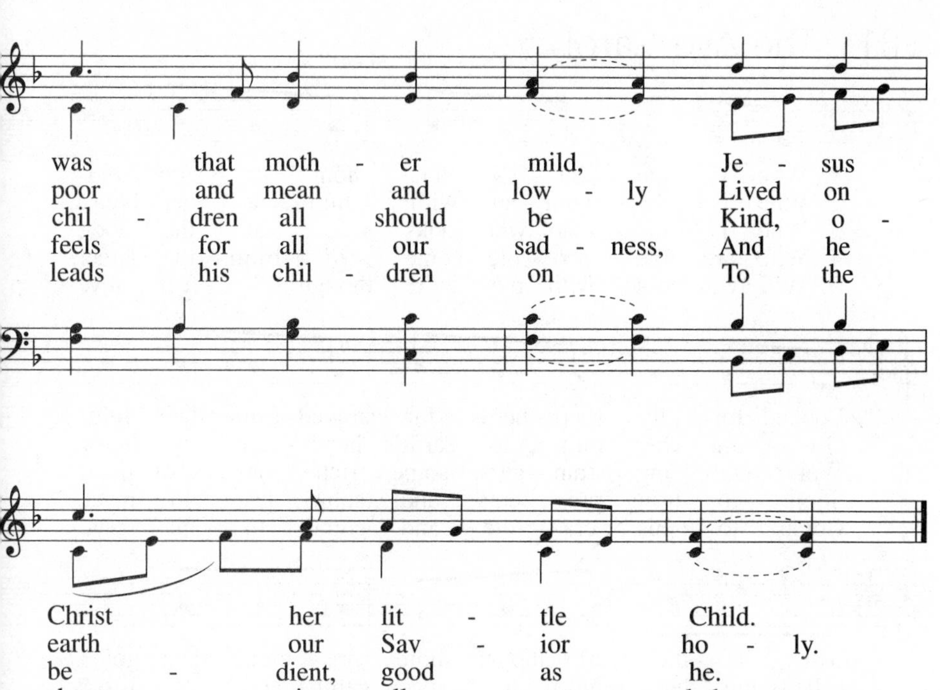
was that moth - er mild, Je - sus
poor and mean and low - ly Lived on
chil - dren all should be Kind, o -
feels for all our sad - ness, And he
leads his chil - dren on To the
Christ her lit - tle Child.
earth our Sav - ior ho - ly.
be - dient, good as he.
shares in all our glad - ness.
place where he has gone.

ext: Cecil Frances Alexander, 1818-1895
une: IRBY, 8 7 8 7 77; Henry J. Gauntlett, 1805-1876; harm. by Arthur H. Mann, 1850-1929.

381 The Aye Carol

1. Who is the ba - by an hour or two old
Looked for by shep - herds far strayed from their fold,
Lost in the world though more pre - cious than gold?
This is God with us in Je - sus.

2. Who is the wom - an with child at her breast,
Giv - ing her milk to earth's heav - en - ly guest,
Tell - ing her mind to be calm and at rest?
Mar - y, the moth - er of Je - sus.

3. Who is the man who looks on at the door,
Wel - com - ing stran - gers, some rich but most poor,
Scan - ning the world as if some - how un - sure?
Jo - seph, the fa - ther of Je - sus.

4. Who are the peo - ple come in from the street,
Some to bring pres - ents and some just to meet,
Join - ing their song to what an - gels re - peat?
These are the new friends of Je - sus.

5. Will you come with me, ev'n though I feel shy,
Come to his cra - dle and come to his cry,
Give him your nod or your "yes" or your "aye,"
Give what you can give to Je - sus?

Final ending

Text: John L. Bell, b.1949
Tune: AYE CAROL, 10 10 10 8; John L. Bell, b.1949

382 We Three Kings of Orient Are

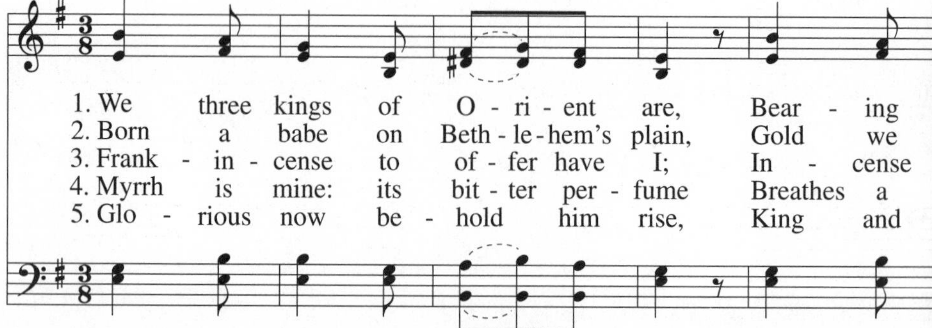

1. We three kings of O - ri - ent are, Bear - ing
2. Born a babe on Beth - le - hem's plain, Gold we
3. Frank - in - cense to of - fer have I; In - cense
4. Myrrh is mine: its bit - ter per - fume Breathes a
5. Glo - rious now be - hold him rise, King and

gifts we trav - erse a - far Field and foun - tain,
bring to crown him a - gain; King for - ev - er,
owns a De - i - ty nigh, Prayer and prais - ing
life of gath - 'ring gloom; Sor - rowing, sigh - ing,
God and sac - ri - fice: Heav'n sings, "Hal - le -
Moor and moun - tain, Fol - low - ing yon - der star.
Ceas - ing nev - er, O - ver us all to reign.
Glad - ly rais - ing, Wor - ship - ing God on high.
Bleed - ing, dy - ing, Sealed in the stone cold tomb.
lu - jah!" "Hal - le - lu - jah!" earth re - plies.
O star of won - der, star of night, Star with
roy - al beau - ty bright, West - ward lead - ing,
still pro - ceed - ing, Guide us to the per - fect Light.

Text: Matthew 2:1-11; John H. Hopkins, Jr., 1820-1891
Tune: KINGS OF ORIENT, 88 44 6 with refrain; John H. Hopkins, Jr., 1820-1891

383 Songs of Thankfulness and Praise

1. Songs of thank-ful-ness and praise, Je-sus, Lord, to
2. Man-i-fest at Jor-dan's stream, Proph-et, Priest, and
3. Man-i-fest in mak-ing whole Pal-sied limbs and
4. Grant us grace to see you, Lord, Mir-rored in your
you we raise, Man-i-fest-ed by the star
King su-preme; And at Ca-na, wed-ding guest,
faint-ing soul; Man-i-fest in val-iant fight,
ho-ly word; May we im-i-tate you now,
To the sag-es from a-far; Branch of roy-al
In your God-head man-i-fest; Man-i-fest in
Quell-ing all the dev-il's might; Man-i-fest in
And on us your grace en-dow; That we like to
Da-vid's stem In your birth at Beth-le-hem;
pow'r di-vine, Chang-ing wa-ter in-to wine;
gra-cious will, Ev-er bring-ing good from ill;
you may be At your great e-piph-a-ny;

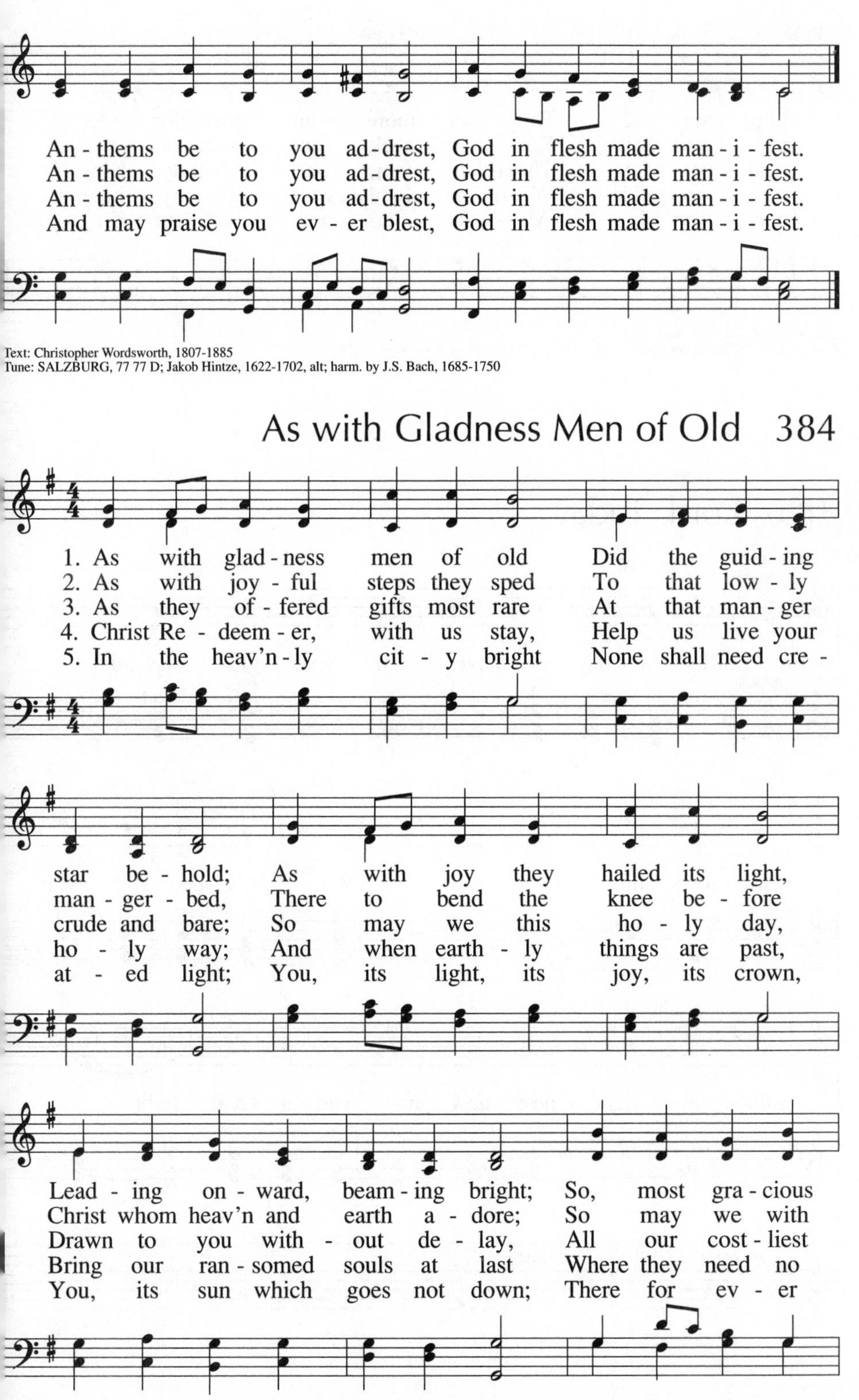
An - thems be to you ad - drest, God in flesh made man - i - fest.
An - thems be to you ad - drest, God in flesh made man - i - fest.
An - thems be to you ad - drest, God in flesh made man - i - fest.
And may praise you ev - er blest, God in flesh made man - i - fest.
Text: Christopher Wordsworth, 1807-1885
Tune: SALZBURG, 77 77 D; Jakob Hintze, 1622-1702, alt; harm. by J.S. Bach, 1685-1750
As with Gladness Men of Old 384
1. As with glad - ness men of old Did the guid - ing star be - hold; As with joy they hailed its light, Lead - ing on - ward, beam - ing bright; So, most gra - cious
2. As with joy - ful steps they sped To that low - ly man - ger - bed, There to bend the knee be - fore Christ whom heav'n and earth a - dore; So may we with
3. As they of - fered gifts most rare At that man - ger crude and bare; So may we this ho - ly day, Drawn to you with - out de - lay, All our cost - liest
4. Christ Re - deem - er, with us stay, Help us live your ho - ly way; And when earth - ly things are past, Bring our ran - somed souls at last Where they need no
5. In the heav'n - ly cit - y bright None shall need cre - at - ed light; You, its light, its joy, its crown, You, its sun which goes not down; There for ev - er

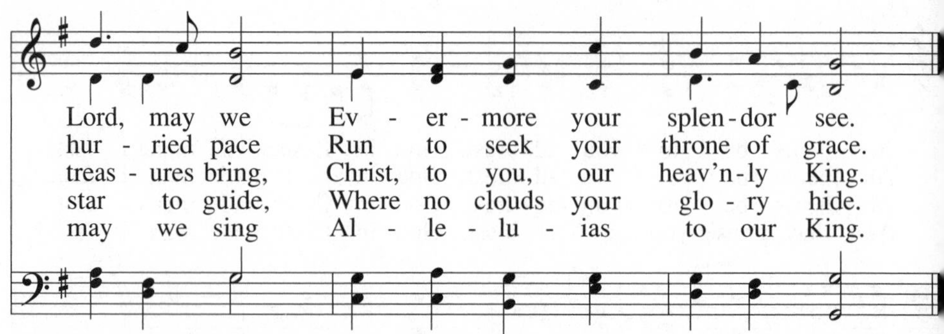
Lord, may we Ev - er - more your splen - dor see.
hur - ried pace Run to seek your throne of grace.
treas - ures bring, Christ, to you, our heav'n - ly King.
star to guide, Where no clouds your glo - ry hide.
may we sing Al - le - lu - ias to our King.

Text: William C. Dix, 1837-1898
Tune: DIX, 77 77 77; arr. from Conrad Kocher, 1786-1872, by William H. Monk, 1823-1889

385 Lord, Today

Refrain

Melody:

Harmony:

Lord, to - day we have seen your glo - ry, dawn fol - lows the night. We, your peo - ple who walked in dark - ness now have seen a great light.

To verses | *Last time*

Verses
1. A child is born, a Son giv - en us,
2. The Lord is king, the na - tions re - joice,
3. O Beth - le - hem, you are from of old,
4. The days will come, the Lord prom - ised us,
5. New light has dawned up - on all the just,
on him do - min - ion shall rest. His name shall
let all God's peo - ple be glad. The heav - ens pro -
too small a - mong Ju - dah's clans. From you shall
when God would raise up a shoot to rule the
glad - ness for up - right of heart. Re - joice in the
Melody:
be Won - der - ful God, Coun - sel - or,
claim jus - tice for all. Glo - ry has
come a rul - er this day, shep - herd to
land, reign as a king, whose name is
Lord, you faith - ful ones. Give thanks to
Harmony:
D.C.
Prince of Peace.
filled the land.
guide the land.
Lord the Just.
God's great name.

Text: Mike Balhoff, b.1946
Tune: Darryl Ducote, b.1945, Gary Daigle, b.1957

386 Epiphany Carol

1. Ev - 'ry na - tion sees the glo - ry Of a
2. Ev - 'ry tongue shall sing the prais - es Of his
3. Once a - gain may we dis - cov - er Word made
4. Gath - er, God, the world to - geth - er In the
star that pierced the night. As we tell the won-drous
birth in deep - est night. He is heal - ing for the
flesh sent from a - bove. In our neigh - bor, sis - ter,
bright - ness of your day. Fill our hearts with joy for -
sto - ry We are bathed in ra - diant light.
a - ges; He is Christ, our God's de - light.
broth - er, In the lone - ly and un - loved.
ev - er; Help us walk the ho - ly way.
Star sent forth from high - est heav - en, Danc-ing
He pro - claims with - in his be - ing All our
May we touch him, may we hold him, May we
May your jus - tice rule the na - tions; May all

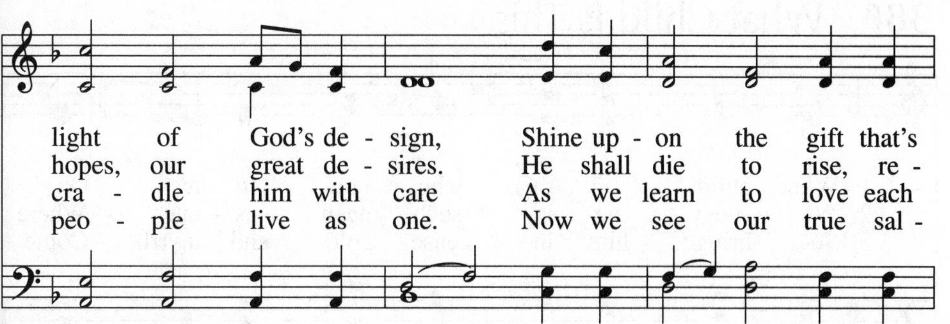
light of God's de - sign, Shine up - on the gift that's
hopes, our great de - sires. He shall die to rise, re -
cra - dle him with care As we learn to love each
peo - ple live as one. Now we see our true sal -

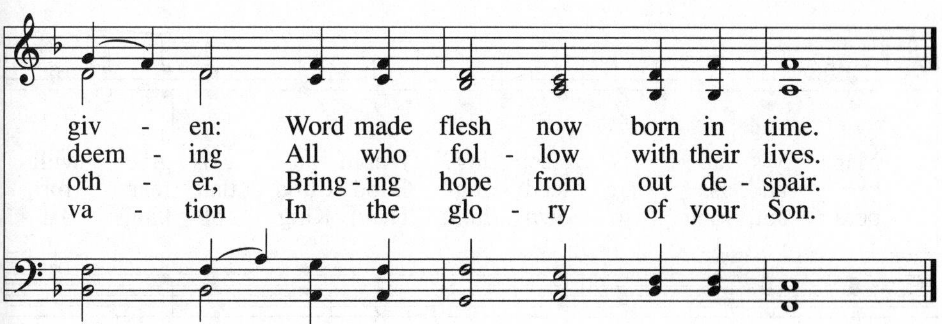
giv - en: Word made flesh now born in time.
deem - ing All who fol - low with their lives.
oth - er, Bring - ing hope from out de - spair.
va - tion In the glo - ry of your Son.

Text: Francis Patrick O'Brien, b.1958,
Tune: BEACH SPRING, 8 7 8 7 D; *The Sacred Harp*, 1844; harm. by Ronald A. Nelson, b.1927,

387 What Child Is This

1. What child is this, who, laid to rest, On Mar - y's lap is sleep - ing? Whom an - gels greet with an - thems sweet, While shep - herds watch are keep - ing?
2. Why lies he in such mean es - tate Where ox and ass are feed - ing? Good Chris - tian, fear; for sin - ners here The si - lent Word is plead - ing.
3. So bring him in - cense, gold and myrrh, Come peas - ant, king to own him; The King of kings sal - va - tion brings, Let lov - ing hearts en - throne him.
This, this is Christ the King, Whom shep - herds guard and an - gels sing;

Haste, haste to bring him laud, The babe, the son of Mar - y.

Text: William C. Dix, 1827-1898
Tune: GREENSLEEVES, 8 7 8 7 with refrain; English Melody, 16th C.; harm. by John Stainer, 1840-1901

The First Nowell 388

1. The first Now - ell, the an - gel did say, Was to
2. They look - ed up and saw a star Shin-ing
3. And by the light of that same star Three
4. This star drew nigh to the north - west, O'er
5. Then en - tered in those wise men three, Full
6. Then let us all with one ac - cord Sing

cer - tain poor shep - herds in fields as they lay; In
in the east, be - yond them far, And
wise men came from coun - try far; To
Beth - le - hem it took its rest; And
rev - 'rent - ly up - on their knee, And
prais - es to our heav - 'nly Lord; Who

fields where they lay keep - ing their sheep, On a
to the earth it gave great light, And
seek for a king was their in - tent, And to
there it did both stop and stay, Right
of - fered there, in his pres - ence, Their
with the Fa - ther we a - dore And
cold win - ter's night that was so deep.
so it con - tin - ued both day and night.
fol - low the star where - ev - er it went.
o - ver the place where Je - sus lay.
gold and myrrh and frank - in - cense.
Spir - it blest for ev - er - more.
Now - ell, Now - ell, Now - ell, Now - ell,
Born is the King of Is - ra - el.

Text: English Carol, 17th C.
Tune: THE FIRST NOWELL, Irregular; English Melody; harm. from *Christmas Carols New and Old,* 1871

What Star Is This 389

1. What star is this with beams so bright, More lovely than the noonday light? 'Tis sent to announce a newborn king, Glad tidings of our God to bring.
2. 'Tis now fulfilled what God decreed, "From Jacob shall a star proceed"; And lo! the eastern sages stand, To read in heav'n the Lord's command.
3. O Jesus, while the star of grace Impels us on to seek your face, Let not our slothful hearts refuse The guidance of your light to use.
4. To God Creator, heav'nly light, To Christ, revealed in earthly night, To God the Spirit blest we raise An endless song of thankful praise!

Text: *Quem stella sole pulchrior,* Charles Coffin, 1676-1749; tr. by John Chandler, 1806-1876, alt.
Tune: PUER NOBIS, LM; adapt. by Michael Praetorius, 1571-1621

390 When John Baptized by Jordan's River

1. When John bap - tized by Jor - dan's riv - er In faith and
2. There as the Lord, bap - tized and pray - ing, Rose from the
3. O Son of Man, our na - ture shar - ing, In whose o -
hope the peo - ple came, That John and Jor - dan might de -
stream, the sin - less one, A voice was heard from heav - en
be - dience all are blest, Sav - ior, our sins and sor - rows
liv - er Their trou - bled souls from sin and shame.
say - ing, "This is my own be - lov - ed Son."
bear - ing, Hear us and grant us this re - quest:
They came to seek a new be - gin - ning, The hu - man
There as the Fa - ther's word was spo - ken, Not in the
Dai - ly to grow, by grace de - fend - ed, Filled with the

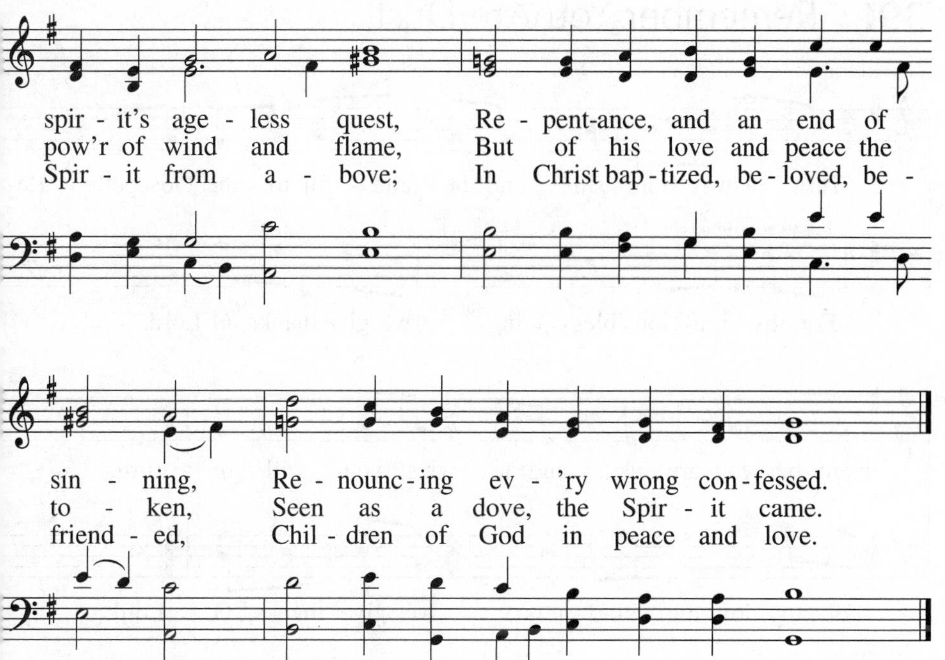
spir - it's age - less quest, Re - pent-ance, and an end of
pow'r of wind and flame, But of his love and peace the
Spir - it from a - bove; In Christ bap - tized, be - loved, be -
sin - ning, Re - nounc - ing ev - 'ry wrong con - fessed.
to - ken, Seen as a dove, the Spir - it came.
friend - ed, Chil - dren of God in peace and love.

Text: Timothy Dudley-Smith, b.1926,
Tune: RENDEZ À DIEU, 9 8 9 8 D; Louis Bourgeois, c.1510-1561

391 Remember You Are Dust

Refrain
Melody:
Turn a-way from sin and be faith - ful to the Gos-pel. Re - mem-ber you are dust, and to dust you will re - turn.
Counter melody (optional):
For thy gra-cious bless - ing we give thanks, O Lord.
For thy lov-ing kind-ness we give thanks, O Lord.
To verses
Cantor:
1.-4. Re-
Last time
Verses
pent, the king-dom is at hand.
All:
Re-pent, the king-dom is at hand.
*Cantor:
1. Rend your hearts, not your gar-ments.
2. Blow the trum - pet in Zi - on.
3. For - give one an - oth - er.
4. Now, the day of sal - va - tion.
Now, the ac-cept-a-ble time.
All:
Now, the ac - cept - a - ble time.
D.C.

Additional verse tropes for the season of Lent:

eek the God of compassion…
.ive in kindness and mercy…
'rust in God and be faithful…
'raise the God of salvation…
.et us bow down in worship…

Dust and Ashes 392

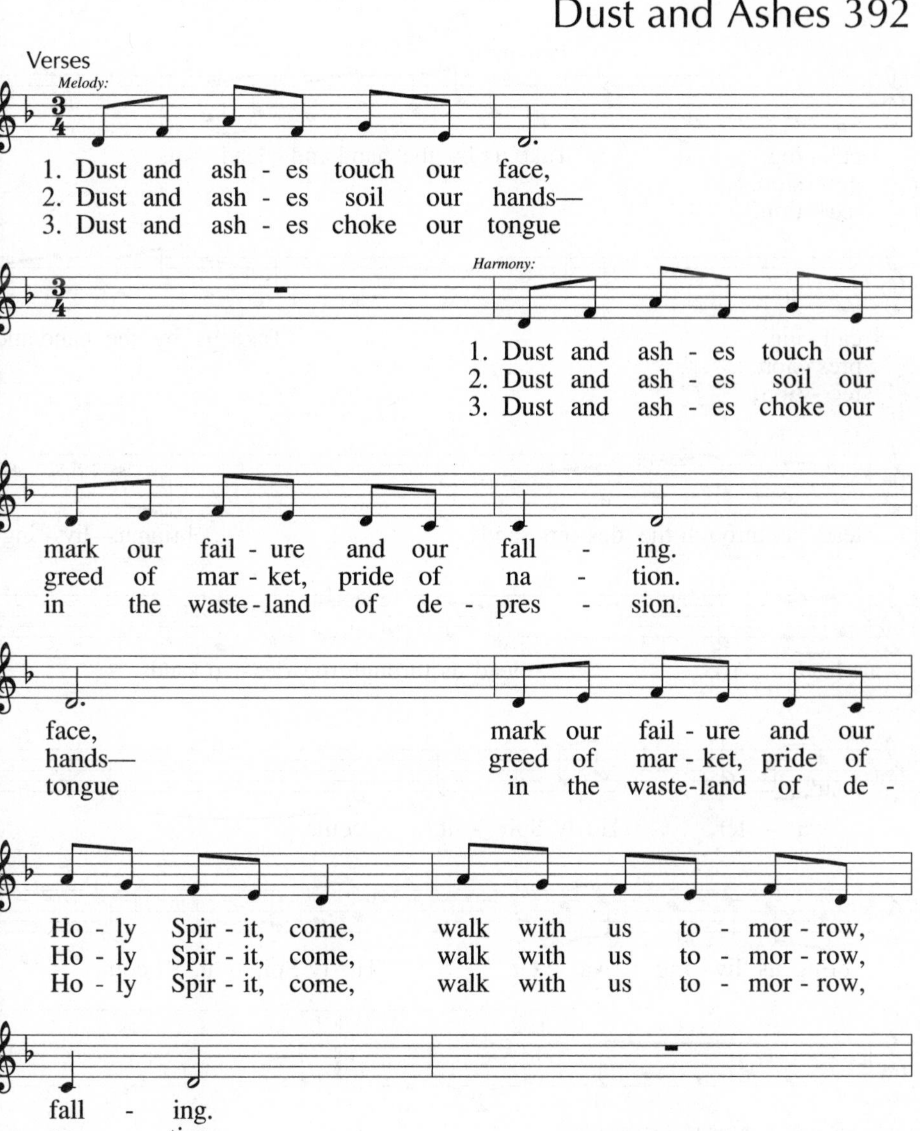
Verses
Melody:
1. Dust and ash - es touch our face,
2. Dust and ash - es soil our hands—
3. Dust and ash - es choke our tongue
Harmony:
1. Dust and ash - es touch our
2. Dust and ash - es soil our
3. Dust and ash - es choke our
mark our fail - ure and our fall - ing.
greed of mar - ket, pride of na - tion.
in the waste-land of de - pres - sion.
face,
hands—
tongue
mark our fail - ure and our
greed of mar - ket, pride of
in the waste-land of de -
Ho - ly Spir - it, come, walk with us to - mor - row,
Ho - ly Spir - it, come, walk with us to - mor - row,
Ho - ly Spir - it, come, walk with us to - mor - row,
fall - ing.
na - tion.
pres - sion.

take us as dis - ci - ples, washed and wak - ened by your
as we pray and strug - gle through the mesh - es of op -
through all gloom and griev - ing to the paths of res - ur -
take us as dis - ci - ples, washed and wak - ened by your
as we pray and strug - gle through the mesh - es of op -
through all gloom and griev - ing to the paths of res - ur -
Refrain
call - ing.
pres - sion.
rec - tion.
Take us by the hand and lead us,
call - ing.
pres - sion.
rec - tion.
Take us by the hand and
lead us through the des - ert sands,
bring us liv - ing
lead us,
lead us through the des - ert sands,
wa - ter, Ho-ly Spir - it, come.
bring us liv - ing wa - ter, Ho-ly Spir - it, come.
1.-2.
3.

Text: Brian Wren, b.1936, © 1989, Hope Publishing Co.
Tune: David Haas, b.1957, © 1991, GIA Publications, Inc.

Crucem Tuam / O Lord, Your Cross 393

Melody:
Cru - cem tu - am a - do - ra - mus Do - mi -
O Lord, your cross, we a - dore and glo - ri -
Harmony:
ne, re - sur - re - cti - o - nem tu - am lau - da - mus Do - mi -
fy, for your ho - ly res - ur - rec - tion, we praise you Lord of
ne. Lau - da - mus et glo - ri - fi - ca - mus.
life. We praise you and we glo - ri - fy you.
Re - sur - re - cti - o - nem tu - am lau - da - mus Do - mi - ne.
For your ho - ly res - ur - rec - tion, we praise you Lord of life.

Text: Taizé Community, 1991
Tune: Jacques Berthier, 1923-1994

394 Somebody's Knockin' at Your Door

Some-bod - y's knock-in' at your door; Some-bod - y's
knock-in' at your door; O sin - ner, why don't you
an-swer? Some-bod - y's knock-in' at your door.
Solo:
All:
1. Knocks like Je - sus,
2. Can't you hear him?
3. Je - sus calls you,
4. Can't you trust him?
Some-bod - y's knock-in' at your door.

Solo:
All:
Knocks like Je - sus,
Can't you hear him?
Je - sus calls you,
Can't you trust him?
Some-bod - y's knock-in' at your door.
O sin - ner, why don't you an - swer?
Some-bod - y's knock - in' at your door.

Text: African-American spiritual
Tune: SOMEBODY'S KNOCKIN', Irregular; African-American spiritual; harm. by Richard Proulx, b.1937,

395 Seek the Lord

Refrain
Descant:
Seek the Lord while he may be found;
Melody:
Seek the Lord while he may be found;
Bass:
call to him while he is still near.
1.- 3. To verses
Last time
call to him while he is still near.
Verses 1, 2
Melody:
1. To-day is the day and now the pro-per hour to for-
2. As high as the sky is a-bove the earth, so
Harmony:

D.C.
sake our sin - ful lives and turn to the Lord.
high a - bove our ways, the ways of the Lord.
Verse 3
3. Find-ing the Lord, let us cling to him. His
words, his ways lead us to life.
D.C.
Verse 4
4. Some day we'll live in the house of God;
gaze on his face and praise his name.
D.C.

Text: Isaiah 55:6-9; Roc O'Connor, SJ, b.1949
Tune: Roc O'Connor, SJ, b.1949; arr. by Peter Felice, alt.

396 The Cross of Jesus

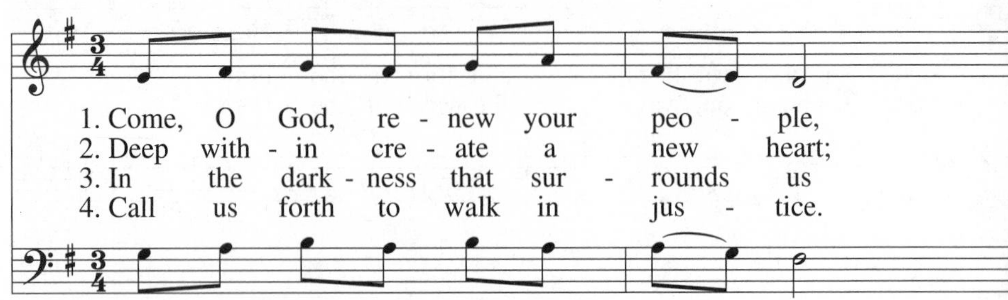
1. Come, O God, re - new your peo - ple,
2. Deep with - in cre - ate a new heart;
3. In the dark - ness that sur - rounds us
4. Call us forth to walk in jus - tice.

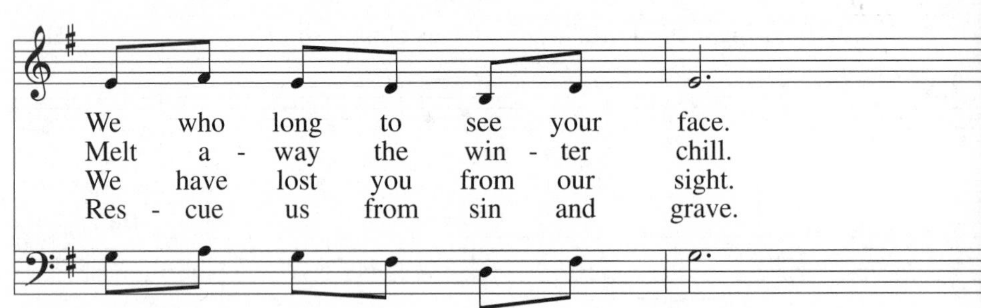
We who long to see your face.
Melt a - way the win - ter chill.
We have lost you from our sight.
Res - cue us from sin and grave.

Strength - en hearts that have grown fee - ble;
Help us now to make a new start,
E - ven though your love has found us,
Through the pow - er of your Spir - it,

Fill our lives with truth and grace.
Help us now to know your will.
We em - brace the powers of night.
Breathe in us the breath that saves.

On - ly you can win our free - dom;
Washed in wa - ters of for - giv - ness,
Scat - ter now our deep - est dark - ness.
Strength - en us in our com - mun - ion,
On - ly you can bring us peace.
Cleansed in wa - ters of new birth,
Guide our hearts in - to the light.
One in Word and cup and bread.
On - ly in the cross of Je - sus
Lead us to the cross of Je - sus,
Join us to the cross of Je - sus.
Here with - in the cross of Je - sus,
Will the cap - tives find re - lease.
Bring - ing life to all the earth.
Help us set our liv - ing right.
All who hun - ger will be fed.
Last time

Text: Francis Patrick O'Brien, b.1958
Tune: Francis Patrick O'Brien, b.1958

397 The Glory of These Forty Days

1. The glo - ry of these for - ty days
2. A - lone and fast - ing Mo - ses saw
3. So Dan - iel trained his mys - tic sight,
4. Then grant that we like them be true,
We cel - e - brate with songs of praise;
The lov - ing God who gave the law;
De - liv - ered from the li - on's might;
Con - sumed in fast and prayer with you;
For Christ, by whom all things were made,
And to E - li - jah, fast - ing, came
And John, the Bride - groom's friend, be - came
Our spir - its strength - en with your grace,
Him - self has fast - ed and has prayed.
The steeds and char - i - ots of flame.
The her - ald of Mes - si - ah's name.
And give us joy to see your face.

Text: Clarum decus jejunii; Gregory the Great, c. 540-604; tr. by Maurice F. Bell, 1862-1947, © Oxford University Press
Tune: OLD HUNDREDTH, LM; Louis Bourgeois, c.1510-1561

Hold Us in Your Mercy: Penitential Litany 398

Cantor:
All:
Hold us in your mer - cy. Hold us in your mer - cy.

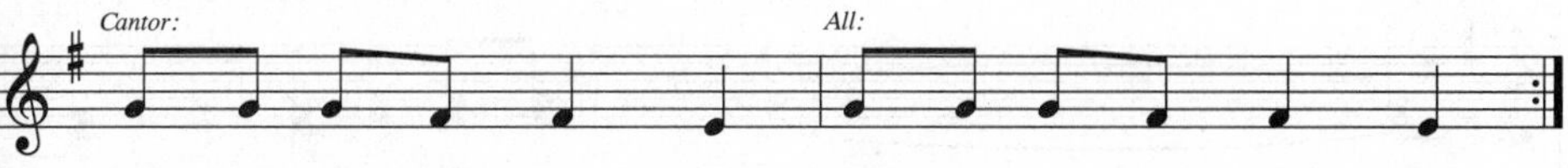
Cantor:
All:
Hold us in your mer - cy. Hold us in your mer - cy.

Verses 1-3

Cantor:
All:
1. Mak - er's love poured out from heav - en.
2. Born as one of home - less pil - grims. Hold us in your mer - cy.
3. You who shared the sin - ner's ta - ble.

Cantor:
All:
Mer - cy's word - made - flesh a - mong us.
Sent to bring the poor good news. Hold us in your mer - cy.
You who cleansed the lep - er's flesh.

Verses 4-7

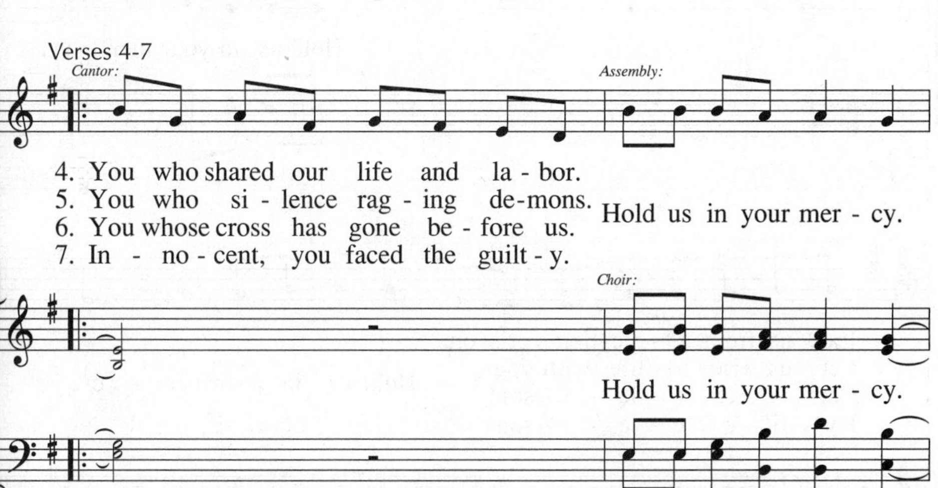
Cantor:
Assembly:
4. You who shared our life and la - bor.
5. You who si - lence rag - ing de-mons. Hold us in your mer - cy.
6. You whose cross has gone be - fore us.
7. In - no - cent, you faced the guilt - y.
Choir:
Hold us in your mer - cy.

Cantor:
Assembly:
You who chose to walk our roads.
You who bid the storm be si-lent.
You who bear our cross with us,
One in death with us for-ev-er.
Hold us in your mer-cy.
Hold us in your mer-cy.
Verses 8-11
Cantor:
Assembly:
8. Come and break the chains that bind us.
9. Break the pow-er of the dark-ness.
10. Ky-ri-e e-le-i-son!
11. Ky-ri-e e-le-i-son!
Hold us in your mer-cy.
Choir:
Hold us in your mer-cy.
Cantor:
Assembly:
Free us from ad-dic-tion's pris-on.
Let us rise to life with you.
Chri-ste e-le-i-son!
Ky-ri-e e-le-i-son!
Hold us in your mer-cy.
Hold us in your mer-cy.

Cantor:
Assembly:
Cantor:
Hold us in your mer-cy. Hold us in your mer-cy. Hold us in your mer-cy.
Hold us in your mer - cy.
Assembly:
Cantor:
Hold us in your mer - cy. Hold us in your mer - cy.
Hold us in your mer - cy.
Assembly:
repeat as desired
Hold us in your mer - cy.
repeat as desired
Hold us in your mer - cy.

Text: Rory Cooney, b.1952
Tune: Gary Daigle, b.1957

399 Jerusalem, My Destiny

Refrain
I have fixed my eyes on your hills, Je - ru - sa - lem, my
des - ti - ny! Though I can - not see the end for me, I
can - not turn a - way. We have set our hearts for the
way; this jour - ney is our des - ti - ny. Let
no - one walk a - lone. The jour - ney makes us one.
Last time
Last time

Verses
1. Oth - er spir - its, less - er gods, have court - ed
2. See, I leave the past be - hind; a new land
3. In my thirst, you let me drink the wa - ters
4. All the worlds I have not seen you o - pen
5. To the tombs I went to mourn the hope I
me with lies. Here a - mong you
calls to me. Here a - mong you
of your life. Here a - mong you
to my view. Here a - mong you
thought was gone. Here a - mong you
D.C.
I have found a truth which bids me rise.
now I find a glimpse of what might be.
I have met the sav - ior, Je - sus Christ.
I have found a vi - sion, bright and new.
I a - woke to un - ex - pect - ed dawn.

Text: Rory Cooney, b.1952
Tune: Rory Cooney, b.1952

400 Adoramus Te Christe

Canon Refrain *

1\. A - do - ra - mus te Chri - ste, 2. a - do - ra - mus te Chri - ste,
3\. a - do - ra - mus te Chri - ste, a - do - ra - mus Chri - ste.

Verses

1\. A - do - ra - mus te Chri - ste, et be - ne - di - ci - mus ti - bi,
2\. Qui - a per san - ctam Cru - cem tu - am re - de - mi - sti mun - dum.

** This refrain can be used as descant to the final verse of "Tree of Life."*

Text: Antiphon from Good Friday Liturgy; *We adore you, O Christ, and we bless you, because by your holy cross you have redeemed the world.*
Tune: Marty Haugen, b.1950, © 1984, GIA Publications, Inc.

401 Tree of Life

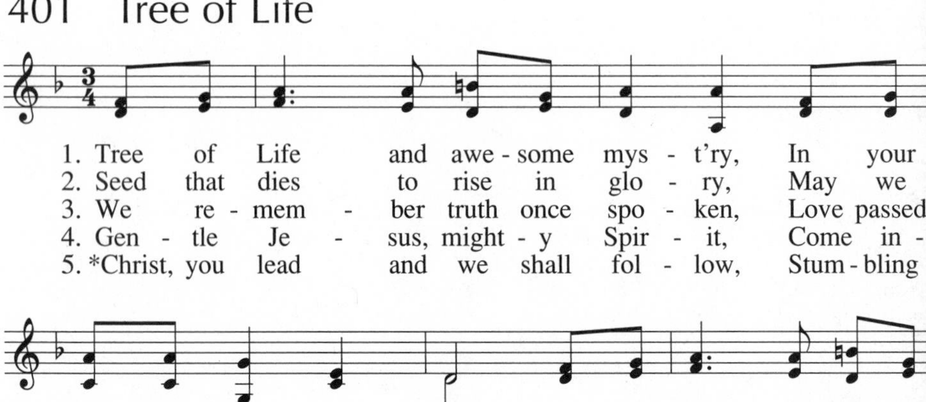
1. Tree of Life and awe - some mys - t'ry, In your
2. Seed that dies to rise in glo - ry, May we
3. We re - mem - ber truth once spo - ken, Love passed
4. Gen - tle Je - sus, might - y Spir - it, Come in -
5. *Christ, you lead and we shall fol - low, Stum - bling

death we are re - born, Though you die in all of
see our - selves in you, If we learn to live your
on through act and word, Ev - 'ry per - son lost and
flame our hearts a - new, We may all your joy in -
though our steps may be, One with you in joy and

**The refrain "Adoramus Te Christe" can be used as a descant to the final stanza of this hymn*

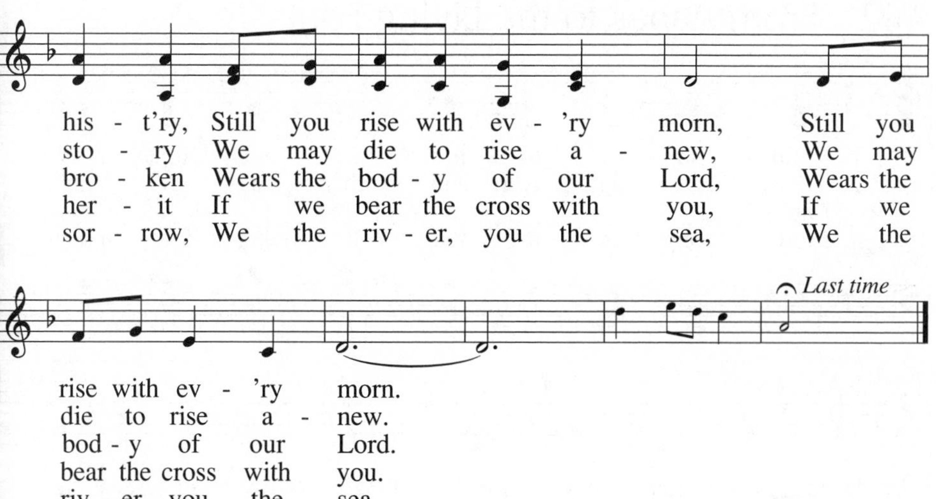
his - t'ry, Still you rise with ev - 'ry morn, Still you
sto - ry We may die to rise a - new, We may
bro - ken Wears the bod - y of our Lord, Wears the
her - it If we bear the cross with you, If we
sor - row, We the riv - er, you the sea, We the
Last time
rise with ev - 'ry morn.
die to rise a - new.
bod - y of our Lord.
bear the cross with you.
riv - er, you the sea.

Lenten Verses:

General: Light of life beyond conceiving, Mighty Spirit of our Lord;
Give new strength to our believing, Give us faith to live your word.

1st Sunday: From the dawning of creation, You have loved us as your own;
Stay with us through all temptation, Make us turn to you alone.

2nd Sunday: In our call to be a blessing, May we be a blessing true;
May we live and die confessing Christ as Lord of all we do.

3rd Sunday: Living Water of salvation, Be the fountain of each soul;
Springing up in new creation, Flow in us and make us whole.

4th Sunday: Give us eyes to see you clearly, Make us children of your light;
Give us hearts to live more nearly As your gospel shining bright.

5th Sunday: God of all our fear and sorrow, God who lives beyond our death;
Hold us close through each tomorrow, Love as near as every breath.

Text: Marty Haugen, b.1950
Tune: THOMAS, 8 7 8 77; Marty Haugen, b.1950

402 From Ashes to the Living Font

1. From ash - es to the liv - ing font Your Church must jour - ney, Lord, Bap - tized in grace, in grace re - newed By your most ho - ly word.
2. Through fast - ing, prayer, and char - i - ty Your voice speaks deep with - in, Re - turn - ing us to ways of truth And turn - ing us from sin.
3. (below)
4. From ash - es to the liv - ing font, Your Church must jour - ney still, Through cross and tomb to Eas - ter joy, In Spir - it - fire ful - filled.

Sundays I & II

3. From desert to the mountaintop
In Christ our way we see,
So, tempered by temptation's might
We might transfigured be.

Sunday III

3. For thirsting hearts let waters flow
Our fainting souls revive;
And at the well your waters give
Our everlasting life.

Sunday IV

3. We sit beside the road and plead,
"Come, save us, David's son!"
Now with your vision heal our eyes,
The world's true Light alone.

Sunday V

3. Our graves split open, bring us back,
Your promise to proclaim;
To darkened tombs call out, "Arise!"
And glorify your name.

Text: Alan J. Hommerding, b.1956,
Tune: ST. FLAVIAN, CM; *John's Day Psalter,* 1562; harm. based on the original *faux-bourdon* setting

Jesus, the Lord 403

Refrain
Descant:
Je - sus. Je - sus.
Melody:
Let all cre - a - tion bend the knee to the
Lord.
1.-3. To verses
4.
Verse 1
1. In him we live, we move and have our be-ing; in him the
Christ, in him the King. Je - sus, the Lord.
D.C.
Verses 2, 3
2. Though Son, he did not cling to god - li - ness; but emp-tied him-
3. He lived o-be-dient-ly his Fa-ther's will ac - cept-ing his
self, be - came a slave!
death, death on a tree!
Je - sus, the Lord.
D.C.

Text: *Jesus Prayer,* Philippians 2:5-11; Acts 17:28; Roc O'Connor, SJ, b.1949
Tune: Roc O'Connor, SJ, b.1949; arr. by Rick Modlin, b.1966

404 Stations of the Cross

*Kneel-ing in the gar - den grass, Je - sus groans a - gainst his death, Let this cup of sor - row pass, While he prays in that same breath: Not my will but yours be done.
1. While the court and priests con-spire How to slant the ev - i - dence Je - sus calm - ly bears their ire As his prayer grows more in - tense:
2. When the mas - sive cross of wood Bends and bruis - es Je - sus' frame Hear him seek e - ter - nal good As he prays in Yah - weh's name:
3. Je - sus falls be - neath the weight Of the cross he's forced to bear Yet its load of sin and hate Do not crush his hope and prayer:

*This stanza begins the devotions. Stanzas 1-14 accompany each station.

1. Jesus is condemned to death

2. Jesus carries his Cross

3. Jesus falls the first time

4. Jesus meets his afflicted mother
Jesus reads in Mary's eyes
all the sorrow mothers bear,
and he prays his friend supplies
grace to strengthen her own prayer:
Not my will but yours be done.

5. Simon of Cyrene helps Jesus to carry his Cross
We with Simon of Cyrene
help the Savior bear the cross.
Step by step we slowly glean
what true faith and prayer will cost:
Not my will but yours be done.

6. Veronica wipes the face of Jesus
Seek the courage and the grace
that Veronica displays
when she wipes the bleeding face
of the one who bravely prays:
Not my will but yours be done.

7. Jesus falls the second time
Jesus trips and falls again
as he struggles through the street
where the mob's unceasing din
mocks the prayer his lips repeat:
Not my will but yours be done.

8. Jesus meets the women of Jersusalem
Christ directs the women's tears
toward the coming judgment day
when God weighs our faithless years
with our willingness to pray:
Not my will but yours be done.

9. Jesus falls a third time
Jesus stumbles one last time
nearly broken by the load
yet by prayer finds strength to climb
Calvary's final stretch of road:
Not my will but yours be done.

10. Jesus is stripped of his clothes
Naked to the sun and clouds
and the jeers and gawking stare
of the soldiers and the crowds
Christ continues with his prayer:
Not my will but yours be done.

11. Jesus is nailed to the Cross
While the soldiers throw their dice
they ignore their victim's groans,
lost to them the sacrifice
and the prayer that Jesus moans:
Not my will but yours be done.

12. Jesus dies on the Cross
Jesus gives one loud last cry
at the moment of his death
while his prayer moves heaven's sky
with his final, parting breath:
Not my will but yours be done.

13. The body of Jesus is taken down from the Cross
As they take the body down
and they wrap it in a sheet
in their hearts they hear the sound
that his lips no more repeat:
Not my will but yours be done.

14. Jesus is laid in the tomb
Quiet is the hollowed cave.
Peace and tears and grief descend.
Mourners offer at the grave
what they learned from Christ their friend:
Not my will but yours be done.

405 Hosea

Verses
1. Come back to me with all your heart.
Trees do bend, 'though straight and tall;
2. The wil - der - ness will lead you
In - teg - ri - ty and jus - tice, With
3. You shall sleep se - cure with peace;
Don't let fear keep us a - part.
so must we to oth - ers' call. (To refrain)
to your heart where I will speak.
ten - der - ness, you shall know. (To refrain)
faith - ful - ness will be your joy. (To refrain)
1.
2. To refrain
Refrain
Long have I wait - ed for your com - ing
home to me and liv - ing deep - ly our new life.
1.- 2.
D.C.
Last time
life.

Text: Hosea 6:1, 3:3, 2:16, 21; Joel 2:12; Gregory Norbet, OSB, b.1940
Tune: Gregory Norbet, OSB, b.1940; arr. by Mary David Callahan, OSB, b.1923

Jesus Walked This Lonesome Valley 406

1. Je - sus walked this lone - some val - ley;
2. We must walk this lone - some val - ley;
3. You must go and stand your tri - al;
He had to walk it by him - self.
We have to walk it by our - selves.
You have to stand it by your - self.
3
Oh, no-bod-y else could walk it for him;
Oh, no-bod-y else can walk it for us;
Oh, no-bod-y else can stand it for you;
He had to walk it by him - self.
We have to walk it by our - selves.
You have to stand it by your - self.

Text: American folk hymn
Tune: LONESOME VALLEY, 8 8 10 8; American folk hymn; harm. by Richard Proulx, b.1937,

407 Again We Keep This Solemn Fast

1. A - gain we keep this sol - emn fast
2. The law and proph - ets from of old
3. More spar - ing, there - fore, let us make
4. Let us a - void each harm - ful way
5. We pray, O bless - ed Three in One,
A gift of faith from a - ges past,
In fig - ured ways this Lent fore - told,
The words we speak, the food we take,
That lures the care - less mind a - stray;
Our God while end - less a - ges run,
This Lent which binds us lov - ing - ly
Which Christ, all a - ges' Lord and Guide,
Our sleep, our laugh - ter, ev - 'ry sense;
By watch - ful prayer our spir - its free
That this, our Lent of for - ty days,
To faith and hope and char - i - ty.
In these last days has sanc - ti - fied.
Learn peace through ho - ly pen - i - tence.
From schem - ing of the En - e - my.
May bring us growth and give you praise.

Text: *Ex more docti mystico;* ascr. to Gregory the Great, c.540-604; tr. by Peter J. Scagnelli, b.1949, ©
Tune: OLD HUNDREDTH, LM; Louis Bourgeois, c.1510-1561

Turn to the Living God 408

Refrain
Turn, turn to the liv - ing God, the God of heal-ing and
Turn, turn, liv - ing God, God of
com - fort, and with de-light, God will turn to
com - fort, with de - light, turn to
you. With de-light, God will turn to
To verses
you.
Final ending
you.
you, de - light, turn to you. you.
Verse 1
1. For now is the time of ful - fill - ment. The
reign of our God is at hand. Re-form your life,
D.C.
turn from sin and be - lieve this glo-rious news.

Verse 2
2. Come, and re - turn to the Lord. All you
wea - ry, bring your griev - ing hearts. With kind - ness and
D.C.
mer - cy God's com - pas - sion will fill your hearts with love.
Verse 3
3. Have mer - cy, O Lord, on your peo - ple. In your
good - ness wipe a - way our guilt. Wash us clean,
D.C.
free us, to be - come your liv - ing song of praise.
Verse 4
4. Come, sing with joy to the Lord.
Lis - ten with an o - pen heart. Hear God's voice and
D.C.
fol - low; our good shep-herd is guid - ing the way.

Text: Lori True, b.1961
Tune: Lori True, b.1961

Lord Jesus Christ 409

Ostinato Refrain
Lord Je - sus Christ, Son of the liv - ing God, have mer - cy on me, a sin - ner, have mer - cy, Lord, have mer - cy.
mer - cy.
Final ending
Verses (Superimposed on Ostinato Refrain)
1. Cre - ate in me a clean heart, O my God. Give me back the joy of your sal - va-tion, Lord.
2. Be mer-ci - ful, O Lord, be mer-ci - ful. Wash me from my guilt. Lord, cleanse me.
3. Re-mem-ber not my of - fen - ses, O God. Cast me not a - way from your pres-ence.
4. You take a - way the sin of the world. Lord, have mer-cy, mer - cy.

Text: *The Jesus Prayer*; verses, Psalm 51 and Agnus Dei, adapt. by Carol E. Browning, b.1956
Tune: Carol E. Browning, b.1956; acc. by Kathy McGrath

410 Return to God

Refrain
Re - turn to God with all your heart, the source of grace and mer - cy; come seek the ten - der faith - ful - ness of
1.
God.
2.
Last time
God.
Last time
Verse 1
1. Now the time of grace has come, the day of sal - va - tion; come and learn now the way of our God.
D.C.
Verse 2
2. I will take your heart of stone and place a heart with - in you, a heart of com - pas - sion and love.
D.C.

Verse 3*
3. If you break the chains of op - pres - sion, if you
if you share your bread with the hun - gry, give pro -
give a shel - ter to the home - less, clothe the
set the pris - 'ner free;
tec - tion to the lost;
na - ked in your midst, then your light shall break
forth like the dawn.
1., 2.
3.
D.C.

Soprano alone first time through repeated section, sopranos and tenors second time, ll third time.

Text: Marty Haugen, b.1950
Tune: Marty Haugen, b.1950

411 Forty Days and Forty Nights

1. For - ty days and for - ty nights You were fast - ing in the wild; For - ty days and for - ty nights Tempt - ed and yet un - de - filed.
2. Shall not we your sor - row share And from world - ly joys ab - stain, Fast - ing with un - ceas - ing prayer, Strong with you to suf - fer pain?
3. Then if Sa - tan on us press, Flesh or spir - it to as - sail, Vic - tor in the wil - der - ness, Grant we may not faint nor fail!
4. So shall we have peace di - vine: Ho - lier glad - ness ours shall be; Round us, too, shall an - gels shine, Such as served you faith - ful - ly.
5. Keep, O keep us, Sav - ior dear, Ev - er con - stant by your side; That with you we may ap - pear At the e - ter - nal East - er - tide.

Text: George H. Smyttan, 1822-1870, alt.
Tune: HEINLEIN, 7 7 7 7; attr. to Martin Herbst, 1654-1681, *Nürnbergisches Gesangbuch*, 1676

Parce Domine 412

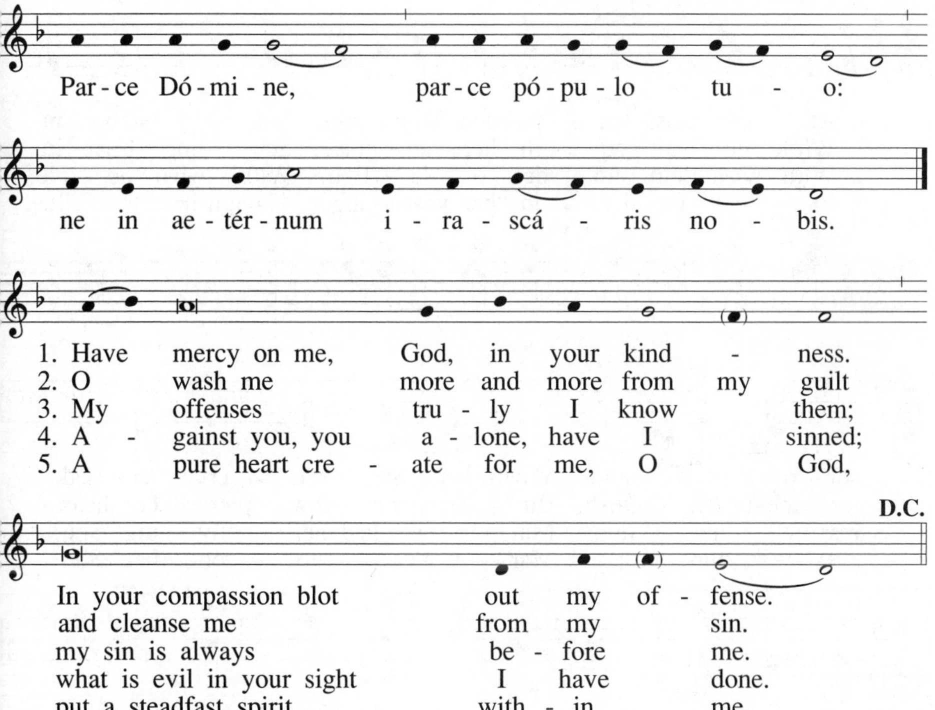
Par - ce Dó - mi - ne, par - ce pó - pu - lo tu - o:
ne in ae - tér - num i - ra - scá - ris no - bis.
1. Have mercy on me, God, in your kind - ness.
2. O wash me more and more from my guilt
3. My offenses tru - ly I know them;
4. A - gainst you, you a - lone, have I sinned;
5. A pure heart cre - ate for me, O God,
D.C.
In your compassion blot out my of - fense.
and cleanse me from my sin.
my sin is always be - fore me.
what is evil in your sight I have done.
put a steadfast spirit with - in me.

Text: *Spare your people, Lord, lest you be angry for ever,* Joel 2:17, Psalm 51:3-6, 12; tr. The Grail, © 1963, The Grail, GIA Publications, Inc., agent
Tune: PARCE DOMINE, Irregular; Mode I with Tonus Peregrinus; acc. by Robert LeBlanc, OSB, b.1948, © 1986, GIA Publications, Inc.

413 At the Cross Her Station Keeping

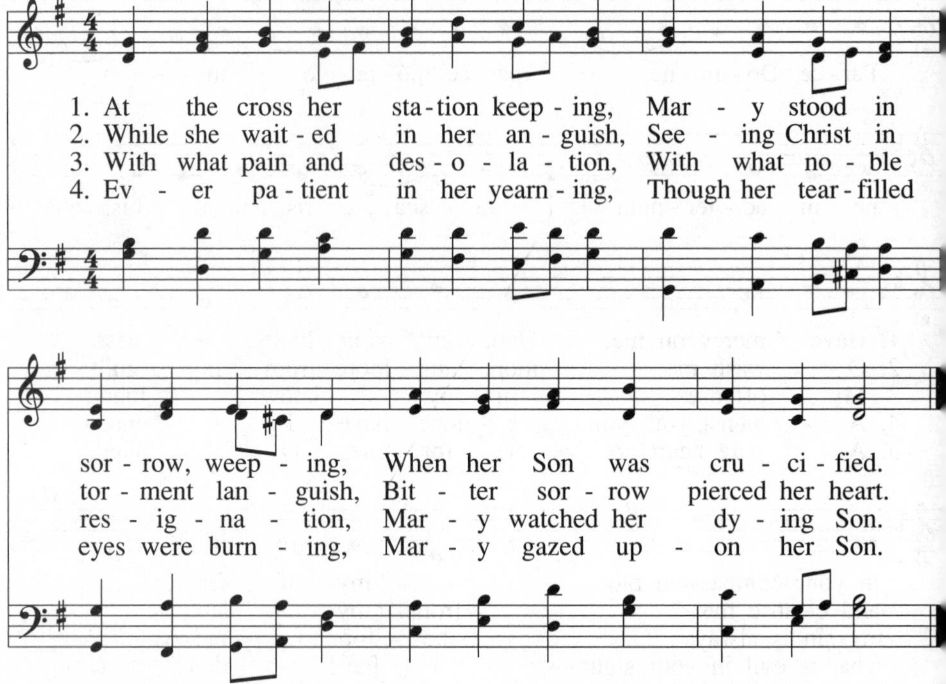
1. At the cross her sta-tion keep-ing, Mar-y stood in sor-row, weep-ing, When her Son was cru-ci-fied.
2. While she wait-ed in her an-guish, See-ing Christ in tor-ment lan-guish, Bit-ter sor-row pierced her heart.
3. With what pain and des-o-la-tion, With what no-ble res-ig-na-tion, Mar-y watched her dy-ing Son.
4. Ev-er pa-tient in her yearn-ing, Though her tear-filled eyes were burn-ing, Mar-y gazed up-on her Son.

5. Who, that sorrow contemplating,
On that passion meditating,
Would not share the Virgin's grief?

6. Christ she saw, for our salvation,
Scourged with cruel acclamation,
Bruised and beaten by the rod.

7. Christ she saw with life-blood failing,
All her anguish unavailing,
Saw him breathe his very last.

8. Mary, fount of love's devotion,
Let me share with true emotion
All the sorrow you endured.

9. Virgin, ever interceding,
Hear me in my fervent pleading:
Fire me with your love of Christ.

10. Mother, may this prayer be granted:
That Christ's love may be implanted
In the depths of my poor soul.

11. At the cross, your sorrow sharing,
All your grief and torment bearing,
Let me stand and mourn with you.

12. Fairest maid of all creation,
Queen of hope and consolation,
Let me feel your grief sublime.

13. Virgin, in your love befriend me,
At the Judgment Day defend me.
Help me by your constant prayer.

14. Savior, when my life shall leave me,
Through your mother's prayers receive me
With the fruits of victory.

15. Let me to your love be taken,
Let my soul in death awaken
To the joys of Paradise.

Text: *Stabat mater dolorosa;* Jacopone da Todi, 1230-1306; trans. by Anthony G. Petti, 1932-1985,
Tune: STABAT MATER, 88 7; *Mainz Gesangbuch,* 1661; harm. by Richard Proulx, b.1937,

Change Our Hearts 414

Refrain
Descant:
Change our hearts,
Melody:
Change our hearts this time, Your word says it can
change our minds.
be. Change our minds, this time, Your life could make us
We are the peo - ple Your call set a - part,
free. We are the peo - ple Your call set a - part,
Last time
To verses
Lord, this time change our hearts.
Last time
Lord, this time change our hearts.
Verses
1. Brought by your hand to the edge of our
2. Now as we watch you stretch out your
3. Show us the way that leads to your

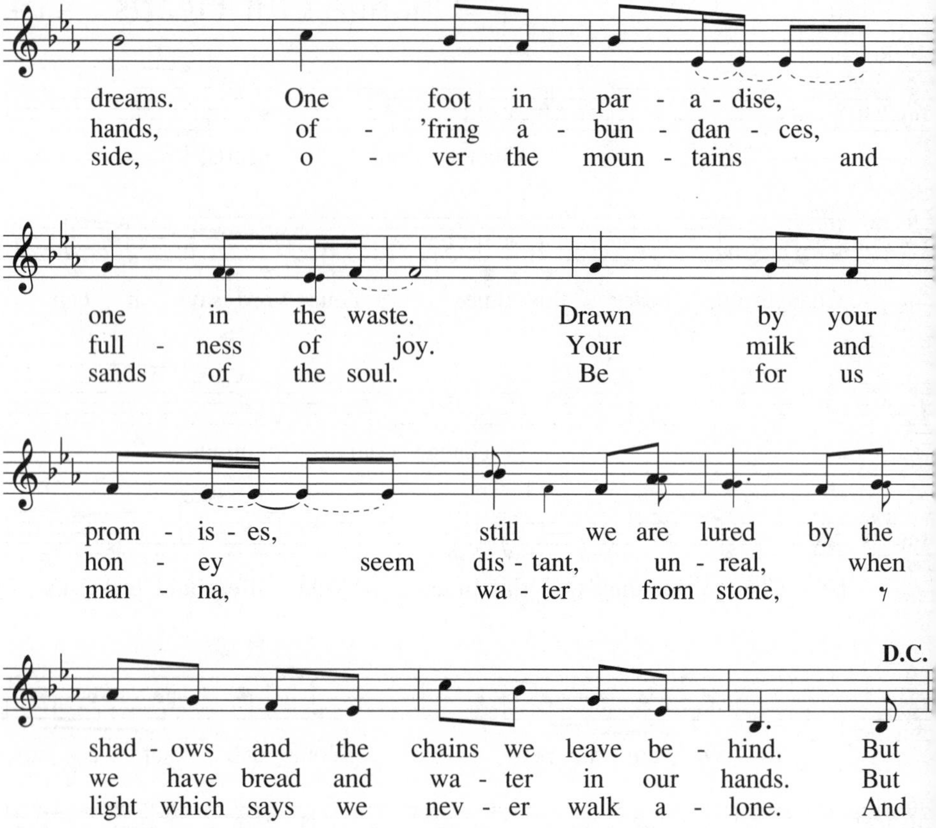

dreams. One foot in par - a - dise,
hands, of - 'fring a - bun - dan - ces,
side, o - ver the moun - tains and

one in the waste. Drawn by your
full - ness of joy. Your milk and
sands of the soul. Be for us

prom - is - es, still we are lured by the
hon - ey seem dis - tant, un - real, when
man - na, wa - ter from stone,

D.C.

shad - ows and the chains we leave be - hind. But
we have bread and wa - ter in our hands. But
light which says we nev - er walk a - lone. And

Text: Rory Cooney, b.1952
Tune: Rory Cooney, b.1952

415 Return to the Lord

Refrain
Cantor:
Re - turn, re - turn to the Lord,
your God.
Assembly:
Re - turn, re - turn to the Lord, your God.

Verse 1
1. Who is gra - cious and mer - ci-ful, and slow to
an - ger, a - bound - ing in love. Re -
D.S.
Verse 2
2. Re - turn with all your heart, with fast - ing and weep-ing,
rend your hearts, and re - turn to God. Re -
D.S.
Verse 3
3. Have mer - cy, O God, in your good-ness,
cleanse me from my sin. Re -
D.S.
Verse 4
4. Cre - ate in me a clean heart, re-new your
spir-it, keep me in your pres - ence. Re -
D.S.
Verse 5
5. Give back to me, the joy of your sal - va-tion, sus -
tain your spir - it with - in me. Re -
D.S.

Text: David Haas, b.1957
Tune: David Haas, b.1957

416 Lord, Who throughout These Forty Days

1. Lord, who through - out these for - ty days, For
2. As you with Sa - tan did con - tend, And
3. As you did hun - ger and did thirst, So
4. And through these days of pen - i - tence, And
5. A - bide with us, that through this life Of
us did fast and pray, Teach us to o - ver -
did the vic - t'ry win, O give us strength in
teach us, gra - cious Lord, To die to self, and
through your Pas - sion - tide, For ev - er - more, in
doubts and hope and pain, An East - er of un -
come our sins, And close by you to stay.
you to fight, In you to con - quer sin.
so to live By your most ho - ly word.
life and death, O Lord! with us a - bide.
end - ing joy We may at last at - tain!

Text: Claudia F. Hernaman, 1838-1898, alt.
Tune: ST. FLAVIAN, CM; *John's Day Psalter,* 1562; harm. based on the original *faux-bourdon* setting

Mercy, O God 417

Refrain
Mer-cy, O God, have mer-cy on us.
Mer - cy, mer - cy.
Send down your mer-cy to set us free.
Mer-cy, O God, have mer-cy on us.
Mer - cy, mer - cy.
Last time
Send down your mer-cy to set us free.
Last time

Verses
1. Gath - er the peo - ple, the chil - dren, the el - ders;
2. Now is the hour, the day of sal - va - tion;
3. Long is the jour - ney and steep are the moun - tains,
4. Wash us a - new in your life - giv - ing wa - ter;
5. Once lost in dark - ness you did not for - sake us, but
6. Wake, O sleep - er, a - wake from your slum - ber;
come now and gath - er be - fore the Lord.
now is the time to re - turn to God.
come now and guide us, O gra - cious God.
come quench the thirst of our yearn - ing hearts.
called us your chil - dren and gave us light.
rise from the chains of the dark, cold tomb.
3
O - pen your hearts to com - pas - sion and mer - cy;
O - pen your lives to for - give - ness and mer - cy;
Show us your face, give us hope for the jour - ney;
Break through the si - lence, the fear and the long - ing; em -
O - pen our eyes, come re - move all our blind - ness.
Walk in the light of com - pas - sion and mer - cy;
3
D.C.
O - pen your hearts to the Lord.
O - pen your lives to the Lord.
Lead us to walk in your love.
brace us with un - end - ing love.
O - pen our eyes to your love.
walk in the light of the Lord.

Text: Francis Patrick O'Brien, b.1958
Tune: Francis Patrick O'Brien, b.1958

Kyrie 418

Ostinato I
Ky-ri-e e-le-i-son, Chri-ste e-le-i-son, Ky-ri-e e-
le-i-son, e-le-i-son, e-le-i-son. le-i-son.
To repeat
Last time
Ostinato II (optional)
(mer-cy,) Christ, have mer-cy, Lord, have
mer-cy, have mer-cy on us. Lord, have
To repeat
Ostinato II enter
Last time
Verses (Superimposed on Ostinato Refrain)
(God.)
Cantor:
1. On my breath and
2. In my song and
3. You who know my
4. No one el-se's
5. Won-drous Love that
6. Sun of Jus-tice,
7. Rock of A-ges,
8. Heal-ing Rain, pour

in my breath - ing: In my laugh - ter
in my si - lence: In my faith and
se - cret fail - ings: You who touch my
love can raise me: No one el - se's
seeks and finds me: Word that rais - es
shin - ing o'er me: Wind of New Life,
still sup - port me: Bread of New Life,
down up - on me: Liv - ing Riv - er,
and my la - bor: Full of joy or
in my doubt - ing: In my cour - age
deep - est feel - ings: Know me well, and
touch can heal me: No one el - se's
and un - binds me: When my sin en -
rush - ing 'round me: Life of ev - 'ry
still sus - tain me: Wine of Mer - cy,
swell a - round me: End - less Sea of
To repeat
Last time
spent in griev - ing: I call up - on you,
and my weak - ness: I call up - on you,
still you love me: I call up - on you,
voice can free me: I call up - on you,
slaves and blinds me: I call up - on you,
twig and blos - som: I call up - on you,
still re - new me: I call up - on you,
Love, sur - round me: I call up - on you,

Text: Marty Haugen, b.1950
Tune: Marty Haugen, b.1950

Deep Within 419

Refrain
Deep with - in I will plant my law,
not on stone, but in your heart.
Fol - low me, I will bring you back, you will
be my own, and I will be your God.
Verses
1. I will give you a new heart, a new spir - it with -
2. Seek my face, and see your
3. Re - turn to me, with all your
D.C.
in you, for I will be your strength.
God, for I will be your hope.
heart, and I will bring you back.

Text: Jeremiah 31:33, Ezekiel 36:26, Joel 2:12; David Haas, b.1957
Tune: David Haas, b.1957; acc. by Jeanne Cotter, b.1964

420 Palm Sunday Processional

Cantor:
1. When they heard that Je - sus was com - ing,
2. Spread their cloaks and branch - es be - fore him,
3. Blest is he, like Da - vid be - fore him.
4. Guid - ing cloud and pil - lar of fire,
5. Word of God, and first - born of peo - ple,
6. Vi - sion blest, and hope for the fu - ture,
7. Won - drous bread, and stream in the des - ert,
8. Eye of God, who see to the heart of us,
9. Ris - ing sun, the light of the world,
10. Friend in death, who weep for our dy - ing,
11. Friend in death, who wake us to new life,
Assembly:
Sing ho - san - na to the cho - sen one!
Choir:
Sing ho - san - na to the cho - sen one!
Cantor:
All the peo - ple went out to meet him.
Chil - dren sang with palm branch - es wav - ing.
Blest is he, God's bless - ing up - on him.
Sa - tan's foe and friend of the sin - ner.
Prom - ise kept, the crown of cre - a - tion.
God's be - lov - ed, ra - diant with glo - ry.
Ho - ly thirst, and God's liv - ing wa - ter.
Heal - ing touch, the sight for our blind - ness.
Word of life, who give us your Spir - it.
Friend in death, who roll back the stone for us.
Friend in life, we sing glad ho - san - nas.

Assembly:
Sing ho - san - na to the cho - sen one!
Choir:
Sing ho - san - na to the cho - sen one!
Sing ho - san - na, sing ho - san - na,
unis.
Sing ho - san - na, sing ho - san - na,
unis.
sing ho - san - na to the cho - sen one!
div.
sing ho - san - na to the cho - sen one!

Text: Rory Cooney, b.1952
Tune: Rory Cooney, b.1952

421 All Glory, Laud, and Honor

All glo - ry, laud, and hon - or To you, Re - deem - er, King!
To whom the lips of chil - dren Made sweet ho - san - nas ring.
1. You are the King of Is - ra - el, And Da - vid's roy - al Son,
2. The com - pa - ny of an - gels Are prais - ing you on high;
3. The peo - ple of the He - brews With palms be - fore you went:
4. To you be - fore your pas - sion They sang their hymns of praise
5. Their prais - es you ac - cept - ed, Ac - cept the prayers we bring,
D.C.
Now in the Lord's Name com - ing, Our King and Bless - ed One.
And mor - tals, joined with all things Cre - a - ted, make re - ply.
Our praise and prayers and an - thems Be - fore you we pre - sent.
To you, now high ex - alt - ed, Our mel - o - dy we raise.
Great source of love and good - ness, Our Sav - ior and our King.

Text: *Gloria, laus et honor;* Theodulph of Orleans, c.760-821; tr. by John M. Neale, 1818-1866, alt.
Tune: ST. THEODULPH, 7 6 7 6 D; Melchior Teschner, 1584-1635

Jesus, Remember Me 422

Ostinato Refrain
Je-sus, re-mem-ber me when you come in-to your King-dom.
Je-sus, re-mem-ber me when you come in-to your King-dom.

Text: Luke 23:42; Taizé Community, 1981
Tune: Jacques Berthier, 1923-1994

423 Hosanna

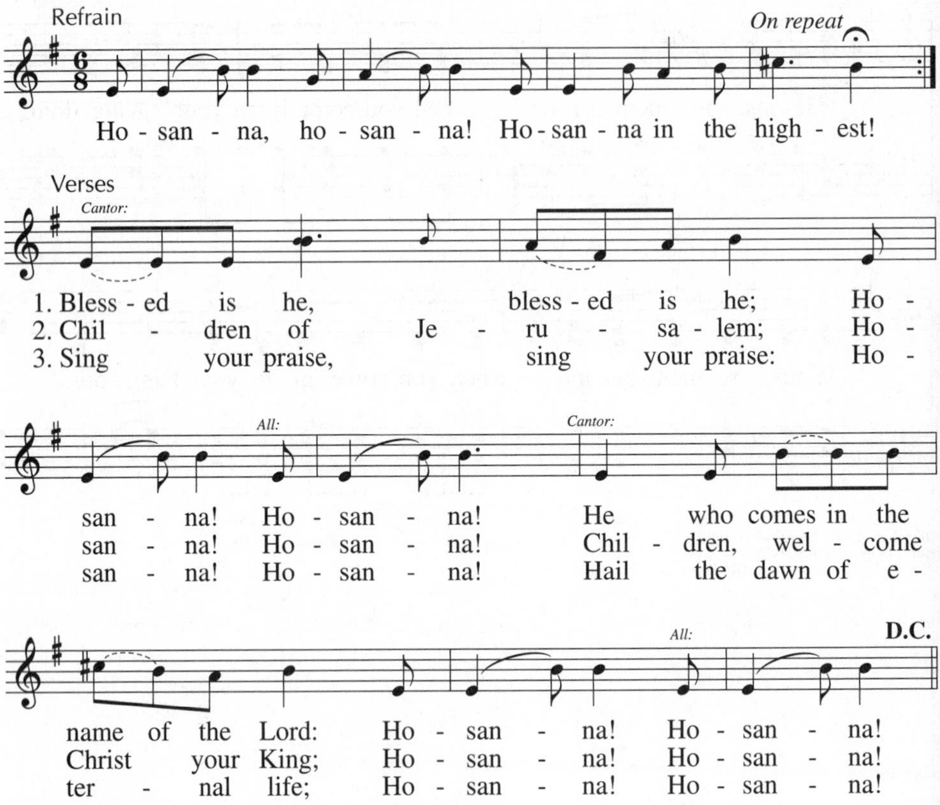

Refrain

On repeat

Ho - san - na, ho - san - na! Ho - san - na in the high - est!

Verses

Cantor:

1. Bless - ed is he, bless - ed is he; Ho - san - na! *All:* Ho - san - na! *Cantor:* He who comes in the name of the Lord: Ho - san - na! *All:* Ho - san - na!
2. Chil - dren of Je - ru - sa - lem; Ho - san - na! Ho - san - na! Chil - dren, wel - come Christ your King; Ho - san - na! Ho - san - na!
3. Sing your praise, sing your praise: Ho - san - na! Ho - san - na! Hail the dawn of e - ter - nal life; Ho - san - na! Ho - san - na!

D.C.

Text: Scott Soper, b.1961
Tune: Scott Soper, b.1961

424 Ride On, Jesus, Ride

Ride on, Je - sus, ride. Ride on, Je - sus, ride.
Ride on, Je - sus, con - quering King, Ride on, Je - sus ride.

1. King Je - sus rides on a milk white horse. Ride on, Je - sus, ride. The riv - er Jor - dan he did cross.
2. My Je - sus lift - ed his throne a - bove. Ride on, Je - sus, ride. See his mer - cy and his love.
3. The chil - dren of Je - ru - sa - lem, Ride on, Je - sus, ride, strewed their branch - es on his way.
4. "Bless - ings on the Ho - ly One!" Ride on, Je - sus, ride. "Bless - ings on the Sav - ing One!"
5. Ride so hum - ble, ride so true, Ride on, Je - sus, ride. Ride to bring the world to you, Ride on, Je - sus,
6. Ride to set your peo - ple free, Ride on, Je - sus, ride. Ride the road to Cal - va - ry,
7. Ride o - be - dient un - to death, Ride on, Je - sus, ride. Ride to break the chains of death,
8. Ride a - gain in the hearts of us, Ride on, Je - sus, ride. Ride a - gain in the hands of us,
9. Now be - yond all time and space, Ride on, Je - sus, ride. Now in ev - 'ry land and race,
ride. Ride on, Je-sus, con-quering King. Ride on, Je-sus ride.

425 Hosanna

Refrain
Ho - san-na, Ho - san-na, Ho - san - na in the high-est!
Ho - san-na, Ho - san-na, Ho - san - na in the high-est!
Verses
1. Chil - dren of Je - ru - sa - lem shout - ing prais - es fol - lowed him. "This is he who comes to save,
2. En - ter - ing Je - ru - sa - lem crowds of peo - ple cov - ered him. "Ho - san - na to the cho - sen One!
3. O - pen wide the sa - cred door the king of glo - ry rides once more. Sing ho - san - nas, shout his name,
4. Bless - ed Christ, who comes in pow'r, saves us all from Sa - tan's hour. Grasp - ing not Di - vin - i - ty he
5. Earth and sea and sky a - bove glo - ry in this sav - ing love. Bless - ed, rich in mer - cy be
6. Ev - 'ry tongue on earth con - fess, Je - sus, rich in ho - li - ness, comes to be our sav - ing Lord;
7. Spir - it of the liv - ing God, pour - ing forth e - ter - nal love, help us praise the bless - ed One,

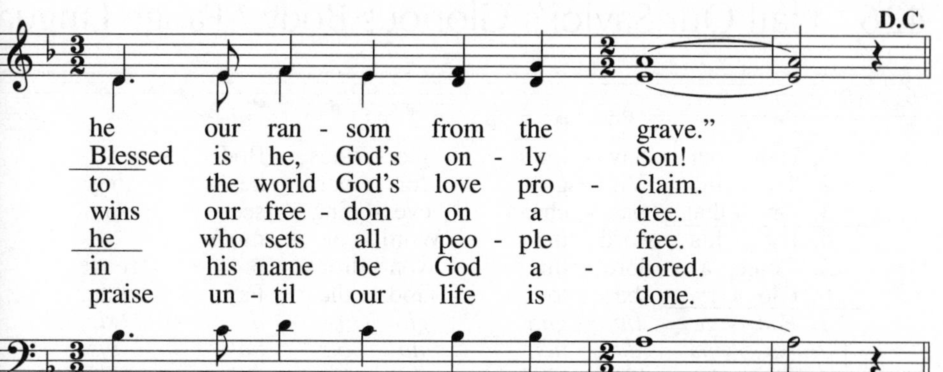
D.C.
he our ran - som from the grave."
Blessed is he, God's on - ly Son!
to the world God's love pro - claim.
wins our free - dom on a tree.
he who sets all peo - ple free.
in his name be God a - dored.
praise un - til our life is done.

Text: Francis Patrick O'Brien, b.1958
Tune: Francis Patrick O'Brien, b.1958

426 Hail Our Savior's Glorious Body / Pange Lingua

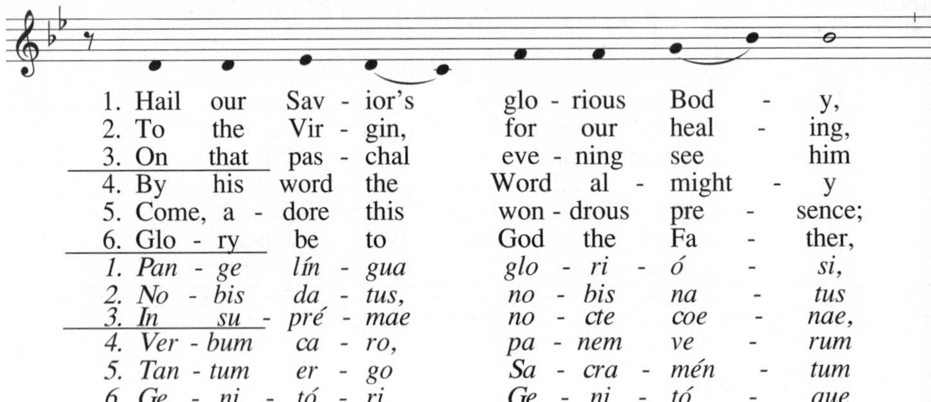
1. Hail our Sav - ior's glo - rious Bod - y,
2. To the Vir - gin, for our heal - ing,
3. On that pas - chal eve - ning see him
4. By his word the Word al - might - y
5. Come, a - dore this won - drous pre - sence;
6. Glo - ry be to God the Fa - ther,
1. Pan - ge lín - gua glo - ri - ó - si,
2. No - bis da - tus, no - bis na - tus
3. In su - pré - mae no - cte coe - nae,
4. Ver - bum ca - ro, pa - nem ve - rum
5. Tan - tum er - go Sa - cra - mén - tum
6. Ge - ni - tó - ri, Ge - ni - tó - que

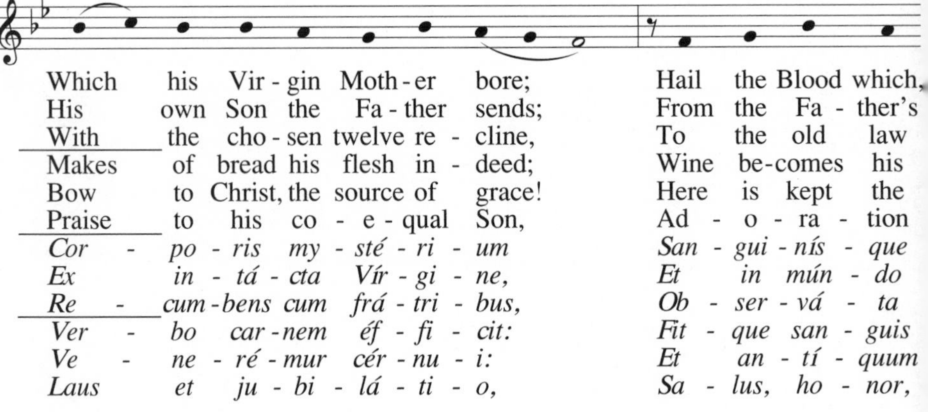
Which his Vir - gin Moth - er bore; Hail the Blood which,
His own Son the Fa - ther sends; From the Fa - ther's
With the cho - sen twelve re - cline, To the old law
Makes of bread his flesh in - deed; Wine be-comes his
Bow to Christ, the source of grace! Here is kept the
Praise to his co - e - qual Son, Ad - o - ra - tion
Cor - po - ris my - sté - ri - um San - gui - nís - que
Ex in - tá - cta Vír - gi - ne, Et in mún - do
Re - cum - bens cum frá - tri - bus, Ob - ser - vá - ta
Ver - bo car - nem éf - fi - cit: Fit - que san - guis
Ve - ne - ré - mur cér - nu - i: Et an - tí - quum
Laus et ju - bi - lá - ti - o, Sa - lus, ho - nor,

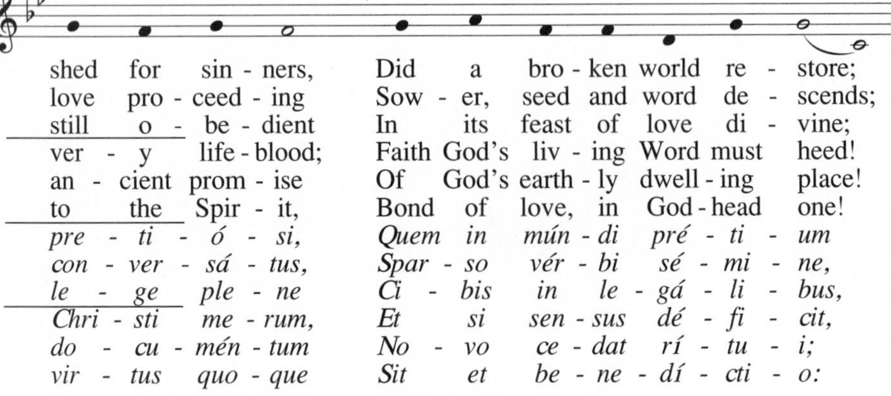
shed for sin - ners, Did a bro - ken world re - store;
love pro - ceed - ing Sow - er, seed and word de - scends;
still o - be - dient In its feast of love di - vine;
ver - y life - blood; Faith God's liv - ing Word must heed!
an - cient prom - ise Of God's earth - ly dwell - ing place!
to the Spir - it, Bond of love, in God - head one!
pre - ti - ó - si, Quem in mún - di pré - ti - um
con - ver - sá - tus, Spar - so vér - bi sé - mi - ne,
le - ge ple - ne Ci - bis in le - gá - li - bus,
Chri - sti me - rum, Et si sen - sus dé - fi - cit,
do - cu - mén - tum No - vo ce - dat rí - tu - i;
vir - tus quo - que Sit et be - ne - dí - cti - o:

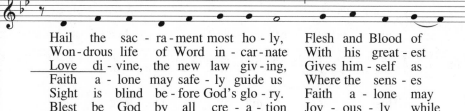

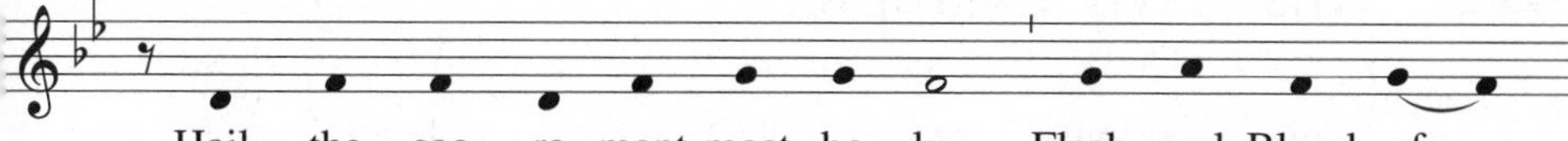

Hail the sac - ra - ment most ho - ly, Flesh and Blood of
Won - drous life of Word in - car - nate With his great - est
Love di - vine, the new law giv - ing, Gives him - self as
Faith a - lone may safe - ly guide us Where the sens - es
Sight is blind be - fore God's glo - ry. Faith a - lone may
Blest be God by all cre - a - tion Joy - ous - ly while
Fru - ctus ven - tris ge - ne - ró - si Rex ef - fú - dit
Su - i mo - ras in - co - lá - tus Mi - ro clau - sit
Ci - bum tur - bae du - o - dé - nae Se dat su - is
Ad fir - mán - dum cor sin - cé - rum So - la fi - des
Prae - stet fi - des sup - ple - mén - tum Sén - su - um de -
Pro - ce - dén - ti ab u - tró - que Com - par sit lau -

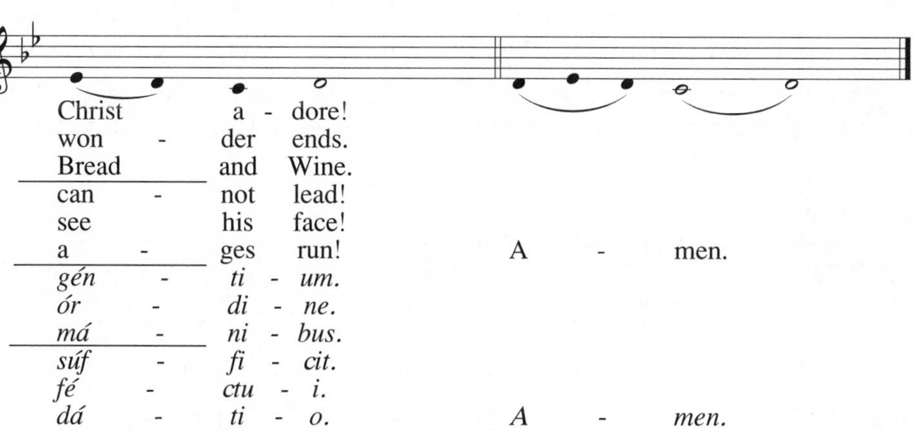
Christ a - dore!
won - der ends.
Bread and Wine.
can - not lead!
see his face!
a - ges run! A - men.
gén - ti - um.
ór - di - ne.
má - ni - bus.
súf - fi - cit.
fé - ctu - i.
dá - ti - o. A - men.

427 This Is My Example

Refrain

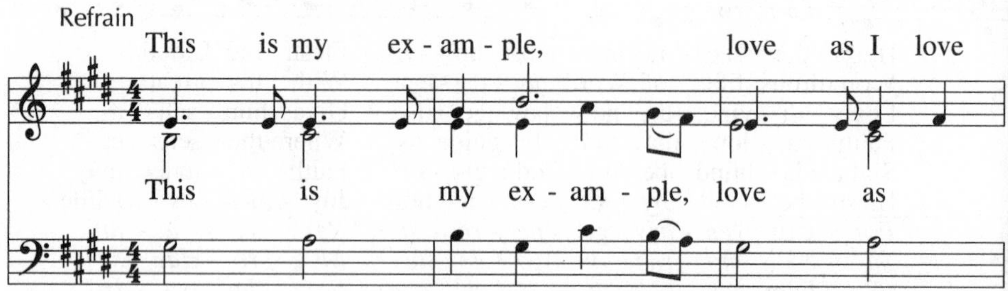
This is my ex - am - ple, love as I love
This is my ex - am - ple, love as

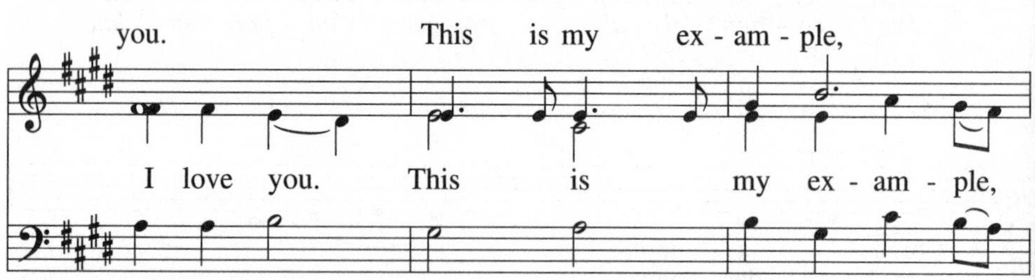
you. This is my ex - am - ple,
I love you. This is my ex - am - ple,

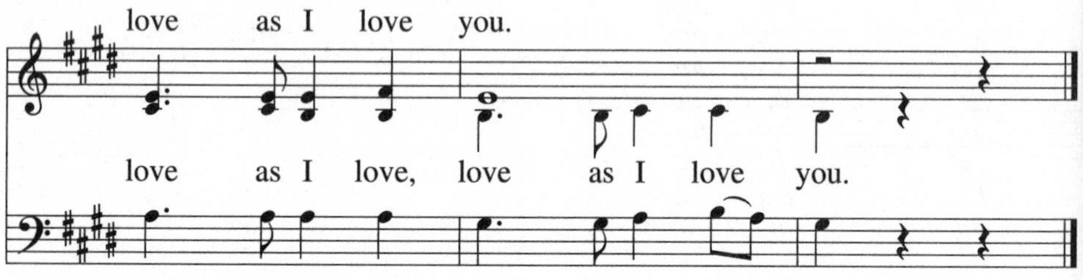
love as I love you.
love as I love, love as I love you.

Verses 1, 4, 6, 7, 10, 12

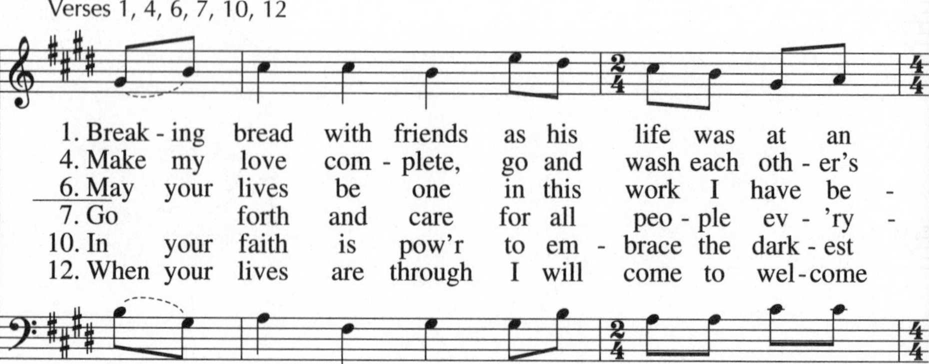
1. Break - ing bread with friends as his life was at an
4. Make my love com - plete, go and wash each oth - er's
6. May your lives be one in this work I have be -
7. Go forth and care for all peo - ple ev - 'ry -
10. In your faith is pow'r to em - brace the dark - est
12. When your lives are through I will come to wel - come

D.C.
end, Je - sus knelt to wash their feet.
feet; what I have done so you must do.
gun; come and fol - low where I lead.
where. Find your strength with - in my love.
hour; go with - out fear to heal and serve.
you. We will be for - ev - er one.
Je - sus knelt to wash their, wash their feet.
what I have done so you must, you must do.
come and fol - low where I, where I lead.
Find your strength with - in my, in my love.
go with - out fear to heal and, heal and serve.
We will be for - ev - er, ev - er one.
Verses 2, 5, 8, 11
2. In a time to come you will know what I have
5. To the poor and weak, be the com - fort that they
8. Speak my words of peace. To the cap - tives, bring re -
11. This my life I give; I must die that you may
serve.
guide.
name.
you.
D.C.
done; let me wash you, let me, let me serve.
seek; let my ex - am - ple be your, be your guide.
lease. Go em-brace them in my, in my name.
live. All this I do for love of, love of you.

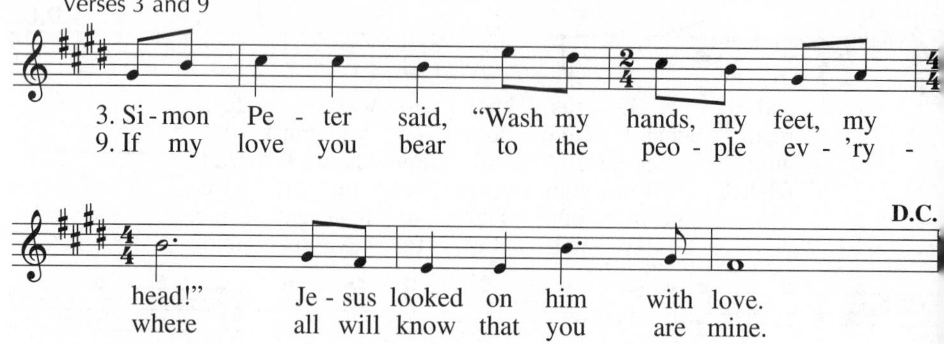
Verses 3 and 9
3. Si - mon Pe - ter said, "Wash my hands, my feet, my
9. If my love you bear to the peo - ple ev - 'ry -
head!" Je - sus looked on him with love.
where all will know that you are mine.
D.C.

Text: Francis Patrick O'Brien, b.1958
Tune: Francis Patrick O'Brien, b.1958

428 Prepare a Room for Me

To be sung in alternating verses by cantor and congregation.

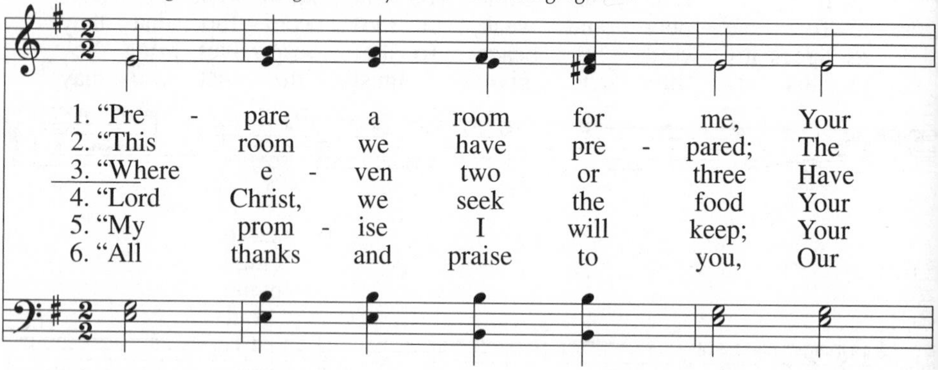

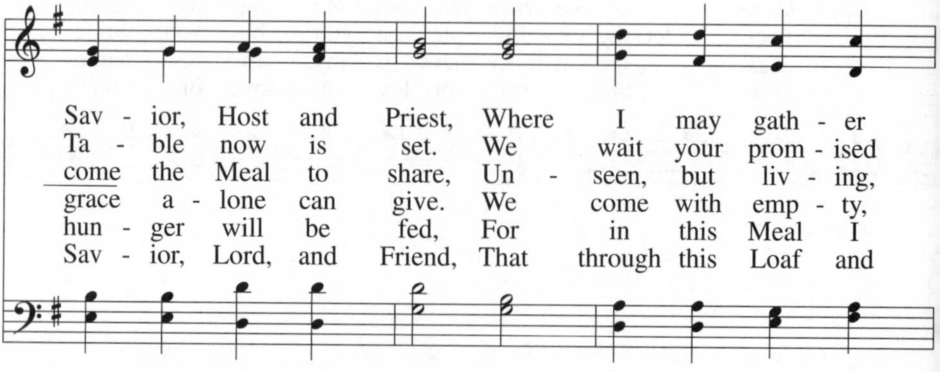

1. "Pre - pare a room for me, Your Sav - ior, Host and Priest, Where I may gath - er
2. "This room we have pre - pared; The Ta - ble now is set. We wait your prom - ised
3. "Where e - ven two or three Have come the Meal to share, Un - seen, but liv - ing,
4. "Lord Christ, we seek the food Your grace a - lone can give. We come with emp - ty,
5. "My prom - ise I will keep; Your hun - ger will be fed, For in this Meal I
6. "All thanks and praise to you, Our Sav - ior, Lord, and Friend, That through this Loaf and

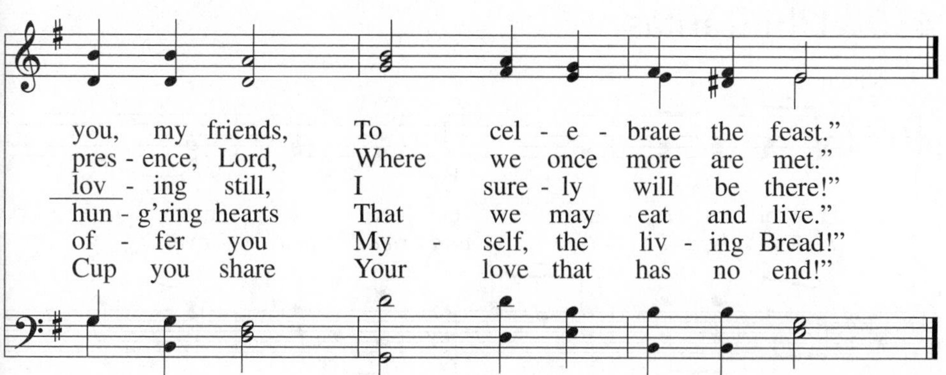
you, my friends, To cel - e - brate the feast."
pres - ence, Lord, Where we once more are met."
lov - ing still, I sure - ly will be there!"
hun - g'ring hearts That we may eat and live."
of - fer you My - self, the liv - ing Bread!"
Cup you share Your love that has no end!"

Text: Herman G. Stuempfle, Jr., b.1923, © 2000, GIA Publications, Inc.
Tune: SOUTHWELL, SM; Damon's *Psalmes,* alt.

Jesu, Jesu 429

Refrain

Je - su Je - su fill us with your love, show
us how to serve the neigh - bors we have from you.

Verses

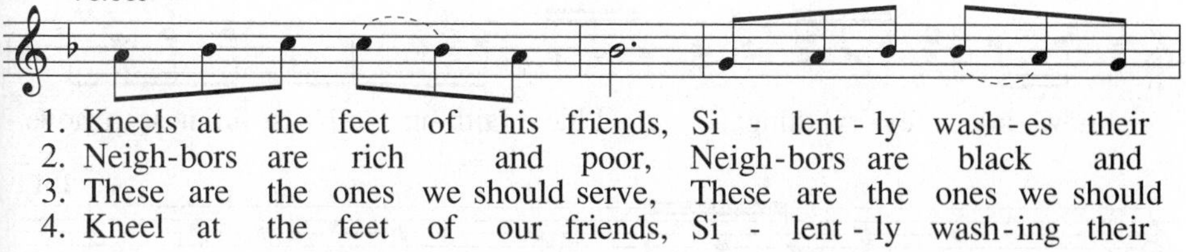

1. Kneels at the feet of his friends, Si - lent - ly wash - es their feet, Mas - ter who pours out him - self for them.
2. Neigh - bors are rich and poor, Neigh - bors are black and white, Neigh - bors are near and far a - way.
3. These are the ones we should serve, These are the ones we should love. All are neigh - bors to us and you.
4. Kneel at the feet of our friends, Si - lent - ly wash - ing their feet, This is the way we should live with you.

D.C.

Text: Tom Colvin, b.1925
Tune: CHEREPONI, Irregular; Ghana folk song; adapt. Tom Colvin, b.1925; acc. by Jane M. Marshall, b.1924

430 Ubi Caritas

Refrain
U - bi ca - ri - tas et a - mor,
Live in char - i - ty and stead - fast love,
u - bi ca - ri - tas De - us i - bi est.
live in char - i - ty; God will dwell with you.
Verse 1
Cantor:
1. If I have the gift of prophecy, understanding all the mysteries there are,
know - ing ev-'ry-thing; if I have faith in all its full-ness to move
moun-tains, but have not love, I am noth-ing at all.
D.C.
Verse 2
Cantor:
2. If I give everything I have to feed the poor, and
let them take my bod - y to be

D.C.
burned, but have not love, I gain noth-ing at all.
Verse 3
Cantor:
3. Love is pa-tient, love is not jeal-ous. Love does not re-
joice in what is wrong, but love re-joic-es in the
truth. Love is al-ways read-y to ex-cuse, to hope, to
D.C.
trust, and to en-dure what-ev-er comes.
Verse 4
Cantor:
4. Love nev-er fails. Prophesies will cease, and tongues will be si-lent,
knowl-edge will pass a-way; but there are on-ly
three things in the end that last: faith, hope and
D.C.
love, and the great-est of these is love.

Text: I Corinthians 13:2-8; *Where charity and love are found, God is there;* Taizé Community, 1978
Tune: Jacques Berthier, 1923-1994

431 So You Must Do

Refrain
Je-sus, our teach-er and our Lord, stooped to
Je-sus, our teach-er, stooped to
wash the feet of his dis-ci-ples, and he
div.
and he
div.
told them, "This is an ex-am-ple; just as I have
Last time to Coda
told them, "This ex-am-ple; as I have
done, so you must do."

Verses
1. When Je - sus had gath - ered with those he loved, as a
2. With tow - el and ba - sin he washed their feet, so that
3. He asked, "Do you know what I have done? I give
4. "As I, your teach - er, have washed your feet, so must
5. "A new com-mand-ment I give to you, that you
D.C.
hum - ble ser-vant he knelt at their feet.
they might share in his pas - sion and death.
you a wit-ness of what you must do."
you be will-ing to serve in my name."
love each oth - er as I have loved you."
Coda
unis.
done, so you must do." And he told them, "This is an ex-
unis.
am-ple; just as I have done, so you must do."

Text: John 13:1-15, adapt. by Marty Haugen, b.1950
Tune: Marty Haugen, b.1950

432 Song of the Lord's Command

Refrain
Descant:
Do you know, you who
Melody:
Do you know what I have done for you, you who
call me your teach-er and your Lord? If I have
call me your teach-er and your Lord? If I have
washed your feet, you must do as I have done for
washed your feet, so you must do as I have done for
To verses
Last time
you.
you.
Verses 1-4
Cantor:
1. What I am do - ing now you do not
2. Don't you un - der - stand what I must
3. I have giv - en to you an ex -
4. There is no great - er love than

know, but af - ter a time has gone
do? If you would be mine, then I must
am - ple; what I have done for you, you must
this: than to lay down your
D.S.
by, you will un - der - stand.
bend to wash your feet.
do for one an - oth - er.
life for a friend.
Refrain
Descant:
D.S.
Do you
Melody:
D.S.
Do you know what I have
Verses 5, 6
5. Go, and live in my love. You will
6. Go, and love as I have shown you.
D.S.
live in my love if you keep my com-mands.
Love one an - oth - er as I have loved you.
Refrain
Descant:
D.S.
Do you
Melody:
D.S.
Do you know what I have

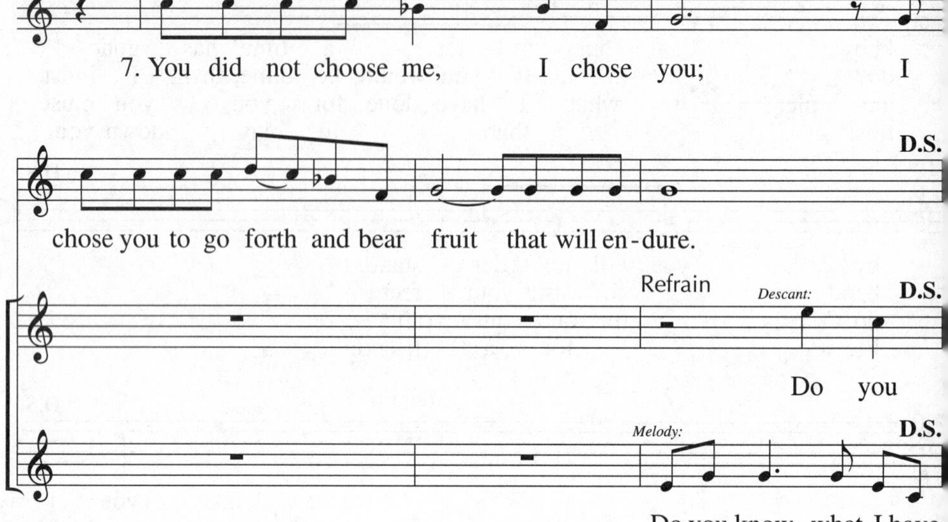
Verse 7
7. You did not choose me, I chose you; I
chose you to go forth and bear fruit that will en - dure.
D.S.
Refrain
Descant:
D.S.
Do you
Melody:
D.S.
Do you know what I have

Text: John 13:1-15, 15:12-14, 16; David Haas, b.1957
Tune: David Haas, b.1957

433 Stay Here and Keep Watch

Ostinato Refrain
Stay here and keep watch with me. The hour has come.
Stay here and keep watch with me. Watch and pray.

Verses

Cantor:

1. My heart is near - ly bro - ken with sor - row. Re - main here, re - main here and stay a - wake with me.

2. Fa - ther, if it is pos - si - ble, let this cup pass me by.

3. Fa - ther, if this can not pass me by with - out my drink - ing it, then your will be done.

Text: from Matthew 26; Taizé Community
Tune: Jacques Berthier, 1923-1994

Song of the Lord's Supper 434

1. We re - mem - ber one who loved us well,
2. We re - mem - ber how he spoke of you,
3. On the night be - fore he suf - fered death,
4. As they sat at ta - ble he took bread,
5. Now we take these gifts of field and vine,
Shared our life, its joy and sor - row, Walked a - mong us as the
Taught us to be - lieve your prom - ise, Showed us all what you are
Je - sus gath - ered his dis - ci - ples, Knelt be - fore them as a
Blest it, broke it, gave it free - ly: "Take this bread and eat it,
Bless and share them in his mem - 'ry: Bread of life and cup of

least of all, Gave him - self in - to our keep - ing.
real - ly like— Faith - ful, ten - der, God of peo - ple:
ser - vant might, Washed their feet and bid them wel - come:
all of you; Take and eat, this is my bod - y."
cov - e - nant, King - dom - feast in pledge and prom - ise.

He is light that dawns for blind - ed eyes,
Not a God to break the wound - ed heart,
"Do you know what I have done for you,
Then he took the cup and passed it round:
When we eat this bread and drink this cup

He is hope for the de - spair - ing; All on earth can find a
Not the thun - der of the might - y, But a God that wel-comes
I who am your Lord and Mas - ter? If I bend to you and
"Take and drink, this is my life - blood, Shed for you and for all
We pro-claim the death of Je - sus, Taste his pres-ence, liv - ing

place with him, Saint and sin - ner at his ta - ble.
sin - ners home, Meets the low - ly with com - pas - sion.
wash your feet, So must you for one an - oth - er."
hu - man - kind, Shed that sins may be for - giv - en."
in our midst, Look for him to come in glo - ry.

Text: Michael Joncas, b.1951
Tune: Michael Joncas, b.1951

435 O Sacred Head Surrounded

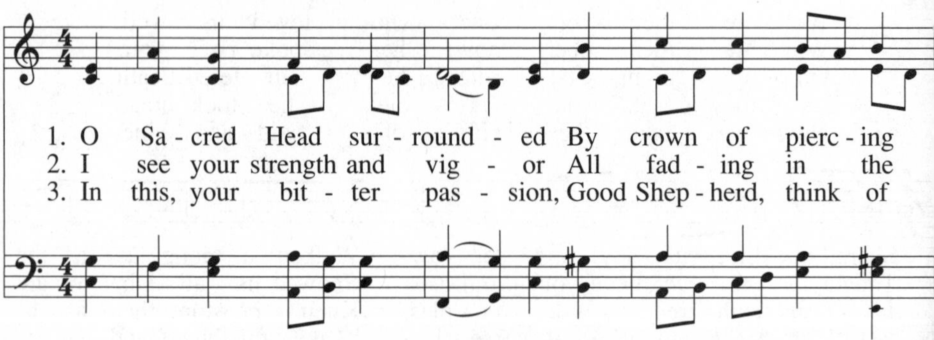
1. O Sa - cred Head sur - round - ed By crown of pierc - ing
2. I see your strength and vig - or All fad - ing in the
3. In this, your bit - ter pas - sion, Good Shep - herd, think of

thorn! O bleed - ing Head, so wound - ed, Re - viled and put to scorn! The pow'r of death comes o'er you, The glow of life de - cays, Yet an - gel hosts a - dore you, And trem - ble as they gaze.
strife, And death with cru - el rig - or, Be - reav - ing you of life; O ag - o - ny and dy - ing! O love to sin - ners free! Je - sus, all grace sup - ply - ing, O turn your face on me.
me With your most sweet com - pas - sion, Un - worth - y though I be: Be - neath your cross a - bid - ing For ev - er would I rest, In your dear love con - fid - ing, And with your pres - ence blest.

Text: *Salve caput cruentatum;* ascr. to Bernard of Clairvaux, 1091-1153; tr. by Henry Baker, 1821-1877
Tune: PASSION CHORALE, 7 6 7 6 D; Hans Leo Hassler, 1564-1612; harm. by J. S. Bach, 1685-1750

436 In the Cross of Christ

Refrain
In the cross of Christ, our glo - ry, Christ, our sto - ry,
Christ, our song, Christ, our song.
To verses
Final ending
Verses 1, 2
1. Let your mind and heart be one with Christ who
2. He was pierced for our in - iq - ui - ties, and
3
emp - tied him - self, for us be-came a slave, ac -
crushed for our sins. He died to make us whole, and
D.C.
cept - ing death up - on the cross.
by his suf - f'ring we are healed.

Verses 3-5
3. Come, be - hold the cross of sac - ri - fice on which
4. May we nev - er boast of an - y - thing save the
5. Now in Christ, we who were a - li - ens have been
Je - sus died– the Sav - ior of us all– to
cross of Christ, by which we die to sin and
rec - on - ciled; as mem-bers of God's house, we
D.C.
save a lost and bro - ken world.
rise to life in Je - sus Christ.
live as God's own dwell - ing place.

Text: Philippians 2:5-8, Ephesians 2:12-13, Galatians 6:14; adapt. by Marty Haugen, b.1950
Tune: Marty Haugen, b.1950

437 Behold the Wood

Refrain
Be - hold, be - hold the wood of the cross,
on which is hung our sal - va - tion. O
come, let us a - dore.
Verses
Slightly faster
1. Un - less a grain of wheat shall fall up -
2. And when my hour of glo - ry comes as
3. For there can be no great - er love
4. My Fa - ther, if it be your plan, this
5. For sure - ly he has borne our tears, is
6. My bod - y now is torn with pain, my

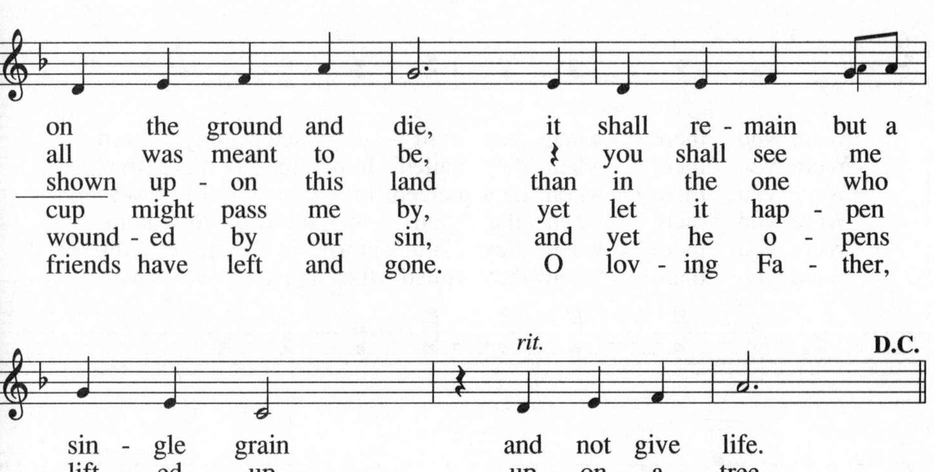
on the ground and die, it shall re - main but a
all was meant to be, you shall see me
shown up - on this land than in the one who
cup might pass me by, yet let it hap - pen
wound - ed by our sin, and yet he o - pens
friends have left and gone. O lov - ing Fa - ther,
rit.
D.C.
sin - gle grain and not give life.
lift - ed up up - on a tree.
came to die that we might live.
as you will if I must die.
not his mouth that we might live.
take my life in - to your hands.

Text: John 12; Dan Schutte, b.1947
Tune: Dan Schutte, b.1947

Were You There 438

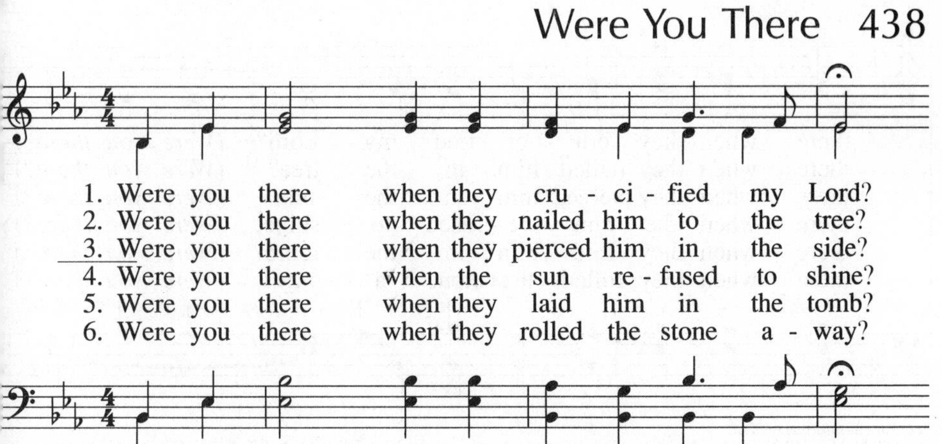
1. Were you there when they cru - ci - fied my Lord?
2. Were you there when they nailed him to the tree?
3. Were you there when they pierced him in the side?
4. Were you there when the sun re - fused to shine?
5. Were you there when they laid him in the tomb?
6. Were you there when they rolled the stone a - way?

Were you there when they cru - ci - fied my Lord?
Were you there when they nailed him to the tree?
Were you there when they pierced him in the side?
Were you there when the sun re - fused to shine?
Were you there when they laid him in the tomb?
Were you there when they rolled the stone a - way?
Oh! Some - times it caus - es me to trem - ble, trem - ble, trem - ble, Were you
there when they cru - ci - fied my Lord? (Were you there?)
there when they nailed him to the tree? (Were you there?)
there when they pierced him in the side? (Were you there?)
there when the sun re - fused to shine? (Were you there?)
there when they laid him in the tomb? (Were you there?)
there when they rolled the stone a - way? (Were you there?)

Text: African-American spiritual
Tune: WERE YOU THERE, 10 10 with refrain; African-American spiritual; harm. by Robert J. Batastini, b.1942,

Christ the Lord Is Risen Today 439

1. Christ the Lord is ris'n to - day, Al - le - lu - ia!
2. Lives a - gain our glo - rious King; Al - le - lu - ia!
3. Love's re - deem - ing work is done, Al - le - lu - ia!
4. Soar we now where Christ has led, Al - le - lu - ia!
All on earth with an - gels say, Al - le - lu - ia!
Where, O death, is now your sting? Al - le - lu - ia!
Fought the fight, the bat - tle won. Al - le - lu - ia!
Fol - l'wing our ex - alt - ed head; Al - le - lu - ia!
Raise your joys and tri - umphs high, Al - le - lu - ia!
Once he died our souls to save, Al - le - lu - ia!
Death in vain for - bids him rise; Al - le - lu - ia!
Made like him, like him we rise, Al - le - lu - ia!
Sing, O heav'ns, and earth re - ply, Al - le - lu - ia!
Where your vic - to - ry, O grave? Al - le - lu - ia!
Christ has o - pened par - a - dise. Al - le - lu - ia!
Ours the cross, the grave, the skies. Al - le - lu - ia!

Text: Charles Wesley, 1707-1788
Tune: LLANFAIR, 77 77 with alleluias; Robert Williams, 1781-1821

440 Alleluia! Alleluia! Let the Holy Anthem Rise

1. Al - le - lu - ia! Al - le - lu - ia! Let the ho - ly an - them rise, And the choirs of heav - en chant it In the tem - ple of the skies; Let the
2. Al - le - lu - ia! Al - le - lu - ia! He en - dured the knot - ted whips, And the jeer - ing of the rab - ble, And the scorn of mock - ing lips, And the
3. Al - le - lu - ia! Al - le - lu - ia! Like the sun from out the wave He has ris - en up in tri - umph From the dark - ness of the grave. He's the
4. Al - le - lu - ia! Al - le - lu - ia! He has burst our pris - on bars; He has lift - ed up the por - tals Of our home be - yond the stars; He has
5. Al - le - lu - ia! Al - le - lu - ia! Bless - ed Je - sus, make us rise From the life of this cor - rup - tion To the life that nev - er dies. May we

moun - tains skip with glad - ness And the
ter - rors of the gib - bet Up - on
splen - dor of the na - tions; He's the
won for us our free - dom— 'Neath his
share with you your glo - ry When the
joy - ful val - leys ring With ho - san - nas in the
which he would be slain, But his death was on - ly
lamp of end - less day; He's the ver - y Lord of
feet our foes are trod; He has pur - chased back our
days of time are past, And the dead shall be a -
high - est To our Sav - ior and our King!
slum - ber; He is ris - en up a - gain!
glo - ry Who is ris - en up to - day!
birth - right To the king - dom of our God!
wak - ened By the trum - pet's might - y blast!

Text: Edward Caswall, 1814-1878
Tune: HOLY ANTHEM, 8 7 8 7 D; traditional melody; harm. by Jerry R. Brubaker, b.1946, © 1975, Romda Ltd.

441 Earth, Earth, Awake!

1. Earth, earth, a - wake! Your prais - es sing! Al - le - lu - ia!
2. All na - ture sings of hope re - born! Al - le - lu - ia!
3. Win - ter is past; the night is gone! Al - le - lu - ia!
4. Praise we the Fa - ther, Spir - it, Son! Al - le - lu - ia!

Greet with the dawn your ris - en King! Al - le - lu - ia!
Christ lives to com - fort those who mourn! Al - le - lu - ia!
Christ's light, tri - um - phant, brings the dawn! Al - le - lu - ia!
Praise we the vic - t'ry God has won! Al - le - lu - ia!

Bright suns and stars, your hom - age pay! Al - le - lu - ia!
First fruit of all the dead who sleep! Al - le - lu - ia!
Cre - a - tion spreads its spring-time bloom! Al - le - lu - ia!
Praise we the Lamb who reigns a - bove! Al - le - lu - ia!

Life reigns a - gain this East - er day! Al - le - lu - ia!
Prom - ise of joy for all who weep! Al - le - lu - ia!
Life bursts like flame from death's cold tomb! Al - le - lu - ia!
Praise we the King whose rule is love! Al - le - lu - ia!

Text: Herman G. Stuempfle, Jr., b.1923
Tune: STUEMPFLE, LM with alleluias; Sally Ann Morris, b.1952

442 Sing with All the Saints in Glory

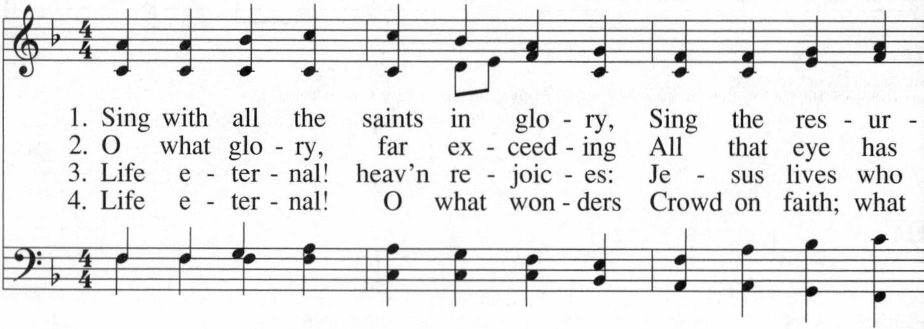
1. Sing with all the saints in glo - ry, Sing the res - ur -
2. O what glo - ry, far ex - ceed - ing All that eye has
3. Life e - ter - nal! heav'n re - joic - es: Je - sus lives who
4. Life e - ter - nal! O what won - ders Crowd on faith; what

rec - tion song! Death and sor - row, earth's dark sto - ry,
yet per-ceived! Ho - liest hearts for a - ges plead - ing,
once was dead; Shout with joy, O death - less voic - es!
joy un-known, When, a - midst earth's clos - ing thun - ders,
To the for - mer days be - long. All a - round the
Nev - er that full joy con-ceived. God has prom - ised,
Child of God, lift up your head! Pa - tri - archs from
Saints shall stand be - fore the throne! O to en - ter
clouds are break - ing, Soon the storms of time shall cease;
Christ pre - pares it, There on high our wel - come waits;
dis - tant a - ges, Saints all long - ing for their heav'n,
that bright por - tal, See that glow - ing fir - ma - ment,
In God's like - ness, we a - wak - en, Know-ing ev - er - last - ing peace.
Ev - 'ry hum - ble spir - it shares it, Christ has passed the e - ter - nal gates.
Proph - ets, psalm - ists, seers, and sag - es, All a - wait the glo - ry giv'n.
Know, with you, O God im - mor - tal, Je - sus Christ whom you have sent!

Text: 1 Corinthians 15:20; William J. Irons, 1812-1883, alt.
Tune: HYMN TO JOY, 8 7 8 7 D; arr. from Ludwig van Beethoven, 1770-1827, by Edward Hodges, 1796-1867

443 Resucitó

Refrain
Descant:
Last time to coda
Re-su-ci-tó, re-su-ci-tó, re-su-ci-tó, a-le-lu-ya.
A-le-lu-ya, a-le-lu-ya, a-le-lu-ya, re-su-ci-tó.
Melody:
Re-su-ci-tó, re-su-ci-tó, re-su-ci-tó, a-le-lu-ya.
A-le-lu-ya, a-le-lu-ya, a-le-lu-ya, re-su-ci-tó.
Verses
1. La muer-te ¿dón-de es-tá la muer-te? ¿Dón-de es-tá mi muer-te? ¿Dón-de su vic-to-ria?
2. Gra-cias se-an da-das al Pa-dre que nos pa-só a su rei-no ¿dón-de se vi-ve de a-mor.
3. A-le-grí-a, a-le-grí-a her-ma-nos, que si hoy nos que-re-mos es que re-su-ci-tó.
4. Si con Él mo-ri-mos, con Él vi-vi-mos, con Él can-ta-mos. ¡A-le-lu-ya.!
1. And death now, van-ished is the fear now, ban-ished are my tears now, death has passed a-way.
2. The king-dom, praise to God, the king-dom! Raised up to the king-dom, we shall live in love.
3. Our glad-ness, bliss-ful in our glad-ness, this will be our glad-ness, that he is a-live.
4. With him then, die and live with him then, rise and sing our hymn then, sing al-le-lu-ia.
D.C.
Coda
A-le-lu-ya.

Text: Kiko Argüello, © 1972, Ediciones Musical PAX, U.S. agent: OCP Publications; trans. by Robert C. Trupia, © 1988, OCP Publications
Tune: Kiko Argüello, © 1972, Ediciones Musical PAX, U.S. agent: OCP Publications; acc. by Diana Kodner

Sequence for Easter 444

1. Chris-tians, praise the pas-chal vic-tim! Of - fer thank-ful sac - ri - fice!
1. Ví - cti - mae Pa-schá - li lau-des im - mó-lent Chri-sti - á - ni.
2. Christ the Lamb has saved the sheep, Christ the just one paid the price, Re - con - cil - ing sin - ners to the Fa-ther.
3. Death and life fought bit - ter - ly For this won-drous vic - to - ry; The Lord of life who died reigns glo - ri - fied!
2. A - gnus ré - de - mit ó - ves: Chri - stus ín - no - cens Pá - tri re - con - ci - li - á - vit pec - ca - tó - res.
3. Mors et vi - ta du - él - lo con - fli - xé - re mi - rán - do: dux vi - tae mór - tu - us re - gnat vi - vus.
4. O Mar - y, come and say what you saw at break of day.
6. Bright an - gels tes - ti - fied, Shroud and grave clothes side by side!
4. Dic no - bis Ma - rí - a, quid vi - dí - sti in vi - a?
6. An - gé - li - cos te - stes, su - dá - ri - um, et ve - stes.
5. "The emp - ty tomb of my liv - ing Lord! I saw Christ Je - sus ri - sen and a - dored!
7. "Yes, Christ my hope rose glo - ri - ous - ly. He goes be - fore you in - to Ga - li - lee."
5. Se - púl - crum Chri - sti vi - vén - tis, et gló - ri - am vi - di re - sur - gén - tis.
7. Sur - ré - xit Chri-stus spes me - a: prae-cé - det su - os in Ga - li - láe - am.
8. Share the good news, sing joy - ful - ly: His death is vic - to - ry! Lord Je - sus, Vic - tor King, Show us mer - cy.
8. Scí - mus Chrí - stum sur - re - xís - se a mór - tu - is ve - re: tu no - bis vi - ctor Rex, mi - se - ré - re.

Text: Sequence for Easter, ascr. to Wipo of Burgundy, d.1048; tr. by Peter J. Scagnelli, b.1949, © 1983
Tune: Mode I; acc. by Richard Proulx, b.1937, © 1975, GIA Publications, Inc.

445 On the Journey to Emmaus

1. On the jour - ney to Em-ma - us with our hearts cold as stone—
2. And our hearts burned with - in us as we talked on the way,
3. And that eve - ning at the ta - ble as he blessed and broke bread,
4. On our jour - ney to Em-ma - us, in our sto - ries and feast,
The One who would save us had left us a - lone.
How all that was prom - ised was ours on that day.
We saw it was Je - sus a - ris'n from the dead;
With Je - sus we claim that the great - est is least:
Then a stran - ger walks with us and, to our sur - prise,
So we begged him, "Stay with us and grant us your word."
Though he van - ished be - fore us we knew he was near—
And his words burn with - in us— let none be ig - nored—
He o - pens our sto - ries and he o - pens our eyes.
We wel - comed the stran - ger and we wel - comed the Lord.
The life in our dy - ing and the hope in our fear.
Who wel - comes the stran - ger shall wel - come the Lord.

Text: Luke 24:13-35; Marty Haugen b.1950
Tune: COLUMCILLE, Irregular; Gaelic, arr. by Marty Haugen, b.1950

O Sons and Daughters 446

Al - le - lu - ia, al - le - lu - ia, al - le - lu - ia.

1. O sons and daugh - ters, let us sing!
2. That East - er morn, at break of day,
3. An an - gel clad in white they see,
4. That night the a - pos - tles met in fear;
5. When Thom - as, first the tid - ings heard,
6. "My wound - ed side, O Thom - as, see;

The King of heav'n the glo - rious King,
The faith - ful wom - en went their way
Who sat, and spoke un - to the three,
A - midst them came their Lord most dear,
How they had seen the ris - en Lord,
Be - hold my hands, my feet," said he,

D.C.

O'er death to - day rose tri - umph - ing. Al - le - lu - ia!
To seek the tomb where Je - sus lay. Al - le - lu - ia!
"Your Lord has gone to Gal - i - lee." Al - le - lu - ia!
And said, "My peace be on all here." Al - le - lu - ia!
He doubt - ed the dis - ci - ples' word. Al - le - lu - ia!
"Not faith - less, but be - liev - ing be." Al - le - lu - ia!

7. No longer Thomas then denied,
He saw the feet, the hands, the side;
"You are my Lord and God," he cried. Alleluia!

8. How blest are they who have not seen,
And yet whose faith has constant been,
For they eternal life shall win. Alleluia!

9. On this most holy day of days,
To God your hearts and voices raise,
In laud, and jubilee and praise. Alleluia!

Text: *O filii et filiae;* Jean Tisserand, d.1494; tr. by John M. Neale, 1818-1866, alt.
Tune: O FILII ET FILIAE, 888 with alleluias; Mode II; acc. by Richard Proulx, b.1937, © 1975, GIA Publications, Inc.

447 Easter Alleluia

Refrain
Last time to coda
Al - le - lu - ia, al - le - lu - ia,
al - le - lu - ia!
Verses
1. Glo - ry to God who does won - drous things,
2. See how sal - va - tion for all has been won,
3. Now in our pres - ence the Lord will ap - pear,
4. Call us, Good Shep - herd, we lis - ten for you,
5. Lord, we are o - pen to all that you say,
6. If we have love, then we dwell in the Lord,
Let all the peo - ple God's prais - es now sing,
Up from the grave our new life has be - gun,
Shine in the fac - es of all of us here,
Want - ing to see you in all that we do,
Read - y to lis - ten and fol - low your way,
God will pro - tect us from fire and sword,
All of cre - a - tion in splen - dor shall ring:
Life now per - fect - ed in Je - sus, the Son:
Fill us with joy and cast out all our fear:
We would the gate of sal - va - tion pass through:
You are the pot - ter and we are the clay:
Fill us with love and the peace of his word:

D.C.
Al - le - lu - ia!
Coda
al - le - lu - ia!

ext: Marty Haugen, b.1950
une: O FILII ET FILIAE; 10 10 10 with alleluias; adapt. by Marty Haugen, b.1950

Come, Ye Faithful, Raise the Strain 448

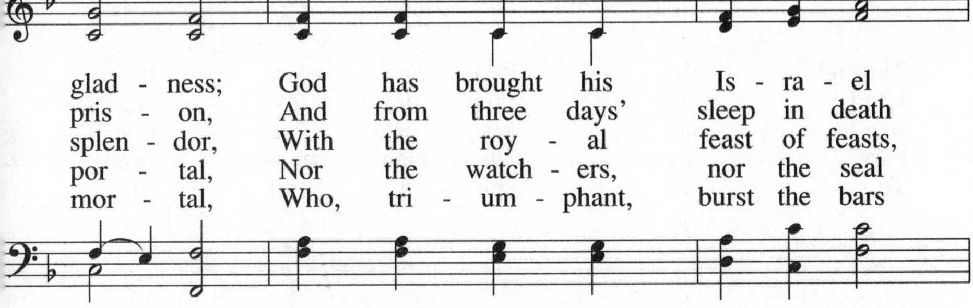

1. Come, ye faith - ful raise the strain Of tri - um - phant glad - ness; God has brought his Is - ra - el
2. 'Tis the spring of souls to - day; Christ has burst the pris - on, And from three days' sleep in death
3. Now the queen of sea - sons, bright With the day of splen - dor, With the roy - al feast of feasts,
4. Nei - ther could the gates of death, Nor the tomb's dark por - tal, Nor the watch - ers, nor the seal
5. "Al - le - lu - ia!" now we cry To our King im - mor - tal, Who, tri - um - phant, burst the bars

In - to joy from sad - ness; Loosed from Phar - aoh's bit - ter yoke Ja - cob's sons and daugh - ters; Led them with un - moist - ened foot Through the Red Sea wa - ters.
As a sun has ris - en; All the win - ter of our sins, Long and dark is fly - ing From his light, to whom we give Laud and praise un - dy - ing.
Comes its joy to ren - der; Comes to glad - den faith - ful hearts Who with true af - fec - tion Wel - come in un - wea - ried strains Je - sus' res - ur - rec - tion.
Hold him as a mor - tal; For to - day a - mong the Twelve Christ ap - peared be - stow - ing Last - ing peace which ev - er - more Pass - es hu - man know - ing.
Of the tomb's dark por - tal; "Al - le - lu - ia!" with the Son, God the Fa - ther prais - ing; "Al - le - lu - ia!" yet a - gain To the Spir - it rais - ing.

Text: Exodus 15; Ασωμεν παντεζ λαοι; John of Damascus, c.675-c.749; tr. by John M. Neale, 1818-1886, alt.
Tune: GAUDEAMUS PARITER, 7 6 7 6 D; Johann Horn, c. 1495-1547

Christ Is Risen! Shout Hosanna! 449

1. Christ is ris - en! Shout Ho - san - na! Cel - e - brate this
2. Christ is ris - en! Raise your spir - its From the cav - erns
3. Christ is ris - en! Earth and heav - en Nev - er - more shall
day of days! Christ is ris - en! Hush in won - der:
of des - pair. Walk with glad - ness in the morn - ing.
be the same. Break the bread of new cre - a - tion
All cre - a - tion is a - mazed. In the des - ert
See what love can do and dare. Drink the wine of
Where the world is still in pain. Tell its grim, de -
all sur - round - ing, See, a spread - ing tree has grown.
res - ur - rec - tion, Not a ser - vant, but a friend.
mon - ic cho - rus: "Christ is ris - en! Get you gone!"
Heal - ing leaves of grace a - bound - ing Bring a taste
Je - sus is our strong com - pan - ion. Joy and peace
God the First and Last is with us. Sing Ho - san -
of love un - known.
shall nev - er end.
na ev - 'ry one!
Last time

Text: Brian Wren, b.1936, © 1986, Hope Publishing Co.
Tune: HOSANNA, 8 7 8 7 D; David Haas, b.1957, © 1991, GIA Publications, Inc.

450 All Things New

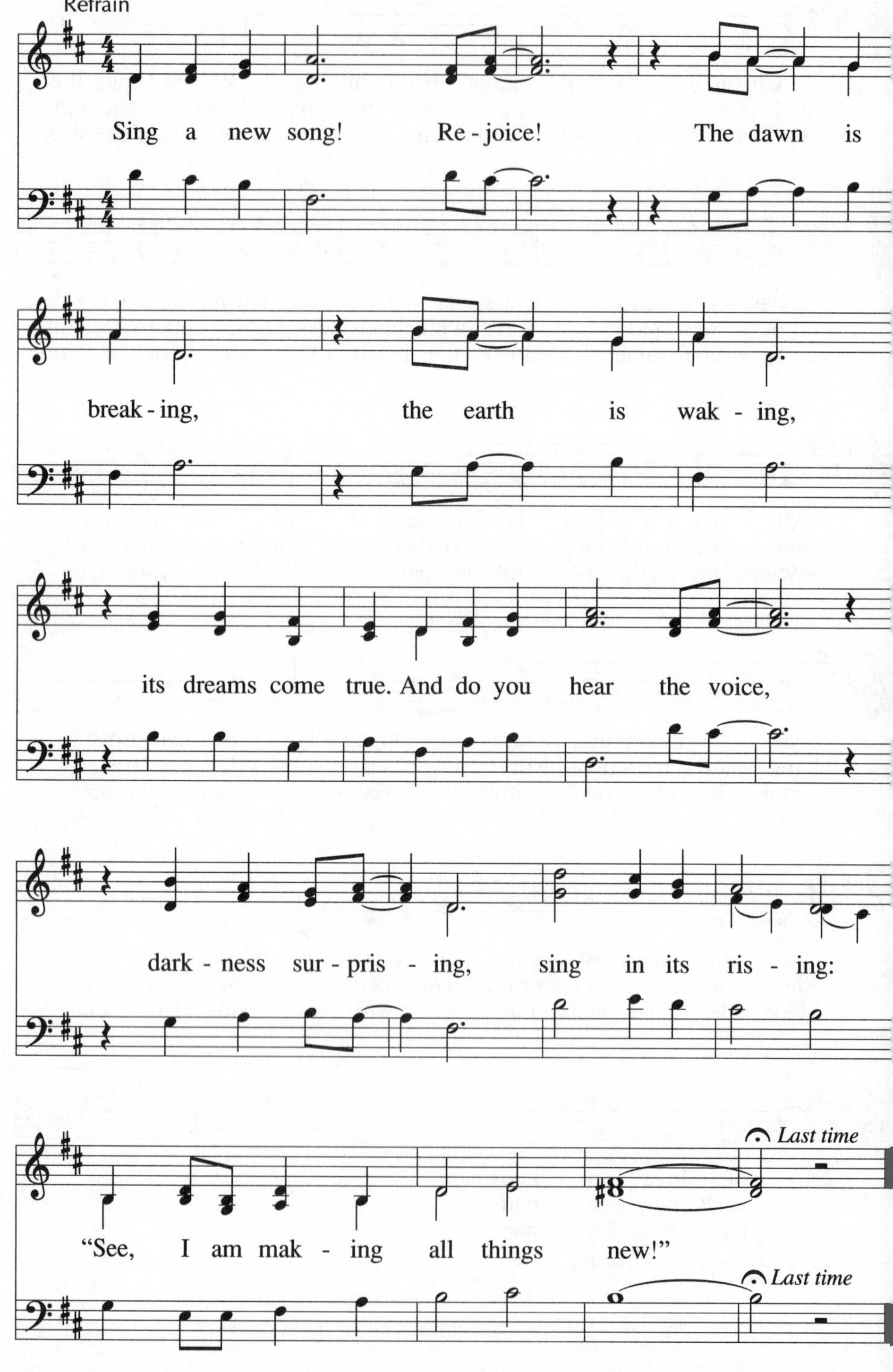
Refrain
Sing a new song! Re - joice! The dawn is
break - ing, the earth is wak - ing,
its dreams come true. And do you hear the voice,
dark - ness sur - pris - ing, sing in its ris - ing:
"See, I am mak - ing all things new!"
Last time
Last time

Verses
1. Whom shall we live for? Whose might-y hand
2. Who found us wan-der-ers, and made us in-to one?
3. Who is known to ev-'ry heart and called by man-y names?
made the moon, the sun and stars on high?
Who is ev-er near with strength to save?
Who has called the low-ly ones "My own,"
Who made a way for us through wa-ter and the sand,
Whose love a-dopt-ed us as daugh-ters and as sons,
Breathes a dream of jus-tice in-to us like tongues of flame?
brought us out of slav-er-y and fed us from the sky?
fam-'ly to the First-born who is ris-en from the grave?
Who is ten-der mer-cy? On-ly God and God a-lone.
D.C.

Text: Rory Cooney, b.1952
Tune: Rory Cooney, b.1952

451 Goodness Is Stronger Than Evil

Good-ness is strong-er than e - vil; love is strong-er than hate; light is strong-er than dark - ness; life is strong-er than death.
Vic-t'ry is ours, vic-t'ry is ours through him who loved us. us.
Oh, vic-t'ry is ours, vic-t'ry is ours through him who loved us. us.
1. 2.

Text: Desmond Tutu, b.1931, ©; adapt. by John L. Bell, b.1949
Tune: GOODNESS IS STRONGER, Irregular; John L. Bell, b.1949, © 1996, Iona Community, GIA Publications, Inc., agent

Sing to the Mountains 452

Refrain
Descant:
Sing to the mountains, sing to the sea.
Melody:
Sing to the mountains, sing to the sea.
Raise your voic - es, lift your hearts.
Raise your voic - es, lift your hearts.
This is the day the Lord has made.
This is the day the Lord has made.
1.-3.
To verses
Let all the earth re - joice.
Let all the earth re - joice.
Last time
joice. Let all the earth re - joice.
joice. Let all the earth re - joice.

Verse 1
1. I will give thanks to you, my Lord.
You have an - swered my plea.
You have saved my soul from death.
D.S.
You are my strength and my song.
Verse 2
2. Ho - ly, ho - ly, ho - ly
Lord, heav - en and earth are
D.S.
full of your glo - ry.

Verse 3
Descant:
3. This is the day that the Lord has made.
Melody:
3. This is the day that the Lord has made.
Let us be glad and re - joice.
Let us be glad and re - joice.
Death has lost and all is life.
Death has lost and all is life.
D.S.
Sing of the glo - ry of God.
D.S.
Sing of the glo - ry of God.

Text: Psalm 118; Bob Dufford, SJ, b.1943
Tune: Bob Dufford, SJ, b.1943; acc. by Randall DeBruyn

453 This Is a Day of New Beginnings

Refrain
Christ is a-live, and goes be-fore us to show and share what
show and
div.
love can do. This is a day of new be-gin-nings;
share what love can do. This day new be-gin - nings;
our God is mak - ing all things new,
our God is mak - ing all things new.

Verses
1. This is a day of new be-gin-ings, time to re-mem-ber,
2. For by the life and death of Je-sus, love's might-y Spir-it,
3. Then let us, with the Spir-it's dar-ing, step from the past, and
div.
and move on, time to be-lieve what love is bring-ing,
now as then, can make for us a world of dif-f'rence,
leave be-hind our dis-a-point-ment, guilt, and griev-ing,
D.C.
lay-ing to rest the pain that's gone.
as faith and hope are born a-gain.
seek-ing new paths, and sure to find.

Text: Brian Wren, b.1936, © 1975, 1995, Hope Publishing Co.
Tune: Lori True, b.1961, © 2003, GIA Publications, Inc.

454 I Know That My Redeemer Lives

1. I know that my Re - deem - er lives;
2. He lives, to bless me with his love;
3. He lives, and grants me dai - ly breath;
4. He lives, all glo - ry to his name;
What joy the blest as - sur - ance gives!
He lives, to plead for me a - bove;
He lives, and I shall con - quer death;
He lives, my Sav - ior still the same;
He lives, he lives, who once was dead;
He lives, my hun - gry soul to feed;
He lives, my man - sion to pre - pare;
What joy the blest as - sur - ance gives;
He lives, my ev - er - last - ing Head!
He lives, to help in time of need.
He lives, to bring me safe - ly there.
I know that my Re - deem - er lives!

Text: Samuel Medley, 1738-1799
Tune: DUKE STREET, LM; John Hatton, c.1710-1793

Surrexit Christus 455

Ostinato Refrain

(hum) Sur - re - xit Chri-stus, al-le-lu - ia!

(hum) Can - ta - te Do - mi - no, al-le-lu - ia!

Verses

Cantor:

1. All you heav-ens, bless the Lord.
Stars of the heav-ens bless the Lord.

2. Sun and moon, bless the Lord. And
you, night and day, bless the Lord.

3. Frost and cold, bless the Lord.

*Choose either part

*
Ice and snow, bless the Lord.
4. Fire and heat, bless the Lord. And
*
you, light and dark-ness, bless the Lord.
5. Spir-its and souls of the just, bless the Lord.
*
Saints and the hum-ble heart-ed, bless the Lord.

*Choose either part

Text: *Christ is risen, sing to the Lord*; Daniel 3; Taizé Community, 1984
Tune: Jacques Berthier, 1923-1994

Now the Green Blade Rises 456

1. Now the green blade ris - es from the bur - ied grain,
2. In the grave they laid him, love by ha - tred slain,
3. Forth he came at East - er, like the ris - en grain,
4. When our hearts are win - try, griev - ing, or in pain,

Wheat that in dark earth man - y days has lain;
Think - ing that he would nev - er wake a - gain,
He that for three days in the grave had lain;
Your touch can call us back to life a - gain,

Love lives a - gain, that with the dead has been;
Laid in the earth like grain that sleeps un - seen;
Raised from the dead, my liv - ing Lord is seen;
Fields of our hearts that dead and bare have been;

Last time
Love is come a - gain like wheat a - ris - ing green.
Last time

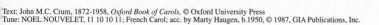

Text: John M.C. Crum, 1872-1958, *Oxford Book of Carols,* © Oxford University Press
Tune: NOEL NOUVELET, 11 10 10 11; French Carol; acc. by Marty Haugen, b.1950, © 1987, GIA Publications, Inc.

457 Jesus Christ Is Risen Today

Descant, verse 4:
4. Sing we to our God a - bove, Al - le - lu - ia!
Praise e - ter - nal as his love; Al - le - lu - ia!
1. Je - sus Christ is ris'n to - day, Al - le - lu - ia!
2. Hymns of praise then let us sing, Al - le - lu - ia!
3. But the pains which he en - dured, Al - le - lu - ia!
4. Sing we to our God a - bove, Al - le - lu - ia!
Our tri - um - phant ho - ly day, Al - le - lu - ia!
Un - to Christ, our heav'n - ly King, Al - le - lu - ia!
Our sal - va - tion have pro - cured; Al - le - lu - ia!
Praise e - ter - nal as his love; Al - le - lu - ia!

Praise him, now his might con - fess, Al - le - lu - ia!
Who did once up - on the cross, Al - le - lu - ia!
Who en - dured the cross and grave, Al - le - lu - ia!
Now a - bove the sky he's King, Al - le - lu - ia!
Praise him, now his might con - fess, Al - le - lu - ia!
Fa - ther, Son, and Spir - it blest. Al - le - lu - ia!
Suf - fer to re - deem our loss. Al - le - lu - ia!
Sin - ners to re - deem and save. Al - le - lu - ia!
Where the an - gels ev - er sing. Al - le - lu - ia!
Fa - ther, Son, and Spir - it blest. Al - le - lu - ia!

Text: St. 1, *Surrexit Christus hodie,* Latin, 14th C.; para. in *Lyra Davidica,* 1708, alt.; st. 2, 3, *The Compleat Psalmodist,* c.1750, alt.; st. 4, Charles Wesley, 1707-1788
Tune: EASTER HYMN, 77 77 with alleluias; *Lyra Davidica,* 1708

458 This Is the Feast of Victory

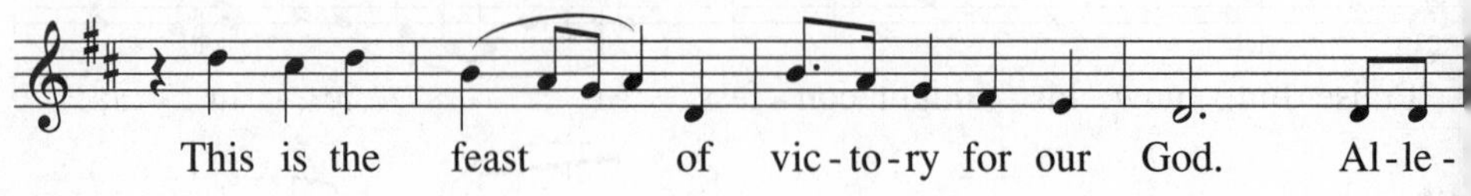
This is the feast of vic-to-ry for our God. Al-le-

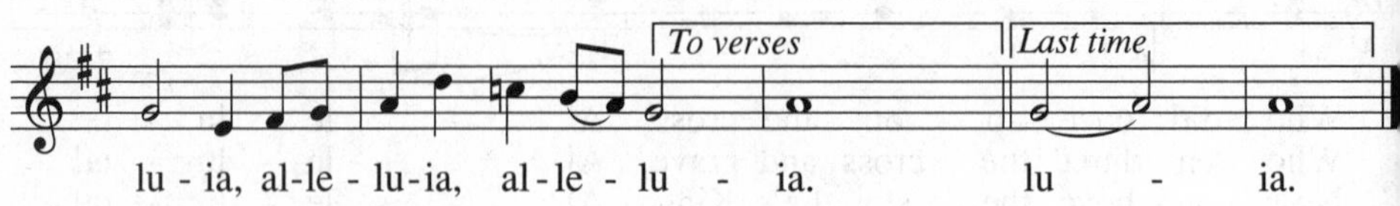
To verses
Last time
lu-ia, al-le-lu-ia, al-le-lu - ia. lu - ia.

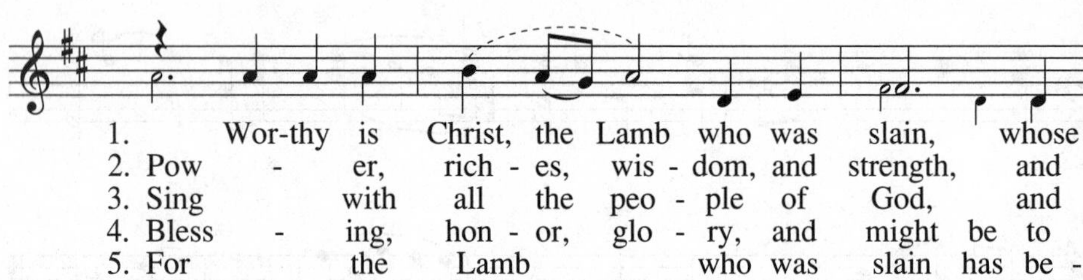
1. Wor-thy is Christ, the Lamb who was slain, whose
2. Pow - er, rich - es, wis - dom, and strength, and
3. Sing with all the peo - ple of God, and
4. Bless - ing, hon - or, glo - ry, and might be to
5. For the Lamb who was slain has be -

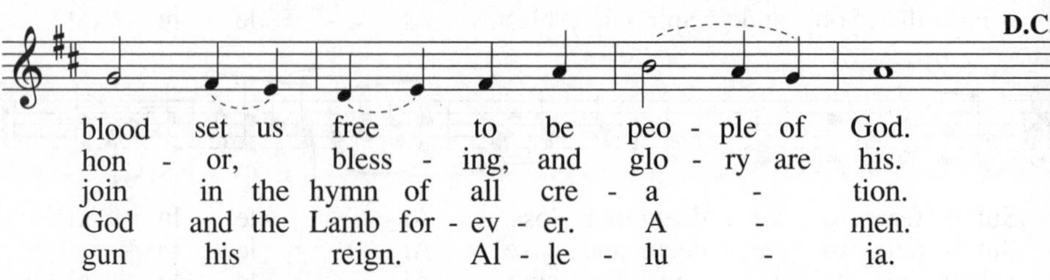
D.C.
blood set us free to be peo - ple of God.
hon - or, bless - ing, and glo - ry are his.
join in the hymn of all cre - a - tion.
God and the Lamb for - ev - er. A - men.
gun his reign. Al - le - lu - ia.

Text: Based on Revelation 5, © 1978, *Lutheran Book of Worship*
Tune: FESTIVAL CANTICLE, Irregular; Richard Hillert, b.1923, © 1975, 1988, Richard Hillert

The Strife Is O′er 459

Refrain

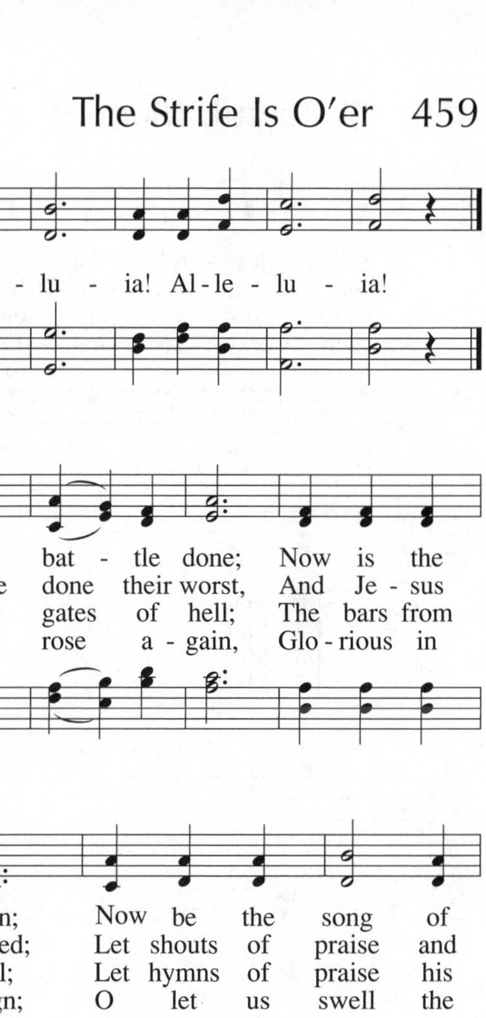
Al - le - lu - ia! Al - le - lu - ia! Al - le - lu - ia!
Verses
1. The strife is o'er, the bat - tle done; Now is the Vic - tor's tri - umph won; Now be the song of
2. Death's might - iest pow'rs have done their worst, And Je - sus has his foes dis - persed; Let shouts of praise and
3. He closed the yawn - ing gates of hell; The bars from heav'n's high por - tals fell; Let hymns of praise his
4. On the third morn he rose a - gain, Glo - rious in maj - es - ty to reign; O let us swell the

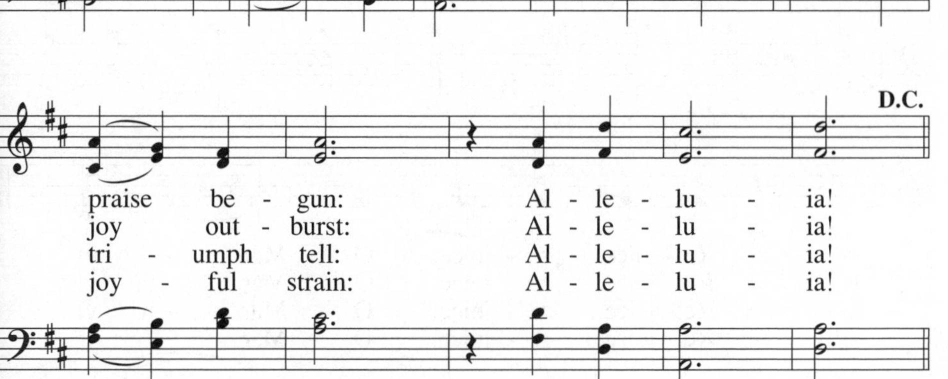
D.C.
praise be - gun: Al - le - lu - ia!
joy out - burst: Al - le - lu - ia!
tri - umph tell: Al - le - lu - ia!
joy - ful strain: Al - le - lu - ia!

Text: *Finita iam sunt praelia;* Latin, 12th C.; tr. by Francis Pott, 1832-1909, alt.
Tune: VICTORY, 888 with alleluias; Giovanni da Palestrina, 1525-1594; adapt. by William H. Monk, 1823-1889

460 Be Joyful, Mary

1. Be joy - ful, Mar - y, heav'n - ly Queen, be joy - ful, Mar - y! Your grief is changed to joy se - rene, Al - le - lu - ia! Re - joice, re - joice, O Mar - y!
2. The Son you bore by heav - en's grace, be joy - ful, Mar - y! Did by his death our guilt e - rase, Al - le - lu - ia! Re - joice, re - joice, O Mar - y!
3. The Lord has ris - en from the dead, be joy - ful, Mar - y! He rose in glo - ry as he said, Al - le - lu - ia! Re - joice, re - joice, O Mar - y!
4. Then pray to God, O Vir - gin fair, be joy - ful, Mar - y! That he our souls to heav - en bear, Al - le - lu - ia! Re - joice, re - joice, O Mar - y!

Text: *Regina caeli, jubila*; Latin, 17th C.; tr. anon. in *Psallite,* 1901
Tune: REGINA CAELI, 8 5 8 4 7; *Leisentritt's Gesangbuch,* 1584, alt.

That Easter Day with Joy Was Bright 461

1. That Eas - ter day with joy was bright, The sun shone out with fair - er light, When to their long - ing eyes re - stored, The a - pos - tles saw their ris - en Lord.
2. His ris - en flesh with ra - diance glowed; His wound - ed hands and feet he showed; Those scars their sol - emn wit - ness gave That Christ was ris - en from the grave.
3. O Je - sus, King of gen - tle - ness, Who with your grace our hearts pos - sess That we may give you all our days The will - ing trib - ute of our praise.
4. O Lord of all, with us a - bide In this our joy - ful East - er - tide; From ev - 'ry weap - on death can wield Your own re - deemed for ev - er shield.
5. All praise, to you, O ris - en Lord, Now both by heav'n and earth a - dored; To God the Fa - ther e - qual praise, And Spir - it blest, our songs we raise.

Text: *Claro paschali gaudio*; Latin 5th C.; tr. by John M. Neale, 1818-1866, alt.
Tune: PUER NOBIS, LM; adapt. by Michael Praetorius, 1571-1621

462 Alleluia No. 1

Refrain
Descant:
Al - le - lu - ia, al - le - lu - ia,
Melody:
Al - le - lu - ia, al - le - lu - ia, give thanks to the ris - en Lord. Al - le -
To verses
Last time
al - le - lu - ia, praise to his Name.
lu - ia, al - le - lu - ia, give praise to his Name.
Verses
1. Je - sus is Lord of all the earth.
2. Spread the good news o'er all the earth:
3. We have been cru - ci - fied with Christ.
4. God has pro - claimed his gra - cious gift:
5. Come, let us praise the liv - ing God,
D.C.
He is the King of cre - a - tion.
Je - sus has died and has ris - en.
Now we shall live for ev - er.
Life e - ter - nal for all who be - lieve.
Joy - ful - ly sing to our Sav - ior.

Text: Donald Fishel, b.1950, © 1973, Word of God Music
Tune: ALLELUIA NO. 1, 8 8 with refrain; Donald Fishel, b.1950, © 1973, Word of God Music; descant harm. by Betty Pulkingham, b.1929, Charles Mallory, b.1953, and George Mims, b.1938, © 1979, Celebration

At the Lamb's High Feast We Sing 463

1. At the Lamb's high feast we sing Praise to our vic -
2. Where the Pas - chal blood is poured, Death's dark an - gel
3. Might - y vic - tim from the sky, Hell's fierce pow'rs be -
4. East - er tri - umph, East - er joy, This a - lone can
to - rious King. Who has washed us in the tide
sheathes his sword; Is - rael's hosts tri - umph - ant go
neath you lie; You have con - quered in the fight,
sin de - stroy; From sin's pow'r, Lord, set us free
Flow - ing from his pierc - ed side; Praise we him, whose
Through the wave that drowns the foe. Praise we Christ, whose
You have brought us life and light: Now no more can
New - born souls in you to be. Fa - ther, who the
love di - vine Gives his sa - cred Blood for wine,
blood was shed, Pas - chal vic - tim, Pas - chal bread;
death ap - pall, Now no more the grave en - thrall;
crown shall give, Sav - ior, by whose death we live,

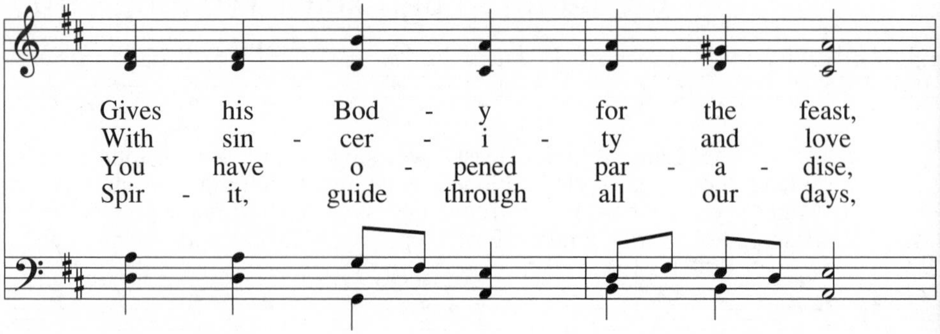

Gives his Bod - y for the feast,
Christ the vic - tim, Christ the priest.

With sin - cer - i - ty and love
Eat we man - na from a - bove.

You have o - pened par - a - dise,
And in you your saints shall rise.

Spir - it, guide through all our days,
Three in One, your name we praise.

Text: *Ad regias agni dapes;* Latin, 4th C.; tr. by Robert Campbell, 1814-1868
Tune: SALZBURG, 77 77 D; Jakob Hintze, 1622-1702; harm. by J.S. Bach, 1685-1750

464 The Tomb Is Empty

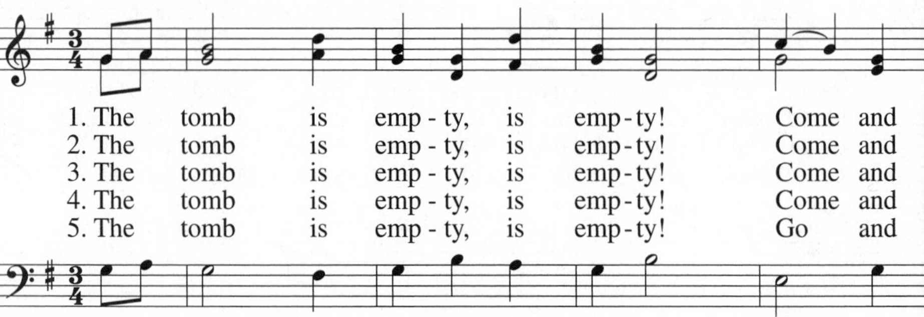
1. The tomb is emp - ty, is emp-ty! Come and
2. The tomb is emp - ty, is emp-ty! Come and
3. The tomb is emp - ty, is emp-ty! Come and
4. The tomb is emp - ty, is emp-ty! Come and
5. The tomb is emp - ty, is emp-ty! Go and

see where once the bod - y lay.
hear these words of life and peace:
touch the stone and fold - ed shroud.
meet the Ris - en Christ our Lord
serve all peo - ple who long to be free!
Can it be true, be true that Je - sus Christ
"He is not here, not here. He lives a - gain
Christ lives in - deed, in - deed. Al - le - lu - ia!
in whom we have, we have our vic - to - ry,
Raise those who sleep, who sleep in tombs of fear,
is raised to life to - day? Sing
in all your Gal - i - lees." Sing
Be - liev - ers shout a - loud. Sing
in whom is life re - stored. Sing
and give them eyes to see! Sing
al - le - lu - ia! Sing al - le - lu - ia!

Text: Sts. 1-4, Sylvia G. Dunstan, 1955-1993, © 1991, GIA Publications, Inc.; St. 5, David Haas, b.1957, © 2003, GIA Publications, Inc.
Tune: David Haas, b.1957; vocal arr. by Robert J. Batastini, b.1942, © 2003, GIA Publications, Inc.

465 Christ Has Risen

1. Christ has ris - en while earth slum - bers, Christ has
2. Christ has ris - en for the peo - ple Whom he
3. Christ has ris - en to com - pan - ion For - mer
4. Christ has ris - en and for ev - er Lives to
ris - en where hope died, As he said and as he
died to love and save; Christ has ris - en for the
friends who fear the night, Sens - ing loss and lim - i -
chal - lenge and to change All whose lives are messed or
prom - ised, As we doubt - ed and de -
wom - en Bring - ing flowers to grace his
ta - tion Where their faith had once burned
man - gled, All who find re - lig - ion
nied. Let the moon em - brace the bless - ing; Let the
grave. Christ has ris - en for dis - ci - ples Hud - dled
bright. They be - moan what is no long - er, They ex -
strange. Christ is ris - en, Christ is pres - ent Mak - ing
sun sus - tain the cheer; Let the world con - firm the
in an up - stairs room. He whose word in - spired cre -
pect no hope - ful sign Till Christ ends their con - ver -
us what he has been— Ev - i - dence of trans - for -
ru - mor: Christ is ris - en, God is here!
a - tion Can't be si - lenced by the tomb.
sa - tion, Break - ing bread and shar - ing wine.
ma - tion In which God is known and seen.

Text: John L. Bell, b.1949
Tune: TRANSFORMATION, 8 7 8 7 D; John L. Bell, b.1949

Lord, You Give the Great Commission 466

1. Lord, you give the great com - mis - sion:
2. Lord, you call us to your serv - ice:
3. Lord, you make the com - mon ho - ly:
4. Lord, you show us love's true meas - ure:
5. Lord, you bless with words as - sur - ing:
"Heal the sick and preach the word."
"In my name bap - tize and teach."
"This my bod - y, this my blood."
"Fa - ther, what they do, for - give."
"I am with you to the end."
Lest the Church ne - glect its mis - sion,
That the world may trust your prom - ise,
Let us all, for earth's true glo - ry,
Yet we hoard as pri - vate treas - ure
Faith and hope and love re - stor - ing,
And the Gos - pel go un - heard,
Life a - bun - dant meant for each,
Dai - ly lift life heav - en - ward,
All that you so free - ly give.
May we serve as you in - tend,

Help us wit - ness to your pur - pose
Give us all new fer - vor, draw us
Ask - ing that the world a - round us
May your care and mer - cy lead us
And, a - mid the cares that claim us,
With re - newed in - teg - ri - ty;
Clos - er in com - mun - i - ty;
Share your chil - dren's lib - er - ty;
To a just so - ci - e - ty;
Hold in mind e - ter - ni - ty;
With the Spir - it's gifts em - pow'r us
For the work of min - is - try.

Text: Jeffery Rowthorn, b.1934, © 1978, Hope Publishing Co.
Tune: ABBOT'S LEIGH, 8 7 8 7 D; Cyril V. Taylor, 1907-1991, © 1942, 1970, Hope Publishing Co.

A Hymn of Glory Let Us Sing 467

1. A hymn of glo - ry let us sing! New
2. The ho - ly ap - os - tol - ic band Up -
3. To whom the shin - ing an - gels cry, "Why
4. O ris - en Christ, as - cend - ed Lord, All
hymns through - out the world shall ring: Al - le - lu - ia! Al - le -
on the Mount of Ol - ives stand. Al - le - lu - ia! Al - le -
stand and gaze up - on the sky?" Al - le - lu - ia! Al - le -
praise to you let earth ac - cord: Al - le - lu - ia! Al - le -
lu - ia! Christ, by a road be - fore un - trod. As -
lu - ia! And with his faith - ful fol - l'wers see Their
lu - ia! "This is the Sav - ior!" Thus they say, "This
lu - ia! You are, while end - less a - ges run, With
cends un - to the throne of God.
Lord as - cend in maj - es - ty. Al - le - lu - ia! Al - le -
is his glo - rious tri - umph day!"
Fa - ther and with Spir - it one.
lu - ia! Al - le - lu - ia! Al - le - lu - ia! Al - le - lu - ia!

Text: *Hymnum canamus gloria*; Venerable Bede, 673-735; tr. *Lutheran Book of Worship*, © 1978
Tune: LASST UNS ERFREUEN, LM with alleluias; *Geistliche Kirchengasange*, Cologne, 1623; harm. by Ralph Vaughan Williams, 1872-1958, © Oxford University Press

468 Hail the Day That Sees Him Rise

1. Hail the day that sees him rise, Al - le - lu - ia!
2. There for him high tri - umph waits; Al - le - lu - ia!
3. High - est heav'n its Lord re - ceives, Al - le - lu - ia!
4. See, he lifts his hands a - bove. Al - le - lu - ia!
5. Still for us he in - ter - cedes, Al - le - lu - ia!
6. There we shall with him re - main, Al - le - lu - ia!
To his throne a - bove the skies; Al - le - lu - ia!
Lift your heads, e - ter - nal gates; Al - le - lu - ia!
Yet he loves the earth he leaves: Al - le - lu - ia!
See, he shows the prints of love. Al - le - lu - ia!
His pre - vail - ing death he pleads, Al - le - lu - ia!
Part - ners of his end - less reign; Al - le - lu - ia!
Christ, a - while to mor - tals giv'n, Al - le - lu - ia!
He has con - quered death and sin; Al - le - lu - ia!
Though re - turn - ing to his throne, Al - le - lu - ia!
Hark, his gra - cious lips be - stow, Al - le - lu - ia!
Near him - self pre - pares our place, Al - le - lu - ia!
There his face un - cloud - ed see. Al - le - lu - ia!

Re - as - cends his na - tive heav'n. Al - le - lu - ia!
Take the King of glo - ry in. Al - le - lu - ia!
Still he calls the world his own. Al - le - lu - ia!
Bless - ings on his church be - low. Al - le - lu - ia!
He the first fruits of our race. Al - le - lu - ia!
Live with him e - ter - nal - ly. Al - le - lu - ia!

Text: Charles Wesley, 1707-1788, alt.
Tune: LLANFAIR, 77 77 with alleluias; Robert Williams, 1781-1821

Go to the World! 469

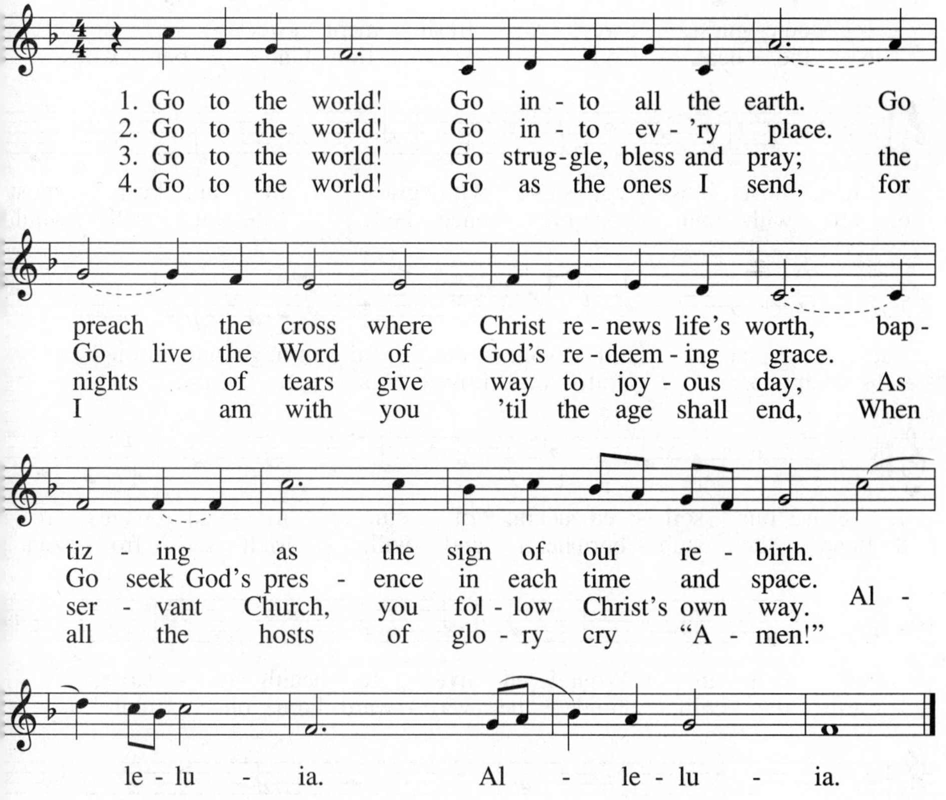

1. Go to the world! Go in - to all the earth. Go
2. Go to the world! Go in - to ev - 'ry place.
3. Go to the world! Go strug - gle, bless and pray; the
4. Go to the world! Go as the ones I send, for

preach the cross where Christ re - news life's worth, bap -
Go live the Word of God's re - deem - ing grace.
nights of tears give way to joy - ous day, As
I am with you 'til the age shall end, When

tiz - ing as the sign of our re - birth.
Go seek God's pres - ence in each time and space.
ser - vant Church, you fol - low Christ's own way.
all the hosts of glo - ry cry "A - men!"

Al - le - lu - ia. Al - le - lu - ia.

Text: Sylvia G. Dunstan, 1955-1993,
Tune: SINE NOMINE, 10 10 10 with alleluias; Ralph Vaughan Williams, 1872-1958,

470 Sequence for Pentecost

1. Ho - ly Spir - it, Lord Di - vine, Come, from heights of heav'n and shine, Come with bless - ed ra - diance bright!
2. Come, O Fa - ther of the poor, Come, whose treas - ured gifts en - dure, Come, our heart's un - fail - ing light!
3. Of con - so - lers, wis - est, best, And our soul's most wel - come guest, Sweet re - fresh - ment sweet re - pose.
4. In our la - bor rest most sweet, Pleas - ant cool - ness in the heat, Con - so - la - tion in our woes.
5. Light most bless - ed, shine with grace In our heart's most se - cret place, Fill your faith - ful through and through.
6. Left with - out your pres - ence here, Life it - self would dis - ap - pear, Noth - ing thrives a - part from you!
7. Cleanse our soil - ed hearts of sin, Ar - id souls re - fresh with - in, Wound - ed lives to health re - store.
8. Bend the stub - born heart and will, Melt the fro - zen, warm the chill, Guide the way - ward home once more!
9. On the faith - ful who are true And pro -
10. Give us vir - tue's sure re - ward, Give us

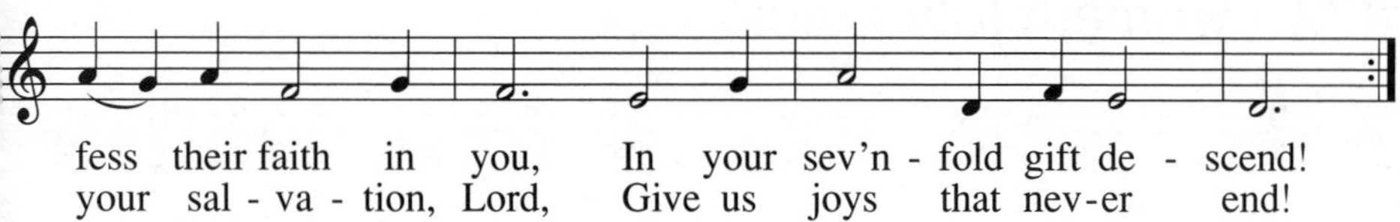
fess their faith in you, In your sev'n - fold gift de - scend!
your sal - va - tion, Lord, Give us joys that nev-er end!

Text: Sequence for Pentecost, 13th. C.; tr. by Peter J. Scagnelli; b.1949, © 1983
Tune: Mode I; acc. by Adriaan Engels, 1906-2003, © Interkerkelijke Stichting voor het Kerklied Den Haag

Come Down, O Love Divine 471

1. Come down, O Love di - vine, Seek now this soul of
2. O let it free - ly burn, Till earth - ly pas - sions
3. And so the yearn - ing strong, With which the soul will

mine, And vis - it it with your own ar - dor glow - ing;
turn To dust and ash - es in its heat con - sum - ing;
long, Shall far out - pass the power of hu - man tell - ing;

O Com - fort - er, draw near, With - in my heart ap -
And let your glo - rious light Shine ev - er on my
For none can guess its grace, Till love cre - ates the

pear, And kin - dle it, your ho - ly flame be - stow - ing.
sight, And clothe me round, the while my path il - lum - ing.
place Where - in the Ho - ly Spir - it makes its dwell - ing.

Text: *Discendi, Amor Santo;* Bianco da Siena, d.c.1434; tr. by Richard F. Littledale, 1833-1890
Tune: DOWN AMPNEY, 66 11 D; Ralph Vaughan Williams, 1872-1958, © Oxford University Press

472 Come, Holy Ghost

1. Come, Ho - ly Ghost, Cre - a - tor blest, And in our
2. O Com-fort - er, to thee we cry, Thou heav'n-ly
3. O Ho - ly Ghost, through thee a - lone, Know we the
4. Praise we the Lord, Fa - ther and Son, And Ho - ly
hearts take up thy rest; Come with thy grace
gift of God most high; Thou fount of life,
Fa - ther and the Son; Be this our firm
Spir - it with them one; And may the Son
and heav'n-ly aid To fill the hearts which thou hast
and fire of love, And sweet a - noint - ing from a -
un - chang-ing creed, That thou dost from them both pro -
on us be - stow All gifts that from the Spir - it
made, To fill the hearts which thou hast made.
bove, And sweet a - noint - ing from a - bove.
ceed, That thou dost from them both pro - ceed.
flow, All gifts that from the Spir - it flow.

Text: *Veni, Creator Spiritus;* attr. to Rabanus Maurus, 776-856; tr. by Edward Caswall, 1814-1878, alt.
Tune: LAMBILLOTTE, LM with repeat; Louis Lambillotte, SJ, 1796-1855, harm. by Richard Proulx, b.1937,

Spirit Wind 473

Refrain
Spir - it Wind, Breath of God, breathe new life in - to the world. Spir - it Wind, Breath of God, breathe new life in - to the world.
To verses
Last time
Verses
1. My soul cries out, "O bless the Lord!" O God, you are the Ho - ly One; so man - y works your hands have made through-out the earth.
2. If you should take a - way our breath, what could we do but fall to dust? When you send forth the breath of life we rise a - gain!
3. All praise and thanks are yours, O God; may you re - joice in all your works. May you find joy in us as we re - joice in you!
D.C.

Text: Psalm 104; Scott Soper, b.1961
Tune: Scott Soper, b.1961

474 Veni Creator Spiritus

1. Ve - ni Cre - á - tor Spí - ri - tus,
2. Qui dí - ce - ris Pa - rá - cli - tus,
3. Tu se - pti - fór - mis mú - ne - re,
4. Ac - cén - de lu - men sén - si - bus,
5. Hó - stem re - pél - las lón - gi - us,
6. Per te sci - á - mus da Pa - trem,
7. De - o Pa - tri sit gló - ri - a,

Men - tes tu - ó - rum ví - si - ta:
Al - tís - si - mi dó - num De - i,
Di - gi - tus pa - tér - nae déx - te - rae,
In - fun - de - a - mó - rem cór - di - bus,
Pa - cém - que do - nes pró - ti - nus:
No - scá - mus at - que Fí - li - um
Et Fí - li - o, qui a mór - tu - is

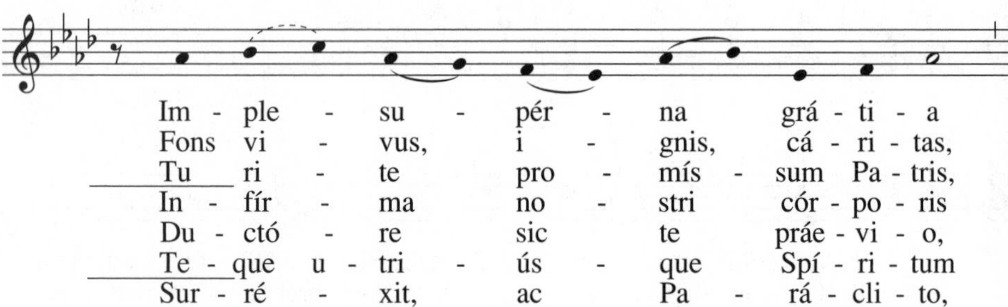
Im - ple - su - pér - na grá - ti - a
Fons vi - vus, i - gnis, cá - ri - tas,
Tu ri - te pro - mís - sum Pa - tris,
In - fír - ma no - stri cór - po - ris
Du - ctó - re sic te práe - vi - o,
Te - que u - tri - ús - que Spí - ri - tum
Sur - ré - xit, ac Pa - rá - cli - to,

Quae tu cre - á - sti pé - cto - ra.
Et spi - ri - tá - lis ún - cti - o.
Ser - mó - ne di - tans gút - tu - ra.
Vir - tú - te fír - mans pér - pe - ti.
Vi - té - mus om - ne nó - xi - um.
Cre - dá - mus om - ni tém - po - re.
In sae - cu - ló - rum sáe - cu - la. A - men.

Text: Attr. to Rabanus Maurus, 776-856
Tune: VENI CREATOR SPIRITUS, LM; Mode VIII; acc. by Richard Proulx, b.1937,

O Holy Spirit, by Whose Breath 475

1. O Ho - ly Spir - it, by whose breath
2. You are the seek - er's sure re - source,
3. In you God's en - er - gy is shown,
4. Flood our dull sens - es with your light;
5. From in - ner strife grant us re - lease;
6. Praise to the Fa - ther, Christ the Word,
3
Life ris - es vi - brant out of death:
Of burn - ing love the liv - ing source,
To us your var - ied gifts made known.
In mu - tual love our hearts u - nite.
Turn na - tions to the ways of peace.
And to the Spir - it, God the Lord;
Come to cre - ate, re - new, in - spire;
Pro - tec - tor in the midst of strife,
Teach us to speak; teach us to hear;
Your pow'r the whole cre - a - tion fills;
To full - er life your peo - ple bring
To whom all hon - or, glo - ry be
Come, kin - dle in our hearts your fire.
The giv - er and the Lord of life.
Yours is the tongue and yours the ear.
Con - firm our weak, un - cer - tain wills.
That as one bod - y we may sing:
Both now and for e - ter - ni - ty.

Text: *Veni, Creator Spiritus;* attr. to Rabanus Maurus, 776-865; tr. by John W. Grant, b.1919, © 1971
Tune: VENI CREATOR SPIRITUS, LM; Mode VIII; setting by Richard J. Wojcik, b.1923, © 1975, GIA Publications, Inc.

476 Send Us Your Spirit

Refrain
*1.
2.
Come Lord Je-sus, send us your Spir-it, re-new the face of the earth.
Come Lord Je-sus, send us your Spir-it, re-new the face of the earth.
To verses
Final ending
Verses
1. Come to us, Spir-it of God, breathe in us now, we sing to-geth-er.
2. Fill us with the fire of your love, burn in us now, bring us to-geth-er.
3. Send us the wings of new birth, fill all the earth with the love you have taught us. Let
Spir-it of hope and of light, fill our lives, come to us, Spir-it of God.
Come to us, dwell in us, change our lives, O Lord, come to us, Spir-it of God.
all cre-a-tion now be shak-en with love, come to us, Spir-it of God.
D.C.

May be sung in canon.

Text: David Haas, b.1957
Tune: David Haas, b.1957; acc. by Jeanne Cotter, b.1964

Send Down the Fire 477

Refrain
Melody (Soprano):
Send down the fire of your jus - tice,
Alto:
Send down the fire of your
Send down the fire of your jus - tice,
Tenor:
Bass:
Send down the fire of your
Send down the rains of your love; Come,
jus - tice, Send down your love;
Send down the rains of your love; Come,
jus - tice, Send down your love;
send down the Spir - it, breathe life in your peo - ple, and
send down the Spir - it, breathe life in your peo - ple, and

Last time to coda
we shall be peo - ple of God.
Last time to coda
we shall be peo - ple of God.
Verses
1. Call us to be your com - pas - sion, Teach us the
2. Call us to learn of your mer - cy, Teach us the
3. Call us to an - swer op - pres - sion, Teach us the
4. Call us to wit - ness your King - dom, Give us the
song of your love; Give us hearts that
way of your peace; Give us hearts that
fire of your truth; Give us right - eous
pres - ence of Christ; May your ho - ly
sing, Give us deeds that ring, Make us ring with the
feel, Give us hands that heal, Make us walk in the
souls, 'Til your jus - tice rolls, Make us burn with the
light Keep us shin - ing bright, Ev - er shine with the
D.C.
Coda
song of your love.
way of your peace.
fire of your truth.
pres - ence of Christ.

Text: Marty Haugen, b.1950
Tune: Marty Haugen, b.1950

Veni Sancte Spiritus 478

Ostinato Refrain
pp Melody:
Ve - ni San - cte Spi - ri - tus.
pp Harmony:
Ve - ni San - cte Spi - ri - tus.

As the ostinato continues, vocal and instrumental verses are sung or played as desired with some space always left between the verses (after the cantor's "Veni Sancte Spiritus").

Verses

Cantor:

1. Come, Ho - ly Spir - it, from heav - en shine forth
with your glo - rious light. Ve - ni San - cte Spi - ri - tus.

2. Come, Fa - ther of the poor, come, gen - er - ous Spir - it,
come, light of our hearts. Ve - ni San - cte Spi - ri - tus.

Text: *Come Holy Spirit;* Verses drawn from the Pentecost Sequence; Taizé Community, 1978
Tune: Jacques Berthier, 1923-1994

479 Holy Spirit, Come to Us

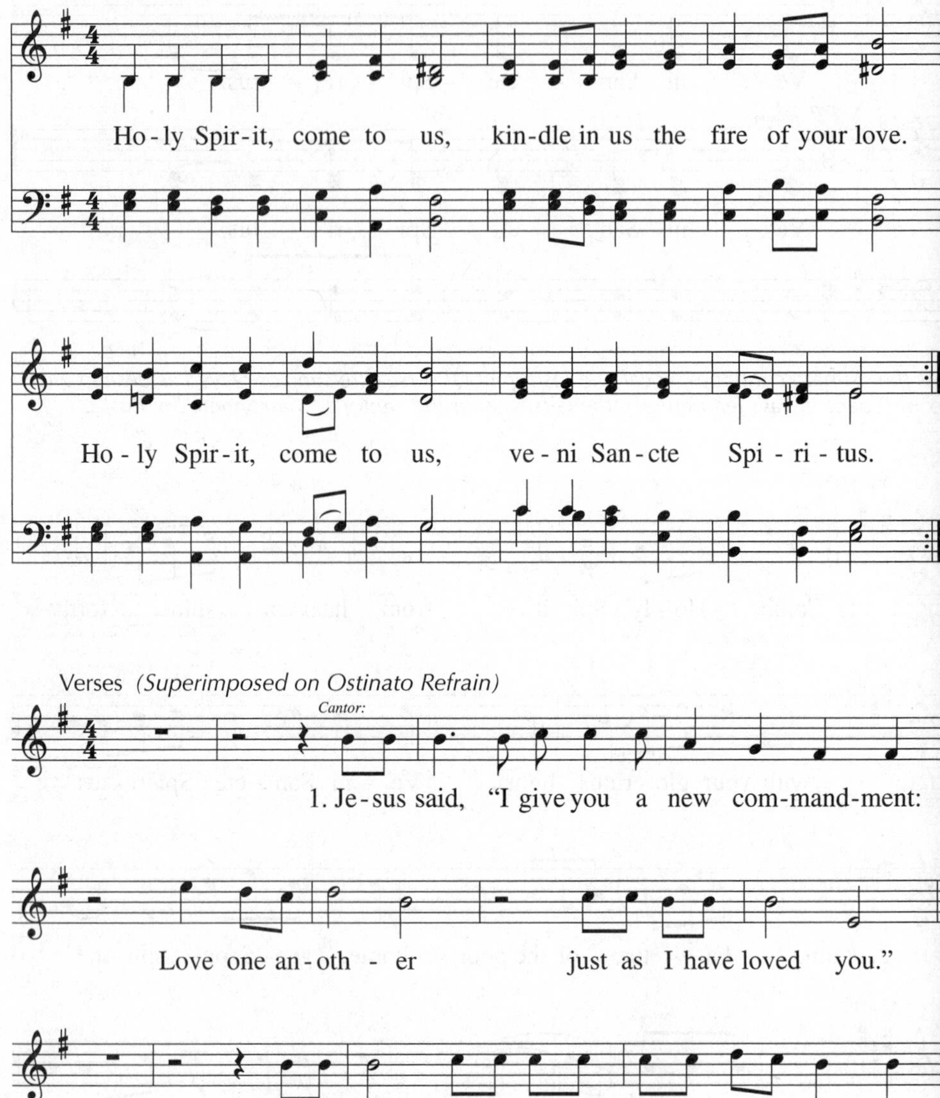
Ostinato Refrain
Ho - ly Spir - it, come to us, kin - dle in us the fire of your love.
Ho - ly Spir - it, come to us, ve - ni San - cte Spi - ri - tus.
Verses (Superimposed on Ostinato Refrain)
Cantor:
1. Je - sus said, "I give you a new com - mand - ment:
Love one an - oth - er just as I have loved you."
2. Je - sus said, "It is by your love for one an - oth - er,

4
3. Je - sus said, "No one has great - er love than this:
to lay down one's life for those one loves."
4. We know love by this, that Christ laid down his
*
life for us. 5. This is love: it is not we who have
3
loved God but God who loved us. 6. God is love,
and those who a - bide in love a - bide in God and God in them.

*Choose either part

Text: John 13:35, 15:12-13, 1 John 3:16, 4:10, 16
Tune: Jacques Berthier, 1923-1994

480 Spirit of God

Refrain

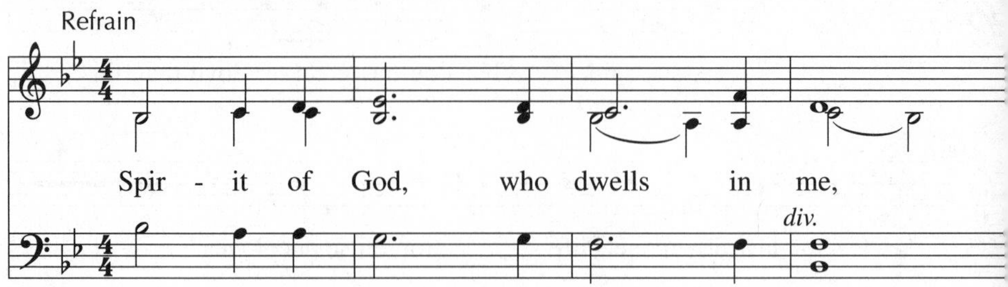
Spir - it of God, who dwells in me,
div.

O - pen my eyes that I may see.

Come fill my heart and make me whole.

Spir - it of God, I am yours.

Verses
1. This is the Spir-it of the liv-ing God,
2. Come, Ho-ly Spir-it, and set me free
Who hears your ev-'ry sin-gle prayer.
To do the best I can.
O this is the Spir-it of the
O come, Ho-ly Spir-it, and
liv-ing God,
set me free
Who is al-
To be all
ways right there.
that I am.
D.C.

Text: James E. Moore, Jr., b.1951
Tune: James E. Moore, Jr., b.1951

481 Spirit Blowing through Creation

Verses
1. Spir - it blow - ing through cre - a - tion, Spir - it burn - ing in the skies, Let the hope of your sal - va - tion fill our eyes; God of splen - dor, God of glo - ry, You who light the stars a - bove, All the heav - ens tell the sto - ry of your love.
2. As you moved up - on the wa - ters, As you ride up - on the wind, Move us all, your sons and daugh - ters deep with - in; As you shaped the hills and moun - tains, Formed the land and filled the deep, Let your hand re - new and wak - en all who sleep.
3. Love that sends the riv - ers danc - ing, Love that wa - ters all that lives, Love that heals and holds and rous - es and for - gives; You are food for all your crea - tures, You are hun - ger in the soul, In your hands the bro - ken - heart - ed are made whole.
4. All the crea - tures you have fash - ioned, All that live and breathe in you, Find their hope in your com - pas - sion, strong and true; You, O Spir - it of sal - va - tion, You a - lone, be - neath, a - bove, Come, re - new your whole cre - a - tion in your love.
To verses 2, 4
To refrain*

*Refrain may be sung after each verse by using this ending.

Refrain
Descant:
Spir-it re-new-ing the earth, re-new-ing the hearts of all
Melody:
Spir-it re-new-ing the earth, re-new-ing the hearts of all
peo-ple; Burn in the wea-ry souls,
peo-ple; Burn in the wea-ry souls,
blow through the si-lent lips, come now a-wake us,
blow through the si-lent lips, come now a-wake us,
Spir-it of God.
Spir-it of God.
To verse 3
Last time

Text: Marty Haugen, b.1950
Tune: Marty Haugen, b.1950

482 We Are One

We are one, we are one. We are
one in the Spir - it, we are one. Hal - le -
lu - jah, Hal - le - lu - jah, we are
one in the Spir - it, we are one.

Text: Timothy Wright, ©
Tune: Congregational Praise Song, arr. Valeria A. Foster, © 2000, GIA Publications, Inc.

Holy, Holy, Holy! Lord God Almighty 483

1. Ho - ly, Ho - ly, Ho - ly! Lord God Al - might - y!
2. Ho - ly, Ho - ly, Ho - ly! all the saints a - dore thee,
3. Ho - ly, Ho - ly, Ho - ly! though the dark - ness hide thee,
4. Ho - ly, Ho - ly, Ho - ly! Lord God Al - might - y!
Ear - ly in the morn - ing our song shall rise to thee:
Cast - ing down their gold - en crowns a - round the glass - y sea;
Though the eye made blind by sin thy glo - ry may not see,
All thy works shall praise thy Name in earth, and sky, and sea;
Ho - ly, Ho - ly, Ho - ly! mer - ci - ful and might - y,
Cher - u - bim and ser - a - phim fall - ing down be - fore thee,
On - ly thou art ho - ly; there is none be - side thee,
Ho - ly, Ho - ly, Ho - ly! mer - ci - ful and might - y,
God in three Per - sons, bless - ed Trin - i - ty.
God ev - er - last - ing through e - ter - ni - ty.
Per - fect in pow'r, in love, and pu - ri - ty.
God in three Per - sons, bless - ed Trin - i - ty.

Text: Reginald Heber, 1783-1826, alt.
Tune: NICAEA, 11 12 12 10; John Bacchus Dykes, 1823-1876

484 The Play of the Godhead

1. The play of the God-head, the Trin - i - ty's dance,
2. The warm mists of sum - mer, cool wa - ters that flow,
3. In God's gra - cious im - age of co - e - qual parts,
Em - brac - es the earth in a sa - cred ro - mance:
Turn crys - tal as ice when the win - try winds blow.
We gath - er as danc - ers, u - nit - ing our hearts.
With God the Cre - a - tor, and Christ the true Son,
The tap - root that nur - tures, the shoot grow - ing free,
Men, wom - en, and chil - dren, and all liv - ing things,
En - twined with the Spir - it, a web dai - ly spun
The life - giv - ing fruit, full and ripe on the tree:
We join in the round of bright na - ture that rings
In span - gles of mys - t'ry the great Three-in - One.
More mys - tic and won-drous, the great One - in - Three.
With rap - ture and rhy - thm: Cre - a - tion now sings!

Text: Mary Louise Bringle, b.1953
Tune: BEDFORD PARK, 11 11 11 11 11; Robert J. Batastini, b.1942

O God, Almighty Father 485

1. O God, al-might-y Fa - ther, Cre - a - tor of all things, The
2. O Je - sus, Word in - car - nate, Re - deem-er most a - dored, All
3. O God, the Ho - ly Spir - it, Who lives with - in our soul, Send
heav-ens stand in won - der, While earth your glo - ry sings.
glo - ry, praise, and hon - or Be yours, O sov-'reign Lord.
forth your light and lead us To our e - ter - nal goal.
O most ho - ly Trin - i - ty, Un - di - vid - ed u - ni - ty,
Ho-ly God, might-y God, God im - mor - tal be a - dored!

Text: *Gott Vater sei gepriesen;* anon; tr. by Irvin Udulutsch, OFM Cap., fl. 1959, alt. © 1959, The Liturgical Press
Tune: GOTT VATER SEI GEPRIESEN, 7 6 7 6 with refrain; *Limburg Gesangbuch,* 1838; harm. by Healey Willan, 1880-1968, © 1958, Ralph Jusko Publications, Inc.

486 Come Now, Almighty King

1. Come now, al - might - y King, Help us your
2. Come now, In - car - nate Son, Your life in
3. Come, ho - ly Com - fort - er, Your sa - cred
4. To the great One in Three E - ter - nal
name to sing, Help us to praise.
us be - gun, Our prayer at - tend.
wit - ness bear In this glad hour.
prais - es be For ev - er - more!
Fa - ther all glo - ri - ous, Ev - er vic - to - ri - ous,
Come and your peo - ple bless And give your Word suc-cess;
Your grace to us im - part, Now rule in ev - 'ry heart
Your sov - 'reign maj - es - ty May we in glo - ry see
Come and reign o - ver us, An - cient of Days.
Strength - en your right - eous - ness, Sav - ior and Friend!
Nev - er from us de - part, Spir - it of Pow'r!
And to e - ter - ni - ty Love and a - dore!

Text: Anon. c.1757
Tune: ITALIAN HYMN, 66 4 666 4; Felice de Giardini, 1716-1796

TRINITY

Stand Up, Friends 487

Verses
1. Praise the God who chang - es plac - es, Leaves the loft - y seat, Wel - comes us with warm em - brac - es, Stoops to wash our feet.
2. Praise the Rab - bi, speak - ing, do - ing All that God in - tends, Dy - ing, ris - ing, faith re - new - ing, Call - ing us his friends.
3. Praise the Breath of Love, whose free - dom Spreads our wak - ing wings, Lift - ing ev - 'ry blight and bur - den Till the spir - it sings;
4. Praise, un - til we join the sing - ing Far be - yond our sight, With the End - ing and Be - gin - ning Danc - ing in the light.
Refrain
Stand up, friends! Hold your heads high! Free - dom is our song! Al - le - lu - ia! Free-dom is our song! Al - le - lu - ia!
1.
2.
ia!
D.C.
Final ending

Text: Brian Wren, b.1936, © 1986, Hope Publishing Co.
Tune: David Haas, b.1957, © 1993, GIA Publications, Inc.

488 How Wonderful the Three-in-One

1. How won - der - ful the Three - in -
2. Be - fore the flow of dawn and
3. The Lov - er's own Be - lov'd, in
4. Their E - qual Friend all life sus -
5. How won - der - ful the Liv - ing
One, Whose en - er - gies of danc - ing
dark, Cre - a - tion's Lov - er dreamed of
time, Be - tween a cra - dle and a
tains With green - ing pow'r and lov - ing
God: Di - vine Be - lov'd Em - pow'r - ing
light Are un - di - vid - ed, pure and
earth, And with a car - ing deep and
cross, At home in flesh, gave love and
care, And calls us, born a - gain by
Friend, E - ter - nal Lov - er, Three - in -
good, Com - mun - ing love in shared de -
wise, All things con - ceived and brought to
life To heal our bro - ken - ness and
grace, In Love's com - mun - ing life to
One, Our hope's be - gin - ning, way and
1.- 4.
light.
birth.
loss.
share.
Final ending
rit.
end.

Text: Brian Wren, b.1936, © 1989, Hope Publishing Co.
Tune: PROSPECT, 8 8 8 8; *Southern Harmony*; arr. by Marty Haugen, b.1950, © 1991, GIA Publications, Inc.

Crown Him with Many Crowns 489

1. Crown him with man - y crowns, The Lamb up - on his
2. Crown him the Lord of life, Who tri - umphed o'er the
3. Crown him the Lord of love, Be - hold his hands and
4. Crown him the Lord of peace, Whose power a scep - ter
5. Crown him the Lord of years, The ris - en Lord sub -
throne; Hark! how the heav'n - ly an - them drowns All
grave, And rose vic - to - rious in the strife For
side, Rich wounds yet vis - i - ble a - bove In
sways From pole to pole, that wars may cease, Ab -
lime, Cre - a - tor of the roll - ing spheres, The
mu - sic but its own. A - wake, my soul, and sing Of
those he came to save. His glo - ries now we sing, Who
beau - ty glo - ri - fied. No an - gel in the sky Can
sorbed in prayer and praise. His reign shall know no end, And
Mas - ter of all time. All hail, Re - deem - er, hail! For

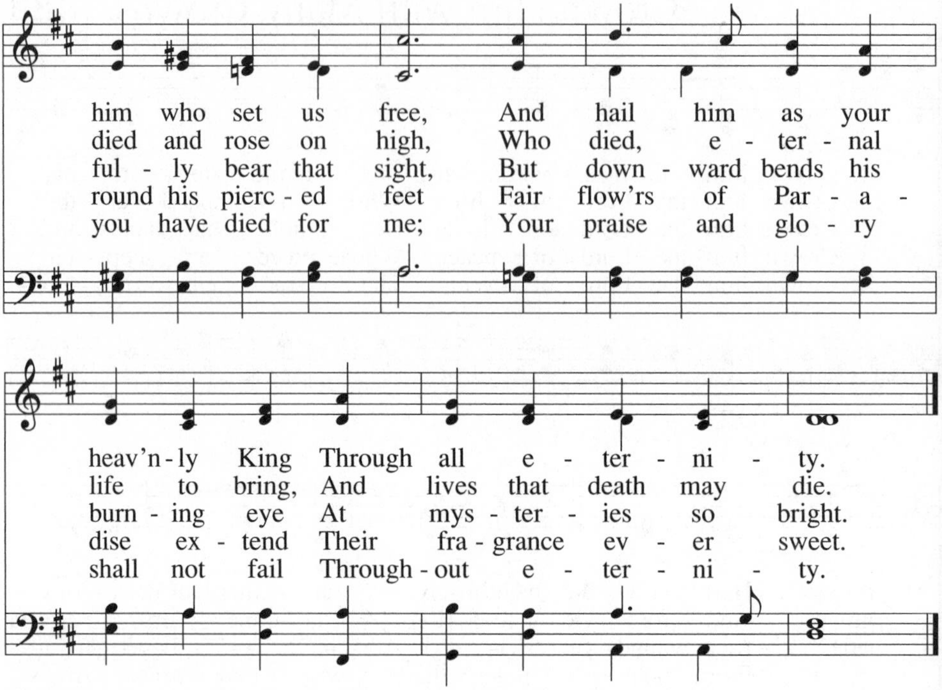

him who set us free, And hail him as your
died and rose on high, Who died, e - ter - nal
ful - ly bear that sight, But down - ward bends his
round his pierc - ed feet Fair flow'rs of Par - a -
you have died for me; Your praise and glo - ry

heav'n - ly King Through all e - ter - ni - ty.
life to bring, And lives that death may die.
burn - ing eye At mys - ter - ies so bright.
dise ex - tend Their fra - grance ev - er sweet.
shall not fail Through - out e - ter - ni - ty.

Text: Revelation 19:12; St. 1, 3-5, Matthew Bridges, 1800-1894; St. 2, Godfrey Thring, 1823-1903
Tune: DIADEMATA, SMD; George J. Elvey, 1816-1893

490 All Hail the Power of Jesus' Name

1. All hail the power of Je - sus' name! Let
2. Crown him, ye mar - tyrs of our God, Who
3. Ye cho - sen seed of Is - rael's race, A
4. O that, with yon - der sa - cred throng, We

an - gels pros - trate fall; Bring forth the roy - al
from his al - tar call; Ex - tol the stem of
rem - nant weak and small, Hail him who saved you
at his feet may fall, Join in the ev - er -

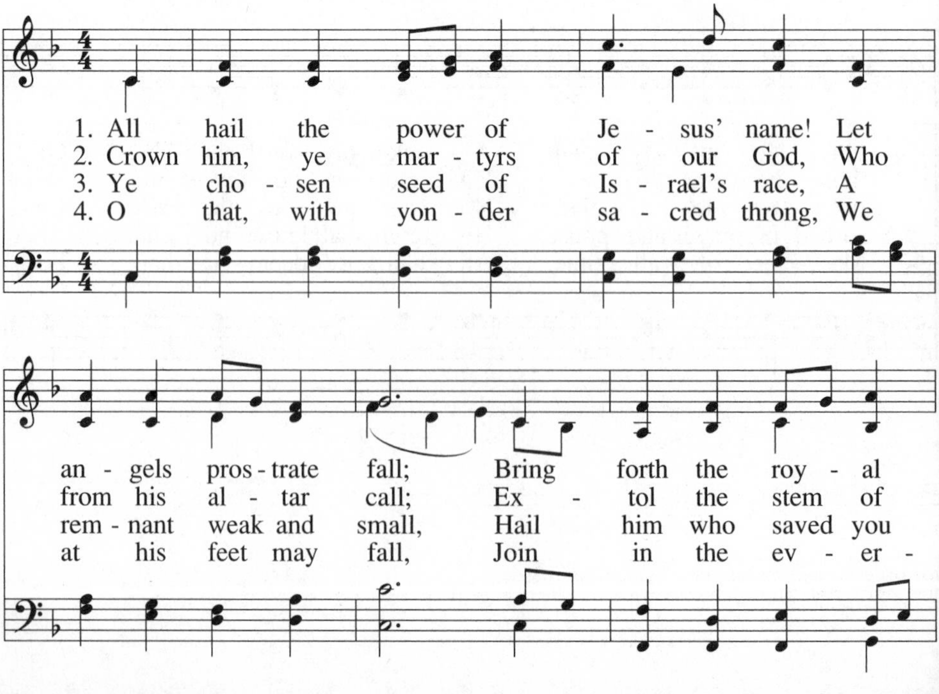

di - a - dem And crown him Lord of all; And crown him Lord of all; And crown him Lord of all; Bring forth the roy - al di - a - dem And crown him Lord of all.
Jes - se's rod, And crown him Lord of all; And crown him Lord of all; And crown him Lord of all; Ex - tol the stem of Jes - se's rod, And crown him Lord of all.
by his grace, And crown him Lord of all; And crown him Lord of all; And crown him Lord of all; Hail him who saved you by his grace, And crown him Lord of all.
last - ing song, And crown him Lord of all; And crown him Lord of all; And crown him Lord of all; Join in the ev - er - last - ing song, And crown him Lord of all.

Text: Edward Perronet, 1726-1792; alt. by John Rippon, 1751-1836, alt.
Tune: DIADEM, CM with repeats; from the *Primitive Baptist Hymn and Tune Book,* 1902; harm. by Richard Proulx, b.1937, © 1975, GIA Publications, Inc.

491 Christ Is the King

1. Christ is the King! O friends, re - joice:
2. O mag - ni - fy the Lord, and raise
3. They with a faith for ev - er new
4. O Chris - tian wom - en, Chris - tian men,
5. Christ through all a - ges is the same:
Broth - ers and sis - ters, with one voice
An - thems of joy and ho - ly praise
Fol - lowed the King, and round him drew
All the world o - ver, seek a - gain
Place the same hope in his great name,
Let the world know he is your choice.
For Christ's brave saints of an - cient days.
Thou - sands of men and wom - en true.
The Way dis - ci - ples fol - lowed then.
With the same faith his word pro - claim.
Al - le - lu - ia, al - le - lu - ia, al - le - lu - ia.

6. Let love's all reconciling might
Your scattered companies unite
In service to the Lord of light.
Alleluia, alleluia, alleluia.

7. So shall God's will on earth be done,
New lamps be lit, new tasks begun,
And the whole Church at last be one.
Alleluia, alleluia, alleluia.

Text: George K. A. Bell, 1883-1958, alt.,
Tune: GELOBT SEI GOTT, 888 with alleluias; Melchior Vulpius, c. 1560-1616

To Jesus Christ, Our Sovereign King 492

1. To Je - sus Christ, our sov - 'reign King, Who
2. Your reign ex - tend, O King be - nign, To
3. To you, and to your church, great King, We
is the world's sal - va - tion, All praise and hom - age
ev - 'ry land and na - tion; For in your King - dom,
pledge our heart's ob - la - tion; Un - til be - fore your
do we bring And thanks and ad - o - ra - tion.
Lord di - vine, A - lone we find sal - va - tion.
throne we sing In end - less ju - bi - la - tion.
Christ Je - sus, Vic - tor! Christ Je - sus, Rul - er!

Christ Je - sus, Lord and Re - deem - er!

Text: Martin B. Hellrigel, 1891-1981, alt., © 1941, Irene C. Mueller
Tune: ICH GLAUB AN GOTT, 8 7 8 7 with refrain; *Mainz Gesangbuch*, 1870; harm. by Richard Proulx, b.1937, © 1986, GIA Publications, Inc.

493 Rejoice, the Lord Is King!

1. Re - joice, the Lord is King! Your Lord and King a - dore!
2. The Lord, our Sav - ior, reigns, The God of truth and love;
3. His king-dom can - not fail, He rules o'er earth and heav'n;
4. Re - joice in glo - rious hope! Our Lord the judge shall come

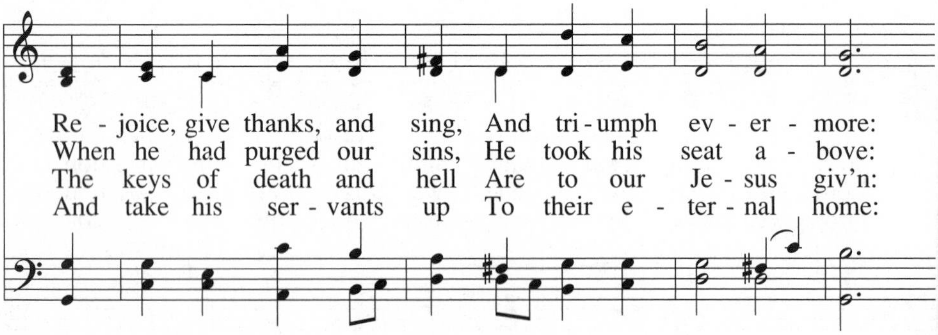

Re - joice, give thanks, and sing, And tri - umph ev - er - more:
When he had purged our sins, He took his seat a - bove:
The keys of death and hell Are to our Je - sus giv'n:
And take his ser - vants up To their e - ter - nal home:

Lift up your heart, lift up your voice!

Re - joice, a - gain I say, re - joice!

Text: Charles Wesley, 1707-1788
Tune: DARWALL'S 148TH, 6 6 6 6 88; John Darwall, 1731-1789; harm. from *The Hymnal 1940*

The King of Glory 494

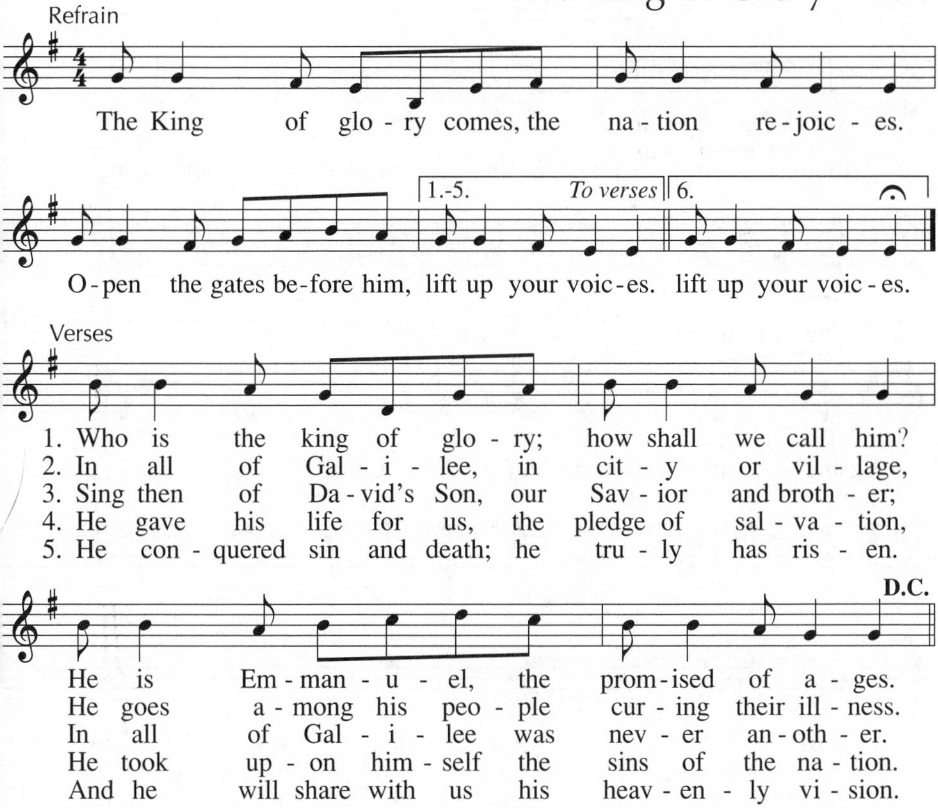

Refrain

The King of glo - ry comes, the na - tion re - joic - es.
O - pen the gates be - fore him, lift up your voic - es.

1.-5. *To verses* lift up your voic - es. 6. lift up your voic - es.

Verses

1. Who is the king of glo - ry; how shall we call him?
He is Em - man - u - el, the prom - ised of a - ges.

2. In all of Gal - i - lee, in cit - y or vil - lage,
He goes a - mong his peo - ple cur - ing their ill - ness.

3. Sing then of Da - vid's Son, our Sav - ior and broth - er;
In all of Gal - i - lee was nev - er an - oth - er.

4. He gave his life for us, the pledge of sal - va - tion,
He took up - on him - self the sins of the na - tion.

5. He con - quered sin and death; he tru - ly has ris - en.
And he will share with us his heav - en - ly vi - sion.

D.C.

Text: Willard F. Jabusch, b. 1930,
Tune: KING OF GLORY, 12 12 with refrain; Israeli; harm. by Richard Proulx, b.1937

495 Canticle of the Sun

Refrain
The heavens are telling the glory of God, and
all creation is shouting for joy. Come, dance in the
forest, come, play in the field, and sing,
sing to the
1.- 6.
To verses
sing the glory of the Lord.
7.
Lord. Sing, sing to the glory

of the Lord.
Verses
1. Praise for the sun, the bring - er of day, He car - ries the light of the Lord in his rays; The moon and the stars who light up the way Un - to your throne.
2. Praise for the wind that blows through the trees, The seas might - y storms, the gen - tl - est breeze; They blow where they will, they blow where they please To please the Lord.
3. Praise for the rain that wa - ters our fields, And bless - es our crops so all the earth yields; From death un - to life her mys - t'ry re - vealed Springs forth in joy.
4. Praise for the fire who gives us his light, The warmth of the sun to bright - en our night; He danc - es with joy, his spir - it so bright, He sings of you.
5. Praise for the earth who makes life to grow, The crea - tures you made to let your life show; The flow - ers and trees that help us to know The heart of love.
6. Praise for our death that makes our life real, The know - ledge of loss that helps us to feel; The gift of your - self, your pres - ence re - vealed To lead us home.
D.C.

Text: Marty Haugen, b.1950
Tune: Marty Haugen, b.1950

496 How Great Thou Art

1. O Lord my God, when I in awe-some won-der Con-sid-er all the worlds Thy hands have made, I see the stars, I hear the roll-ing thun-der, Thy pow'r thru-out the un-i-verse dis-played!
2. When thru the woods and for-est glades I wan-der And hear the birds sing sweet-ly in the trees, When I look down from loft-y moun-tain gran-deur And hear the brook and feel the gen-tle breeze.
3. And when I think that God, His Son not spar-ing, Sent Him to die, I scarce can take it in That on the cross, my bur-den glad-ly bear-ing, He bled and died to take a-way my sin!
4. When Christ shall come with shout of ac-cla-ma-tion And take me home, what joy shall fill my heart! Then I shall bow in hum-ble ad-o-ra-tion And there pro-claim, my God, how great Thou art!

Then sings my soul, my Sav - ior God, to
Thee; How great Thou art, how great Thou
art! Then sings my soul, my Sav - ior God, to
Thee; How great Thou art, How great Thou art!

ext: Stuart K. Hine, 1899-1989
une: O STORE GUD, 11 10 11 10 with refrain; Stuart K. Hine, 1899-1989

497 Sing Out, Earth and Skies

Verses

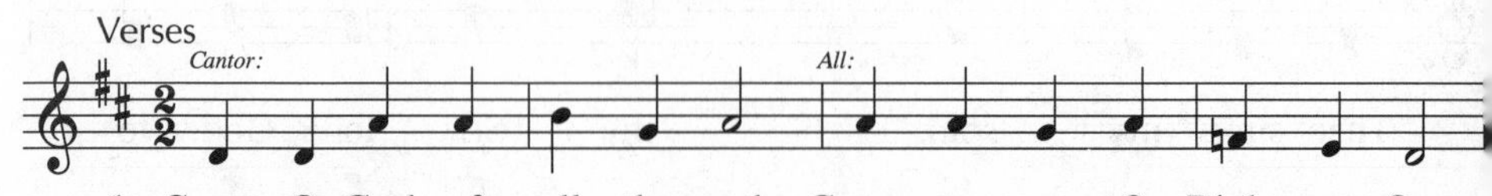
Cantor:
All:

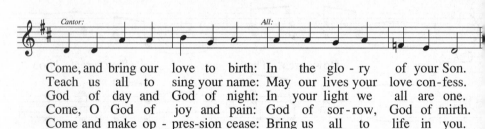

1. Come, O God of all the earth: Come to us, O Right-eous One;
2. Come, O God of wind and flame: Fill the earth with right-eous-ness;
3. Come, O God of flash-ing light: Twin-kling star and burn-ing sun;
4. Come, O God of snow and rain: Show-er down up-on the earth;
5. Come, O Jus-tice, Come, O Peace: Come and shape our hearts a-new;

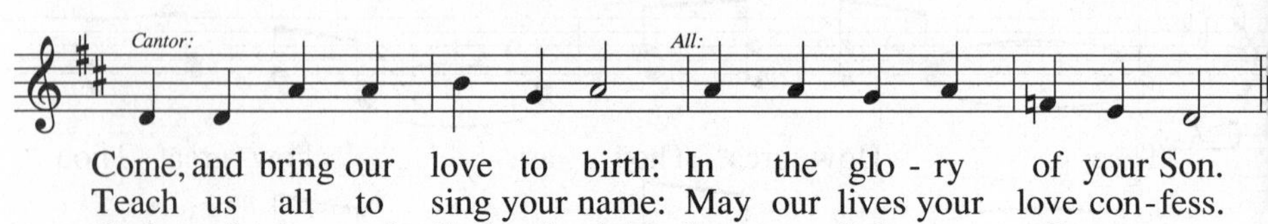
Cantor:
All:

Come, and bring our love to birth: In the glo-ry of your Son.
Teach us all to sing your name: May our lives your love con-fess.
God of day and God of night: In your light we all are one.
Come, O God of joy and pain: God of sor-row, God of mirth.
Come and make op-pres-sion cease: Bring us all to life in you.

Refrain

Sing out, earth and skies! Sing of the God who
Tenor:
Alto:
Sing out, earth and skies!

loves you! Raise your joy-ful cries!
Sing of the God who loves you! Raise your

Dance to the life a-round you!
dance to the life a-round you!

Text: Marty Haugen, b.1950
Tune: SING OUT, 7 7 7 7 with refrain; Marty Haugen, b.1950

All You Works of God 498

Refrain
unis.
div.
All you works of God, ev - 'ry moun - tain, star and
tree, bless the One who shapes your beau - ty, who has
3
caused you all to be one great song of love and
grace, ev - er an - cient, ev - er new. Raise your
voic - es, all you works of God!
To verses
Last time
God!
Verses
Soloist:
All:
1. Sun and moon:
2. Winds of God:
3. Night and day:
4. All the earth:
5. Wells and springs:
6. Fly - ing birds:
7. All who live:
Bless your Mak - er!

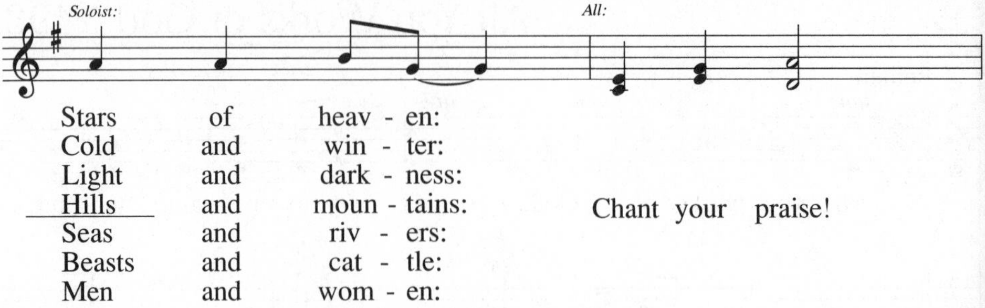

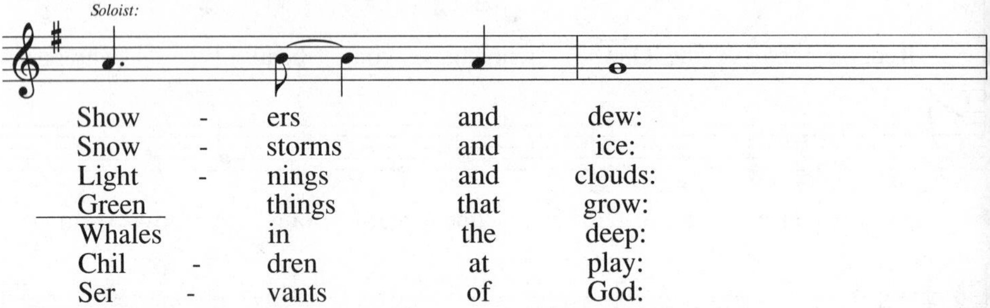

Soloist: | All:

Stars of heav - en:
Cold and win - ter:
Light and dark - ness:
Hills and moun - tains: Chant your praise!
Seas and riv - ers:
Beasts and cat - tle:
Men and wom - en:

Soloist:

Show - ers and dew:
Snow - storms and ice:
Light - nings and clouds:
Green things that grow:
Whales in the deep:
Chil - dren at play:
Ser - vants of God:

All: D.C.

Raise up your joy - ful song.

Text: Marty Haugen, b.1950
Tune: Marty Haugen, b.1950

499 Come to the Feast

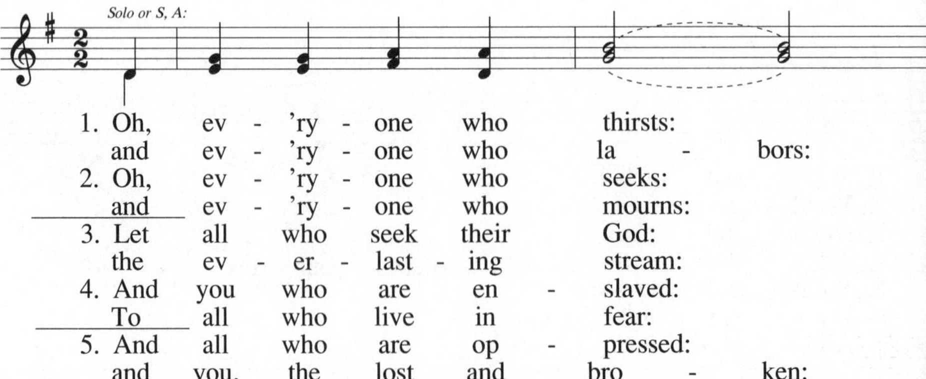
Solo or S, A:
1. Oh, ev - 'ry - one who thirsts:
and ev - 'ry - one who la - bors:
2. Oh, ev - 'ry - one who seeks:
and ev - 'ry - one who mourns:
3. Let all who seek their God:
the ev - er - last - ing stream:
4. And you who are en - slaved:
To all who live in fear:
5. And all who are op - pressed:
and you, the lost and bro - ken:

PROVIDENCE

All:
Solo or S, A:
Come to the wa-ters!
here is an end to hun-ger:
all you who have no mon-ey:
hear me and share the rich-es:
now is an end to sad-ness:
heed now the One who calls you:
drink deep the Cup that saves you:
this is the feast of free-dom:
join in the feast with cour-age:
this is the feast of jus-tice:
this is the feast of heal-ing:
1. All:
2. All:
Come to the feast!
Come
Come to the feast!
Come
For this is life:
this is life:
For this is life:
Solo or S, A:
1. the wa-ters of the
2. the streams of joy and
3. the floods that o-ver-
4. the wa-ters that have
5. to die and rise in

PROVIDENCE

All:
For this is life:
Solo or S, A:
Jor - dan: this is life: the wa - ters of your
glad - ness: the rains that bring you
whelm you: the streams of death and
freed you: the sav - ing stream of
Je - sus: to share the life of
For this is life:
All:
For this is life:
Solo or S, A:
birth: this is life: the wa - ters that re -
joy: the wa - ters that re -
life: the wa - ters that sus -
God: to share a - round the
Christ: the bread and wine of
For this is life:
All:
new you:
store you:
tain you:
ta - ble:
jus - tice:
O come to the feast! O come to the
come
1.- 4.
D.C.
5.
feast! feast! O come to the feast!
come

Text: Isaiah 55; Marty Haugen, b.1950
Tune: Marty Haugen, b.1950

Wisdom, My Road 500

1. Long be - fore my jour - ney's start, When in my youth I searched in my heart, I would pray for her, wait for her, Wis - dom, my road, my goal, and my star.
2. From the blos - som to the seed, Long has she filled my cup in need, May I cling to her vine, taste of her wine, Wis - dom, my life, my per - fect de - sign.
3. When I stretched my hands to the sky, When in de - spair my soul raised a cry, I was saved by her gaze, led in her ways, Wis - dom, my love, the light of my days.

Text: Based on Ecclesiasticus 51:13-22; Steven C. Warner, b.1954
Tune: Leslie Palmer Barnhart

501 Over My Head

Refrain
O-ver my head, I hear mu-sic in the air; o-ver my head,
I hear mu-sic in the air; o-ver my head, I hear
mu-sic in the air; there must be a God some-where.
Verses
Cantor:
1. Oh when the world is si-lent, oh
2. And when I'm feel-ing lone-ly, and
3. Now when I think on Je-sus, now
(hum)
I hear mu-sic in the air;

when the world is si - lent,
when I'm feel - ing lone - ly,
when I think on Je - sus,
oh
and
now
(hum)
I hear mu - sic in the air;
when the world is si - lent,
when I'm feel - ing lone - ly,
when I think on Je - sus,
(hum)
I hear mu - sic in the air;
D.C.
there must be a God some - where.
D.C.
there must be a God some - where.

502 Come to the Water

Descant:
1. O let all who thirst, let them come
2. And let all who seek, let them come
3. And let all who toil, let them come
4. And let all the poor, let them come
Melody:
1. O let all who thirst, let them come
2. And let all who seek, let them come
3. And let all who toil, let them come
4. And let all the poor, let them come
to the wa - ter. And let all who have
to the wa - ter. And let all who have
to the wa - ter. And let all who are
to the wa - ter. Bring the ones who are
to the wa - ter. And let all who have
to the wa - ter. And let all who have
to the wa - ter. And let all who are
to the wa - ter. Bring the ones who are
noth - ing, let them come to the Lord:
noth - ing, let them come to the Lord:
wea - ry, let them come to the Lord:
lad - en, bring them all to the Lord:
noth - ing, let them come to the Lord:
noth - ing, let them come to the Lord:
wea - ry, let them come to the Lord:
lad - en, bring them all to the Lord:

PROVIDENCE

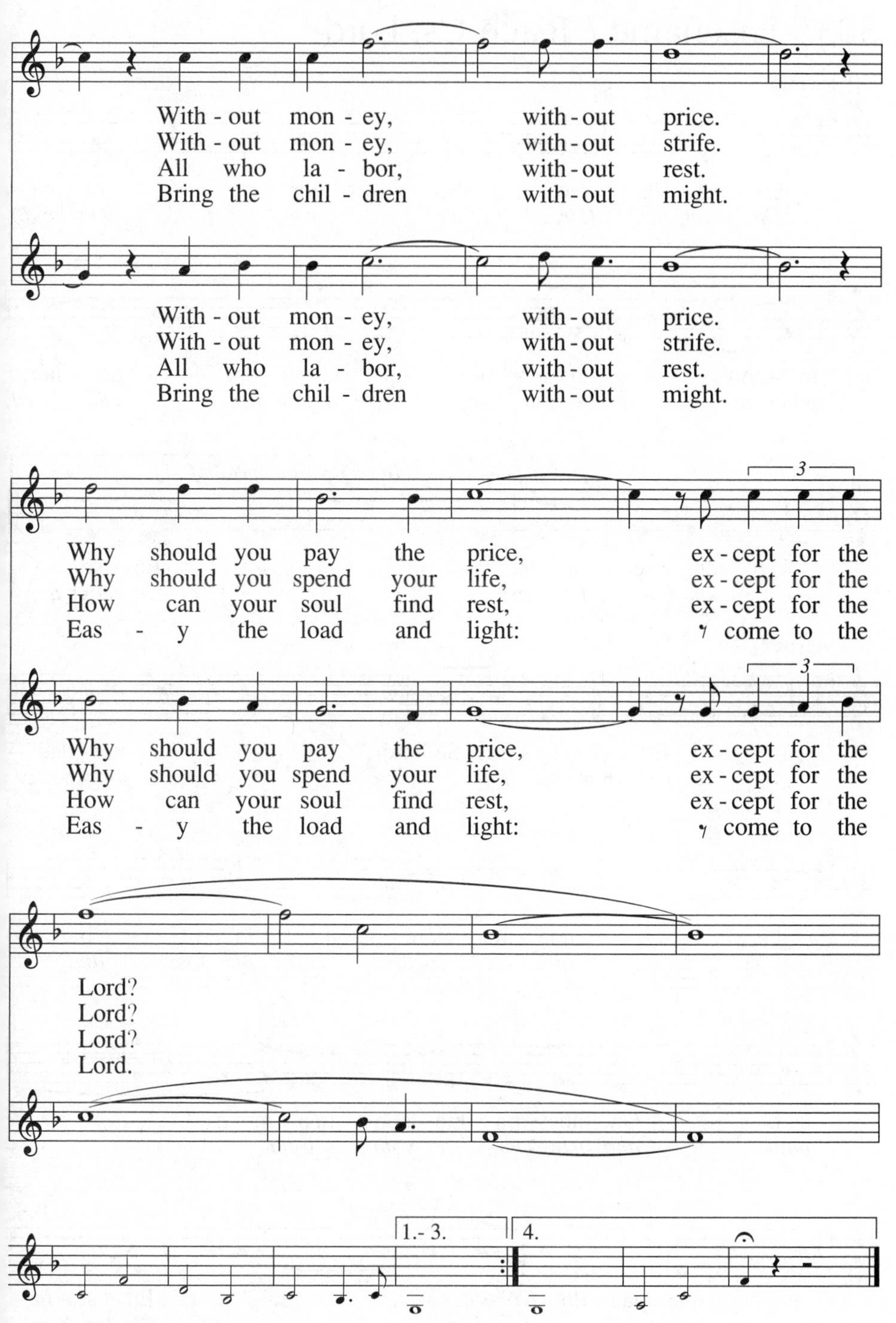

With - out mon - ey, with - out price.
With - out mon - ey, with - out strife.
All who la - bor, with - out rest.
Bring the chil - dren with - out might.
With - out mon - ey, with - out price.
With - out mon - ey, with - out strife.
All who la - bor, with - out rest.
Bring the chil - dren with - out might.
3
Why should you pay the price, ex - cept for the
Why should you spend your life, ex - cept for the
How can your soul find rest, ex - cept for the
Eas - y the load and light: come to the
3
Why should you pay the price, ex - cept for the
Why should you spend your life, ex - cept for the
How can your soul find rest, ex - cept for the
Eas - y the load and light: come to the
Lord?
Lord?
Lord?
Lord.
1.- 3.
4.

Text: Isaiah 55:1, 2; Matthew 11:28-30; John Foley, SJ, b.1939
Tune: John Foley, SJ, b.1939

503 Enséñame / Teach Us, Lord

Refrain
En - sé - ña - me, Se - ñor, el ca -
Oh, teach us, Lord, we pray, come and
mi - no y guí - a - me por la vi - da, Se - ñor,
guide us in your way to a new life. Oh Lord,
Last time
To verses
To repeat refrain
en - sé - ña - me.
show us the way.
En - sé - ña -
Oh, teach us,
Verses 1, 2
1. En - sé - ña - me, Se - ñor, tu ver - dad
2. Oh, show me how to live in your peace
no i - llu - sión, la rea - li -
in a world of loss and
dad. Oh, mués - tra - me con tu a - mor
pain, and bring me to your light
D.S.
que pue - do vi - vir.
when all is done.
En - sé - ña -
Oh, teach us,

PROVIDENCE

Verses 3, 4
3. Da - me, Se - ñor, tu fuer - za y va - lor
4. Oh, teach me how to pray with - out end.
cuan - do el mun - do te re - cha -
Spir - it, blow with - out, with -
za y dé - ja - me a - cla - mar
in, and whis - per to my heart
tu glo - ria y po - der.
that life may be - gin.
D.S.
En - sé - ña -
Oh, teach us,

Text: Donna Peña, b.1955
Tune: Donna Peña, b.1955; acc. by William Gokelman

504 I Have Loved You

Refrain
Melody:
I have loved you with an ev-er-last-ing love, I have called you and you are mine; I have loved you with an ev-er-last-ing love, I have called you and you are mine.
Harmony:
I have loved you with an ev-er-last-ing love, I have called you and you are mine; I have loved you with an ev-er-last-ing love, I have called you and you are mine.
I have loved you with an ev-er-last-ing love, I have called you and you are mine.

PROVIDENCE

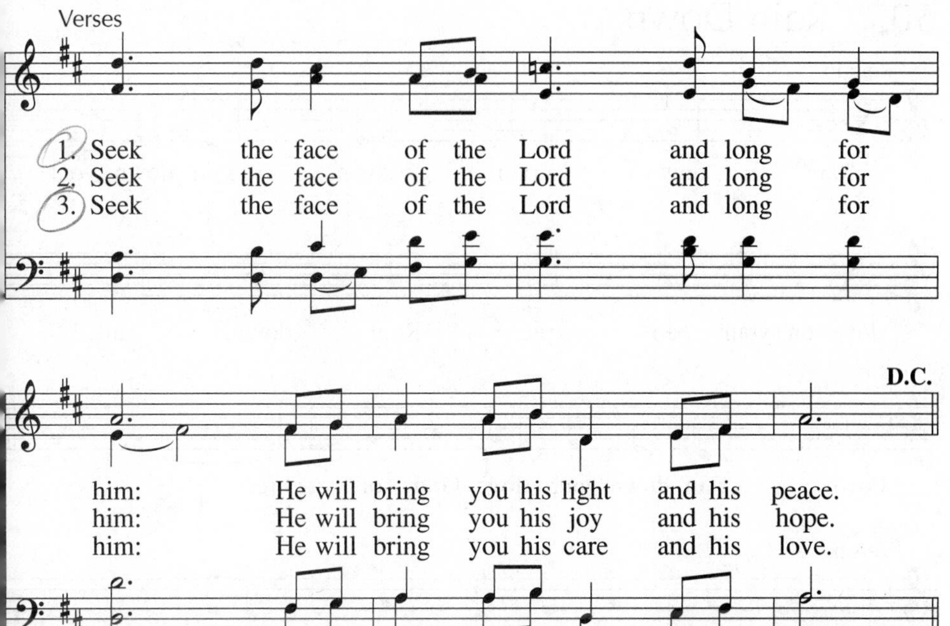
Verses
1. Seek the face of the Lord and long for him: He will bring you his light and his peace.
2. Seek the face of the Lord and long for him: He will bring you his joy and his hope.
3. Seek the face of the Lord and long for him: He will bring you his care and his love.
D.C.

Text: Jeremiah 31:3, Psalm 24:3; Michael Joncas, b.1951
Tune: Michael Joncas, b.1951

505 Rain Down

Refrain
Rain down, rain down, rain down your love on your peo - ple. Rain down, rain down, rain down your love, God of life.
Verses
1. Faith - ful and true is the word of our God. All of God's works are so wor - thy of trust. God's mer - cy falls on the just and the right; full of God's love is the earth.
2. We who re - vere and find hope in our God live in the kind - ness and joy of God's wing. God will pro - tect us from dark - ness and death; God will not leave us to starve.
3. God of cre - a - tion, we long for your truth; you are the wa - ter of life that we thirst. Grant that your love and your peace touch our hearts, all of our hope lies in you.
D.C.

Text: Based on Psalm 33; Jaime Cortez, b.1963
Tune: Jaime Cortez, b.1963; acc. by Craig S. Kingsbury, b.1952

You Are Our Center 506

Refrain
You are our cen - ter, you are our hope.
You are our hope.
This we know and be - lieve.
This we be - lieve.
You are our an - swer, you bring us home.
You bring us home.
To verses
Final ending
You are all we need.
You are all we need.

Verses
1. When pain - ful mem - 'ries haunt our minds, and
2. When dreams are shat - tered by name - less pow'rs, and
3. When our in - dif - f'rence feeds pov - er - ty, and
4. When faith is ques - tioned by doubt and fear, we
sor - row dark - ens our heart; when
hope seems far from our sight; when
greed leaves us want - ing more; when
wan - der lost and a - lone; when
chil - dren lie bro - ken from vio - lent ways, and
truth is shak - en by those we love, and
we have fall - en in sin and shame, and
death and bro - ken - ness tear our hearts, we
D.C.
hate and jeal - ous - y reign:
walls are built by fear:
dark - ness rules our days:
cry to you in our grief:

Text: Lori True, b.1961
Tune: Lori True, b.1961

Fresh as the Morning 507

Verses
1. God of the Bi - ble, God in the Gos - pel,
2. God in our strug - gles, God in our hun - ger,
3. Those with - out sta - tus, those who are noth - ing,
4. Not by your fin - ger, not by your an - ger
5. Hope we must car - ry, shin - ing and cer - tain
hope seen in Je - sus, hope yet to come,
suf - fer - ing with us, tak - ing our part,
you have made roy - al, gift - ed with rights,
will our world or - der change in a day,
through all our tur - moil, ter - ror and loss,
you are our cen - ter, day - light or dark - ness,
still you em - pow'r us, moth - er - ing Spir - it,
cho - sen as part - ners, mid - wives of jus - tice,
but by your peo - ple, fear - less and faith - ful,
bond - ing us glad - ly one to the oth - er,
free - dom or pris - on, you are our home.
feed - ing, sus - tain - ing, from your own heart.
birth - ing new sys - tems, light - ing new lights.
small pa - per lan - terns, light - ing the way.
till our world chang - es fac - ing the Cross.

Refrain
S + Assembly:
Fresh as the morn - ing, sure as the sun - rise,
A
Fresh as the sun - rise,
T,B
God al - ways faith - ful, you do not change.
al - ways faith - ful, you do not change.
Fresh as the morn - ing, sure as the sun - rise,
Fresh as the sun - rise,

PROVIDENCE

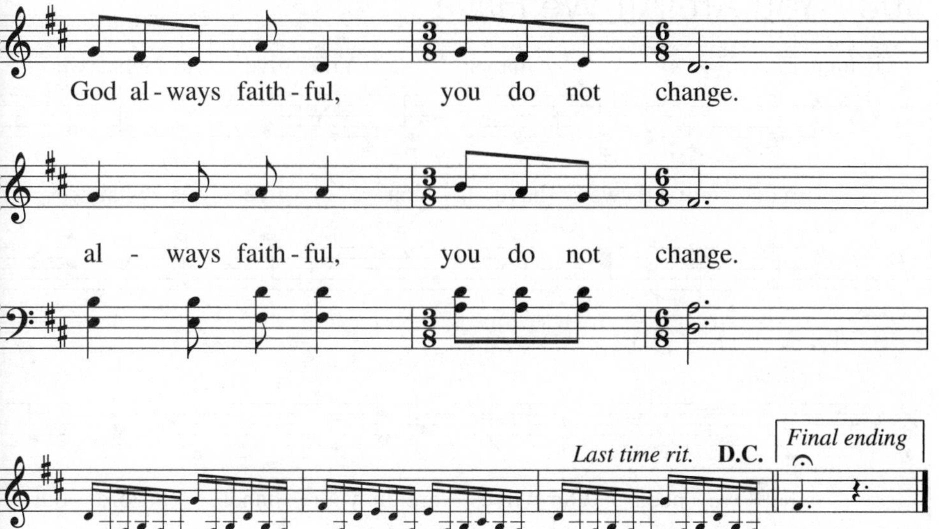
God al - ways faith - ful, you do not change.
al - ways faith - ful, you do not change.
Last time rit.
D.C.
Final ending

508 You Are All We Have

Refrain
You are all we have. You give us what we need.
have. You give us what we
need.
what we need. Our lives are in your hands, O Lord, our lives are in your hands.
To verses
Last time
hands.
hands.
Verse 1
1. Pro-tect me, Lord; I come to you for safe-ty. I say, "You are my God." All good things, Lord, all good things that I have come from you, the God of my sal-va-tion.
D.C.

PROVIDENCE
Verse 2
Melody:
Harmony:
2. How won-der-ful are your gifts to me, how good they are! I praise the Lord who guides me and teach-es me the way of truth and life.
D.C.
Verse 3
3. You are near, the God I seek. Noth-ing can take me from your side. All my days I rest se-cure; you will show me the path that leads to life.
D.C.

Text: Francis Patrick O'Brien, b.1958
Tune: Francis Patrick O'Brien, b.1958

509 O God, You Search Me

1. O God, you search me and you know me. All my
2. You know my rest - ing and my ris - ing. You dis -
3. Be - fore a word is on my tongue, Lord, You have
4. Al - though your Spir - it is up - on me, Still I
5. For you cre - at - ed me and shaped me, Gave me
thoughts lie o - pen to your gaze. When I
cern my pur - pose from a - far, And with
known its mean - ing through and through. You are
search for shel - ter from your light. There is
life with - in my moth - er's womb. For the
walk or lie down you are be - fore me: Ev - er the
love ev - er - last - ing you be - siege me: In ev - 'ry
with me be - yond my un - der - stand - ing: God of my
no - where on earth I can es - cape you: E - ven the
won - der of who I am I praise you: Safe in your
3
3
3
3

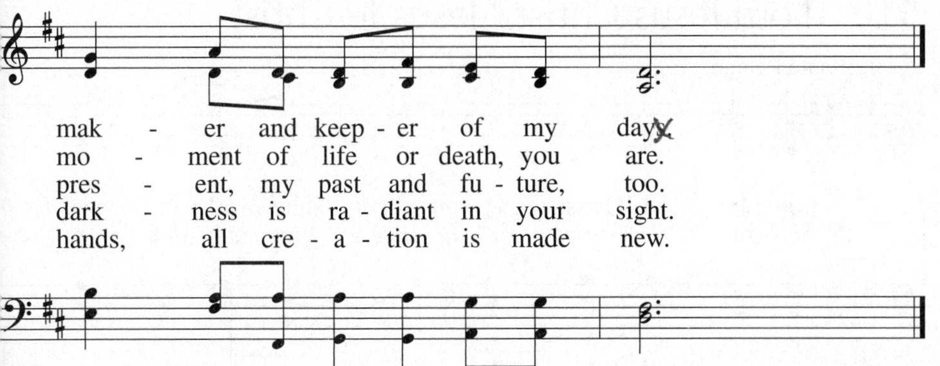
mak - er and keep - er of my days.
mo - ment of life or death, you are.
pres - ent, my past and fu - ture, too.
dark - ness is ra - diant in your sight.
hands, all cre - a - tion is made new.

Text: Based on Psalm 139; Bernadette Farrell, b.1957
Tune: Bernadette Farrell, b.1957

510 Lord Jesus Christ / Jesus le Christ

Ostinato Refrain
Lord Je - sus Christ, your light shines with - in us.
Jé - sus le Christ, lu - mière in - té - rieu - re,
Let not my doubts nor my dark - ness speak to me.
ne lais - se pas mes té - nè - bres me par - ler.
Lord Je - sus Christ, your light shines with - in us.
Jé - sus le Christ, lu - mière in - té - rieu - re,
Let my heart al - ways wel - come your love.
don - ne - moi d'ac-cueil - lir ton a - mour.

Verses *(Superimposed on Ostinato Refrain)*

Cantor:
1. Lord, you have searched me and known me;
you know when I sit down, when I rise up.
You are ac-quaint-ed with all my ways.
2. If I take the wings of the morn-ing, and set-tle
at the far-thest lim-its of the sea,
e-ven there your hand shall hold me fast. 3. If I say, "Let the
dark-ness cov-er me," e-ven the dark-ness is not dark to
you, and night is as bright as the day.
4. Search me, God, and know my heart
and lead me in the ev-er-last-ing way.

*Choose either part.

Text: Psalm 139
Tune: Jacques Berthier, 1923-1994

511 Be Light for Our Eyes

Refrain
Come and be light for our eyes; be the
air we breathe, be the voice we speak!
Come, be the song we sing, be the
path we seek!
To verses
Final ending
Verses
1. Your life was giv - en; food for all peo - ple,
2. We hold your pres - ence, ris - en for ev - er!
3. Lead us to jus - tice, light in the dark - ness;

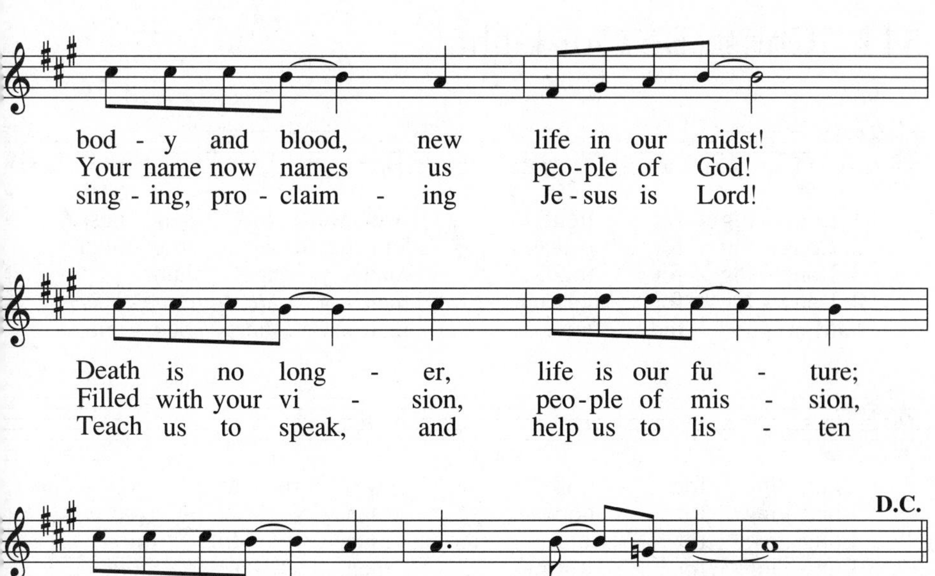
bod - y and blood, new life in our midst!
Your name now names us peo-ple of God!
sing - ing, pro - claim - ing Je - sus is Lord!
Death is no long - er, life is our fu - ture;
Filled with your vi - sion, peo-ple of mis - sion,
Teach us to speak, and help us to lis - ten
D.C.

Je - sus, Mes-si - ah, name of all names!
heal-ing, for-giv - ing; light for the world!
for when your truth and our dreams em-brace!

Text: David Haas, b.1957
Tune: David Haas, b.1957; keyboard arr. by David Haas, b.1957, and Marty Haugen, b.1950

512 Christ, Be Our Light

Verses
1. Long - ing for light, we wait in dark - ness.
2. Long - ing for peace, our world is trou - bled.
3. Long - ing for food, man - y are hun - gry.
4. Long - ing for shel - ter, man - y are home - less.
5. Man - y the gifts, man - y the peo - ple,
Long - ing for truth, we turn to you.
Long - ing for hope, man - y de - spair.
Long - ing for wa - ter, man - y still thirst.
Long - ing for warmth, man - y are cold.
man - y the hearts that yearn to be - long.
Make us your own, your ho - ly peo - ple,
Your word a - lone has pow'r to save us.
Make us your bread, bro - ken for oth - ers,
Make us your build - ing, shel - ter - ing oth - ers,
Let us be ser - vants to one an - oth - er,
light for the world to see.
Make us your liv - ing voice.
shared un - til all are fed.
walls made of liv - ing stone.
mak - ing your king - dom come.
Refrain
Descant:
Christ, be our light! Shine
Melody:
Christ, be our light! Shine in our

out through the dark, shine!
hearts. Shine through the dark - ness.
Christ, be our light! Shine in your church
Christ, be our light! Shine in your church
1.- 4.
5.
gath-ered to - day.
gath-ered to - day.

ext: Bernadette Farrell, b.1957
une: Bernadette Farrell, b.1957

513 I Want to Walk as a Child of the Light

1. I want to walk as a child of the light.
2. I want to see the bright-ness of God.
3. I'm look - ing for the com - ing of Christ.
I want to fol - low Je - sus.
I want to look at Je - sus.
I want to be with Je - sus.
God set the stars to give light to the world. The
Clear sun of right - eous - ness shine on my path, And
When we have run with pa - tience the race, We
star of my life is Je - sus.
show me the way to the Fa - ther.
shall know the joy of Je - sus.
In him there is no dark - ness at all. The
night and the day are both a - like. The
Lamb is the light of the cit - y of God.
Shine in my heart, Lord Je - sus.

Text: Ephesians 5:8-10, Revelation 21:23, John 12:46, 1 John 1:5, Hebrews 12:1; Kathleen Thomerson, b.1934, © 1970, 1975, Celebration
Tune: HOUSTON, 10 7 10 8 9 9 10 7; Kathleen Thomerson, b.1934, © 1970, 1975, Celebration; acc. by Robert J. Batastini, b.1942, © 1987, GIA Publications, Inc.

This Little Light of Mine 514

1. This lit - tle light of mine I'm gon - na let it shine,
2. Ev - 'ry - where I go, I'm gon - na let it shine,
3. Je - sus gave it to me, I'm gon - na let it shine,
Oh, Oh,
This lit - tle light of mine I'm gon - na let it shine;
Ev - 'ry - where I go, I'm gon - na let it shine;
Je - sus gave it to me, I'm gon - na let it shine;
Oh,
This lit - tle light of mine I'm gon - na let it shine,
Ev - 'ry - where I go, I'm gon - na let it shine,
Je - sus gave it to me, I'm gon - na let it shine,
Oh,
Let it shine, let it shine, let it shine.
Let it shine, let it shine, let it shine.
Let it shine, let it shine, let it shine.

ext: African-American spiritual
une: African-American spiritual; harm. by Horace Clarence Boyer, b.1935, © 1992

515 We Are the Light of the World

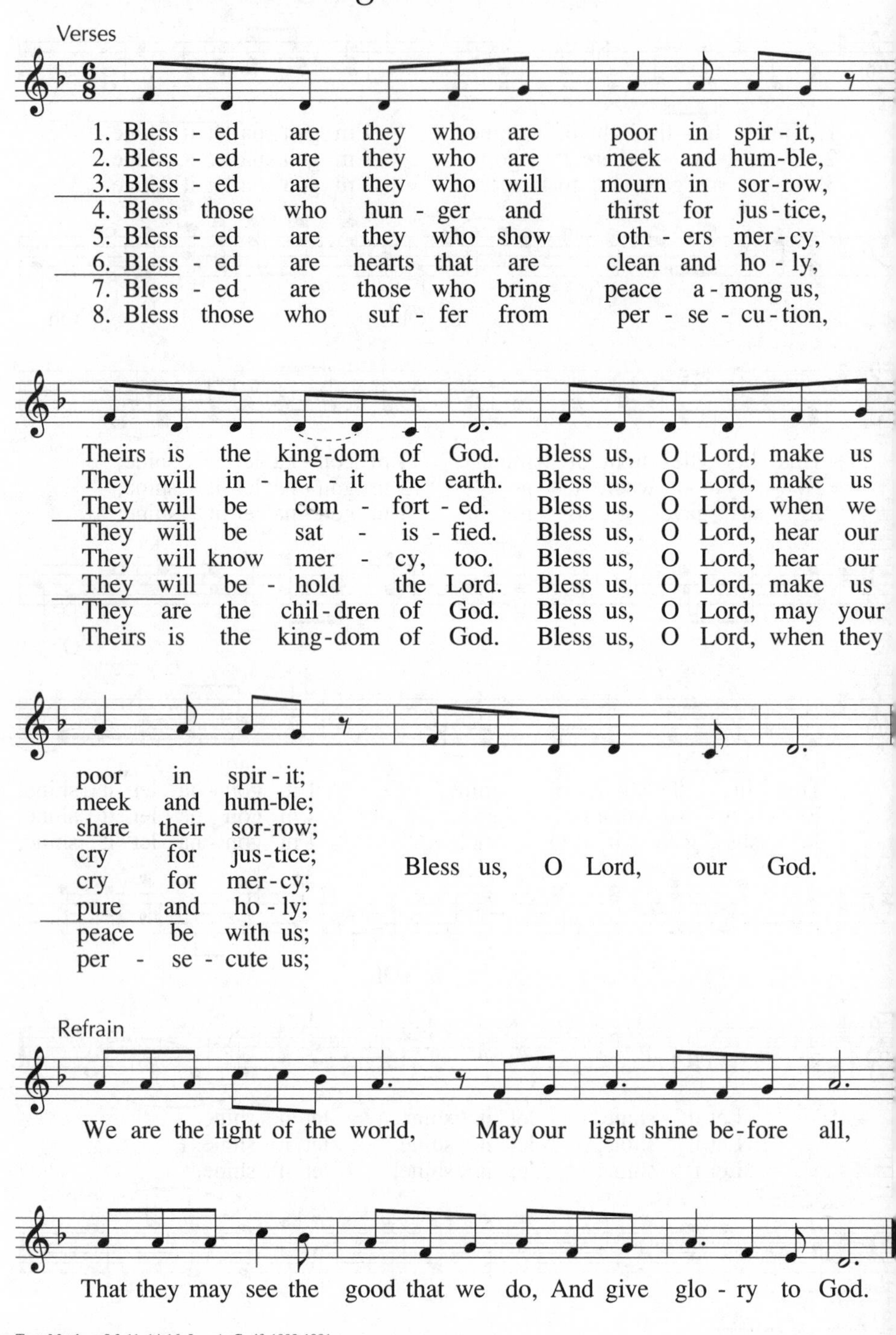
Verses
1. Bless - ed are they who are poor in spir - it,
2. Bless - ed are they who are meek and hum-ble,
3. Bless - ed are they who will mourn in sor-row,
4. Bless those who hun - ger and thirst for jus-tice,
5. Bless - ed are they who show oth - ers mer-cy,
6. Bless - ed are hearts that are clean and ho - ly,
7. Bless - ed are those who bring peace a - mong us,
8. Bless those who suf - fer from per - se - cu-tion,
Theirs is the king-dom of God. Bless us, O Lord, make us
They will in - her - it the earth. Bless us, O Lord, make us
They will be com - fort - ed. Bless us, O Lord, when we
They will be sat - is - fied. Bless us, O Lord, hear our
They will know mer - cy, too. Bless us, O Lord, hear our
They will be - hold the Lord. Bless us, O Lord, make us
They are the chil-dren of God. Bless us, O Lord, may your
Theirs is the king-dom of God. Bless us, O Lord, when they
poor in spir - it;
meek and hum-ble;
share their sor-row;
cry for jus-tice;
cry for mer-cy;
pure and ho - ly;
peace be with us;
per - se - cute us;
Bless us, O Lord, our God.
Refrain
We are the light of the world, May our light shine be-fore all,
That they may see the good that we do, And give glo - ry to God.

Text: Matthew 5:3-11, 14-16; Jean A. Greif, 1898-1981
Tune: Jean A. Greif, 1898-1981

We Are Marching 516

We are march - ing* in the light of God, we are
1.
march-ing in the light of God.
2.
march-ing in the light of God,
march-ing in the light of the
march-ing in the light of God,
we are march - ing,
light of God, we are march-ing, march-ing, we are
Oo we are
march-ing, march-ing, we are march-ing in the light of God.

* Alternate text: dancing, singing, praying

ext: South African
une: South African

517 Praise to You, O Christ, Our Savior

Refrain
Praise to you, O Christ, our Sav-ior, Word of the Fa-ther, call-ing us to life;
Son of God who leads us to free-dom: glo-ry to you, Lord Je-sus Christ!
Verses
1. You are the Word who calls us out of dark - ness;
2. You are the one whom proph - ets hoped and longed for;
3. You are the Word who calls us to be ser - vants;
4. You are the Word who binds us and u - nites us;
you are the Word who leads us in - to light;
you are the one who speaks to us to - day;
you are the Word whose on - ly law is love;
you are the Word who calls us to be one;
you are the Word who brings us through the des - ert:
you are the one who leads us to our fu - ture:
you are the Word - made - flesh who lives a - mong us:
you are the Word who teach - es us for - give - ness:
glo - ry to you, Lord Je - sus Christ!
glo - ry to you, Lord Je - sus Christ!
glo - ry to you, Lord Je - sus Christ!
glo - ry to you, Lord Je - sus Christ!
D.C.

Text: Bernadette Farrell, b.1957
Tune: Bernadette Farrell, b.1957

Tell It! Tell It Out with Gladness 518

1. Tell it! Tell it out with glad-ness— God's good news to ev - 'ry land, Sin for - giv - en, lives trans - fig - ured, All in God's great lov - ing plan. In the Book is found the wit - ness To his might - y acts of yore: Lis - ten, heed, o - bey, and serve him, Kneel be - fore him and a - dore.
2. Lord, we thank thee for the treas - ure Hid with - in the sa - cred page. We would be thy faith - ful her - alds To our deep - ly trou - bled age; We would pub - lish thy sal - va - tion, Ev - er on thy side to stand, Liv - ing, serv-ing, giv-ing, send - ing Life to quick-en ev - 'ry land.
3. "Go and teach," thus spoke the Mas - ter, Ris - en vic - tor from the grave. Still he gives this great com - mis - sion To his faith - ful ones, and brave. Go and tell the gos - pel sto - ry Of what all through Christ can be. Send it! Send it to the na - tions That God's love may set us free.

Text: Georgia Harkness, 1891-1974, © 1966, The Hymn Society. (Administered by Hope Publishing Co.)
Tune: HYMN TO JOY, 8 7 8 7 D; arr. from Ludwig van Beethoven, 1770-1827, by Edward Hodges, 1796-1867.

519 Holy God, We Praise Thy Name

1. Ho - ly God, we praise thy name! Lord of all, we bow be - fore thee; All on earth thy scep - ter claim, All in heav'n a - bove a - dore thee;
2. Hark! the loud ce - les - tial hymn An - gel choirs a - bove are rais - ing; Cher - u - bim and Ser - a - phim In un - ceas - ing cho - rus prais - ing,
3. Ho - ly Fa - ther, Ho - ly Son, Ho - ly Spir - it, Three we name thee, While in es - sence on - ly One, Un - di - vid - ed God we claim thee,

In - fi - nite thy vast do - main,
Fill the heav'ns with sweet ac - cord:
And a - dor - ing bend the knee,
Ev - er - last - ing is thy reign.
Ho - ly, ho - ly, ho - ly Lord!
While we own the mys - ter - y.
Optional repeat of last eight measures
In - fi - nite thy vast do - main,
Fill the heav'ns with sweet ac - cord:
And a - dor - ing bend the knee,
Ev - er - last - ing is thy reign.
Ho - ly, ho - ly, ho - ly Lord!
While we own the mys - ter - y.

Text: *Grosser Gott, wir loben dich;* ascr. to Ignaz Franz, 1719-1790; tr. by Clarence Walworth, 1820-1900
Tune: GROSSER GOTT, 7 8 7 8 77; *Katholisches Gesangbuch*, Vienna, c.1774

520 Joyful, Joyful, We Adore You

1. Joy - ful, joy - ful, we a - dore you, God of glo - ry,
2. All your works with joy sur - round you, Earth and heav'n re -
3. Al - ways giv - ing and for - giv - ing, Ev - er bless - ing,
4. Mor - tals join the might - y cho - rus, Which the morn - ing
Lord of love; Hearts un - fold like flowers be - fore you,
flect your rays, Stars and an - gels sing a - round you,
ev - er blest, Well - spring of the joy of liv - ing,
stars be - gan; God's own love is reign - ing o'er us,
Open - ing to the sun a - bove. Melt the clouds of
Cen - ter of un - bro - ken praise; Field and for - est,
O - cean depth of hap - py rest! Lov - ing Fa - ther,
Join - ing peo - ple hand in hand. Ev - er sing - ing,
sin and sad - ness; Drive the dark of doubt a - way;
vale and moun - tain, Flow - ery mead - ow, flash - ing sea,
Christ our broth - er, Let your light up - on us shine;
march we on - ward, Vic - tors in the midst of strife;

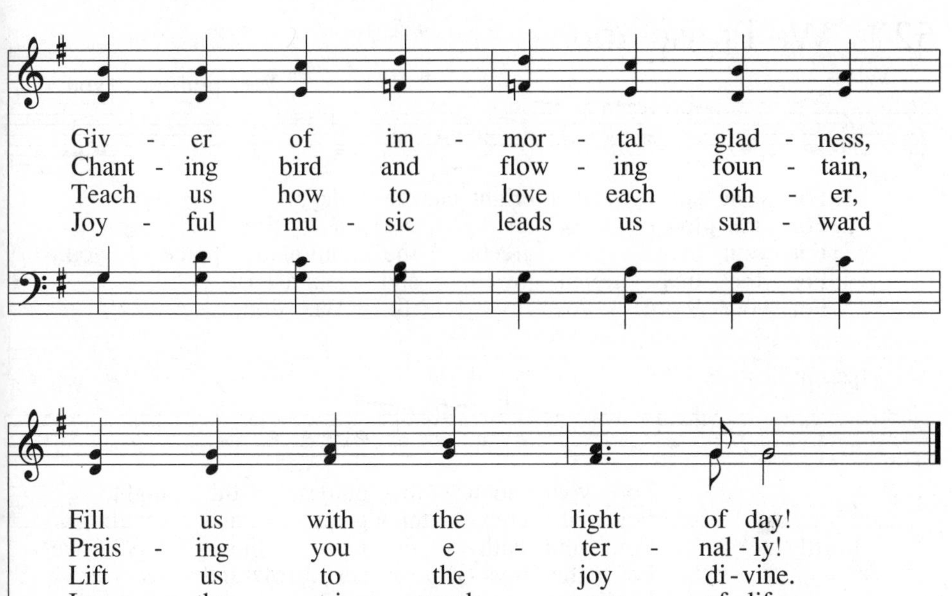
Giv - er of im - mor - tal glad - ness,
Chant - ing bird and flow - ing foun - tain,
Teach us how to love each oth - er,
Joy - ful mu - sic leads us sun - ward

Fill us with the light of day!
Prais - ing you e - ter - nal - ly!
Lift us to the joy di - vine.
In the tri - umph song of life.

Text: Henry van Dyke, 1852-1933, alt.
Tune: HYMN TO JOY, 8 7 8 7 D; arr. from Ludwig van Beethoven, 1770-1827, by Edward Hodges, 1796-1867

521 We Praise You

Verses

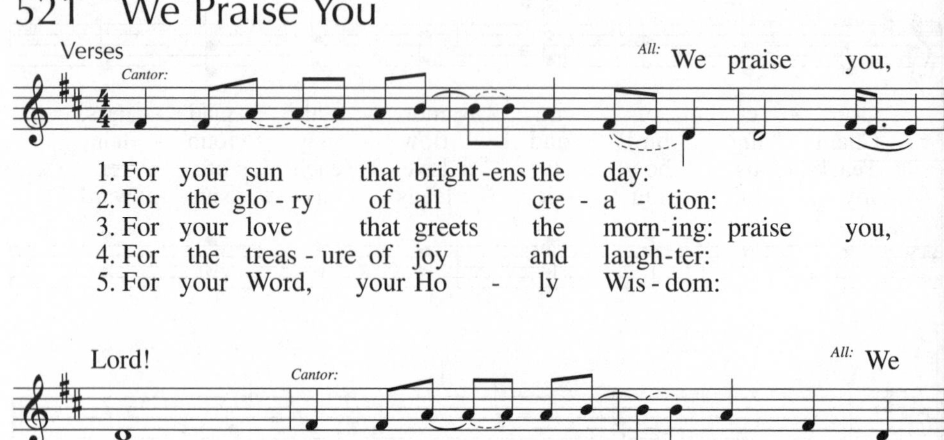
Cantor:
All: We praise you,
1. For your sun that bright-ens the day:
2. For the glo - ry of all cre - a - tion:
3. For your love that greets the morn-ing: praise you,
4. For the treas - ure of joy and laugh-ter:
5. For your Word, your Ho - ly Wis - dom:
Lord!
Cantor:
All: We
For your moon that guides the night:
For all crea - tures great and small:
Lord! For your faith - ful - ness through night: We
For the mys - t'ry of sor - row and tears:
For the bread, the work of our hands:

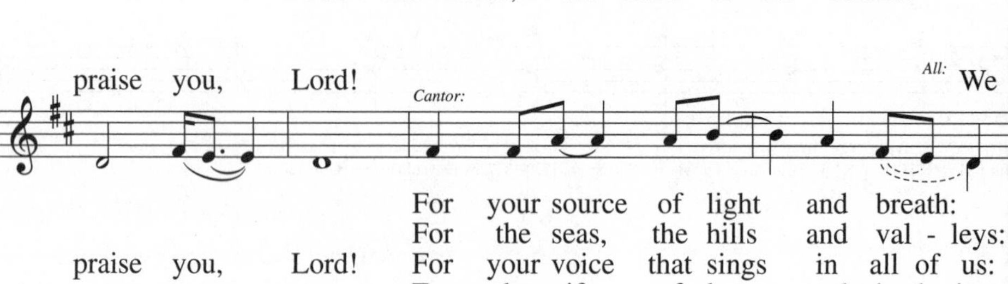
praise you, Lord!
Cantor:
All: We
For your source of light and breath:
For the seas, the hills and val - leys:
praise you, Lord! For your voice that sings in all of us:
For the gift of love and heal - ing:
For the wine, the cup of bless - ing,

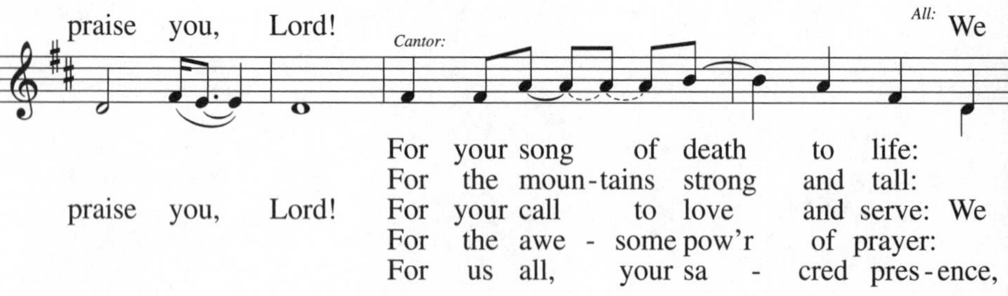
praise you, Lord!
Cantor:
All: We
For your song of death to life:
For the moun-tains strong and tall:
praise you, Lord! For your call to love and serve: We
For the awe - some pow'r of prayer:
For us all, your sa - cred pres-ence,

praise you, Lord!
All:
praise you, Lord! We praise you,

Refrain

Lord! You hear our cry! We praise you, Lord! You are the an - swer! We praise you, Lord! You are al-ways near! With all our be-ing we praise you, Lord!

div. SA: *unis.*

div. TB: *unis.*

Text: David Haas, b.1957
Tune: David Haas, b.1957

Magnificat 522

Canon

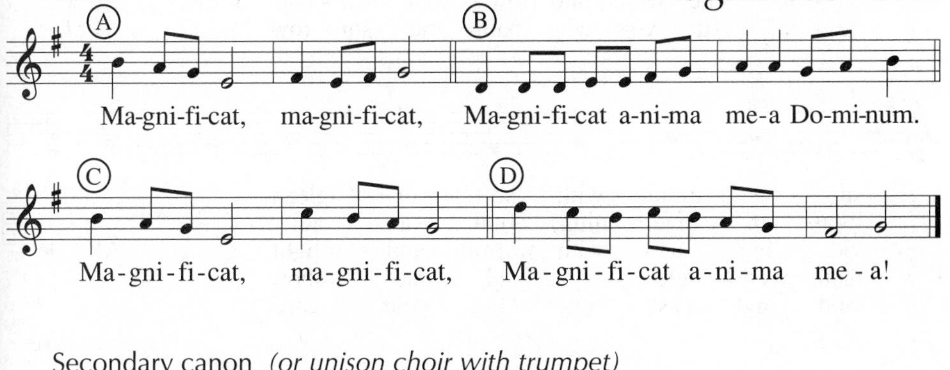
A
B
Ma-gni-fi-cat, ma-gni-fi-cat, Ma-gni-fi-cat a-ni-ma me-a Do-mi-num.
C
D
Ma-gni-fi-cat, ma-gni-fi-cat, Ma-gni-fi-cat a-ni-ma me-a!

Secondary canon *(or unison choir with trumpet)*

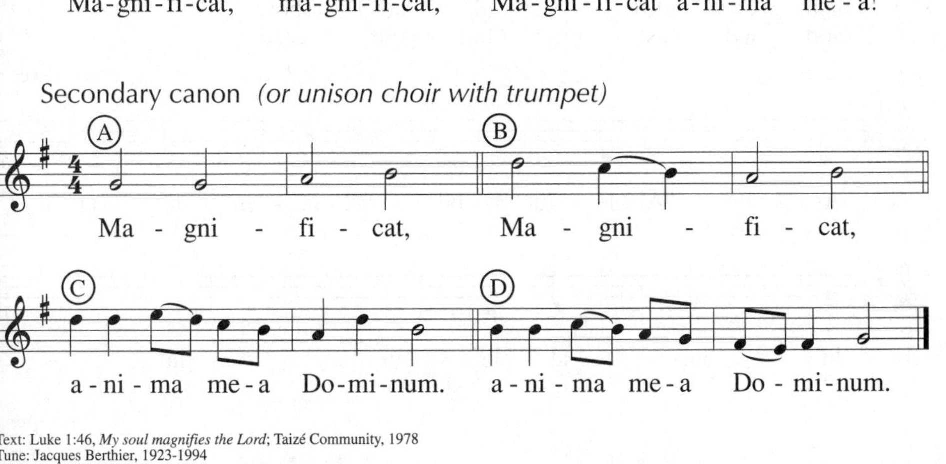
A
B
Ma - gni - fi - cat, Ma - gni - fi - cat,
C
D
a-ni-ma me-a Do-mi-num. a-ni-ma me-a Do-mi-num.

Text: Luke 1:46, *My soul magnifies the Lord*; Taizé Community, 1978
Tune: Jacques Berthier, 1923-1994

523 All Creatures of Our God and King

1. All crea - tures of our God and King, Lift
2. O rush - ing wind and breez - es soft, O
3. O flow - ing wa - ters, pure and clear, Make
4. Dear moth - er earth, who day by day Un -
5. O ev - 'ry one of ten - der heart, For -
up your voice and with us sing: Al - le - lu - ia! Al - le -
clouds that ride the winds a - loft: Al - le - lu - ia! Al - le -
mu - sic for your Lord to hear. Al - le - lu - ia! Al - le -
folds rich bless - ings on our way, Al - le - lu - ia! Al - le -
giv - ing oth - ers, take your part, Al - le - lu - ia! Al - le -
lu - ia! O burn - ing sun with gold - en beam And
lu - ia! O ris - ing morn, in praise re - joice, O
lu - ia! O fire so mas - ter - ful and bright, Pro -
lu - ia! The fruits and flow'rs that ver - dant grow, Let
lu - ia! All you who pain and sor - row bear, Praise
sil - ver moon with soft - er gleam:
lights of eve - ning, find a voice.
vid - ing us with warmth and light, Al - le -
them God's glo - ry al - so show.
God and cast on God your care.
lu - ia! Al - le - lu - ia! Al - le - lu - ia, al - le -
lu - ia, al - le - lu - ia!

6. And you, most kind and gentle death,
Waiting to hush our final breath,
Alleluia! Alleluia!
You lead to heav'n the child of God,
Where Christ our Lord the way has trod.
Alleluia! Alleluia!
Alleluia, alleluia, alleluia!

7. Let all things their Creator bless,
And worship God in humbleness,
Alleluia! Alleluia!
Oh praise the Father, praise the Son,
And praise the Spirit, Three in One!
Alleluia! Alleluia!
Alleluia, alleluia, alleluia!

Text: *Laudato si, mi Signor;* Francis of Assisi, 1182-1226; tr. by William H. Draper, 1855-1933, alt.
Tune: LASST UNS ERFREUEN, LM with alleluias; *Geistliche Kirchengesänge,* 1623; harm. by Ralph Vaughan Williams, 1872-1958, © Oxford University Press

All Glory Is Yours 524

Verse 1
1. How deep are your rich - es, your
wis - dom pro - found. Your know - ledge sur -
pass - es all we dare i - mag - ine. You are
God: all glo - ry is yours!
Refrain
To you, O God, all glo - ry be, all glo - ry for -
for -

ev - er. To you, O God, all glo - ry be, all glo - ry for -
ev - er. To you, O God, all glo - ry for -
To Verses 2 and 3
Last time
ev - er, a - men.
men.
ev - er, a - men.
men.
Verse 2
2. God, how can we know you?
Who knows your mind? What more can
we do but serve you and love you? You are
D.S.
God: all glo - ry is yours!

Verse 3
3. God, all things are from you,
3. God, all things are from you,
con - ceived and brought forth. Through
you all things move, move and have be - ing. Cre-
a - tion ex - ults: all glo - ry is yours!
D.S.

Text: Romans 11:33-36; Bob Moore, b.1962
Tune: Bob Moore, b.1962

525 You, Lord, Are Both Lamb and Shepherd

1. You, Lord, are both Lamb and Shep - herd.
2. Clothed in light up - on the moun - tain,
3. You, who walk each day be - side us,
4. Wor - thy is our earth - ly Je - sus!
You, Lord, are both prince and slave.
Stripped of might up - on the cross,
Sit in pow - er at God's side.
Wor - thy is our cos - mic Christ!
You, peace - mak - er and sword - bring - er
Shin - ing in e - ter - nal glo - ry,
You, who preach a way that's nar - row,
Wor - thy your de - feat and vic - t'ry.
Of the way you took and gave.
Beg - gar'd by a sol - dier's toss,
Have a love that reach - es wide.
Wor - thy still your peace and strife.
You, the ev - er - last - ing in - stant;
You, the ev - er - last - ing in - stant;
You, the ev - er - last - ing in - stant;
You, the ev - er - last - ing in - stant;
You, whom we both scorn and crave.
You, who are our gift and cost.
You, who are our pil - grim guide.
You, who are our death and life.

Text: *Christus Paradox,* Sylvia Dunstan, 1955-1993, © 1991, GIA Publications, Inc.
Tune: PICARDY, 8 7 8 7 8 7; French Carol; harm. by Richard Proulx, b.1937, © 1986, GIA Publications, Inc.

All the Ends of the Earth 526

Refrain
All the ends of the earth, all you crea - tures of the sea,
lift up your eyes to the won - ders of the Lord.
For the Lord of the earth, the Mas - ter of the sea,
Last time
has come with jus - tice for the world.
Verse 1
1. Break in - to song at the deeds of the Lord, the
D.C.
won - ders he has done in ev - 'ry age.
Verse 2
2. Heav - en and earth shall re - joice in his might;
D.C.
ev - 'ry heart, ev - 'ry na - tion call him Lord.
Verse 3
3. The Lord has made sal - va - tion known,
faith - ful to the prom - is - es of old.

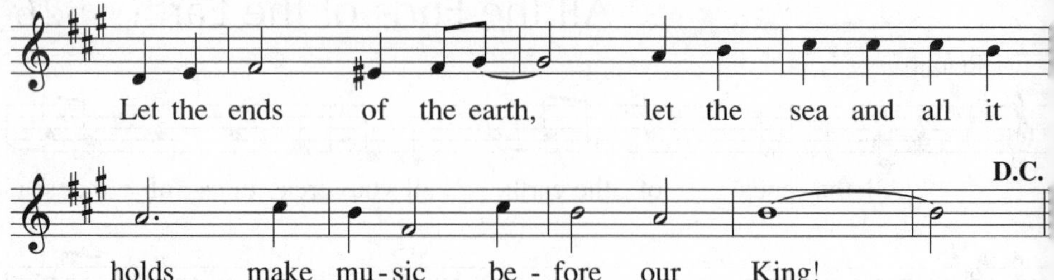
Let the ends of the earth, let the sea and all it
holds make mu-sic be - fore our King!
D.C.

Text: Psalm 98; Bob Dufford, SJ, b.1943
Tune: Bob Dufford, SJ, b.1943; acc. by Bob Dufford and Chris Morash, alt.

527 Canticle of the Turning

Verses

1. My soul cries out with a joy - ful shout that the
2. Though I am small, my God, my all, you
3. From the halls of power to the for - tress tower, not a
4. Though the na - tions rage from age to age, we re -

God of my heart is great, And my spir - it sings of the
work great things in me, And your mer - cy will last from the
stone will be left on stone. Let the king be - ware for your
mem - ber who holds us fast: God's mer - cy must de -

won - drous things that you bring to the ones who wait.
depths of the past to the end of the age to be.
jus - tice tears ev - 'ry ty - rant from his throne.
liv - er us from the con - quer - or's crush - ing grasp.

You fixed your sight on your ser - vant's plight, and my
Your ver - y name puts the proud to shame, and to
The hun - gry poor shall weep no more, for the
This sav - ing word that our fore - bears heard is the

weak - ness you did not spurn, So from east to west shall my
those who would for you yearn, You will show your might, put the
food they can nev - er earn; There are ta - bles spread, ev - 'ry
prom - ise which holds us bound, 'Til the spear and rod can be
name be blest. Could the world be a - bout to turn?
strong to flight, for the world is a - bout to turn.
mouth be fed, for the world is a - bout to turn.
crushed by God, who is turn - ing the world a - round.
Refrain
My heart shall sing of the day you bring. Let the
fires of your jus - tice burn. Wipe a - way all tears, for the
fires of your jus - tice burn. Wipe a - way all tears, for the
dawn draws near, and the world is a-bout to turn!
dawn draws near, and the world is a - bout to turn!

Text: Luke 1:46-58; Rory Cooney, b.1952
Tune: STAR OF THE COUNTY DOWN; Irish traditional; arr. by Rory Cooney, b.1952

528 Laudate Dominum

Ostinato Refrain
Lau-da - te Do-mi-num, lau-da - te Do-mi-num om-nes
gen-tes, al - le - lu - ia. al - le - lu - ia.
1. 2.
Verses
Cantor:
Praise the Lord, all you na - tions, praise him
all you peo - ples. Al - le - lu - ia.
Strong is his love and mer - cy. He is
faith - ful for ev - er. Al - le - lu - ia. Al - le -
lu - ia, al - le - lu - ia. Let ev - 'ry thing
liv - ing give praise to the Lord. Al - le - praise to the Lord.
*

**Choose either part*

Text: Psalm 117, *Praise the Lord, all you peoples;* Taizé Community, 1980
Tune: Jacques Berthier, 1923-1994

Halleluya! We Sing Your Praises 529

Refrain
Hal - le - lu - ya! We sing your prais-es, all our
hearts are filled with glad - ness. Hal - le - lu - ya! We sing your
prais - es, all our hearts are filled with glad - ness.
Verses
1. Christ the Lord to us said: I am
wine, I am bread, I am wine, I am
bread, give to all who thirst and hun - ger.
2. Now he sends us all out, strong in
faith, free of doubt, strong in faith, free of
doubt, to pro - claim the joy - ful Gos - pel.

Text: South African
Tune: South African

530 Let Us Sing to the Lord / Bénissez le Seigneur

Ostinato Refrain
Let us sing to the Lord!
Bé-nis-sez le Sei-gneur!
O
O
Let us sing to the Lord!
Bé-nis-sez le Sei-gneur!
O
Let us sing to the Lord! Let us sing to the Lord!
Bé-nis-sez le Sei-gneur! Bé-nis-sez le Sei-gneur!
Let us sing to the Lord! Let us sing to the Lord!
Bé-nis-sez le Sei-gneur! Bé-nis-sez le Sei-gneur!

*Choose either part

Verses *(Superimposed on ostinato refrain)*

Cantor:
1. All cre - a - tion bless the Lord; and
you, an-gels of the Lord, praise and
glo - ri - fy the Lord.
4
2. Sun and moon, bless the
Lord; and you, night and day, bless the
Lord; and you, light and dark-ness, bless the
Lord.
4
3. Praise the Lord all the earth.
Birds of the air, bless the Lord. All
crea-tures of the sea, bless the Lord.
4
4. Fire and
hail, bless the Lord. Snow and frost, bless the
Lord. Moun-tains and hills, bless the Lord.

3
5. My soul glo - ri - fies the Lord.
My spir - it re - joic - es in God.
The Lord has done won - ders for me.
3
6. The glo - ry of the Lord fills the earth.
Let all peo - ple bless God's name.
Let ev - 'ry - thing that breathes bless the Lord.
4
7. Sing a - loud to the Lord.
Praise our God for his won - der - ful deeds.
Shout for joy to our God.
4

Text: Daniel 3:57-75, Luke 1:46-47, 49, Psalm 5:1-2; Taizé Community
Tune: Jacques Berthier, 1923-1994

Praise, My Soul, the King of Heaven 531

1. Praise, my soul, the King of heav - en; To his
2. Praise him for his grace and fa - vor To his
3. Fa - ther - like he tends and spares us; Well our
4. Frail as sum-mer's flow'r we flour - ish, Blows the
5. An - gels, help us to a - dore him; You be -
feet your trib-ute bring; Ran-somed, healed, re - stored, for -
peo - ple in dis - tress; Praise him still the same as
fee - ble frame he knows; In his hands he gen - tly
wind and it is gone; But while mor - tals rise and
hold him face to face; Sun and moon, bow down be -
giv - en, Ev - er - more his prais - es sing: Al - le - lu-ia!
ev - er, Slow to chide, and swift to bless: Al - le - lu-ia!
bears us, Res - cues us from all our foes. Al - le - lu-ia!
per - ish, God en - dures un - chang-ing on; Al - le - lu-ia!
fore him, Dwell-ers all in time and space: Al - le - lu-ia!
Al - le - lu - ia! Praise the ev - er - last - ing King.
Al - le - lu - ia! Glo - rious in his faith - ful - ness.
Al - le - lu - ia! Wide - ly yet his mer - cy flows.
Al - le - lu - ia! Praise the high e - ter - nal one!
Al - le - lu - ia! Praise with us the God of grace.

Text: Psalm 103; Henry F. Lyte, 1793-1847, alt.
Tune: LAUDA ANIMA, 8 7 8 7 8 7; John Goss, 1800-1880

532 Sing of the Lord's Goodness

Verses
1. Sing of the Lord's good - ness, Fa - ther of all wis - dom,
2. Pow - er he has wield - ed, hon - or is his gar - ment,
3. Cour - age in our dark - ness, com - fort in our sor - row,
4. Praise him with your sing - ing, praise him with the trum - pet,
come to him and bless his name.
ris - en from the snares of death.
Spir - it of our God most high;
praise God with the lute and harp;
Mer - cy he has shown us, his love is for - ev - er,
His word he has spo - ken, one bread he has bro - ken,
sol - ace for the wea - ry, par - don for the sin - ner,
praise him with the cym - bals, praise him with your danc - ing,
faith - ful to the end of days.
new life he now gives to all.
splen - dor of the liv - ing God.
praise God till the end of days.
Refrain
Descant:
Come, then, all you na - tions, sing of your Lord's good - ness,
Melody:
Come, then, all you na - tions, sing of your Lord's good - ness,

mel - o - dies of praise and thanks to God. Ring out the Lord's glo - ry,
mel - o - dies of praise and thanks to God. Ring out the Lord's glo - ry,
praise him with your mu - sic, wor - ship him and bless his name.
praise him with your mu - sic, wor - ship him and bless his name.
Final ending

Text: Ernest Sands, b.1949, © 1981, Ernest Sands
Tune: Ernest Sands, b.1949, © 1981, Ernest Sands; acc. by Paul Inwood, b.1947, © 1986, Paul Inwood
Published by OCP Publications.

533 Sing to God / Singt dem Herrn

Refrain
A
Sing to God with joy-ful hearts. Praise the Lord for ev-er-more, praise the Lord for ev-er-more.
Singt dem Herrn ein neu-es Lied. Lob-singt ihm al-le-zeit, lob-singt ihm al-le-zeit!
Verses
B
D.C.
O
Verses (Superimposed on B section)
B
Cantor:
1. Sing to the Lord all the earth, sing and bless God's ho-ly name.
2. Sing a new song to the Lord, for God has done mar-vel-ous deeds.

*Choose either part

B
3. The Lord has made known his sal - va - tion for all peo-ples to be - hold.
B
4. The Lord has re - mem-bered his faith - ful - ness, his stead-fast love for all peo-ples.
B
5. Make a joy - ful noise to the Lord! Break forth in - to songs of praise!
B
6. Sing prais - es to the Lord with sounds of mu - sic, with trum - pet and horn, re - joice in the Lord.
B
7. Let the sea roar, let the floods clap their hands, and the hills sing to - geth-er for joy in the Lord.
B
8. The heav-ens pro - claim the Lord's right - eous - ness and all peo - ples be - hold his

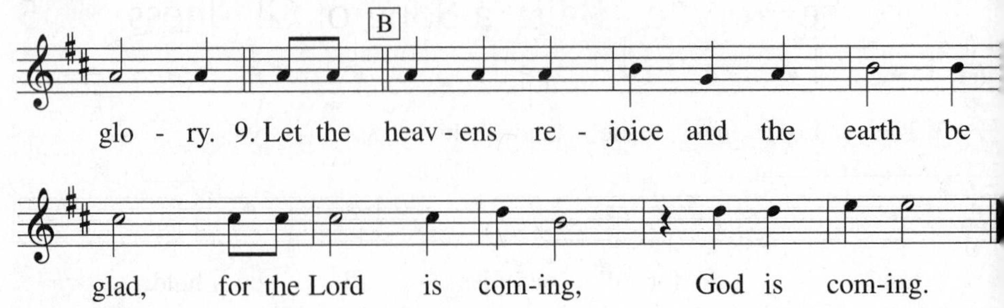
B
glo - ry. 9. Let the heav - ens re - joice and the earth be
glad, for the Lord is com-ing, God is com-ing.

Text: Psalm 96:2, 97:6, 98:1-8
Tune: Jacques Berthier, 1923-1994

534 Holy God

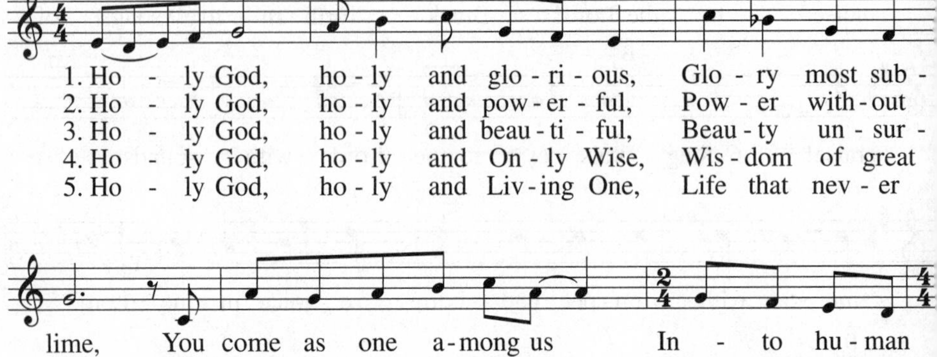
1. Ho - ly God, ho - ly and glo - ri - ous, Glo - ry most sub -
2. Ho - ly God, ho - ly and pow - er - ful, Pow - er with - out
3. Ho - ly God, ho - ly and beau - ti - ful, Beau - ty un - sur -
4. Ho - ly God, ho - ly and On - ly Wise, Wis - dom of great
5. Ho - ly God, ho - ly and Liv - ing One, Life that nev - er
lime, You come as one a - mong us In - to hu - man
peer, You bend to us in weak - ness, Emp - tied you draw
passed, You are de - spised, re - ject - ed; Scorned you hold us
price, You choose the way of fol - ly: God the cru - ci -
ends, You show your love by dy - ing, Dy - ing for your

time, And we be - hold your glo - ry.
near, And we be - hold your pow - er.
fast, And we be - hold your beau - ty.
fied, Yet we be - hold your wis - dom.
friends, And we be - hold you liv - ing.

Text: Susan R. Briehl, b.1952
Tune: MAGDALENA, 9 5 7 5 7; Marty Haugen, b.1950

Jubilate, Servite / Raise a Song of Gladness 535

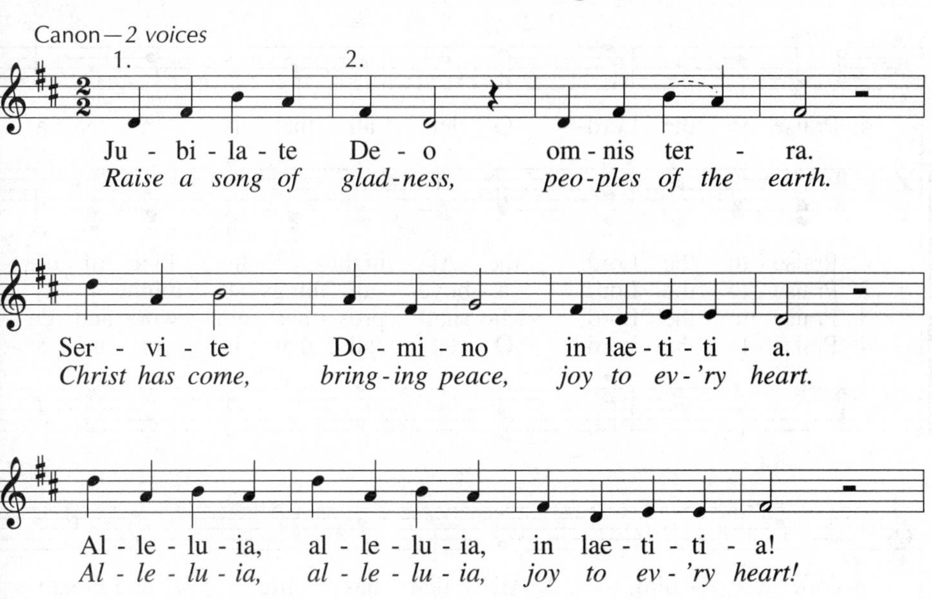
Canon—2 voices
1.
2.
Ju - bi - la - te De - o om - nis ter - ra.
Raise a song of glad - ness, peo - ples of the earth.
Ser - vi - te Do - mi - no in lae - ti - ti - a.
Christ has come, bring - ing peace, joy to ev - 'ry heart.
Al - le - lu - ia, al - le - lu - ia, in lae - ti - ti - a!
Al - le - lu - ia, al - le - lu - ia, joy to ev - 'ry heart!

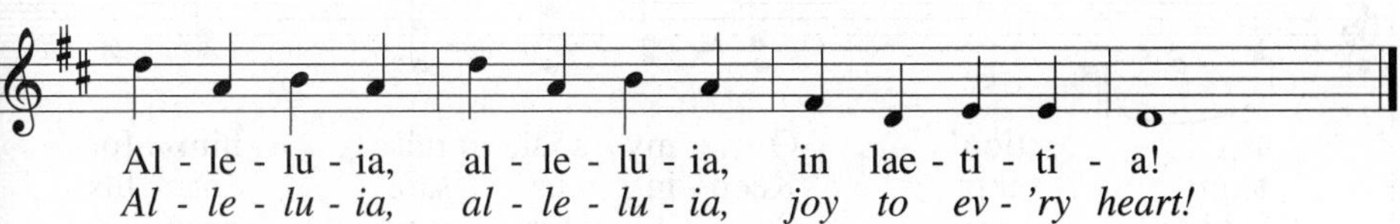
Al - le - lu - ia, al - le - lu - ia, in lae - ti - ti - a!
Al - le - lu - ia, al - le - lu - ia, joy to ev - 'ry heart!

Text: Psalm 100, *Rejoice in God, all the earth, Serve the Lord with gladness;* Taizé Community, 1978
Tune: Jacques Berthier, 1923-1994

536 Praise to the Lord, the Almighty

Descant:
4. Praise to the Lord— O let all that is in us a - dore him! All that has life and breath come now with prais - es be - fore him!
1. Praise to the Lord, the Al - might - y, the king of cre - a - tion! O my soul, praise him, for he is your health and sal - va - tion!
2. Praise to the Lord, a - bove all things so might - i - ly reign - ing; Keep - ing us safe at his side, and so gent - ly sus - tain - ing.
3. Praise to the Lord, who shall pros - per our work and de - fend us; Sure - ly his good - ness and mer - cy shall dai - ly at - tend us.
4. Praise to the Lord— O let all that is in us a - dore him! All that has life and breath come now with prais - es be - fore him!

Let the "A - men!" Sound from his peo - ple a - gain—
Come, all who hear: Broth - ers and sis - ters, draw near,
Have you not seen All you have need - ed has been
Pon - der a - new What the Al - might - y can do,
Let the "A - men!" Sound from his peo - ple a - gain—
Glad - ly with praise we a - dore him!
Praise him in glad ad - o - ra - tion!
Met by his gra - cious or - dain - ing?
Who with his love will be - friend us.
Glad - ly with praise we a - dore him!

Text: *Lobe den Herren, den mächtigen König;* Joachim Neander, 1650-1680; tr. by Catherine Winkworth, 1827-1878, alt.
Tune: LOBE DEN HERREN, 14 14 47 8; *Stralsund Gesangbuch,* 1665; descant by C.S. Lang, 1891-1971, © 1953, Novello and Co. Ltd.

537 Glory and Praise to Our God

Refrain

Melody:

Glo - ry and praise to our God, who a - lone gives light to our days. Man - y are the bless-ings he bears to those who trust in his ways.

Harmony:

Glo - ry and praise to our God, who a - lone gives light to our days. Man - y are the bless-ings he bears to those who trust in his ways.

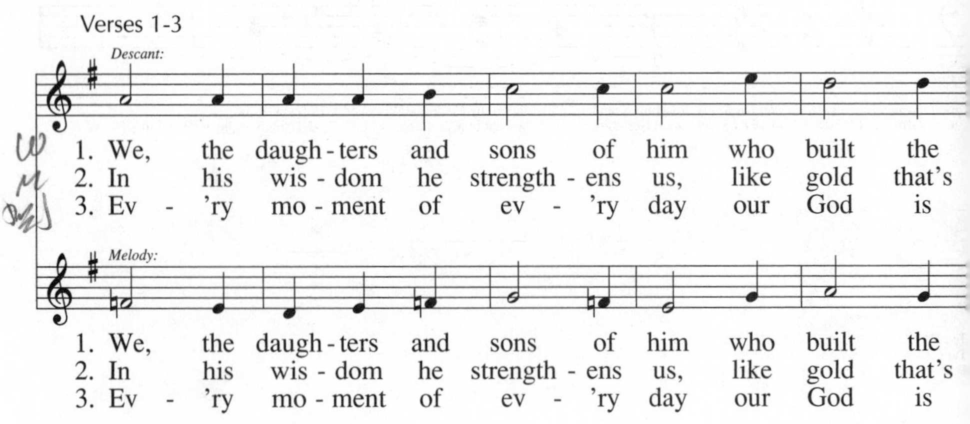
Verses 1-3
Descant:
1. We, the daugh - ters and sons of him who built the
2. In his wis - dom he strength - ens us, like gold that's
3. Ev - 'ry mo - ment of ev - 'ry day our God is
Melody:
1. We, the daugh - ters and sons of him who built the
2. In his wis - dom he strength - ens us, like gold that's
3. Ev - 'ry mo - ment of ev - 'ry day our God is

val - leys and plains, Praise the won-ders our God has
test - ed in fire. Though the pow - er of sin pre -
wait-ing to save, Al - ways read - y to seek the
val - leys and plains, Praise the won-ders our God has
test - ed in fire. Though the pow - er of sin pre -
wait-ing to save, Al - ways read - y to seek the
D.C.
done in ev - 'ry heart that sings.
vails, our God is there to save.
lost, to an - swer those who pray.
done in ev - 'ry heart that sings.
vails, our God is there to save.
lost, to an - swer those who pray.
Verse 4
4. God has wa - tered our bar - ren land and spent his
mer - ci - ful rain. Now the riv - ers of life run
D.C.
full for an - y - one to drink.

Text: Psalm 65, 66; Dan Schutte, b.1947
Tune: Dan Schutte, b.1947; acc. by Sr. Theophane Hytrek, OSF, 1915-1992, alt.

538 You Are the Voice

Refrain

Melody:
You are the voice of the liv - ing
Harmony:
You, you are the voice of the the liv - ing
God, call - ing us now to live in your
God, call - ing us now to live,
love, to be chil - dren of God once a -
live in your love, to be chil - dren of God once a -
To verses
Final ending
gain!
gain!

Verses
Cantor:
1. Praise for the light that shines through the night, from dark - ness to light, from death to new life, and praise to the morn - ing that brings forth the sun, to o - pen our eyes to the Lord! To o - pen our eyes to the Lord! For
2. Praise for the wa - ter that springs from the sea, the seed that gives life to all who be - lieve, God's love o - ver - flow - ing, our hearts know the joy to be daugh - ters and sons of the Lord! To be daugh - ters and sons of the Lord! For
3. Praise for the sing - ing and praise for the dance, with new heart and voice, all raise the song of praise to cre - a - tion; all heav - en and earth, come sing of the glo - ry of God! Come sing of the glo - ry of God! For
All:
D.C.

Text: David Haas, b.1957
Tune: David Haas, b.1957; acc. by Jeanne Cotter, b.1964

539 When, in Our Music, God Is Glorified

1. When, in our music, God is glorified,
And adoration leaves no room for pride,
It is as though the whole creation cried:
Alleluia!

2. How often, making music, we have found
A new dimension in the world of sound,
As worship moved us to a more profound
Alleluia!

3. So has the Church, in liturgy and song,
In faith and love, through centuries of wrong,
Borne witness to the truth in ev'ry tongue:
Alleluia!

4. And did not Jesus sing a psalm that night
When utmost evil strove against the Light?
Then let us sing, for whom he won the fight:
Alleluia!

5. Let ev'ry instrument be tuned for praise!
Let all rejoice who have a voice to raise!
And may God give us faith to sing always:
Alleluia!

Text: Mark 14:26; Fred Pratt Green, 1903-2000, © 1972, Hope Publishing Co.
Tune: ENGELBERG, 10 10 10 with alleluia; Charles V. Stanford, 1852-1924

540 We Praise You

Refrain
We praise you, O Lord, for all your works are won-der-ful.
We praise you, O Lord, for ev-er is your love.

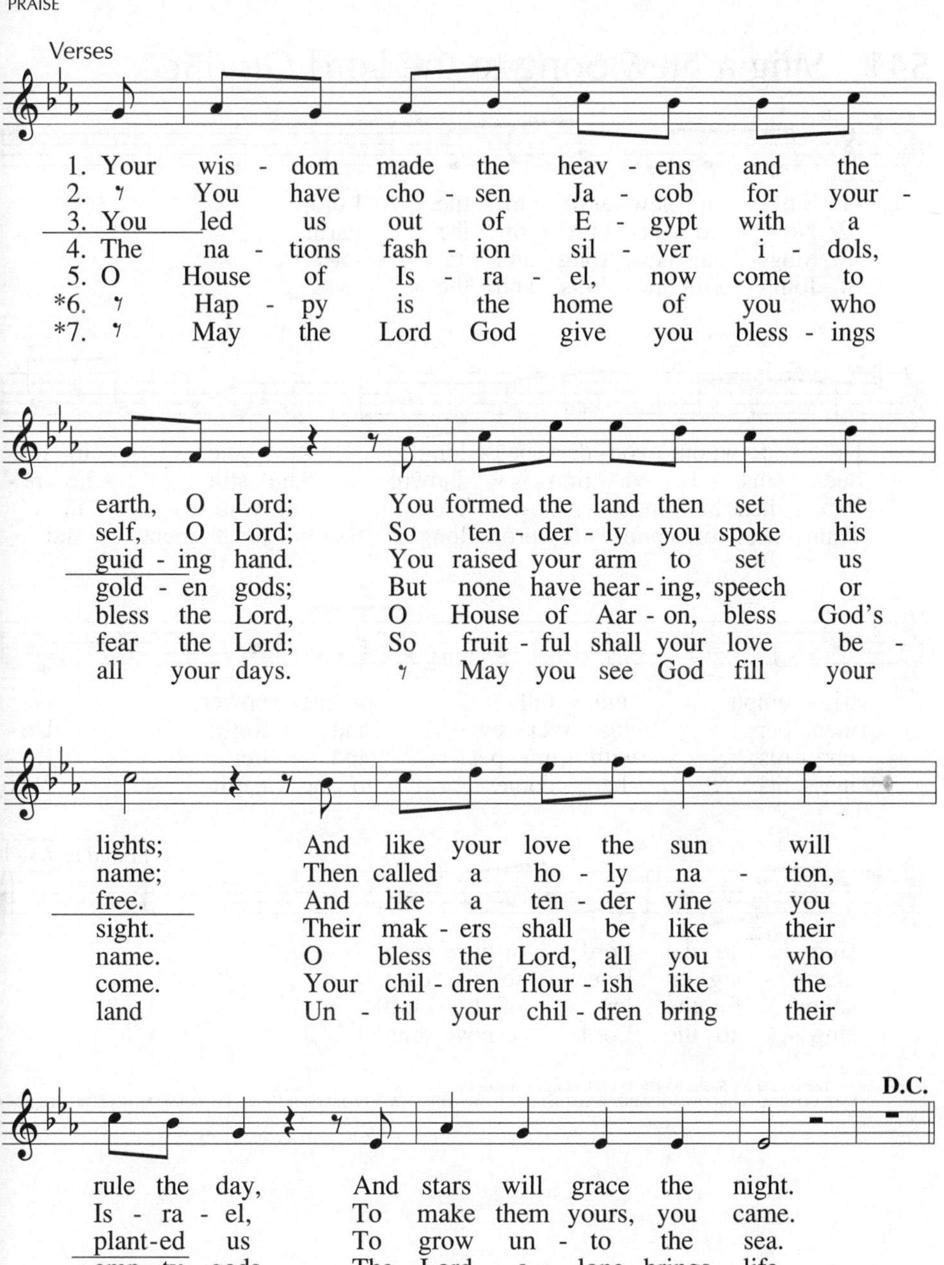
Verses
1. Your wis - dom made the heav - ens and the
2. You have cho - sen Ja - cob for your -
3. You led us out of E - gypt with a
4. The na - tions fash - ion sil - ver i - dols,
5. O House of Is - ra - el, now come to
*6. Hap - py is the home of you who
*7. May the Lord God give you bless - ings
earth, O Lord; You formed the land then set the
self, O Lord; So ten - der - ly you spoke his
guid - ing hand. You raised your arm to set us
gold - en gods; But none have hear - ing, speech or
bless the Lord, O House of Aar - on, bless God's
fear the Lord; So fruit - ful shall your love be -
all your days. May you see God fill your
lights; And like your love the sun will
name; Then called a ho - ly na - tion,
free. And like a ten - der vine you
sight. Their mak - ers shall be like their
name. O bless the Lord, all you who
come. Your chil - dren flour - ish like the
land Un - til your chil - dren bring their
D.C.
rule the day, And stars will grace the night.
Is - ra - el, To make them yours, you came.
plant-ed us To grow un - to the sea.
emp - ty gods, The Lord a - lone brings life.
hon - or God, And praise his ho - ly name.
ol - ive plants, For ev - er are you one.
chil-dren home To show God's love a - gain.

**wedding verses*

Text: Mike Balhoff, b.1946
Tune: Darryl Ducote, b.1945, Gary Daigle, b.1957

541 Sing a New Song to the Lord

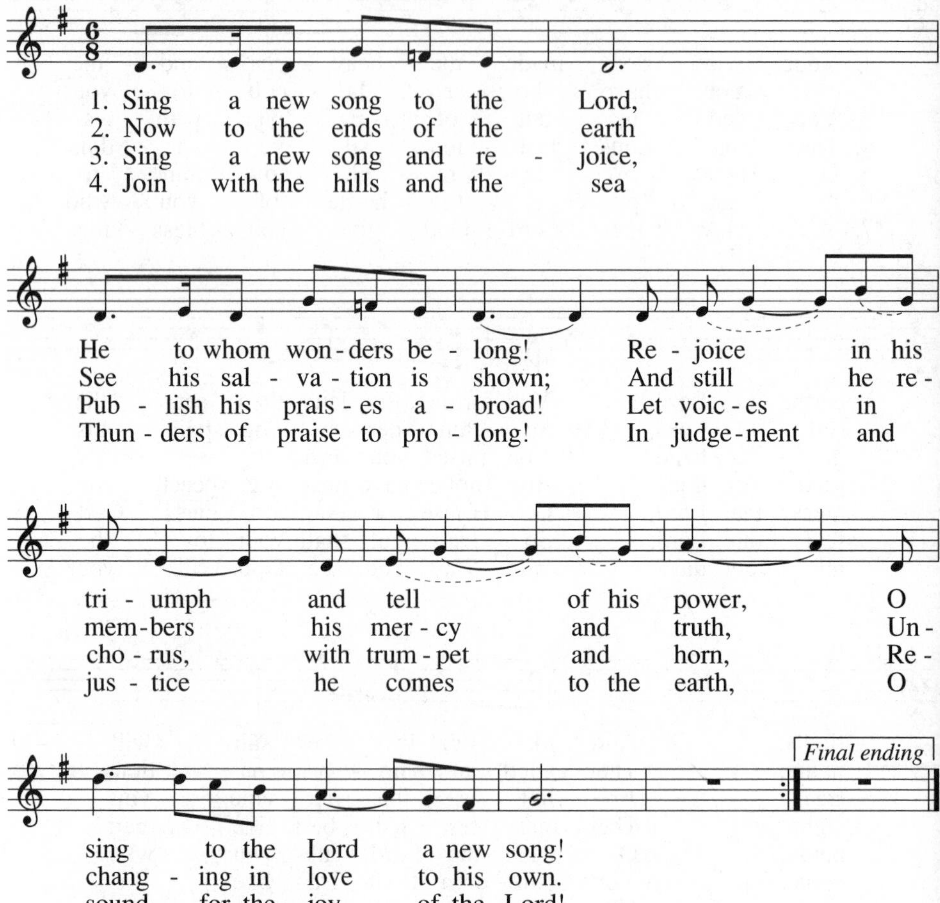
1. Sing a new song to the Lord,
He to whom won-ders be - long!
Re - joice in his tri - umph and tell of his power,
O sing to the Lord a new song!
2. Now to the ends of the earth
See his sal - va - tion is shown;
And still he re - mem-bers his mer - cy and truth,
Un - chang - ing in love to his own.
3. Sing a new song and re - joice,
Pub - lish his prais - es a - broad!
Let voic - es in cho - rus, with trum - pet and horn,
Re - sound for the joy of the Lord!
4. Join with the hills and the sea
Thun - ders of praise to pro - long!
In judge-ment and jus - tice he comes to the earth,
O sing to the Lord a new song!
Final ending

Text: Psalm 98; Timothy Dudley-Smith, b.1926, © 1973, Hope Publishing Co.
Tune: CANTATE DOMINO (ONSLOW SQUARE), Irregular; David G. Wilson, b.1940, © 1973, Jubilate Hymns, Ltd. (admin. by Hope Publishing Co.)

Let All Mortal Flesh Keep Silence 542

1. Let all mor - tal flesh keep si - lence,
2. King of kings, yet born of Mar - y,
3. Rank on rank the host of heav - en
4. At his feet the six - winged ser - aph,
And with fear and trem - bling stand;
As of old on earth he stood,
Spreads its van - guard on the way,
Cher - u - bim with sleep - less eye,
Pon - der noth - ing earth - ly mind - ed,
Lord of lords in hu - man ves - ture,
As the Light of Light de - scend - ing
Veil their fac - es to the Pres - ence,
For with bless - ing in his hand
In the Bod - y and the Blood
From the realms of end - less day,
As with cease - less voice they cry,
Christ our God to earth de - scend - ing,
He will give to all the faith - ful
That the pow'rs of hell may van - ish
"Al - le - lu - ia, al - le - lu - ia,
Our full hom - age to de - mand.
His own self for heav'n - ly food.
As the dark - ness clears a - way.
Al - le - lu - ia, Lord, most high!"

Text: Liturgy of St. James, 5th C.; para. by Gerard Moultrie, 1829-1885
Tune: PICARDY, 8 7 8 7 8 7; French Carol; harm. by Richard Proulx, b.1937, © 1986, GIA Publications, Inc.

543 Lift Up Your Hearts

Refrain
Descant:
Lift up your hearts, praise God's all gra - cious mer - cy, sing! Sing out to God, whose love is en - dur - ing. ing.
Melody:
Lift up your hearts to the Lord, praise God's gra-cious mer - cy! Sing out your joy to the Lord, whose love is en - dur - ing. ing.
To verses
Last time
Verses
1. Shout with joy to the Lord, all the earth! Praise the name a - bove all names!
2. Let the earth wor - ship, sing - ing your praise. Praise the glo - ry of your name!
3. God's right hand made a path through the night, split the wa - ters of the sea.
4. Lis - ten now, all you ser - vants of God, As I tell of these great works.

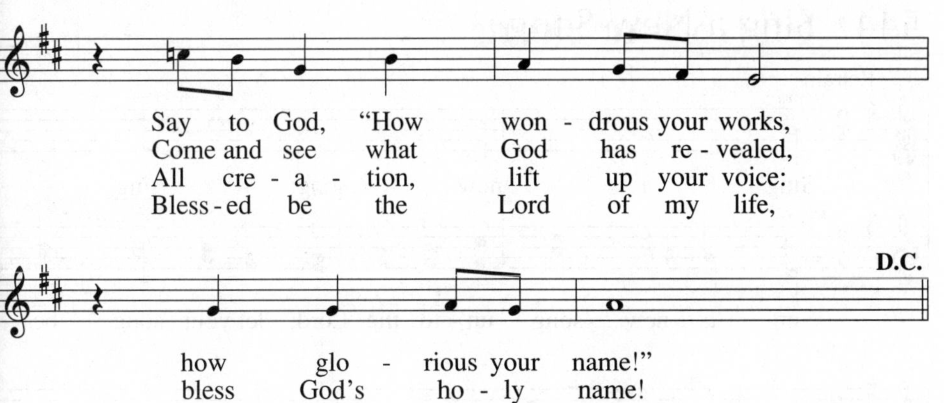
D.C.
Say to God, "How won - drous your works,
Come and see what God has re - vealed,
All cre - a - tion, lift up your voice:
Bless - ed be the Lord of my life,
how glo - rious your name!"
bless God's ho - ly name!
Our God set us free.
whose love shall en - dure!

Text: Psalm 66; Roc O'Connor, SJ, b.1949
Tune: Roc O'Connor, SJ, b.1949; acc. by Robert J. Batastini, b.1942

544 Sing a New Song

Refrain
Descant:
Melody:
Harmony:
Sing a new song; sing al - le - lu - ia. Sing a new song al - le - lu - ia.
Sing a new song un - to the Lord; let your song be sung from moun - tains high. Sing a new song un - to the Lord, sing - ing al - le - lu - ia.
Verses
1. Yah - weh's peo - ple dance for joy. O come be - fore the Lord. And play for him on glad tam - bou - rines, and let your trum - pet sound.
2. Rise, O chil - dren, from your sleep; your Sav - ior now has come. He has turned your sor - row to joy, and filled your soul with song.
3. Glad my soul for I have seen the glo - ry of the Lord. The trum - pet sounds; the dead shall be raised. I know my Sav - ior lives.
D.C.

Text: Psalm 98; Dan Schutte, b.1947
Tune: Dan Schutte, b.1947

Now Thank We All Our God 545
1. Now thank we all our God With hearts and hands and
2. O may this gra - cious God Through all our life be
3. All praise and thanks to God The Fa - ther now be
voic - es, Who won - drous things has done, In
near us, With ev - er joy - ful hearts And
giv - en, The Son, and Spir - it blest, Who
whom his world re - joic - es; Who, from our moth-ers'
bless - ed peace to cheer us; Pre - serve us in his
reigns in high - est heav - en, E - ter - nal, Tri - une
arms, Hath blest us on our way With
grace, And guide us in dis - tress, And
God, Whom earth and heav'n a - dore; For
count - less gifts of love, And still is ours to - day.
free us from all sin, Till heav - en we pos - sess.
thus it was, is now, And shall be ev - er - more.

ext: *Nun danket alle Gott*; Martin Rickart, 1586-1649; tr. by Catherine Winkworth, 1827-1878, alt.
une: NUN DANKET, 6 7 6 7 6 6 6 6; Johann Crüger, 1598-1662; harm. by A. Gregory Murray, OSB, 1905-1992

546 In the Lord I'll Be Ever Thankful

Ostinato Refrain
In the Lord I'll be ev - er thank - ful, in the Lord I will re - joice! Look to God, do not be a - fraid; lift up your voic - es, the Lord is near; lift up your voic - es, the Lord is near.
Verse (In the Lord)
Cantor:
With joy you will draw wa - ter at the foun-tain of sal - va - tion.
Give thanks to the Lord. Ac - claim God's name.

Text: Taizé Community
Tune: Jacques Berthier, 1923-1994

547 Father, We Thank Thee, Who Hast Planted

1. Fa - ther, we thank thee, who hast plant - ed Thy ho - ly
2. Watch o'er thy Church, O Lord, in mer - cy, Save it from

Name with - in our hearts. Knowl - edge and faith and life im -
e - vil, guard it still, Per - fect it in thy love, u -
mor - tal Je - sus, thy Son, to us im - parts.
nite it, Cleansed and con - formed un - to thy will.
Thou, Lord, didst make all for thy pleas - ure,
As grain, once scat - tered on the hill - sides,
Didst give us food for all our days, Giv - ing in Christ
Was in this bro - ken bread made one, So from all lands
the Bread e - ter - nal; Thine is the pow'r, be thine the praise.
thy Church be gath - ered In - to thy king-dom by thy Son.

Text: From the *Didache,* c.110; tr. by F. Bland Tucker, 1895-1984, alt., © 1940, The Church Pension Fund
Tune: RENDEZ À DIEU, 9 8 9 8 D; *Genevan Psalter,* 1551; attr. to Louis Bourgeois, c.1510-1561

548 For the Beauty of the Earth

1. For the beau - ty of the earth, For the glo - ry of the skies, For the love which from our birth O - ver and a - round us lies:
2. For the beau - ty of each hour Of the day and of the night, Hill and vale, and tree and flow'r, Sun and moon, and stars of light:
3. For the joy of ear and eye, For the heart and mind's de - light, For the mys - tic har - mo - ny Link - ing sense to sound and sight:
4. For the joy of hu - man love, Broth - er, sis - ter, par - ent, child, Friends on earth, and friends a - bove; For all gen - tle thoughts and mild:
5. For your church, that ev - er - more Lifts its ho - ly hands a - bove, Off - 'ring up on ev - 'ry shore Its pure sac - ri - fice of love:
6. For your - self, best Gift Di - vine! To this world so free - ly giv'n; Word In - car - nate, God's de - sign, Peace on earth and joy in heav'n:
Lord of all, to you we raise This our hymn of grate - ful praise.

Text: Folliot S. Pierpont, 1835-1917
Tune: DIX, 7 7 7 7 77; arr. from Conrad Kocher, 1786-1872, by William H. Monk, 1823-1889

We Gather Together 549

1. We gath - er to - geth - er to ask the Lord's bless - ing;
2. Be - side us to guide us, our God with us join - ing,
3. We all do ex - tol you our lead - er tri - um - phant,
He chas - tens and has - tens his will to make known;
Whose king - dom calls all to the love which en - dures.
And pray that you still our de - fend - er will be.
The wick - ed op - press - ing now cease from dis - tress - ing:
So from the be - gin - ning the fight we were win - ning:
Let your con - gre - ga - tion es - cape trib - u - la - tion:
Sing prais - es to his name; he for - gets not his own.
You, Lord, were at our side; all glo - ry be yours!
Your name be ev - er praised! O Lord, make us free!

Text: *Wilt heden nu treden*, Netherlands folk hymn; tr. by Theodore Baker, 1851-1934, alt.
Tune: KREMSER, 12 11 12 11; *Neder-landtsch Gedenckclanck*, 1626; harm. by Edward Kremser, 1838-1914

550 Confitemini Domino / Come and Fill

Ostinato Refrain

Con - fi - te - mi - ni Do - mi - no
Come and fill our hearts with your peace.

quo - ni - am bo-nus. Con - fi - te - mi - ni
You a - lone, O Lord, are ho - ly. Come and fill our hearts

Do - mi - no, Al - le - lu - ia!
with your peace, Al - le - lu - ia!

Text: Psalm 137, *Give thanks to the Lord for he is good;* Taizé Community, 1982
Tune: Jacques Berthier, 1923-1994

551 Let All Things Now Living

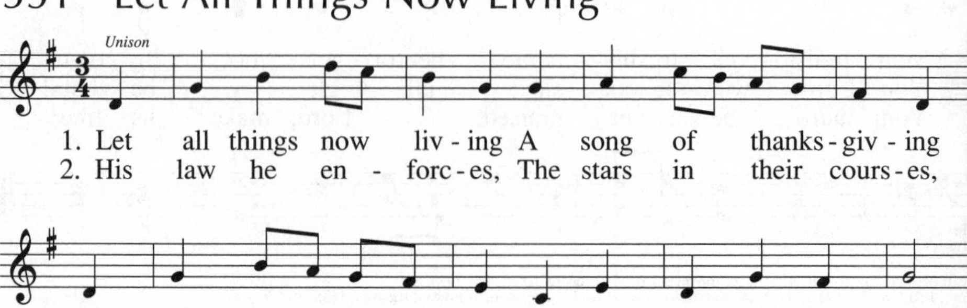
Unison
1. Let all things now liv - ing A song of thanks - giv - ing
2. His law he en - forc - es, The stars in their cours - es,
To God our Cre - a - tor tri - um - phant - ly raise;
The sun in its or - bit o - be - dient - ly shine,

Who fash - ioned and made us, Pro - tect - ed and stayed us,
The hills and the moun - tains, The riv - ers and foun-tains,
By guid - ing us on to the end of our days.
The depths of the o - cean pro - claim God di - vine.
Harmony
God's ban - ners are o'er us, Pure light goes be - fore us,
We, too, should be voic - ing Our love and re - joic - ing
A pil - lar of fire shin - ing forth in the night:
With glad ad - o - ra - tion, a song let us raise:
Unison
Till shad - ows have van - ished And dark - ness is ban - ished,
Till all things now liv - ing U - nite in thanks - giv - ing,
As for - ward we trav - el from light in - to Light.
To God in the high - est, ho - san - na and praise.

Text: Katherine K. Davis, 1892-1980, © 1939, 1966, E. C. Schirmer Music Co.
Tune: ASH GROVE, 66 11 66 11 D; Welsh; harm. by Gerald H. Knight, 1908-1979, © The Royal School of Church Music

552 Come, Ye Thankful People, Come

1. Come, ye thank - ful peo - ple, come, Raise the song of har - vest - home: All is safe - ly gath - ered in, Ere the win - ter storms be - gin; God, our Mak - er, does pro - vide For our wants to be sup - plied;
2. All the world is God's own field, Fruit un - to God's praise to yield; Wheat and tares to - geth - er sown, Un - to joy or sor - row grown; First the blade, and then the ear, Then the full corn shall ap - pear:
3. For the Lord our God shall come, And shall take the har - vest home; From the field shall in that day All of - fens - es purge a - way, Giv - ing an - gels charge at last In the fire the tares to cast,
4. E - ven so, Lord, quick - ly come To your fi - nal har - vest home; Gath - er all your peo - ple in, Free from sor - row, free from sin; There, for ev - er pu - ri - fied, In your pres - ence to a - bide:

Come to God's own tem - ple, come,
Lord of har - vest, grant that we
But the fruit - ful ears to store
Come, with all your an - gels, come,
Raise the song of har - vest - home.
Whole - some grain and pure may be.
In God's gar - ner ev - er - more.
Raise the glo - rious har - vest - home.

Text: Henry Alford, 1810-1871, alt.
Tune: ST. GEORGE'S WINDSOR, 77 77 D; George J. Elvey, 1816-1893; harm. by Richard Proulx, b.1937,

553 We Give You Thanks

Verses
1. For the bread and wine we share here, for the friends that we em - brace, for the peace we find in heal-ing, for all who gath-er in this place,
2. For the move-ment deep with - in us, for the sto - ries that we bring, for the signs of God's com - pas-sion, for the jour-ney that we sing,
3. For the wa - ter bring-ing new life, for the fra - grance of re - lease, for the fire that blaz - es for-ward, for the call to bring forth peace,
for the faith of those a - round us, for the dead and all those here, for the hope we find in mem - 'ry, for the love that draws us near:
for the Word that holds our prom-ise, for the gifts that we can claim, for the won - ders that sur - round us, for the song that sings our name:
for the blind-ness now en - light-ened, for the bound that are now free, for the bright-ness of your new day, for the king - dom we will be:

Refrain
We give you thanks, we give you thanks
for the grace to re-ceive,
for the grace, re - ceive, in you we be - lieve. We
give you thanks, we give you thanks. With
we give you thanks.
D.S.
faith and hope and love, we give you, give you thanks.
we give you thanks.
Final ending

Text: David Haas, b.1957
Tune: WE GIVE YOU THANKS, 8 7 8 7 D; David Haas, b.1957

554 A Celtic Rune

Descant:
Lord, hear our prayer. Lord, hear our prayer.
Lord, hear our prayer. Lord, hear our prayer.
Lord, in your mer - cy, Lord, hear our prayer.
Lord, in your mer - cy, Lord, hear our prayer.

Text: Liam Lawton, b.1959
Tune: Liam Lawton, b.1959; arr. by Ian Callanan, OP

Lead Me, Guide Me 555

Refrain
Lead me, guide me, a - long the way,
For if you lead me, I can - not stray.
Lord, let me walk each day with thee.
Lead me, oh Lord, lead me.
Verses
1. I am weak and I need thy strength and pow'r to help me o - ver my weak - est hour. Help me through the dark - ness thy face to see, Lead me, oh Lord, lead me.
2. Help me tread in the paths of right - eous - ness, Be my aid when Sa - tan and sin op - press. I am put - ting all my trust in thee. Lead me, oh Lord, lead me.
3. I am lost if you take your hand from me, I am blind with - out thy Light to see, Lord, just al - ways let me thy ser - vant be. Lead me, oh Lord, lead me.
D.C.

Text: Doris M. Akers, 1922-1995
Tune: Doris M. Akers, 1922-1995, harm. by Richard Smallwood

556 O Lord, the Guardian of My Heart

Refrain
O Lord, the guard - ian of my heart, who
rules the day and night, you guide me through my
dark - est hours and lead me in - to light.
Last time
Last time
Verses
1. Teach me the way of your truth,
2. Take my weak - ness, O God.
3. Wipe a - way my fear,
Ooh

help me to know your wis - dom.
Build my strength in faith.
lift me from my sor - row.
Keep me in your pres - ence, Lord,
Save me in your mer - cy, Lord,
Wash a - way my bro - ken - ness,
show me how to love.
clothe me with your grace.
heal my wound - ed soul.
O
O
O
D.S.

Text: Carol E. Browning, b.1956
Tune: Carol E. Browning, b.1956

557 Make Us Worthy

Refrain
Lord, make us wor - thy. Make us wor - thy to see your face. Fill us with your word, O Lord, and heal us with your grace.
Last time
Last time
Verses
1. O - pen up your ten - der arms
2. Of - fer all your praise to God
3. You are strength when we are weak.
4. Fash - ion plough - shares from our swords.
5. Lord, you sent your heal - ing word

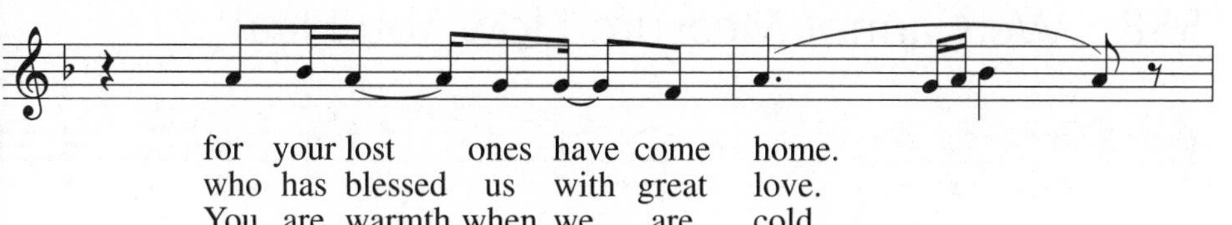
for your lost ones have come home.
who has blessed us with great love.
You are warmth when we are cold.
Rip the ha - tred from our minds.
to re - deem us from our sins.

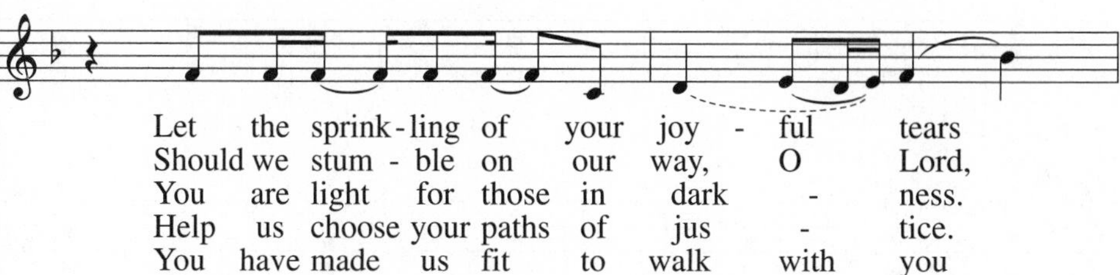
Let the sprink - ling of your joy - ful tears
Should we stum - ble on our way, O Lord,
You are light for those in dark - ness.
Help us choose your paths of jus - tice.
You have made us fit to walk with you

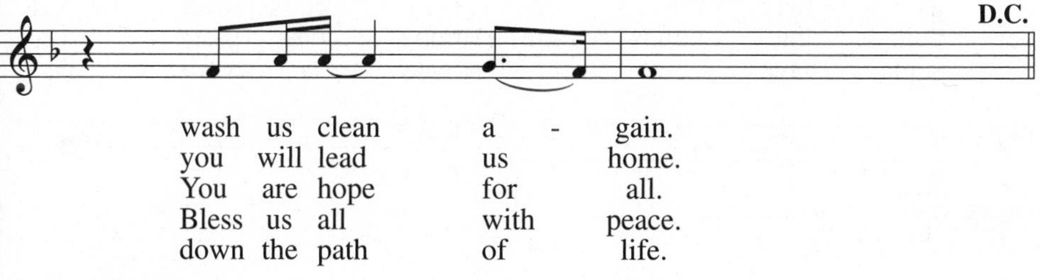
D.C.
wash us clean a - gain.
you will lead us home.
You are hope for all.
Bless us all with peace.
down the path of life.

Text: Michael Mahler, b.1981
Tune: Michael Mahler, b.1981

558 We Cannot Measure How You Heal

1. We can - not meas - ure how you heal Or an - swer ev - 'ry suf - f'rer's prayer, Yet we be - lieve your grace re - sponds Where faith and doubt u - nite to care. Your
2. The pain that will not go a - way, The guilt that clings from things long past, The fear of what the fu - ture holds, Are pres - ent as if meant to last. But
3. So some have come who need your help And some have come to make a - mends, As hands which shaped and saved the world Are pres - ent in the touch of friends. Lord,

hands, though blood - ied on the cross, Sur - vive to hold and heal and warn, To car - ry all through death to life And cra - dle chil - dren yet un - born.
pres - ent too is love which tends The hurt we nev - er hoped to find, The pri - vate ag - o - nies in - side, The mem - o - ries that haunt the mind.
let your Spir - it meet us here To mend the bod - y, mind, and soul, To dis - en - tan - gle peace from pain, And make your bro - ken peo - ple whole.

Text: John L. Bell, b.1949
Tune: YE BANKS AND BRAES, 8 8 8 8 D; Scottish traditional; arr. by John L. Bell, b.1949

559 Song over the Waters

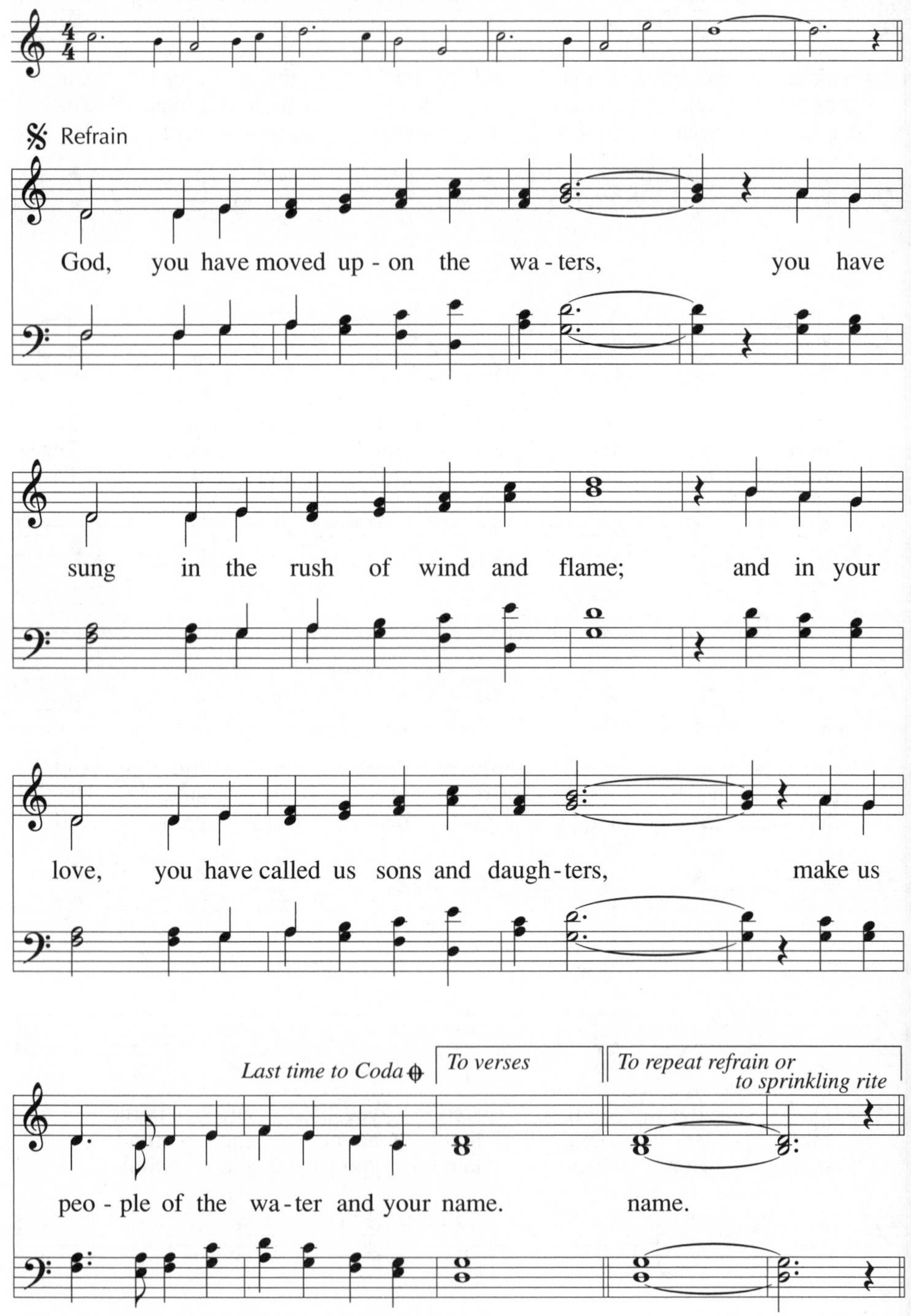
Refrain
God, you have moved up - on the wa - ters, you have
sung in the rush of wind and flame; and in your
love, you have called us sons and daugh - ters, make us
Last time to Coda
To verses
To repeat refrain or to sprinkling rite
peo - ple of the wa - ter and your name.
name.

Verses
1. Come fill our wait-ing hearts with the spir-it of
2. Give us a thirst for love, give us a hun-ger for
3. You are the breath of life, you are the hope of the
4. Come, o-pen ev-'ry heart, come now and wake us to
D.S.
Je-sus, let us shine with your light and peace.
jus-tice, make us one with the mind of Christ.
hope-less, come and fill us with light and peace.
won-der, make us ves-sels of light and peace.
Coda
unis.
rit.
name. Make us peo-ple of the wa-ter and your name.
Sprinkling Rite*
Cantor:
Wa-ters of the sea, wa-ters of the earth:
Riv-ers of the earth, gen-tle flow-ing streams:
Wa-ters of the clouds, wa-ters of the wind:
Might-y blow-ing storms, gen-tle fall-ing rains:

Additional verses for Sprinkling Rite:

1. You who give us life,
   you who give us breath:
   You beyond our fears,
   you beyond our death:

2. You who are the truth,
   you who are the way:
   You who give us light,
   lead us in the day:

3. Springing from the earth,
   dancing from the sky:
   Springing from our hearts,
   welling up within:

4. Spirit of all hope,
   spirit of all peace:
   Spirit of all joy,
   spirit of all life:

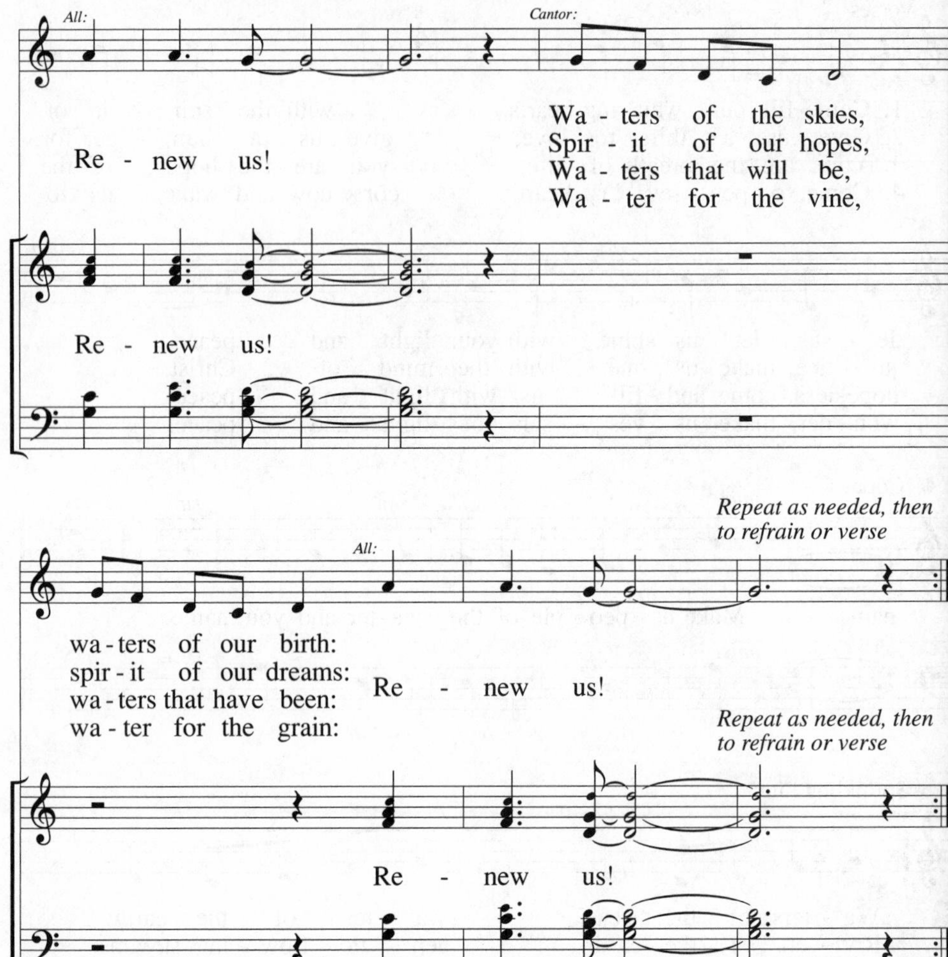
All:
Cantor:
Re - new us!
Wa - ters of the skies,
Spir - it of our hopes,
Wa - ters that will be,
Wa - ter for the vine,
Re - new us!
Repeat as needed, then to refrain or verse
All:
wa - ters of our birth:
spir - it of our dreams:
wa - ters that have been:
wa - ter for the grain:
Re - new us!
Repeat as needed, then to refrain or verse
Re - new us!

Text: Marty Haugen, b.1950
Tune: Marty Haugen, b.1950

Lord of All Hopefulness 560

1. Lord of all hope - ful - ness, Lord of all joy, Whose
2. Lord of all ea - ger - ness, Lord of all faith, Whose
3. Lord of all kind - li - ness, Lord of all grace, Your
4. Lord of all gen - tle - ness, Lord of all calm, Whose
trust, ev - er child - like, no cares can de - stroy, Be
strong hands were skilled at the plane and the lathe, Be
hands swift to wel - come, your arms to em - brace, Be
voice is con - tent - ment, whose pres-ence is balm, Be
there at our wak - ing, and give us, we pray, Your
there at our la - bors, and give us, we pray, Your
there at our hom - ing, and give us, we pray, Your
there at our sleep - ing, and give us, we pray, Your
bliss in our hearts, Lord, at the break of the day.
strength in our hearts, Lord, at the noon of the day.
love in our hearts, Lord, at the eve of the day.
peace in our hearts, Lord, at the end of the day.

Text: Jan Struther, 1901-1953, © Oxford University Press
Tune: SLANE, 10 11 11 12; Gaelic; harm. by Erik Routley, 1917-1982, © 1975, Hope Publishing Co.

561 Turn My Heart, O God

Refrain
God.
Turn my heart, O God. Turn my heart, O turn my heart.
God.
Take my pain and bro-ken-ness; shape my life for you. Come and
turn my heart, O God.
To repeat refrain
Final ending
God.
To verses
Cantor:
Verses
1. From all that leads to death, to
2. From bit - ter - ness and hate, to
3. O let your Spir - it come and
4. O bring me home to you, Most
turn my heart, O God.

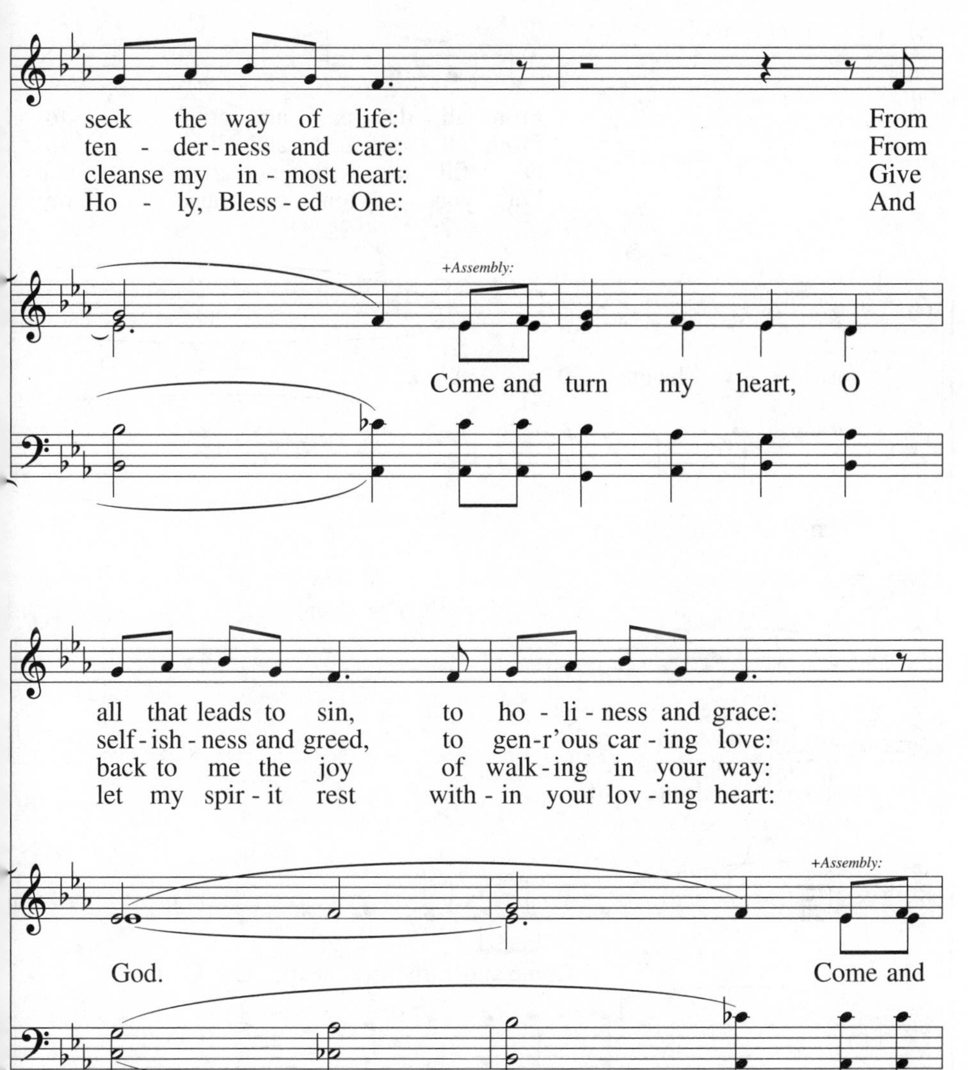
seek the way of life: From
ten - der - ness and care: From
cleanse my in - most heart: Give
Ho - ly, Bless - ed One: And
+Assembly:
Come and turn my heart, O
all that leads to sin, to ho - li - ness and grace:
self - ish - ness and greed, to gen-r'ous car - ing love:
back to me the joy of walk - ing in your way:
let my spir - it rest with - in your lov - ing heart:
God.
+Assembly:
Come and

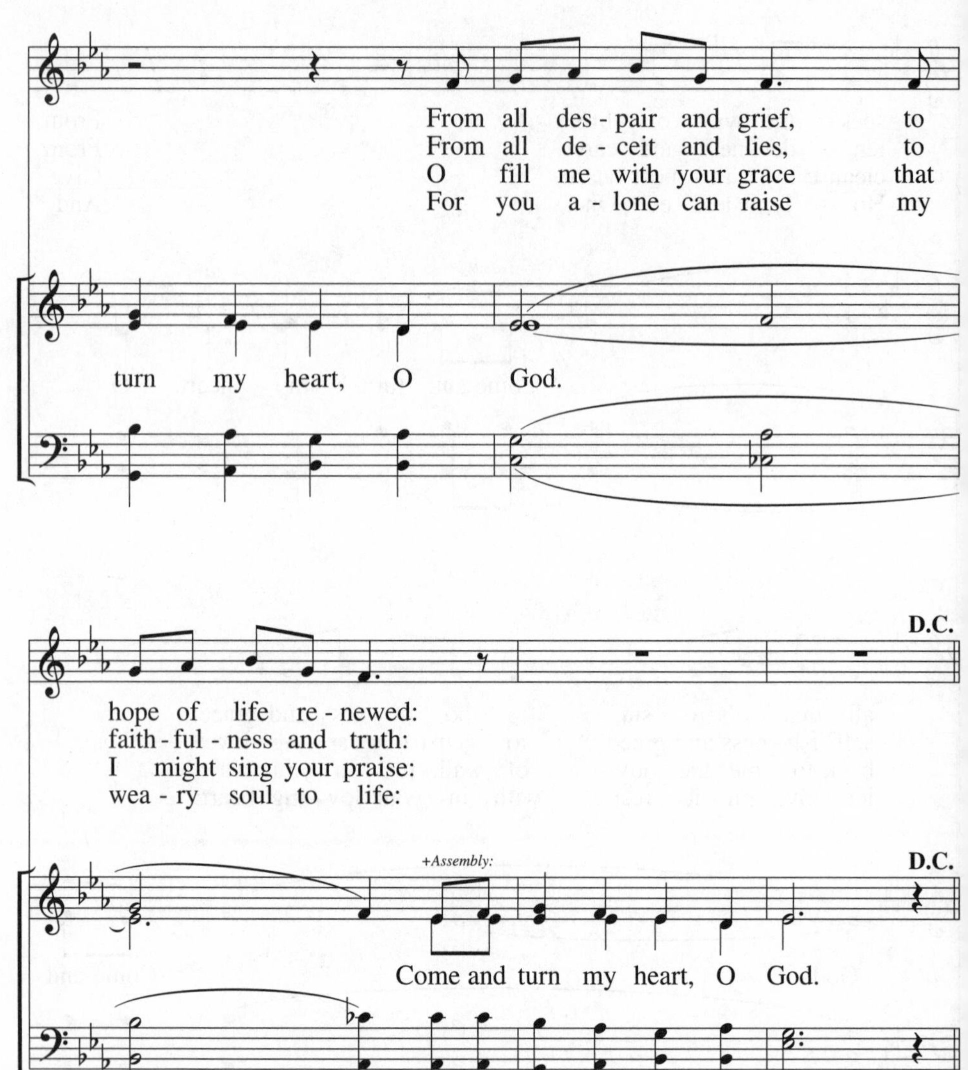
From all des - pair and grief, to
From all de - ceit and lies, to
O fill me with your grace that
For you a - lone can raise my
turn my heart, O God.
D.C.
hope of life re - newed:
faith - ful - ness and truth:
I might sing your praise:
wea - ry soul to life:
+Assembly:
Come and turn my heart, O God.

Text: Marty Haugen, b.1950
Tune: Marty Haugen, b.1950

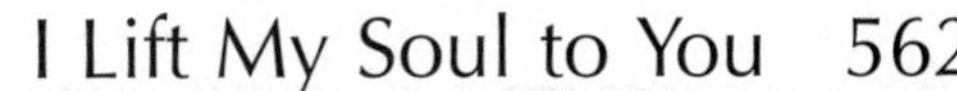
I Lift My Soul to You 562

Refrain

I lift my soul to you, O Lord. To you I lift my hands, I lift my heart, my soul. I lift my soul to you, O Lord. To you I lift my hands, I lift my heart, my soul.

Last time

Last time

Verses 1, 2
1. Lord, make me know your ways, keep me on your path.
2. Your ways are good and just. You find the lost,
Walk with me in your truth and teach me. You save my
you lead the hum-ble to right - eous - ness. You help the
life, you are my song.
poor to find the way.
D.C.
Verse 3
3. You hold true to your prom-ise, your
friend - ship is with those who keep your cov - e - nant.
Let us hum - bly walk in your name. For-
give the past and wash a - way our guilt.
D.C.

Text: Psalm 25; Lori True, b.1961
Tune: Lori True, b.1961; acc. by Paul A. Tate, b.1968

How Shall We Name God? 563

Verses
1. Source and Sov-'reign, Rock and Cloud, For-tress, Foun-tain, Shel-ter, Light, Judge, De-fend-er, Mer-cy, Might,
2. Word and Wis-dom, Root and Vine, Shep-herd, Sav-ior, Ser-vant, Lamb, Well and Wa-ter, Bread and Wine,
3. Storm and Still-ness, Breath and Dove, Thun-der, Tem-pest, Whirl-wind, Fire, Com-fort, Coun-sel-or, Pres-ence,
1., 2.
To refrain
Life whose life all life en-dowed:
Way who leads us to I AM:
3.
To refrain
En-er-gies that nev-er tire:
Refrain
May the church at prayer re-call That no sin-gle ho-ly name But the truth be-hind them all Is the God whom we pro-claim.
To verses
D.C.
Last time
claim.

564 Healing River

Cantor:*
1., 4. O heal - ing riv - er, send down your wa - ters, Send down your wa - ters up - on this land. O heal - ing riv - er, send down your wa - ters, And wash the blood from off the
2. This land is thirst - ing, this land is parch-ing, No seed is grow - ing in the bar - ren ground. This land is thirst-ing, this land is parch - ing, O heal - ing riv-er, send your wa - ters
1., 3.
Last time
sand.
2.
down.
3. Let the seed of free - dom, a-wake and flour-ish, Let the deep roots nour - ish, let the tall stalks rise. Let the seed of free-dom, a - wake and flour-ish, Proud leaves un - curl - ing a - gainst the skies.
D.C.

The assembly echoes each phrase of the cantor at the interval of one half measure.

Text: Fran Minkoff
Tune: Fred Hellerman; arr. by Michael Joncas, b.1951

Increase Our Faith 565

Refrain

With all our
Lord, in-crease our faith. With all our

heart, may we al-ways fol-low you.
heart, fol - low you. Teach us to pray

al - ways.
To verses
Final ending
al - ways, al-ways.
VERSE 2 - NEXT PAGE
al - ways.

Verses 1, 3

1. So I say to you: "ask, you will re-ceive; seek and you will
3. If you, with all your sins, know how to give, how much more will

D.C.

find. Knock, it shall be o-pened to you."
God give to all those who cry from their hearts!

Verse 2
2. Who-ev-er asks, they shall re-ceive; who - ev-er seeks shall
D.C.
find. Who - ev-er knocks, the door will be o - pened.

Text: Based on Luke 11:1-13, 17:5; David Haas, b.1957
David Haas, b.1957

566 O Lord, Hear My Prayer

Ostinato Chorale

O Lord, hear my prayer, O Lord, hear my prayer:
*The Lord is my song, the Lord is my praise:

when I call an - swer me. O Lord, hear my prayer, O
all my hope comes from God. The Lord is my song, the

Last time

Lord, hear my prayer. Come and lis - ten to me. O
Lord is my praise: God, the well-spring of life. The

Last time

Alternate text

Text: Psalm 102; Taizé Community, 1982
Tune: Jacques Berthier, 1923-1994

Down to the River to Pray 567

As I went down to the riv-er to pray, stud-y-ing a-bout that
good old way. And who shall wear the star - ry crown, good
Lord, show me the way. Oh *broth-er let's go down,
come on down, don't you want to go down? Oh broth-er,
let's go down, down to the riv-er to pray.

Sister, father, mother.

Text: American folk song
Tune: American folk song; arr. by Robert J. Batastini, b.1942, © 2003, GIA Publications, Inc.

568 Ubi Caritas

Refrain

U-bi cá-ri-tas et a-mor De-us i-bi est.

Last time

U - bi cá-ri-tas et a-mor

Last time

Verses

1. We feel your pres-ence here, your love and com-fort near.
*2a. And now we break this bread, our souls and bod-ies fed.
2b. And so we come to you, we need to be re-newed.
3. Bless us, your peo-ple, Lord, that we may serve the world.
4. So as we live each day, Lord, help us, that we may

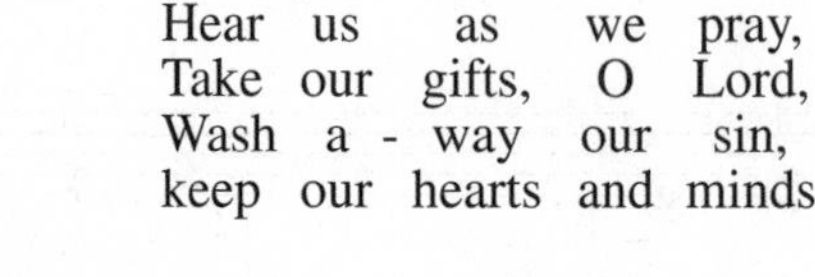

As you wel-come us, fill our ev-'ry need,
Hear us as we pray, from this ta-ble, Lord,
Take our gifts, O Lord, use us for your good.
Wash a-way our sin, cleanse us from with-in.
keep our hearts and minds o-pen to your love that

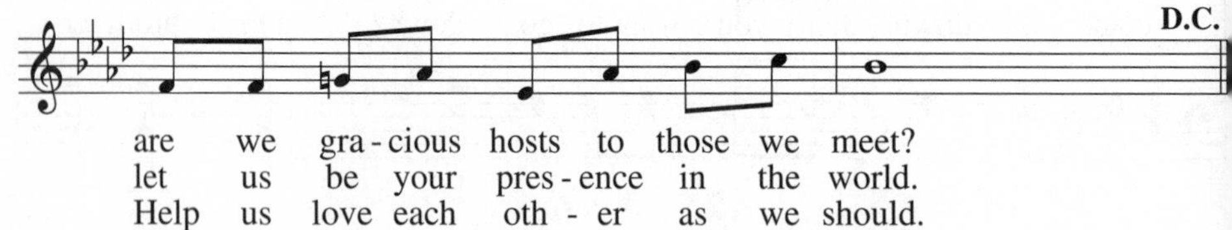
D.C.

are we gra-cious hosts to those we meet?
let us be your pres-ence in the world.
Help us love each oth-er as we should.
Send us forth with strength to do your will.
char-i-ty and love in us a-bound.

**Verse 2a for Communion, verse 2b for other occasions.*

Text: 1 Corinthians 13:2-8; *Where charity and love are found, God is there*; verses, Carol E. Browning, b.1956, © 1998, GIA Publications, Inc.
Tune: Carol E. Browning, b.1956, © 1998, GIA Publications, Inc.

Open My Eyes 569

Verses
1. O - pen my eyes, Lord. Help me to see your face.
2. O - pen my ears, Lord. Help me to hear your voice.
3. O - pen my heart, Lord. Help me to love like you.
O - pen my eyes, Lord. Help me to see. (To verse 2)
O - pen my ears, Lord. Help me to hear. (To bridge)
O - pen my heart, Lord. Help me to love.
Bridge
And the first shall be last, and our eyes are o - pened, and we'll hear like nev - er be - fore. And we'll speak in new ways, and we'll see God's face in plac - es we've nev - er known.
D.C.

Text: Based on Mark 8:22-25; Jesse Manibusan, b.1958
Tune: Jesse Manibusan, b.1958

570 O God, Why Are You Silent?

1. O God, why are you si - lent? I can - not hear your voice. The proud and strong and vio - lent All claim you and re - joice.
2. Now lost with - in my griev - ing, I fall and lose my way, My frag - ile, faint be - liev - ing So swift - ly swept a - way.
3. My hope lies bruised and bat - tered, My wound - ed heart is torn; My spir - it spent and shat - tered By life's re - lent - less storm.
4. Through end - less nights of weep - ing, Through wea - ry days of grief, My heart is in your keep - ing, My com - fort, my re - lief.
5. May pain draw forth com - pas - sion, Let wis - dom rise from loss. O take my heart and fash - ion The im - age of your cross.

LAMENT

You prom - ised you would hold me With
O God of pain and sor - row, My
Will you not bend to hear me, My
Come, share my tears and sad - ness, Come,
Then may I know your heal - ing Through
ten - der - ness and care. Draw near, O Love, en -
com - pass and my guide, I can - not face the
cries from deep with - in? Have you no word to
suf - fer in my pain; O bring me home to
heal - ing that I share, Your grace and love re -
fold me, And ease the pain I bear.
mor - row With - out you by my side.
cheer me When night is clos - ing in?
glad - ness, Re - store my hope a - gain.
veal - ing Your ten - der - ness and care.

Text: Marty Haugen, b.1950, © 2003, GIA Publications, Inc.
Tune: PASSION CHORALE, 7 6 7 6 D; Hans Leo Hassler, 1564-1612; harm. by Marty Haugen, b.1950, © 2003, GIA Publications, Inc.

571 We Await with Wakeful Care

Verses
Cantor:
1. Sit - ting with a child in sick - ness,
2. Yearn - ing for a graced for - give - ness;
3. Thirst - ing for a day of jus - tice,
All:
We a - wait with wake-ful care.
list - 'ning for a cry of pain,
sore, re - pent - ing; deep in need;
hun - g'ring, plead - ing, now we kneel;
We a - wait with wake - ful care.
bear - ing with a friend through sor - row,
wan - d'ring through a maze of ques - tions,
griev - ing for a world that's bro - ken,
We a - wait with wake-ful care.

Cantor:
keep - ing vig - il we re - main.
won - d'ring where our paths will lead.
pray - ing for its wounds to heal.
Refrain
More than watch - ers for the morn - ing, we a - wait with wake - ful
Watch - ers, a - wait with
care, hop - ing through the night of weep - ing our
care, through the night, our
God will lift us from de - spair.
God will lift de - spair.
D.C.
Final ending

Text: Mary Louise Bringle, b.1953, © 2002, GIA Publications, Inc.
Tune: Lori True, b.1961, © 2003, GIA Publications, Inc.

572 God Remembers

1. God re-mem-bers pain: Nail by nail, thorn by thorn,
2. God re-mem-bers joy: Touch of love, taste of food,
3. God re-mem-bers us: All we were, all we are,
Hun - ger, thirst, and mus - cles torn. Time may dull our griefs And
All our sens - es know is good. Love and life flow by And
Lives with - in our Lov - er's care. Time may dull our minds And
heal our less - er wounds, But in e - ter - nal Love
pre - cious days are gone, But in e - ter - nal Love
death will take us all, But in e - ter - nal Love
Yes-ter-day is now, And pain is in the heart of God.
Ev - 'ry day is now, And joy is in the heart of God.
Ev - 'ry life is now: Our life is hid with Christ in God.
1., 2.
3.

Text: Colossians 3:3-4; Brian Wren, b.1936, © 1993, Hope Publishing Co.
Tune: GOD REMEMBERS, 5 6 7 5 6 6 5 8; Marty Haugen, b.1950, © 2003, GIA Publications, Inc.

By the Waters of Babylon 573

Refrain

By the wa-ters of

Descant:

We shall cry

Bab-y-lon,

Melody:

we shall cry, we shall rest, and re-

To verses *Last time*

and re-mem-ber Zi-on. Zi-on.

mem-ber Zi-on. Zi-on.

Verses

Sopranos and basses:

1. We long to play our harps
2. May we not for - get
3. Lord, we need your strength!

Altos:

Tenors:

By the wa - ters.

and raise a song to you.
be-lov-ed Je-ru - sa - lem!
Fill us with your spir - it!

By the wa - ters.

But how can we sing our song in a
Lord, help us to sing our song in this
In - spire us to bring your song to this
By the wa - ters.
D.S.
for-eign land?
for-eign land!
for-eign land!
D.S.
By the wa - ters.

Text: Psalm 137; Paul A. Tate, b.1968
Tune: Paul A. Tate, b.1968

LAMENT

God Weeps with Us Who Weep and Mourn 574

1. God weeps with us who weep and mourn,
God's tears flow down with ours,
And God's own heart is bruised and worn
From all the heavy hours
Of watching while the soul's bright fire
Burned lower day by day,
And pulse and breath and love's desire
Dimmed down to ash and clay.

2. Through tears and sorrow, God, we share
A sense of your vast grief;
The weight of bearing ev'ry prayer
For healing and relief,
The burden of our questions why,
The doubts that they engage,
And as our friends and *lovers die,
Our hopelessness and rage.

3. And yet, because, like us, you weep,
We trust you will receive
And in your tender heart will keep
The ones for whom we grieve,
While with your tears our hearts will taste
The deep, dear core of things
From which both life and death are graced
By love's renewing springs.

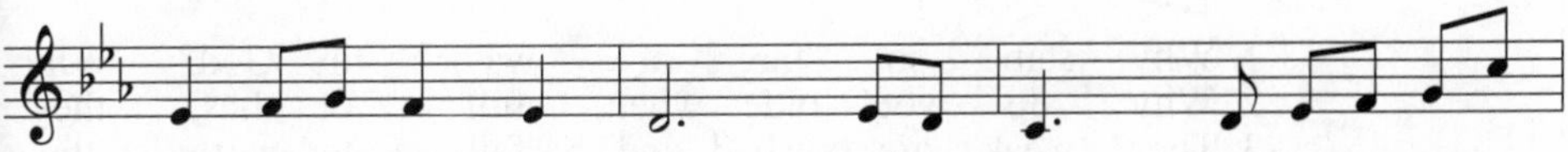

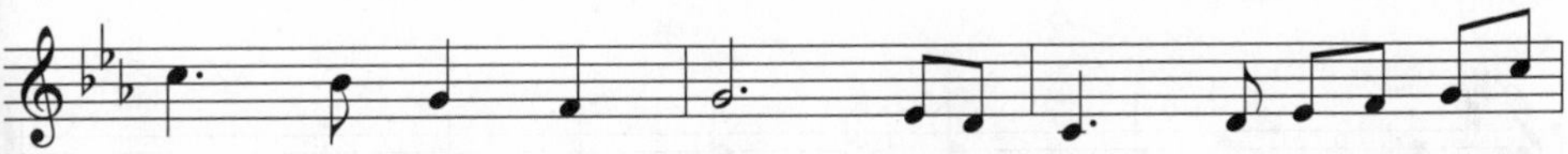

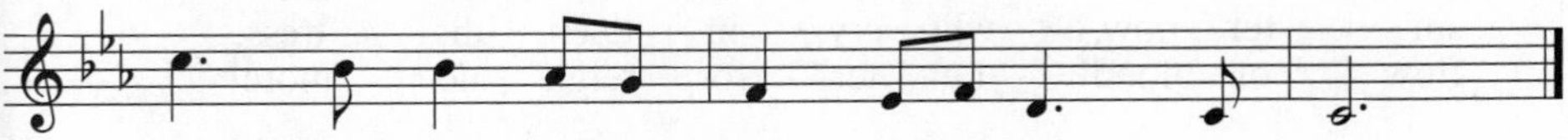

*Or "loved ones"

Text: Thomas H. Troeger, b.1945, © 1996, Oxford University Press
Tune: MOSHIER, CMD; Sally Ann Morris, b.1952, © 1998, GIA Publications, Inc.

LAMENT

575 Why Stand So Far Away

1. Why stand so far a - way, my God? Why
2. Why do you hide when, full of lies, they
3. The weak are crushed and fall to earth; the
4. In a - ges past you heard the voice of
5. A - rise, O God, and lift your hand; bring
hide in times of need? The proud, un - bri - dled,
mur - der and be - tray? They wait to pounce up -
wick - ed strut and preen. Why in these cruel, cha -
those the proud op - press. Re - mem - ber those who
jus - tice to the poor. Come, help us stop the
chase the poor, and curse you in their greed.
on the weak as li - ons stalk their prey.
ot - ic times can - not your face be seen?
suf - fer now, who cry in deep dis - tress.
flow of blood! Let ter - ror reign no more!

Text: Based on Psalm 10, Ruth Duck, b.1947, © 1992, GIA Publications, Inc.
Tune: Michael Mahler, b.1981, © 2003, GIA Publications, Inc.

Bless the Lord 576

Ostinato Refrain
Bless the Lord, my soul, and bless God's ho - ly name.
Bless the Lord, my soul, who leads me in - to life.
Verses (Superimposed on Ostinato Refrain)
Cantor:
1. For-get not my soul all God's good deeds.
2. The Lord is for-give-ness and re-deems our life from the grave.
3. The Lord is com-pas-sion-ate and gra-cious, a - bound-ing in love.
4. It is God who for-gives all your guilt, who

*Choose either part

heals ev-'ry-one of your ills, who re-deems your life from the
grave, who crowns you with love and com-pas-sion.
3
5. The Lord is com-pas-sion and love, the Lord is pa-tient and
rich in mer-cy. God does not treat us ac-cord-ing to our
sins nor re-pay us ac-cord-ing to our faults.
6. As a Fa-ther has com-pas-sion on his chil-dren, the Lord has
mer-cy on those who re-vere him; for God knows of what we are
made, and re-mem-bers that we are dust.
7. As the heav-ens are high a-bove the earth, so is
God's way a-bove our way, so is God's love for us.

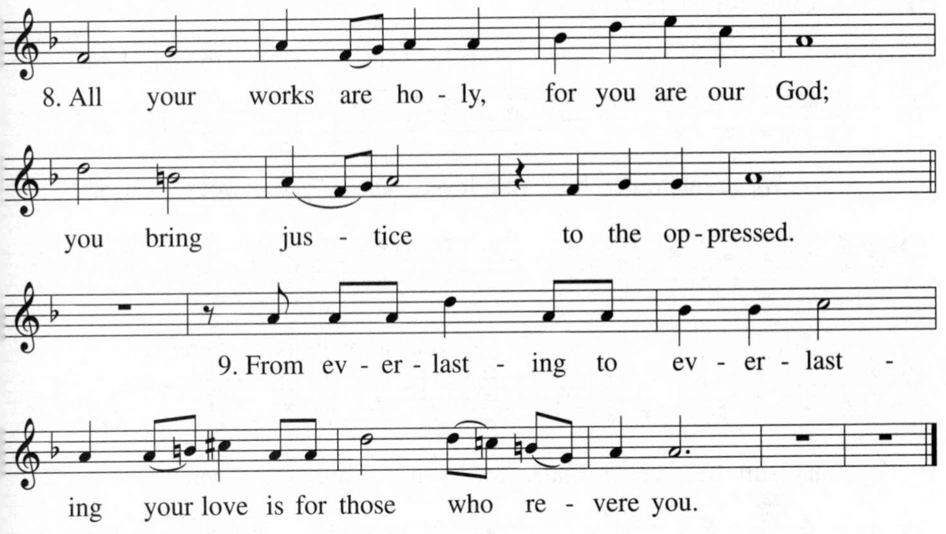
8. All your works are ho - ly, for you are our God;
you bring jus - tice to the op - pressed.
9. From ev - er - last - ing to ev - er - last -
ing your love is for those who re - vere you.

Text: Psalm 103
Tune: Jacques Berthier, 1923-1994

May God Bless and Keep You 577

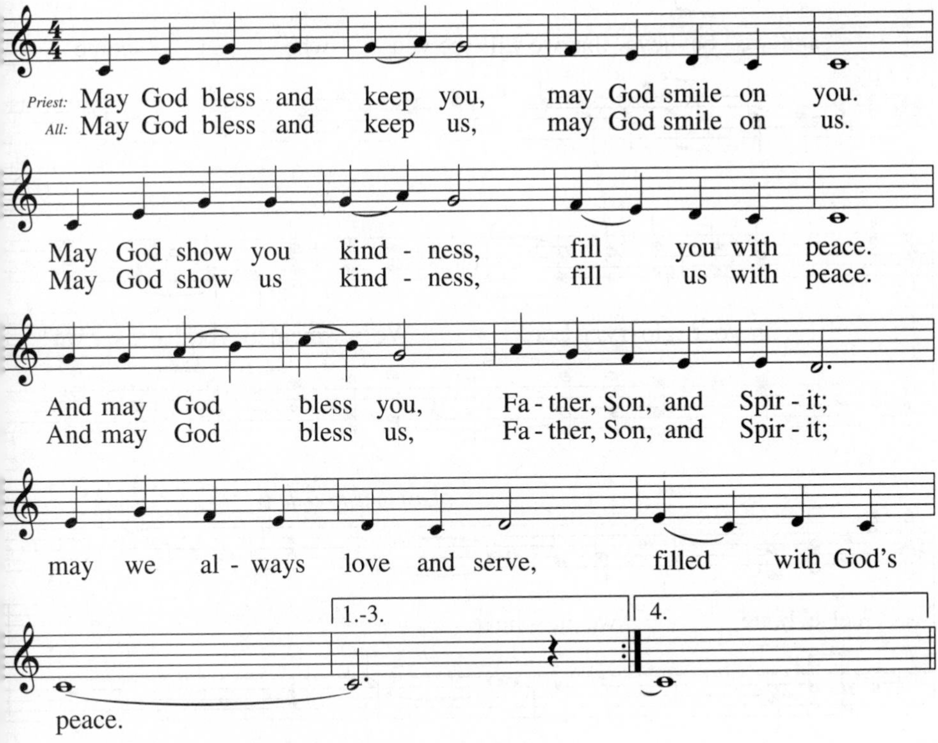

Priest: May God bless and keep you, may God smile on you.
All: May God bless and keep us, may God smile on us.

May God show you kind - ness, fill you with peace.
May God show us kind - ness, fill us with peace.

And may God bless you, Fa - ther, Son, and Spir - it;
And may God bless us, Fa - ther, Son, and Spir - it;

may we al - ways love and serve, filled with God's

peace.

1.-3. 4.

Text: Numbers 6:24-26; David Haas, b.1957, © 1997, GIA Publications, Inc.
Tune: ADORO TE DEVOTE, Mode V; adapt. by David Haas, b.1957, © 1997, GIA Publications, Inc.

578 We Remember

Refrain
us
to your death,
We re-mem-ber how you loved us to your death,
you are with us here;
and still we cel-e-brate, for you are here;
you
when you come
and we be-lieve that we will see you when you come
in your glo-ry, Lord. We re-mem - ber, we
Last time to coda
cel-e-brate, we be - lieve.

Verses
1. Here, a mil - lion wound - ed souls are yearn - ing just to touch you and be healed.
2. Now we re - cre - ate your love, we bring the bread and wine to share a meal.
3. Christ, the Fa - ther's great "A - men" to all the hopes and dreams of ev - 'ry heart,
4. See the face of Christ re - vealed in ev - 'ry per - son stand - ing by your side,
Gath - er all your peo - ple, and hold them to your heart.
Sign of grace and mer - cy, the pres - ence of the Lord.
Peace be - yond all tell - ing, and free - dom from all fear.
Gift to one an - oth - er, and tem - ples of your love.
D.C.
Coda

Text: Marty Haugen, b.1950
Tune: Marty Haugen, b.1950

579 A Living Faith

1. Faith of our fa - thers, liv - ing still
2. Faith of our moth - ers, dar - ing faith,
3. Faith of our broth - ers, sis - ters too,
4. Faith born of God, O call us yet;
In spite of dun - geon, fire and sword;
Your work for Christ is love re - vealed,
Who still must bear op - pres - sion's might,
Bind us with all who fol - low you,
O how our hearts beat high with joy,
Spread - ing God's word from pole to pole,
Rais - ing on high, in pris - ons dark,
Shar - ing the strug - gle of your cross
When - e'er we hear that glo - rious word:
Mak - ing love known and free - dom real:
The cross of Christ still burn - ing bright:
Un - til the world is made a - new,

FAITH

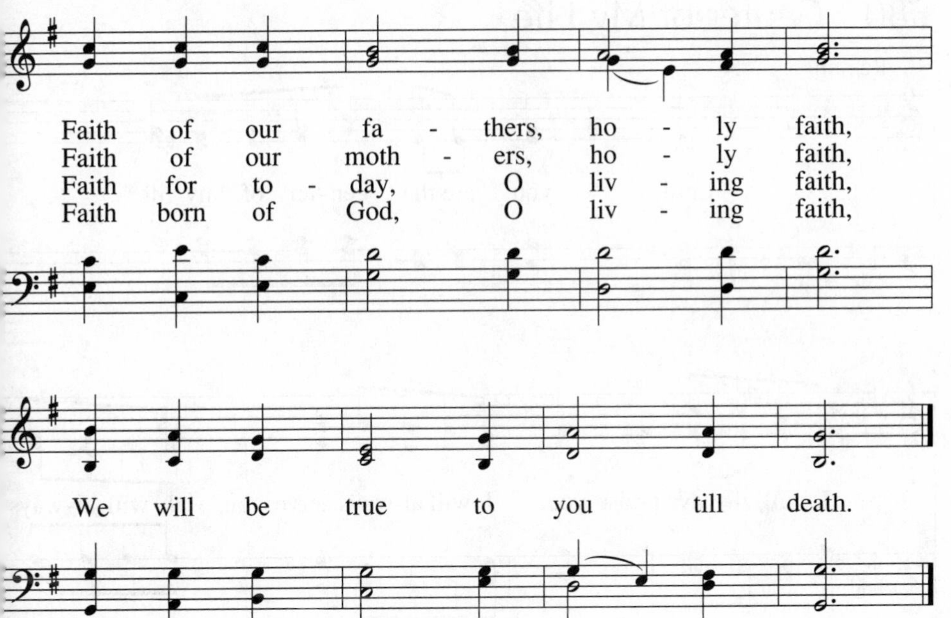
Faith of our fa - thers, ho - ly faith,
Faith of our moth - ers, ho - ly faith,
Faith for to - day, O liv - ing faith,
Faith born of God, O liv - ing faith,
We will be true to you till death.

Text: St. 1, Frederick W. Faber, 1814-1863, alt.; Sts. 2-4, Joseph R. Alfred, © 1981, alt.
Tune: ST. CATHERINE, LM with refrain; Henry F. Hemy, 1818-1888; adapt. by James G. Walton, 1821-1905

580 Center of My Life

Refrain
O Lord, you are the cen-ter of my life:
I will al-ways praise you, I will al-ways serve you, I will al-ways
keep you in my sight. O sight. sight.
First time only
To verses
Last time
3. And
Verses 1-3
1. Keep me safe, O God, I take ref-uge in you. I
2. I will bless the Lord who gives me coun - sel, who
(3.) so my heart re - joic - es, my soul is glad;
say to the Lord, "You are my God. My
e - ven at night di - rects my heart. I
e - ven in safe - ty shall my bod - y rest. For

hap - pi - ness lies in you a - lone; my
keep the Lord ev - er in my sight: since
you will not leave my soul a - mong the dead, nor
1., 2.
D.S.
hap - pi - ness lies in you a - lone." O
he is at my right hand, I shall stand firm. O
3.
D.S.
let your be - lov - ed know de - cay. O
Verse 4
4. You will show me the path of life, the full - ness of
joy in your pres - ence, at your right hand,
D.S.
at your right hand hap-pi-ness for ev - er. O

581 I Say "Yes," Lord / Digo "Sí," Señor

Verses

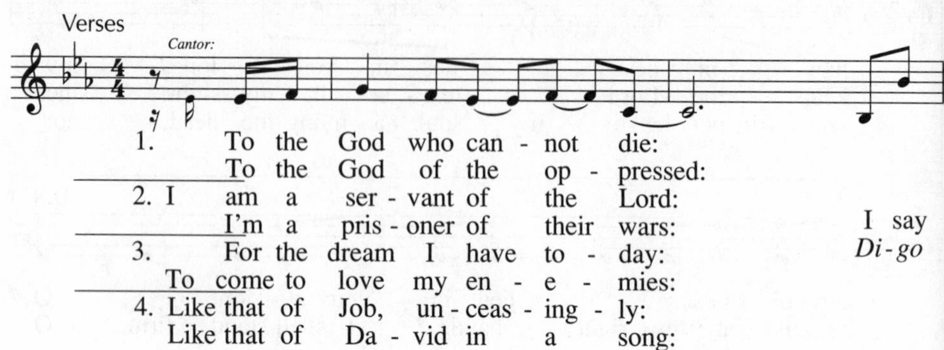
Cantor:
1. To the God who can - not die:
To the God of the op - pressed:
2. I am a ser - vant of the Lord:
I'm a pris - oner of their wars:
3. For the dream I have to - day:
To come to love my en - e - mies:
4. Like that of Job, un - ceas - ing - ly:
Like that of Da - vid in a song:
I say
Di - go

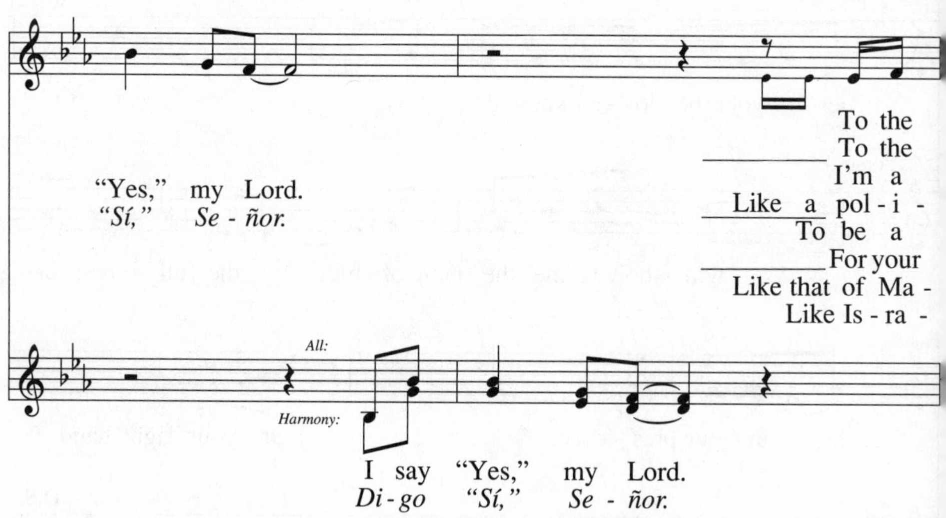
"Yes," my Lord.
"Sí," Se - ñor.
To the
To the
I'm a
Like a pol - i -
To be a
For your
Like that of Ma -
Like Is - ra -
All:
Harmony:
I say "Yes," my Lord.
Di - go "Sí," Se - ñor.

One who hears me cry:
God of all jus - tice:
work - er in the fields:
ti - cian, in - e - vi - ta - bly:
heal - er of all pain:
peace in all the world:
ri - a whole - heart - ed - ly:
el, for you I long:
I say
Di - go

1.
2.
"Yes," my Lord.
"Sí," Se - ñor.
All:
Harmony:
I say "Yes," my Lord. "Yes," my Lord.
Di - go "Sí," Se - ñor. "Sí," Se - ñor.
Refrain
Descant:
I say "Yes," my Lord, in all the good times, through
Di - go "Sí," Se - ñor, en tiem - pos ma - los, en
Melody:
I say "Yes," my Lord, in all the good times, through
Di - go "Sí," Se - ñor, en tiem - pos ma - los, en
all the bad times, I say "Yes," my Lord, to
tiem - pos bue - nos, Di - go "Sí," Se - ñor, a
all the bad times, I say "Yes," my Lord, to
tiem - pos bue - nos, Di - go "Sí," Se - ñor, a
Last time to coda
D.C. Coda
ev - 'ry word you speak.
to - do lo que_ha - blas.
ev - 'ry word you speak.
to - do lo que_ha - blas.

Text: Donna Peña, b.1955
Tune: Donna Peña, b.1955; arr. by Marty Haugen, b.1950

582 Dwelling Place

Verses 1, 2, 4
1., 4. I fall on my knees to the Fa - ther of Je - sus, the Lord who has shown us the glo - ry of God.
2. May Christ in his love give us strength for our liv - ing, the strength of the Spir - it the glo - ry of God.
(To verse 2)
Refrain
May Christ find a dwell - ing place of faith in our hearts. May our lives be root - ed in love, root - ed in love.
Last time to coda
Verse 3
3. May grace and peace be yours in

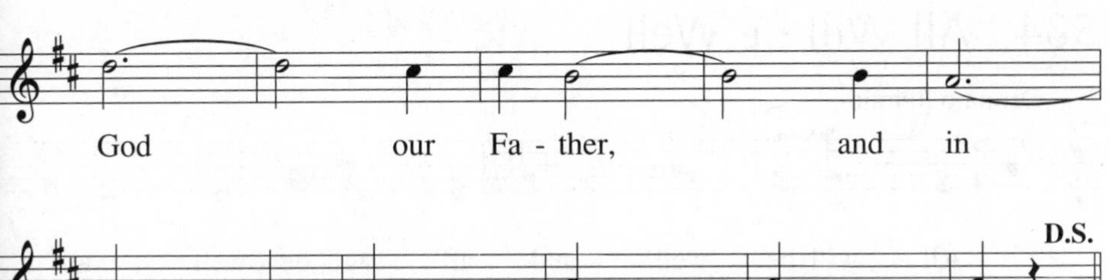
God our Fa - ther, and in

D.S.
the Son.

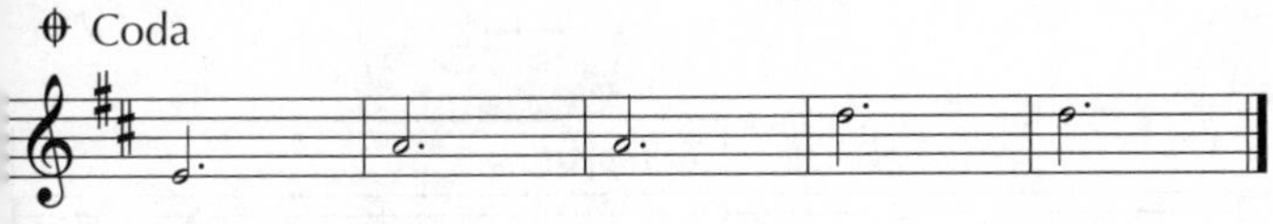
Coda

Text: Ephesians 3:14-17; 1:2; John Foley, SJ, b.1939
Tune: John Foley, SJ, b.1939

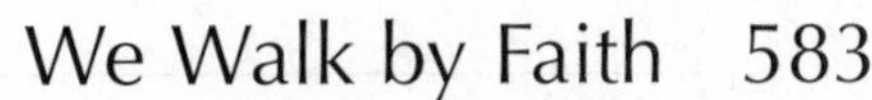
We Walk by Faith 583

1., 5. We walk by faith, and not by sight: No gracious words we hear Of him who spoke as none e'er spoke, But we believe him near.

2. We may not touch his hands and side, Nor follow where he trod; Yet in his promise we rejoice, And cry "My Lord and God!"

3. Help then, O Lord, our unbelief, And may our faith abound; To call on you when you are near, And seek where you are found:

4. That when our life of faith is done In realms of clearer light We may behold you as you are In full and endless sight.

div.

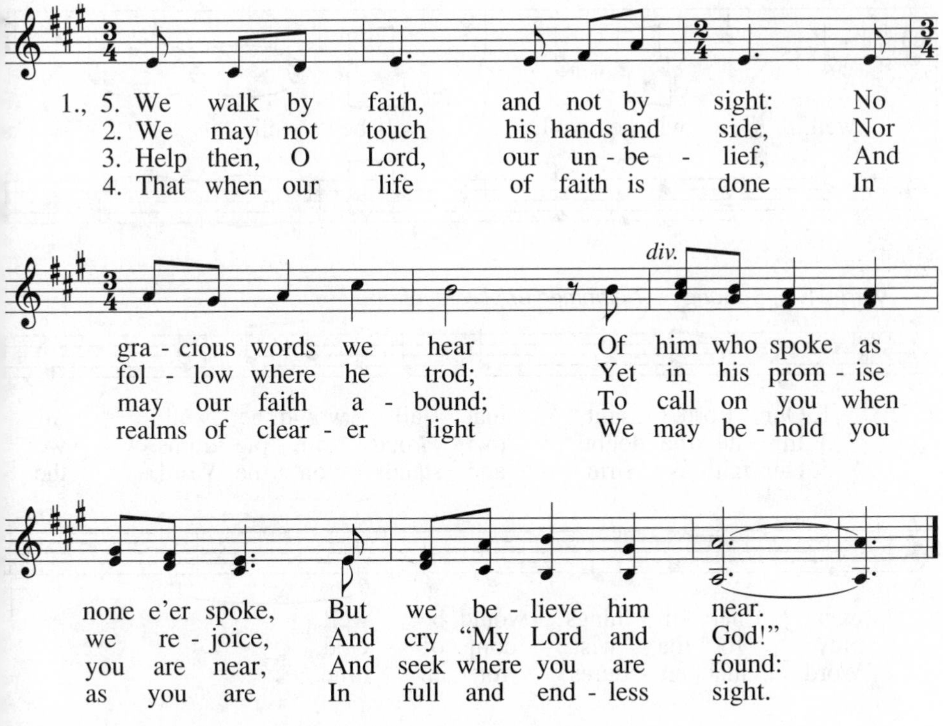

Text: Henry Alford, 1810-1871, alt.
Tune: SHANTI, CM; Marty Haugen, b.1950, © 1984, GIA Publications, Inc.

584 All Will Be Well

Ostinato Refrain
All will be well, and all will be well, all man - ner of things will be well.
To repeat
Last time
well, will be well, will be well.
Verses 1, 3, 5 (Sung over hummed or played refrain)
Cantor:
1. Our Lord said that all would be well, all man - ner of things would be well.
3. In all the doubts that shroud sim - ple truths, we pray for the wis - dom of God.
5. Our faith is firm and stands on the Word, the Word that en - dures for all time.
D.C.

Verses 2, 4, 6 (Sung over hummed or played refrain)
Cantor:
2. With all the sad - ness wrought in this world, the good shall al - ways pre - vail.
4. Give us the faith to trust in your love, when things are con - cealed from our view.
6. And so we pray to trust in the hope that all man - ner of things shall be well.
D.C.
Text: The Revelations of Divine Love, Julian of Norwich; adapt. by Steven C. Warner, b.1954
Tune: Steven C. Warner, b.1954
© 1993, World Library Publications
Blest Be the Lord 585
Refrain
Melody:
Blest be the Lord; blest be the Lord, the God of mer - cy, the God who saves. I shall not
Harmony:
Blest be the Lord; blest be the Lord, the God of mer - cy, the God who saves.

fear the dark of night,
I shall not fear the dark of
nor the ar - row that flies by day.
night, nor the ar - row that flies by day.
Verse 1
1. He will re - lease me from the nets of all my foes
He will pro - tect me from their wick-ed hands.
Be-neath the shad-ow of his wings I will re-joice
D.C.
to find a dwell-ing place se - cure.
Verse 2
2. I need not shrink be - fore the ter-rors of the night
nor stand a - lone be - fore the light of day.

No harm shall come to me, no ar-row strike me down,
no e - vil set-tle in my soul.
D.C.
Verse 3
3. Al - though a thou - sand strong have fall-en at my side,
I'll not be shak-en with the Lord at hand.
His faith-ful love is all the ar-mor that I
need to wage my bat-tle with the foe.
D.C.

Text: Psalm 91; Dan Schutte, b.1947
Tune: Dan Schutte, b.1947; arr. by Sr. Theophane Hytrek, OSF, 1915-1992

586 Amazing Grace

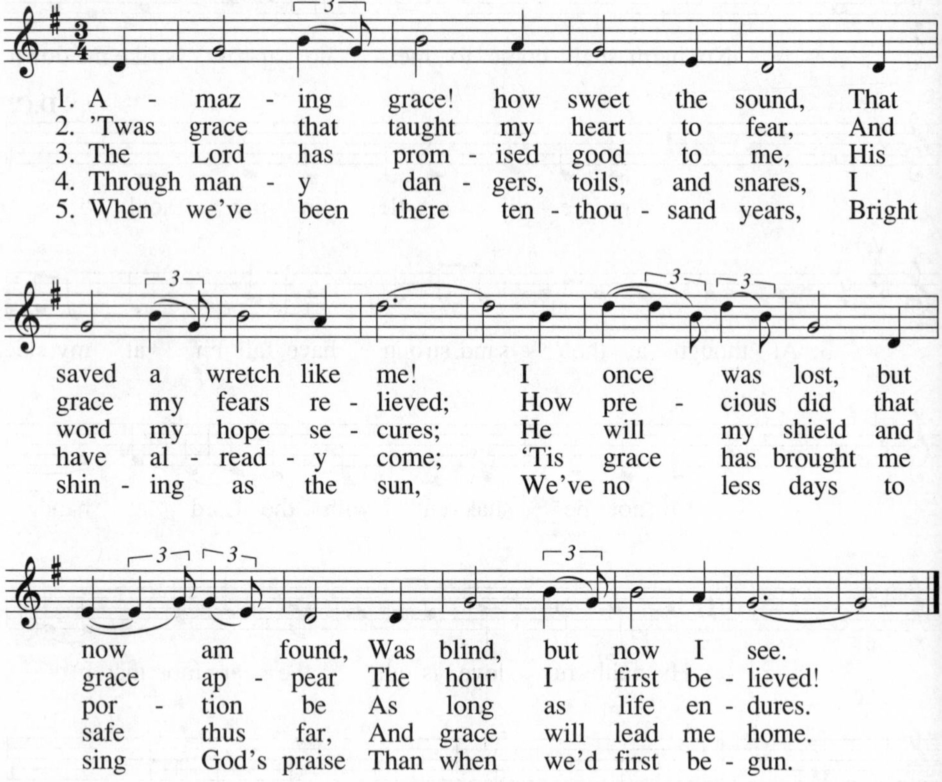
3
1. A - maz - ing grace! how sweet the sound, That
2. 'Twas grace that taught my heart to fear, And
3. The Lord has prom - ised good to me, His
4. Through man - y dan - gers, toils, and snares, I
5. When we've been there ten - thou - sand years, Bright
saved a wretch like me! I once was lost, but
grace my fears re - lieved; How pre - cious did that
word my hope se - cures; He will my shield and
have al - read - y come; 'Tis grace has brought me
shin - ing as the sun, We've no less days to
now am found, Was blind, but now I see.
grace ap - pear The hour I first be - lieved!
por - tion be As long as life en - dures.
safe thus far, And grace will lead me home.
sing God's praise Than when we'd first be - gun.

Text: St. 1-4, John Newton, 1725-1807; st. 5, attr. to John Rees, fl.1859
Tune: NEW BRITAIN, CM; *Virginia Harmony,* 1831; acc. by Diana Kodner, b.1957, © 1993, GIA Publications, Inc.

How Firm a Foundation 587

1. How firm a foun - da - tion, you saints of the Lord,
2. "Fear not, I am with you, O be not dis - mayed,
3. "When through the deep wa - ters I call you to go,
4. "The soul that on Je - sus still leans for re - pose,
Is laid for your faith in this ex - cel - lent Word!
For I am your God, and will still give you aid;
The riv - ers of woe shall not you o - ver - flow;
I will not, I will not de - sert to its foes;
What more can God say than to you has been said,
I'll strength - en you, help you, and cause you to stand,
For I will be with you, your trou - bles to bless,
That soul, though all hell should en - deav - or to shake,
To you who for ref - uge to Je - sus have fled?
Up - held by my right - eous, om - nip - o - tent hand.
And sanc - ti - fy to you, your deep - est dis - tress.
I'll nev - er, no nev - er, no nev - er for - sake!"

Text: 2 Peter 1:4; "K" in Rippon's *A Selection of Hymns*, 1787
Tune: FOUNDATION, 11 11 11 11; Funk's *Compilation of Genuine Church Music,* 1832; harm. by Richard Proulx, b.1937,

588 O God, Our Help in Ages Past

1. O God, our help in a - ges past, Our hope for years to come, Our shel - ter from the storm - y blast, And our e - ter - nal home.
2. Un - der the shad - ow of your throne Your saints have dwelt se - cure; Suf - fi - cient is your arm a - lone, And our de - fense is sure.
3. Be - fore the hills in or - der stood, Or earth re - ceived its frame, From ev - er - last - ing you are God, To end - less years the same.
4. A thou - sand a - ges in your sight Are like an eve - ning gone, Short as the watch that ends the night Be - fore the ris - ing sun.
5. Time, like an ev - er - roll - ing stream, Soon bears us all a - way; We fly for - got - ten, as a dream Dies at the o - p'ning day.
6. O God, our help in a - ges past, Our hope for years to come, Still be our guard while trou - bles last, And our e - ter - nal home.

Text: Psalm 90; Isaac Watts, 1674-1748
Tune: ST. ANNE, CM; attr. to William Croft, 1678-1727; harm. composite from 18th C. versions

Psalm of Hope 589

Refrain
A - maz - ing grace! how sweet the sound that
saved and set me free. I once was lost, but
now am found; was blind, but now I see.
Verses
1. My God, my God, why have you a - ban - doned me? Far from my prayers,
2. But here am I, the scorn of all my peo - ple. They say, "if God
3. The e - vil - do - ers cir - cle in a - round me. I am en - slaved
4. I shall pro - claim your name to the full as - sem - bly. Those who fear God,
*1. You did not turn your face from all your peo - ple. You res - cued them
*2. And so my soul shall live for you, O Lord of hope. My chil - dren shall

*Alternate Easter verses used with v.4 above.

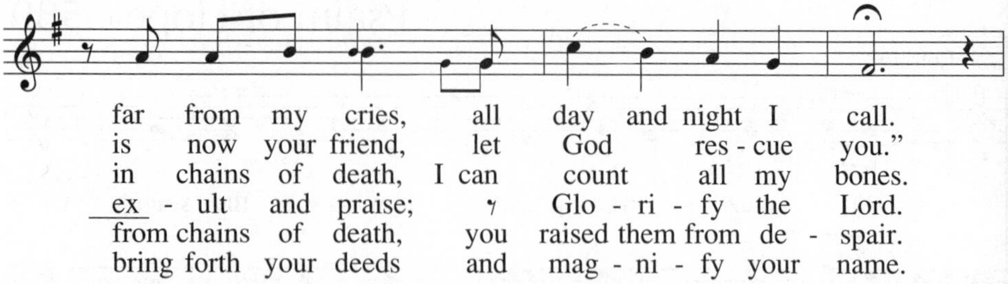

far from my cries, all day and night I call.
is now your friend, let God res - cue you."
in chains of death, I can count all my bones.
ex - ult and praise; Glo - ri - fy the Lord.
from chains of death, you raised them from de - spair.
bring forth your deeds and mag - ni - fy your name.

Yet, our an - ces - tors put their trust in
From my moth - er's womb you are my
O my strength, has - ten to my
All gen - er - a - tions, all chil - dren of the
Ev - 'ry na - tion on earth from end to
All my de - scen-dants shall know your ways, O

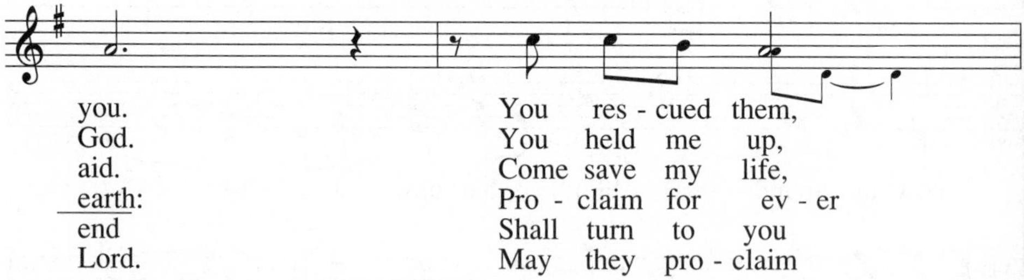

you. You res - cued them,
God. You held me up,
aid. Come save my life,
earth: Pro - claim for ev - er
end Shall turn to you
Lord. May they pro - claim

D.C.

you saved them from all foes.
you placed me in your arms.
come quick - ly to my help.
the won - drous deeds of God.
and bow be - fore your throne.
the jus - tice you have shown.

Text: Refrain, John Newton, 1725-1807; Verses, Psalm 22, adapted by Felix Goebel-Komala, b.1961
Tune: PSALM OF HOPE; Irregular with refrain; Felix Goebel-Komala, b.1961

590 You Are Near

Refrain

Descant:
Yah - weh, I know you are near, stand-ing
Melody:
Yah - weh, I know you are near, stand-ing

al - ways at my side. You guard me from the
al - ways at my side. You guard me from the
foe, and you lead me in ways ev - er - last-ing.
foe, and you lead me in ways ev - er - last-ing.
Verses
1. Lord, you have searched my heart,
2. Where can I run from your love?
3. You know my heart and its ways,
4. Mar - vel - ous to me are your works;
and you know when I sit and when I stand.
If I climb to the heav - ens you are there;
you who formed me be - fore I was born
how pro - found are your thoughts, my Lord.
Your hand is up - on me pro - tect - ing me from death,
if I fly to the sun - rise or sail be - yond the sea,
in the se - cret of dark - ness be - fore I saw the sun,
E - ven if I could count them, they num - ber as the stars,
D.C.
keep - ing me from harm.
still I'd find you there.
in my moth - er's womb.
you would still be there.

Text: Psalm 139; Dan Schutte, b.1947
Tune: Dan Schutte, b.1947; acc. by Sr. Theophane Hytrek, OSF, 1915-1992

591 Only in God

Refrain

Descant:
On - ly in God will my soul be at rest. From
Melody:
On - ly in God will my soul be at rest. From

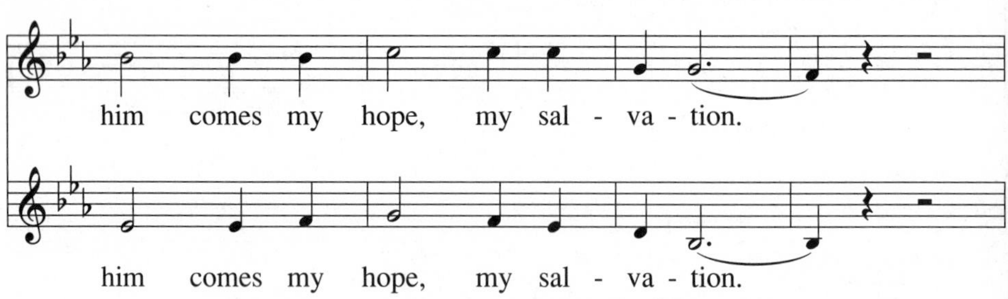
him comes my hope, my sal - va - tion.
him comes my hope, my sal - va - tion.

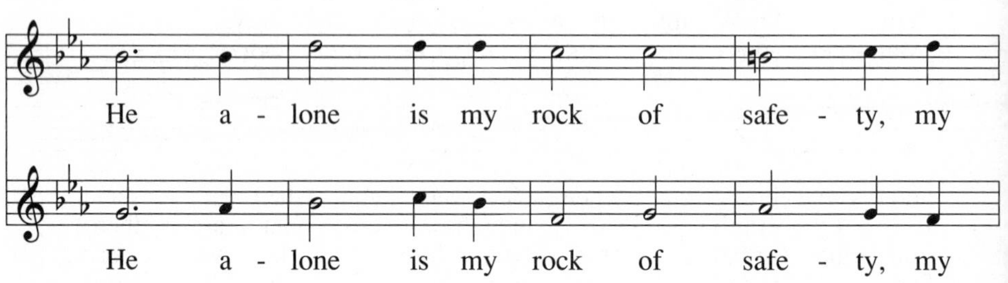
He a - lone is my rock of safe - ty, my
He a - lone is my rock of safe - ty, my

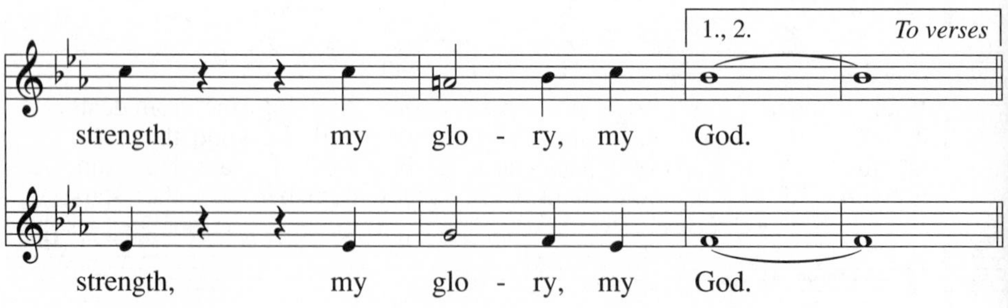
1., 2.
To verses
strength, my glo - ry, my God.
strength, my glo - ry, my God.

TRUST

Last time
God.
God.
Verses
1. Trust in him at all times, O peo - ple, and
2. Man - y times have I heard him tell of his
pour out your hearts.
long last - ing love.
God him - self is a ref - uge for us and a
You your - self, Lord, re - ward all who la - bor for
D.C.
strong - hold for our fear.
love of your name.

Text: Psalm 62:1, 2, 8, 11, 12; John Foley, SJ, b.1939
Tune: John Foley, SJ, b.1939

592 The Lord Is My Light

Verses 1, 3
1. The Lord is my light and my sal - va - tion, the Lord is my light and my sal - va - tion, the Lord is my light and my sal - va - tion; whom shall I fear?
3. Wait on the Lord and be of good cour - age, O wait on the Lord and be of good cour - age, wait on the Lord and be of good cour - age. He shall strength-en thine heart.
Refrain
Whom shall I fear, whom shall I fear?

TRUST

The Lord is the strength of my
life; whom shall I fear?
Verse 2
2. In the time of trou-ble he shall hide me, O
in the time of trou-ble, he shall hide me,
in the time of trou-ble, he shall hide me;
whom shall I fear?
D.S.

Text: Lillian Bouknight
Tune: Lillian Bouknight; arr. by Paul Gainer

593 On Eagle's Wings

Verse 1
1. You who dwell in the shel-ter of the Lord, who a-bide in his shad-ow for life, say to the Lord: "My ref-uge, my rock in whom I trust!"
Refrain
Descant:
Melody:
And he will raise you up on ea-gle's wings, bear you on the breath of dawn, make you to shine like the sun, and hold you in the palm of his hand.
Last time to coda
of his hand.
To verses
2. The
Verse 2
snare of the fowl-er will nev-er cap-ture you, and fam-ine will bring you no fear: un-der his wings your ref-uge, his faith-ful-ness your shield.
3
D.S.

Verse 3
3
3. You need not fear the ter - ror of the night, nor the
ar - row that flies by day; though thou - sands fall a -
bout you, near you it shall not come.
D.S.
Verse 4
3
4. For to his an - gels he's giv - en a com - mand to
guard you in all of your ways; up - on their hands they will
bear you up, lest you dash your foot a - gainst a stone.
D.S.
Coda
And hold you, hold you in the
palm of his hand.

Text: Psalm 91; Michael Joncas, b.1951
Tune: Michael Joncas, b.1951

594 A Mighty Fortress Is Our God

1. A might - y for - tress is our God, A
2. No strength of ours can match his might! We
3. Though hordes of dev - ils fill the land All
4. God's Word for - ev - er shall a - bide, No
sword and shield vic - to - rious, Who breaks the
would be lost, re - ject - ed. But now a
threat - n'ing to de - vour us, We trem - ble
thanks to foes, who fear it; For God, our
cruel op - pres - sor's rod And wins sal - va - tion
cham - pion comes to fight, Whom God a - lone e -
not, un - moved we stand; They can - not o - ver -
Lord, fights by our side With weap - ons of the
glo - rious. The old sa - tan - ic foe
lect - ed. You ask who this may be?
pow'r us. Let this world's ty - rant rage;
Spir - it. Were they to take our house,

Has sworn to work us woe! With craft and
The Lord of hosts is he! Christ Je - sus,
In bat - tle we'll en - gage! His might is
Goods, hon - or, child, or spouse, Though life be
dread - ful might He arms him - self to fight.
might - y Lord, God's on - ly Son, a - dored.
doomed to fail; God's judge - ment must pre - vail!
wrenched a - way, They can - not win the day.
On earth he has no e - qual.
He holds the field vic - to - rious.
One lit - tle word sub - dues him.
The King - dom's ours for - ev - er!

Text: Psalm (45) 46; *Ein' feste Burg ins unser Gott*; Martin Luther, 1483-1546; tr. © 1978, *Lutheran Book of Worship*
Tune: EIN' FESTE BURG, 8 7 8 7 66 66 7; Martin Luther, 1483-1546; harm. by J.S. Bach, 1685-1750

595 Though the Mountains May Fall

Refrain
Descant:
Though the moun - tains may fall and the hills turn to dust,
Melody:
Though the moun - tains may fall and the hills turn to dust,
yet the love of the Lord will stand
yet the love of the Lord will stand
as a shel - ter for all who will call on his name.
as a shel - ter for all who will call on his name.
Sing the praise and the glo - ry of God.
Sing the praise and the glo - ry of God.
Verses
Descant:
1. Could the Lord ev - er leave you?
2. Should you turn and for - sake him,
3. Go to him when you're wea - ry;
4. As he swore to your fa - thers,
Melody:
1. Could the Lord ev - er leave you?
2. Should you turn and for - sake him,
3. Go to him when you're wea - ry;
4. As he swore to your fa - thers,

Could the Lord for - get his love?
he will gent - ly call your name.
he will give you ea - gle's wings.
when the flood de - stroyed the land;
Could the Lord for - get his love?
he will gent - ly call your name.
he will give you ea - gle's wings.
when the flood de - stroyed the land;
Though a moth - er for - sake her child, he will
Should you wan - der a - way from him, he will
You will run, nev - er tire, for your
he will nev - er for - sake you; he will
Though a moth - er for - sake her child, he will
Should you wan - der a - way from him, he will
You will run, nev - er tire, for your
he will nev - er for - sake you; he will
D.C.
not a - ban - don you.
al - ways take you back.
God will be your strength.
swear to you a - gain.
D.C.
not a - ban - don you.
al - ways take you back.
God will be your strength.
swear to you a - gain.

Text: Isaiah 54:6-10, 49:15, 40:31-32; Dan Schutte, b.1947
Tune: Dan Schutte, b.1947; acc. by Michael Pope, SJ

596 Be Not Afraid

Verse 1
1. You shall cross the bar-ren des-ert, but you shall not die of thirst. You shall wan-der far in safe-ty though you do not know the way. You shall speak your words in for-eign lands and all will un-der-stand. You shall see the face of God and live.
Refrain
Melody:
Be not a-fraid. I go be-fore you al-ways. Come, fol-low me, and
Harmony:
Be not a-fraid. I go be-fore you al-ways. Come, fol-low me,

I will give you rest.
I will give you rest.
Verse 2
2. If you pass through rag - ing wa-ters in the sea, you shall not drown. If you walk a-mid the burn-ing flames, you shall not be harmed. If you stand be-fore the pow'r of hell and death is at your side, know that I am with you through it all.
D.S.
Verse 3
Descant:
Ooh king - dom shall be
3. Bless - ed are your poor, for the king - dom shall be

theirs. Bless - ed are the
theirs. Blest are you that weep and mourn, for
ones who mourn. If they
one day you shall laugh. And if wick-ed tongues in -
hate you all be - cause of me,
sult and hate you all be - cause of me,
D.S.
bless - ed, bless - ed are you!
bless - ed, bless - ed are you!

Text: Isaiah 43:2-3, Luke 6:20ff; Bob Dufford, SJ, b.1943
Tune: Bob Dufford, SJ, b.1943; acc. by Sr. Theophane Hytrek, OSF, 1915-1992

All That We Have 597

Refrain
All that we have and all that we of - fer
Comes from a heart both fright-ened and free.
Take what we bring now and give what we need,
Last time
All done in his name.
Verses
1. Some would re - ly on their pow - er,
2. Some - times the road may be lone - some,
3. Some - times when trou - bles are man - y,
Oth - ers put trust in their gold.
Of - ten we may lose our way;
Life can seem emp - ty, it's true,
Some have on - ly their Sav - ior,
Take cour - age and al - ways re - mem - ber
But look at the life of the Mas - ter,
D.C.
Whose faith - ful - ness nev - er grows old.
Love is - n't just for a day.
Who lov - ing - ly suf - fered for you.

Text: Gary Ault, b.1944
Tune: Gary Ault, b.1944; acc. by Gary Daigle, b.1957, alt.

598 How Can I Keep from Singing

1. My life flows on in end-less song A - bove earth's lam - en - ta - tion. I hear the real though far - off hymn That hails a new cre - a - tion.
2. Through all the tu - mult and the strife, I hear that mu - sic ring - ing; It sounds and ech - oes in my soul; How can I keep from sing-ing?
3. What, though my joys and com-fort die, The Lord, my sav - ior liv - eth. What though the dark - ness gath - er 'round? Songs in the night it giv - eth.
4. The peace of Christ makes fresh my heart, A foun - tain ev - er spring-ing. All things are mine since I am his; How can I keep from sing-ing?
No storm can shake my in-most calm, While to that rock I'm cling - ing.
Since Christ is Lord of heav-en and earth,
How can I keep from sing-ing?

Text: Robert Lowry, 1826-1899
Tune: HOW CAN I KEEP FROM SINGING, 8 7 8 7 with refrain; Robert Lowry, 1826-1899; harm. by Robert J. Batastini, b.1942, © 1988, GIA Publications, Inc.

The Lord Is Near 599

*Refrain
O the Lord is near to all who call on him; he is close to all who seek his face, slow to an - ger and full of com - pas-sion and a - bound - ing in mer-ci-ful love.
**May the an - gels lead you in - to par - a - dise; may the mar - tyrs come to wel - come you, and take you to the ho - ly cit - y, the new and e - ter - nal Je - ru - sa-lem.
Verse 1
1. The Lord is my light and my sal - va - tion, there is noth-ing at all I fear; the Lord is the ref - uge of my life; of whom should I be a - fraid?
D.C.
Verse 2
2. One thing I ask of the Lord; there is on - ly one thing I seek: to dwell in the house of the Lord all the days of my life.
D.C.

*The refrain may be sung in a two-voice canon at a distance of one measure, or a three-voice canon at a distance of one-half measure.

**Alternate refrain for funerals

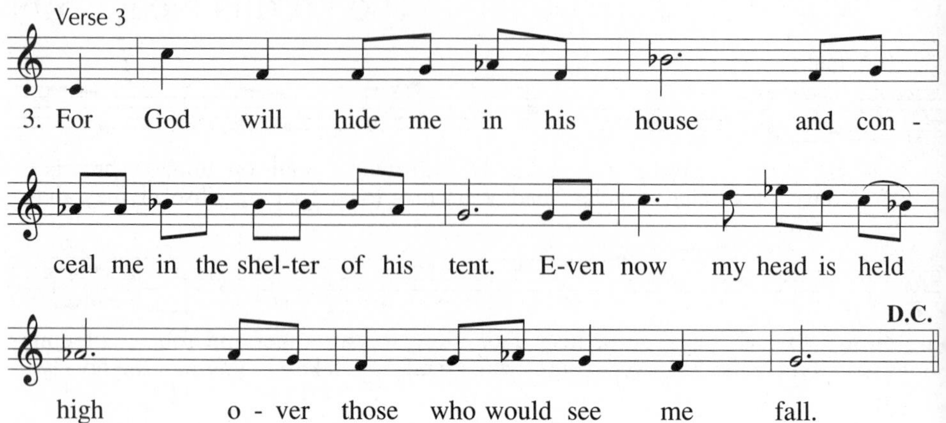
Verse 3
3. For God will hide me in his house and con -
ceal me in the shel-ter of his tent. E-ven now my head is held
high o - ver those who would see me fall.
D.C.

Text: Psalm 27; Michael Joncas, b.1951
Tune: Michael Joncas, b.1951

600 Seek Ye First

Canon

1.

1. Seek ye first the king-dom of God and His right - eous - ness, and all these things shall be add - ed un - to you;

2. Man shall not live by bread a - lone, but by ev - 'ry word that pro - ceeds from the mouth of God;

3. Ask, and it shall be giv-en un-to you, seek, and ye shall find, knock, and the door shall be o-pened un - to you;

Al - le - lu, al-le - lu - ia.

2.

Al - le - lu - ia, al - le - lu - ia, al - le - lu - ia, al - le - lu, al-le - lu - ia.

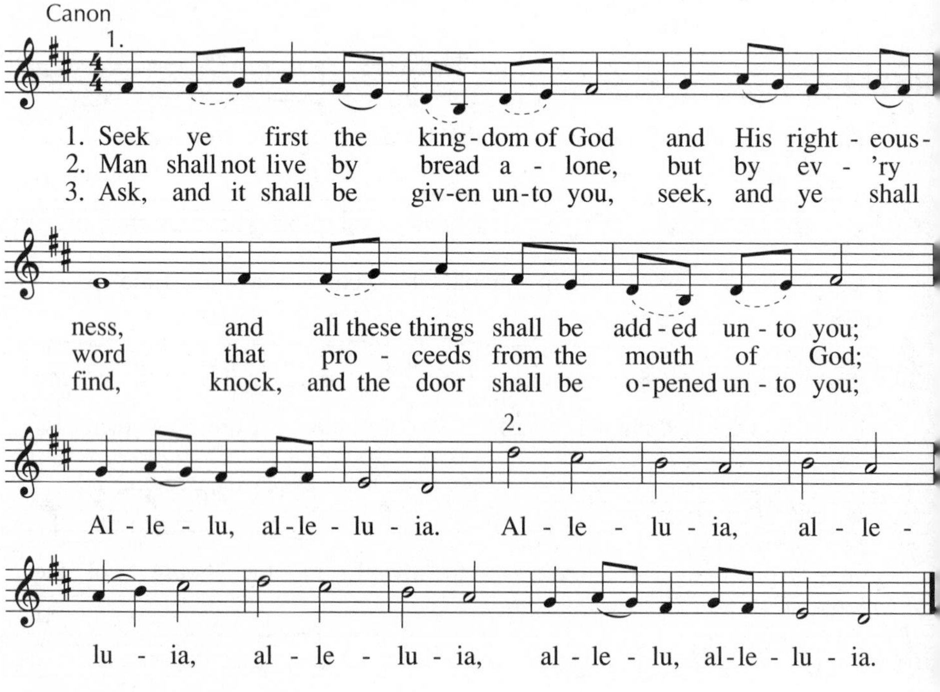

Text: Matthew 6:33, 7:7; adapt. by Karen Lafferty, b.1948
Tune: SEEK YE FIRST, Irregular; Karen Lafferty, b.1948

Where True Love and Charity Are Found / Ubi Caritas 601

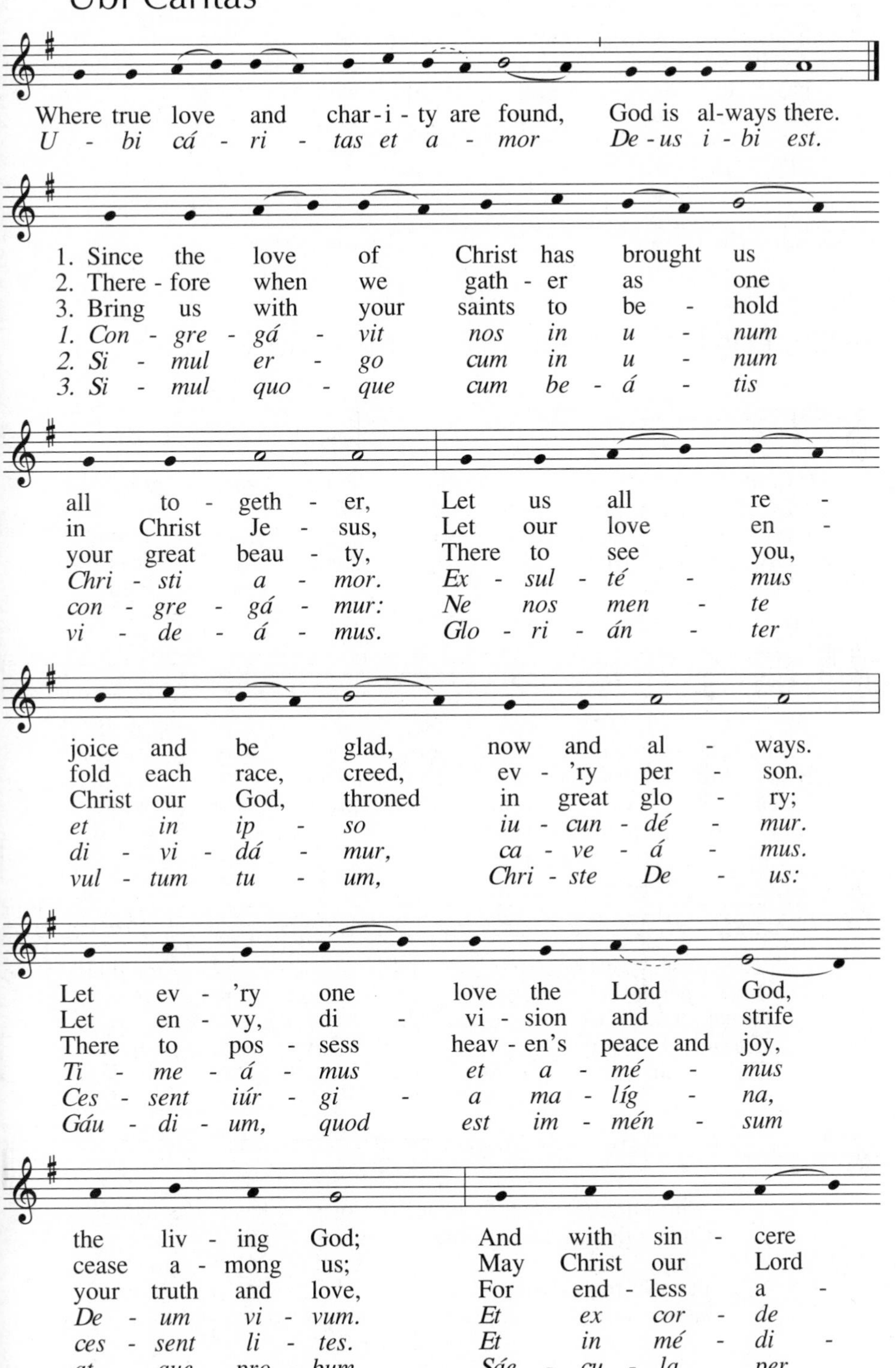
Where true love and char-i-ty are found, God is al-ways there.
U - bi cá - ri - tas et a - mor De-us i-bi est.
1. Since the love of Christ has brought us
2. There-fore when we gath - er as one
3. Bring us with your saints to be - hold
1. Con - gre - gá - vit nos in u - num
2. Si - mul er - go cum in u - num
3. Si - mul quo - que cum be - á - tis
all to - geth - er, Let us all re -
in Christ Je - sus, Let our love en -
your great beau - ty, There to see you,
Chri - sti a - mor. Ex - sul - té - mus
con - gre - gá - mur: Ne nos men - te
vi - de - á - mus. Glo - ri - án - ter
joice and be glad, now and al - ways.
fold each race, creed, ev - 'ry per - son.
Christ our God, throned in great glo - ry;
et in ip - so iu - cun - dé - mur.
di - vi - dá - mur, ca - ve - á - mus.
vul - tum tu - um, Chri - ste De - us:
Let ev - 'ry one love the Lord God,
Let en - vy, di - vi - sion and strife
There to pos - sess heav - en's peace and joy,
Ti - me - á - mus et a - mé - mus
Ces - sent iúr - gi - a ma - líg - na,
Gáu - di - um, quod est im - mén - sum
the liv - ing God; And with sin - cere
cease a - mong us; May Christ our Lord
your truth and love, For end - less a -
De - um vi - vum. Et ex cor - de
ces - sent li - tes. Et in mé - di -
at - que pro - bum. Sáe - cu - la per

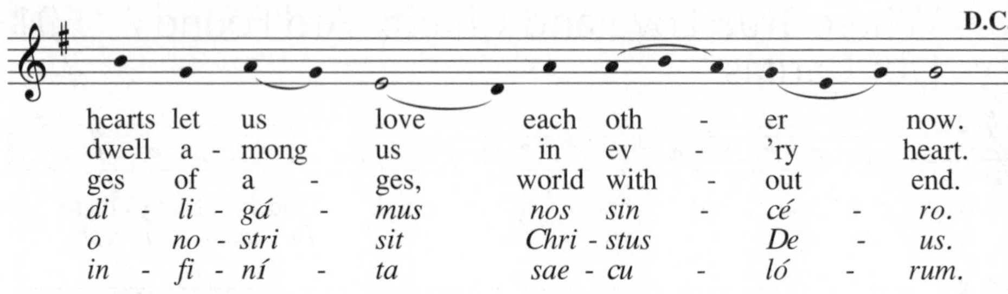
D.C.
hearts let us love each oth - er now.
dwell a - mong us in ev - 'ry heart.
ges of a - ges, world with - out end.
di - li - gá - mus nos sin - cé - ro.
o no - stri sit Chri - stus De - us.
in - fi - ní - ta sae - cu - ló - rum.

Text: Latin, 9th C.; tr. by Richard Proulx, b.1937, © 1975, 1986, GIA Publications, Inc.
Tune: UBI CARITAS, 12 12 12 12 with refrain; Mode VI; acc. by Richard Proulx, b.1937, © 1986, GIA Publications, Inc.

602 Lord of All Nations, Grant Me Grace

1. Lord of all na - tions, grant me grace
2. Break down the wall that would di - vide
3. For - give me, Lord, where I have erred
4. Give me your cour - age, Lord, to speak
5. With your own love may I be filled

To love all peo - ple, ev - 'ry race
Your chil - dren, Lord, on ev - 'ry side.
By love - less act and thought - less word.
When - ev - er strong op - press the weak.
And by your Ho - ly Spir - it willed,

To see each mor - tal as I ought,
My neigh - bor's good let me pur - sue,
Make me to see the wrong I do
Should I my - self as vic - tim live,
That all whose lives are touched by mine,

My kin - dred, whom your love has bought.
Let Chris - tian love bind warm and true.
Will cru - ci - fy my Lord a - new.
Re - mem - b'ring you, may I for - give.
May know your heal - ing touch di - vine.

Text: Philippians 2:1-18; Olive W. Spannus, b.1916, © 1969, Concordia Publishing House
Tune: VENI CREATOR SPIRITUS, LM; Mode VIII; setting by Richard J. Wojcik, b.1923, © 1975, GIA Publications, Inc.

There's a Wideness in God's Mercy 603

1. There's a wide - ness in God's mer - cy Like the wide - ness of the sea; There's a kind - ness in God's jus - tice Which is more than lib - er - ty. There is plen - ti - ful re - demp - tion In the blood that has been shed;
2. For the love of God is broad - er Than the meas - ures of our mind, And the heart of the E - ter - nal Is most won - der - ful - ly kind. If our love were but more sim - ple We should take him at his word,
3. Trou - bled souls, why will you scat - ter Like a crowd of fright - ened sheep? Fool - ish hearts, why will you wan - der From a love so true and deep? There is wel - come for the sin - ner And more grac - es for the good;

There is joy for all the mem - bers
And our lives would be thanks - giv - ing
There is mer - cy with the Sav - ior,
In the sor - rows of the Head.
For the good - ness of our Lord.
There is heal - ing in his blood.

Text: Frederick W. Faber, 1814-1863, alt.
Tune: IN BABILONE, 8 7 8 7 D; *Oude en Nieuwe Hollanste Boerenlities,* c.1710

604 The Call Is Clear and Simple

1. The call is clear and sim - ple: "Love God and hu - man -
2. God, help us sort our mo - tives, That lov - ing may be
3. God, teach us strength and wis - dom When false love takes the
4. O wise and ho - ly Lov - er, Teach us as sea - sons

kind," But love de - mands much wis - dom And
whole. High aims or base am - bi - tion? Com -
lead. Too well we learn sub - mis - sion And
turn To know our - selves and oth - ers— Deep,
clar - i - ty of mind. "Be wi - ly as a
pas - sion or con - trol? Then help us clear our
si - lence our own need. When oth - ers would mis -
hon - est love to learn. So may we nur - ture
ser - pent, Though gen - tle as a dove," For
sched - ules Of ev - 'ry fran - tic task That
use us Or lure us t'ward the wrong, God,
liv - ing In all we say and do, In
man - y are the dan - gers Up - on the path of love.
leads a - way from do - ing The one thing that you ask.
tem - per love with cour - age To keep our bound - 'ries strong.
strong and gen - tle giv - ing To hu - man - kind and you.

Text: Ruth Duck, b.1947, © 1992, GIA Publications, Inc.
Tune: PASSION CHORALE, 7 6 7 6 D; Hans Leo Hassler, 1564-1612; harm. by J. S. Bach, 1685-1750

605 Neither Death nor Life

Refrain
Nei-ther death, nor life, nor an-gels, nor rul-ers, nor
trials in the pres-ent, nor an-y trial to come, nei-ther
height, nor depth, nor all of cre - a-tion can
ev - er sep-a-rate us from the love of God poured
out in Christ Je-sus, in Je-sus our Lord.
our Lord.
Last time
Last time
our Lord.

Verse 1
1. Dwell in the One who raised Christ from the dead; Though your
bod-y shall die, in Christ you shall rise through the
D.C.
Spir - it who brings you to life.
Verse 2
2. All who are led by the Spir-it shall live as
chil - dren of God, and heirs with Christ Je - sus, God's a -
D.C.
dopt - ed and cho - sen and loved.
Verse 3
3. All of the suf - f'ring we now must en - dure is
noth - ing to the glo - ry so soon to be re -
D.C.
vealed when cre - a - tion it - self is set free.

Verse 4
4. All of cre - a - tion a - waits the new birth, the
full - ness of re - demp-tion, through la - bor pains of
love, and so we wait in pa - tience and hope.
D.C.
Verse 5
5. All things work for good for the ones who love God, and if
God is for us, then who can be a - gainst us? God's
jus - ti-fied can - not be con - demned.
D.C.
Verse 6
6. Who can sep - a - rate us from the love of Christ? Will
hard-ship or dis - tress, per - se - cu - tion or fam - ine, or
na - ked-ness or per - il or sword?
D.C.

Text: Romans 8:11-19, 22-25, 28-35, 38; Marty Haugen, b.1950
Tune: Marty Haugen, b.1950

Koinonia 606

1.
2.
D.C.
How can I say that I love the Lord whom I've
get to say that I love the one whom I
nev - er, ev - er seen be-fore; and for -
walk be - side each and
ev - 'ry day? How can I look up -
on your face and ig - nore God's love? You I
must em - brace! You're my broth - er; you're my
sis-ter; and I love you with the love of my
Lord. Love of my Lord!

Koinonia, *derived from the original* κοινωνια, *is a Greek word meaning* fellowship.

Text: V. Michael McKay
Tune: V. Michael McKay

607 No Greater Love

Refrain
There is no great-er love, says the Lord, than to
lay down your life for a friend; there is no great-er love,
no great-er love, than to lay down your life for a friend.
Verse 1
1. As the Fa-ther has loved me, so I have loved you.
Live on in my love. You will live in my love if you
keep my com-mands, e-ven as I have kept my Fa-ther's.
D.C.

Verse 2
2. All this I tell you that my joy may be yours and your joy may be com-plete. Love one an-oth-er as I have loved you: This is my com-mand.
3
D.C.
Verse 3
3. You are my friends if you keep my com-mands; no long-er slaves but friends to me. All I heard from my Fa-ther, I have made known to you: Now I call you friends.
3
D.C.
Verse 4
4. It was not you who chose me, it was I who chose you, chose you to go forth and bear fruit. Your fruit must en-dure, so you will re-ceive all you ask the Fa-ther in my name.
3
D.C.

Text: John 15: 9-17; Michael Joncas, b.1951
Tune: Michael Joncas, b.1951

608 God Is Love

Refrain
God is love, and all who live in love, live in
1. God.
2. God. To verses
Last time God.
Verse 1
1. God is light, in God there is no dark - ness. Come
live in the love of the Lord.
D.C.
Verse 2
2. Come to the Lord, re - ceive the light, and
live in the love of the Lord.
D.C.
Verse 3
3. We are called to be God's own chil - dren, to
live in the love of the Lord.
D.C.

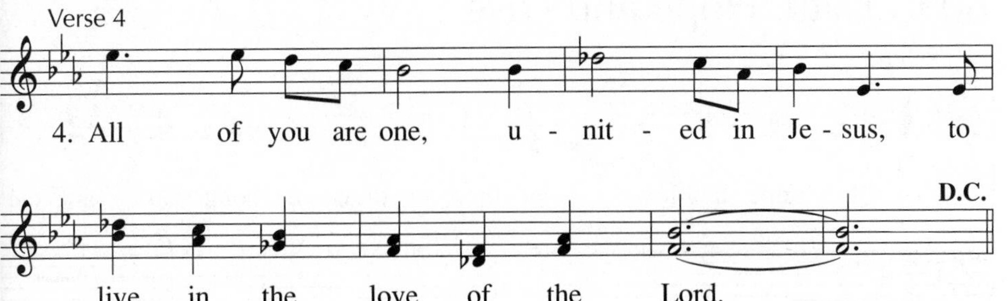
Verse 4
4. All of you are one, u - nit - ed in Je - sus, to
live in the love of the Lord.
D.C.

Text: 1 John 1:5, 3:2, 4:15, Psalm 33:6, Galatians 3:28; David Haas, b.1957
Tune: David Haas, b.1957

609 Faith, Hope and Love

Refrain
Faith, hope and love, let these en-dure a-mong you; and the
great-est of these is love, the great-est of these is love.
Verse 1
1. If I speak with the voice of an - gels but do not
love, I am like a nois-y gong, a clang-ing cym - bal.
I am noth - ing, I am noth - ing with-out love.
D.C.
Verse 2
Melody:
Harmony:
2. If I see all that's held in mys - ter - y,
feed and clothe the poor, if my faith should call me on
to move a moun-tain, still I'm noth-ing, I am noth-ing with-out love.
D.C.

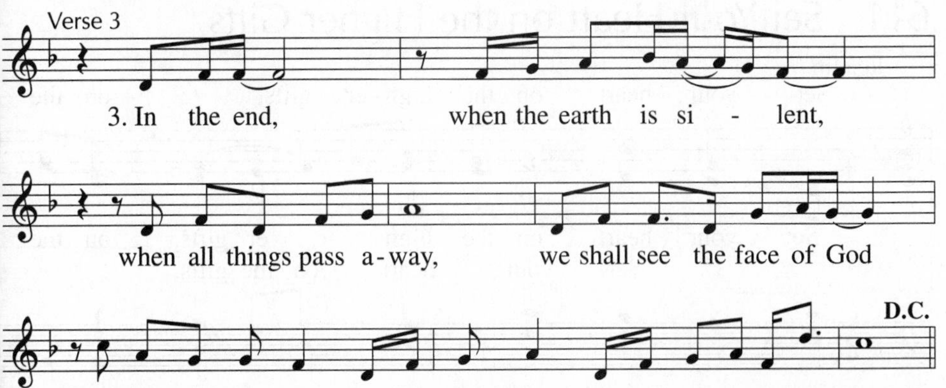
Verse 3
3. In the end, when the earth is si - lent,
when all things pass a-way, we shall see the face of God
in shin-ing splen-dor; there are three things that will lead us to that day.
D.C.

Text: Francis Patrick O'Brien, b.1958
Tune: Francis Patrick O'Brien, b.1958

Where Charity and Love Prevail 610

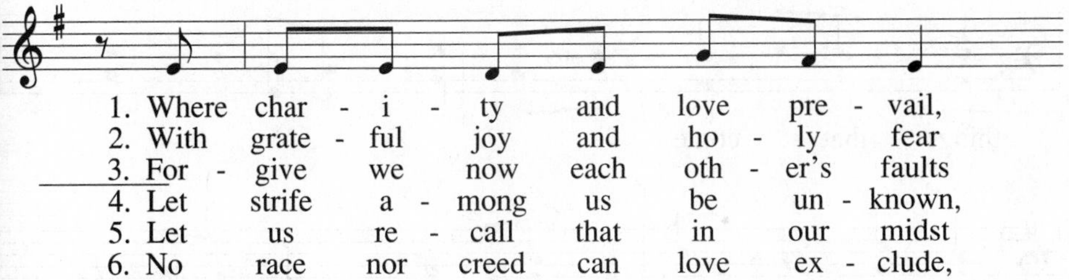

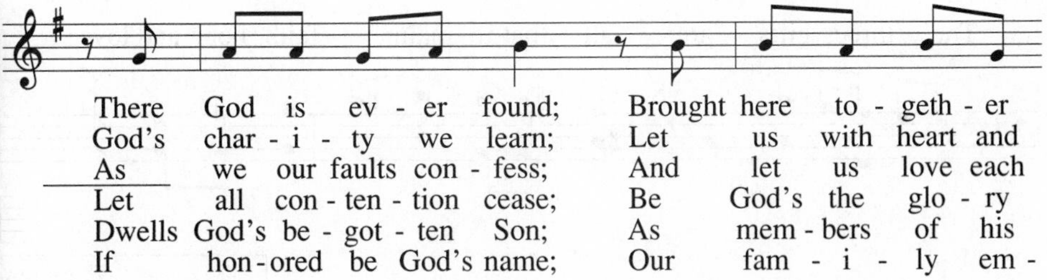

1. Where charity and love prevail,
There God is ever found;
Brought here together by Christ's love,
By love are we thus bound.

2. With grateful joy and holy fear
God's charity we learn;
Let us with heart and mind and soul
Now love God in return.

3. Forgive we now each other's faults
As we our faults confess;
And let us love each other well
In Christian holiness.

4. Let strife among us be unknown,
Let all contention cease;
Be God's the glory that we seek,
Be ours God's holy peace.

5. Let us recall that in our midst
Dwells God's begotten Son;
As members of his body joined,
We are in Christ made one.

6. No race nor creed can love exclude,
If honored be God's name;
Our family embraces all
Whose Father is the same.

Text: *Ubi caritas;* trans. by Omer Westendorf, 1916-1998
Tune: CHRISTIAN LOVE, CM; Paul Benoit, OSB, 1893-1979

611 Set Your Heart on the Higher Gifts

Refrain
Set your heart on the high-er gifts, on the
Set your heart on the high - er gifts, on the
Set your heart on the gifts,
Set your heart on the high - er gifts, on the
things that come
from your Mak - er in heav - en.
on the things
things that come
These three gifts are all that re-main: faith, hope and love,
and the great-est is love.
1.-3.
To verses

4.
Verses
Cantor:
1. If I speak with the tongues of the liv - ing, and of
2. And if I un - der - stand ev-'ry mys - t'ry, hav-ing
3. And if I should re - nounce all my rich - es, feed the
an - gels, but speak with - out love, I am on - ly
wis - dom, but think with - out love, had I faith to
hun - gry, give o - ver my life; with - out love my
D.C.
brass with - out song, an emp - ty noise on the wind.
scat - ter the hills, I am noth - ing at all.
prof - it is loss, my car - ing finds no re - ward.

Text: 1 Corinthians 12:31–13:13; Steven C. Warner, b.1954
Tune: Steven C. Warner, b.1954

612 Not for Tongues of Heaven's Angels

Intro-Coda
To verses
Last time
Verses
1. Not for tongues of heav-en's an-gels, Not for wis-dom to dis-cern, Not for faith that mas-ters moun-tains, For this bet-ter gift we yearn:
2. Love is hum-ble, love is gen-tle, Love is ten-der, true, and kind; Love is gra-cious, ev-er pa-tient, Gen-er-ous of heart and mind—
3. Nev-er jeal-ous, nev-er self-ish, Love will not re-joice in wrong; Nev-er boast-ful nor re-sent-ful, Love be-lieves and suf-fers long—
4. Soon will fade the word of wis-dom, Faith and hope be one day past: When we see our Sav-ior clear-ly, Love it is a-lone will last—
Refrain
May love be ours, Lord; may love be ours.
May love be ours, O Lord.
Last time D.C.

Text: Timothy Dudley-Smith, b.1926, © 1985, Hope Publishing Co.
Tune: COMFORT, 8 7 8 7 with refrain; Michael Joncas, b.1951, © 1988, GIA Publications, Inc.

LOVE

Love Divine, All Loves Excelling 613

1. Love di - vine, all loves ex - cel - ling, Joy of
2. Come, al - might - y to de - liv - er, Let us
3. Fin - ish then your new cre - a - tion, Pure and
heav'n to earth come down! Fix in us your
all your life re - ceive; Sud - den - ly re -
spot - less, gra - cious Lord, Let us see your
hum - ble dwell - ing, All your faith - ful mer - cies crown.
turn and nev - er, Nev - er more your tem - ples leave.
great sal - va - tion Per - fect - ly in you re - stored.
Je - sus, source of all com - pas - sion, Love un -
Lord, we would be al - ways bless - ing, Serve you
Changed from glo - ry in - to glo - ry, Till in

bound - ed, love all pure; Vis - it us with
as your hosts a - bove, Pray, and praise you
heav'n we take our place, Till we sing be -
your sal - va - tion, Let your love in us en - dure.
with - out ceas - ing, Glo - ry in your pre - cious love.
fore the al - might - y Lost in won - der, love and praise.

Text: Charles Wesley, 1707-1788, alt.
Tune: HYFRYDOL, 8 7 8 7 D; Rowland H. Prichard, 1811-1887

What Wondrous Love Is This 614

1. What won - drous love is this, O my soul, O my soul?
2. To God and to the Lamb I will sing, I will sing;
3. And when from death I'm free, I'll sing on, I'll sing on;

What won - drous love is this, O my soul?
To God and to the Lamb, I will sing;
And when from death I'm free, I'll sing on;

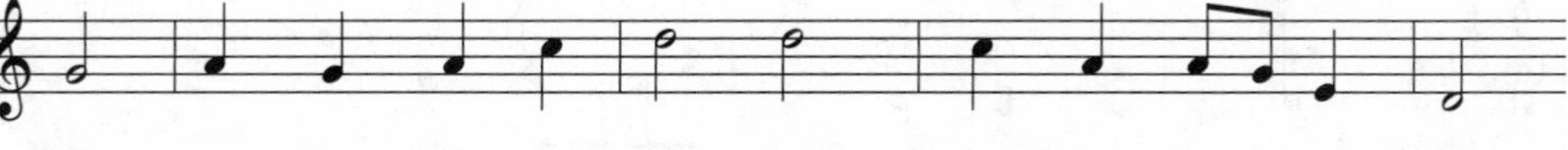

What won - drous love is this that caused the Lord of bliss
To God and to the Lamb who is the great I Am,
And when from death I'm free, I'll sing and joy - ful be,

To bear the dread - ful curse for my soul, for my soul;
While mil - lions join the theme, I will sing, I will sing;
And through e - ter - ni - ty I'll sing on, I'll sing on!

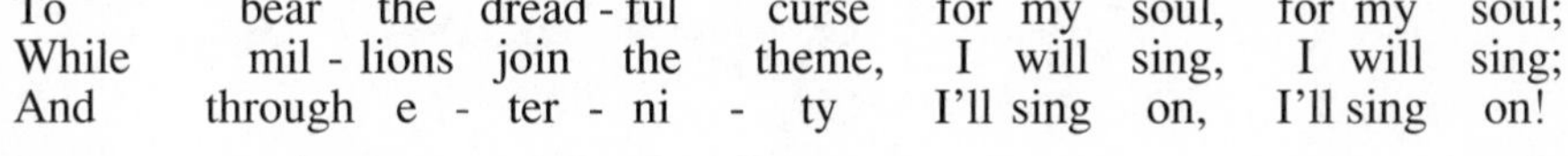

To bear the dread - ful curse for my soul?
While mil - lions join the theme, I will sing.
And through e - ter - ni - ty I'll sing on.

Text: Alexander Means, 1801-1853
Tune: WONDROUS LOVE, 12 9 12 12 9; *Southern Harmony,* 1835; harm. from *Cantate Domino, 1980,* © 1980, World Council of Churches

615 My Song Will Be for You Forever

Verses
1. My song will be for you for - ev - er, you, the mu - sic in my heart, For your love is all a - round me, and your good - ness al - ways here.
2. You have clothed me in your prom - ise, you, my love, my light, my friend. You, the way and path be - fore me, you will lead and guide me home.
3. I am here to be your ser - vant, you a - noint me with your love. You will hold me in my long - ing, all my hope in your em - brace.
4. With your voice, you sing with - in me, you, the one who knows me well. You, my joy, my life and bless - ing, when you call, you know my name.
5. I will pledge my love for - ev - er, I will call your name out loud. I will reach my hand out to you, and I know you'll reach for me.

LOVE

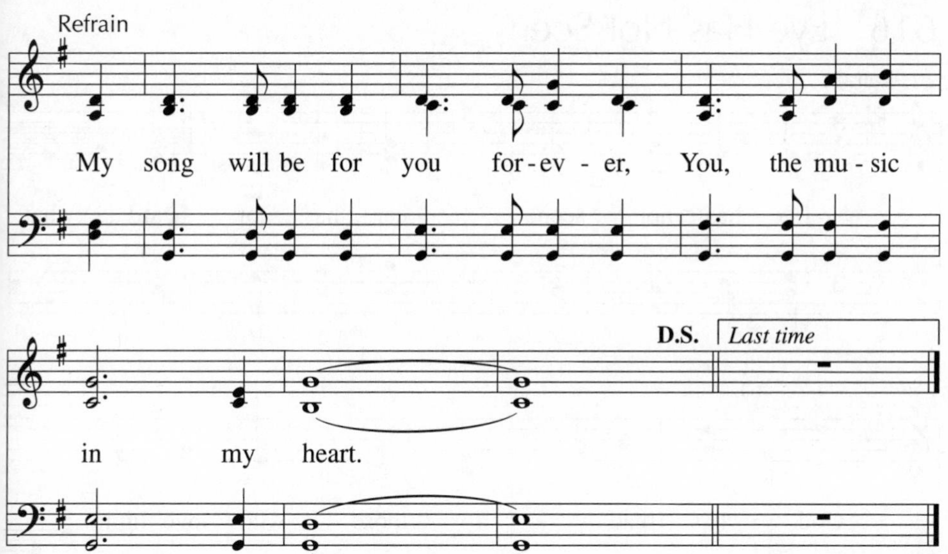
Refrain
My song will be for you for-ev - er, You, the mu - sic
in my heart.
D.S.
Last time

Text: David Haas, b.1957
Tune: David Haas, b.1957

616 Eye Has Not Seen

Refrain
Eye has not seen, ear has not heard what
God has read - y for those who love him;
Spir - it of love, come, give us the mind of
Je - sus, teach us the wis - dom of God.
Last time
Last time
Verses 1-3
1. When pain and sor - row weigh us down, be
2. Our lives are but a sin - gle breath, we
3. To those who see with eyes of faith, the

near to us, O Lord, for - give the weak - ness
flow - er and we fade, yet all our days are
Lord is ev - er near, re - flect - ed in the
of our faith, and bear us up with - in your peace - ful
in your hands, so we re - turn in love what love has
fac - es of all the poor and low - ly of the
word.
made.
world.
D.C.
Verse 4
4. We sing a mys - t'ry from the past in halls where saints have
trod, yet ev - er new the mu-sic rings to Je-sus, Liv - ing
Song of God.
D.C.

Text: 1 Corinthians 2:9-10; Marty Haugen, b.1950
Tune: Marty Haugen, b.1950

617 There Is a Balm in Gilead

Refrain
There is a balm in Gil - e - ad To
make the wound-ed whole, There is a balm in
Gil - e - ad To heal the sin - sick soul.
Last time
Last time
Verses
1. Some - times I feel dis - cour - aged And
2. If you can - not preach like Pe - ter, If you
3. Don't ev - er feel dis - cour - aged, For

think my work's in vain, But then the Ho - ly
can - not pray like Paul, You can tell the love of
Je - sus is your friend; And if you lack for

D.C.
Spir - it Re - vives my soul a - gain.
Je - sus, And say, "He died for all!"
knowl-edge He'll ne'er re - fuse to lend.

Text: Jeremiah 8:22, African-American spiritual
Tune: BALM IN GILEAD, Irregular; African-American spiritual; acc. by Marty Haugen, b.1950,

618 Only You, O God

Refrain
On - ly you, O God, and you a - lone, the
bro - ken heart con - sole; On - ly you, O God, and
you a - lone, the wound - ed world make whole.
Last time
Last time
Verses
1. O God, our rock and ha - ven, Our
2. You guard us, faith - ful fa - ther, With -
3. We pray do not a - ban - don The

strong - hold, safe and sure, Though earth be torn and
in your shel - t'ring palm; You nurse us, lov - ing
ones you call your own; Our com - fort and com -
shak - en, In you we stand se - cure.
moth - er, With milk and heal - ing balm.
pan - ion, We trust in you a - lone.
D.C.

Text: Susan R. Briehl, b.1952, © 2003, GIA Publications, Inc.
Tune: BALM IN GILEAD, 7 6 7 6 with refrain; African-American spiritual; acc. by Marty Haugen, b.1950, © 2003, GIA Publications, Inc.

619 The Clouds' Veil

Refrain
E-ven though the rain hides the stars, e - ven though the
E-ven though the rain hides the stars, e - ven though the
e - ven when the dark clouds
mist swirls the hills, e - ven when clouds
mist swirls the hills, e - ven when clouds
veil the sky,
veil the sky, God is by my side. E - ven when the
veil the sky, God is by my side.
e - ven when at dawn the sky shall
sun shall fall in sleep, e - ven when the sky shall
weep, e - ven in the night when storms shall rise,
weep, e - ven when the storms shall rise,

Last time
God is by my side. God is by my side.
Last time
Verses
1. Bright the stars at night that
2. Deep the feast of life where
3. Blest are they who sing the
mir - ror heav - en's way to you.
saints shall gath - er in deep peace.
fel - low - ship of saints in light.
Bright the stars in light where
Deep in heav - en's light where
Blest is heav - en's King. All
D.C.
dwell the saints in love and truth.
sor - rows pass be - yond death's sleep.
saints a - dore the Lord, Most High.

Text: Liam Lawton, b.1959
Tune: Liam Lawton, b.1959; arr. by John McCann, b.1961

620 Our God Is Rich in Love

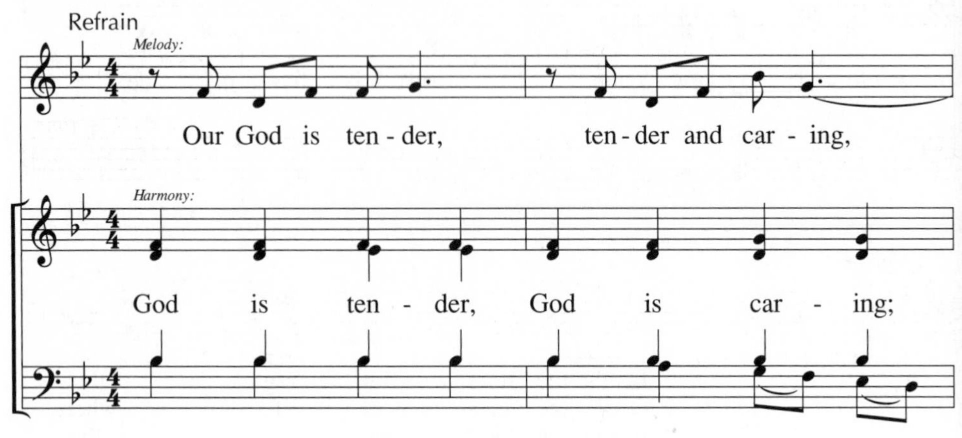
Refrain
Melody:
Our God is ten - der, ten - der and car - ing,
Harmony:
God is ten - der, God is car - ing;

slow to an - ger so rich in love.
slow to an - ger; rich in love.

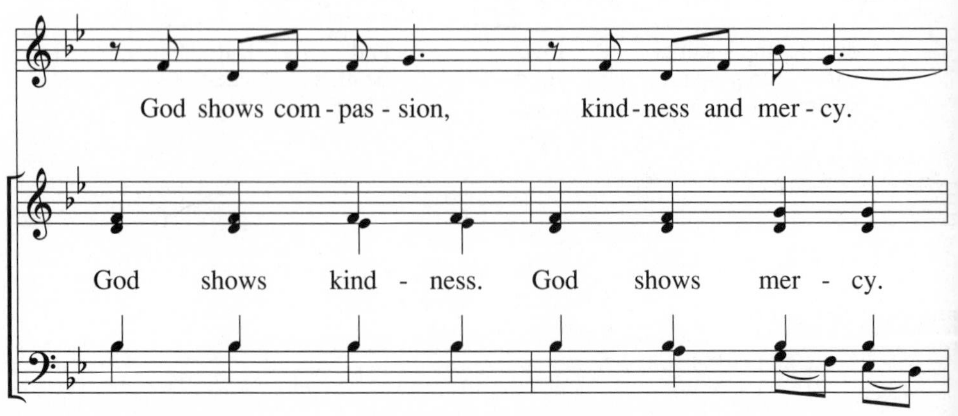
God shows com - pas - sion, kind - ness and mer - cy.
God shows kind - ness. God shows mer - cy.

God is gen - tle. Our God is rich in love.
God is gen - tle. God is rich in love.
Verse 1
1. Our God is mer - ci - ful. God's gen-tle kind-ness knows no end.
D.C.
And though our sins be great or small, God's love is our re-ward.
Verse 2
2. Our God is ten - der as a par - ent to a child.
D.C.
God re-mem-bers how we were made, re-mem-bers that we are dust.
Verse 3
3. God's love is e - ter - nal for those who live the law;
D.C.
for those who live the cov - e - nant; for those who keep the faith.

Text: Psalm 103: Bob Moore, b.1962
Tune: Bob Moore, b.1962

621 The Lord Will Heal the Broken Heart

Refrain
Melody:
The Lord will heal the bro - ken heart. God will
Harmony:
Heal the bro - ken heart. God will
Heal the bro - ken heart. God will
seek the lost and find them.
seek the lost and find them.
Verses
Cantor:
1. I will bless the Lord all of my days, I will
2. When the poor shall cry, they shall be saved. God will
3. You who live in love shall nev - er die. You who
bless the Lord and give God praise, For the hum - ble
hear your cry, live not in shame. God will guard your
keep your word need nev - er hide. For the Lord will

COMFORT

heart the Lord will guard. In the
life from sin's dis - tress. Let us
seek the right - eous soul. May the
D.C.
Fa - ther's care may you rest from harm.
fear the Lord, may God's name be blessed.
peace of God be your life and hope.

Text: Psalm 34; Liam Lawton, b.1959
Tune: Liam Lawton, b.1959; arr. John McCann, b.1961

622 I Heard the Voice of Jesus Say

1. I heard the voice of Je - sus say, "Come un - to me and rest; Lay down, O wea - ry one, lay down Your head up - on my breast." I came to Je - sus as I was, So
2. I heard the voice of Je - sus say, "Be - hold, I free - ly give The liv - ing wa - ter; thirst - y one, Stoop down, and drink, and live." I came to Je - sus, and I drank Of
3. I heard the voice of Je - sus say, "I am this dark world's light; Look un - to me, your morn shall rise, And all your day be bright." I looked to Je - sus, and I found In

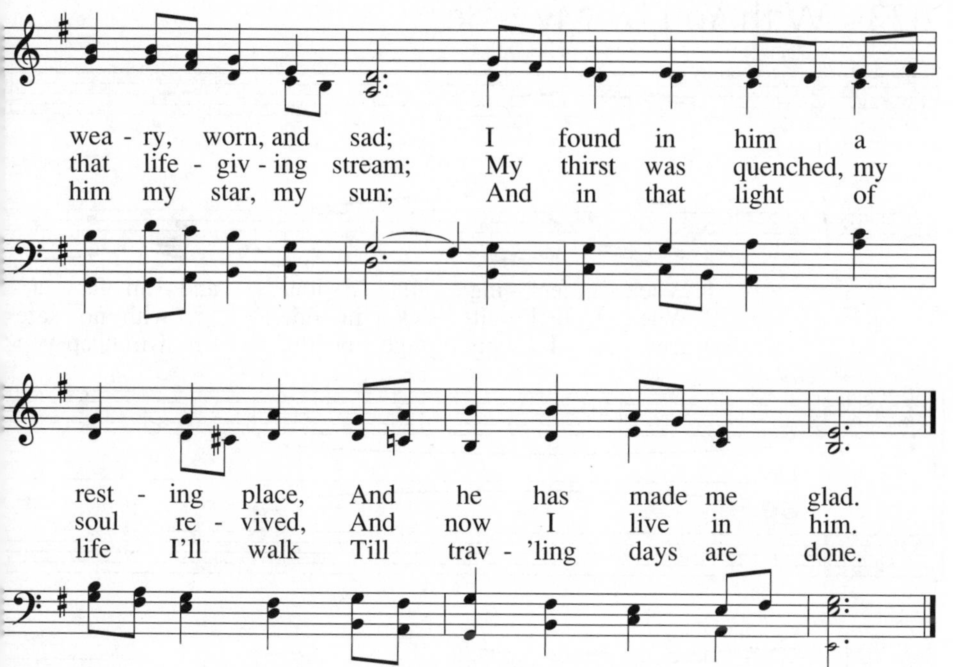
wea - ry, worn, and sad; I found in him a
that life - giv - ing stream; My thirst was quenched, my
him my star, my sun; And in that light of
rest - ing place, And he has made me glad.
soul re - vived, And now I live in him.
life I'll walk Till trav - 'ling days are done.

Text: Horatius Bonar, 1808-1889
Tune: KINGSFOLD, CMD; English; harm. by Ralph Vaughan Williams, 1872-1958, © Oxford University Press

623 With You by My Side

Verses
Cantor:
Choir:
div.
1. When I'm feel - ing all a - lone, and I'm far a - way from home, God, I need you to hear me.
2. When I feel all sick in - side, with no safe place to hide, God, I need you to lis - ten.
3. And as I go through my life, I will keep you in my sight to walk with me and be my strength.
Ooh
When my friends all turn a - way, then I ache to hear you say
When it seems I can't go on, then I long to hear the song
God, I know your plan for me: to help all those in need.

that you are with me through it all.
re - mind - ing me you are my friend.
To you a - lone I give my life!
Refrain
You are the light, you're the song that I'm sing - ing;
whom should I fear when you are with me? For
you are my God, and with you there is noth - ing I can't
do, with you by my side.
Last time

Text: David Haas, b.1957
Tune: David Haas, b.1957; choral arr. by David Haas, and Kate Cuddy, b.1953

624 Shepherd of My Heart

Verses
Melody:
Harmony:
1. My shep-herd is the Lord, for noth-ing shall I want;
2. If I should walk one day in - to the vale of dark-ness,
3. You a-noint my head with oil; my cup is o-ver-flow-ing;
green are the pas - tures where I'm led to re - pose.
no e - vil shall I fear with God at my side.
good-ness and kind-ness crown the days of my life.
Near wa - ters still and deep God will re - fresh my soul.
There with your crook and staff you give me strength and com-fort;
With - in the Lord's own house I dwell in peace for ev - er;
I am led on-ward in ways true to the Name.
you spread a ban-quet in the sight of my foes.
with - in the house of God my soul is at rest.

Refrain
Guide me, O shep-herd of my heart; lead me home-ward through the
day.
dark, in - to ev - er - last - ing, ev - er - last - ing.
Show me the way of truth and light; keep me al-ways in your
sight. May my life nev-er part from the shep-herd of my
heart.
Final ending

Text: Psalm 23; Francis Patrick O'Brien, b.1958
Tune: Francis Patrick O'Brien, b.1958

625 You Are All I Want

Refrain
You are all I want, you are all I need, you a - lone are my de - light. You shep-herd me with love, you lead me through the dark-ness of night. In you my heart shall rest.
You are all I want, are all I need, are my de - light. You shep - herd me with love, you lead me through the night. In you my heart shall rest.
Last time
Last time

COMFORT

Verse 1
1. O Lord, you are my God, my shep - herd and my
life. There's noth - ing I shall want. As I
lie in fields of green, near cool and gen - tle streams, my
heart is calm, my spir - it re - freshed.
D.C.
Verses 2, 3
2. With your staff, strong and true, you
3. You have spread a lav - ish feast, for
guide my life for you. Faith - ful is your name.
all my foes to see. You give me all I need. You a -
You are al - ways near, you com - fort all my fears. In the
noint my head with oil, you soothe and heal my soul. My
face of death, I shall not hide.
heart is full. I sing for joy.
D.C.

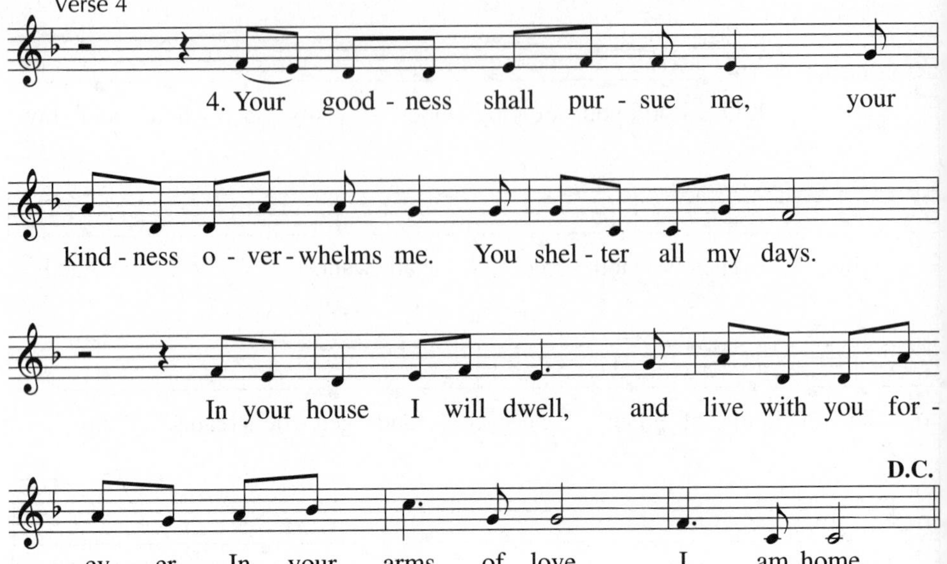
Verse 4
4. Your good - ness shall pur - sue me, your
kind - ness o - ver - whelms me. You shel - ter all my days.
In your house I will dwell, and live with you for -
ev - er. In your arms of love, I am home.
D.C.

Text: Psalm 23; Lori True, b.1961
Tune: Lori True, b.1961; acc. by David Haas, b.1957

Nada Te Turbe / Nothing Can Trouble 626

Ostinato Refrain
1.
Na - da te tur - be, na - da te es - pan - te. Quien a Dios tie - ne
Noth - ing can trou - ble, noth - ing can fright - en. Those who seek God shall
na - da le fal - ta.
nev - er go want - ing.
2.
So - lo Dios bas - ta.
God a - lone fills us.
Verses (Superimposed on Ostinato Refrain)
1
Cantor:
Ya no dur - máis, no dur - máis, pues que no hay
Stay a - wake, keep watch, there is no
paz en la tie - rra.
peace on the earth.
2
No hay a nin - gún co - bar - de,
Noth - ing can fright - en those
a - ven - tu - re - mos la vi - da.
who make the jour - ney and seek God.
No hay que te -
Noth - ing can
mer, no dur - máis, a - ven - tu - re - mos la vi - da.
fright - en those who make the jour - ney and seek God.

*Choose either part

Text: St. Teresa of Jesus; Taizé Community, 1986, 1991
Tune: Jacques Berthier, 1923-1994

627 You Are Mine

Verses

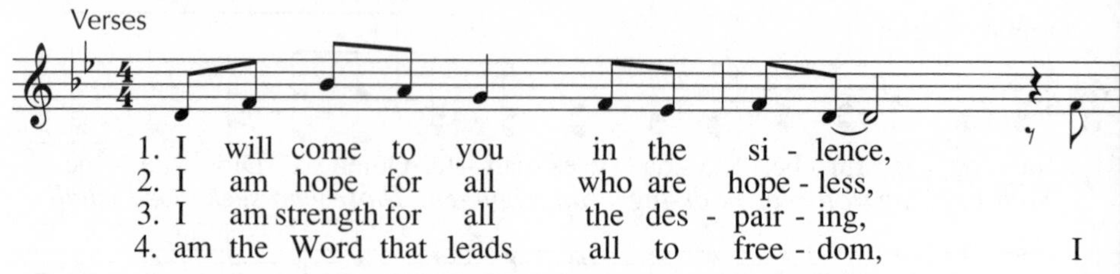
1. I will come to you in the si - lence,
2. I am hope for all who are hope - less,
3. I am strength for all the des - pair - ing,
4. am the Word that leads all to free - dom, I

I will lift you from all your fear.
I am eyes for all who long to see. In the
heal - ing for the ones who dwell in shame.
am the peace the world can - not give.

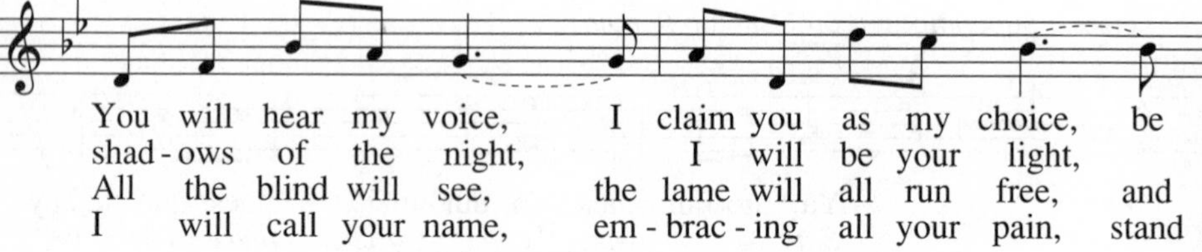
You will hear my voice, I claim you as my choice, be
shad - ows of the night, I will be your light,
All the blind will see, the lame will all run free, and
I will call your name, em - brac - ing all your pain, stand

still and know I am here. (To verse 2)
come and rest in me. (To refrain)
all will know my name. (To refrain)
up, now walk, and live! (To refrain)

Refrain

Melody:
Do not be a - fraid, I am with you.
Harmony:

I have called you each by name. Come and fol-low me,
I will bring you home; I love you and you are
mine.
D.C.
Final ending
4. I

Text: David Haas, b.1957
Tune: David Haas, b.1957

628 With a Shepherd's Care

Refrain

With a shep-herd's care, God leads us.
With a shep-herd's care, God leads us.
With a shep-herd's care,
With a shep-herd's

With a fa-ther's strength, God guides us.
With a fa-ther's strength, God guides us.
With a fa-ther's strength,
care,
With a fa-ther's

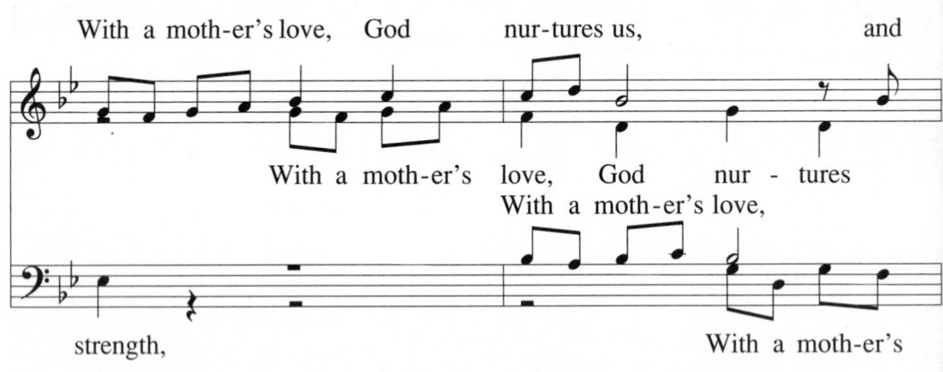
With a moth-er's love, God nur-tures us, and
With a moth-er's love, God nur - tures
With a moth-er's love,
strength,
With a moth-er's

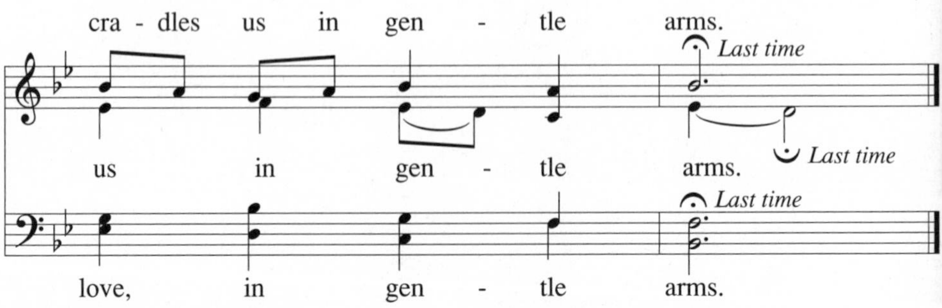
cra - dles us in gen - tle arms.
Last time
us in gen - tle arms.
Last time
Last time
love, in gen - tle arms.

COMFORT
Verses
unis.
div.
1. When we are lost, and can-not find the way, God cares for us and keeps us safe.
2. When we are weak, and cares press all a-round, God strength-ens us to face each day.
3. When we are scared, and feel so all a-lone, God loves us and is by our side.
God cares for us. For
God strength-ens us. For
God loves us. For
God is our light and our faith-ful guide, and leads us with a shep-herd's care.
God is our rock and our sav-ing help, and guides us with a fa-ther's strength.
God is our hope and our con-stant friend, and nur-tures with a moth-er's love.
with a shep-herd's care.
with a fa-ther's strength.
with a moth-er's love.
D.C.

Text: James J. Chepponis, b.1956
Tune: James J. Chepponis, b.1956

629 Live in the Light

Refrain

Melody:
Let your love be a light for our days, and a fire to keep us warm in the night.
Harmony:
Let your love be a guide on our way. May we learn to al - ways live in the light.
Last time
Last time
Verses 1, 2
Cantor:
1. When I'm a - lone or when I lose my way.
2. When I'm a - fraid of do-ing what is right,

Yours is the hand I can hold on
when there is no one who will help
to. When I was fall - en you
me. When I am sti - fled by
lift - ed me up. I was weak Lord, and you
fear and re - gret, your com - pas - sion and strength
div.
D.C.
pulled me through!
set me free!
Verse 3
Cantor:
3. God of all cre - a - tion,
God be - yond all time and all space,
God, look down with mer - cy and
keep me al - ways in your em - brace.
D.C.

Text: Michael Mahler, b.1981
Tune: Michael Mahler, b.1981

630 Come to Me, O Weary Traveler

1. Come to me, O wea - ry trav - 'ler; Come to me with your dis - tress; Come to me, you heav - y bur - dened; Come to me and find your rest.
2. Do not fear, my yoke is eas - y; Do not fear, my bur - den's light; Do not fear the path be - fore you; Do not run from me in fright.
3. Take my yoke and leave your trou - bles; Take my yoke and come with me. Take my yoke, I am be - side you; Take and learn hu - mil - i - ty.
4. Rest in me, O wea - ry trav - 'ler; Rest in me and do not fear. Rest in me, my heart is gen - tle; Rest and cast a - way your care.
1.- 3.
4.

Text: Matthew 11:28-30; Sylvia G. Dunstan, 1955-1993, © 1991, GIA Publications, Inc.
Tune: DUNSTAN, 8 7 8 7; Bob Moore, b.1962, © 1993, GIA Publications, Inc.

The King of Love My Shepherd Is 631

1. The King of love my shep - herd is, Whose good-ness
2. Where streams of liv - ing wa - ter flow My ran-somed
3. Con - fused and fool - ish oft I strayed, But yet in
4. In death's dark vale I fear no ill With you, dear
5. You spread a ta - ble in my sight; Your sav - ing
6. And so through all the length of days Your good-ness
3
fails me nev - er; I noth - ing lack if
soul he's lead - ing, And where the ver - dant
love he sought me; And on his shoul - der
Lord, be - side me, Your rod and staff my
grace be - stow - ing; And O what trans - port
fails me nev - er; Good Shep - herd, may I
I am his, And he is mine for ev - er.
pas - tures grow With food ce - les - tial feed - ing.
gent - ly laid, And home, re - joic - ing, brought me.
com - fort still, Your cross be - fore to guide me.
of de - light From your pure chal - ice flow - ing!
sing your praise With - in your house for ev - er.

Text: Psalm 23; Henry W. Baker, 1821-1877, alt.
Tune: ST. COLUMBA, 8 7 8 7; Gaelic; harm. by A. Gregory Murray, OSB, 1905-1992, © Downside Abbey

632 Jesus, Lead the Way

1. Je - sus, lead the way Through our life's long day, When at
2. Je - sus be our light, In the midst of night, Let not
3. When in deep - est grief, Strength - en our be - lief. When temp -
4. Je - sus, still lead on 'Til our rest be won: If you

times the way is cheer - less, Help us fol - low, calm and
faith - less fear o'er - take us, Let not faith and hope for-
ta - tions come al - lur - ing, Make us pa - tient and en-
lead us through rough plac - es, Grant us your re - deem - ing

fear - less; Guide us by your hand To the prom - ised land.
sake us; May we feel you near As we wor - ship here.
dur - ing; Lord we seek your grace In this ho - ly place.
grac - es. When our course is o'er, O - pen heav - en's door.

Text: *Jesu, geh voran;* Nicholas L. von Zinzendorf, 1700-1760; tr. by Jane Borthwick, 1813-1897, alt.
Tune: ROCHELLE, 55 88 55; Adam Drese, 1620-1701; harm. alt.

633 Come to Me

Refrain

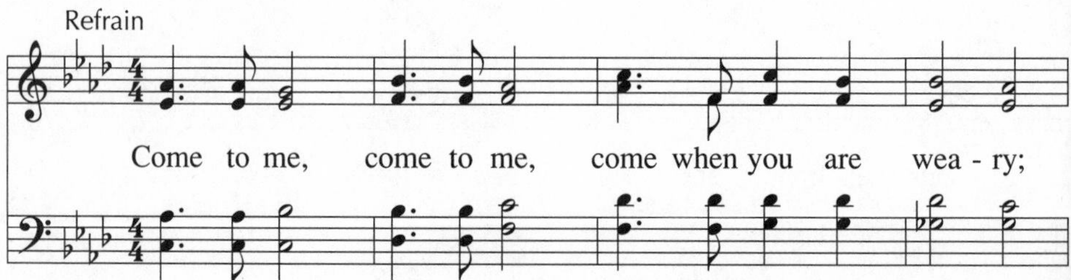
Come to me, come to me, come when you are wea - ry;

COMFORT

Last time
come to me, come to me, and I will give you rest.
Last time
Last time
Verses 1, 2
1. All who la - bor and are bur - dened,
2. Take my yoke up - on your shoul - ders,
all who la - bor and are bur - dened, let them
take my yoke up - on your shoul - ders, come and
come to me, come to me, and
learn from me, learn from me, for
D.C.
I will give them rest.
I am gen - tle of heart.
Verse 3
3. For the heart I hold is hum - ble, yes, the heart I hold is
hum - ble, and my yoke is eas - y, my
3
3
D.C.
bur - den light, and you will find rest for your souls.

Text: Matthew 11:28-30; Michael Joncas, b.1951
Tune: Michael Joncas, b.1951

634 Shelter Me, O God

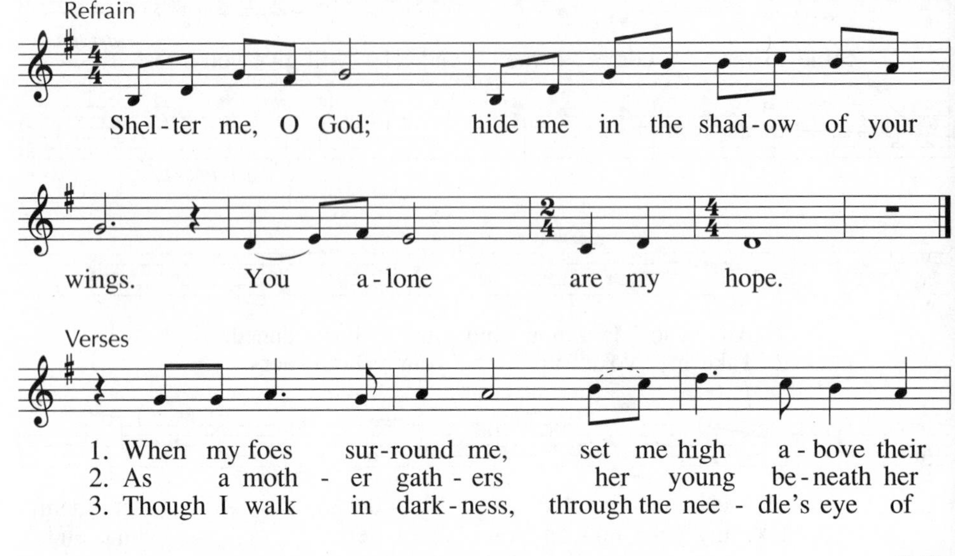
Refrain
Shel-ter me, O God; hide me in the shad-ow of your
wings. You a-lone are my hope.
Verses
1. When my foes sur-round me, set me high a-bove their
2. As a moth - er gath - ers her young be-neath her
3. Though I walk in dark-ness, through the nee - dle's eye of

D.C.
reach. Hear me when I call your name.
care, gath - er me in - to your arms.
death, you will nev - er leave my side.

Text: Psalm 16:1, 61:5, Luke 13:34; Bob Hurd, b.1950, © 1984, Bob Hurd
Tune: Bob Hurd, b.1950, © 1984, Bob Hurd; harm. by Craig S. Kingsbury, b.1952, © 1984, OCP Publications
Published by OCP Publications.

635 We Will Walk with God

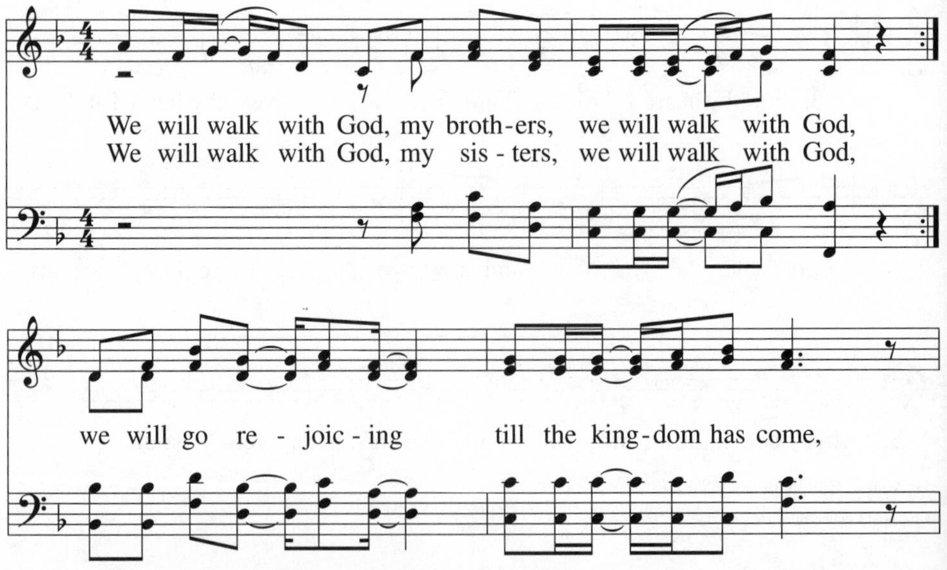
We will walk with God, my broth-ers, we will walk with God,
We will walk with God, my sis - ters, we will walk with God,
we will go re - joic - ing till the king-dom has come,

we will go re - joic - ing till the king-dom has come.

Text: Swaziland traditional, trans. by John L. Bell, b.1949, © 2002, The Iona Community, GIA Publications, Inc., agent
Tune: Swaziland traditional

Blest Are They 636

Verses 1-3

1. Blest are they, the poor in spir - it,
theirs is the king - dom of God.
Blest are they, full of sor - row,
they shall be con - soled.

2. Blest are they, the low - ly ones,
they shall in - her - it the earth.
Blest are they who hun - ger and thirst,
they shall have their fill.

3. Blest are they who show mer - cy,
mer - cy shall be theirs.
Blest are they, the pure of heart,
they shall see God!

Refrain

Descant:
Re - joice and be glad!
Melody:
Re - joice and be glad!
Men's voices:
Re - joice and be glad!

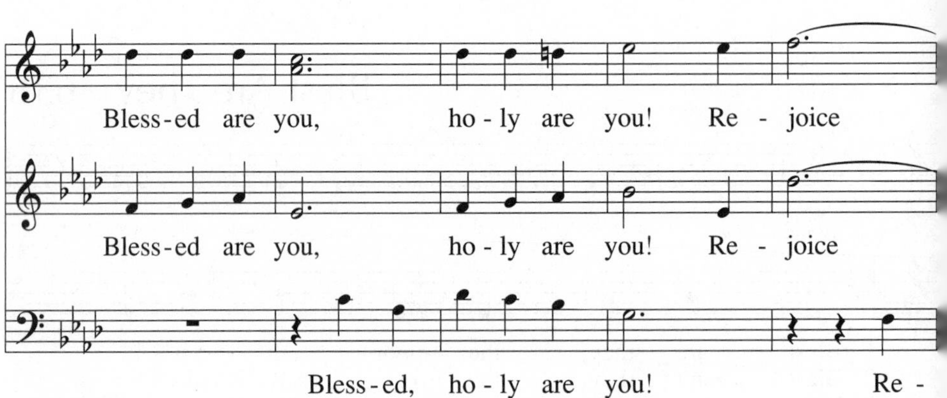
Bless-ed are you, ho - ly are you! Re - joice
Bless-ed are you, ho - ly are you! Re - joice
Bless-ed, ho - ly are you! Re -

and be glad! Yours is the king-dom of
and be glad! Yours is the king-dom of
joice and be glad! Yours is the king-dom of

1.- 4.
To verses
Last time
God!
God!
God!
God!
God!
God!
Verses 4, 5
4. Blest are they who seek peace;
5. Blest are you who suf - fer hate,
they are the chil - dren of God.
all be - cause of me. Re -
Blest are they who suf - fer in faith, the
joice and be glad, yours is the king-dom;
To refrain
glo - ry of God is theirs.
shine for all to see.

Text: Matthew 5:3-12; David Haas, b.1957
Tune: David Haas, b.1957; vocal arr. by David Haas and Michael Joncas, b.1951

637 The Kingdom of God

Ostinato Refrain

The king - dom of God is jus - tice and peace and
joy in the Ho - ly Spir - it. Come, Lord, and
o - pen in us the gates of your king - dom.
Last time
Last time

Text: Community of Taizé
Tune: Community of Taizé

Within the Reign of God 638

Verses

Cantor:

1. Come now, the feast is spread; in Je - sus' name we break the bread.
2. Stand up and do not fear, for Christ is tru - ly pres - ent here.
3. Wel - come the weak and poor, the sin - ner finds an o - pen door,
4. All fear and ha - tred ends and foes be - come our faith - ful friends,
5. Sing out the ju - bi - lee when those en - slaved are all set free,
6. One earth, one ho - ly band, one fam - 'ly as our God has planned,

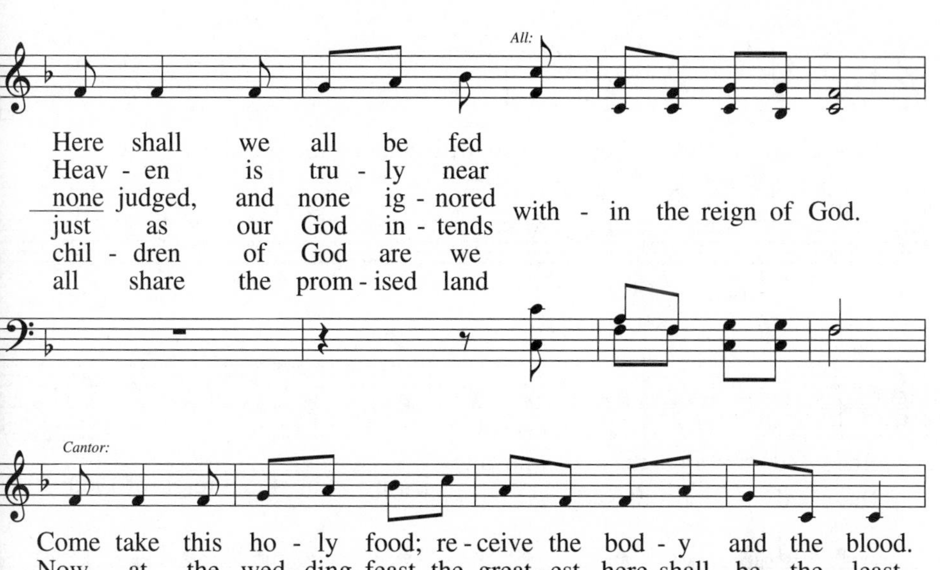
All:
Here shall we all be fed
Heav - en is tru - ly near
none judged, and none ig - nored
just as our God in - tends
chil - dren of God are we
all share the prom - ised land
with - in the reign of God.
Cantor:

Come take this ho - ly food; re - ceive the bod - y and the blood.
Now at the wed - ding feast, the great - est here shall be the least.
Here shall the wea - ry rest, the stran - ger be a wel-come guest.
All you who seek God's face are wel-come in this ho - ly place;
No more can we for - get the ones who bear life's crush-ing debt;
Come now, the feast is spread, in Je - sus' name we break the bread;

All:
Grace is a might - y flood
All bonds shall be re - leased
So shall we all be blest
join in the feast of grace
God's jus - tice guides us yet
here shall we all be fed
with - in the reign of God.

Refrain
Bless-ed are they who will feast in the reign of God.
Bless-ed, oh bless - ed,
oh bless - ed,
Bless-ed are they who will share the bread of life.
oh bless - ed,
Bless - ed are they who are least in the reign of God;
Bless - ed, oh bless - ed,
oh bless - ed,
Last time
they shall re - joice at the feast of life.
Last time
re - joice

Text: Marty Haugen, b.1950
Tune: Marty Haugen, b.1950

The Kingdom of God 639

1. The king - dom of God is jus - tice and joy;
2. The king - dom of God is mer - cy and grace;
3. The king - dom of God is chal - lenge and choice:
4. God's king - dom is come, the gift and the goal;
For Je - sus re - stores what sin would de - stroy.
The cap - tives are freed, the sin - ners find place,
Be - lieve the good news, re - pent and re - joice!
In Je - sus be - gun, in heav - en made whole.
God's pow - er and glo - ry in Je - sus we know;
The out - cast are wel - comed God's ban - quet to share;
God's love for us sin - ners brought Christ to his cross:
The heirs of the king - dom shall an - swer his call;
And here and here - af - ter the king - dom shall grow.
And hope is a - wak - ened in place of de - spair.
Our cri - sis of judge - ment for gain or for loss.
And all things cry "Glo - ry!" to God all in all.

Text: Bryn A. Rees, 1911-1983,
Tune: LAUDATE DOMINUM, 10 10 11 11; Charles H. H. Parry, 1848-1918

640 Bring Forth the Kingdom

Verses
Cantor:
1. You are salt for the earth, O peo - ple:
2. You are a light on the hill, O peo - ple:
3. You are a seed of the Word, O peo - ple:
4. We are a blest and a pil - grim peo - ple:
All:
Salt for the King - dom of God!
Light for the Cit - y of God!
Bring forth the King - dom of God!
Bound for the King - dom of God!
Cantor:
Share the fla - vor of life, O peo - ple:
Shine so ho - ly and bright, O peo - ple:
Seeds of mer - cy and seeds of jus - tice,
Love our jour - ney and love our home - land:
All:
Life in the King - dom of God!
Shine for the King - dom of God!
Grow in the King - dom of God!
Love is the King - dom of God!
Refrain
Melody:
Harmony:
Bring forth the King - dom of mer - cy, Bring forth the King - dom of peace; Bring forth the King - dom of jus - tice, Bring forth the Cit - y of God!

Text: Marty Haugen, b.1950
Tune: Marty Haugen, b.1950

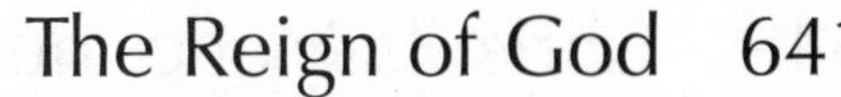

The Reign of God 641

1. The reign of God, like farm - er's field, Bears weeds a - long with wheat; The good and bad are in - ter - twined Till har - vest is com - plete.
2. Like mus - tard tree, the reign of God From ti - ny seed will spread, Till birds of ev - 'ry feath - er come To nest, and there be fed.
3. Though hid - den now, the reign of God May, yet un - no - ticed, grow; From deep with - in it ris - es up, Like yeast in swell - ing dough.
4. The reign of God is come in Christ; The reign of God is near. A - blaze a - mong us, kind - ling hearts, The reign of God is here!

Text: Delores Dufner, OSB, b.1939, © 1995, 2003, GIA Publications, Inc.
Tune: MCKEE, CM; African American; adapt. by Harry T. Burleigh, 1866-1949

642 Christ Is Made the Sure Foundation

1. Christ is made the sure foun - da - tion, Christ the head and cor - ner - stone; Cho - sen of the Lord, and pre - cious, Bind - ing all the Church in one; Ho - ly Zi - on's help for ev - er, And her con - fi - dence a - lone.
2. To this tem - ple where we call you, Come, O Lord of hosts, to - day; With your wont - ed lov - ing kind - ness Hear your ser - vants as they pray, And your full - est ben - e - dic - tion Shed in all its bright ar - ray.
3. Grant, we pray, to all your peo - ple, All the grace they ask to gain; What they gain from you for ev - er With the bless - ed to re - tain, And here - af - ter in your glo - ry Ev - er - more with you to reign.

Text: *Angularis fundamentum*; 11th C.; tr. by John M. Neale, 1818-1866, alt.
Tune: ST. THOMAS, 8 7 8 7 8 7; John Wade, 1711-1786

As a Fire Is Meant for Burning 643

1. As a fire is meant for burn - ing With a
2. We are learn - ers; we are teach - ers; We are
3. As a green bud in the spring - time Is a
bright and warm-ing flame, So the church is meant for
pil - grims on the way. We are seek - ers; we are
sign of life re-newed, So may we be signs of
mis - sion, Giv-ing glo - ry to God's name.
giv - ers; We are ves - sels made of clay.
one - ness 'Mid earth's peo - ples, man - y hued.
Not to preach our creeds or cus - toms, But to
By our gen - tle, lov-ing ac - tions, We would
As a rain - bow lights the heav - ens When a
build a bridge of care, We join hands a - cross the
show that Christ is light. In a hum - ble, lis-t'ning
storm is past and gone, May our lives re - flect the
na - tions, Find-ing neigh - bors ev - 'ry - where.
Spir - it, We would live to God's de - light.
ra - diance Of God's new and glor-ious dawn.

Text: Ruth Duck, b.1947, © 1992, GIA Publications, Inc.
Tune: BEACH SPRING, 8 7 8 7 D; *The Sacred Harp,* 1844; harm. by Marty Haugen, b.1950, © 1985, GIA Publications, Inc.

644 Sing a New Church

1. Sum - moned by the God who made us Rich in
2. Ra - diant ris - en from the wa - ter; Robed in
3. Trust the good - ness of cre - a - tion; Trust the
4. Bring the hopes of ev - 'ry na - tion; Bring the
5. Draw to - geth - er at one ta - ble All the
our di - ver - si - ty, Gath - ered in the name of
ho - li - ness and light, Male and fe - male in God's
Spir - it strong with - in. Dare to dream the vi - sion
art of ev - 'ry race. Weave a song of peace and
hu - man fam - i - ly; Shape a cir - cle ev - er
Je - sus, Rich - er still in u - ni - ty:
im - age, Male and fe - male, God's de - light:
prom - ised Sprung from seed of what has been.
jus - tice: Let it sound through time and space.
wid - er And a peo - ple ev - er free.

Let us bring the gifts that dif - fer And, in
splen - did, var - ied ways, Sing a new church in - to
be - ing, One in faith and love and praise.

Text: Delores Dufner, OSB, b.1939, © 1991, Sisters of St. Benedict. Published by OCP Publications.
Tune: NETTLETON, 8 7 8 7 D, from *Wyeth's Repository of Sacred Music, Pt. II*, 1813

645 Somos el Cuerpo de Cristo / We Are the Body of Christ

Refrain
So-mos el cuer-po de Cris-to. We are the bod-y of Christ.
So-mos el cuer-po de Cris-to. We are the bod-y of Christ.
He-mos o-í-do el lla-ma-do; we've an-swered "Yes," to the call of the Lord. (*Oh!)
Tra-e-mos su san-to men-sa-je. We come to bring the good news to the
1.
2.
To verses
world.
3. Que
Final ending
world. (*Oh!)

*Sing after Verse 2 (optional)

Verses
Cantor:
All:
1. Dios vie-ne al mun-do a tra - vés de no - so-tros.
mun-do a cum-plir la mi - sión de la I-gle-sia,
2. Ca - da per - so - na es par - te del rei - no;
To - das las ra - zas que ha - bi - tan la tie - rra,
3. nues-tras ac - cio - nes re - fle-jen jus - ti - cia;
Va - mos al mun-do a cui - dar su re - ba - ño.
So-mos el cuer-po de
Cris-to.
God is re-vealed when we love one an-oth - er.
Bring-ing the light of God's mer - cy to oth - ers,
Put - ting a stop to all dis-crim - i - na - tion,
All are in - vit - ed to feast in the ban - quet.
Stop - ping a - buse and re - liev - ing the hun - gry,
Serv - ing each oth - er we build up the king-dom;
We are the bod - y of Christ.
1.
2.
(1.) Al
(2.) Christ.
(3.)
D.C.

Text: Jaime Cortez, b.1963, and Bob Hurd, b.1950
Tune: Jaime Cortez, b.1963; acc. by Jeffrey Honoré, b.1956

646 O Christ the Great Foundation

1. O Christ the great foun - da - tion On
2. Bap - tized in one con - fes - sion, One
3. Where ty - rants' hold is tight - ened, Where
4. This is the mo - ment glo - rious When
which your peo - ple stand To preach your true sal -
church in all the earth, We bear our Lord's im -
strong de - vour the weak, Where in - no - cents are
he who once was dead Shall lead his church vic -
va - tion In ev - 'ry age and land: Pour
pres - sion, The sign of sec - ond birth: One
fright - ened The right - eous fear to speak, There
to - rious, Their cham - pion and their head. The
out your Ho - ly Spir - it To make us strong and
ho - ly peo - ple gath - ered In love be - yond our
let your church a - wak - ing At - tack the pow'rs of
Lord of all cre - a - tion His heav'n - ly kingdom

pure, To keep the faith un - bro - ken As
own, By grace we were in - vit - ed, By
sin And, all their ram - parts break - ing, With
brings The fi - nal con - sum - ma - tion, The
long as worlds en - dure.
grace we make you known.
you the vic - tory win.
glo - ry of all things.

Text: Timothy T'ingfang Lew, 1891-1947, alt., © Christian Conference of Asia
Tune: AURELIA, 7 6 7 6 D; Samuel Sebastian Wesley, 1810-1876

647 Where Your Treasure Is

Refrain
Where your treas-ure is, there your heart shall be. All that
there your heart shall be.
you pos-sess will nev-er set you free. Seek the
things that last; come and learn from me. Where your
Fourth time to Vs. 4
1.-3. To verses 1-3
Last time
treas-ure is, your heart shall be. be.

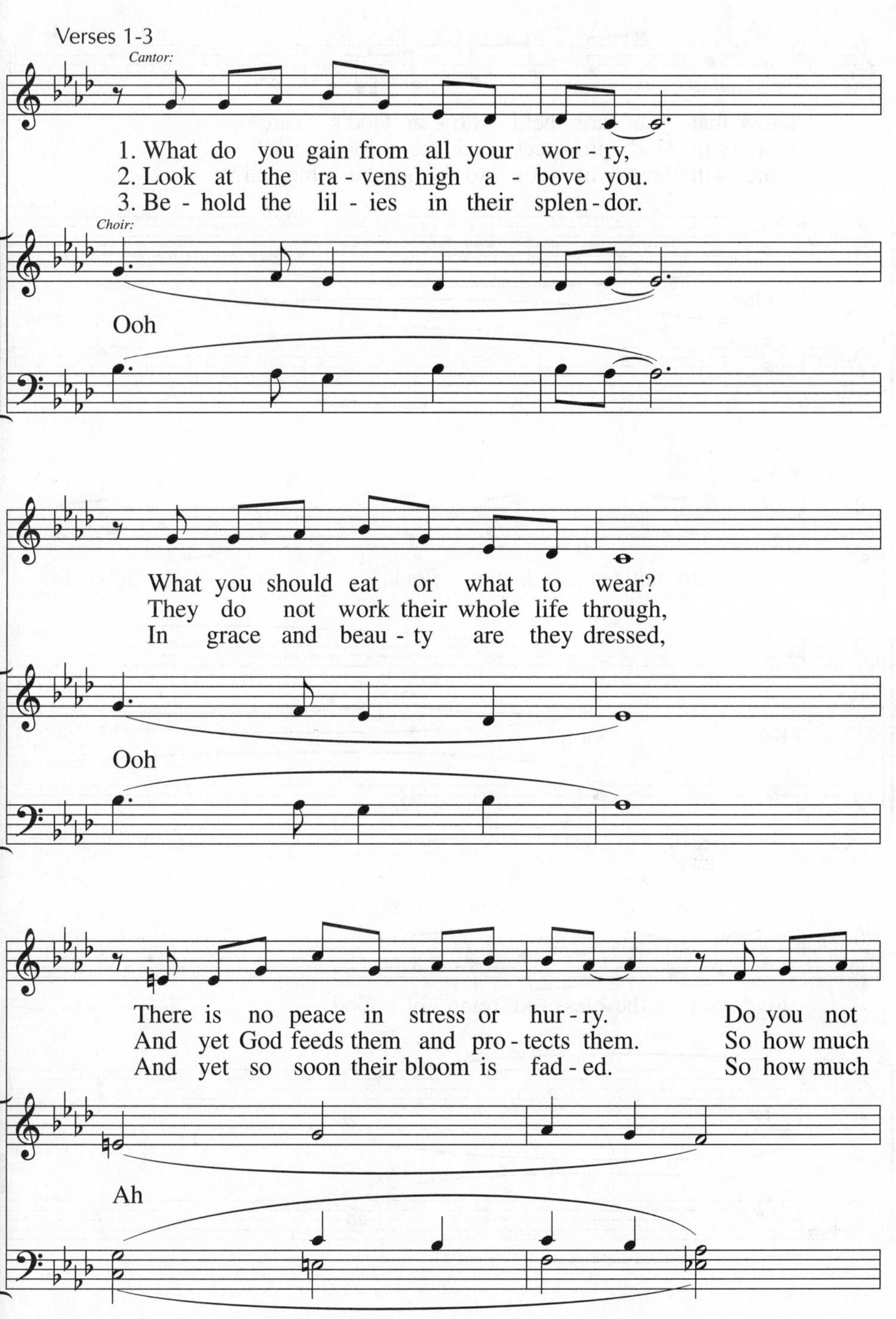
Verses 1-3
Cantor:
1. What do you gain from all your wor - ry,
2. Look at the ra - vens high a - bove you.
3. Be - hold the lil - ies in their splen - dor.
Choir:
Ooh
What you should eat or what to wear?
They do not work their whole life through,
In grace and beau - ty are they dressed,
Ooh
There is no peace in stress or hur - ry.
And yet God feeds them and pro - tects them.
And yet so soon their bloom is fad - ed.
Do you not
So how much
So how much
Ah

D.C.
know that you are held with - in God's care?
more will God pro - tect and care for you?
more will those who look to God be blessed?
D.C.
Ooh
Verse 4
Cantor:
4. Do not fear, lit-tle flock, for God de-lights to
Choir:
be.
Ooh
give you the bless - ed reign of God.

Give your pos-ses-sions to the need-y; gain a
Ah
gain a
D.C.
treas - ure that will not fade.
fade.
D.C.
treas - ure that will not, will not fade.
fade.

Text: Luke 12:22-34; Marty Haugen, b.1950
Tune: Marty Haugen, b.1950

648 Jesus, Your Spirit in Us

Ostinato Refrain
Je - sus, your Spir - it in us is a well-spring of life ev-er-last-ing.
Verses (Superimposed over Ostinato Refrain)
1. O God, you are my God, for you I long, my soul thirsts for
you. I wish to gaze up-on you, Lord, in your dwell-ing, be-
hold - ing your pow-er and your glo - ry. 2. Your stead-fast love is
bet - ter than life, my mouth will sing your praise. I will
bless you, O Lord, as long as I live, in your name, lift up my
hands. 3. You have been my help, Lord; in the
shad-ow of your wings I sing for joy. My soul clings to you,
O God, your right hand holds me fast.

Text: Psalm 63:1-4, 7-8; Taizé Community
Tune: Taizé Community

Your Wonderful Love 649

Cantor:
1. From
Verse 1
dark - ness to light, from sad-ness to joy,
lead us, lead us O God. The
way may be cloud-y, the storms give us fright, but to-
geth - er we con - quer the night.
Refrain
We will walk through the dark - ness, ev-er close by your
side. We will car - ry each oth - er, your com-

pas - sion our guide. We will share in the sto - ry of
bod - y and blood. We will live in your
Last time to coda
won - der - ful love.
won - der - ful, won - der - ful love.
To verses 2 and 3
Verse 2
Cantor:
2. Called as com - pan - ions, called to be free,
sis - ters and broth - ers as one.
Shar - ing the bur - den, light - 'ning the load as we

D.S.
bring forth the day of your Son.
Verse 3
Cantor:
3. One day we'll rise and, healed of our pain, we'll
walk, walk in the sun.
No more con - fu - sion, we'll be whole a - gain, We will
D.S.
fol - low 'til king - dom comes.
Coda
unis.
won - der - ful love. We will
live in your won - der - ful love.

Text: Francis Patrick O'Brien, b.1958
Tune: Francis Patrick O'Brien, b.1958

650 Pues Si Vivimos / When We Are Living

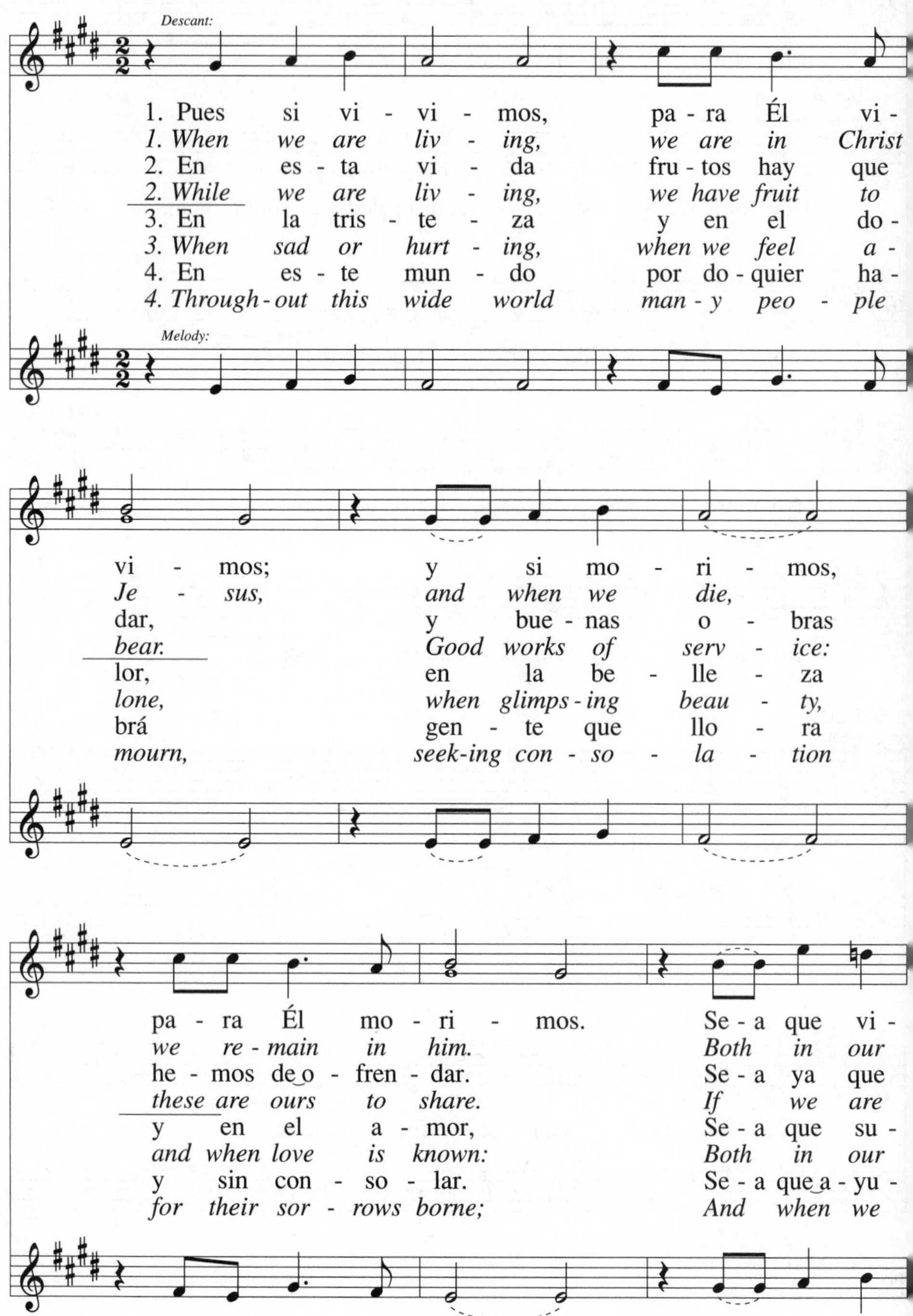
Descant:
Melody:
1. Pues si vi - vi - mos, pa - ra Él vi - vi - mos; y si mo - ri - mos, pa - ra Él mo - ri - mos. Se - a que vi -
1. When we are liv - ing, we are in Christ Je - sus, and when we die, we re - main in him. Both in our
2. En es - ta vi - da fru - tos hay que dar, y bue - nas o - bras he - mos de‿o - fren - dar. Se - a ya que
2. While we are liv - ing, we have fruit to bear. Good works of serv - ice: these are ours to share. If we are
3. En la tris - te - za y en el do - lor, en la be - lle - za y en el a - mor, Se - a que su -
3. When sad or hurt - ing, when we feel a - lone, when glimps - ing beau - ty, and when love is known: Both in our
4. En es - te mun - do por do - quier ha - brá gen - te que llo - ra y sin con - so - lar. Se - a que‿a - yu -
4. Through - out this wide world man - y peo - ple mourn, seek-ing con - so - la - tion for their sor - rows borne; And when we

va - mos o que mu - ra - mos,
liv - ing, and in our dy - ing,
de - mos o que re - ci - ba - mos,
giv - ing or are re - ceiv - ing,
fra - mos o que go - ce - mos,
suf - f'ring and our re - joic - ing,
de - mos o que a - li - men - te - mos,
help them or when we feed them,
so-mos del Se -
we are the
D.C.
Last time
ñor, so - mos del Se - ñor.
Lord's, we be - long to him.

651 Bambelela / Never Give Up

Leader (beginning second time):
O bam - be - le - la, O bam - be - le - la,
no nev - er give up, no nev - er give up,
Bam - be - le - la, bam - be - le - la, O
Nev - er give up, nev - er give up, no
O bam - be - le - la, O
no nev - er give up, no
bam - be - le - la, bam - be - le - la,
nev - er give up, nev - er give up,
bam - ba, bam - ba, bam - ba, bam - ba, O
nev - er, nev - er, nev - er, nev - er, no
bam - ba, bam - ba, bam - ba, bam - ba, bam - ba, O
nev - er, nev - er, nev - er, nev - er, nev - er, no

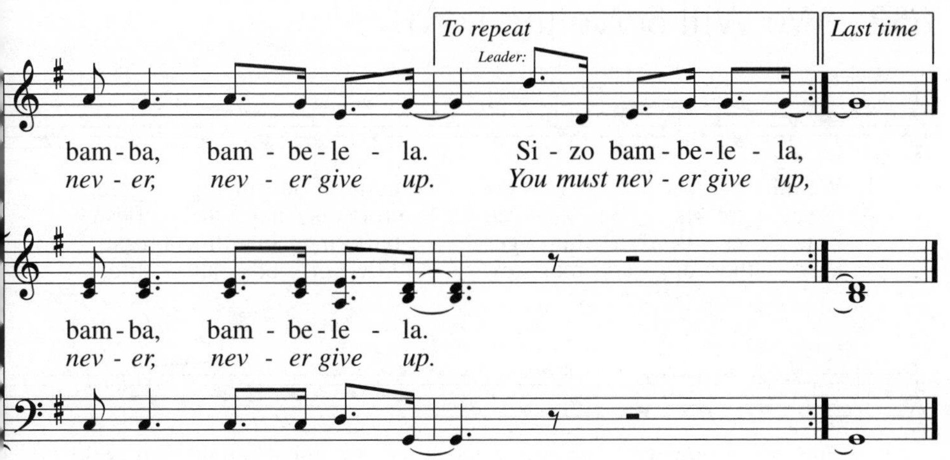
To repeat
Last time
Leader:
bam - ba, bam - be - le - la. Si - zo bam - be - le - la,
nev - er, nev - er give up. You must nev - er give up,
bam - ba, bam - be - le - la.
nev - er, nev - er give up.

Text: Traditional South African
Tune: Traditional South African; tr. by Mairi Munro and Martine Stemerick; adapt. by Mairi Munro and Philip Jakob

652 We Will Serve the Lord

Verses

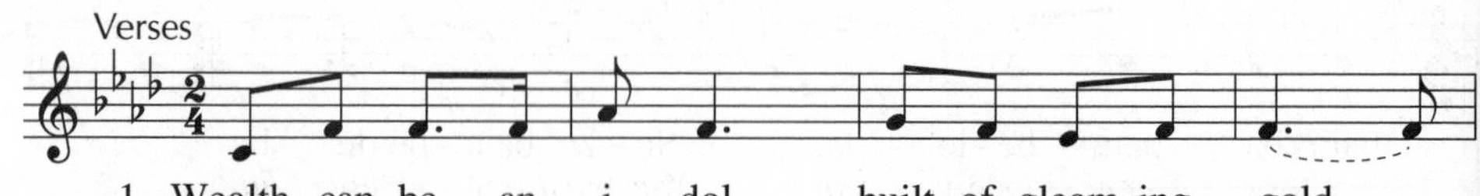

1. Wealth can be an i - dol built of gleam-ing gold,
2. Pleas - ure is a si - ren, prom - is - ing the flesh
3. Pow - er is a hun - ger, burn-ing in the breast, to
4. Fa - ther of all mer - cy, Giv - er of all life,

bring-ing dreams of par - a - dise, fu - tures bought and sold.
brief re - lief from emp - ti - ness, a hid - ing place from death.
walk a - mong the might-y and tram - ple on the rest.
here we speak our cov - e - nant a - bove the nois - y strife.

Some will choose to gath - er it, all that they can hoard, but
Some will choose to chase it, un - til it leaves them bored, but
Some will choose to gain it by lie or guile, or sword, but
Hear us shout in glo - ry a - bove the pa - gan horde:

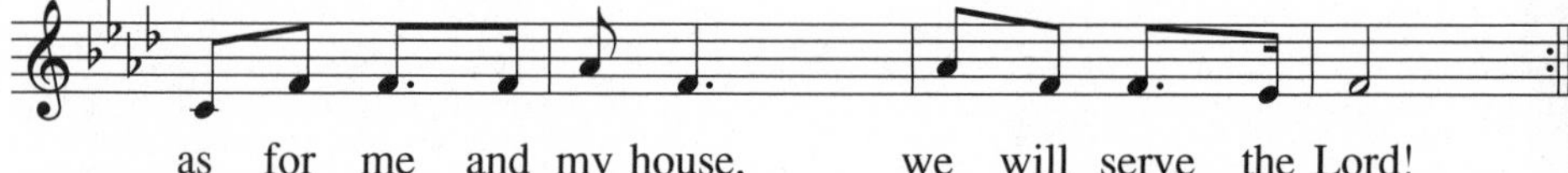

as for me and my house, we will serve the Lord!

Refrain

Melody:
Tenor:
Alto:

As for me and my house, we will serve the Lord,

we will serve the Lord, we will serve the Lord!

Text: Rory Cooney, b.1952
Tune: Rory Cooney, b.1952

On a Journey Together 653

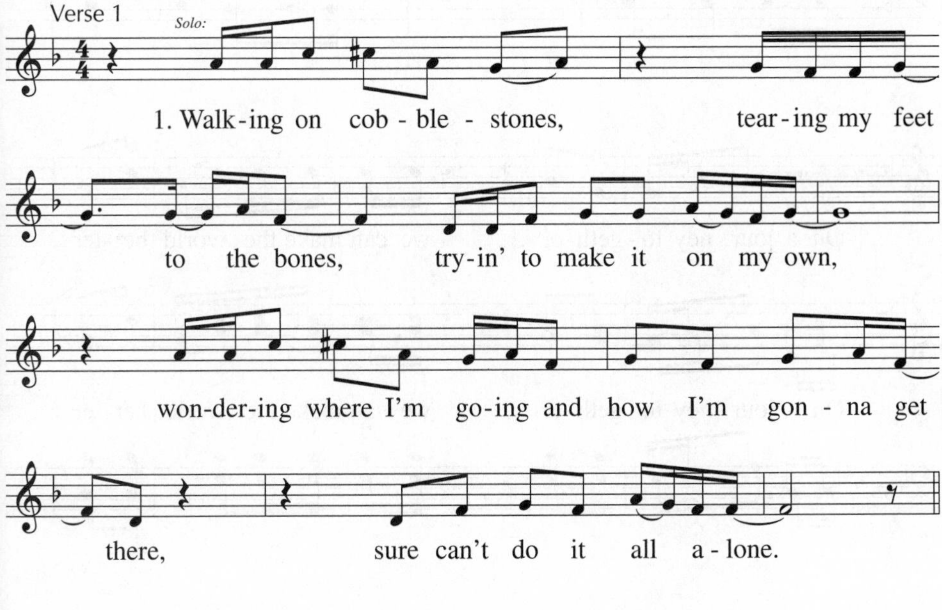

Verse 1

Solo:

1. Walk-ing on cob - ble - stones, tear-ing my feet to the bones, try-in' to make it on my own,

won-der-ing where I'm go-ing and how I'm gon - na get there, sure can't do it all a-lone.

Refrain
Melody:
On a jour - ney to - geth - er we can fare an - y weath - er,
On a jour - ney to - geth - er we can fare an - y weath - er,
keep - ing Christ the cen - ter of our com - mu - ni - ty.
keep - ing Christ the cen - ter of our com - mu - ni - ty.
On a jour - ney to - geth - er we can make the world bet - ter
On a jour - ney to - geth - er we can make the world bet - ter

Last time to Coda
To verses 2 and 3
by for-giv-ing and lov-ing start-ing with you and me.
Last time to Coda
To verses 2 and 3
by for-giv-ing and lov - ing, you and me.
Verse 2
Solo:
2. All of the mis-takes I made, tak-ing man-y wrong turns,
are real-ly les - sons that I learned. So ev-'ry time I
D.S.
start to stum - ble I re-main hum - ble to God's love and his word.
Verse 3
Solo:
3. Trav-'ling on this road to Je-sus, know-ing that
vi-sion is the key to un-der-stand where we've been and
D.S.
where we are and want to be, now it starts with you and me.

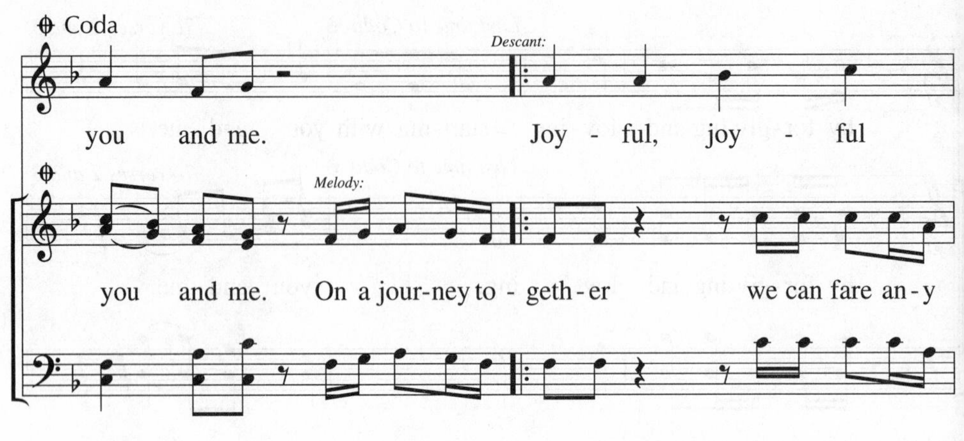
Coda
Descant:
you and me. Joy - ful, joy - ful
Melody:
you and me. On a jour-ney to - geth - er we can fare an - y

we a - dore you, God of glo - ry,
weath-er, keep-ing Christ the cen - ter of our com-

Lord of love; Hearts un - fold like
mun - i - ty. On a jour-ney to-geth - er we can make the world

flow'rs be - fore you, O - p'ning to the
bet - ter by for - giv - ing and lov - ing, start - ing with
sun a - bove.
you and me. On a jour - ney to - geth - er.

Text: John Angotti
Tune: John Angotti

654 All That Is Hidden

Verses

1. If you would fol-low me, fol - low where life will lead:
2. If you would hon - or me, hon - or the least of these:
3. If you would speak of me, live all your life in me:
4. If you would rise with me, rise through your des - ti - ny:

do not look for me a - mong the dead, for I am
you will not find me dressed in fin - er - y. My Word cries
my ways are not the ways that you would choose; my thoughts are
do not re-fuse the death which brings you life, for as the

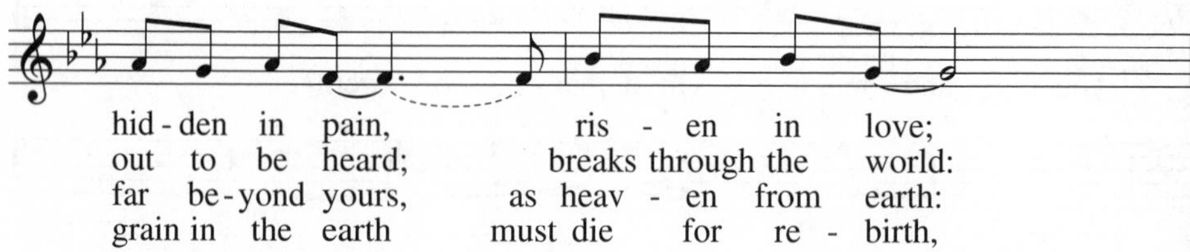

hid-den in pain, ris - en in love;
out to be heard; breaks through the world:
far be-yond yours, as heav - en from earth:
grain in the earth must die for re - birth,

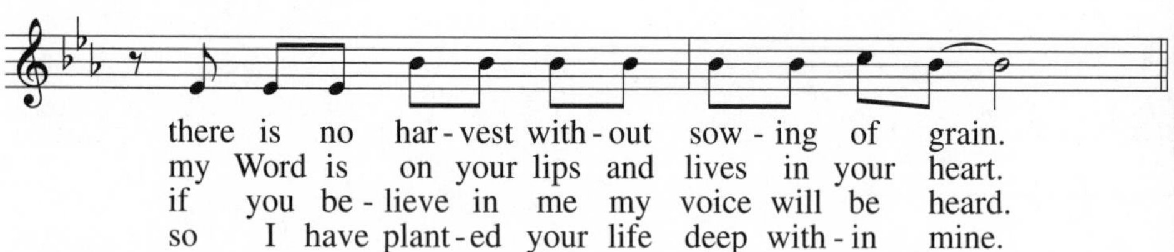

there is no har-vest with-out sow - ing of grain.
my Word is on your lips and lives in your heart.
if you be - lieve in me my voice will be heard.
so I have plant-ed your life deep with-in mine.

Refrain

All that is hid-den will be made clear.

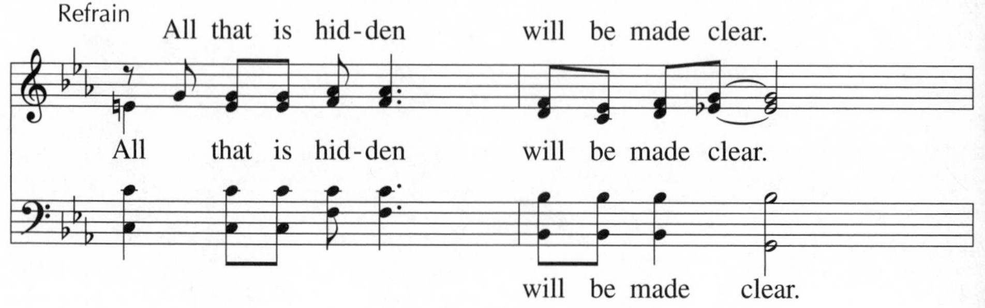

All that is hid-den will be made clear.

will be made clear.

All that is dark now will be re-vealed.
All that is dark now will be re-vealed.
What you have heard in the dark pro-claim in the light;
What you have heard in the dark pro-claim in the
what you hear in whis - pers
light; what you hear in whis-pers
hear in whis-pers
pro-claim from the house - tops.
Last time
pro - claim from the house-tops.
Last time

Text: Refrain based on Luke 12:2-3, Bernadette Farrell, b.1957
Tune: Bernadette Farrell, b.1957; choral arr. by Paul Inwood, b.1947

655 Take This Moment

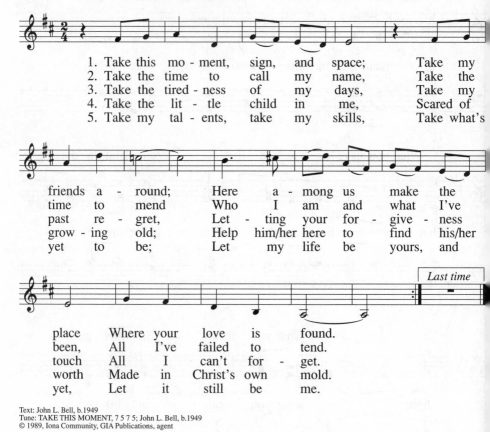

1. Take this moment, sign, and space;
Take my friends around;
Here among us make the place
Where your love is found.

2. Take the time to call my name,
Take the time to mend
Who I am and what I've been,
All I've failed to tend.

3. Take the tiredness of my days,
Take my past regret,
Letting your forgiveness touch
All I can't forget.

4. Take the little child in me,
Scared of growing old;
Help him/her here to find his/her worth
Made in Christ's own mold.

5. Take my talents, take my skills,
Take what's yet to be;
Let my life be yours, and yet,
Let it still be me.

Last time

Text: John L. Bell, b.1949
Tune: TAKE THIS MOMENT, 7 5 7 5; John L. Bell, b.1949

656 Whatsoever You Do

Refrain
What-so-ev-er you do to the least of my peo-ple,
that you do un-to me.

Verses
1. When I was hun - gry, you gave me to eat;
2. When I was home - less, you o - pened your door;
3. When I was wea - ry, you helped me find rest;
4. When I was lit - tle, you taught me to read;
5. When in a pris - on, you came to my cell;
6. In a strange coun - try, you made me at home;
7. Hurt in a bat - tle, you bound up my wounds;
8. When I was Black, or La - ti - no, or white;
9. When I was a - ged, you both - ered to smile;
10. You saw me cov - ered with spit - tle and blood;
11. When I was laughed at, you stood by my side;
When I was thirst - y, you gave me to drink.
When I was na - ked, you gave me your coat.
When I was anx - ious, you calmed all my fears.
When I was lone - ly, you gave me your love.
When on a sick - bed, you cared for my needs.
Seek - ing em - ploy - ment, you found me a job.
Search - ing for kind - ness, you held out your hand.
Mocked and in - sult - ed, you car - ried my cross.
When I was rest - less, you lis - tened and cared.
You knew my fea - tures, though grim - y with sweat.
When I was hap - py, you shared in my joy.
D.C.
Now en - ter in - to the home of my Fa - ther.

Text: Matthew 5:3-12; Willard F. Jabusch, b.1930
Tune: WHATSOEVER YOU DO, 10 10 11 with refrain; Willard F. Jabusch, b.1930; harm. by Robert J. Batastini, b.1942

657 'Tis the Gift to Be Simple

'Tis the gift to be sim-ple, 'tis the gift to be free, 'tis the
gift to come down where we ought to be, and
when we find our-selves in the place just right, 'twill
be in the val - ley of love and de - light.
When true sim - plic - i - ty is gained to bow and to bend we
shan't be a-shamed, to turn, turn, will be our de-light till by
turn - ing, turn - ing we come round right.

Text: Shaker Song, 18th. C.
Tune: SIMPLE GIFTS; acc. Margaret W. Mealy, b.1922, © 1984

Keep in Mind 658

Refrain
Keep in mind that Je - sus Christ has died for
us and is ris - en from the dead. He
is our sav-ing Lord, he is joy for all a - ges.
Verse 1
D.C.
1. If we die with the Lord, we shall live with the Lord.
If we en - dure with the Lord, we shall reign with the Lord.
Verses 2, 3
D.C.
2. In Christ all our sor - row, in Christ all our joy.
In him hope of glo - ry, in him all our love.
3. In Christ our re - demp - tion, in Christ all our grace.
In him our sal - va - tion, in him all our peace.

Text: 2 Timothy 2:8-12, Lucien Deiss, CSSp, b.1921
Tune: Lucien Deiss, CSSp, b.1921

659 Jesus in the Morning

1. Je - sus, Je - sus, Je - sus in the morn - ing,
2. Praise him, Praise him, Praise him in the morn - ing,
3. Love him, Love him, Love him in the morn - ing,
4. Serve him, Serve him, Serve him in the morn - ing,
5. Je - sus, Je - sus, Je - sus in the morn - ing,
Je - sus in the noon - time; Je - sus,
Praise him in the noon - time; Praise him,
Love him in the noon - time; Love him,
Serve him in the noon - time; Serve him,
Je - sus in the noon - time; Je - sus,
Je - sus, Je - sus when the sun goes down!
Praise him, Praise him when the sun goes down!
Love him, Love him when the sun goes down!
Serve him, Serve him when the sun goes down!
Je - sus, Je - sus when the sun goes down!
(goes down!)

Text: African-American folk song
Tune: African-American folk song

Deliver Us, O Lord of Truth 660

1. De - liv - er us, O Lord of Truth, From speech un - backed by deed, From lives that by their faith - less - ness De - ny our spo - ken creed.
2. For you have taught that weight - less words Are like the shift - ing sand. When storm and flood come rag - ing in, They give no place to stand.
3. When we with bold, fa - mil - iar phrase Con - fess that you are Lord, You ask for lives whose faith - ful - ness Sup - ports our spo - ken word.
4. Lord, help us build on sol - id rock No floods can un - der - mine. May ac - tions fol - low words we speak; Let creed with deed com - bine.

Text: Herman G. Stuempfle, Jr., b.1923, © 1997, GIA Publications, Inc.
Tune: LAND OF REST, CM; American; harm. by Annabel M. Buchanan, 1888-1983, © 1938, J. Fisher and Bro.

661 The Servant Song

1., 6. Will you let me be your ser - vant,
2. We are pil - grims on a jour - ney,
3. I will hold the Christ - light for you
4. I will weep when you are weep - ing;
5. When we sing to God in heav - en
Let me be as Christ to you; Pray that I may
We are trav - 'lers on the road; We are here to
In the night - time of your fear; I will hold my
When you laugh I'll laugh with you. I will share your
We shall find such har - mo - ny, Born of all we've
have the grace to Let you be my ser - vant, too.
help each oth - er Walk the mile and bear the load.
hand out to you, Speak the peace you long to hear.
joy and sor - row 'Til we've seen this jour - ney through.
known to - geth - er Of Christ's love and ag - o - ny.

Text: Richard Gillard, b.1953
Tune: Richard Gillard, b.1953; harm. by Betty Pulkingham, b.1929

You Have Anointed Me 662

Verse 1
1. To bring glad tid - ings to the low - ly, to heal the bro - ken heart,
You have a - noint - ed me.
To pro - claim lib - er - ty to cap - tives, re - lease to pris - on - ers,
You have a - noint - ed me.
Refrain
Melody:
Your Spir - it, O God, is up - on me,
Harmony:
on
Your Spir - it, O God, is up - on me,
To verse 2
Last time
me,
You have a - noint - ed me.

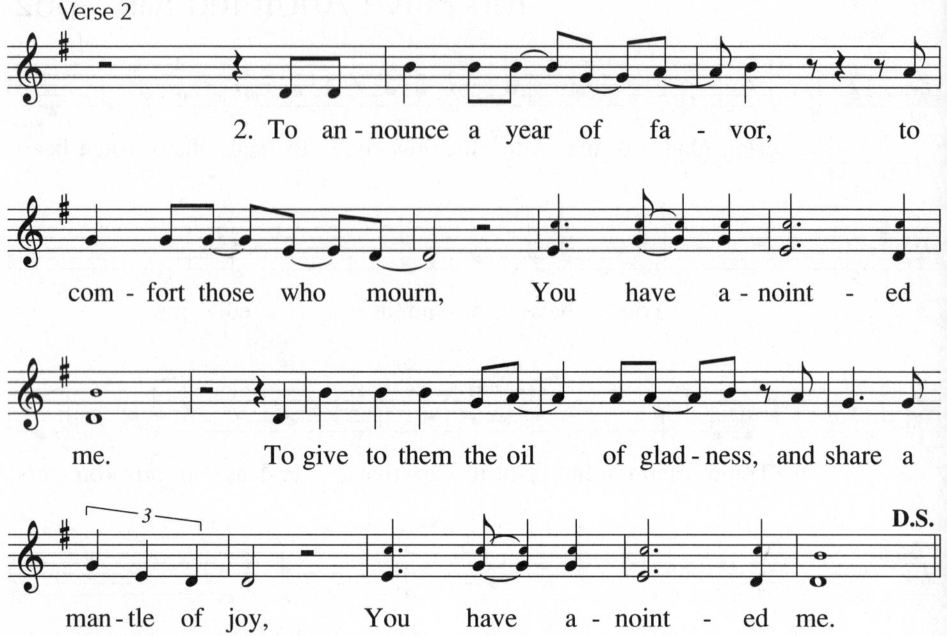
Verse 2
2. To an - nounce a year of fa - vor, to
com - fort those who mourn, You have a - noint - ed
me. To give to them the oil of glad - ness, and share a
3
man - tle of joy, You have a - noint - ed me.
D.S.

Text: Mike Balhoff, b.1946, Gary Daigle, b.1957, Darryl Ducote, b.1945
Tune: Mike Balhoff, b.1946, Gary Daigle, b.1957, Darryl Ducote, b.1945; acc. by Gary Daigle

City of God 663

Verses 1, 2
1. Awake from your slumber! Arise from your sleep! A new day is dawning for all those who weep. The people in darkness have seen a great light. The Lord of our longing has conquered the night.
2. We are sons of the morning; we are daughters of day. The One who has loved us has brightened our way. The Lord of all kindness has called us to be a light for his people to set their hearts free.
Refrain
Descant:
Let us build the city of God. May our
Melody:
Let us build the city of God. May our tears be

tears be turned to dance! For the Lord, our
turned in - to danc - ing! For the Lord, our light and our
light and our love, has turned the night in - to day!
love, has turned the night in - to day!
1.
2. To next section (v.3)
3. D.S. (v.4)
4.
Verse 3
3. God is light; in him there is no
dark - ness. Let us walk in his light, his
chil - dren, one and all.

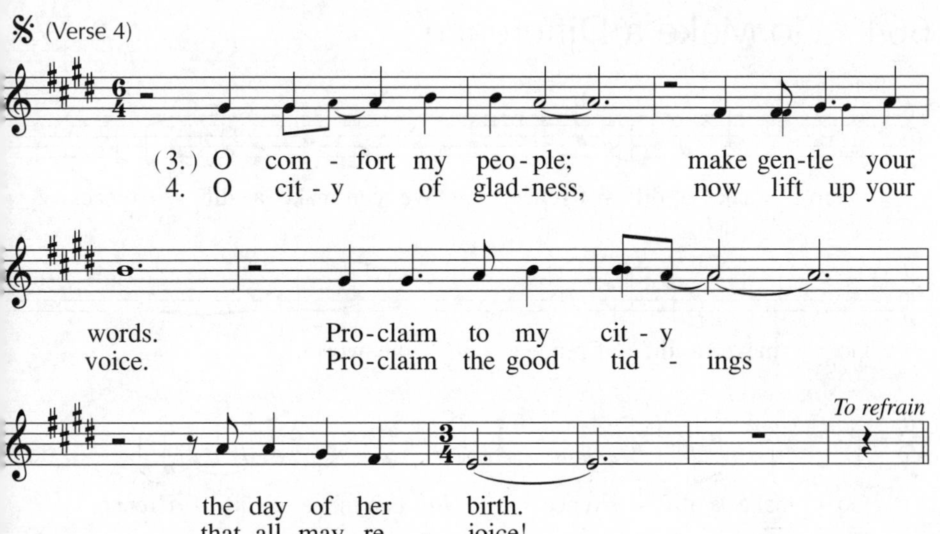
(Verse 4)
(3.) O com - fort my peo-ple; make gen-tle your
4. O cit - y of glad-ness, now lift up your
words. Pro-claim to my cit - y
voice. Pro-claim the good tid - ings
To refrain
the day of her birth.
that all may re - joice!

ext: Dan Schutte, b.1947
une: Dan Schutte, b.1947; acc. by Robert J. Batastini, b.1942

664 Go Make a Difference

Refrain
Go make a dif - f'rence. We can make a dif - f'rence.
Go make a dif - f'rence in the world.
Go make a dif - f'rence. We can make a dif - f'rence.
To verses
To repeat refrain
Last time
Go make a dif-f'rence in the world.
Verses 1, 2
1. We are the salt of the earth, called to let the peo - ple
2. We are the hands of Christ reach-ing out to those in
see the love of God in you and me.
need, the face of God for all to see.
We are the light of the world, not to be hid - den but be
We are the spir - it of hope; we are the voice of
D.C.
seen. Go make a dif - f'rence in the world.
peace. Go make a dif - f'rence in the world.

Verse 3
3. So let your love shine on, let it shine for all to see.
Go make a dif - f'rence in the world. And the
spir - it of Christ will be with us as we go.
D.C.
Go make a dif - f'rence in the world.

Text: Matthew 5:13-16; Steve Angrisano, b.1965, and Tom Tomaszek, b.1950
Tune: Steve Angrisano, b.1965, and Tom Tomaszek, b.1950; acc. by Rick Modlin, b.1966

The Church of Christ 665

1. The Church of Christ in ev - 'ry age Be - set by
2. A - cross the world, a - cross the street, The vic - tims
3. Then let the ser - vant Church a - rise, A car - ing
4. For he a - lone, whose blood was shed, Can cure the
5. We have no mis - sion but to serve In full o -

change but Spir - it led, Must claim and test its
of in - jus - tice cry For shel - ter and for
Church that longs to be A part - ner in Christ's
fe - ver in our blood, And teach us how to
be - dience to our Lord: To care for all, with -

her - i - tage And keep on ris - ing from the dead.
bread to eat, And nev - er live un - til they die.
sac - ri - fice, And clothed in Christ's hu - man - i - ty.
share our bread And feed the starv - ing mul - ti - tude.
out re - serve, And spread his lib - er - at - ing Word.

Text: Fred Pratt Green, 1903-2000, © 1971, Hope Publishing Co.
Tune: O WALY, WALY, LM; arr. by John L. Bell, b.1949, © 1989, The Iona Community, GIA Publications, Inc., agent

666 Go Make of All Disciples

1. "Go make of all dis - ci - ples:" We hear the call, O
2. "Go make of all dis - ci - ples:" Bap - tiz - ing in the
3. "Go make of all dis - ci - ples:" We at your feet would
4. "Go make of all dis - ci - ples:" We wel-come your com -
Lord, That comes from you, our Fa - ther, In
name Of Fa - ther, Son, and Spir - it— From
stay Un - til each life's vo - ca - tion Ac -
mand; "Lo, I am with you al - ways:" We
your e - ter - nal Word. In - spire our ways of
age to age the same. We call each new dis -
cents your ho - ly way. We cul - ti - vate the
take your guid - ing hand. The task looms large be -
learn - ing Through earn - est, fer - vent prayer, And
ci - ple To fol - low you, O Lord, Re -
na - ture God plants in ev - 'ry heart, Re -
fore us— We fol - low with - out fear. In

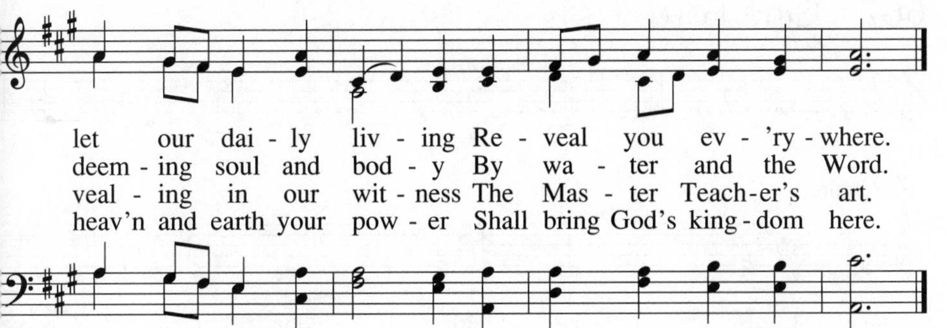
let our dai - ly liv - ing Re - veal you ev - 'ry - where.
deem - ing soul and bod - y By wa - ter and the Word.
veal - ing in our wit - ness The Mas - ter Teach-er's art.
heav'n and earth your pow - er Shall bring God's king - dom here.

Text: Matthew 28:19-20; Leon M Adkins, 1896-1986, alt. © 1964, Abingdon Press
Tune: ELLACOMBE, 7 6 7 6 D; *Gesangbuch der Herzogl,* Wirtemberg, 1784

667 One Lord

Refrain
One Lord, one faith, one call to serve each oth - er. One heart, one mind, one com - mon ground; we stand all as one.
To verses
Last time
Verses
1. Give us new hands, o - pen and free,
2. Give us new eyes, lov - ing and wise,
3. Give us new hearts, hum - ble yet strong
4. Breathe out your Spir - it up - on the land.

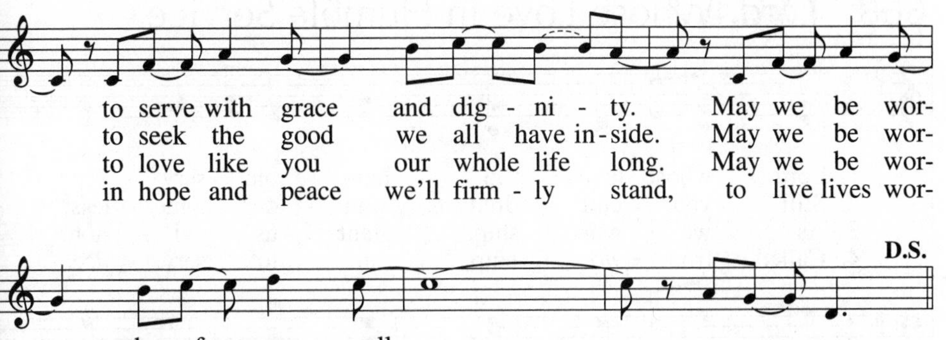
to serve with grace and dig - ni - ty. May we be wor-
to seek the good we all have in - side. May we be wor-
to love like you our whole life long. May we be wor-
in hope and peace we'll firm - ly stand, to live lives wor-

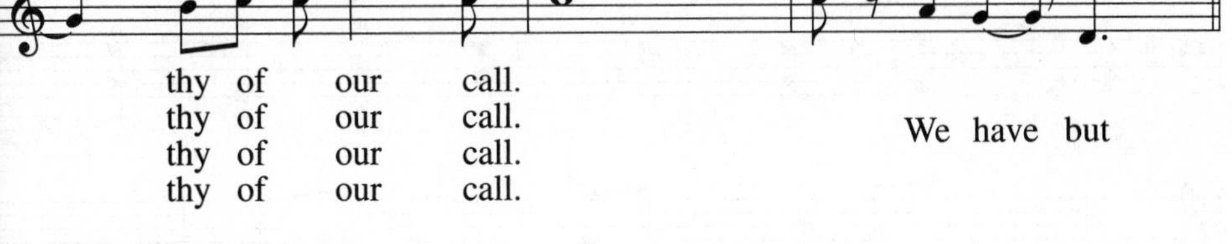
D.S.
thy of our call.
thy of our call.
thy of our call.
thy of our call.
We have but

Text: Ephesians 4:1-24; Lori True, b.1961
Tune: Lori True, b.1961

668 Lord, Whose Love in Humble Service

1. Lord, whose love in hum - ble serv - ice
2. Still your chil - dren wan - der home - less;
3. As we wor - ship, grant us vi - sion,
4. Called from wor - ship in - to serv - ice
Bore the weight of hu - man need,
Still the hun - gry cry for bread;
Till your love's re - veal - ing light,
Forth in your great name we go,
Who did on the Cross for - sak - en,
Still the cap - tives long for free - dom;
Till the height and depth and great - ness
To the child, the youth, the a - ged,
Show us mer - cy's per - fect deed;
Still in grief we mourn our dead.
Dawns up - on our hu - man sight:
Love in liv - ing deeds to show;

We, your ser - vants, bring the wor - ship
As, O Lord, your deep com - pas - sion
Mak - ing known the needs and bur - dens
Hope and health, good - will and com - fort,
Not of voice a - lone, but heart:
Healed the sick and freed the soul,
Your com - pas - sion bids us bear,
Coun - sel, aid, and peace we give
Con - se - crat - ing to your pur - pose
Use the love your Spir - it kin - dles
Stir - ring us to faith - ful serv - ice,
That your chil - dren, Lord, in free - dom,
Ev - 'ry gift which you im - part.
Still to save and make us whole.
Your a - bun - dant life to share.
May your mer - cy know and live.

Text: Albert F. Bayly, 1901-1984, © Oxford University Press
Tune: IN BABILONE, 8 7 8 7 D; *Oude en Nieuwe Hollanste Boerenlities,* c.1710

669 God Has Chosen Me

Verses
1. God has cho - sen me, God has cho - sen me to
2. God has cho - sen me, God has cho - sen me to
3. God is call - ing me, God is call - ing me in
bring good news to the poor. God has cho - sen me,
set a - light a new fire. God has cho - sen me,
all whose cry is un - heard. God is call - ing me,
God has cho - sen me to bring new sight to those
God has cho - sen me to bring to birth a new
God is call - ing me to raise up the voice with no
search - ing for light: God has cho - sen me, cho - sen me:
king - dom on earth: God has cho - sen me, cho - sen me:
pow - er or choice: God is call - ing me, call - ing me:

Refrain
And to tell the world that God's king-dom is near, to re -
move op - pres - sion and break down fear, yes, God's
time is near, God's time is near, God's time is near.
1.
2.

Text: Bernadette Farrell, b.1957
Tune: Bernadette Farrell, b.1957

670 How Can We Be Silent

Verses
Tenors:
1. How can we be si-lent when we know our God is near, bring-ing light to those in dark-ness, to the worth-less, end-less worth?
2. How can we be si-lent when our God has con-quered death, stretch-ing out his arms to suf-fer so that we might have new life?
3. How can we be si-lent as we turn our eyes a-way and ig-nore the poor and bro-ken who lie bleed-ing in the street?
4. How can we be si-lent, not give praise with all our hearts, for Christ Je-sus is our Sav-ior and com-pas-sion is our king?
5. How can we be si-lent when our souls are filled with awe at the beau-ty of cre-a-tion and the mer-cy of our Lord?
How can we be si-lent when we are the voice of Christ, speak-ing
How can we be si-lent when we know that Je-sus rose, and will
How can we be si-lent when we're called to heal and serve in the
How can we be si-lent when God gave us life to be vi-brant
How can we be si-lent when we yearn to sing new songs? In our

jus - tice to the na - tions, breath - ing love to all the earth?
come a - gain in glo - ry, end - ing suf - fer - ing and strife?
im - age of Lord Je - sus, who has stooped to wash our feet?
in - stru - ments of wor - ship, made to laugh and dance and sing?
hearts a fire is burn - ing and it will not be ig - nored!
Refrain*
1.
None can stop the Spir - it
2.
burn - ing now in - side us.
3.
We will shape the fu - ture.
4.
We will not be si - lent!
Last time

*May be sung as a canon.

Text: Michael Mahler, b.1981
Tune: Michael Mahler, b.1981

671 Here I Am, Lord

Verses
Descant:
3. Ah
Ah
Melody:
1. I, the Lord of sea and sky, I have heard my
2. I, the Lord of snow and rain, I have borne my
3. I, the Lord of wind and flame, I will tend the

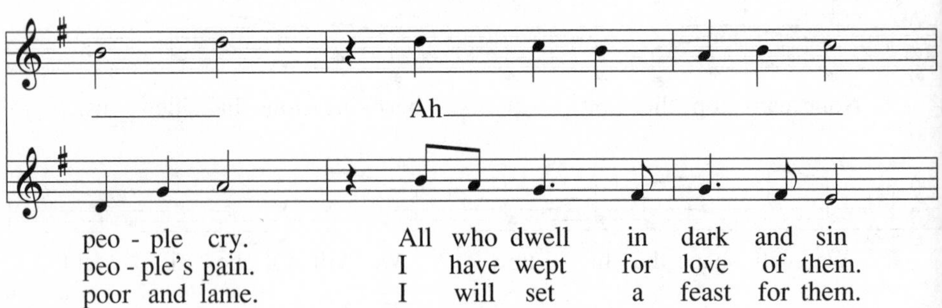
Ah
peo - ple cry. All who dwell in dark and sin
peo - ple's pain. I have wept for love of them.
poor and lame. I will set a feast for them.

My hand will save. Fin - est bread I
My hand will save. I who made the
They turn a - way. I will break their
My hand will save. Fin - est bread I

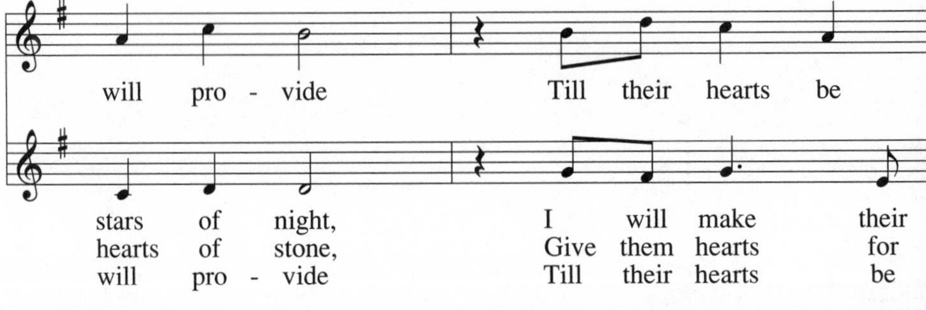
will pro - vide Till their hearts be
stars of night, I will make their
hearts of stone, Give them hearts for
will pro - vide Till their hearts be

sat - is - fied. I will give my
dark - ness bright. Who will bear my
love a - lone. I will speak my
sat - is - fied. I will give my
life to them. Whom shall I send?
light to them? Whom shall I send?
word to them. Whom shall I send?
life to them. Whom shall I send?
Refrain
Here I am, Lord. Is it I, Lord?
I have heard you call-ing in the night. I will
go, Lord, if you lead me. I will hold your
peo - ple in my heart. heart.
1., 2.
3.

ext: Isaiah 6; Dan Schutte, b.1947
'une: Dan Schutte, b.1947; arr. by Michael Pope, SJ, and John Weissrock

672 Good News

Verses
1. When Je - sus worked here on earth he preached in his home - town, I - sa - iah's hopes now ful - filled, those claims of great re - nown.
2. The eld - ers of the syn - a - gogue were shocked by Mar - y's son, That he was des - tined to be the Christ for ev - 'ry - one.
3. The way he lived was proof of it: he qui - et - ed our strife. The cross it - self he would not flee e'en though it cost his life.
4. So pass it on to - day, good friend: the mes - sage is the same. De - liv - 'rance Christ a - lone can give, for this to earth he came.
Refrain
To bring good news to the need - y, to make the blind to see, the bro - ken hearts healed a - gain, to

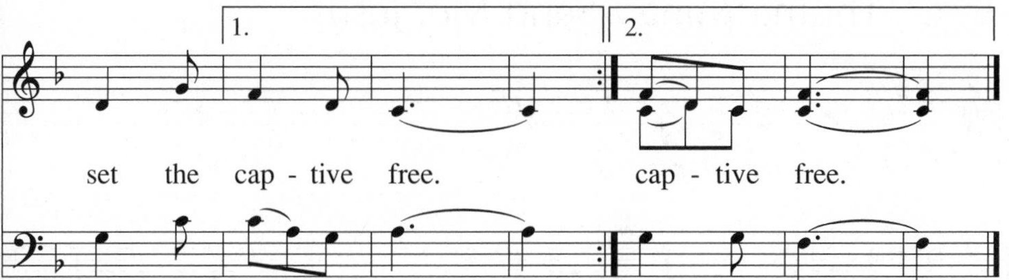
1.
2.
set the cap - tive free.
cap - tive free.

Text: Howard S. Olson
Tune: Almaz Belihu; Yemissrach Dimts Literature Program, Ethiopia

Stand Firm 673

Stand, O stand firm; stand, O stand firm;

div.

stand, O stand firm and see what the Lord can

unis.

Cantor:

O my sis - ters,
O my broth - ers,
All you chil - dren,
Let God's peo - ple,
stand ver - y firm!

D.C.

Last time

do.

div. *Last time*

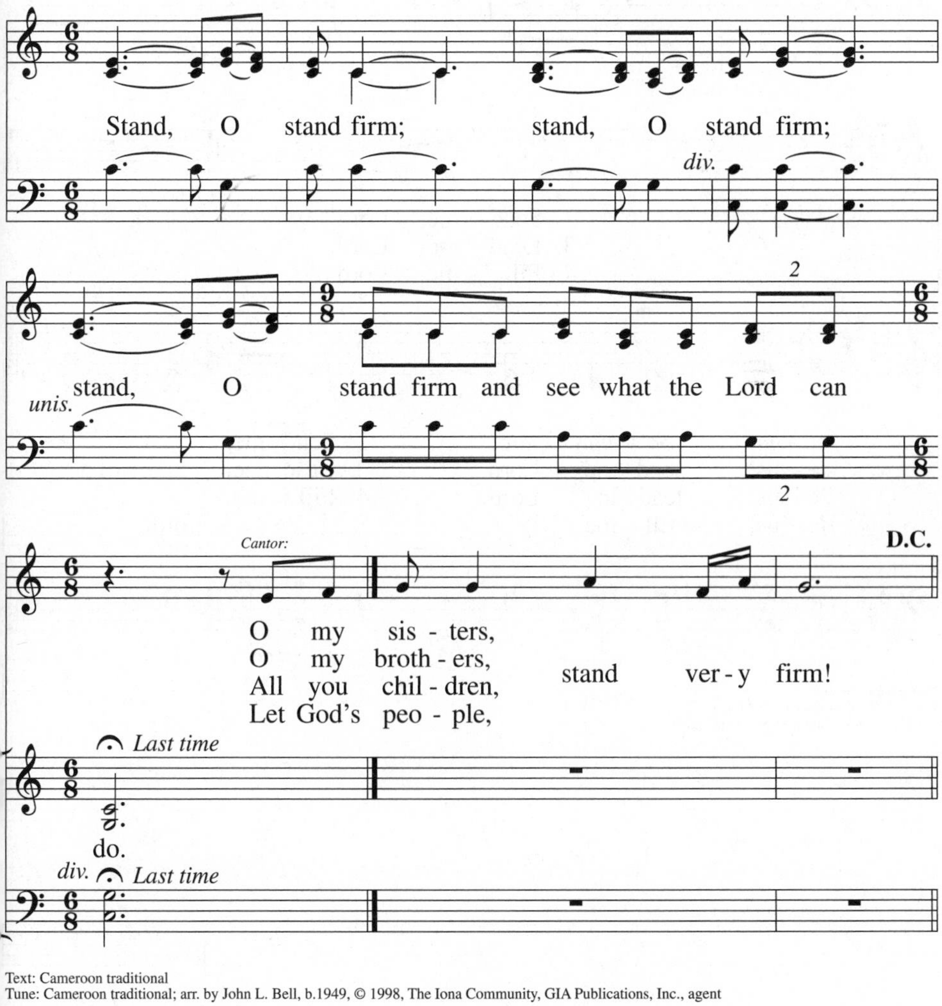

Text: Cameroon traditional
Tune: Cameroon traditional; arr. by John L. Bell, b.1949,

674 Thuma Mina / Send Me, Jesus

Solo:
1. Thu - ma mi - na.
All:
1. Thu-ma mi-na, Thu-ma mi - na, Thu-ma
Je-sus, send me, Je - sus, send me,
Je-sus, lead me, Je - sus, lead me,
Je-sus, fill me, Je - sus fill me,
1.- 3.
4.
2. Send me, Lord.
3. Lead me, Lord.
4. Fill me, Lord.
mi-na So - man - dla. 2. Send me,
Je-sus, send me, Lord. 3. Lead me,
Je-sus, lead me, Lord. 4. Fill me,
Je-sus, fill me, Lord.

Text: South African
Tune: THUMA MINA, South African

You Are Called to Tell the Story 675

1. You are called to tell the sto - ry, Pass - ing words of life a - long, Then to blend your voice with oth - ers (ers) As you sing the sa - cred song. Christ be known in all our sing - ing, Fill - ing all with songs of love.
2. You are called to teach the rhy - thm Of the dance that nev - er ends, Then to move with - in the cir - cle, (cle,) Hand in hand with stran - gers, friends. Christ be known in all our danc - ing, Touch-ing all with hands of love.
3. You are called to set the ta - ble, Bless-ing bread as Je - sus blessed, Then to come with thirst and hun - ger, (ger,) Need-ing care like all the rest. Christ be known in all our shar - ing, Feed - ing all with signs of love.
4. May the One whose love is broad-er Than the meas - ure of all space Give us words to sing the sto - ry, (ry,) Move a - mong us in this place. Christ be known in all our liv - ing, Fill - ing all with gifts of love.

Text: Ruth Duck, b.1947, © 1992, GIA Publications, Inc.
Tune: ROSEMARY, 8 7 8 7 8 7; Marty Haugen, b.1950, © 2002, GIA Publications, Inc.

676 I Am for You

3
3
1. There is a moun - tain there is a sea.
2. There was a wom - an small as a star,
3. There was a man who walked in the storm,
4. We are a - noint - ed, ser - vants of God;
5. There is a world that waits in the womb;
3
3
There is a wind with - in all breath - ing,
Full of the pa - tient dreams of her na - tion,
Caught in be - tween the waves and the light - ning,
We have been born a - gain of Spir - it.
There is a hope un - born God is bear - ing,
3
3
There is an arm to break ev - 'ry chain,
Wel - com - ing in an an - gel of God,
Shar - ing his bread with those cast a - side,
We are the word God speaks to the world,
Though the powers of death prowl the night,
3
3
There is a fire in all things liv - ing.
Wel - com - ing in God's bold in - vi - ta - tion.
Heal - ing by touch the lost and the dy - ing.
Free - dom and light to all who will hear it.
There is a day our God is pre - par - ing.
3
There is a voice that speaks from the flame:
"Let it be done," she sang, "un - to me.
Send - ing us forth, he says to his friends:
So let us be the word of the Lord:
Sing 'round the fire to wak - en the dawn:
3
"I am for you, I am for you, I am for you is my name."
I am for you, I am for you, I am for you: let it be."
"I am for you, I am for you, I am for you to the end."
I am for you, I am for you, I am for you ev - er - more.
I am for you, I am for you, I am for you: We are one.

Text: Rory Cooney, b.1952
Tune: Rory Cooney, b.1952

Come and Follow Me 677

Verses
1. Come, be my light,
2. Go, take your gift
be my voice to the na - tions. Be my hands,
to the poor and the lone - ly. As you love,
be my heart for the world. Would you
so will I live in you. Will you
go where I go? Where I lead, will you fol -
feed, feed my lambs? Share your hope with the hope-
low? Would you leave ev-'ry - thing for my sake?
less? Bring new sight to the blind in my name?
By the pow - er of the Spir-
With a tow - el and a ba -
it, ev - 'ry - one with ears to hear it will em -
sin, t'ward the king - dom we will has - ten, through the
brace the call to love with - in their heart.
nar - row gate that leads to Cal - va - ry.

Refrain
If an-y-one would come and fol-low me, my dis-ci-ple you would be. Leave the past be-hind, seek and you will find all you're called to be. If an-y-one would come and fol-low me, know the truth will make you free. Give and you re-ceive. Trust me and be-lieve. Come and fol-low me.
1., 3.
Final ending
2.
me.
With a tow-el and a ba-sin, t'ward the king-dom we will has-ten, through the nar-row gate that leads to Cal-va-ry.
D.S.

Text: Tom Franzak, b.1954
Tune: Tom Franzak, b.1954; acc. by Gerard Chiusano, b.1953

Lord, When You Came / Pescador de Hombres 678

Verses
1. Lord, when you came to the sea - shore
2. Lord, you knew what my boat car - ried:
3. Lord, have you need of my la - bor,
4. Lord, send me where you would have me,
1. Tú has ve - ni - do‿a la‿o - ri - lla,
2. Tú sa - bes bien lo que ten - go,
3. Tú ne - ce - si - tas mis ma - nos,
4. Tú pes - ca - dor de‿o - tros, ma - res,
You weren't seek - ing the wise or the wealth - y,
Nei - ther mon - ey nor weap - ons for fight - ing,
Hands for serv - ice, a heart made for lov - ing,
To a vil - lage, or heart of the cit - y;
no‿has bus - ca - do ni‿a sa - bios, ni‿a ri - cos,
en mi bar - ca no‿hay o - ro ni‿es - pa - das,
mi can - san - cio que‿a o - tros des - can - se,
an - sia‿e - ter - na, al - mas que es - pe - ran.
But on - ly ask - ing that I might fol - low.
But nets for fish - ing, my dai - ly la - bor.
My arms for lift - ing the poor and bro - ken?
I will re - mem - ber that you are with me.
tan só - lo quie - res que yo te si - ga.
tan só - lo re - des y mi tra - ba - jo.
a - mor que quie - ra se - guir a - man - do.
A - mi - go bue - no, que‿a - sí me lla - mas.
Refrain
O Lord, in my eyes you were gaz - ing,
Se - ñor me‿has mi - ra - do‿a los o - jos,
Kind - ly smil - ing, my name you were
son - ri - en - do has di - cho mi

say - ing; All I treas - ured,
nom - bre, en la a - re - na
I have left on the sand there; Close to
he de - ja - do mi bar - ca, jun - to a
you, I will find oth - er seas.
ti bus - ca - ré o - tro mar.

Text: *Pescador de Hombres*, Cesáreo Gabaráin, © 1979, published by OCP Publications; trans. by Willard Francis Jabusch, b.1930, © 1982, administered by OCP Publications
Tune: Cesáreo Gabaráin, © 1979, published by OCP Publications; acc. by Diana Kodner, b.1957

679 You Walk along Our Shoreline

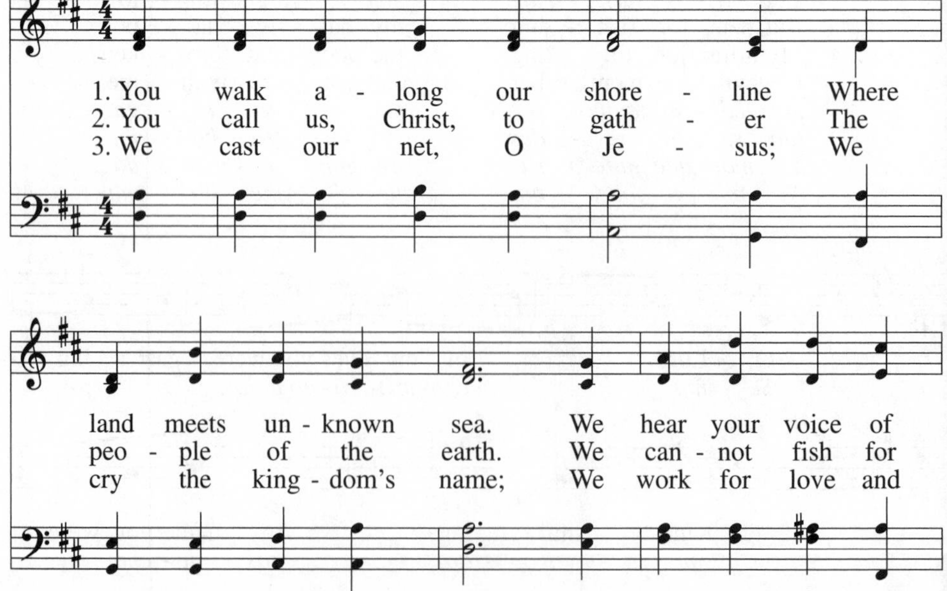
1. You walk a - long our shore - line Where
2. You call us, Christ, to gath - er The
3. We cast our net, O Je - sus; We
land meets un - known sea. We hear your voice of
peo - ple of the earth. We can - not fish for
cry the king - dom's name; We work for love and

pow - er, "Now come and fol - low me. And
on - ly Those lives we think have worth. We
jus - tice; We learn to hope through pain. You
if you still will fol - low Through storm and wave and
spread your net of gos - pel A - cross the wa - ter's
call us, Lord, to gath - er God's daugh - ters and God's
shoal, Then I will make you fish - ers But
face, Our boat a com - mon shel - ter For
sons, To let your judg - ment heal us So
of the hu - man soul."
all found by your grace.
that all may be one.

Text: Sylvia Dunston, 1955-1993,
Tune: AURELIA, 7 6 7 6 D; Samuel Sebastian Wesley, 1810-1876

680 The Love of the Lord

Intro-Coda
To verses
Last time
Verses
1. All that I count - ed as gain
2. Rich - es and hon - ors will fade,
3. Sil - ver and gold have I none,
4. Faith is the wealth I pos - sess
now I con - sid - er as loss,
earth - ly de - light dis - ap - pear,
no land to count as my home, yet
Find - ing its source in my God:
emp - ty and worth - less to me in the
fade like the grass of the field in the
wealth be - yond meas - ure I own in the
faith in the prom - ise of Christ is my
1., 3.
2., 4.
light of the love of the Lord.
light of the love of the Lord.
light of the love of the Lord.
life and my love of the Lord.

Refrain
What more could bring us hope than to know the pow'r of his life?
life, of his life? What more could bring us peace than to
share in his suf - f'ring and death? What
more could be our fi - nal wish than to
live in the love of the Lord?
Last time D.C.

Text: Philippians 3:7-11; Michael Joncas, b.1951
Tune: Michael Joncas, b.1951

681 Anthem

Refrain

Descant:
We are called, we are cho - sen. We are Christ for one an-oth-er. We are
Melody:
We are called, we are cho - sen. We are Christ for one an-oth-er. We are

prom - ised to to - mor - row, while we are for him to - day. We are
prom - ised to to - mor - row, while we are for him to - day. We are

sign, we are won - der. We are sow - er, we are seed. We are
sign, we are won - der. We are sow - er, we are seed. We are

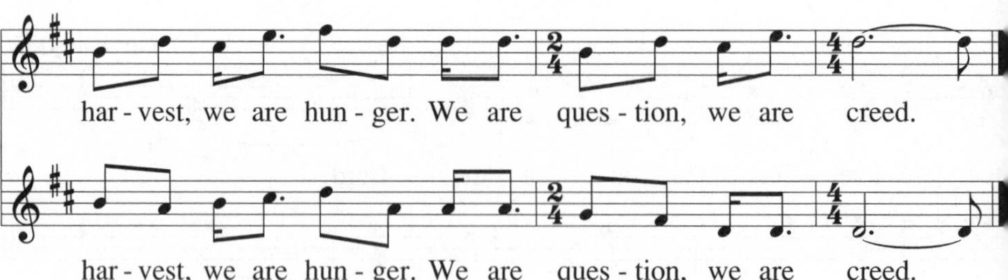
har - vest, we are hun - ger. We are ques - tion, we are creed.
har - vest, we are hun - ger. We are ques - tion, we are creed.

Verses

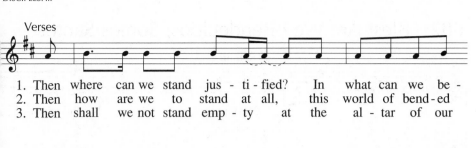

1. Then where can we stand jus - ti - fied? In what can we be -
2. Then how are we to stand at all, this world of bend - ed
3. Then shall we not stand emp - ty at the al - tar of our

lieve? In no one else but Christ who suf - fered, noth - ing
knee? In noth - ing more than bar - ren shad - ows. No one
dreams: When Christ prom - ised us our - selves. Who mark

more than Christ who rose. Who was jus - tice for the poor.
else but Christ could save us. Who was jus - tice for the poor.
time a - gainst to - mor - row. Who are jus - tice for the poor.

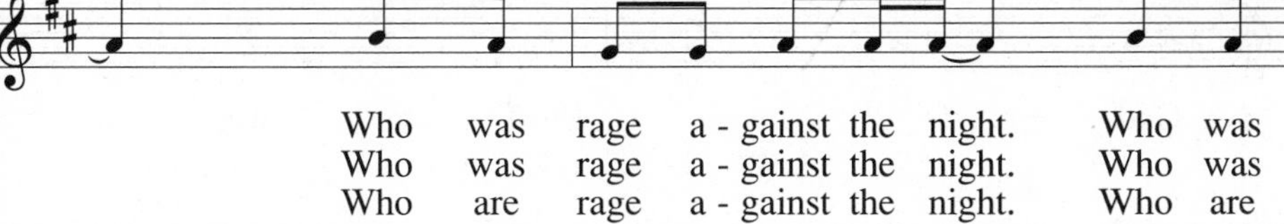

Who was rage a - gainst the night. Who was
Who was rage a - gainst the night. Who was
Who are rage a - gainst the night. Who are

D.C.

hope for peace - ful peo - ple. Who was light.
hope for peace - ful peo - ple. Who was light.
hope for peace - ful peo - ple. Who are light.

Text: Tom Conry, b.1951
Tune: Tom Conry, b.1951; acc. by Robert J. Batastini, b.1942

682 Blest Are We / Bendecidos, Somos Santos

Refrain
Blest are we, holy children of light are we! Blest are we, chosen people of God. Blest are we, God has plans for you and me.
¡Bendecidos, somos santos hijos de la luz! Bendecidos, y elegidos por Dios. Bendecidos, Dios nos quiere ser cual Jesús.

Blest are we! We are the chil-dren of God!
¡Ben-de-ci-dos, so-mos los hi-jos de Dios!
Verses
Cantor:
All:
1. For our world, each sis-ter and broth-er: We are called,
2. For the poor, the meek and the low-ly: We are called,
3. For all those who yearn for free-dom: We are called,
1. Por el mun-do, por to-dos sus pue-blos: ¡So-mos lla-ma-
2. Por los po-bres, los man-sos y hu-mil-des: ¡So-mos lla-ma-
3. Por los que su-fren y quie-ren ser li-bra-dos: ¡So-mos lla-ma-
Cantor:
called to serve! We are here to love one an-
called to serve! For the weak, the sick and the
called to serve! For the world, to be God's
dos pa-ra ser-vir! Nos a-me-mos los u-nos a los
dos pa-ra ser-vir! Por los en-fer-mos, ham-brien-tos, y
dos pa-ra ser-vir! Ven-ga a no-so-tros el Rei-no de los
All:
D.S.
oth-er: We are called, called to serve!
hun-gry: We are called, called to serve!
king-dom: We are called, called to serve!
D.S.
o-tros; ¡So-mos lla-ma-dos pa-ra ser-vir!
dé-bi-les: ¡So-mos lla-ma-dos pa-ra ser-vir!
Cie-los: ¡So-mos lla-ma-dos pa-ra ser-vir!

**Last time, repeat final 4 bars.*

Text: David Haas, b.1957, Spanish tr. by Ronald F. Krisman, b.1946
Tune: David Haas, b.1957

683 I Will Choose Christ

Refrain
I will choose Christ, I will choose love, I choose to serve.
I give my heart, I give my life,
I give my all to you.
To verses
Final ending
I give my all to you.
Verse 1
1. How man-y times must he call my name and show to me that he is God?
And as a ser - vant he calls to me, "You must serve too."
D.C.
Verse 2
2. Christ, my teach - er and heal - er, teach my heart and heal my soul.
And as I walk this road with you, teach me to love.
D.C.

Verse 3
3. As I look up - on your cross, so too must I
die with you. And with the death of my
own de - sires, I'll rise with you.
D.C.

Text: Tom Booth, b.1961
Tune: Tom Booth, b.1961; acc. by Ed Bolduc

684 Guide My Feet

1., 6. Guide my feet while I run this race,
O Lord
Guide my feet while I run this race,
O Lord
Guide my feet while I run this race, for I
don't want to run this race in vain! (race in vain!)

2. Hold my hand… 3. Stand by me... 4. I'm your child... 5. Search my heart...

Text: African-American spiritual
Tune: African-American spiritual; harm. by Diana Kodner, b. 1957,

Song of St. Patrick 685

Refrain
May the Spir - it of Christ be our hope through the day,
be our guard through the night, our com - pan - ion on the way.
unis.
To verses
Last time
rit.
Verse 1
1. Christ be ev - er be - fore us, Christ be ev - er be - hind us,
Christ be ev - er with - in.
D.C.
Verses 2-5
2. Christ up - on our left hand watch - ing, At our right hand guid - ing, Christ a - bove, be - neath us guard - ing, Near to us a - bid - ing.
3. Christ be in each ho - ly si - lence, Christ be in our speak - ing, Christ in ev - 'ry work we of - fer, Ev - er in our seek - ing.
4. Let us be God's light in the dark - ness, Let us be God's kind - ness; Let us be God's jus - tice and mer - cy, Hands and feet of Christ.
5. God Cre - a - tor, bless and keep us, Christ, be ev - er near us; Spir - it be the light be - fore us, Gen - tle be our path - way.
D.C.

Text: Based on *St. Patrick's Breastplate*; Marty Haugen, b.1950
Tune: Marty Haugen, b.1950

686 Come and Journey with a Savior

1. Come and jour - ney with a Sav - ior Who has
2. Come and jour - ney jour - ney in - ward, Come and
3. Come and jour - ney, jour - ney out - ward, Tell - ing
4. Come and jour - ney, jour - ney out - ward, Where that
5. Come and jour - ney, jour - ney up - ward, Sing his
6. Come and jour - ney, jour - ney on - ward, All our
Descant:
6. All our gifts we bring To the build - ing of a
cit - y That is ho - ly, Christ its king.
called us from our birth, Who has washed us in the
seek him deep with - in, Where he meets us in our
oth - ers of his name, Tell - ing oth - ers of his
cross calls us to care, Where in - jus - tice and where
prais - es, of - fer prayer. In the storm and in the
gifts we now shall bring, To the build - ing of a
wa - ters, And who loved us on the earth.
liv - ing, In our striv - ing and our sin.
glo - ry, Of his cross and of the shame.
hun - ger And the poor call us to share.
still - ness, Find his pres - ence ev - 'ry - where.
cit - y That is ho - ly, Christ its king.

Descant:
Come and journey, come and journey With a
Melody:
Come and journey, come and journey With a
Savior who has come. We are all God's sons and
Savior who has come. We are all God's sons and
daughters. In the
daughters. In the Spirit we are one. In the
Last time
Spirit we are one.
Last time
Spirit we are one.

Text: Herbert O'Driscoll, b.1928, ©
Tune: COME AND JOURNEY, 8 7 8 7 with refrain; Marty Haugen, b.1950, © 1998, GIA Publications, Inc.

687 The Summons

1. Will you come and fol - low me If I but
2. Will you leave your - self be - hind If I but
3. Will you let the blind - ed see If I but
4. Will you love the 'you' you hide If I but
5. Lord, your sum - mons ech - oes true When you but
call your name? Will you go where
call your name? Will you care for
call your name? Will you set the
call your name? Will you quell the
call my name. Let me turn and
you don't know And nev - er be the same?
cruel and kind And nev - er be the same?
pris - 'ners free And nev - er be the same?
fear in - side And nev - er be the same?
fol - low you And nev - er be the same.
Will you let my love be shown, Will you
Will you risk the hos - tile stare Should your
Will you kiss the lep - er clean, And do
Will you use the faith you've found To re -
In your com - pa - ny I'll go Where your
let my name be known, Will you let my
life at - tract or scare? Will you let me
such as this un - seen, And ad - mit to
shape the world a - round, Through my sight and
love and foot - steps show. Thus I'll move and
life be grown In you and you in me?
an - swer prayer In you and you in me?
what I mean In you and you in me?
touch and sound In you and you in me?
live and grow In you and you in me.

Text: John L. Bell, b.1949, © 1987, Iona Community, GIA Publications, Inc., agent
Tune: KELVINGROVE, 7 6 7 6 777 6; Scottish traditional; arr. by John L. Bell, b.1949, © 1987, Iona Community, GIA Publications, Inc., agent

Take Up Your Cross 688

Refrain
Descant:
If you want to save your life, then
Melody:
If you lose your life for my sake, you will find it;
if you want to save your life, let it go.
take up your cross, de - ny your - self.
Take up your cross, de - ny your - self: Come, fol - low
1., 2. To verses
3.
Fol - low me, fol - low me. me.
me, fol - low me.

Verse 1
1. How will you prof - it by gain - ing the
world, while you for - feit all of your life?
What will you give in re - turn?
D.C.
What will you give in re - turn?
Verse 2
2. Be - fore I re - turn in glo - ry, I will
give you the gift of my love:
you will nev - er taste death, you will
D.C.
nev - er taste death.

Text: Matthew 16:24-28; David Haas, b.1957
Tune: David Haas, b.1957

I Danced in the Morning 689

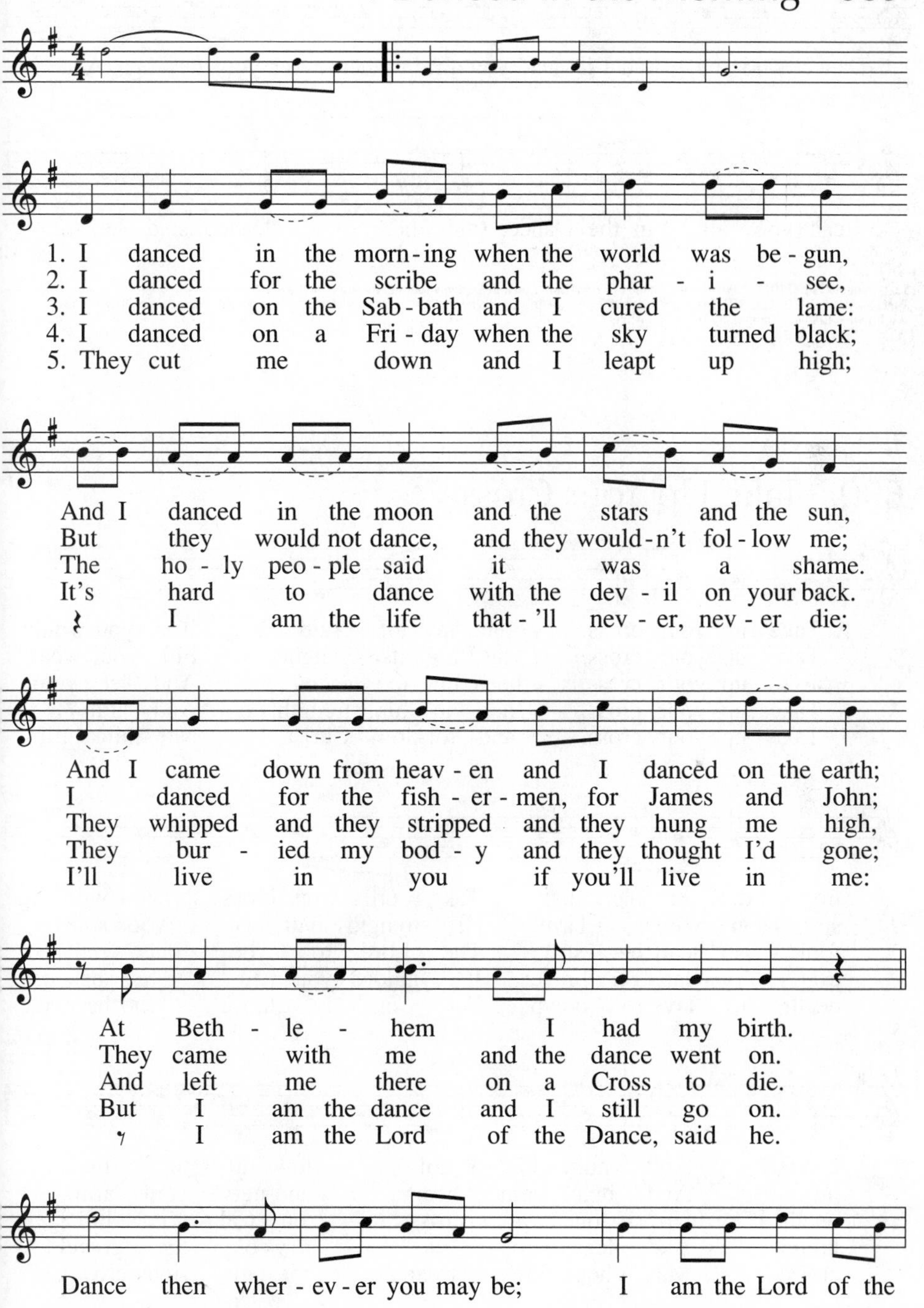
1. I danced in the morn-ing when the world was be-gun,
2. I danced for the scribe and the phar - i - see,
3. I danced on the Sab-bath and I cured the lame:
4. I danced on a Fri-day when the sky turned black;
5. They cut me down and I leapt up high;
And I danced in the moon and the stars and the sun,
But they would not dance, and they would-n't fol-low me;
The ho-ly peo-ple said it was a shame.
It's hard to dance with the dev-il on your back.
I am the life that-'ll nev-er, nev-er die;
And I came down from heav-en and I danced on the earth;
I danced for the fish-er-men, for James and John;
They whipped and they stripped and they hung me high,
They bur-ied my bod-y and they thought I'd gone;
I'll live in you if you'll live in me:
At Beth-le-hem I had my birth.
They came with me and the dance went on.
And left me there on a Cross to die.
But I am the dance and I still go on.
I am the Lord of the Dance, said he.
Dance then wher-ev-er you may be; I am the Lord of the

Dance, said he, And I'll lead you all, wher-ev-er you may be, And I'll

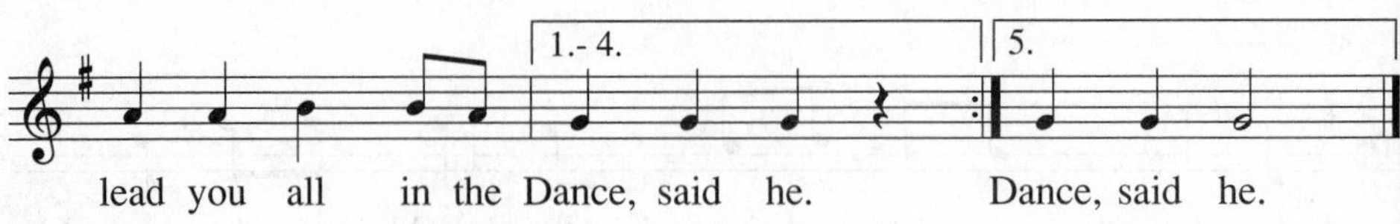

lead you all in the Dance, said he. Dance, said he.

Text: Sydney Carter, 1915-2004,
Tune: LORD OF THE DANCE, Irregular; adapted from a traditional Shaker melody by Sydney Carter, 1915-2004,

690 Take Up Your Cross

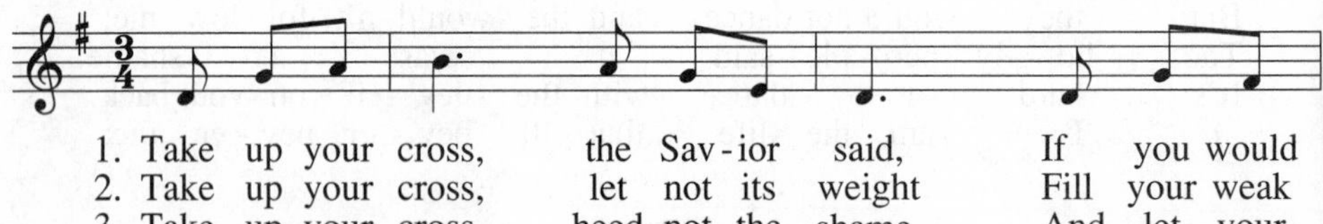

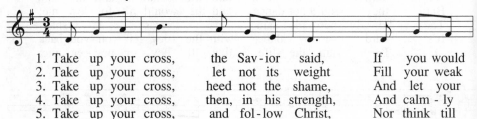

1. Take up your cross, the Sav-ior said, If you would
2. Take up your cross, let not its weight Fill your weak
3. Take up your cross, heed not the shame, And let your
4. Take up your cross, then, in his strength, And calm-ly
5. Take up your cross, and fol-low Christ, Nor think till

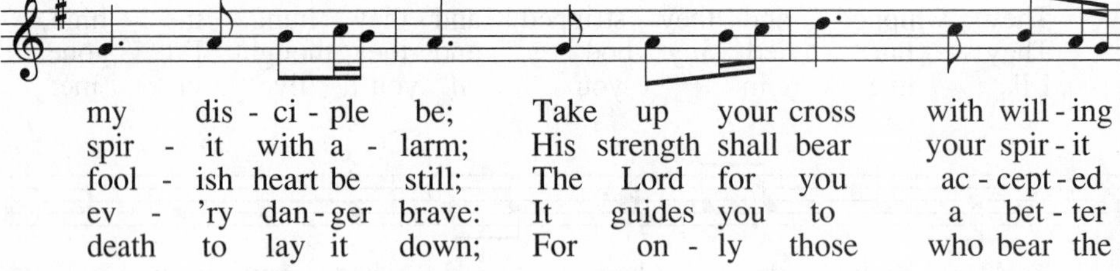

my dis-ci-ple be; Take up your cross with will-ing
spir-it with a-larm; His strength shall bear your spir-it
fool-ish heart be still; The Lord for you ac-cept-ed
ev-'ry dan-ger brave: It guides you to a bet-ter
death to lay it down; For on-ly those who bear the

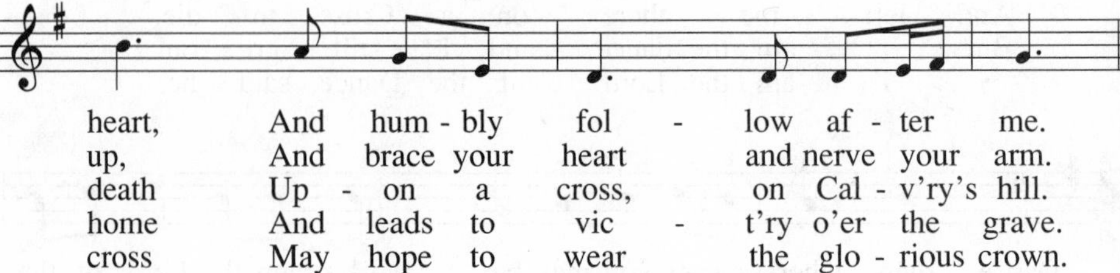

heart, And hum-bly fol-low af-ter me.
up, And brace your heart and nerve your arm.
death Up-on a cross, on Cal-v'ry's hill.
home And leads to vic-t'ry o'er the grave.
cross May hope to wear the glo-rious crown.

Text: Charles W. Everest, 1814-1877, alt.
Tune: O WALY WALY, LM; English; harm. by Martin West, b.1929,

Give the Lord Your Heart 691

Verses

1. If you want to see the king -
2. You can store your wealth in barns
3. If you spend your life - time sow -
Si tú quie - res un te - so -

dom God has planned for you you must
or banks or prop - er - ty, but you'll
ing seeds of world - ly gain you will
ro en el Rei - no, a los

give all your pos - ses - sions to the poor.
leave this world with - out one sin - gle cent.
har - vest on - ly hard - ship and dis - tress.
po - bres da - les to - do y lo ten - drás.

For a per - son rich in goods,
In the mid - dle of the night,
You will nev - er learn the joys
Pa - ra los ri - cos, !qué di - fí -

it seems im - pos - si - ble. The de -
our God may call for you and you
of sim - ple ser - vi - tude, and your
cil es es - te di - cho! Su de -

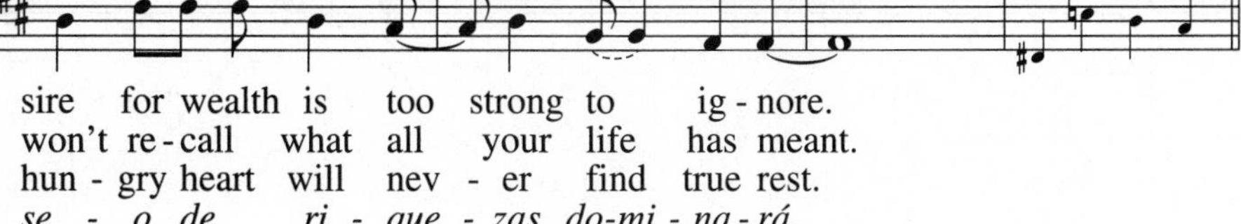

sire for wealth is too strong to ig - nore.
won't re - call what all your life has meant.
hun - gry heart will nev - er find true rest.
se - o de ri - que - zas do-mi - na - rá.

Refrain
Melody:
Un-less you love the Lord, un-less you thank
Si-no a-mas al Se-ñor, si-no das gra-cias al
Harmony:
Love the Lord. Thank the Lord.
Á - ma - lo. Dá - se - lo.
the Lord, un-less you give the Lord your heart.
Se-ñor, si-no le das tu co - ra-zón.
Give the Lord your heart.
Da - le el co - ra - zón.
Un-less you love the Lord,
Si-no a-mas al Se-ñor,
Love the Lord.
Á - ma - lo.

un - less you thank the Lord, un-less you give
si-no das gra-cias al Se - ñor, si - no le das
Thank the Lord. Give the Lord
Dá - se - lo. Da - le el co -
D.C.
Final ending
the Lord your heart.
tu co - ra - zón.
your heart.
ra - zón.

Text: Based on Luke 12:16-21, Matthew 19:21-23; Michael Mahler, b.1981
Tune: Michael Mahler, b.1981

692 Take, O Take Me As I Am

Ostinato Refrain

Take, O take me as I am; sum - mon out what I shall
be; set your seal up - on my heart and live in me.

Text: John L. Bell, b.1949
Tune: John L. Bell, b.1949

693 Two Fishermen

1. Two fish - er - men, who lived a - long The Sea of Gal - i -
2. And as he walked a - long the shore 'Twas James and John he'd
3. O Si - mon Pe - ter, An - drew, James And John be - lov - ed
4. And you, good Chris - tians, one and all Who'd fol - low Je - sus'

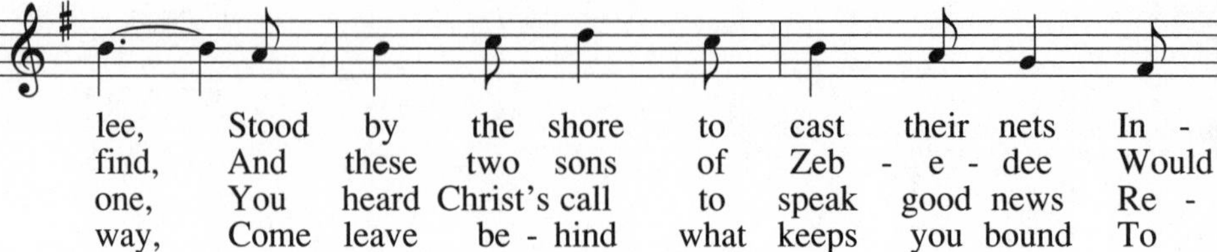
lee, Stood by the shore to cast their nets In -
find, And these two sons of Zeb - e - dee Would
one, You heard Christ's call to speak good news Re -
way, Come leave be - hind what keeps you bound To

to an age - less sea. Now Je - sus watched them
leave their boats be - hind. Their work and all they
vealed to God's own Son. Su - san - na, Mar - y,
trap - pings of our day, And lis - ten as he
from a - far Then called them each by name; It
held so dear They left be - side their nets. Their
Mag - da - lene Who trav - eled with your Lord, You
calls your name To come and fol - low near, For
changed their lives, these sim - ple men; They'd nev - er be the same.
names they'd heard as Je - sus called; They came with-out re - gret.
min - is - tered to him with joy For he is God a - dored.
still he speaks in var - ied ways To those his call will hear.
Leave all things you have And come and fol - low
me, And come and fol - low me.

Text: Suzanne Toolan, SM, b.1927, © 1986, GIA Publications, Inc.
Tune: LEAVE ALL THINGS, CMD with refrain; Suzanne Toolan, SM, b.1927, © 1970, GIA Publications, Inc.

694 We Have Been Told

Refrain
We have been told, we've seen his face, and heard his voice a - live in our hearts;
"Live in my love with all your heart, as the Fa - ther has loved me, so I have loved you."
1.- 3. To verses
4.

Verse 1
1. "I am the vine, you are the branch-es, and
all who live in me will bear great fruit."
D.C.
Verses 2, 3
2. "You are my friends, if you keep my com-mands,
3. "No great-er love is there than this: to
no long-er slaves, I call you friends."
lay down one's life, for a friend."
D.C.

Text: David Haas, b.1957
Tune: David Haas, b.1957; vocal arr. by David Haas and Marty Haugen, b.1950

695 Here Am I, Lord

Refrain
Here am I, Lord, that you send me;
I have come, I have come, I have come to do your will.
come,
come
My de - light, Lord, is your wis -
dom in the still - ness of my
1., 2.
To verses
Last time
heart.
heart, of my heart.
heart.
heart.

Verses

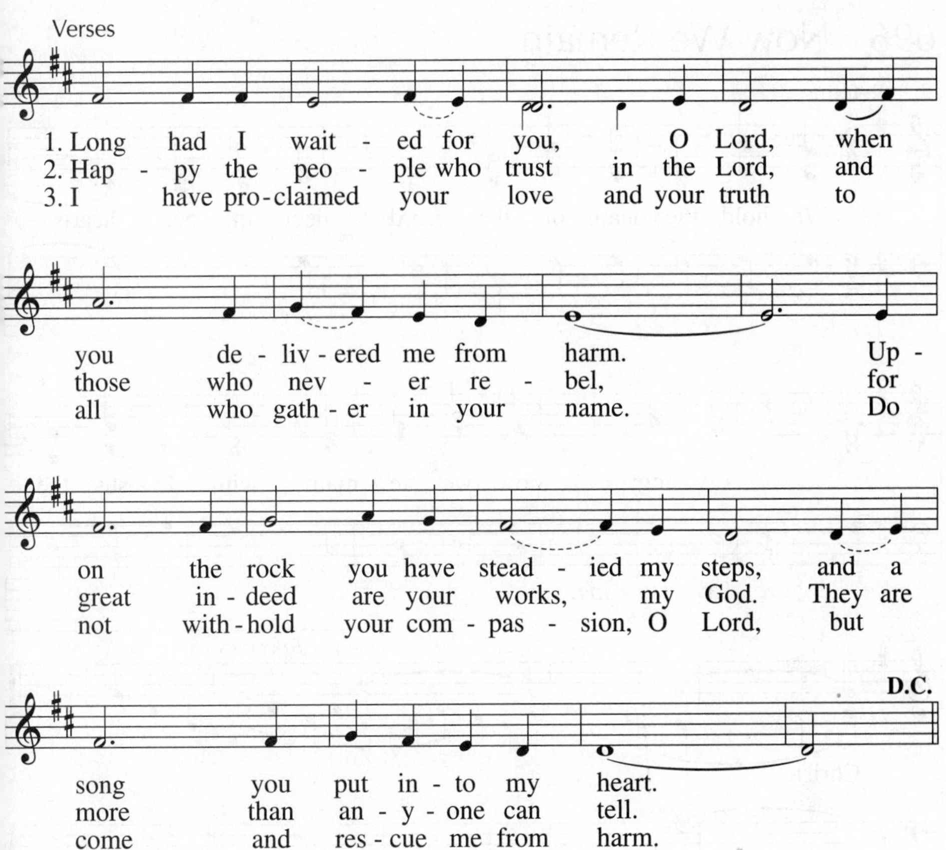
1. Long had I wait - ed for you, O Lord, when you de - liv - ered me from harm. Up - on the rock you have stead - ied my steps, and a song you put in - to my heart.
2. Hap - py the peo - ple who trust in the Lord, and those who nev - er re - bel, for great in - deed are your works, my God. They are more than an - y - one can tell.
3. I have pro - claimed your love and your truth to all who gath - er in your name. Do not with - hold your com - pas - sion, O Lord, but come and res - cue me from harm.
D.C.

Text: Psalm 40, Timothy Valentine, S.J., b.1959
Tune: Timothy Valentine, S.J., b.1959

696 Now We Remain

Refrain
We hold the death of the Lord deep in our hearts.
Liv - ing; now we re - main with Je - sus the
Liv - ing;
1.- 4. To verses
5.
Christ.
Verses 1, 4
1. Once we were peo - ple a - fraid, lost in the
4. We are the pres - ence of God; this is our
night.
call.
Then by your cross we were saved;
Now to be - come bread and wine:
To Coda, Verse 4
D.C.
Dead be - came liv - ing, Life from your giv - ing.
Food for the hun-gry, Life for the wea - ry,

Verse 2
2. Some - thing which we have known, some - thing we've touched,
What we have seen with our eyes: This we have heard; Life giv - ing word.
D.C.
Verse 3
3. He chose to give of him - self, be - came our bread.
Bro - ken, that we might live.
Love be - yond love, Pain for our pain.
D.C.

Coda

for to live with the Lord, we must die with the Lord.

D.C.

Text: Corinthians, 1 John, 2 Timothy; David Haas, b.1957
Tune: David Haas, b.1957

697 Sing Yes for the Carpenter

Verses
1. Come with me, come wan - der, come wel - come the
2. Come walk in my com - p'ny, come sleep by my
3. Come share in my laugh - ter, come close to my
4. Come leave your pos - ses - sions, come share out your
world Where stran - gers might smile or where
side, Come sa - vor a life - style with
fears, Come find your - self washed with the
treas - ure. Come give and re - ceive with - out
stones may be hurled; Come leave what you
noth - ing to hide; Come sit at my
kiss of my tears; Come stand close at
meth - od or meas - ure; Come loose ev - 'ry
cling to, lay down what you clutch And
ta - ble and eat with my friends, Dis -
hand while I suf - fer and die And
bond that's re - sist - ing the Spir - it, En -
find, with hands emp - ty, that hearts can hold much.
cov - 'ring that love which the world nev - er ends.
find in three days how I nev - er will lie.
a - bling the earth to be yours to in - her - it.
Refrain
Sing yes for the car - pen - ter leav - ing his
tools! Sing yes for the Phar - i - sees leav - ing their

rules! Sing yes for the fish - er - men leav - ing their
nets! Sing yes for the peo - ple who leave their re - grets!
ext: John L. Bell, b.1949
une: SING HEY, Irregular, John L. Bell, b.1949
) 1987, The Iona Community, GIA Publications, Inc., agent
Embrace My Way and Cross 698
Refrain
Will you come and fol - low in my steps to serve the poor and
lost? Can you leave all things with - out re - gret, em -
brace my way and cross?
Verses
1. In a wel-come place is my a - bode, In all hearts both
2. In the serv - ing line I will be found, On the streets of
3. Wheth-er lone - ly rich or gra - cious poor, You will find me
young and old. There I en - ter in and will be known
an - y town. For I have no bounds of time and space,
at your door. I will call you from your wan-d'ring ways
As com - pas - sion, gent - ly shown.
But am found in ev - 'ry face.
In - to Gos - pel liv - ing days.
D.C.

'ext: Rob Glover, b.1950
'une: ROCKY POINT, 9 7 9 7 with refrain; Rob Glover, b.1950

699 Unless a Grain of Wheat

Refrain
Unless a grain of wheat shall fall upon the ground and die, it remains but a single grain with no life.
on the ground and die, it remains a single grain, a grain with no life.
1.- 6. To verses
Last time
2. If
Verses
1. If we have died with him then we shall
2. anyone serves me then they must
3. Make your home in me as I make
4. If you remain in me and my word
5. Those who love me are loved by my
6. Peace I leave with you, my peace I

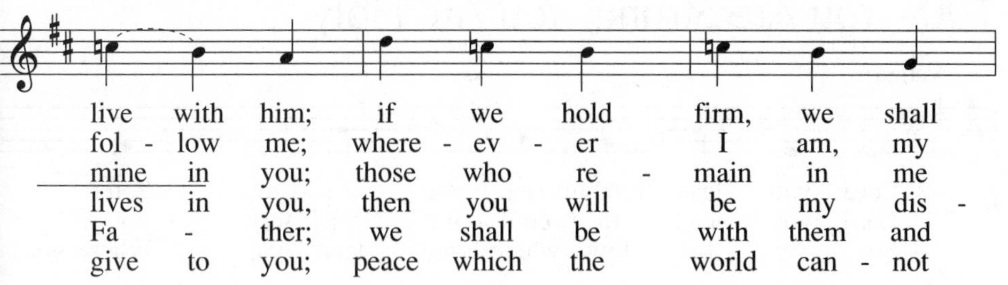
live with him; if we hold firm, we shall
fol - low me; where - ev - er I am, my
mine in you; those who re - main in me
lives in you, then you will be my dis -
Fa - ther; we shall be with them and
give to you; peace which the world can - not

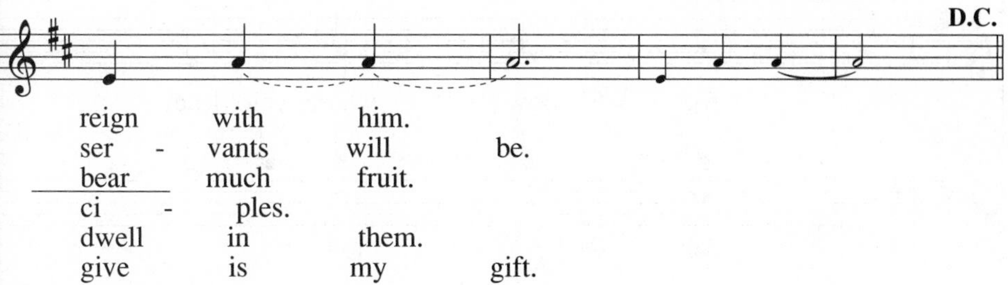
D.C.
reign with him.
ser - vants will be.
bear much fruit.
ci - ples.
dwell in them.
give is my gift.

Text: John 12:24; Bernadette Farrell, b.1957
Tune: Bernadette Farrell, b.1957

700 You Are Strong, You Are Holy

Verses
Melody:
1. Lord, you lead through sea and des - ert, You lead to prom - ised lands. We are your own ho - ly peo - ple, In your cov - e - nant we stand!
2. Lord, you lead to cool - ing wa - ters, You lead to green - ing fields. Lord, you lead to deep - 'ning val - leys Where your com - fort is re - vealed!
3. So we fol - low where you lead us, Where you walk a - long the shore, Where you suf - fer in the gar - den, When you rise to die no more!
Harmony (verse 3):
fol - low where you lead, walk the shore, suf - fer in the gar - den no more.
fol - low

Refrain
You are strong, you are ho - ly,
ho - ly, you are
mer - cy and
ev - er - last - ing peace. You are love, you are
jus - tice. Your
jus - tice, grace and fa - vor nev - er cease!

This may be used as an introduction.

Last time

701 Only This I Want

Refrain

On-ly this I want: but to know the Lord,
and to bear his cross so to wear the crown he wore.

Last time

Verses

1. All but this is loss, worth-less ref - use to me,
for to gain the Lord is to gain all I need.
2. I will run the race; I will fight the good fight,
so to win the prize of the King-dom of my Lord.
3. Let your heart be glad, al - ways glad in the Lord,
so to shine like stars in the dark - ness of the night.

D.C.

Text: Philippians 3:7-16; 2:15, 18; Dan Schutte, b.1947
Tune: Dan Schutte, b.1947; arr. by Michael Pope, SJ

702 Voices That Challenge

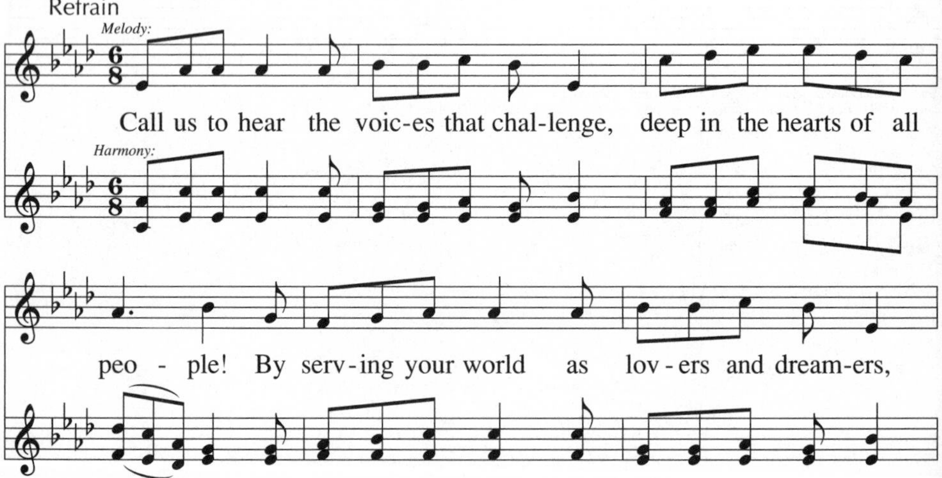
Refrain
Melody:
Call us to hear the voic-es that chal-lenge, deep in the hearts of all
Harmony:
peo - ple! By serv-ing your world as lov - ers and dream-ers,

Last time
we be-come voic-es that chal - lenge, for we are the voice of God!
Last time
Verses 1, 2
All:
Cantor:
1. Voic-es that chal-lenge: the chil - dren who long to be
the low - ly and bro - ken de -
the old and the fear - ful who
2. Voic-es that chal-lenge: the lives and the cries of the
the young ones who dream of a
the sick and the dy - ing who
1., 2., 4., 5.
3., 6.
D.C.
(1.) heard and re - spec - ted!
stroyed by op - pres - sion!
hope for a new day!
(2.) poor and the si - lenced!
world free of ha - tred!
cry for com - pas - sion!
Verse 3
All:
Cantor:
3. Voic-es that chal-lenge: the ones who seek
the wom - en who
the peo - ple with
the proph - ets and
the heal - ers who
the vic - tims of
the Christ who
1.- 6.
7.
D.C.
peace by their wit - ness and cour - age!
suf - fer the pain of in - jus - tice!
AIDS and those plagued with ad - dic - tion!
he - roes who call us to ques - tion!
teach us for - give - ness and mer - cy!
vio - lent a - buse and a - gres - sion!
gave his life that we might live!

Text: David Haas, b.1957
Tune: David Haas, b.1957

703 Abundant Life

1. We can - not own the sun - lit sky, The
2. When bod - ies shiv - er in the night And
3. God calls hu - man - i - ty to join As
moon, the wild - flow'rs grow - ing, For we are
wea - ry, wait for morn - ing, When chil - dren
part - ners in cre - at - ing A fu - ture
part of all that is With - in life's
have no bread but tears, And war - horns
free from want or fear, Life's good - ness
riv - er flow - ing. With o - pen
sound their warn - ing, God calls hu -
cel - e - brat - ing, That new world
hands re - ceive and share The gifts of God's cre -
man - i - ty to wake, To join in com - mon
beck - ons from a - far, In - vites our shared en -
a - tion, That all may have a - bun - dant
la - bor, That all may have a - bun - dant
deav - or, That all may have a - bun - dant
life In ev - 'ry earth - ly na - tion.
life In one - ness with their neigh - bor.
life And peace en - dure for - ev - er.

Text: Ruth Duck, b.1947, © 1992, GIA Publications, Inc.
Tune: LA GRANGE, 8 7 8 7 D; Marty Haugen, b.1950, © 1994, GIA Publications, Inc.

God, Whose Purpose Is to Kindle 704

1. God, whose pur - pose is to kin - dle: Now ig - nite us with your fire; While the earth a - waits your burn - ing, With your pas - sion us in - spire. O - ver - come our sin - ful calm - ness, Stir us with your sav - ing name; Bap - tize with your fier - y Spir - it, Crown our lives with tongues of flame.
2. God, who in your ho - ly gos - pel Wills that all should tru - ly live, Make us sense our share of fail - ure, Our tran - quil - li - ty for - give. Teach us cour - age as we strug - gle In all lib - er - at - ing strife; Lift the small - ness of our vi - sion By your own a - bun - dant life.
3. God, who still a sword de - liv - ers Rath - er than a plac - id peace, With your sharp - ened word dis - turb us, From com - pla - cen - cy re - lease! Save us now from sat - is - fac - tion, When we pri - vate - ly are free, Yet are un - dis - turbed in spir - it By our neigh - bor's mis - er - y.

Text: Luke 12:49; David E. Trueblood, 1900-1994, © 1967, David Elton Trueblood
Tune: HYMN TO JOY, 8 7 8 7 D; arr. from Ludwig van Beethoven, 1770-1827, by Edward Hodges, 1796-1867

705 A Place at the Table

Verses
1. For ev - 'ry - one born, a place at the ta -
2. For wom - an and man, a place at the ta -
3. For young and for old, a place at the ta -
4. For just and un - just, a place at the ta -
5. For ev - 'ry - one born, a place at the ta -
ble, for ev - 'ry - one born, clean wa - ter and
ble, re - vis - ing the roles, de - cid - ing the
ble, a voice to be heard, a part in the
ble, a - bus - er, a - bused, with need to for -
ble, to live with - out fear, and sim - ply to
bread, a shel - ter, a space, a
share, with wis - dom and grace, di -
song, the hands of a child in
give, in an - ger, in hurt, a
be, to work, to speak out, to
safe place for grow - ing, for ev - 'ry - one
vid - ing the pow - er, for wom - an and
hands that are wrin - kled, for young and for
mind - set of mer - cy, for just and un -
wit - ness and wor - ship, for ev - 'ry - one
born, a star o - ver - head.
man, a sys - tem that's fair.
old, the right to be - long. And
just, a new way to live.
born, the right to be free.

Refrain
Descant:
And God will de-light,
Melody:
God will de - light when we are cre-a-
jus-tice, com - pas-sion and peace!
tors of jus-tice and joy, yes, God
Yes, God will de-light,
will de - light when we are cre-a - tors of
jus - tice and joy!
jus - tice, jus - tice and joy!
div.
To verses
D.C.
Final ending
jus-tice and joy!

Text: Shirley Erena Murray, b.1931, © 1998, Hope Publishing Co.
Tune: Lori True, b.1961, © 2001, GIA Publications, Inc.

706 We Come with Joy

1. We come with joy in Je - sus Christ, Who knows our hu - man need, Who, moved with pit - y for the world, Would ev - 'ry hun - ger feed, Who blessed the fish and bar - ley loaves Till
2. A lit - tle bread is all we have, So mea - ger our sup - ply— A lit - tle time, a lit - tle love Can hard - ly sat - is - fy. But let us bring the best we have De -
3. Like rip - ples in a pool, our gifts, How - ev - er small they are, Will reach and heal a need - y world, Will com - fort near and far. For Christ will bless our bit of bread, The

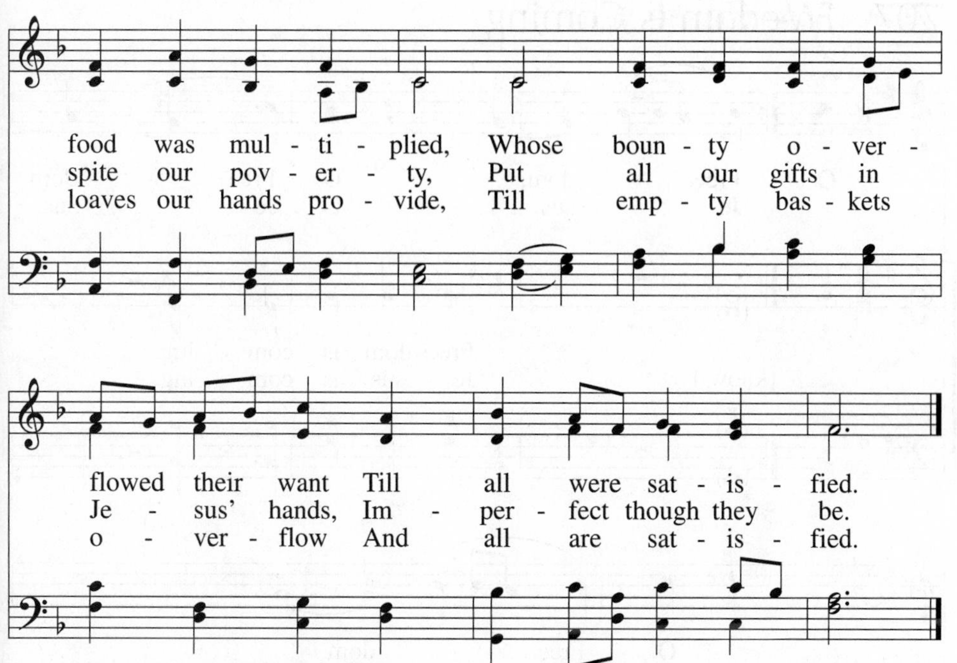
food was mul - ti - plied, Whose boun - ty o - ver -
spite our pov - er - ty, Put all our gifts in
loaves our hands pro - vide, Till emp - ty bas - kets
flowed their want Till all were sat - is - fied.
Je - sus' hands, Im - per - fect though they be.
o - ver - flow And all are sat - is - fied.

707 Freedom Is Coming

Solo:
O Free - dom, O Free - dom,
Je - sus, O Je - sus,
(know.)
Free-dom is com - ing.
Je - sus is com - ing.
O Free - dom.
O Je - sus.
Free-dom is com - ing.
Je - sus is com - ing.
Free-dom is
Je - sus is
O yes, I know.
O
com - ing. O yes, I know.
com - ing. O yes, I know. O

O yes, I know. O yes, I know.
O yes, I know. O yes, I know.
yes, I know. O yes, I know. O
O yes, I know. O yes, I know.
1.
2.
O
O yes,
yes, I know. O yes, I yes, I know.
O yes, I know.

Text: South African
Tune: South African

708 If You Believe and I Believe

If you be-lieve and I be-lieve And we to-geth-er pray,
The Ho-ly Spir-it must come down And set God's peo-ple free,
And set God's peo-ple free,
And set God's peo-ple free;
The Ho-ly Spir-it must come down And set God's peo-ple free.

Text: Zimbabwean traditional
Tune: Zimbabwean traditional; adapt. of English traditional; as taught by Tarasai; arr. by John L. Bell, b.1949, © 1991, Iona Community, GIA Publications, Inc., agent

Let Justice Roll Like a River 709

Refrain
Let jus - tice roll like a riv - er, and
wash all op - pres - sion a - way; Come, O
God, and take us, move and shake us,
Come now, and make us a - new, that
we might live just - ly like you.
Last time
Last time

Verse 1
1. Take from me your ho - ly feasts, all your
of - f'rings and your mu - sic; Let
jus - tice flow like wa - ters, and in -
teg - ri - ty like an ev - er - flow - ing
D.C.
stream.
Verse 2
2. How long shall we wait, O God, for the
day of your mer - cy to dawn, the
day we beat our swords in - to ploughs, when your
D.C.
peace reigns o - ver the earth?

Verses 3, 4
3. Hear this, all of you who use the poor in your
4. E - ven now re - turn to me, let your
thirst of pow - er and rich - es: the
hearts be bro - ken and hum - ble, for
Lord will turn your laugh - ter to tears, on the
I am gra - cious, gen - 'rous and kind; come and
D.C.
won - drous Day of our God.
seek the mer - cies of God.
Verse 5
5. You have been told the way of life, the
way of jus - tice and peace; to
act just - ly, to love gen - tly, and
D.C.
walk hum - bly with God.

Text: Amos 5:21-24, 8:4, Micah 4:3-4, 6:8, Joel 2:12-14; Marty Haugen, b.1950
Tune: Marty Haugen, b.1950

710 We Are Called

1. Come! Live in the light! Shine with the
2. Come! O - pen your heart! Show your
3. Sing! Sing a new song! Sing of that
joy and the love of the Lord! We are called
mer - cy to all those in fear! We are called
great day when all will be one! God will reign,
to be light for the king - dom, to
to be hope for the hope - less so all
and we'll walk with each oth - er as
live in the free - dom of the cit - y of God!
ha - tred and blind - ness will be no more!
sis - ters and broth - ers u - nit - ed in love!
We are called to act with jus - tice, we are
called to love ten - der - ly, we are called to
serve one an - oth - er; to walk hum - bly with
God!
1., 2.
3.

Text: Micah 6:8; David Haas, b.1957
Tune: David Haas, b.1957

We Shall Overcome 711

1. We shall o - ver - come, we shall o - ver - come, we shall o - ver - come some - day.
2. We'll walk hand in hand, we'll walk hand in hand, we'll walk hand in hand some - day.
3. We shall live in peace, we shall live in peace, we shall live in peace some - day.
4. We are not a - fraid, we are not a - fraid, we are not a - fraid to - day.
Oh, deep in my heart I do be - lieve we shall o - ver - come some - day.
3
3

5. We shall stand together...
6. The truth will make us free...
7. The Lord will see us through...
8. We shall be like him...
9. The whole wide world around...

Text: adapt. by Zilphia Horton, Frank Hamilton, Guy Carawan, and Pete Seeger, © 1960, 1963, Ludlow Music
Tune: adapt. by Zilphia Horton, Frank Hamilton, Guy Carawan, and Pete Seeger, © 1960, 1963, Ludlow Music; harm. by J. Jefferson Cleveland, b.1937, © 1981, by Abingdon Press

712 For the Healing of the Nations

1. For the heal - ing of the na - tions, Lord, we pray with one ac - cord; For a just and e - qual shar - ing Of the things that earth af - fords. To a life of love and ac - tion Help us rise and pledge our word.
2. Lead us now, Lord, in - to free - dom, From de - spair your world re - lease; That re - deemed from war and ha - tred, All may come and go in peace. Show us how through care and good - ness Fear will die and hope in - crease.
3. All that kills a - bun - dant liv - ing, Let it from the earth be banned; Pride of stat - us, race or school - ing, Dog - mas that ob - scure your plan. In our com - mon quest for jus - tice May we hal - low life's brief span.
4. You, cre - a - tor God, have writ - ten Your great name on hu - man - kind; For our grow - ing in your like - ness Bring the life of Christ to mind: That by our re - sponse and serv - ice Earth its des - ti - ny may find.

Text: Fred Kaan, b. 1929, alt., © 1968, Hope Publishing Co.
Tune: ST. THOMAS, 8 7 8 7 8 7; John Wade, 1711-1786

Here Am I 713

1. Here am I, Where un-der-neath the bridg - es
2. Here am I, With peo-ple in the line - up,
3. Here am I, Where two or three are gath - ered,

Of our win-ter cit - ies Home-less peo-ple sleep.
Anx-ious for a hand - out, Ach - ing for a job.
Read-y to be al - tered, Shar - ing wine and bread.

Here am I, Where in de - cay-ing hous - es Lit - tle
Here am I, When pen - sion - ers and strik - ers Sing and
Here am I, Where those who hear the preach-ing Change their

chil-dren shiv - er, Cry - ing at the cold. Where are you?
march to - geth - er, Want - ing some-thing new. Where are you?
way of liv - ing, Find the way to life. Where are you?

Text: Brian Wren, b.1936
Tune: STANISLAUS, 3 7 6 5 D 3; Daniel Charles Damon, b.1955

714 What You Have Done for Me

Verse 1
1. I am the hun - gry, I am the poor, I am the stran - ger out - side your door. So when you feed the hun - gry, when you clothe the poor I will no long - er be just a stran - ger at your door.
Refrain
What you have
What you have done for the least of my chil - dren
What you have done,
you have
you have done for me.

What you have giv - en, with noth-ing left to
What you have giv - en, with noth - ing to
What you have giv - en,
you have
Last time to coda
give, you have giv - en me.
To verses 2, 3
Verse 2
2. Come all you bless - ed, come and re - joice. In -
her - it the king - dom pre - pared for you. For
you are my chil - dren, called to serve as
keep-ers of the vi - sion and speak-ers of the word.
D.S.

Verse 3
3. I will look to you when life on earth has end - ed.
Those who give will re-ceive, those who seek will find; so
seek my face in ev-'ry face and see the eyes of God!
D.S.
Coda
me.
poco rit.

Text: Based on Matthew 25:24-41; Tony E. Alonso, b.1980
Tune: Tony E. Alonso, b.1980

On Holy Ground 715

Verses
1. The heav - ens em - brace the earth, as they
2. Á - bran - se los cie - los, en el
3. Let heav - en and earth sing praise to the
4. Bless earth, wa - ter, fire, and wind. Bless your
5. La his - to - ria de los pue - blos se - rá
6. U - nit - ed we join the light. We are
sing of the new birth. The
nom - bre de Cris - to Dios. Trans -
one who from death was raised. Let
peo - ple with - out, with - in. Let
li - bre por la ver - dad. La
born of the same right. We've
earth ech - oes and re - sounds that
for - men la tie - rra cau - ti - va en u - na
hearts ut - ter words pro - found in pro -
beau - ty and birth sur - round in re -
cau - sa es jus - ti - fi - ca - da. San - ta
come to re - lease what's bound, for
we are on ho - ly ground.
tie - rra con li - ber - tad.
claim - ing this ho - ly ground.
claim - ing this ho - ly ground.
tie - rra nues - tra se - rá.
we are on ho - ly ground.

Refrain
Assembly:
Yes, we do Lord!
Soli:
Descant:
Do you be-lieve in free - dom?
Melody:
Do you be-lieve in free - dom?
3
Jus - tice for all!
Do you be - lieve in jus - tice?
Do you be - lieve in jus - tice?
¡En su es - pí - ri - tu!
¿Yen la nue-va vi - da?
¿Yen la nue-va vi - da?

¡Tú, Se - ñor!
¿Quién es su li-be-ra - ción?
¿Quién es su li-be-ra - ción?
All:
Descant:
3
¡A - rri - ba! ¡Pro - cla - men! ¡San - ta Tie - rra!
Melody:
3
¡A - rri - ba! ¡Pro - cla - men! ¡San - ta Tie - rra!
1.- 5.
D.C.
Final ending
3
We are on ho - ly ground! ground!
3
We are on ho - ly ground! ground!

Text: Donna Peña, b.1955
Tune: Donna Peña, b.1955; acc. by Diana Kodner, b.1957

716 The Harvest of Justice

(Refrain) May we find rich - ness in the har - vest of jus - tice which Christ Je - sus has ripened for us.
1. Gath - er with pa - tience for those who have noth - ing. Leave them your rich - es, and you will re - ceive.
2. For to have mer - cy on those for - got - ten, this is my true law, this is my com - mand:
3. For to have lit - tle is to be in a - bun - dance. To give what re - mains, to give all we have,
(Bass on Refrain only)
Bread for the jour - ney,
Make room for the poor ones, make
Clothe the na - ked, be
is to walk with the poor ones, and be -

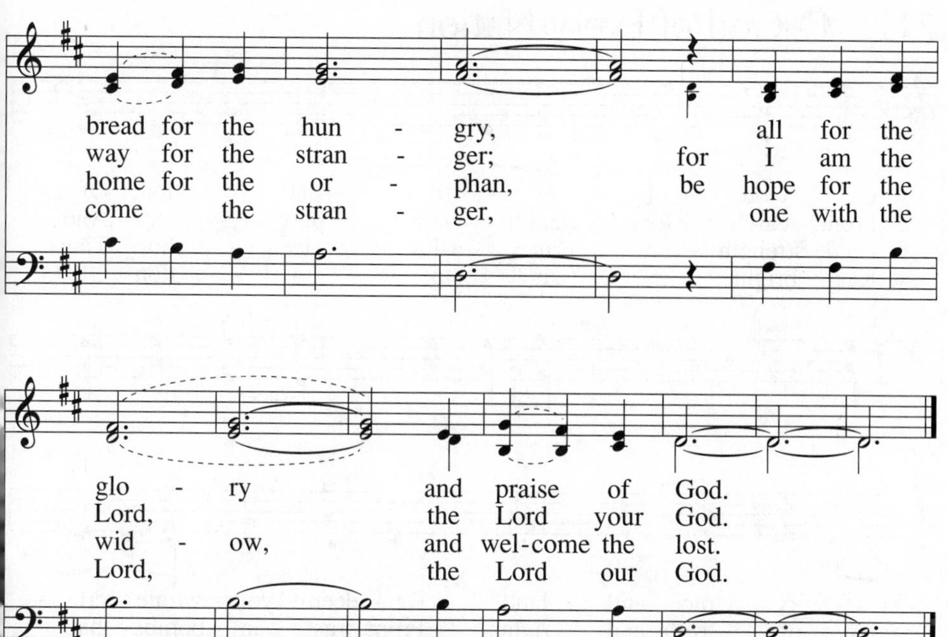
bread for the hun - gry, all for the
way for the stran - ger; for I am the
home for the or - phan, be hope for the
come the stran - ger, one with the
glo - ry and praise of God.
Lord, the Lord your God.
wid - ow, and wel-come the lost.
Lord, the Lord our God.

Text: Philippians 1:11, Leviticus 19:9, 23:22, Deuteronomy 24:19; David Haas, b.1957
Tune: David Haas, b.1957

717 O God of Every Nation

1. O God of ev - 'ry na - tion, Of
2. From search for wealth and pow - er And
3. Lord, strength - en all who la - bor That
4. Keep bright in us the vi - sion Of
ev - 'ry race and land, Re - deem your whole cre -
scorn of truth and right, From trust in bombs that
we may find re - lease From fear of rat - tling
days when wars shall cease, When ha - tred and di -
a - tion With your al - might - y hand; Where
show - er De - struc - tion through the night, From
sa - ber, From dread of war's in - crease; When
vi - sion Give way to love and peace, Till

hate and fear di - vide us And bit - ter threats are hurled, In love and mer - cy guide us And heal our strife - torn world.
pride of race and sta - tion And blind - ness to your way, De - liv - er ev - 'ry na - tion, E - ter - nal God, we pray.
hope and cour - age fal - ter, Your still small voice be heard; With faith that none can al - ter, Up - hold us by your word.
dawns the morn - ing glo - rious When Christ a - lone shall reign And he shall rule vic - to - rious O'er all the world's do - main.

Text: William W. Reid, b.1923, alt., © 1958, 1986, The Hymn Society (Administered by Hope Publishing Co.)
Tune: PASSION CHORALE, 7 6 7 6 D; Hans Leo Hassler, 1564-1612; harm. by J. S. Bach, 1685-1750

718 World Peace Prayer

Refrain
Descant:
Lead us from death to life, from false-hood to
Melody:
Lead us from death to life, from false-hood to
truth, from des - pair to hope, from fear to
truth, from des - pair to hope, from fear to
trust. Lead us from hate to love, from
trust. Lead us from hate to love, from
war to peace; let peace fill our hearts, let
war to peace; let peace fill our hearts, let
peace fill our world, let peace fill our u - ni - verse.
peace fill our world, let peace fill our u - ni - verse.

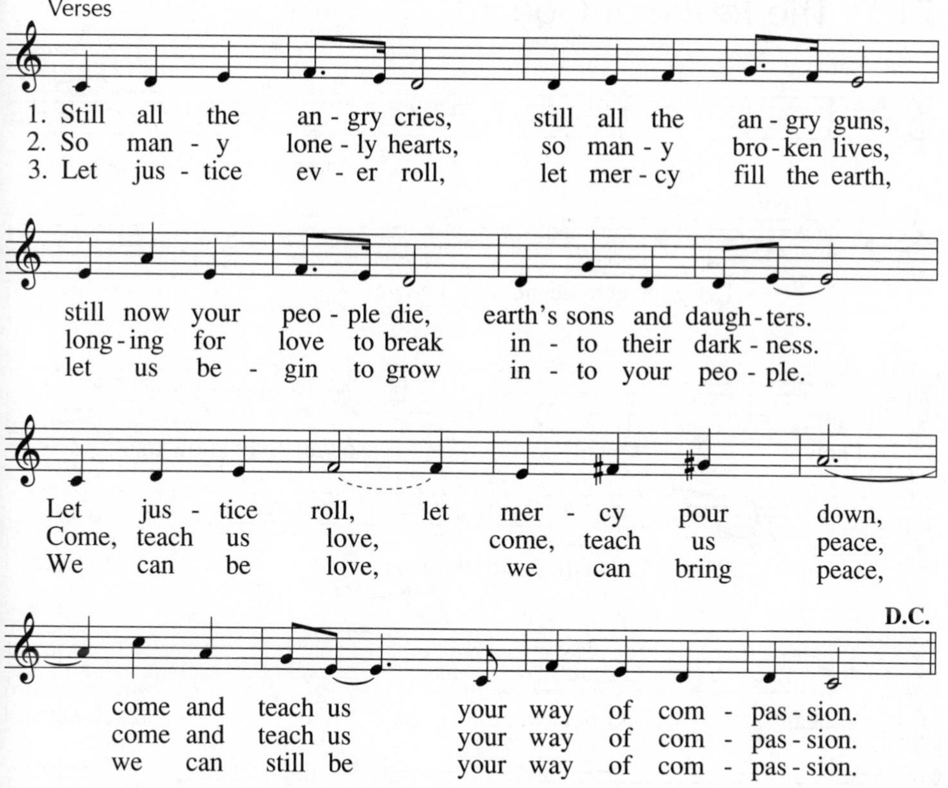
Verses
1. Still all the an - gry cries, still all the an - gry guns,
2. So man - y lone - ly hearts, so man - y bro - ken lives,
3. Let jus - tice ev - er roll, let mer - cy fill the earth,
still now your peo - ple die, earth's sons and daugh - ters.
long - ing for love to break in - to their dark - ness.
let us be - gin to grow in - to your peo - ple.
Let jus - tice roll, let mer - cy pour down,
Come, teach us love, come, teach us peace,
We can be love, we can bring peace,
come and teach us your way of com - pas - sion.
come and teach us your way of com - pas - sion.
we can still be your way of com - pas - sion.
D.C.

Text: Refrain, Upanishads, Satish Kumar; verses, Marty Haugen, b.1950, © 1985, GIA Publications, Inc.
Tune: Marty Haugen, b.1950, © 1985, GIA Publications, Inc.

719 The Peace of God

Refrain
Descant:
Melody:
Let your gen-tle-ness be known,
so all may know the Lord is near.
Do not wor-ry;
reach out in prayer, in prayer.
Stay with all that you have learned,
the peace of
Let your gen-tle-ness be known,
so all may know the Lord is near.
Do not wor-ry, do not wor-ry;
reach out to God in prayer.
Stay with all that you have learned,
and all that you have heard and seen,
and the

1., 2. To verses
God will be with you.
peace of God, the peace of God will be with you.
3.
you.
you.
Verse 1
1. What - ev - er is true, what - ev - er is just,
all that is pure and pleas - ing and all that is
D.C.
wor - thy of praise: think on these things.
Verse 2
2. And the peace of God, the peace of God be -
yond all un - der - stand - ing will guard your hearts, and
D.C.
guide your minds in Christ Je - sus.

Text: Based on Philippians 4:5-9; David Haas, b.1957
Tune: David Haas, b.1957

720 Prayer of Peace

1. Peace be - fore us, peace be - hind us, peace
2. Love be - fore us, love be - hind us, love
3. Light be - fore us, light be - hind us, light
4. Christ be - fore us, Christ be - hind us, Christ
5. Al - le - lu - ia, al - le - lu - ia, al - le -
6. Peace be - fore us, peace be - hind us, peace
un - der our feet. Peace with - in us, peace
un - der our feet. Love with - in us, love
un - der our feet. Light with - in us, light
un - der our feet. Christ with - in us, Christ
lu - ia, Al - le - lu - ia, al - le -
un - der our feet. Peace with - in us, peace
o - ver us, let all a - round us be peace.
o - ver us, let all a - round us be love.
o - ver us, let all a - round us be light.
o - ver us, let all a - round us be Christ.
lu - ia, al - le - lu - ia.
o - ver us, let all a - round us be peace.

Text: Based on a Navajo prayer; David Haas, b.1957
Tune: David Haas, b.1957

Make Me a Channel of Your Peace 721

Verses 1, 2, 4
1. Make me a chan-nel of your peace. Where there is ha-tred, let me bring your love. Where there is in-ju-ry, your par-don, Lord, And where there's doubt, true faith in you.
2. Make me a chan-nel of your peace. Where there's de-spair in life, let me bring hope. Where there is dark-ness, on-ly light, And where there's sad-ness, ev-er joy.
4. Make me a chan-nel of your peace. It is in par-don-ing that we are par-doned, in giv-ing of our-selves that we re-ceive, and in dy-ing that we're born to e-ter-nal life.
1.
2., 4.
Verse 3
3. Oh, Mas-ter, grant that I may nev-er seek So much to be con-soled as to con-sole. To be un-der-stood as to un-der-stand. To be loved as to love with all my soul.
D.C.

Text: *Prayer of St. Francis;* adapt. by Sebastian Temple, 1928-1997
Tune: Sebastian Temple, 1928-1997; acc. by Robert J. Batastini, b.1942

Dedicated to Mrs. Frances Tracy

722 Give Us Your Peace

Refrain
Je - sus, give us your peace. Bring us to - geth - er. Let all the fight - ing cease. Shat - ter all our hearts of stone. Give us a heart for love a - lone
Break our hearts of stone.
Repeat each time
Oh woh
To verses
Final ending

Verses
1. Some days the road I walk is lone - ly,
2. Some days the walk - ing makes me wea - ry
3. Some days the strength I need is fail - ing,
and it's so hard to find a friend.
and my soul yearns to be re - lieved.
and then, O Lord, I turn to you.
E - ven then I know,
You, my Lord, are strong.
I need nev - er fear,
some - where in my soul,
You pull me a - long.
you are al - ways near.
your love is far
Your love is far
What - ev - er hap -
too great to com - pre - hend.
too great to be be - lieved.
pens, you will pull me through.
D.S.
Oh woh
Oh woh
Oh woh

Text: Michael Mahler, b.1981
Tune: Michael Mahler, b.1981

723 Let There Be Peace on Earth

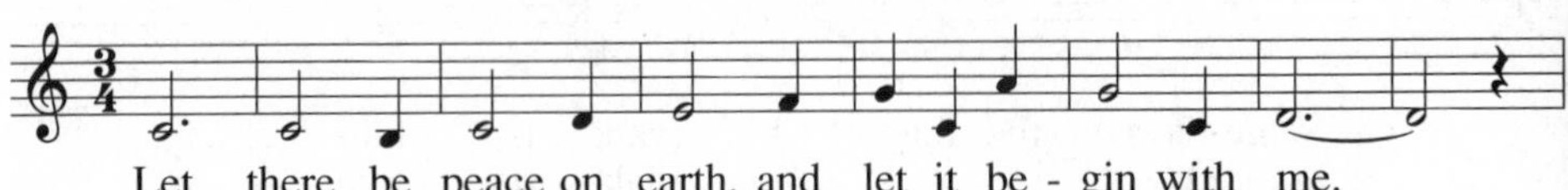
Let there be peace on earth, and let it be - gin with me.

Let there be peace on earth, the peace that was meant to be. With

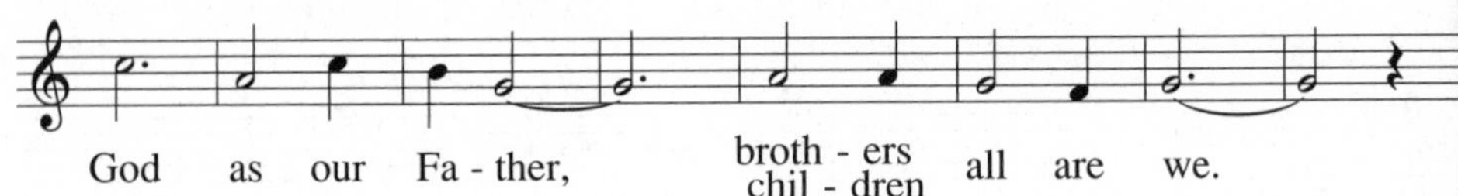
God as our Fa - ther, broth - ers / chil - dren all are we.

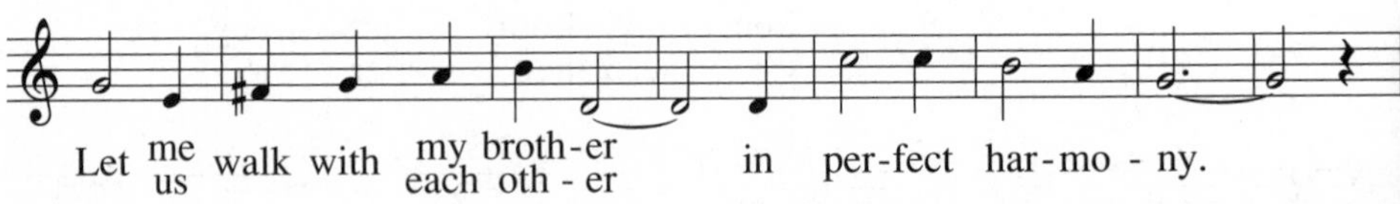
Let me / us walk with my broth-er / each oth - er in per-fect har-mo - ny.

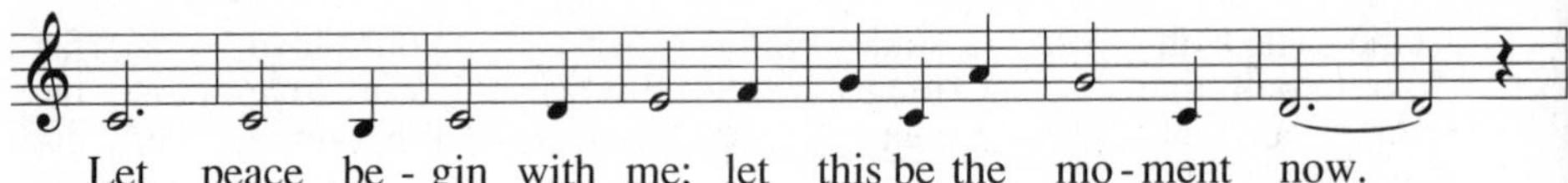
Let peace be - gin with me; let this be the mo-ment now.

With ev - 'ry step I take, let this be my sol-emn vow; To

take each mo-ment, and live each mo-ment in peace e - ter-nal - ly!

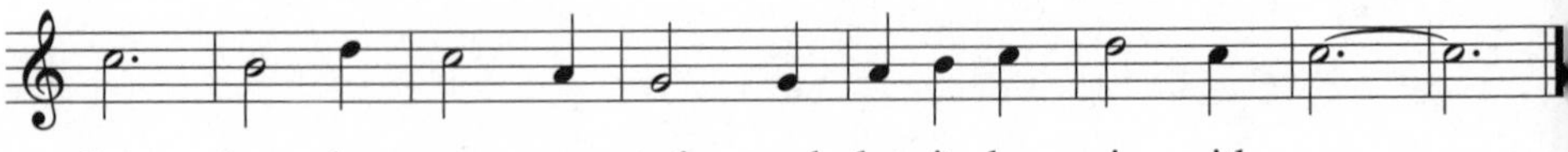
Let there be peace on earth, and let it be - gin with me.

Text: Sy Miller, 1908-1941, Jill Jackson, b.1913, © 1955, 1983, Jan-Lee Music
Tune: Sy Miller, 1908-1941, Jill Jackson, b.1913, © 1955, 1983, Jan-Lee Music; acc. by Diana Kodner, b.1957, © 1993, GIA Publications, Inc.
Used with permission

Dona Nobis Pacem 724

Canon
1.
Do - na no - bis pa - cem, pa - cem.
Do - na no - bis pa - cem.
2.
Do - na no - bis pa - cem.
Do - na no - bis pa - cem.
3.
Do - na no - bis pa - cem.
Do - na no - bis pa - cem.

Text: *Grant us peace*; Unknown
Tune: Traditional; acc. by Diana Kodner, b.1957,

725 Peace Is Flowing Like a River

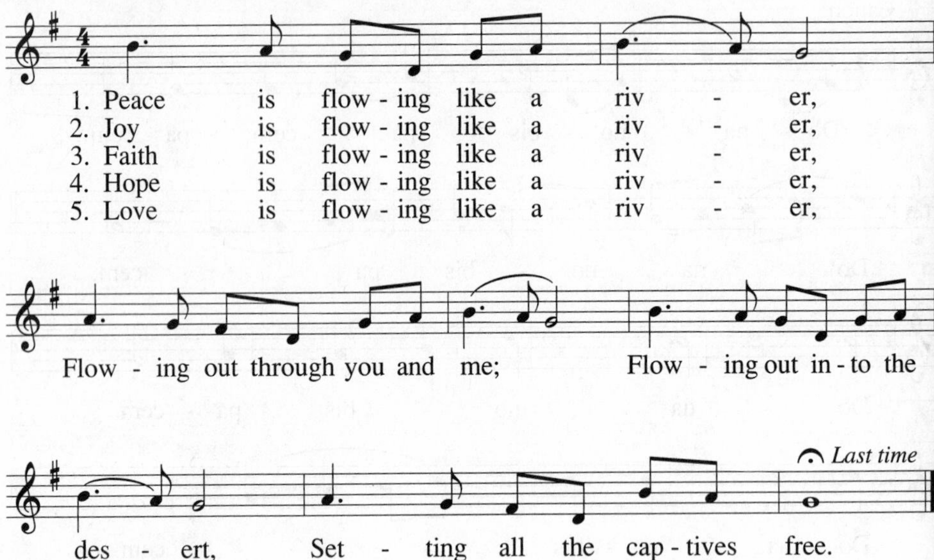
1. Peace is flow - ing like a riv - er,
2. Joy is flow - ing like a riv - er,
3. Faith is flow - ing like a riv - er,
4. Hope is flow - ing like a riv - er,
5. Love is flow - ing like a riv - er,
Flow - ing out through you and me;
Flow - ing out in - to the des - ert,
Set - ting all the cap - tives free.
Last time

Text: Unknown
Tune: Unknown; acc. by Diana Kodner, b.1957, © 1993, GIA Publications, Inc.

In Christ There Is No East or West 726

1. In Christ there is no east or west, In
2. In him shall true hearts ev - 'ry - where Their
3. Join hands, dis - ci - ples in the faith, What-
4. In Christ now meet both east and west, In
him no south or north, But one great fam - 'ly
high com - mun - ion find; His serv - ice is the
e'er your race may be! Who serve each oth - er
him meet south and north, All Christ - ly souls are
bound by love Through - out the whole wide earth.
gold - en cord Close - bind - ing hu - man - kind.
in Christ's love Are sure - ly kin to me.
one in him, Through - out the whole wide earth.

Text: Galatians 3:23; John Oxenham, 1852-1941
Tune: MC KEE, CM; African-American; adapt. by Harry T. Burleigh, 1866-1949

727 We Are Many Parts

Refrain
We are man - y parts, we are all one
bod - y, and the gifts we have
we are giv - en to share. May the Spir - it of
love make us one in - deed; one, the love that we
share, one, our hope in de - spair,
3
3

Last time
one, the cross that we bear.
Last time
Verses
unis.
1. God of all, we look to you,
2. So my pain is pain for you,
3. All you seek - ers, great and small,
we would be your ser - vants true,
in your joy is my joy, too;
seek the great - est gift of all;
div.
D.C.
let us be your love to all the world.
all is brought to - geth - er in the Lord.
if you love, then you will know the Lord.
div.

Text: 1 Corinthians 12, 13; Marty Haugen, b.1950
Tune: Marty Haugen, b.1950

728 They'll Know We Are Christians

1. We are one in the Spir - it, we are
2. We will walk with each oth - er, we will
3. We will work with each oth - er, we will
4. All praise to the Fa - ther, from
one in the Lord, We are one in the
walk hand in hand, We will walk with each
work side by side, We will work with each
whom all things come, And all praise to Christ
Spir - it, we are one in the Lord, And we
oth - er, we will walk hand in hand, And to -
oth - er, we will work side by side, And we'll
Je - sus, his on - ly Son, And all
pray that all u - ni - ty may one day be re -
geth - er we'll spread the news that God is in our
guard hu - man's dig - ni - ty and save hu - man's
praise to the Spir - it, who makes us
stored:
land:
pride:
one:
And they'll know we are Chris - tians by our
love, by our love, Yes, they'll know we are
Chris - tians by our love.

Text: Peter Scholtes, b.1938
Tune: ST. BRENDAN'S, 7 6 7 6 8 6 with refrain; Peter Scholtes, b.1938

Diverse in Culture, Nation, Race 729

*1.
2.
3.
4.
1. Di - verse in cul - ture, na - tion, race, We come to - geth - er by your grace. God, let us be a meet - ing ground Where hope and heal - ing love are found.
2. God, let us be a bridge of care Con - nect - ing peo - ple ev - 'ry - where. Help us con - front all fear and hate And lust for pow'r that sep - a - rate.
3. When cha - sms wid - en, storms a - rise, O Ho - ly Spir - it, make us wise. Let our re - solve, like steel, be strong To stand with those who suf - fer wrong.
4. God, let us be a ta - ble spread With gifts of love and bro - ken bread, Where all find wel - come, grace at - tends, And en - e - mies a - rise as friends.

*May be sung as a two or four-voice canon.

Text: Ruth Duck, b.1947,
Tune: TALLIS' CANON, LM; Thomas Tallis, c.1510-1583

730 Jesus Christ, Yesterday, Today and for Ever

Ostinato Refrain
Je - sus Christ, Je - sus Christ,
Je - su - cris - to a - yer, Je - su - cris - to hoy,
yes - ter - day, to - day and for ev - er.
siem - pre se - rá el Se - ñor.
Verses
Cantor:
1. O ra - diant light, O sun di - vine of our
Spanish
1. Oh luz go - zo - sa del san - to ros - tro de
God's death - less face.
Dios in - mor - tal.
3
2. You are al - pha and o - me - ga,
Spanish
2. Tú e - res al - fa y o - me - ga,

3
you are sav - ior and friend.
3
tú_e - res el Sal - va - dor.
3. Im - age of light sub - lime that
fills the heav-en - ly dwell - ing place.
4. At noon - time / eve - ning / morn - ing we praise you,
Spanish
4. Du - ran - te to - do el dí - a
ev - er - liv - ing Lord.
te_a - la - ba - mos, Se - ñor.
5. Son of God; source of light.
Spanish
5. Hi - jo de Dios, mues - tra luz.

6. At the light of ev - en - tide we
joy in your pres-ence.
3
7. Je - sus, com - pas-sion - ate one, friend of the op - pressed.
3
Spanish
8. Cris - to, da - nos la li - ber - tad;
Cris - to, da - nos tu sal - va - ción.
(Christ, give us freedom; Christ, give us salvation.)
3
Spanish
9. Da - me, Se-ñor, tu pa - la - bra; o - ye mi o - ra - ción.
(Lord, give me your word, hear my prayer.)
3
French
10. Joie a-bon-dan-te de l'É-gli-se, et la sour-ce de la vi - e.
(Abundant joy of the Church; fountain of life.)
3
11. You are our way and our truth; You are our life.
3
Vietnamese
12. Chúa sống Lai tràn dầy sù sống.
(Jesus Christ rose with full life.)
3

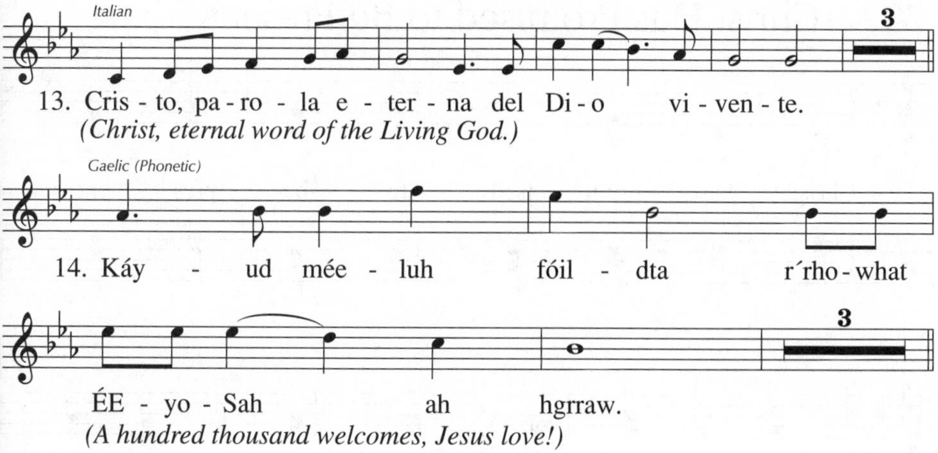

Italian

13. Cris - to, pa - ro - la e - ter - na del Di - o vi - ven - te.
(Christ, eternal word of the Living God.)

Gaelic (Phonetic)

14. Káy - ud mée - luh fóil - dta r´rho - what ÉE - yo - Sah ah hgrraw.
(A hundred thousand welcomes, Jesus love!)

Text: Suzanne Toolan, SM, b.1927, Spanish tr. by Ronald F. Krisman, b.1946
Tune: Suzanne Toolan, SM, b.1927

Jesus Is the Resurrection 731

Refrain

Je-sus is the res-ur - rec-tion and the life.
All who be - lieve will live.

To repeat and last time | *To verses*

Verse 1

1. We come to this house, we gath - er in his name. We know that our Sav - ior lives.

1. | 2. D.C.

Verse 2

2. Just as Laz - a - rus rose and Mar - tha be - lieved, the glo - ry of the Lord shall be re - vealed.

1. | 2. D.C.

Text: Derek Campbell, b.1963
Tune: Derek Campbell, b.1963

732 Christ Has Promised to Be Present

1.-4. Christ has prom - ised to be pres - ent
When we gath - er in his name. He, the Ho - ly
When God's mer - cy we pro - claim. He, the Guid - ing
When in pain we cry his name. He, the Wound - ed
In our fail - ures, joys, or fame. He, the Ris - en
One, will cleanse us From our sin - ful - ness and shame.
One, will teach us Words of wis - dom in his name.
One, will touch us With his Spir - it's heal - ing flame.
One, will save us Through his pow'r - ful, glo - rious name.

Text: Rae E. Whitney, © 1994, Selah Publishing Co., Inc.
Tune: STUTTGART, 8 7 8 7; *Psalmodia Sacra,* 1715; adapt. and harm. by William Henry Havergal, 1793-1870, alt.

Alleluia! Give the Glory 733

Refrain
Descant (last time only):
Al-le-lu - ia!
Al-le-lu - ia!
Al-le - lu - ia!
Al-le-lu - ia!
Al-le-
Ooh
lu - ia!
Give the
Give the glo - ry
and the hon - or,
glo - ry
and the hon - or
to the

give glo - ry to the Lord!
Lord!
Al-le -
Al-le-lu - ia!
Al-le-lu - ia!
Al-le -
lu - ia!
Al-le - lu - ia!
Al-le -
Al-le -
Al-le-lu - ia!
lu - ia!
lu - ia!
Al-le-lu!
Give the
lu - ia!

glo - ry and the hon - or to the
Lord!
To verses
Last time
Verses
1. Where two or three are gath - ered in my
2. I am the vine and you are the
name,
branch - es.
there I am in the midst of them; there I'll
A - bide in me and
be.
bear much fruit.
D.C.

xt: Matthew 18:20, John 15:5; adapt. by Ken Canedo, b.1953, and Bob Hurd, b.1950
ne: Ken Canedo, b.1953; choral arr. by Craig S. Kingsbury, b.1952; acc. by Dominic MacAller, b.1959

734 Come to the Feast / Ven al Banquete

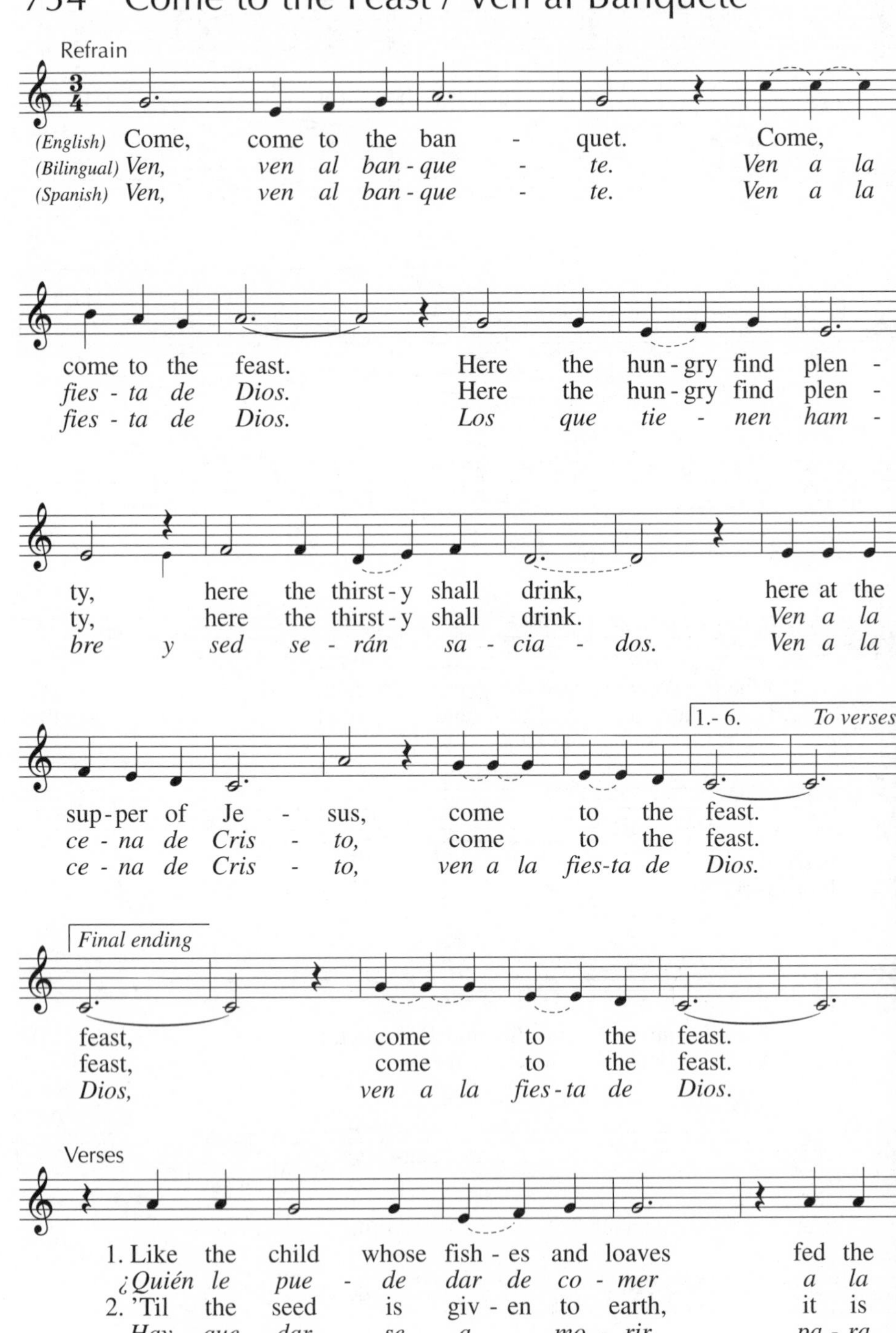
Refrain
(English) Come, come to the ban - quet. Come, come to the feast. Here the hun-gry find plen - ty, here the thirst-y shall drink, here at the sup-per of Je - sus, come to the feast.
(Bilingual) Ven, ven al ban-que - te. Ven a la fies-ta de Dios. Here the hun-gry find plen - ty, here the thirst-y shall drink. Ven a la ce-na de Cris - to, come to the feast.
(Spanish) Ven, ven al ban-que - te. Ven a la fies-ta de Dios. Los que tie - nen ham - bre y sed se - rán sa - cia - dos. Ven a la ce-na de Cris - to, ven a la fies-ta de Dios.
1.- 6.
To verses
Final ending
feast, come to the feast.
feast, come to the feast.
Dios, ven a la fies-ta de Dios.
Verses
1. Like the child whose fish-es and loaves fed the
¿Quién le pue - de dar de co - mer a la
2. 'Til the seed is giv-en to earth, it is
Hay que dar - se a mo - rir pa - ra
3. In the stran - ger by our side, in the
Los des - am - pa - ra-dos ven - drán a par -

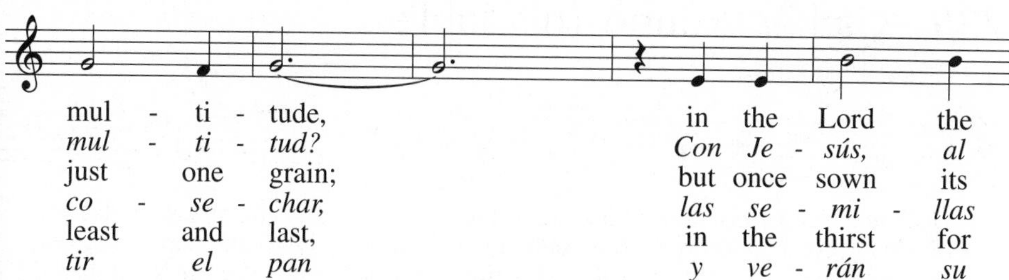
mul - ti - tude, in the Lord the
mul - ti - tud? Con Je - sús, al
just one grain; but once sown its
co - se - char, las se - mi - llas
least and last, in the thirst for
tir el pan y ve - rán su

lit - tle we have, bro - ken and shared, be -
com - par - tir lo po - co que hay, re - ci -
death brings new birth, the har - vest is rich; what's
de li - ber - tad y re - su - rrec - ción, la pro -
jus - tice we share, Christ is here in the
dig - ni - dad de nue - vo en Je - sús, Sal - va -

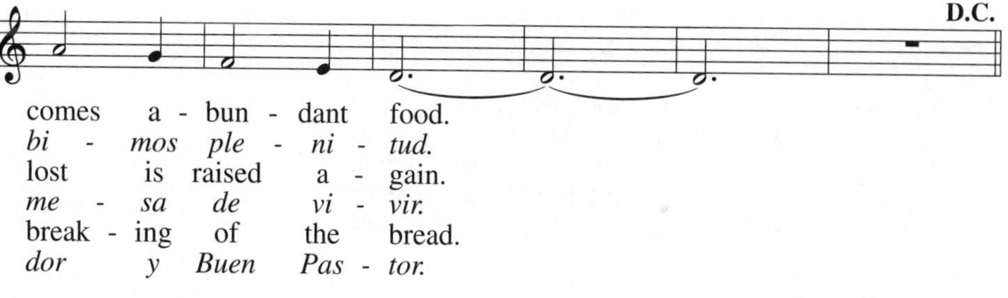
D.C.
comes a - bun - dant food.
bi - mos ple - ni - tud.
lost is raised a - gain.
me - sa de vi - vir.
break - ing of the bread.
dor y Buen Pas - tor.

Text: Bob Hurd, b.1950, Pia Moriarty, b.1948, Jaime Cortez, b.1963
Tune: Bob Hurd, b.1950; acc. by Dominic MacAller, b.1959, alt.

735 Gather 'Round This Table

Verses
Cantor:
1. Come, gath - er 'round this ta - ble, all you from far and near,
(2. O) come and join the ban - quet, ho - ly and hap - py feast,
(3. And) here we taste sal - va - tion, break now the bless - ed bread;
(4. The) cup of God's own glad - ness, sweet and a - bun - dant wine,
(5. And) here we share the sto - ries an - cient and ev - er new,
gath - er 'round this ta - ble, for all are wel - come
God has spread a ban - quet where the great - est shall be
joined with all cre - a - tion, ev - 'ry hun - ger shall be
saved from sin and sad - ness, let your spir - its bright - ly
cross and crown and glo - ry, our death and life a -
All:
here, yes all are wel - come here.
least, the great - est shall be least.
fed, all hun - gers shall be fed.
shine, all spir - its bright - ly shine.
new, our death and life a - new.
Refrain
Bless - ed are they who will feast in the Reign of God.
Bless - ed are they who will share the bread of life.

Bless-ed are they who are least in the Reign of God;
they shall re-joice at the feast of life.
1.- 4.
Cantor:
D.S.
5.
2. O
3. And
4. The
5. And

Text: Marty Haugen, b.1950
Tune: Marty Haugen, b.1950

736 What Is This Place

1. What is this place where we are meet - ing?
2. Words from a - far, stars that are fall - ing,
3. And we ac - cept bread at his ta - ble,
On - ly a house, the earth its floor, Walls and a roof
Sparks that are sown in us like seed. Names for our God,
Bro - ken and shared, a liv - ing sign. Here in this world,
shel - ter - ing peo - ple, Win - dows for light, an o - pen door.
dreams, signs and won - ders Sent from the past are all we need.
dy - ing and liv - ing, We are each oth - er's bread and wine.
Yet it be - comes a bod - y that lives When
We in this place re - mem - ber and speak A -
This is the place where we can re - ceive What
we are gath - ered here, And know our God is near.
gain what we have heard: God's free re - deem - ing word.
we need to in - crease: Our jus - tice and God's peace.

Text: *Zomaar een dak boven wat hoofen;* Huub Oosterhuis, b.1933; trans. by David Smith, b.1933,
Tune: KOMT NU MET ZANG, 9 8 9 8 9 66; Valerius' *Neder-landtsche gedenck-klanck;* acc. by Robert J. Batastini, b.1942,

God Is Here! As We His People 737

1. God is here! As we his people
2. Here are sym - bols to re - mind us
3. Here our chil - dren find a wel - come
4. Lord of all, of church and king - dom,
Meet to of - fer praise and prayer,
Of our life - long need of grace;
In the Shep - herd's flock and fold;
In an age of change and doubt,
May we find in ful - ler meas - ure
Here are ta - ble, font and pul - pit,
Here, as bread and wine are tak - en,
Keep us faith - ful to the gos - pel,
What it is in Christ we share:
Here the cross has cen - tral place:
Christ sus - tains us as of old:
Help us work your pur - pose out:

Here, as in the world a - round us,
Here in hon - es - ty of preach - ing,
Here the ser - vants of the Ser - vant
Here, in this day's ded - i - ca - tion,
All our var - ied skills and arts
Here in si - lence as in speech,
Seek in wor - ship to ex - plore
All we have to give, re - ceive;
Wait the com - ing of his Spir - it
Here in new - ness and re - new - al
What it means in dai - ly liv - ing
We who can - not live with - out you,
In - to o - pen minds and hearts.
God the Spir - it comes to each.
To be - lieve and to a - dore.
We a - dore you! We be - lieve!

Text: Fred Pratt Green, 1903-2000, © 1979, Hope Publishing Co.
Tune: ABBOT'S LEIGH, 8 7 8 7 D; Cyril V. Taylor, 1907-1991, © 1942, 1970, Hope Publishing Co.

As We Gather at Your Table 738

1. As we gath - er at your Ta - ble,
2. Turn our wor - ship in - to wit - ness
3. Gra - cious Spir - it, help us sum - mon
As we lis - ten to your Word,
In the sac - ra - ment of life;
Oth - er guests to share that feast
Help us know, O God, your pres - ence:
Send us forth to love and serve you,
Where tri - um - phant Love will wel - come
Let our hearts and minds be stirred. Nour - ish us with
Bring - ing peace where there is strife. Give us, Christ, your
Those who had been last and least. There no more will
sa - cred sto - ry Till we claim it as our own;
great com - pas - sion To for - give as you for - gave;
en - vy blind us Nor will pride our peace de - stroy,
Teach us through this ho - ly ban - quet
May we still be - hold your im - age
As we join with saints and an - gels
How to make Love's vic - t'ry known.
In the world you died to save.
To re - peat the sound - ing joy.

Text: Carl P. Daw, Jr., b.1944, © 1989, Hope Publishing Co.
Tune: HOLY MANNA, 8 7 8 7 D; William Moore, fl.1830; acc. by Kelly Dobbs Mickus, b.1966, © 2003, GIA Publications, Inc.

739 Come, Let Us Sing with Joy to the Lord

Refrain
Soloist (after vs. 2):
Come, let us sing!
Melody:
Come, let us sing with joy to the Lord! Shout to the rock of our
Come, let us sing and greet him with a song of praise!
sal - va - tion! Come, let us greet him with a song of praise, for
Great is our God, King of all kings!
great is our God, the King of all kings!
Come, let us sing to the Lord!
Come, let us sing with joy to the Lord!
To verses

Last time
Come, let us sing with joy to the Lord! Come, let us sing with joy
to the Lord! Come, let us sing with joy to the
Lord!
Verses
Cantor:
1. Let us bow down and wor - ship the Lord:
2. Great is the Lord and wor - thy of praise:
3. All that has life and breath shall re - joice:
4. Heav-en and earth re - joice in his name:
All:
Come, let us sing
with joy to the Lord!
Cantor:
For this is our God, whose
Sing to the Lord and
The great and the small, all
He gov-erns the world with
peo - ple we are:
bless his name:
crea-tures of God:
jus - tice and truth:
All:
Come, let us sing with joy to the Lord!
Come, let us sing with joy to the Lord!
D.C.

Text: Psalms 95 and 96; Paul A. Tate, b.1968
Tune: Paul A. Tate, b.1968

740 Come to Us

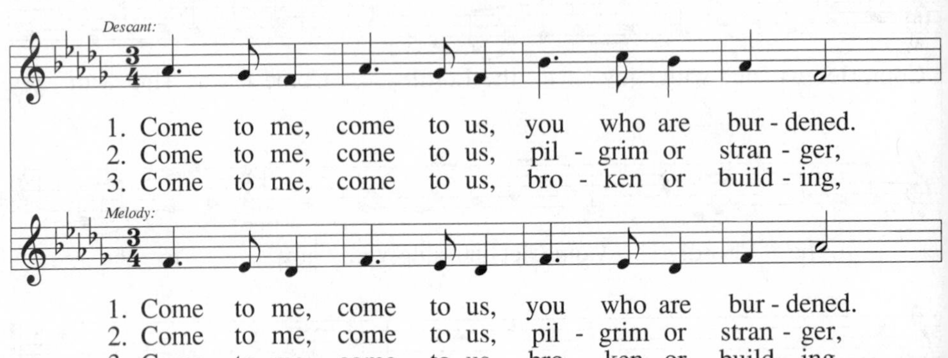
Descant:
1. Come to me, come to us, you who are bur-dened.
2. Come to me, come to us, pil-grim or stran-ger,
3. Come to me, come to us, bro-ken or build-ing,
Melody:
1. Come to me, come to us, you who are bur-dened.
2. Come to me, come to us, pil-grim or stran-ger,
3. Come to me, come to us, bro-ken or build-ing,

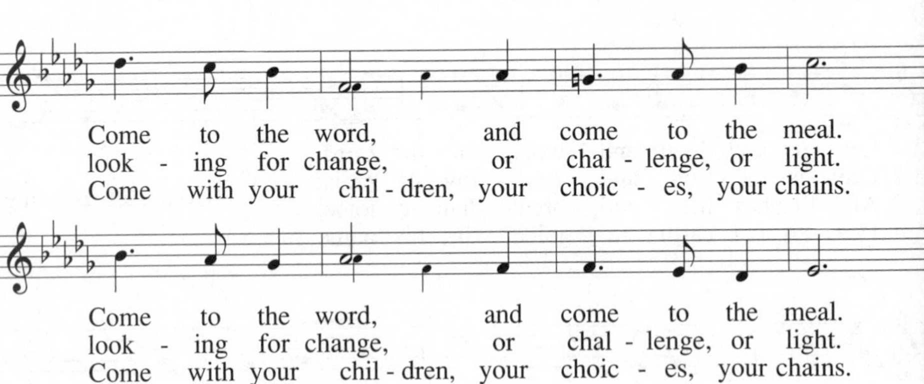
Come to the word, and come to the meal.
look-ing for change, or chal-lenge, or light.
Come with your chil-dren, your choic-es, your chains.
Come to the word, and come to the meal.
look-ing for change, or chal-lenge, or light.
Come with your chil-dren, your choic-es, your chains.

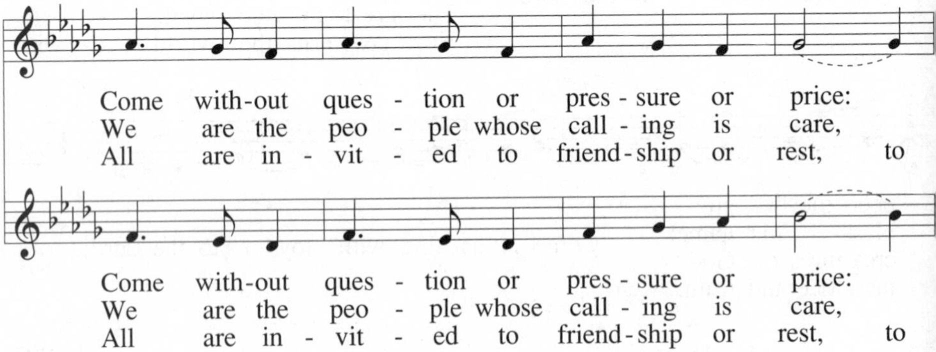
Come with-out ques-tion or pres-sure or price:
We are the peo-ple whose call-ing is care,
All are in-vit-ed to friend-ship or rest, to
Come with-out ques-tion or pres-sure or price:
We are the peo-ple whose call-ing is care,
All are in-vit-ed to friend-ship or rest, to

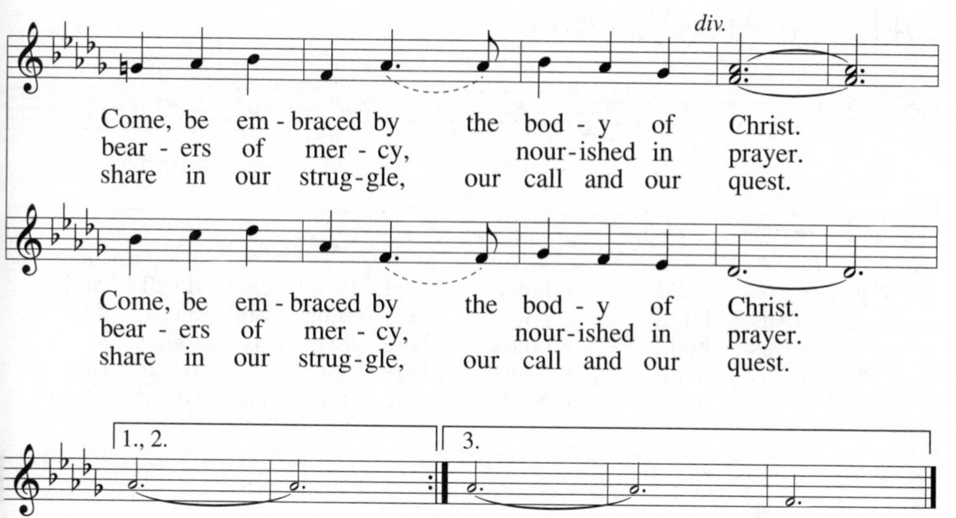
div.
Come, be em - braced by the bod - y of Christ.
bear - ers of mer - cy, nour-ished in prayer.
share in our strug-gle, our call and our quest.
Come, be em - braced by the bod - y of Christ.
bear - ers of mer - cy, nour-ished in prayer.
share in our strug-gle, our call and our quest.
1., 2.
3.

Text: Rory Cooney, b.1952
Tune: Rory Cooney, b.1952

741 All Are Welcome

Descant (verse 5):
5. Let us build so all are named,
Melody:
1. Let us build a house where love can dwell And
2. Let us build a house where proph - ets speak, And
3. Let us build a house where love is found In
4. Let us build a house where hands will reach Be -
5. Let us build a house where all are named, Their
their songs and vi-sions heard,
all can safe - ly live, A place where saints and
words are strong and true, Where all God's chil - dren
wa - ter, wine and wheat: A ban - quet hall on
yond the wood and stone To heal and strength-en,
songs and vi - sions heard And loved and treas - ured,
taught and claimed As words with - in the
chil - dren tell How hearts learn to for -
dare to seek To dream God's reign a -
ho - ly ground, Where peace and jus - tice
serve and teach, And live the Word they've
taught and claimed As words with - in the
Word. Built of tears and cries and laugh - ter,
give. Built of hopes and dreams and vi - sions, Rock of
new. Here the cross shall stand as wit - ness And as
meet. Here the love of God, through Je - sus, Is re -
known. Here the out - cast and the stran - ger Bear the
Word. Built of tears and cries and laugh - ter, Prayers of

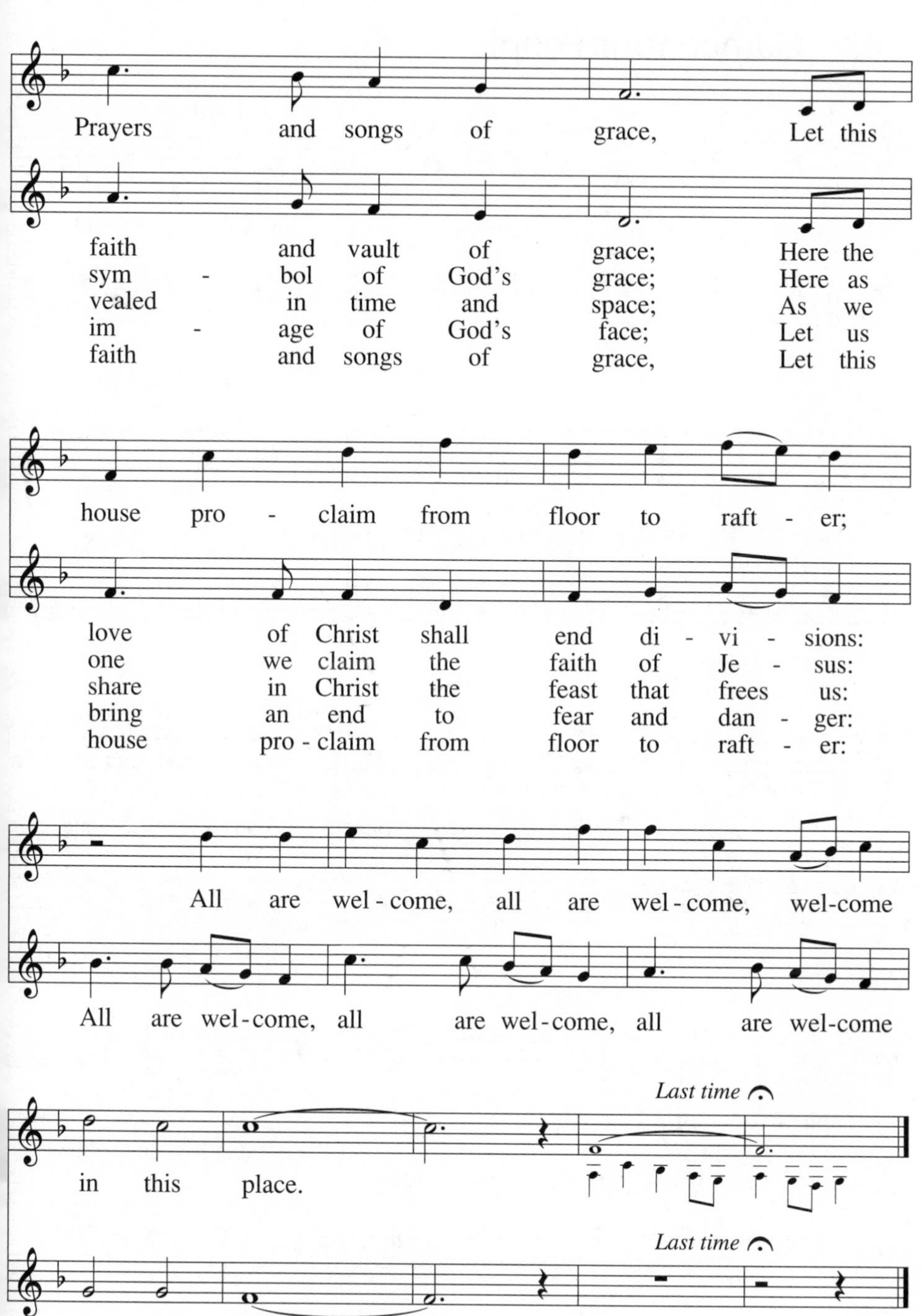
Prayers and songs of grace, Let this
faith and vault of grace; Here the
sym - bol of God's grace; Here as
vealed in time and space; As we
im - age of God's face; Let us
faith and songs of grace, Let this
house pro - claim from floor to raft - er;
love of Christ shall end di - vi - sions:
one we claim the faith of Je - sus:
share in Christ the feast that frees us:
bring an end to fear and dan - ger:
house pro - claim from floor to raft - er:
All are wel - come, all are wel - come, wel-come
All are wel - come, all are wel - come, all are wel - come
in this place.
Last time
in this place.
Last time

Text: Marty Haugen, b.1950
Tune: TWO OAKS, 9 6 8 6 8 7 10 with refrain; Marty Haugen, b.1950

742 Gather Your People

Refrain
Lord.
Gath - er your peo - ple, O Lord, O
Lord. Gath - er your peo - ple, O Lord.
One bread, one bod - y, one
spir - it of love.
Gath - er your
spir - it, one spir - it of love.
of love.

1.- 4.
To verses
Last time
peo - ple, O Lord. (O Lord.) Lord.
Verses
1. Draw us forth to the ta - ble of life:
2. We are parts of the bod - y of Christ,
3. No more harm on the moun - tain of God;
4. Wash us, Lord, in the wa - ters of life;
broth - ers and sis - ters, each of us called to
need - ing each oth - er, each of the gifts the
swords in - to plow - shares. Free us, O Lord, from
wa - ters of mer - cy, wa - ters of hope that
walk in your light.
Spir - it pro - vides.
hard - ness of heart.
flow from your side.
3
D.C.

Text: 1 Corinthians 12, Isaiah 2:3-4, 11:9; Bob Hurd, b.1950
Tune: Bob Hurd, b.1950; choral arr. by Craig S. Kingsbury, b.1952; acc. by Dominic MacAller, b.1959

743 Gather Us In

6/8
1. Here in this place new light is stream - ing,
2. We are the young— our lives are a mys - t'ry,
3. Here we will take the wine and the wa - ter,
4. Not in the dark of build-ings con - fin - ing,
Now is the dark - ness van - ished a - way,
We are the old— who yearn for your face,
Here we will take the bread of new birth,
Not in some heav - en, light - years a - way, But
See in this space our fears and our dream-ings,
We have been sung through - out all of his - t'ry,
Here you shall call your sons and your daugh-ters,
here in this place the new light is shin - ing,
Brought here to you in the light of this
Called to be light to the whole hu - man
Call us a - new to be salt for the
Now is the King - dom, now is the
3/8
6/8
day.
race.
earth.
day.
Gath - er us in— the
Gath - er us in— the
Give us to drink the
Gath - er us in and
lost and for - sak - en,
rich and the haugh - ty,
wine of com - pas - sion,
hold us for ev - er,
Gath - er us in— the
Gath - er us in— the
Give us to eat the
Gath - er us in and

blind and the lame; Call to us now, and
proud and the strong; Give us a heart so
bread that is you; Nour - ish us well, and
make us your own; Gath - er us in— all
we shall a - wak - en, We shall a - rise at the
meek and so low - ly, Give us the cour - age to
teach us to fash - ion Lives that are ho - ly and
peo - ples to - geth - er, Fire of love in our
sound of our name.
en - ter the song.
hearts that are true.
flesh and our bone.

Text: Marty Haugen, b.1950
Tune: GATHER US IN, Irregular; Marty Haugen, b.1950

744 Come All You People

Cantor:
Come all you peo - ple, come and
Come all you peo - ple, come and praise your
Ahom
Ahom
praise your Mak - er, Come all you peo - ple,
Mak - er, Come all you peo - ple,
Ahom
come and praise your Mak - er, Come
come and praise your Mak - er, Come all you
Ahom
Ahom

all you peo - ple, come and praise your Mak - er,
peo - ple, come and praise your Mak - er,
Ahom
3
Last time
Come now and wor - ship the Lord. Come and praise your Mak - er.
3
Last time
Come now and wor - ship the Lord.
3
Last time
Ahom Ahom Ahom

Text: Alexander Gondo
Tune: Alexander Gondo; arr. by John L. Bell, b.1949,

745 Gathered as One

Verses
Cantor:
1. Man-y fac-es, the young and the old,
2. Man-y pil-grims, shar-ing at feast,
3. Man-y voic-es, raised up in song,
Choir and assembly:
gath-ered as one in our God!
Cantor:
Through-out his-t'ry the sto-ry's re-told,
All are wel-come the great-est and least,
In one fam-'ly where all can be-long,
Choir and assembly:
gath-ered as one in our God!
Cantor:
Like those come be-fore us, we lis-ten and learn. We re-mem-ber the prom-ise and a-wait your re-turn. So with-out hes-i-ta-tion a new gen-er-a-tion pro-claims the sal-va-tion of God!

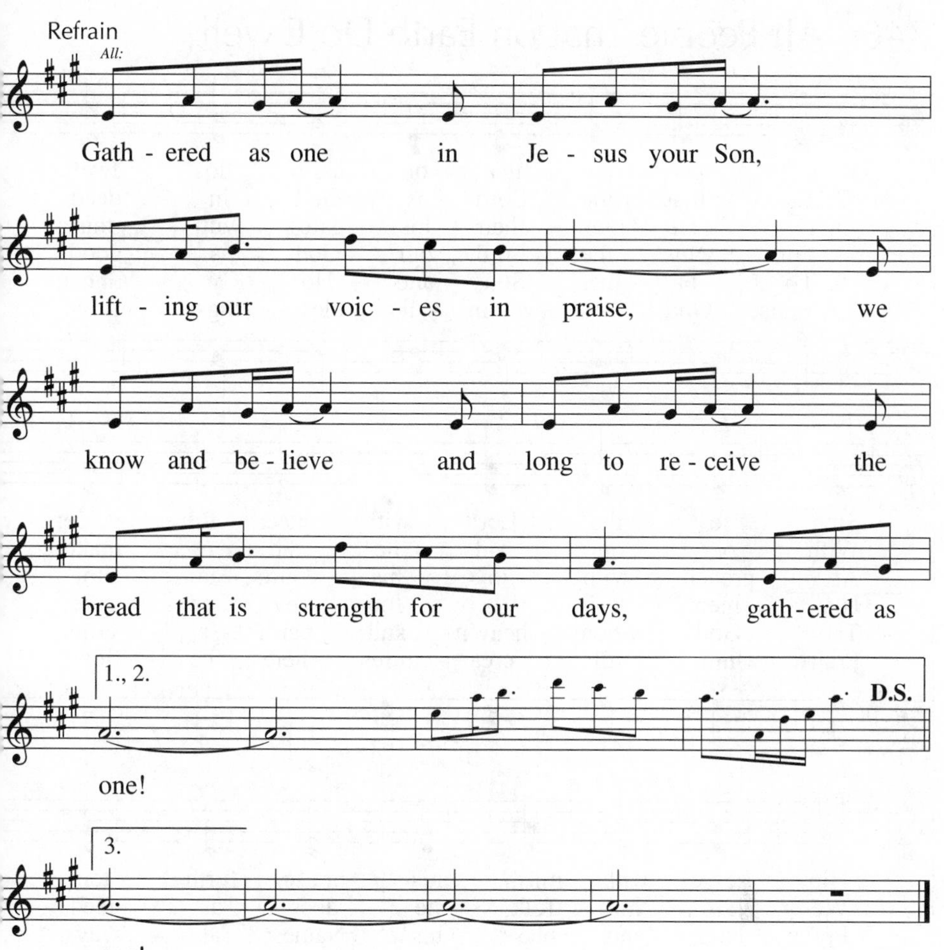
Refrain
All:
Gath - ered as one in Je - sus your Son,
lift - ing our voic - es in praise, we
know and be - lieve and long to re - ceive the
bread that is strength for our days, gath - ered as
1., 2.
one!
D.S.
3.
one!

Text: Deanna Light and Paul A. Tate, b.1968
Tune: Deanna Light and Paul A. Tate, b.1968

746 All People That on Earth Do Dwell

1. All people that on earth do dwell, Sing to the Lord with cheerful voice; Him serve with mirth, his praise forth tell, Come we before him, and rejoice.
2. Know that the Lord is God indeed; Without our aid he did us make; We are his folk, he does us feed, And for his sheep he does us take.
3. O enter then his gates with praise; Approach with joy his courts unto; Praise, laud, and bless his Name always, For it is seemly so to do.
4. For why? the Lord our God is good: His mercy is for ever sure; His truth at all times firmly stood, And shall from age to age endure.
5. To Father, Son, and Holy Ghost, The God whom heav'n and earth adore, From us and from the angel host Be praise and glory evermore.
* Praise God, from whom all blessings flow; Praise him, all creatures here below; Praise him above, you heav'nly host: Praise Father, Son and Holy Ghost.

May be sung alone or as an alternate to stanza 5.

Text: Psalm (99)100; William Kethe, d. c.1593; Doxology, Thomas Ken, 1637-1711
Tune: OLD HUNDREDTH, LM; Louis Bourgeois, c.1510-1561

Come, Host of Heaven's High Dwelling Place 747

1. Come, Host of Heav'n's high dwell - ing place, Come,
2. Sur - round these walls with faith and love That
3. Bless and in - spire those gath - ered here With
4. Here may the los - er find his worth, The
5. Build, from the hu - man fab - ric, signs Of
6. So, to the Lord whose care en - folds The
earth's dis - put - ed guest; Find where we meet a
through the nights and days, When hu - man tongues from
pa - tience, hope, and peace, And all the joys that
stran - ger find a friend; Here may the hope - less
how your king - dom thrives, Of how the Ho - ly
world held in his hands, Be glo - ry, hon - or,
wel - come home, Stay here and take your rest.
speak - ing cease, These stones may ech - o praise.
know the depth In which all sor - rows cease.
find their faith And aim - less find an end.
Spir - it chang - es life By chang - ing lives.
pow'r and praise For which this com - p'ny stands.
3

748 Morning Has Broken

1. Morn - ing has bro - ken Like the first morn - ing,
2. Sweet the rain's new fall Sun - lit from heav - en,
3. Mine is the sun - light! Mine is the morn - ing
Black - bird has spo - ken Like the first bird.
Like the first dew - fall On the first grass.
Born of the one light E - den saw play!
Praise for the sing - ing! Praise for the morn - ing!
Praise for the sweet - ness Of the wet gar - den,
Praise with e - la - tion, Praise ev - 'ry morn - ing,
Praise for them, spring - ing Fresh from the Word!
Sprung in com - plete - ness Where his feet pass.
God's re - cre - a - tion Of the new day!

Text: Eleanor Farjeon, 1881-1965, *The Children's Bells,* © David Higham Assoc. Ltd.
Tune: BUNESSAN, 5 5 5 4 D; Gaelic; acc. by Robert J. Batastini, b.1942, © 1999, GIA Publications, Inc.

This Day God Gives Me 749

1. This day God gives me Strength of high
2. This day God sends me Strength as my
3. God's way is my way, God's shield is
4. Ris - ing I thank you, Might - y and
heav - en, Sun and moon shin - ing,
guard - ian, Might to up - hold me,
'round me, God's host de - fends me,
strong One, King of cre - a - tion,
Flame in my hearth, Flash - ing of light - ning,
Wis - dom as guide. Your eyes are watch - ful,
Sav - ing from ill. An - gels of heav - en,
Giv - er of rest, Firm - ly con - fess - ing
Wind in its swift - ness, Depths of the
Your ears are lis - t'ning, Your lips are
Drive from me al - ways All that would
God in three Per - sons, One - ness of
o - cean, Firm - ness of earth.
speak - ing, Friend at my side.
harm me, Stand by me still.
God - head, Trin - i - ty blest.
Last time

Text: Ascribed to St. Patrick; James Quinn, S.J., b.1919, © 1969. Used by permission of Selah Publishing Co., Inc.
Tune: ANDREA, 5 5 5 4 D; David Haas, b.1957, © 1993, GIA Publications, Inc.

750 God of Day and God of Darkness

1. God of day and God of dark - ness, Now we
2. Still the na - tions curse the dark - ness, Still the
3. Show us Christ in one an - oth - er, Make us
4. You shall be the path that guides us, You the
5. Praise to you in day and dark - ness, You our
stand be - fore the night; As the shad - ows stretch and
rich op - press the poor; Still the earth is bruised and
ser - vants strong and true; Give us all your love of
light that in us burns; Shin - ing deep with - in all
source and you our end; Praise to you who love and
deep - en, Come and make our dark - ness bright. All cre -
bro - ken By the ones who still want more. Come and
jus - tice So we do what you would do. Let us
peo - ple, Yours the love that we must learn, For our
nur-ture us As a fa - ther, moth - er, friend. Grant us
a - tion still is groan - ing For the dawn - ing of your
wake us from our sleep - ing, So our hearts can - not ig -
call all peo - ple ho - ly, Let us pledge our lives a -
hearts shall wan - der rest - less 'Til they safe to you re -
all a peace - ful rest - ing, Let each mind and bod - y
might, When the Sun of peace and jus - tice
nore All your peo - ple lost and bro - ken,
new, Make us one with all the low - ly,
turn; Find - ing you in one an - oth - er,
mend, So we rise re - freshed to - mor - row,
Fills the earth with ra - diant light.
All your chil - dren at our door.
Let us all be one in you.
We shall all your face dis - cern.
Hearts re - newed to King - dom tend.

Day Is Done 751

1. Day is done, but love un - fail - ing Dwells ev - er here; Shad - ows fall, but hope, pre - vail - ing, Calms ev - 'ry fear. God, our Mak - er, none for - sak - ing, Take our hearts, of Love's own mak - ing, Watch our sleep - ing,
2. Dark de - scends, but light un - end - ing Shines through our night; You are with us, ev - er lend - ing New strength to sight: One in love, your truth con - fess - ing, One in hope of heav - en's bless - ing, May we see, in
3. Eyes will close, but you un - sleep - ing Watch by our side; Death may come, in love's safe keep - ing Still we a - bide. God of love, all e - vil quell - ing, Sin for - giv - ing, fear dis - pel - ling, Stay with us, our

guard our wak - ing, Be al - ways near.
love's pos - sess - ing, Love's end - less light!
hearts in - dwell - ing, This e - ven - tide.

Text: James Quinn, SJ, b.1919, © 1969, Used by permission of Selah Publishing Co., Inc.
Tune: AR HYD Y NOS, 8 4 8 4 888 4; Welsh

752 At Evening

1. Now it is eve - ning: Lights of the cit - y
2. Now it is eve - ning: Lit - tle ones sleep - ing
3. Now it is eve - ning: Food on the ta - ble
4. Now it is eve - ning: Here in our meet - ing

Bid us re - mem - ber Christ is our Light.
Bid us re - mem - ber Christ is our Peace.
Bids us re - mem - ber Christ is our Life.
May we re - mem - ber Christ is our Friend.

Man - y are lone - ly, Who will be neigh - bor?
Some are ne - glect - ed, Who will be neigh - bor?
Man - y are hun - gry, Who will be neigh - bor?
Some may be stran - gers, Who will be neigh - bor?

Where there is car - ing Christ is our Light.
Where there is car - ing Christ is our Peace.
Where there is shar - ing Christ is our Life.
Where there's a wel - come Christ is our Friend.

Text: Fred Pratt Green, 1903-2000, © 1974, Hope Publishing Co.
Tune: EVENING HYMN, 5 5 5 4 D; David Haas, b.1957, © 1985, GIA Publications, Inc.

Watch, O Lord 753

Refrain
Watch, O Lord, with all those a - wake this night,
Watch, O Lord, with all those who weep; Give your
Last time to Coda
an - gels and saints charge o - ver all who sleep.
Verses
Cantor:
1. Tend your ail - ing ones:
2. Soothe your suf - f'ring ones:
3. Hold your griev - ing ones:
4. Guard your lit - tle ones:
in your love, Lord;
Rest your
Heal af -
Raise your
Guide your
S,A + Assembly:
in your love, Lord;
B:
wea - ry ones:
flict - ed ones:
fal - len ones:
search - ing ones:
in your love, Lord;
Bless your
Shield your
Mend your
Grant us
in your love, Lord;

D.C.
dy - ing ones:
joy - ous ones:
bro - ken ones:
all your peace:
in your love, O Lord of all.
D.C.
in your love, O Lord of all.

Coda *(Coda may also be used as an introduction.)*

Text: St. Augustine; adapt. Marty Haugen, b.1950
Tune: Marty Haugen, b.1950

Praise and Thanksgiving 754

1. Praise and thanks - giv - ing, Fa - ther, we of - fer,
2. Lord, bless the la - bor We bring to serve you,
3. Fa - ther, pro - vid - ing Food for your chil - dren,
4. Then will your bless - ing Reach ev - 'ry peo - ple,
For all things liv - ing You have made good.
That with our neigh - bor We may be fed.
Your wis - dom guid - ing Teach - es us share
Free - ly con - fess - ing Your gra - cious hand.
Har - vest of sown fields, Fruits of the or - chard,
Sow - ing or till - ing, We would work with you,
One with an - oth - er, So that re - joic - ing
Where you are reign - ing No one will hun - ger,
Hay from the mown fields, Blos - som and wood.
Har - vest - ing, mill - ing, For dai - ly bread.
With us, all oth - ers May know your care.
Your love sus - tain - ing, Fruit - ful the land.

Text: Albert F. Bayly, 1901-1984,
Tune: BUNESSAN, 5 5 5 4 D; Gaelic; harm. Robert J. Batastini, b.1942,

755 The Trumpet in the Morning

Verses

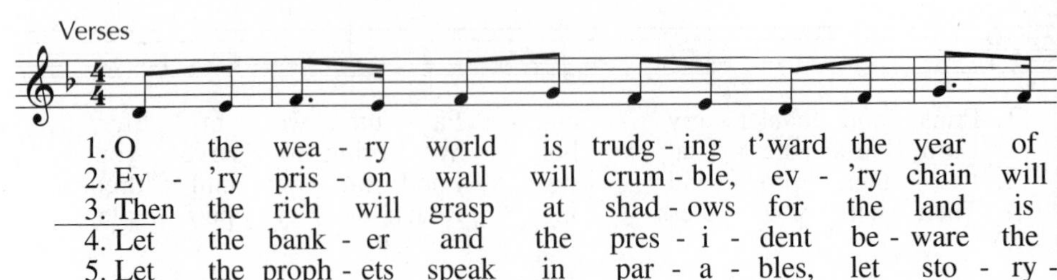
1. O the wea - ry world is trudg - ing t'ward the year of
2. Ev - 'ry pris - on wall will crum - ble, ev - 'ry chain will
3. Then the rich will grasp at shad - ows for the land is
4. Let the bank - er and the pres - i - dent be - ware the
5. Let the proph - ets speak in par - a - bles, let sto - ry -
6. Come and join the great thanks - giv - ing, take your neigh - bor

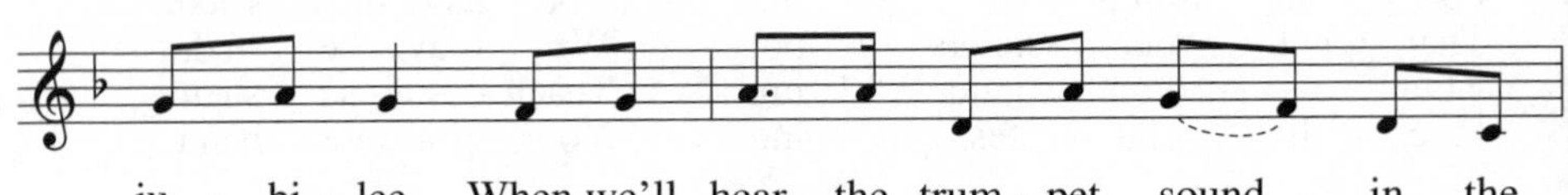
ju - bi - lee, When we'll hear the trum - pet sound in the
fall a - way When we hear the trum - pet sound in the
God's a - lone, When we hear the trum - pet sound in the
trum - pet's call, And beat swords of greed and com - merce in - to
tell - ers spin Tales of faith - ful - ness and res - cue 'til the
by the hand And be - come the voice of free - dom that will

morn - ing. Far and wide we hear the
morn - ing. And the debts that stole our
morn - ing. Ev - 'ry im - mi - grant be
e - qual shares for all. Let the teach - ers speak in
ban - quet shall be - gin; How God wove the world with
thun - der through the land. Let the earth re - pose in

clar - i - on an - nounce that all are free When we
dream - ing we will no more have to pay When we
wel - come, all the home - less find a home, When we
wis - dom, let the mu - sic - mak - ers play, Let the
won - der, how God led us through the sea, Why we
sab - bath while her chil - dren's hearts re - new, And give

hear the trum - pet sound in the morn - ing.
hear the trum - pet sound in the morn - ing.
hear the trum - pet sound in the morn - ing.
weav - ers weave the tent where we shall gath - er on that day.
keep a day of rest and call a year of ju - bi - lee!
back to God in jus - tice what God's boun - ty gave to you.
Refrain
Descant:
Low - ly eyes shall be lift - ed, while the ty - rants taste their fear,
Melody:
Low - ly eyes shall be lift - ed, while the ty - rants taste their fear,
For that sound is both a gos - pel and a warn - ing.
For that sound is both a gos - pel and a warn - ing.
When we rise as a peo - ple who pro - claim that God is near,
When we rise as a peo - ple who pro - claim that God is near,
Who will dare to sound the trum - pet in the morn -
Who will dare to sound the trum - pet in the morn -

To repeat
Last time
ing?
ing?

Text: Leviticus 25, Deuteronomy 15, Joel 2; Rory Cooney, b.1952,
Tune: MORNING TRUMPET, 15 11 15 11 with refrain; B.F. White, 1800-1879, from *Southern Harmony,* 1835, arr. by Rory Cooney, b.1952,

756 On That Day

Refrain

On that day, on that hal - le - lu - ja day

On that day,

on that day, on that hal-le-lu - ja day

on that day,

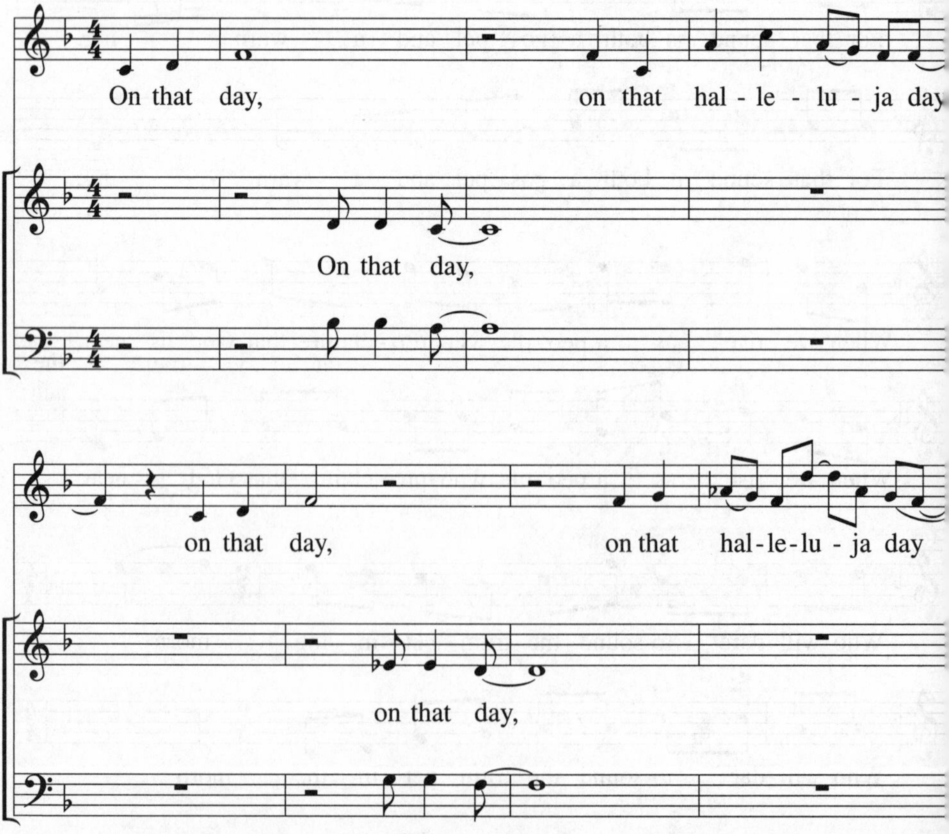

there'll be sing - in', there'll be shout - in', and
ooh
Last time to coda
joy flows like a foun - tain on that day.
Last time to coda
foun - tain, ooh
Verses
1. We'll see the ho - ly cit - y there; the
2. Twelve gates to the king - dom we shall see; all
3. No need of the sun or moon to shine; the
div.
new Je - ru - sa - lem. No more
na - tions will walk as one. Lift - ing our
glo - ry of God is there. Dark - ness to
unis.

sor - row, no more cry - in'.
voic - es, claim - ing our choic - es.
light, God's face in our sight.

D.C.
No more death, no more pain.
Glo - ry and hon - or shall be:
Joy from God's love we will share:
div.

Coda
day, on that day.
on that day, on that day.

Text: Kate Cuddy, b.1953
Tune: Kate Cuddy, b.1953

O Holy City, Seen of John 757

1. O Ho - ly Cit - y, seen of John, Where
2. O shame to us who rest con - tent While
3. Give us, O God, the strength to build The
4. Al - read - y in the mind of God That
Christ, the Lamb, does reign, With - in those four - square
lust and greed for gain In street and shop and
Cit - y that has stood Too long a dream, whose
Cit - y ris - es fair: Lo, how its splen - dor
walls shall come No night, nor need, nor pain, And
ten - e - ment Wring gold from hu - man pain, And
laws are love, Whose ways, the com - mon good, And
chal - leng - es The souls that great - ly dare: Yea,
where the tears are wiped from eyes That shall not weep a - gain.
bit - ter lips in blind de - spair Cry, "Christ has died in vain."
where the shin - ing sun be - comes God's grace for hu - man good.
bids us seize the whole of life And build its glo - ry there.

xt: Revelation 21; W. Russell Bowie, 1882-1969, © Harper and Row
ne: MORNING SONG, 8 6 8 6 8 6; *Kentucky Harmony*, 1816; harm. by C. Winfred Douglas, 1867-1944, © 1940, The Church Pension Fund

758 Soon and Very Soon

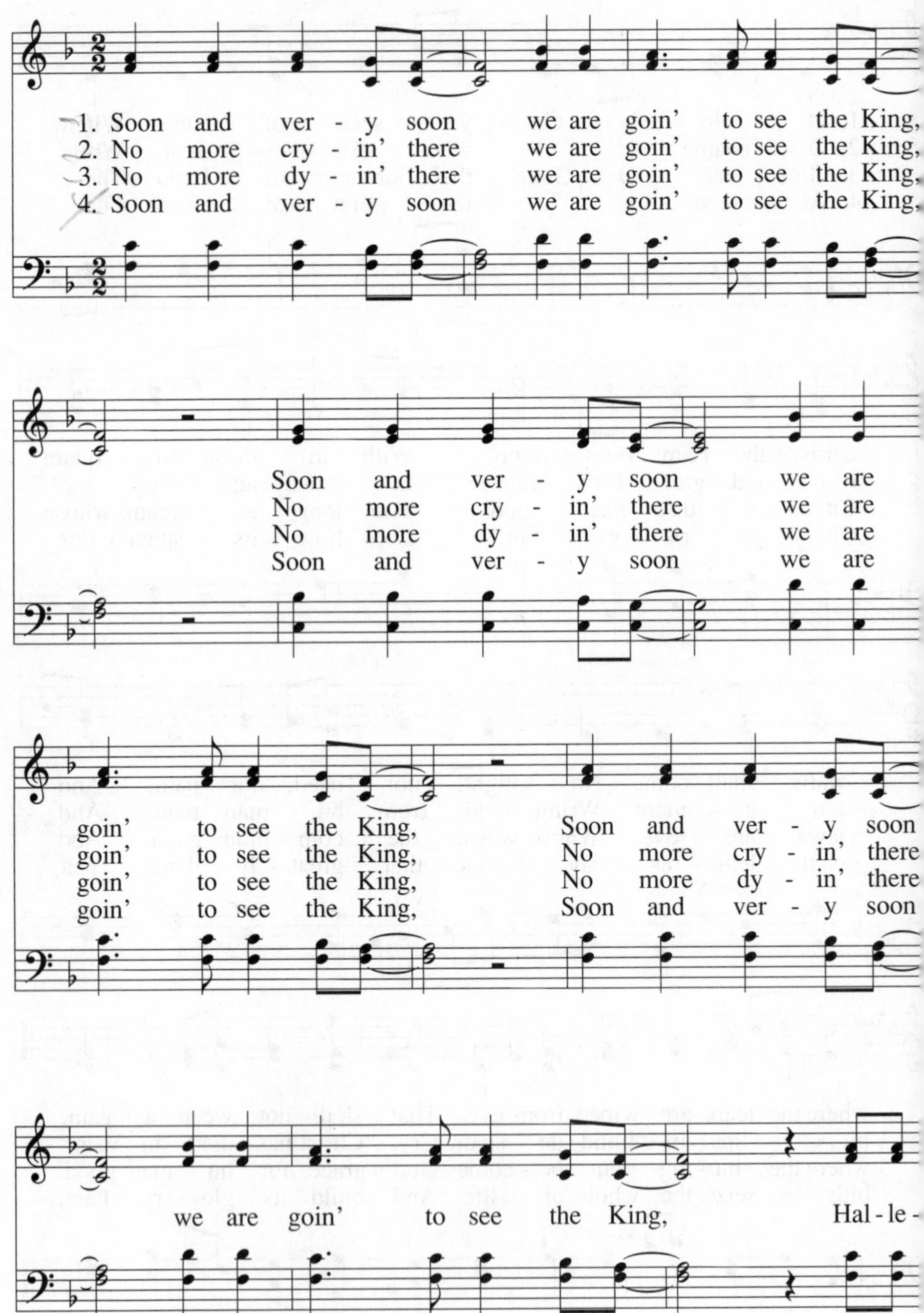
1. Soon and ver - y soon we are goin' to see the King,
2. No more cry - in' there we are goin' to see the King,
3. No more dy - in' there we are goin' to see the King,
4. Soon and ver - y soon we are goin' to see the King,
Soon and ver - y soon we are goin' to see the King,
No more cry - in' there we are goin' to see the King,
No more dy - in' there we are goin' to see the King,
Soon and ver - y soon we are goin' to see the King,
Soon and ver - y soon
No more cry - in' there
No more dy - in' there
Soon and ver - y soon
we are goin' to see the King,
Hal - le -

lu - jah, Hal - le - lu - jah, we're goin' to see the King!
1., 2.
3.,4.
Hal - le - lu - jah, Hal - le -
lu - jah, Hal - le - lu - jah, Hal - le - lu - jah.

Text: Andraé Crouch, b.1945
Tune: Andraé Crouch, b.1945

759 Mine Eyes Have Seen the Glory

1. Mine eyes have seen the glo - ry of the
2. I have seen him in the watch - fires of a
3. He has sound - ed forth the trum - pet that shall
4. In the beau - ty of the lil - ies Christ was
com - ing of the Lord; He is tram - pling out the
hun - dred cir - cling camps; They have build - ed him an
nev - er call re - treat; He is sift - ing out all
born a - cross the sea, With a glo - ry in his
vin - tage where the grapes of wrath are stored; He hath
al - tar in the eve - ning dews and damps; I can
hu - man hearts be - fore his judg - ment seat; O be
bos - om that trans - fig - ures you and me; As he
loosed the fate - ful light - ning of his ter - ri - ble swift
read the right - eous sen - tence by the dim and flar - ing
swift, my soul, to an - swer him; be ju - bi - lant, my
died to make us ho - ly, let us die that all be

sword; His truth is march - ing on.
lamps; His day is march - ing on.
feet! Our God is march - ing on.
free! While God is march - ing on.
Glo - ry! Glo - ry! Hal - le - lu - jah! Glo - ry!
Glo - ry! Hal - le - lu - jah! Glo - ry! Glo - ry!
Hal - le - lu - jah! His truth is march - ing on.

Text: Julia W. Howe, 1819-1910
Tune: BATTLE HYMN OF THE REPUBLIC, 15 15 15 6 with refrain; attr. to William Steffe, d.1911

760 Take Me Home

Refrain
Take me home, to your dwell-ing place, in your sweet em-
Take me home, take me home, take me
brace, read-y to hold me in your arms. Take me
home, hold me, in your arms. Take me
home, home,
home, to your lov-ing eyes, with you a-lone I'll
home, take me home, with you I'll
with you I'll
rise, sing-ing for-ev-er, in your arms, take me
rise, for-ev-er, in your arms, take me
rise, rise,

home.
Last time
home.
Verses
1. O my God, you've led me through it all,
2. With you all pain is left be - hind, no
3. O my God, the road is long and hard,
through all the hurt and my shame.
sor - row or death, on that day.
o - pen your heart, come to me.
O my God, I have trav-eled far to meet you, to
O my God, how I've longed to know your love, come
God, with you, my sor - row turns to danc - ing, reach
D.C.
see your face and call up - on your name!
wipe my tears, and take my fear a - way!
out your hand and set my spir - it free!

Text: David Haas, b.1957
Tune: David Haas, b.1957

761 Shall We Gather at the River

1. Shall we gath - er at the riv - er, Where bright an - gel feet have trod; With its crys - tal tide for ev - er Flow - ing by the throne of God?
2. On the mar - gin of the riv - er, Wash - ing up its sil - ver spray, We will walk and wor - ship ev - er, All the hap - py gold - en day.
3. Ere we reach the shin - ing riv - er, Lay we ev - 'ry bur - den down; Grace our spir - its will de - liv - er, And pro - vide a robe and crown.
4. Soon we'll reach the shin - ing riv - er, Soon our pil - grim - age will cease, Soon our hap - py hearts will quiv - er With the mel - o - dy of peace.

Yes, we'll gath - er at the riv - er, The
beau - ti - ful, the beau - ti - ful riv - er;
Gath - er with the saints at the riv - er That
flows by the throne of God.

Text: Robert Lowry, 1826-1899
Tune: HANSON PLACE, 8 7 8 7 with refrain, Robert Lowry, 1826-1899

762 We Shall Rise Again

1. Come to me, all you wea - ry,
2. Though we walk through the dark - ness,
3. We de - pend on God's mer - cy,
4. Do not fear death's do - min - ion,
5. At the door there to greet us,
with your bur - dens and pain. Take my yoke on your
e - vil we do not fear. You are walk - ing be -
mer - cy which nev - er fades. We re - mem - ber our
look be - yond earth and grave. See the bright - ness of
mar - tyrs, an - gels, and saints, And our fam - 'ly and
shoul - ders and learn from
side us with your rod and your
cov - e - nant and the prom - ise Je - sus
Je - sus shin - ing out to light our
loved ones, ev - 'ry - one freed from their
me: I am gen - tle and hum - ble,
staff. On - ly good - ness and kind - ness
made: If we die with Christ Je - sus,
way. Lov - ing Fa - ther and Spir - it,
chains. We shall feel their ac - cep - tance,
and your soul will find rest, For my yoke is
fol - low us all our lives. We shall dwell in the
we shall live with him, And if we are
lov - ing Je - sus the Son, All God's peo - ple to -
and the joy of new life. We shall join in the
eas - y and my bur - den is light.
Lord's house for so man - y years to come!
faith - ful, we shall reign with him!
geth - er, we shall live on as one!
gath - er - ing, re - u - nit - ed in God's love!

We shall rise a-gain on the last day with the
with the
faith - ful, rich and poor. Com - ing
Com - ing
faith - ful, rich and poor, Com - ing
to the house of Lord Je - sus, we will find an o - pen
to the house of Je - sus,
door there, we will find an o - pen door.
1.-4.
5.

Text: Matthew 11:29-30, Psalm 23, John 11, 2 Timothy 2; Jeremy Young, b.1948
Tune: RESURRECTION, Irregular with refrain; Jeremy Young, b.1948

763 I Will Be the Vine

Refrain
branch-es. All
I will be the vine and you will be the branch - es. All
you who live in me will nev - er, nev - er die.
you who live in me will nev - er die.
I will be the sign, I will of - fer man - y chanc - es; so
I will be the sign, I will of - fer man - y chanc - es; so
oh
live, oh live in me and you shall have new life.
oh

Verses 1, 2
1. Re - main in me, as I re-main in you. You may ask what you will, ask what you will, and you shall re - ceive.
2. As the Fa - ther loved me, so have I loved you. Re - main in my love, re - main in my love, and I will give you life.
D.C.
Verse 3
3. If you are my friends, you will live my com - mands. There is no great - er love, no great - er love than to lay down your life for your friends.
3. You are my friends, live my com - mands.
D.C.

Text: Liam Lawton, b.1959
Tune: Liam Lawton, b.1959; arr. by John McCann, b.1961

764 Jerusalem, My Happy Home

1. Je - ru - sa - lem, my hap - py home, When
2. Your saints are crowned with glo - ry great; They
3. There Da - vid stands with harp in hand As
4. Our La - dy sings Mag - nif - i - cat With
5. There Mag - da - lene has left her tears, And
6. Je - ru - sa - lem, Je - ru - sa - lem, God
shall I with you be? When shall my sor - rows
see God face to face; They tri - umph still, they
mas - ter of the choir: Ten thou - sand times that
tune sur - pass - ing sweet; And all the vir - gins
cheer - ful - ly does sing With bless - ed saints, whose
grant that I may see Your end - less joy, and

have an end? Your joys when shall I see?
still re - joice: In that most ho - ly place.
we were blest That might this mu - sic hear.
join the song While sit - ting at her feet.
har - mo - ny In ev - 'ry street does ring.
of the same Par - tak - er ev - er be!

Text: Joseph Bromehead, 1747-1826, alt.
Tune: LAND OF REST, CM; American; harm. by Richard Proulx, b.1937, © 1975, GIA Publications, Inc.

Do Not Let Your Hearts Be Troubled 765

Refrain
Do not let your hearts be troubled, have faith in God and faith in me.
I will go forth to prepare a place for you, then I'll come back to take you with me, that where I am, you may also be.
To verses
be.
Last time
be.

Verse 1
1. In God's house there are man - y plac - es for you a - lone to dwell in safe - ty. You know the way to where I'll lead you, if you are lost, I will show the way.
D.C.
Verse 2
2. I am the way, the truth and the life, on - ly through me can you know what I know. If you knew me, you would see the vi - sion, if you see me, you see your God.
D.C.
Verse 3
Descant:
3. The words I speak are not on - ly of my-self, it is your God who lives with - in me. If you be - lieve that your God and I are one, I will pro - vide when you call my name.
D.C.

Text: John 14:1-3, 6-7, 10-14; David Haas, b.1957
Tune: David Haas, b.1957

Steal Away to Jesus 766

Refrain
Steal a-way, steal a-way, steal a-way to Je-sus!
Steal a-way, steal a-way home, I ain't got long to stay here.
Verses
1. My Lord, he calls me, He calls me by the thun-der; The
2. Green trees are bend-ing, Poor sin-ners stand a trem-bling; The
3. My Lord, he calls me, He calls me by the light-ning; The
trum-pet sounds with-in my soul; I ain't got long to stay here.
D.C.

Text: African-American spiritual
Tune: African-American spiritual

767 Now Let Your Servant Go

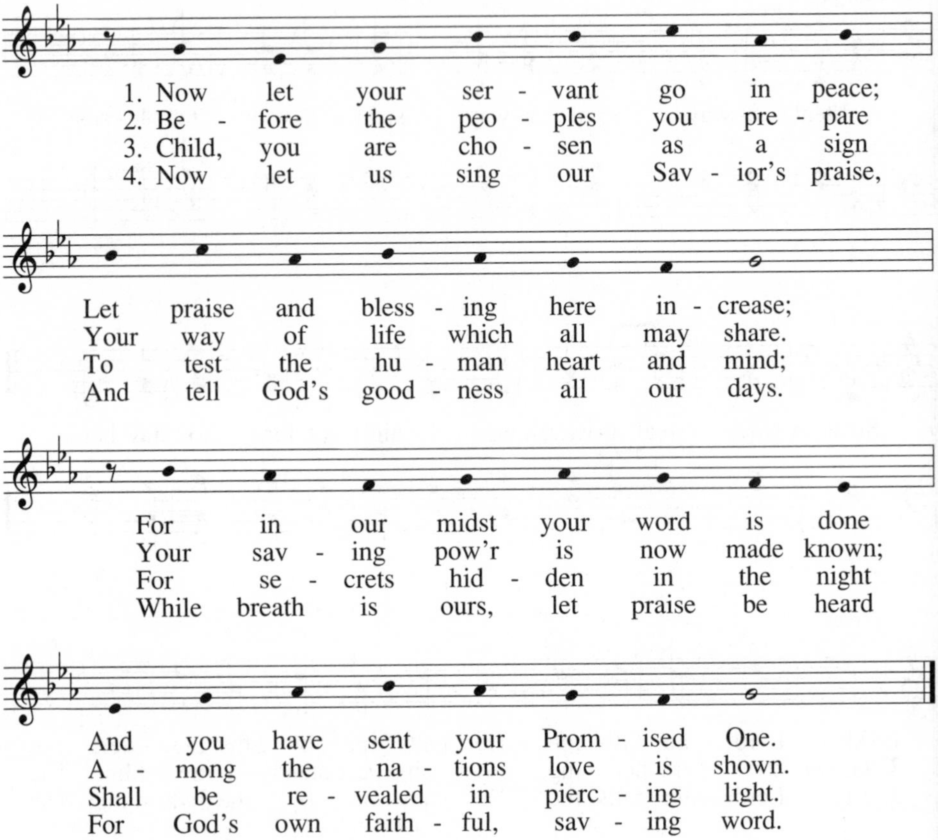

1. Now let your ser - vant go in peace;
2. Be - fore the peo - ples you pre - pare
3. Child, you are cho - sen as a sign
4. Now let us sing our Sav - ior's praise,

Let praise and bless - ing here in - crease;
Your way of life which all may share.
To test the hu - man heart and mind;
And tell God's good - ness all our days.

For in our midst your word is done
Your sav - ing pow'r is now made known;
For se - crets hid - den in the night
While breath is ours, let praise be heard

And you have sent your Prom - ised One.
A - mong the na - tions love is shown.
Shall be re - vealed in pierc - ing light.
For God's own faith - ful, sav - ing word.

Text: *Nunc dimittis,* Luke 2:29-35; Ruth Duck, b.1947, © 1992, GIA Publications, Inc.
Tune: CONDITOR ALME SIDERUM, LM; Mode IV; acc. by Gerard Farrell, OSB, b.1919, © 1986, GIA Publications, Inc.

768 No Wind at the Window

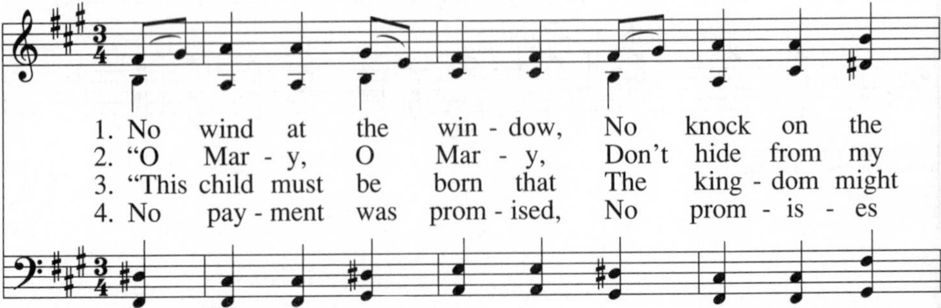

1. No wind at the win - dow, No knock on the
2. "O Mar - y, O Mar - y, Don't hide from my
3. "This child must be born that The king - dom might
4. No pay - ment was prom - ised, No prom - is - es

door; No light from the lamp-stand, No foot on the
face. Be glad that you're fa - vored And filled with God's
come: Sal - va - tion for man - y, De - struc - tion for
made; No wed - ding was dat - ed, No blue - print dis -
floor; No dream born of tired - ness, No
grace. The time for re - deem - ing The
some; Both end and be - gin - ning, Both
played. Yet Mar - y, con - sent - ing To
ghost raised by fear: Just an an - gel and a
world has be - gun; And you are re -
mes - sage and sign; Both vic - tor and
what none could guess, Re - plied with con -
wom - an And a voice in her ear.
quest - ed To moth - er God's son.
vic - tim, Both yours and di - vine."
vic - tion, "Tell God I say yes."

Text: John L. Bell, b.1949
Tune: COLUMCILLE, Irregular; Gaelic, arr. by John L. Bell, b.1949

769 Praise We the Lord This Day

1. Praise we the Lord this day, This
2. The Proph - et gave the sign For
3. Ask not how this should be, But
4. She meek - ly bowed her head To
5. Bless - ed shall be her name In
6. O Christ, the Vir - gin's Son, We
day so long fore - told, Whose prom - ise shone with
faith - ful folk to read: A vir - gin, born of
wor - ship and a - dore Like her whom God's own
hear the gra - cious word, Mar - y, the pure and
all the Church on earth Through whom that won - drous
praise you and a - dore, You are with God the
cheer - ing ray On wait - ing saints of old.
Da - vid's line, Shall bear the prom - ised Seed.
maj - es - ty Came down to shad - ow o'er.
low - ly maid, The fa - vored of the Lord.
mer - cy came, The in - car - nate Sav - ior's birth.
Fa - ther One And Spir - it ev - er - more.

Text: Matthew 1:23; *Hymns for the Festivals and Saints' Days*, 1846
Tune: SWABIA, SM; Johann M. Speiss, 1715-1772; adapt. by William H. Havergal, 1793-1870

Transform Us 770

1. Trans - form us as you, trans - fig - ured,
2. Trans - form us as you, trans - fig - ured,
3. Trans - form us as you, trans - fig - ured,
Stood a - part on Ta - bor's height.
Once spoke with those ho - ly ones.
Would not stay with - in a shrine.
Lead us up our sa - cred moun - tains,
We, sur - round - ed by the wit - ness
Keep us from our great temp - ta - tion—
Search us with re - veal - ing light.
Of those saints whose work is done,
Time and truth we quick - ly bind,
Lift us from where we have fall - en,
Live in this world as your Bod - y,
Lead us down those dai - ly path - ways
Full of ques - tions, filled with fright.
Cho - sen daugh - ters, cho - sen sons.
Where our love is not con - fined.

Text: Sylvia Dunstan, 1955-1993, © 1993, GIA Publications, Inc.
Tune: PICARDY, 8 7 8 7 8 7; French Carol; harm. by Richard Proulx, b.1937, © 1986, GIA Publications, Inc.

771 'Tis Good, Lord, to Be Here

1. 'Tis good, Lord, to be here! Your glo - ry fills the night; Your face and gar - ments, like the sun, Shine with un - bor - rowed light.
2. 'Tis good, Lord, to be here, Your beau - ty to be - hold, Where Mo - ses and E - li - jah stand, Your mes - sen - gers of old.
3. Ful - fill - er of the past! Prom - ise of things to be! We hail your bod - y glo - ri - fied, And our re - demp - tion see.
4. Be - fore we taste of death, We see your king - dom come; We long to hold the vi - sion bright, And make this hill our home.
5. 'Tis good, Lord, to be here! Yet we may not re - main; But since you bid us leave the mount, Come with us to the plain.

Text: Luke 9:32-33; Joseph A. Robinson, 1858-1933, alt., © Esme. D. E. Bird
Tune: SWABIA, SM; Johann M. Speiss, 1715-1772; adapt. by William H. Havergal, 1793-1870

Ave Maria 772

Verses
Melody:
1. Hail Mar - y full of grace, the Lord is with you. Bless - ed are you a - mong all wom - en, Blest is the fruit of your womb.
2. Ho - ly Mar - y moth - er of God, the Lord is with you. Pray for us sin - ners, pray for us sin - ners, Now and at the hour of our death.
Harmony:
A - ve Ma - ri - a, gra - ti - a ple - na, Do - mi - nus te - cum, be - ne - di - cta in mu - li - e - ri - bus. Je - sus.

Refrain
Melody:
Je - sus, formed in your faith, A - ve Ma - ri - a al - le - lu - ia.
Al - le - lu - ia.
Harmony:
Je - sus formed, Je - sus, Al - le - lu - ia. Al - le - lu - ia,
Je - sus, formed in your faith, A - ve Ma - ri - a al - le - lu - ia.
Je - sus, born in your love, A - ve Ma -
Je - sus born, Al - le - lu - ia.
Je - sus, born in your love, A - ve Ma -

ri - a al - le - lu - ia.
Al - le - lu - ia,
A - ve Ma - ri -
ri - a al - le - lu - ia.
a, gra - ti - a ple - na.
1.
2.

Text: Hail Mary; additional text by Dan Kantor, b.1960
Tune: Dan Kantor, b.1960; arr. by Rob Glover, b.1950

773 Magnificat

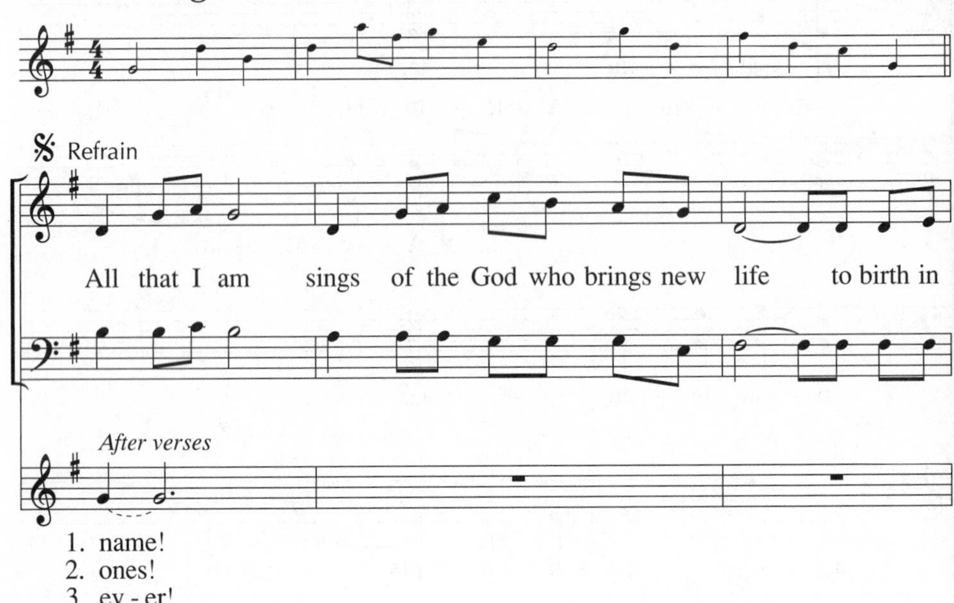
Refrain
All that I am sings of the God who brings new life to birth in
After verses
1. name!
2. ones!
3. ev - er!

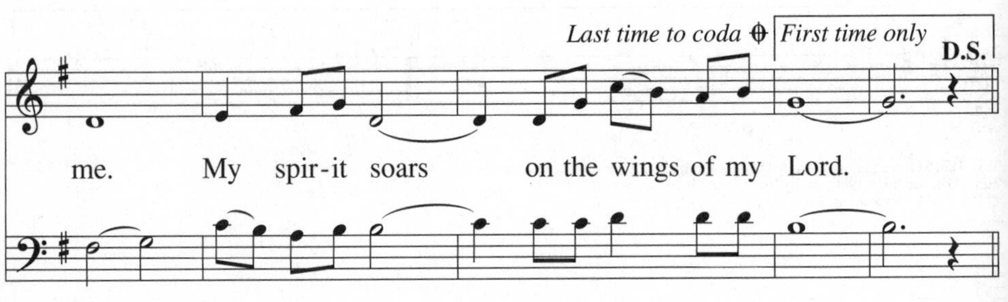
Last time to coda
First time only
D.S.
me. My spir-it soars on the wings of my Lord.

To verses
Lord.
Verses
Cantor 1:
1. My soul gives glo - ry to the
2. God's mer - cy is from age to
3. God fills the starv - ing with good

Lord, re - joic - ing in my sav - ing
age, on those who fol - low in
things, the rich are left with emp - ty
Cantor 2:
God, Who looks up - on me in my
fear; Whose arm is pow - er and
hands; Pro - tect - ing all the faith - ful
state, and all the world will call me
strength, and scat - ters all the proud of
ones, re - mem - b'ring Is - ra - el with
Cantor 1:
blest; For God works mar - vels in my
heart; Who casts the might - y from their
mer - cy,/The prom - ise known to those be -
Both cantors:
D.S.
sight, and ho - ly, ho - ly is God's
thrones and rais - es up the low - ly
fore and to their chil - dren for -
Coda
Lord.

Text: Luke 1:46-55; David Haas, b.1957
Tune: David Haas, b.1957

774 Ave Maria

A - ve Ma - rí - a, grá - ti - a ple - na,

Dó - mi - nus te - cum, be - ne - di - cta tu in mu - li - é -

ri - bus, et be - ne - dí - ctus fru - ctus ven - tris tu - i, Je - sus.

San - cta Ma - rí - a, Ma - ter De - i, o - ra pro no - bis pec - ca -

tó - ri - bus, nunc et in ho - ra mor - tis no - strae. A - men.

Text: *Hail, Mary, full of grace,* Luke 1:29; Latin, 13th C.
Tune: AVE MARIA, Irregular; Mode I; acc. by Robert LeBlanc, b.1948, © 1986, GIA Publications, Inc.

775 O Sanctissima / O Most Virtuous

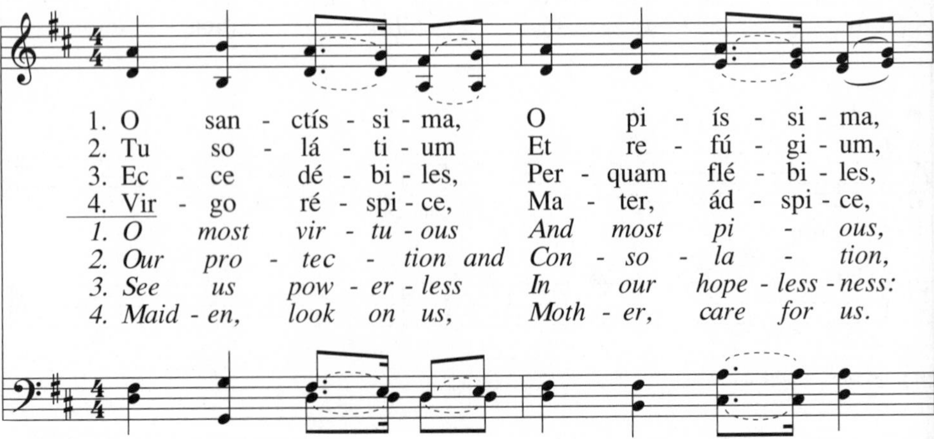
1. O san - ctís - si - ma, O pi - ís - si - ma,
2. Tu so - lá - ti - um Et re - fú - gi - um,
3. Ec - ce dé - bi - les, Per - quam flé - bi - les,
4. Vir - go ré - spi - ce, Ma - ter, ád - spi - ce,
1. O most vir - tu - ous And most pi - ous,
2. Our pro - tec - tion and Con - so - la - tion,
3. See us pow - er - less In our hope - less - ness:
4. Maid - en, look on us, Moth - er, care for us.

Dul - cis vir - go Ma - rí - a!
Vir - go ma - ter Ma - rí - a!
Sal - va nos, Ma - rí - a!
Au - di nos, Ma - rí - a!
Dear - est maid - en, sweet Mar - y,
Vir - gin moth - er, good Mar - y,
Aid us, save us, Mar - y!
Hear our pleas, O Mar - y!
Ma - ter a - má - ta, In - te - me - rá - ta,
Quid - quid op - tá - mus, Per te spe - rá - mus,
Tol - le lan - guó - res, Sa - na do - ló - res,
Tu me - di - cí - nam, Por - tas di - ví - nam;
Moth - er af - fec - tion - ate, Vir - gin in - vi - o - late,
What - e'er our souls de - sire, May you help us to ac - quire.
Wipe a - way the tears we shed, Heal us of our grief and dread.
Balm and our sur - e - ty, Gate - way to di - vin - i - ty,
O - ra, o - ra pro no - bis.
O - ra, o - ra pro no - bis.
O - ra, o - ra pro no - bis.
O - ra, o - ra pro no - bis.
In - ter - cede and pray for us, O Mar - y!
In - ter - cede and pray for us, O Mar - y!
In - ter - cede and pray for us, O Mar - y!
In - ter - cede and pray for us, O Mar - y!

Text: St. 1, *Stimmen der Völker in Liedern*, 1807; st. 2, *Arundel Hymnal*, 1902; tr. Neil Borgstrom, b.1953,
Tune: O DU FRÖLICHE, 55 7 55 7; Tattersall's *Improved Psalmody*, 1794

776 Sing We of the Blessed Mother

1. Sing we of the bless-ed Moth-er Who re-ceived the an-gel's word, And o-be-dient to the sum-mons Bore in love the in-fant Lord; Sing we of the
2. Sing we, too, of Mar-y's sor-rows, Of the sword that pierced her through, When be-neath the cross of Je-sus She his weight of suf-f'ring knew, Looked up-on her
3. Sing a-gain the joys of Mar-y When she saw the ris-en Lord, And in prayer with Christ's a-pos-tles, Wait-ed on his prom-ised word: From on high the
4. Sing the great-est joy of Mar-y When on earth her work was done, And the Lord of all cre-a-tion Brought her to his heav'n-ly home: Vir-gin Moth-er,

joys of Mar - y At whose breast that child was fed
Son and Sav - ior Reign - ing from the aw - ful tree,
blaz - ing glo - ry Of the Spir - it's pres - ence came,
Mar - y bless - ed, Raised on high and crowned with grace,
Who is Son of God e - ter - nal
Saw the price of our re - demp - tion
Heav'n - ly breath of God's own be - ing,
May your Son, the world's re - deem - er,
And the ev - er - last - ing Bread.
Paid to set the sin - ner free.
To - kened in the wind and flame.
Grant us all to see his face.

Text: George B. Timms, 1910-1997, © 1975, Oxford University Press
Tune: OMNE DIE, 8 7 8 7 D; *Trier Gesängbuch*, 1695

777 I Sing a Maid

1. I sing a maid of ten - der years To
2. She watched him grow to man - hood's strength To
3. And if the song had end - ed then, Our
whom an an - gel came, And knelt, as to a
meet his des - ti - ny. And when the dan - ger
eyes would fill with tears, But ah! the song had
might - y queen, And bowed bright wings of
of his truth Brought him to Cal - va -
just be - gun To ech - o down the
flame: A na - tion's hope in her re - ply, This
ry, She stood by him all pow - er - less To
years! Now lift your voic - es, hearts and souls, To
maid of match - less grace; For God's own son be -
ease his dy - ing pain, 'Til in the dark - est
sing with one ac - cord To hon - or Mar - y,
came her child, And she his rest - ing place.
hour of all, She held her son a - gain.
Moth - er of The Christ, the Ris - en Lord!

Text: M. D. Ridge, b.1938, © 1987, GIA Publications, Inc.
Tune: THE FLIGHT OF THE EARLS, CMD; traditional Celtic melody; harm. by Michael Joncas, b.1951, © 1987, GIA Publications, Inc.

Sing of Mary, Meek and Lowly 778

1. Sing of Mar - y meek and low - ly, Vir - gin - moth - er
2. Sing of Je - sus, son of Mar - y, In the home at
3. *Sing of Jo - seph, strong and gen - tle, No - bly born of
4. Glo - ry be to God the Fa - ther; Glo - ry be to

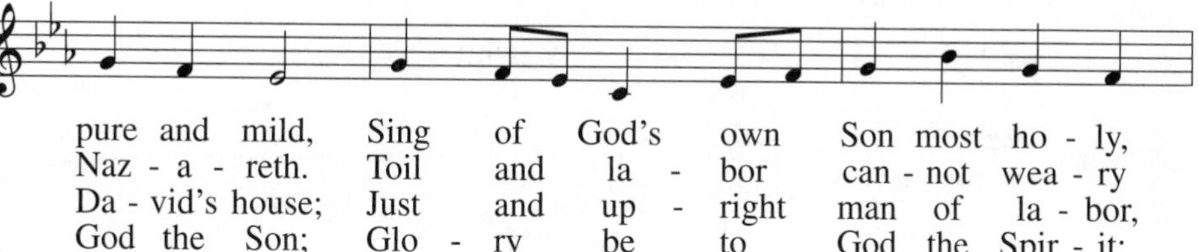
pure and mild, Sing of God's own Son most ho - ly,
Naz - a - reth. Toil and la - bor can - not wea - ry
Da - vid's house; Just and up - right man of la - bor,
God the Son; Glo - ry be to God the Spir - it;

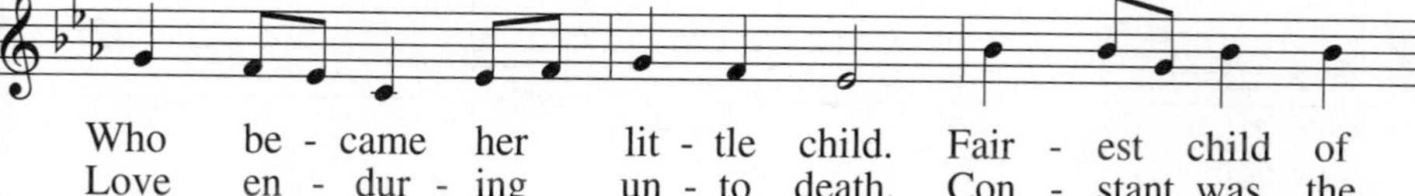
Who be - came her lit - tle child. Fair - est child of
Love en - dur - ing un - to death. Con - stant was the
Whom God chose as Mar - y's spouse; Cho - sen, too, as
Glo - ry to the Three in One. From the heart of

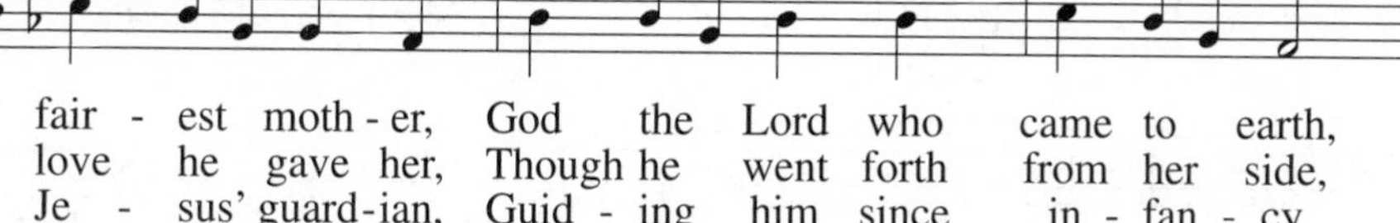
fair - est moth - er, God the Lord who came to earth,
love he gave her, Though he went forth from her side,
Je - sus' guard - ian, Guid - ing him since in - fan - cy.
bless - ed Mar - y, From all saints the song as - cends,

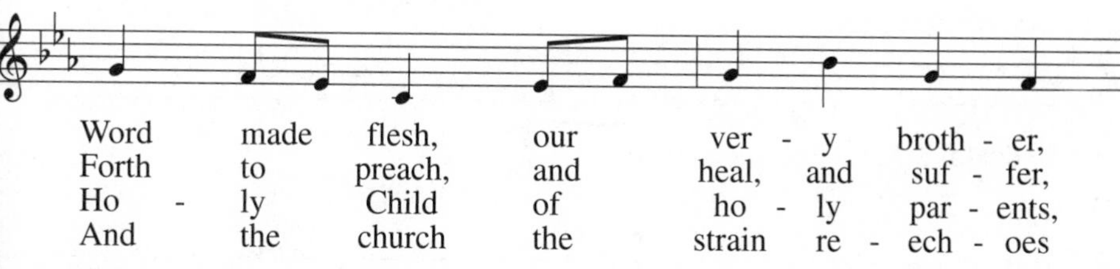
Word made flesh, our ver - y broth - er,
Forth to preach, and heal, and suf - fer,
Ho - ly Child of ho - ly par - ents,
And the church the strain re - ech - oes

Takes our na - ture by his birth.
Till on Cal - va - ry he died.
Ho - ly is their fam - i - ly.
Un - to earth's re - mot - est ends.

**For the Feast of the Holy Family, otherwise may be omitted.*

779 Hail Mary: Gentle Woman

Hail Mar - y, full of grace, the
Lord is with you.
Bless-ed are you a-mong wom-en, and blest is the fruit of your
womb, Je - sus.
Ho-ly Mar - y, Moth-er of God,
pray for us sin - ners now and at the hour of
death. A - men.
Refrain
Gen - tle wom-an, qui-et light,
morn - ing star, so strong and bright,

gen-tle Moth-er, peace-ful dove,
teach us wis-dom; teach us love.
Verse 1
1. You were cho - sen by the Fa-ther; you were
cho - sen for the Son. You were
cho - sen from all wom-en and for
wom-an, shin-ing one.
D.S.
Verse 2
2. Bless-ed are you a-mong wom-en,
blest in turn all wom-en, too.
Bless-ed they with peace - ful spir-its.
Bless - ed they with gen - tle hearts.
D.S.

Text: *Hail Mary,* alt.; Carey Landry, b.1944
Tune: Carey Landry, b.1944; arr. by Martha Lesinski, alt.

780 Salve, Regína / Hail, Queen of Heaven

Sal - ve, Re - gí - na, ma - ter mi - se - ri - cór - di - ae:
Hail, Queen of Heav - en, hail, our Moth - er com-pas-sion-ate,
Vi - ta, dul - cé - do et spes no - stra sal - ve.
True life and com - fort and our hope, we greet you!
Ad te cla - má - mus, éx - su - les fí - li - i He - vae.
To you we ex - iles, chil - dren of Eve, raise our voic - es.
Ad te sus - pi - rá - mus, ge - mén - tes et flen - tes
We send up sighs to you, as mourn-ing and weep-ing,
in hac la - cri - má - rum val - le. E - ia er - go,
we pass through this vale of sor - row. Then turn to us,
ad - vo - cá - ta no - stra, il - los tu - os mi - se - ri -
O most gra - cious Wom - an, those eyes of yours, so full of
cór - des ó - cu - los ad nos con - vér - te. Et Je - sum,
love and ten - der-ness, so full of pit - y. And grant us
be - ne - dí - ctum fru - ctum ven - tris tu - i, no - bis post
af - ter these, our days of lone - ly ex - ile, the sight of

hoc ex - sí - li - um o - stén - de. O cle - mens,
your blest Son and Lord, Christ Je - sus. O gen - tle,

O pi - a, O dul - cis Vir - go Ma - rí - a.
O lov-ing, O ho - ly, sweet Vir-gin Mar - y.

Text: Latin, c.1080, tr. by John C. Selner, SS, 1904-1992, © 1954, GIA Publications, Inc.
Tune: SALVE REGINA, Irregular; Mode V; acc. by Gerard Farrell, OSB, b.1919, © 1986, GIA Publications, Inc.

O Mary of Promise 781

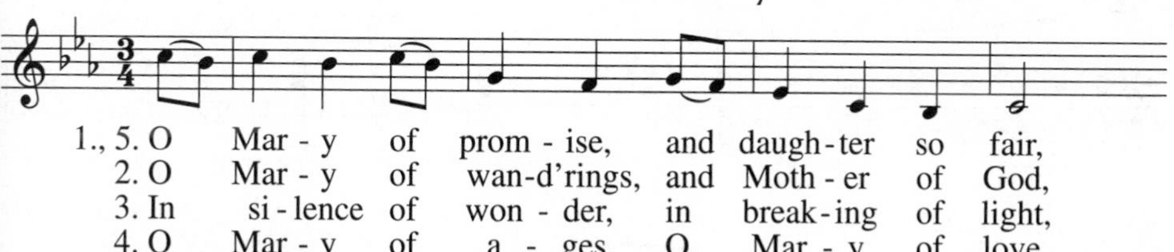
1., 5. O Mar - y of prom - ise, and daugh-ter so fair,
2. O Mar - y of wan-d'rings, and Moth - er of God,
3. In si - lence of won - der, in break-ing of light,
4. O Mar - y of a - ges, O Mar - y of love,

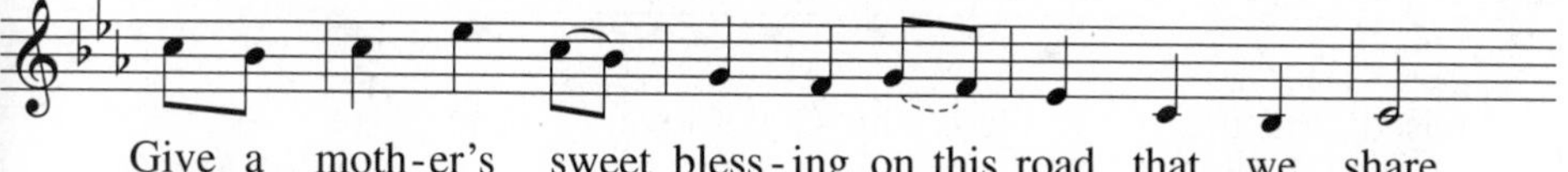
Give a moth-er's sweet bless-ing on this road that we share.
May we walk on the path that the faith - ful have trod.
May we rise to God's will as a bird takes to flight.
May we soar to your wis - dom on the wings of a dove.

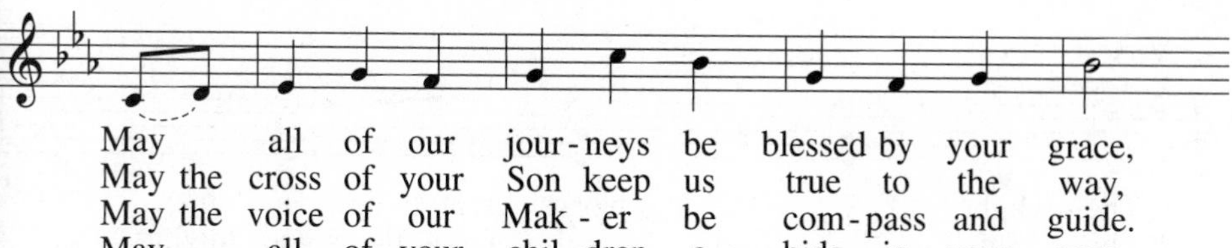
May all of our jour - neys be blessed by your grace,
May the cross of your Son keep us true to the way,
May the voice of our Mak - er be com - pass and guide.
May all of your chil - dren a - bide in your gaze,

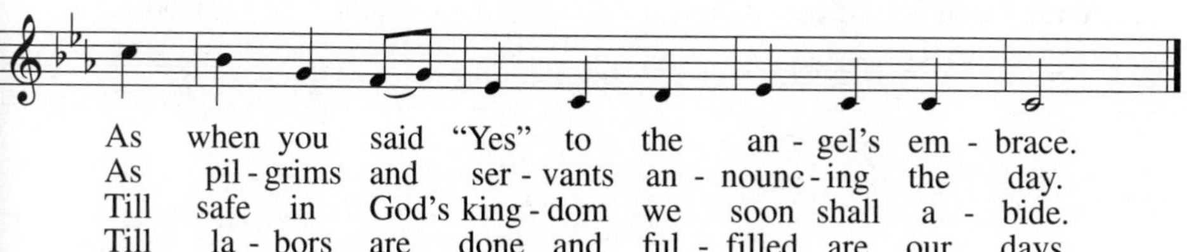
As when you said "Yes" to the an - gel's em - brace.
As pil - grims and ser - vants an - nounc - ing the day.
Till safe in God's king - dom we soon shall a - bide.
Till la - bors are done and ful - filled are our days.

Text: Steven C. Warner, b.1954, © 1993, 2001, World Library Publications
Tune: SIOBHAN NI LAOGHAIRE, 11 12 11 11; Gaelic folk hymn; arr. by Steven C. Warner, b.1954, © 1993, 2001, World Library Publications

782 My Soul Proclaims

Refrain
My soul pro-claims the great-ness of God, re-
Sav - ior,
joic - ing in God, my Sav - ior, the Ho - ly One has
fa - vor.
Last time
raised me up, I live in God's love and fa - vor.
Last time
Verses
Cantor or Section:
All:
1. The Might - y One works great things in me:
2. The arm of God is jus - tice and might:
3. God top - ples ev - 'ry ty - rant and crown:
4. With won - drous things, God's ban - quet is spread:
My

in God.
Cantor or Section:
re - joic - es in God.
soul re - joic - es
in God
All
God
The
The
re - joic - es in God.
All:
faith - ful ser - vants God's mer - cy shall see:
puts the proud and the schem - ing to flight:
low - ly raised and the might - y brought down:
rich go hun - gry, the hun - gry are fed:
My
sings and re - joic - es,
soul re - joic - es, sing, re - joic - es,
glad - ly re - joic - es in God.
D.C.
glad, re - joic - es, re - joic - es in God.
glad, re - joic - es in God.

Text: *Magnificat,* Luke 1:46-55; Marty Haugen, b.1950
Tune: Marty Haugen, b.1950

783 Immaculate Mary

1. Im - mac - u - late Mar - y, your prais - es we sing;
2. Pre - des - tined for Christ by e - ter - nal de - cree,
3. To you by an an - gel, the Lord God made known
4. Most blest of all wom - en, you heard and be - lieved,
5. The an - gels re - joiced when you brought forth God's Son;
You reign now in splen - dor with Je - sus our King.
God willed you both vir - gin and moth - er to be.
The grace of the Spir - it, the gift of the Son.
Most blest in the fruit of your womb then con - ceived.
Your joy is the joy of all a - ges to come.
A - ve, A - ve, A - ve, Ma - ri - a.

A - ve, A - ve, Ma - ri - a.

6. Your child is the Savior, all hope lies in him:
He gives us new life and redeems us from sin.

7. In glory for ever now close to your Son,
All ages will praise you for all God has done.

Text: St. 1, Jeremiah Cummings, 1814-1866, alt.; St. 2-7, Brian Foley, b.1919, © 1971, Faber Music Ltd.
Tune: LOURDES HYMN, 11 11 with refrain; *Grenoble*, 1882

784 Hail, Holy Queen Enthroned Above

1. Hail, ho - ly Queen en - throned a - bove, O Ma - ri - a. Hail, Queen of mer - cy and of love, O Ma - ri - a. Tri - umph, all ye
2. The cause of joy to all be - low, O Ma - ri - a. The spring through which all grac - es flow, O Ma - ri - a. An - gels, all your
3. O gen - tle, lov - ing, ho - ly one, O Ma - ri - a. The God of light be - came your Son, O Ma - ri - a. Tri - umph, all ye

Cher - u - bim, Sing with us, ye Ser - a - phim,
prais - es bring, Earth and heav - en, with us sing,
Cher - u - bim, Sing with us, ye Ser - a - phim,
Heav'n and earth re - sound the hymn: Sal - ve,
All cre - a - tion ech - o - ing: Sal - ve,
Heav'n and earth re - sound the hymn: Sal - ve,
Sal - ve, Sal - ve, Re - gi - na.
Sal - ve, Sal - ve, Re - gi - na.
Sal - ve, Sal - ve, Re - gi - na.

Text: *Salve, Regina, mater misericordia*; c.1080; tr. *Roman Hymnal*, 1884; st. 2-3 adapt. by M. Owen Lee, CSB, b.1930
Tune: SALVE REGINA COELITUM, 8 4 8 4 777 4 5; *Choralmelodien zum Heiligen Gesänge,* 1808; harm. by Healey Willan, 1880-1968,

785 Lift High the Cross

Unison:
Lift high the cross, the love of Christ pro - claim till
all the world a - dore his sa - cred name.
Harmony:
1. Come, Chris - tians, fol - low where the Mas - ter trod, Our
2. Led on their way by this tri - um - phant sign, The
3. Each new - born fol - l'wer of the Cru - ci - fied Bears
4. O Lord, once lift - ed on the glo - rious tree, Your
5. So shall our song of tri - umph ev - er be: Praise
D.C.
King vic - to - rious, Christ, the Son of God.
hosts of God in con - quering ranks com - bine.
on the brow the seal of him who died.
death has bought us life e - ter - nal - ly.
to the Cru - ci - fied for vic - to - ry!

Text: 1 Corinthians 1:18; George W. Kitchin, 1827-1912, and Michael R. Newbolt, 1874-1956, alt.
Tune: CRUCIFER, 10 10 with refrain; Sydney H. Nicholson, 1875-1947

For All the Saints Who've Shown Your Love 786

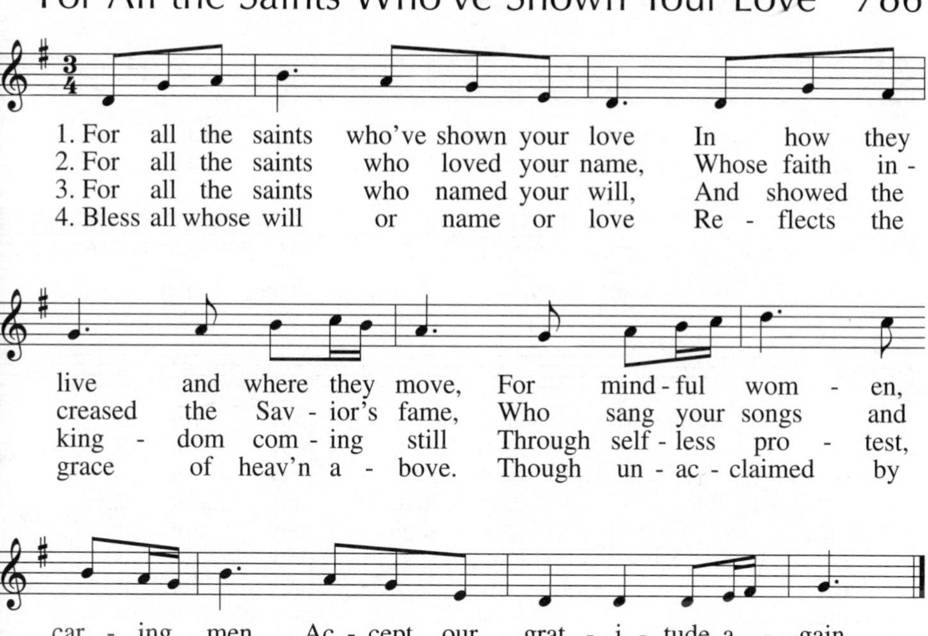
1. For all the saints who've shown your love In how they
2. For all the saints who loved your name, Whose faith in -
3. For all the saints who named your will, And showed the
4. Bless all whose will or name or love Re - flects the
live and where they move, For mind - ful wom - en,
creased the Sav - ior's fame, Who sang your songs and
king - dom com - ing still Through self - less pro - test,
grace of heav'n a - bove. Though un - ac - claimed by
car - ing men, Ac - cept our grat - i - tude a - gain.
shared your word, Ac - cept our grat - i - tude, good Lord.
prayer and praise, Ac - cept the grat - i - tude we raise.
earth - ly pow'rs, Your life through theirs has hal - lowed ours.

787 Litany of the Saints

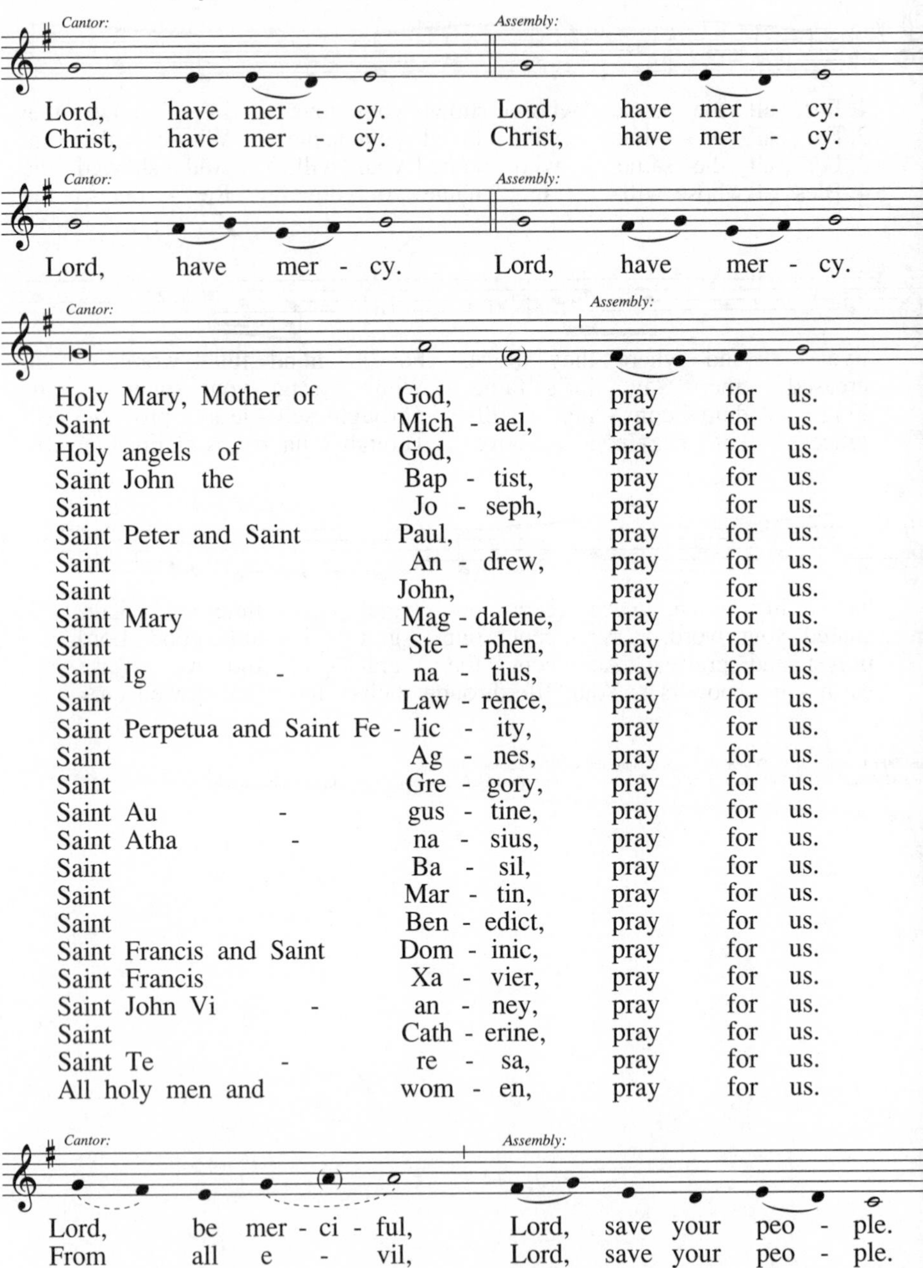
Cantor:
Assembly:
Lord, have mercy. Lord, have mercy.
Christ, have mercy. Christ, have mercy.
Cantor:
Assembly:
Lord, have mercy. Lord, have mercy.
Cantor:
Assembly:
Holy Mary, Mother of God, pray for us.
Saint Michael, pray for us.
Holy angels of God, pray for us.
Saint John the Baptist, pray for us.
Saint Joseph, pray for us.
Saint Peter and Saint Paul, pray for us.
Saint Andrew, pray for us.
Saint John, pray for us.
Saint Mary Magdalene, pray for us.
Saint Stephen, pray for us.
Saint Ignatius, pray for us.
Saint Lawrence, pray for us.
Saint Perpetua and Saint Felicity, pray for us.
Saint Agnes, pray for us.
Saint Gregory, pray for us.
Saint Augustine, pray for us.
Saint Athanasius, pray for us.
Saint Basil, pray for us.
Saint Martin, pray for us.
Saint Benedict, pray for us.
Saint Francis and Saint Dominic, pray for us.
Saint Francis Xavier, pray for us.
Saint John Vianney, pray for us.
Saint Catherine, pray for us.
Saint Teresa, pray for us.
All holy men and women, pray for us.
Cantor:
Assembly:
Lord, be merciful, Lord, save your people.
From all evil, Lord, save your people.
From ev'ry sin, Lord, save your people.
From everlasting death, Lord, save your people.

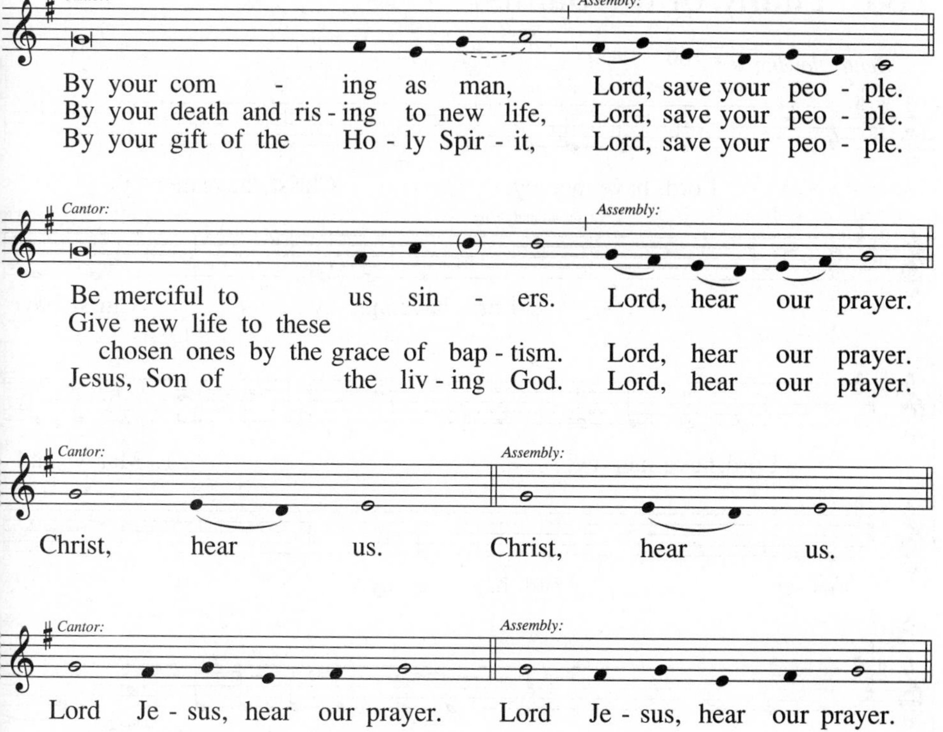
Cantor:
Assembly:
By your com - ing as man, Lord, save your peo - ple.
By your death and ris - ing to new life, Lord, save your peo - ple.
By your gift of the Ho - ly Spir - it, Lord, save your peo - ple.
Cantor:
Assembly:
Be merciful to us sin - ers. Lord, hear our prayer.
Give new life to these chosen ones by the grace of bap - tism. Lord, hear our prayer.
Jesus, Son of the liv - ing God. Lord, hear our prayer.
Cantor:
Assembly:
Christ, hear us. Christ, hear us.
Cantor:
Assembly:
Lord Je - sus, hear our prayer. Lord Je - sus, hear our prayer.

Text: *Litany of the Saints, Roman Missal*
Music: *Litany of the Saints, Roman Missal*

788 Litany of the Saints

Gently flowing ♩ = 100
Priest or cantor:
Lord, have mer-cy. Christ, have mer-cy.
Assembly and choir:
Lord, have mer-cy. Christ, have mer-cy.
Lord, have mer-cy.
Lord, have mer-cy.
1. Mar-y and
1. Jo-seph, Mi-chael and all an-gels,
2. An-drew, James, John and all a-pos-tles,
3. so-go-nus, In-no-cent, and Bon-i-face,
4. se-bi-us, Scho-las-ti-ca and Ben-e-dict,
5. mer-ci-ful. From all e-vil.
6. new life. To these cho-sen.
1.-4. Pray for us.
5. Save your peo-ple.
6. Hear our prayer.
An-na, Jo-a-chim, E-liz-a-beth,
Mar-y Mag-de-lene, Ve-ron-i-ca,
Hip-po-ly-tus and Or-i-gen,
Am-brose, Mon-i-ca, Au-gus-tine,
From ev-'ry sin.
By the grace of bap-tism.
Pray for us.
Save your peo-ple.
Hear our prayer.

E - li - jah, Mo - ses, John the Bap - tist,
Bar - na - bas, Mat - thi - as,
A - tha - na - sius and Ba - sil,
Mar - tin and Greg - o - ry,
From ev - er - last - ing death,
O Je - sus, Son of the liv - ing God.
Pray for us.
Save your peo - ple.
Hear our prayer.
I - saac, Sa - rah, A - bra - ham,
Ste - phen, Phi - lip, and Cor - ne - li - us,
Fel - li - ci - ty, Per - pe - tu - a,
Clare, Fran - cis, and Dom - i - nic,
By your in - car - na - tion,
Send your Spir - it,
Pray for us.
Save your peo - ple.
Hear our prayer.
Ja - cob, Jo - seph, Sam - u - el,
Pris - ca and A - qui - la,
Cos - mos and Da - mi - an,
Fran - cis Xa - vier, Ig - na - tius,
By your death and re - sur - rec - tion,
In its full - ness
Pray for us.
Save your peo - ple.
Hear our prayer.

Ruth, Da - vid, and Sol - o - mon,
Tim - o - thy and Ti - tus,
John Chry - so - stom and Jus - tin,
E - liz - a - beth and Cath - e - rine,
By your gift of the Spir - it,
On your sons and daugh - ters,
Pray for us.
Save your peo - ple.
Hear our prayer.
I - sai - ah, Jer - e - mi - ah,
Li - nus, Cle - tus, and Cle - ment,
Lu - cy, A - ga - tha and Ag - nes,
Lou - is and Wen-ce - slaus,
Have mer - cy on us sin - ners.
Who be - lieve and pro - fess you.
Pray for us.
Save your peo - ple.
Hear our prayer.
All:
1.-4. All you ho - ly men and
5.-6. Christ, hear us; Lord
Pray for us.
Save your peo-ple.
Hear our prayer.
1.-5.
Priest or cantor:
D.S.
Last time
wom-en, pray for us.
Je - sus, hear our prayer.
2. Pe - ter, Paul,
3. Law - rence and Chry -
4. Je - rome and Eu -
5. Lord, be
6. Lord, give

For the Faithful Who Have Answered 789

Verses
1. For the faith - ful who have an - swered When they heard your call to serve, For the man - y ways you led them Test - ing will and stretch - ing nerve, For their work and for their wit - ness As they strove a - gainst the odds, For their cour - age and o - be - dience We give thanks and praise, O God.
2. Man - y eyes have glimpsed the prom - ise. Man - y hearts have yearned to see. Man - y ears have heard you call - ing Us to great - er lib - er - ty. Some have fal - len in the strug - gle. Oth - ers still are fight - ing on. You are not a - shamed to own us. We give thanks and praise, O God.
3. For this cloud of faith - ful wit - ness, For the com - mon life we share, For the work of peace and jus - tice, For the gos - pel that we bear, For the vi - sion that our home - land Is your love— deep, high and broad— For the dif - f'rent roads we trav - el We give thanks and praise, O God.

Refrain
We give you thanks, we give you thanks
for the gos - pel we bear
for the gos - pel bear, the faith we share. We
give you thanks, we give you thanks. With
With
thanks.
D.S.
faith and hope and love, we give you give you thanks.
faith, hope and love, we give you thanks.
Final ending

Text: Verses, Sylvia Dunstan, 1955-1993, © 1991, GIA Publications, Inc.; refrain, David Haas, b.1957, © 1998, GIA Publications, Inc., alt.
Tune: WE GIVE YOU THANKS, 8 7 8 7 D with refrain; David Haas, b.1957, © 1998, GIA Publications, Inc.

Ye Watchers and Ye Holy Ones 790

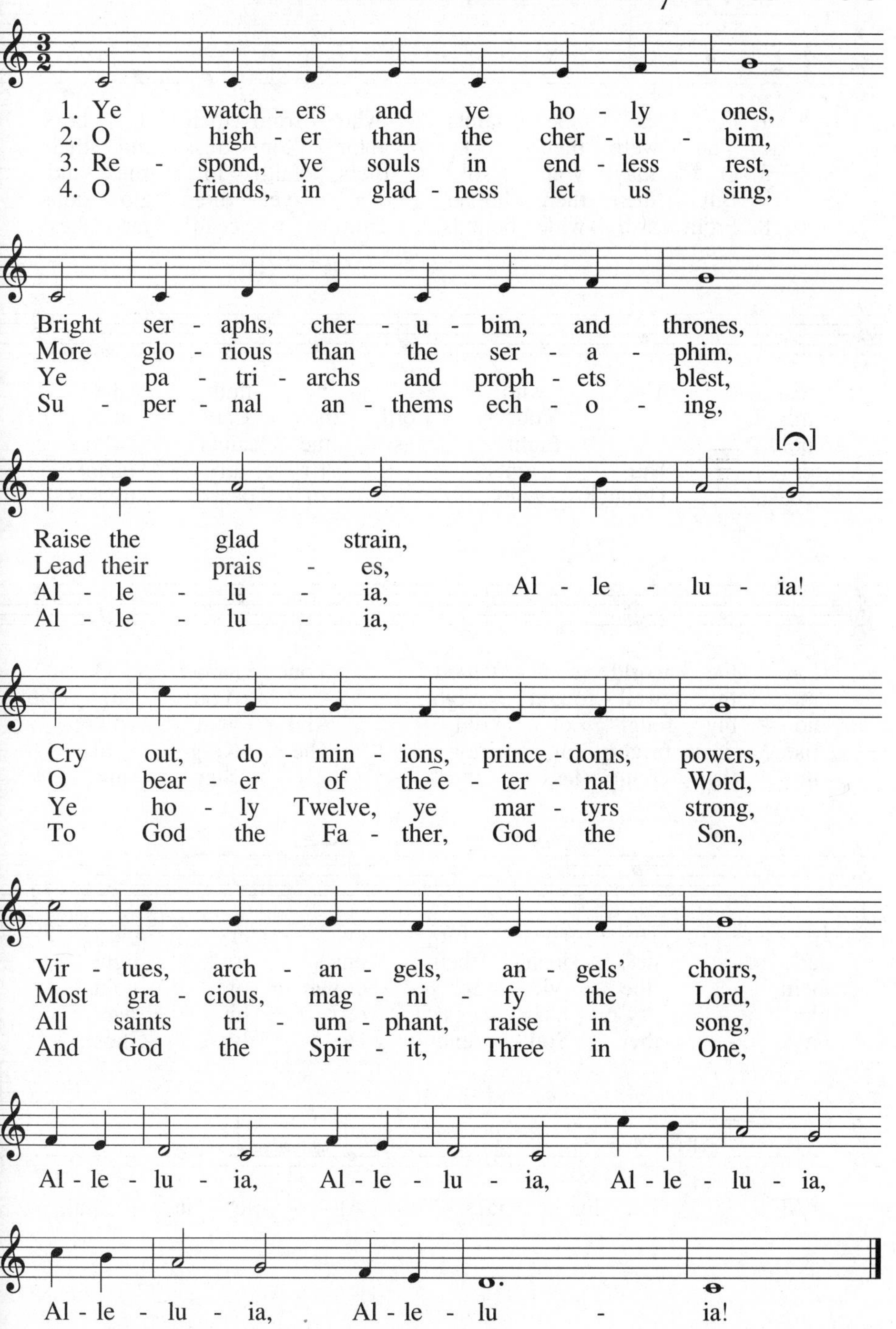
1. Ye watch - ers and ye ho - ly ones,
2. O high - er than the cher - u - bim,
3. Re - spond, ye souls in end - less rest,
4. O friends, in glad - ness let us sing,
Bright ser - aphs, cher - u - bim, and thrones,
More glo - rious than the ser - a - phim,
Ye pa - tri - archs and proph - ets blest,
Su - per - nal an - thems ech - o - ing,
Raise the glad strain,
Lead their prais - es,
Al - le - lu - ia,
Al - le - lu - ia,
Al - le - lu - ia!
Cry out, do - min - ions, prince - doms, powers,
O bear - er of the e - ter - nal Word,
Ye ho - ly Twelve, ye mar - tyrs strong,
To God the Fa - ther, God the Son,
Vir - tues, arch - an - gels, an - gels' choirs,
Most gra - cious, mag - ni - fy the Lord,
All saints tri - um - phant, raise in song,
And God the Spir - it, Three in One,
Al - le - lu - ia, Al - le - lu - ia, Al - le - lu - ia,
Al - le - lu - ia, Al - le - lu - ia!

ext: Athelstan A. Riley, 1858-1945, © Oxford University Press
une: LASST UNS ERFREUEN, LM with alleluias; *Geistliche Kirchengasänge,* Cologne, 1623; harm. by Ralph Vaughan Williams, 1872-1958, © Oxford University Press

791 For All the Saints

1. For all the saints who from their la - bors
2. You were their rock, their for - tress and their
3. O may your sol - diers, faith - ful, true and
7. But then there breaks a yet more glo - rious
8. From earth's wide bounds, from o - cean's far - thest
rest, All who by faith be -
might; You, Lord, their Cap - tain
bold, Fight as the saints who
day: The saints tri - um - phant
coast, Through gates of pearl streams
fore the world con - fessed, Your name, O
in the well - fought fight; You in the
no - bly fought of old, And win with
rise in bright ar - ray; The King of
in the count - less host, Sing - ing to
Je - sus, be for ev - er blest.
dark - ness drear, their one true light.
them, the vic - tor's crown of gold.
glo - ry pass - es on his way.
Fa - ther, Son, and Ho - ly Ghost:
Al - le - lu - ia! Al - le - lu - ia!

Harmony:
4. O blest com - mun - ion, fam - i - ly di - vine!
5. And when the strife is fierce, the war - fare long,
6. The gold - en eve - ning bright - ens in the west;
We fee - bly strug - gle, they in glo - ry shine;
Steals on the ear the dis - tant tri - umph song,
Soon, soon to faith - ful war - riors comes their rest;
Yet all are one with - in your great de - sign.
And hearts are brave a - gain, and arms are strong.
Sweet is the calm of par - a - dise the blest.
Al - le - lu - ia!
Al - le - lu - ia! Al - le - lu - ia!

Text: William W. How, 1823-1897
Tune: SINE NOMINE, 10 10 10 with alleluias; Ralph Vaughan Williams, 1872-1958, © Oxford University Press

792 For the Life of the World

Refrain
world,
For the life of the world, of the world,
we will stand to - geth - er,
we will stand, we will serve the Lord. For the
world,
life of the world, of the world,
we will cry for jus - tice, and
we will cry, and ev - 'ry heart will sing that
Last time
Je - sus Christ is Lord!

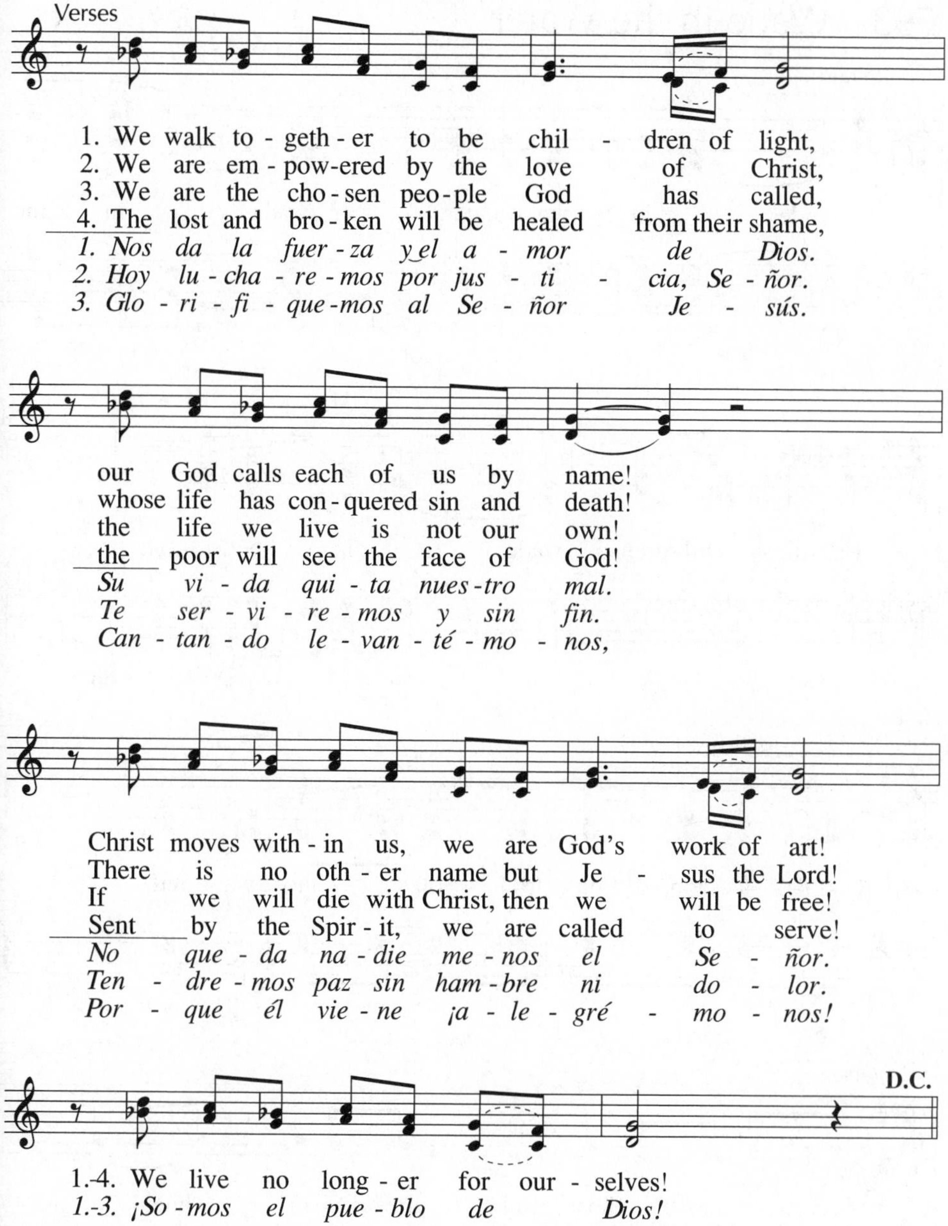

Verses

1. We walk to - geth - er to be chil - dren of light,
2. We are em - pow-ered by the love of Christ,
3. We are the cho - sen peo - ple God has called,
4. The lost and bro - ken will be healed from their shame,
1. Nos da la fuer - za y el a - mor de Dios.
2. Hoy lu - cha - re - mos por jus - ti - cia, Se - ñor.
3. Glo - ri - fi - que-mos al Se - ñor Je - sús.

our God calls each of us by name!
whose life has con - quered sin and death!
the life we live is not our own!
the poor will see the face of God!
Su vi - da qui - ta nues-tro mal.
Te ser - vi - re - mos y sin fin.
Can - tan - do le - van - té - mo - nos,

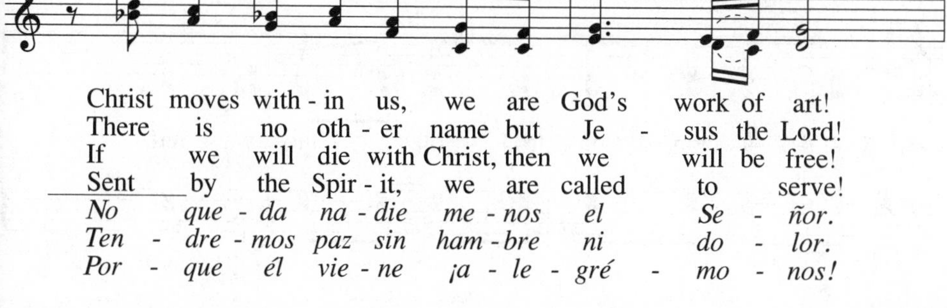
Christ moves with - in us, we are God's work of art!
There is no oth - er name but Je - sus the Lord!
If we will die with Christ, then we will be free!
Sent by the Spir - it, we are called to serve!
No que - da na - die me - nos el Se - ñor.
Ten - dre - mos paz sin ham - bre ni do - lor.
Por - que él vie - ne ¡a - le - gré - mo - nos!

D.C.
1.-4. We live no long - er for our - selves!
1.-3. ¡So - mos el pue - blo de Dios!

Text: David Haas, b.1957; Spanish verses by Jeffrey Judge
Tune: David Haas, b.1957; acc. by Jeanne Cotter, b.1964

793 Wade in the Water

Refrain
Wade in the wa - ter, wade in the
oh,
wa - ter, chil - dren, wade in the wa - ter,
oh,
God's a gon - na trou - ble the wa - ter.
Verses
Cantor:
1. See that host all dressed in white,
2. See that band all dressed in red,
3. Look o - ver yon - der, what do I see?
4. If you don't be - lieve I've been re - deemed,
ooh

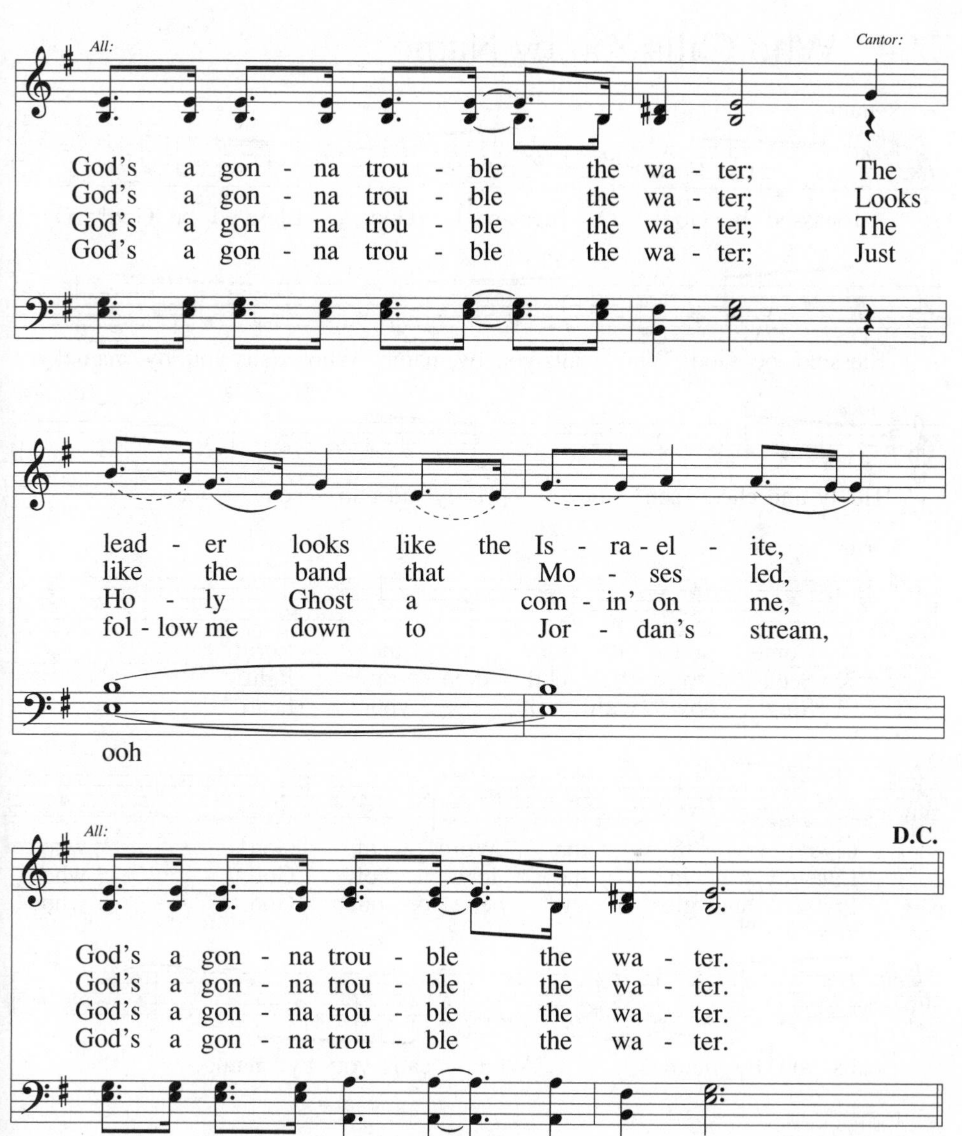
All:
Cantor:
God's a gon - na trou - ble the wa - ter; The
God's a gon - na trou - ble the wa - ter; Looks
God's a gon - na trou - ble the wa - ter; The
God's a gon - na trou - ble the wa - ter; Just
lead - er looks like the Is - ra - el - ite,
like the band that Mo - ses led,
Ho - ly Ghost a com - in' on me,
fol - low me down to Jor - dan's stream,
ooh
All:
D.C.
God's a gon - na trou - ble the wa - ter.
God's a gon - na trou - ble the wa - ter.
God's a gon - na trou - ble the wa - ter.
God's a gon - na trou - ble the wa - ter.

Text: African-American spiritual
Tune: African-American spiritual; harm. by Diana Kodner, b.1957, © 1994, GIA Publications, Inc.

794 Who Calls You by Name

Refrain

Cantor: Bless-ed be God! O Bless-ed be God! *All:* Bless-ed be God! O Bless-ed be God! *Cantor:* Who calls you by name! *All:* Who calls you by name!

Cantor: Ho-ly and cho - sen one! *All:* Ho-ly and cho - sen one! *Last time*

Verses

1. Come, and re - turn to the Lord! Live by the Word of God, who calls you by name! Who calls you by name!
2. Seek to be chil - dren of light! Live in the love of God, who
3. Sing now with all your heart! Praise and glo - ry be to our God, who

D.C.

Text: David Haas, b.1957
Tune: David Haas, b.1957

795 Christ Will Be Your Strength

Christ will be your strength! Learn to know and fol-low him!

Text: David Haas, b.1957
Tune: David Haas, b.1957

There Is One Lord 796

Ostinato Refrain
There is one Lord, one faith, one bap - tis-m,
There is one God who is Fa - ther of all.
Verses
Cantor:
1. Bear with one an - oth - er in love and char-i - ty, be
hum - ble, be pa - tient, be self - less, be as one.
2. There is one bod - y, there is one Spir - it,
there is one hope to which we are called.
3. We are all to come to u - ni - ty, in our
faith and knowl - edge of the Son of God, un - til
we be-come per - fect-ed in the full - ness of Christ.

Text: Ephesians 4; Taizé Community, 1984
Tune: Jacques Berthier, 1923-1994

797 Baptized in Water

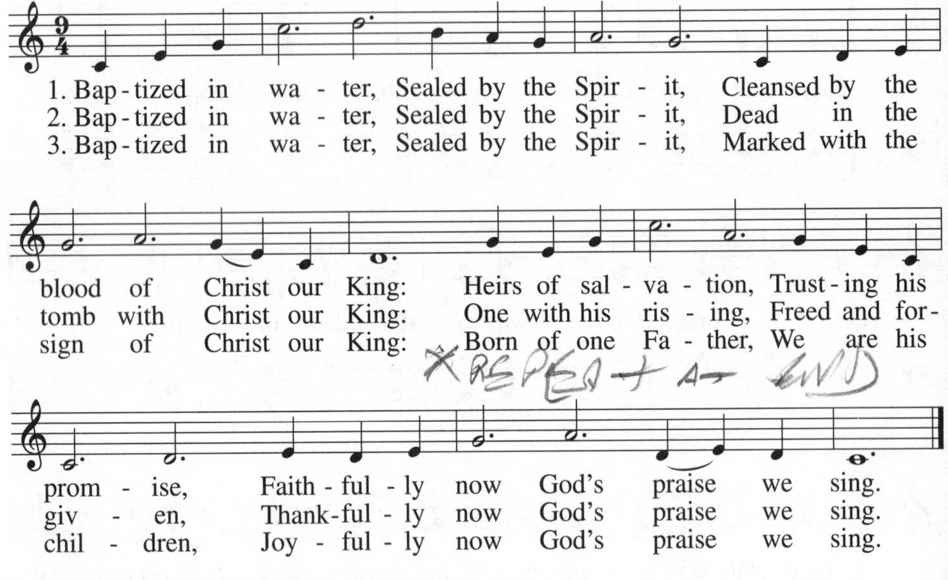
1. Bap-tized in wa - ter, Sealed by the Spir - it, Cleansed by the blood of Christ our King: Heirs of sal - va - tion, Trust-ing his prom - ise, Faith-ful - ly now God's praise we sing.
2. Bap-tized in wa - ter, Sealed by the Spir - it, Dead in the tomb with Christ our King: One with his ris - ing, Freed and for-giv - en, Thank-ful - ly now God's praise we sing.
3. Bap-tized in wa - ter, Sealed by the Spir - it, Marked with the sign of Christ our King: Born of one Fa - ther, We are his chil - dren, Joy - ful - ly now God's praise we sing.

Text: Michael Saward, b.1932, © 1982, Jubilate Hymns, Ltd. (admin. by Hope Publishing Co.)
Tune: BUNESSAN, 5 5 8 D; Gaelic melody; acc. by Marty Haugen, b.1950, © 1987, GIA Publications, Inc.

798 Covenant Hymn

1. Wher - ev - er you go, I will fol - low, Wher-ev - er you live is my home. Though
2. What - ev - er you dream, I am with you, When stars call your name in the night. Though
3. And though you should fall, you will find me, When no oth - er friend can you claim, When
4. Wher - ev - er you die, I will be there To sing you to sleep with a psalm, To
5. Wher - ev - er you go, I will fol - low, Be - hold! The ho - ri - zon shines clear. The

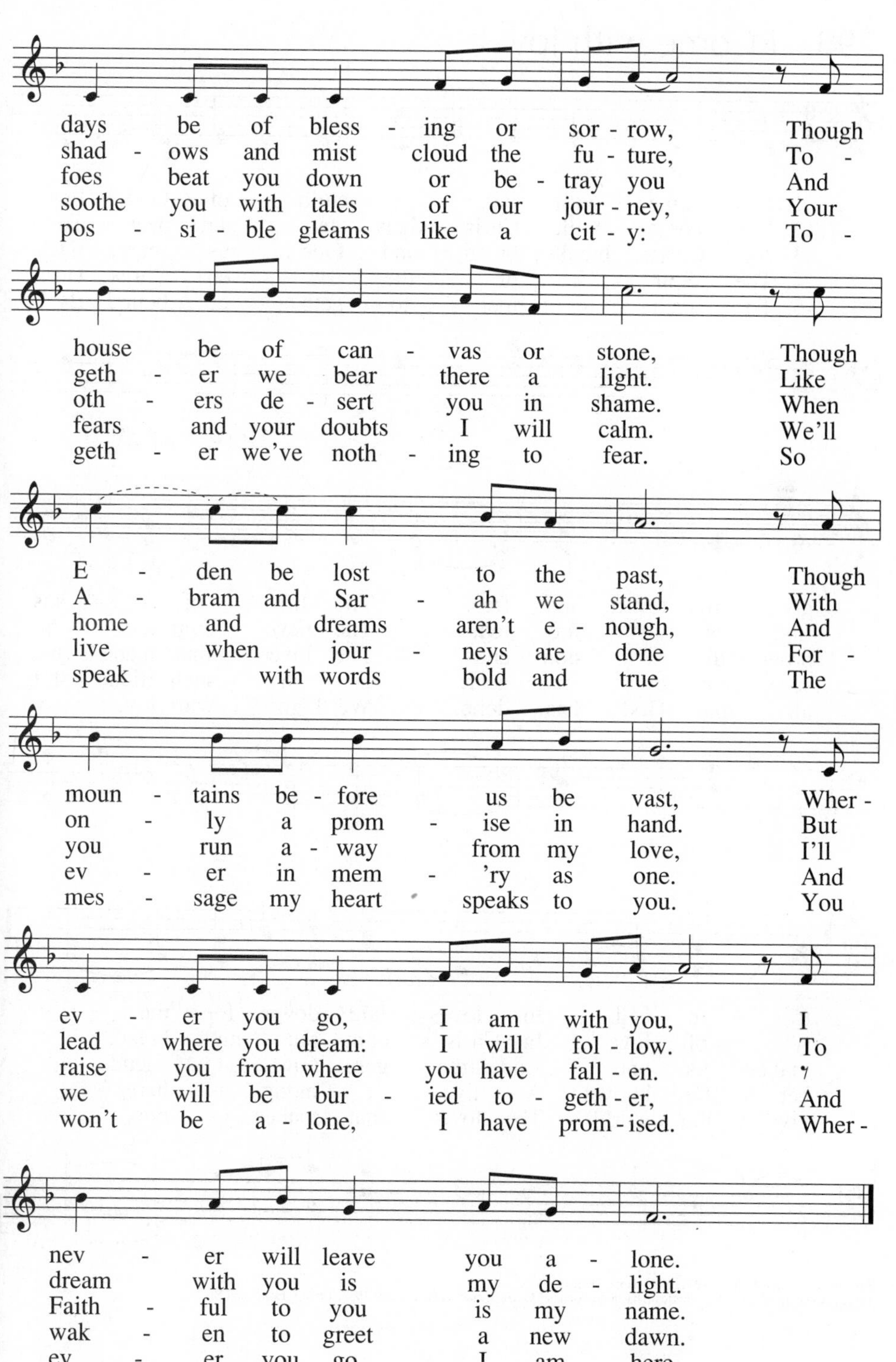
days be of bless - ing or sor - row, Though
shad - ows and mist cloud the fu - ture, To -
foes beat you down or be - tray you And
soothe you with tales of our jour - ney, Your
pos - si - ble gleams like a cit - y: To -
house be of can - vas or stone, Though
geth - er we bear there a light. Like
oth - ers de - sert you in shame. When
fears and your doubts I will calm. We'll
geth - er we've noth - ing to fear. So
E - den be lost to the past, Though
A - bram and Sar - ah we stand, With
home and dreams aren't e - nough, And
live when jour - neys are done For -
speak with words bold and true The
moun - tains be - fore us be vast, Wher -
on - ly a prom - ise in hand. But
you run a - way from my love, I'll
ev - er in mem - 'ry as one. And
mes - sage my heart speaks to you. You
ev - er you go, I am with you, I
lead where you dream: I will fol - low. To
raise you from where you have fall - en.
we will be bur - ied to - geth - er, And
won't be a - lone, I have prom - ised. Wher -
nev - er will leave you a - lone.
dream with you is my de - light.
Faith - ful to you is my name.
wak - en to greet a new dawn.
ev - er you go, I am here.

Text: Ruth 1:16; Rory Cooney, b.1952
Tune: Gary Daigle, b.1957

799 I Come with Joy

1. I come with joy, a child of God, For - giv - en, loved, and free, The life of Je - sus to re - call, In love laid down for me.
2. I come with Chris - tians far and near To find, as all are fed, The new com - mu - ni - ty of love In Christ's com - mu - nion bread.
3. As Christ breaks bread, and bids us share, Each proud di - vi - sion ends. The love that made us, makes us one, And stran - gers now are friends.
4. The Spir - it of the ris - en Christ, Un - seen, but ev - er near, Is in such friend - ship bet - ter known, A - live a - mong us here.
5. To - geth - er met, to - geth - er bound By all that God has done, We'll go with joy, to give the world The love that makes us one.

Text: Brian Wren, b.1936, © 1971, 1995, Hope Publishing Co.
Tune: LAND OF REST, CM; American; harm. by Annabel M. Buchanan, 1888-1983, © 1938, 1966, J. Fisher and Bro.

O Breathe on Me, O Breath of God 800

1. O breathe on me, O breath of God,
Fill me with life anew,
That I may love the things you love,
And do what you would do.

2. O breathe on me, O breath of God,
Until my heart is pure;
Until my will is one with yours,
To do and to endure.

3. O breathe on me, O breath of God,
My will to yours incline,
Until this selfish part of me
Glows with your fire divine.

4. O breathe on me, O breath of God,
So shall I never die,
But live with you the perfect life
Of your eternity.

Text: Edwin Hatch, 1835-1889
Tune: ST. COLUMBA, CM; Gaelic; harm. by A. Gregory Murray, OSB, 1905-1992,

801 Christ Be in Your Senses

1. Christ be in your sens - es, marked with sa - cred sign.
2. Christ be in your vi - sion, guard you day and night;
3. Christ be in your breath-ing, con - stant - ly im - part

In the In - car - na - tion, flesh be - came di - vine.
Keep your feet from stum - bling, shine God's ho - ly light.
Grace to ev - 'ry move - ment, peace with - in your heart.

Christ be in your hear - ing, tune you to re - joice;
Christ be in your speak - ing, train your ev - 'ry word.
Christ be in your sens - es, marked with sa - cred sign.

Last time

In each shout or whis - per, hear God's call - ing voice.
In your dai - ly wit - ness let God's truth be heard.
In the Spir - it's pres - ence, flesh be - comes di - vine.

Text: Mary Louise Bringle, b.1953
Tune: APPALACHIAN FALL, 11 11 11 11; William P. Rowan, b.1951

Sweet Refreshment 802

Refrain
Cantor:
Come to the wa - ter.
All:
Come to the wa-ter.
Cantor:
Drink of it free-ly.
All:
Drink of it free-ly.
Cantor:
Taste God's own Spir - it.
All:
Taste God's Spir - it.
Taste God's own Spir - it.
Taste God's Spir - it.
Cantor:
Sweet re - fresh-ment.
All:
Sweet re - fresh-ment.
To verses
Last time
fresh - ment.

Verses
Cantor:
1. At the dawn of cre - a - tion, your
2. When your peo - ple were cap - tive, you
3. In the wa - ters of Jor - dan, your
4. Liv - ing wa - ters, e - ter - nal,
Spir - it, O God, moved on the wa - ters. You
led them, O God, led them from bond - age. You
Son was bap - tized; with Spir - it a - noint - ed, that
quench ev - 'ry thirst, cleanse ev - 'ry soul.
S,A
Ooo
T,B
D.S.
breathed and the wa - ters were life.
led them through wa - ters to life.
we might be raised to new life.
You are the foun - tain of life.
D.S.
Oh, wa - ters of life.

Text: Based on *Blessing of Water*, Easter Vigil; adapt. by Bob Moore, b.1962
Tune: Bob Moore, b.1962

Bread of Life from Heaven / Pan de Vida Eterna 803

Refrain
Bread of life from heav - en, your blood and bod - y
Pan de vi - da e - ter - na, nos das tu cuer - po y
we eat this
Has - ta que
giv - en, we eat this bread and
san - gre. Has - ta que vuel - vas
Last time
drink this cup un - til you come a - gain.
tú, Se - ñor, co - me - mos en tu a - mor.
Last time

Verses

1. Break now the bread of Christ's sac - ri - fice; Giv - ing
2. Seek not the food that will pass a - way; Set your
3. Love as the One who, in love for you, Gave him -
4. Take in the light that will nev - er dim, Taste the
5. Dwell in the One who now dwells in you; Make your
6. Drink of this cup and de - clare his death; Eat this
7. Ven y com - par - te el di - vi - no pan; De - mos
8. Es - te mis - te - rio es el máx - i - mo sa - cri -
9. Ven a la me - sa de com - pa - sión, re - cor -
10. Hoy que co - me - mos del pan de a - mor so - mos
11. Ce - na que nos re - pre - sen - ta hoy la vi - da,

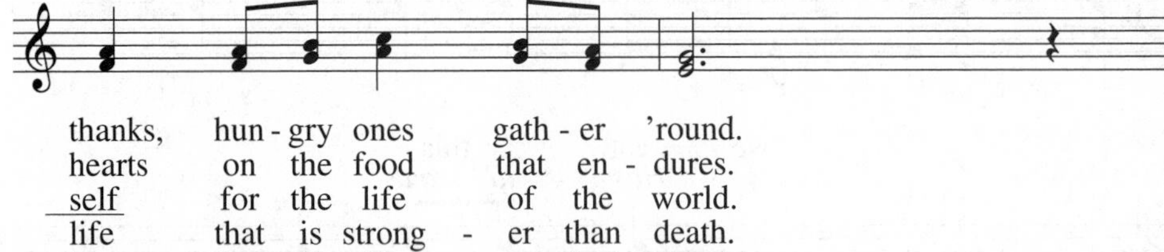
thanks, hun - gry ones gath - er 'round.
hearts on the food that en - dures.
self for the life of the world.
life that is strong - er than death.
home in the life - giv - ing Word.
bread and be - lieve Eas - ter morn;
gra - cias con gran co - ra - zón.
fi - cio de fe y de a - mor.
de - mos a Cris - to Je - sús.
u - no en Cris - to Je - sús.
muer - te y re - su - rrec - ción

Eat all of you, and be sat - is - fied; in Christ's
Come, learn the true and the liv - ing way, that the
Come to the One who is food for you, that your
Live in the One who will come and then raise you
Know on - ly Christ, Ho - ly One of God, and be -
Trust his re - turn and, with ev - 'ry breath, praise the
Cris - to es sus - ten - to que u - ni - rá a los
Pan que nos lla - ma a con - me - mo - rar y a se -
Él nos da vi - da con ple - ni - tud; Nos pro -
Ce - na que es fuen - te de in - spi - ra - ción pa - ra
de Je - su - cris - to que es nues - tro Dios quien nos

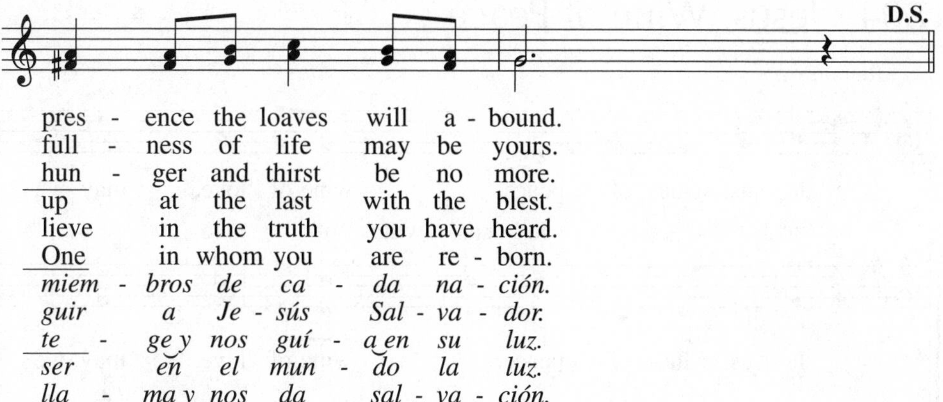
D.S.
pres - ence the loaves will a - bound.
full - ness of life may be yours.
hun - ger and thirst be no more.
up at the last with the blest.
lieve in the truth you have heard.
One in whom you are re - born.
miem - bros de ca - da na - ción.
guir a Je - sús Sal - va - dor.
te - ge y nos guí - a en su luz.
ser en el mun - do la luz.
lla - ma y nos da sal - va - ción.

Text: Based on John 6; adapt. by Susan R. Briehl, b.1952; Spanish by Jaime Cortez, b.1963
Tune: Argentine folk melody; adapt. and verses by Marty Haugen, b.1950

804 Jesus, Wine of Peace

Refrain

Melody:
Je - sus, wine of peace, wine of love, may we
Je - sus, wine of love,
Je - sus, wine of peace, wine of love, may we

drink of you; may we taste your
drink of you; may we taste your

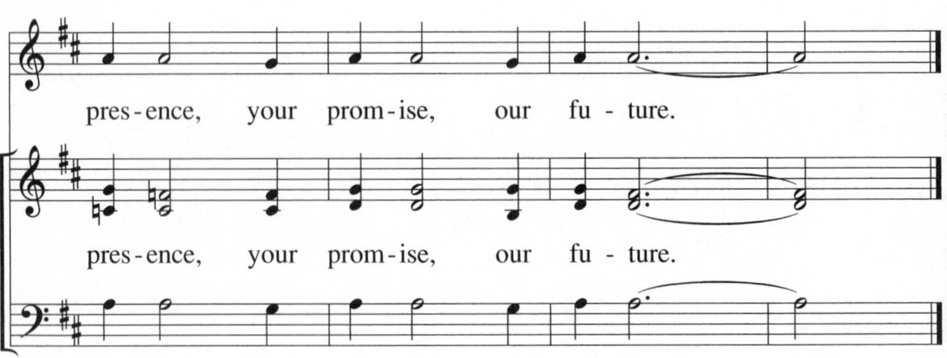
pres - ence, your prom - ise, our fu - ture.
pres - ence, your prom - ise, our fu - ture.

Verses

1. I will be the path that guides you, I will save you.
2. You will nev - er be a - lone, I am with you.
3. You will nev - er thirst a - gain, I will fill you.
4. You will laugh and sing a - gain in my pres - ence.
5. You will live in fear no more, peace be with you.
6. I have come that you may live, I am with you.
7. You will rise and live a - new in my king - dom.
8. I will be your one true shep - herd, I will guide you.
9. I will be your light in dark - ness, I will save you.
10. No more weep - ing, no more pain in my king - dom.

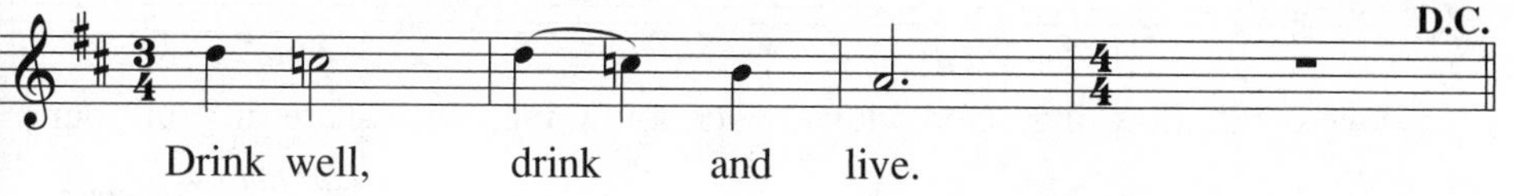
D.C.
Drink well, drink and live.

Text: David Haas, b.1957
Tune: David Haas, b.1957

805 With This Bread

Refrain
With this bread we will walk with each oth - er,
with this cup we will fol-low the Lord. Com- pas - sion,
love o-ver-flow-ing, God's love ev-er know-ing, we share it in our
song.
Last time
To verses
Verses 1, 2
Cantor:
1. To of - fer as - sis - tance when oth - ers are blind to the need,
2. Wash-ing the wounds of di - vi - sion, we seek to ease pain.
Choir: (verse 2 only)
Oo Oo Oo Oo Oo
to give lov-ing care to each oth -
Shar-ing the bur - den of oth -
Oo Oo Oo

er is plant - ing God's seed.
ers, like God's gen - tle rain.
Be -
Oo
Oo
Be -
Walk - ing the prom - ise and fall - ing on mer - cy, be -
friend - ing the one who is lone - ly and lost, be -
friend - ing the one who is lone - ly and lost, be -
liev - ing we'll walk with you.
liev - ing we'll walk with you.
D.C.
liev - ing we'll walk with you.
D.C.

Verse 3
3. We hold the key to our fu - ture as we share our souls,
unis.
3. We hold the key to our fu - ture as we share our souls,
unis.
nur - tur - ing love in a time
div.
nur - tur - ing love in a time
div.
when com - pas - sion un- folds.
when com - pas - sion un- folds.

Danc-ing in joy, shar-ing in won - der the
Oo
Oo
D.C.
prayer that we sing to you.
D.C.
Oo
Oo

Text: Kate Cuddy, b.1953
Tune: Kate Cuddy, b.1953

806 Eat This Bread

Refrain
Eat this bread, drink this cup, come to him and nev-er be hun-gry.
Eat this bread, drink this cup, trust in him and you will not thirst.
Verse 1
1. Christ is the bread of life, the
true bread sent from the Fa - ther.
D.C.
Verse 2
2. Our an - ces - tors ate man - na in the des - ert, but
this is the bread come down from heav - en.
D.C.
Verse 3
3. Eat his flesh and drink his blood, and
Christ will raise you up on the last day.
*
D.C.

*Choose either part

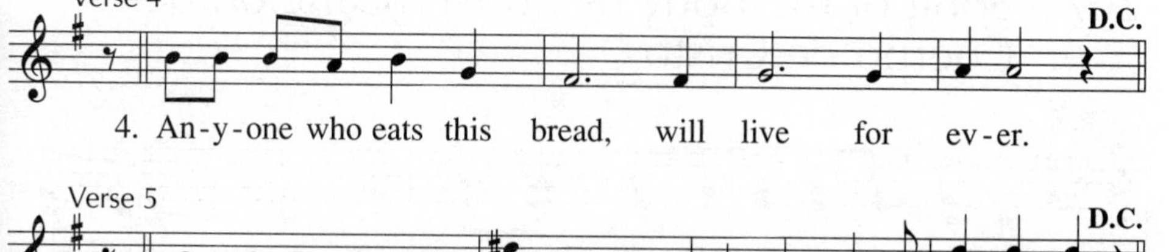
Verse 4
D.C.
4. An-y-one who eats this bread, will live for ev-er.

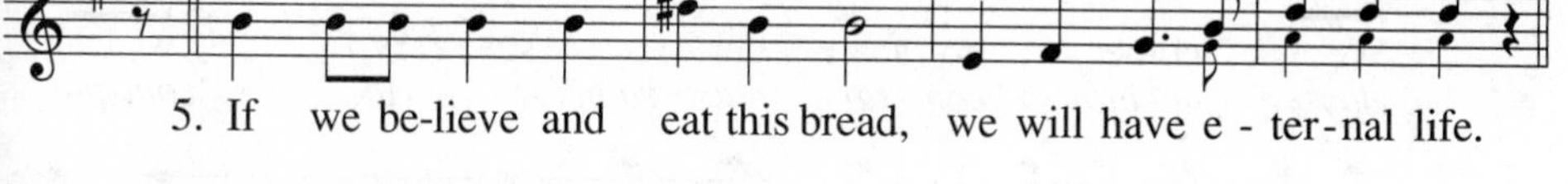
Verse 5
D.C.
5. If we be-lieve and eat this bread, we will have e - ter-nal life.

Text: John 6; adapt. by Robert J. Batastini, b.1942, and the Taizé Community
Tune: Jacques Berthier, 1923-1994

807 Song of the Body of Christ / Canción del Cuerpo de Cristo

Refrain

We come to share our sto - ry, we
Hoy ve - ni - mos a con - tar nues-tra his - to - ria, com-par -

come to break the bread, We
tien - do el pan ce - les - tial. Hoy ve -

Last time
come to know our ris - ing from the dead.
ni - mos jun - tos a ce - le - brar tu mis - te - rio pas - cual.
Last time

Verses

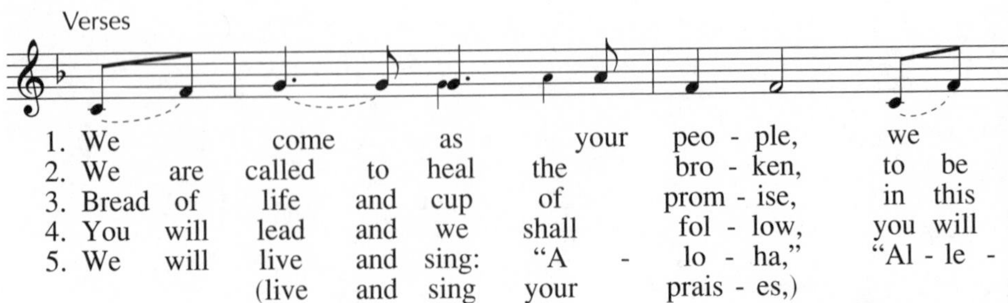
1. We come as your peo - ple, we
2. We are called to heal the bro - ken, to be
3. Bread of life and cup of prom - ise, in this
4. You will lead and we shall fol - low, you will
5. We will live and sing: "A - lo - ha," "Al - le -
(live and sing your prais - es,)

come as your own, u - nit - ed with each
hope for the poor, we are called to feed the
meal we all are one. In our dy - ing and our
be the breath of life; liv - ing wa - ter, we are
lu - ia" is our song. May we live in love and
D.C.
oth - er, love finds a home.
hun - gry at our door.
ris - ing, may your king-dom come.
thirst - ing for your light.
peace our whole life long.
Estrofas
1. Hoy ve - ni - mos por - que so - mos tu pue - blo, re - na -
2. A sa - nar al en - fer - mo nos lla - mas, al an -
3. Pan de vi - da y san - gre de la a - lian - za, haz - nos
4. Nos guia - rás y te se - gui - re - mos. Nues - tro a -
5. Vi - vi - re - mos can - tan - do "A - lo - ja." "A - le -
ci - dos por tu per - dón, re - u - ni - dos en
sio - so, tu es - pe - ran - za tra - er, y al ham - brien - to, nues -
u - no en es - ta co - mu - nión. Que tu rei - no ven -
lien - to vi - tal tú se - rás. Nues - tra luz, en el dí - a
lu - ya" es nues - tra can - ción. Que vi - va - mos por siem -
D.C.
tu a - mor, y de un co - ra - zón.
tro a - li - men - to o - fre - cer.
ga en nues - tra trans - for - ma - ción.
y en la no - che bri - lla - rás.
pre en paz y fra - ter - na u - nión.

Text: David Haas, b.1957, Spanish translation by Donna Peña, b.1955, and Ronald F. Krisman, b.1946
Tune: NO KE ANO' AHI AHI, Irregular, Hawaiian traditional, arr. by David Haas, b.1957

808 Let Us Be Bread

Refrain
Descant:
One faith, one hope, one symbol of love given to us in this one bread, one cup. O let us be one in the Lord.
Melody:
Let us be bread, blessed by the Lord, broken and shared, life for the world. Let us be wine, love freely poured. Let us be one in the Lord.
Last time
Verse 1
1. I am the bread of life, broken for all. Eat now and hunger no more.
D.C.

Verse 2
2. You are my friends if you keep my com-mands,
D.C.
no long-er ser-vants but friends.
Verse 3
3. See how my peo-ple have noth-ing to eat.
D.C.
Give them the bread that is you.
Verse 4
4. As God has loved me so I have loved you.
D.C.
Go and live on in my love.

Text: Thomas J. Porter, b.1958
Tune: Thomas J. Porter, b.1958

809 I Received the Living God

Refrain
I re - ceived the liv - ing God, and my heart is full of joy. I re - ceived the liv - ing God, and my heart is full of joy.
Verses
1. Je - sus said: "I am the Bread Knead - ed long to give you life; You who will par - take of
2. Je - sus said: "I am the Vine, And my branch - es you shall be; Come and drink the sav - ing
3. Je - sus said: "I am the Way; And my Fa - ther longs for you; So I come to bring you
4. Je - sus said: "I am the Truth; If you fol - low close to me, You will know me in your
5. Je - sus said: "I am the Life Far from whom no thing can grow, But re - ceive this liv - ing

D.C.
me Need not ev - er fear to die."
cup, Till the King - dom you shall see."
home To be one with him a - new."
heart, And my word shall make you free."
bread, And my Spir - it you shall know."

Text: Anonymous; verse 2, Alan J. Hommerding, b.1956, © 1994, World Library Publications, Inc.
Tune: LIVING GOD, 7 7 7 7 with refrain; Anonymous; harm. by Richard Proulx, b.1937, © 1986, GIA Publications, Inc.

810 Come to the Banquet

Refrain
Descant:
Come to the ban - quet, come to the
Melody:
Come to the ban - quet, come to the feast. Eat the bread of
feast. Share in the sing - ing, share in the
life! Share in the sing - ing, share in the joy. Drink the cup of
To verses
div.
Last time
div.
joy, share the joy! joy! Share the joy!
love! love! Share the joy!
Verses
1. Draw near and take the bod - y of the
2. Sal - va - tion's giv - er, Christ, the on - ly
3. Come for - ward then with faith - ful hearts sin -
4. With heav'n - ly bread makes those who hun - ger
Descant:
and drink the ho - ly blood for
who by his cross and blood the
and take the prom - ise of sal -
gives liv - ing wa - ters to the
Lord. and drink the ho - ly blood for you out -
Son, who by his cross and blood the vic - t'ry
cere, and take the prom - ise of sal - va - tion
whole, gives liv - ing wa - ters to the thirst - ing

you out - poured.
vic - t'ry won.
va - tion here.
thirst - ing soul.
poured.
won.
here.
soul.
Saved by his bod - y,
Gave up his life for
The Lord, who faith - ful
Be - fore your pres - ence,
with souls re - freshed, we
Him - self the vic - tim
to all be - lieve - ers
In this your feast of
hal - lowed by his blood,
great - est and for least,
ser - vants loves and shields,
Lord, all peo - ple bow.
with souls re - freshed, we
Him - self the vic - tim
to all be - liev - ers
In this your feast of
D.C.
give our thanks to God.
and him - self the priest.
life e - ter - nal yields.
love be with us now.
give our thanks to God.
and him - self the priest.
life e - ter - nal yields.
love be with us now.

Text: *Sancti, venite, corpus sumite,* 7th C., tr. John Mason Neale, 1818-1866, alt.; refrain, James J. Chepponis, b.1956,
Tune: James J. Chepponis, b.1956,

811 Pan de Vida

Refrain
*Pan de Vi - da, cuer-po del Se - ñor,
cup of bless - ing, blood of Christ the
Lord. At this ta - ble the
last shall be first, **po - der es ser - vir,
por-que Dios es a - mor.
To verses
Last time

*Bread of Life, body of the Lord,
**power is for service, because God is Love.

Verses
1. We are the dwell - ing of God,
***2. Us - te - des me lla - man "Se - ñor," me in -
3. There is no Jew or Greek,
fra - gile and wound - ed and weak. We are the
cli - no a la - var - les los pies: Ha - gan lo
there is no slave or free: there is no
bod - y of Christ, called to be
mis - mo, hu - mil - des, sir - vién -
wom - an or man; on - ly heirs
the com - pas - sion of God.
do - se u - nos a o - tros.
of the prom - ise of God.
D.C.

****You call me "Lord", and I bow to wash your feet: you must do the same, humbly serving each other.*

Text: John 13:1-15, Galatians 3:28-29; Bob Hurd, b.1950, and Pia Moriarty, b.1948
Tune: Bob Hurd, b.1950; acc. by Craig S. Kingsbury, b.1952

812 Take and Eat

Refrain
Take and eat; take and eat: this is my bod - y
giv-en up for you. Take and drink; take and drink:
this is my blood giv - en up for you.
Verses

1. I am the Word that spoke and light was made;
2. I am the way that leads the ex - ile home;
3. I am the Lamb that takes a - way your sin;
4. I am the cor - ner - stone that God has laid;
5. I am the light that came in - to the world;
6. I am the first and last, the Liv - ing One;

I am the seed that died to be re - born;
I am the truth that sets the cap - tive free;
I am the gate that guards you night and day;
A cho - sen stone and pre - cious in his eyes;
I am the light that dark - ness can - not hide;
I am the Lord who died that you might live;
I am the bread that comes from heav'n a - bove;
I am the life that rais - es up the dead;
You are my flock: you know the shep - herd's voice;
You are God's dwell - ing place, on me you rest;
I am the morn - ing star that nev - er sets;
I am the bride - groom, this my wed - ding song;
D.C.
I am the vine that fills your cup with joy.
I am your peace, true peace my gift to you.
You are my own: your ran - som is my blood.
Like liv - ing stones, a tem - ple for God's praise.
Lift up your face, in you my light will shine.
You are my bride, come to the mar - riage feast.

813 One Bread, One Body

Refrain
Descant:
Melody:
One bread, one bod-y, one Lord of all, one cup of bless - ing which we bless.
And we, though man-y, through-out the earth, we are one bod - y in this one Lord.
Last time to coda

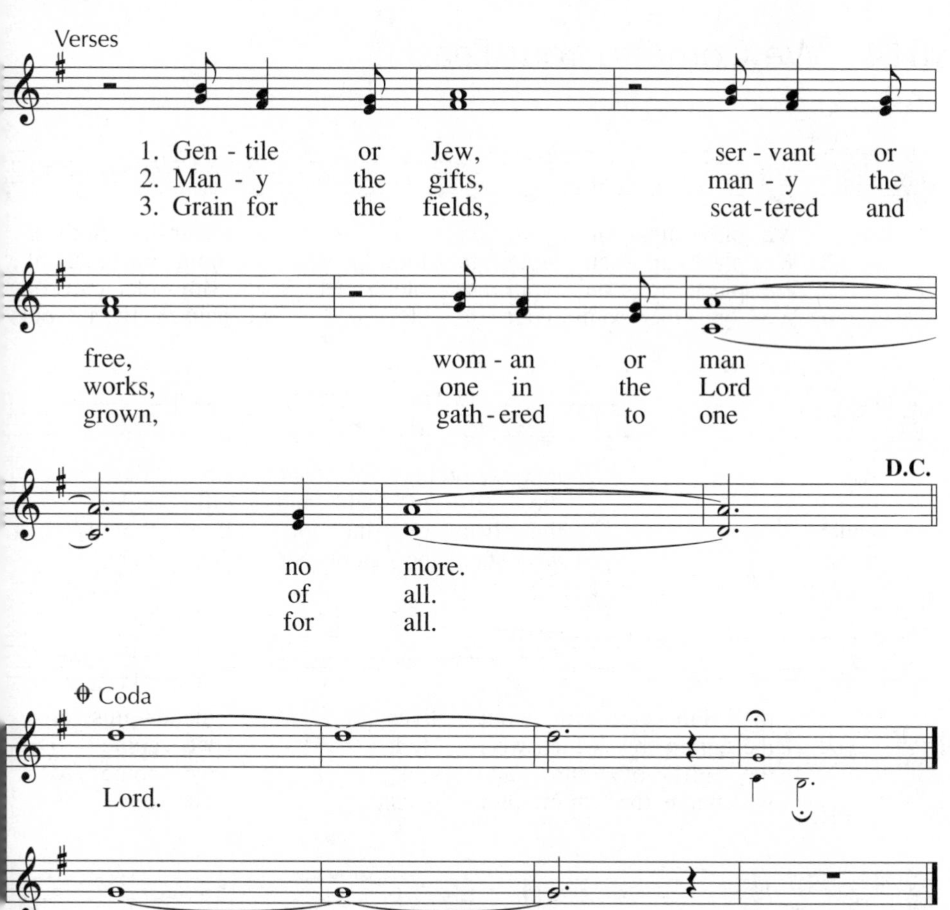
Verses
1. Gen - tile or Jew, ser - vant or free, wom - an or man no more.
2. Man - y the gifts, man - y the works, one in the Lord of all.
3. Grain for the fields, scat - tered and grown, gath - ered to one for all.
D.C.
Coda
Lord.
Lord.

Text: 1 Corinthians 10:16; 17, 12:4, Galatians 3:28; the *Didache* 9; John Foley, SJ, b.1939
Tune: John Foley, SJ, b.1939

814 We Come to Your Feast

Verses
Cantor or choir:
1. We place up - on your ta - ble a gleam-ing cloth of
2. We place up - on your ta - ble a hum - ble loaf of
3. We place up - on your ta - ble a sim - ple cup of
4. We ga - ther 'round your ta - ble, we pause with - in our
white: the weav - ing of our sto - ries,
bread: the gift of field and hill - side,
wine: the fruit of hu - man la - bor,
quest, we stand be - side our neigh - bors,
the fab - ric of our lives; the dreams of
the grain by which we're fed; we come to
the gift of sun and vine; we come to
we name the stran - ger "guest." The feast is
those be - fore us, the an - cient hope - ful cries,
taste the pres - ence of him on whom we feed,
taste the pres - ence of him we claim as Lord,
spread be - fore us; you bid us come and dine:
the prom - ise of our fu - ture: our need - ing and our
to strength - en and con - nect us, to chal - lenge and cor -
his dy - ing and his liv - ing, his lead - ing and his
in bless - ing we'll un - cov - er, in shar - ing we'll dis -
nur - ture lie here be - fore our eyes.
rect us, to love in word and deed.
giv - ing, his love in cup out - poured.
cov - er your sub - stance and your sign.

Refrain
All:
Descant:
We come to your feast, we come to your feast:
Melody:
unis.
the young and the old, the fright-ened, the bold, the great-est
div.
and the least. We come to your feast, we come to your
unis.
feast with the fruit of our lands and the work of our
div.
hands, we come to your feast.

Text: Michael Joncas, b.1951
Tune: Michael Joncas, b.1951

815 Joyous Cup: A Processional for the Easter Season

Verses
Cantor:
All:
1. Slaves and chil - dren, take a stand:
2. Sea, stand straight! And riv - ers, flee:
3. Trem - ble, earth, to see God's face:
4. Heav - ens, sing! O earth, in - tone:
5. Eve and A - dam, tell it plain: Al - le - lu -
6. God, our lov - er, long be - trayed
7. O hap - py fault, O need - ful sin:
8. Go pro - claim a ju - bi - lee:
9. Go pro - claim a ju - bi - lee:
Cantor:
All:
Come to milk and hon - ey land:
Moun-tains, skip like lambs to see:
Flint shall flow with wa - ter's grace:
Death and hell now wail and groan:
ia! All was lost but more's the gain: Al - le - lu -
Pas - sion has our wed - ding made:
O Christ our sav - ior, Christ our kin:
Nei - ther rich nor poor shall be:
Now from ev - 'ry debt set free:
Refrain
ia! Christ has died and death is dead: earth and heav - en
bold - ly wed. Joy - ous cup and heart - y bread.
Last time
Al - le - lu - ia.

Text: Based on Psalm 114 and the Exsultet; Gabe Huck, b.1941, © 2004
Tune: Tony E. Alonso, b.1980, © 2004, GIA Publications, Inc.

You Satisfy the Hungry Heart 816

Refrain
You sat-is-fy the hun-gry heart With gift of fin-est wheat;
Come give to us, O sav-ing Lord, The bread of life to eat.
Verses
1. As when the shep - herd calls his sheep, They know and heed his voice; So when you call your fam - 'ly, Lord, We fol - low and re - joice.
2. With joy - ful lips we sing to you Our praise and grat - i - tude, That you should count us wor - thy, Lord, To share this heav'n - ly food.
3. Is not the cup we bless and share The blood of Christ out-poured? Do not one cup, one loaf, de - clare Our one - ness in the Lord?
4. The mys - t'ry of your pres-ence, Lord, No mor - tal tongue can tell: Whom all the world can - not con - tain Comes in our hearts to dwell.
5. You give your - self to us, O Lord; Then self - less let us be, To serve each oth - er in your name In truth and char - i - ty.
D.C.

Text: Omer Westendorf, 1916-1998
Tune: BICENTENNIAL, CM, with refrain; Robert E. Kreutz, 1922-1996

817 All Who Hunger

Verses
Cantor(s):
1. All who hun - ger, gath - er glad - ly;
2. All who hun - ger, nev - er stran - gers,
3. All who hun - ger, sing to - geth - er;
ho - ly man - na is our bread.
seek - er, be a wel - come guest.
Je - sus Christ is liv - ing bread.
Come from wil - der - ness and wan - d'ring.
Come from rest - less - ness and roam - ing.
Come from lone - li - ness and long - ing.
Here, in truth, we will be fed. You that
Here, in joy, we keep the feast. We that
Here, in peace, we have been led. Blest are
yearn for days of full - ness, all a -
once were lost and scat - tered in com -
those who from this ta - ble live their
round us is our food.
mun - ion's love have stood.
lives in grat - i - tude.
Refrain
All:
Taste and see the grace e - ter - nal. Taste and

see that God is good.

Text: Sylvia G. Dunstan, 1955-1993, © 1991, GIA Publications, Inc.
Tune: Bob Moore, b. 1962, © 1993, GIA Publications, Inc.

Shepherd of Souls 818

1. Shep-herd of souls, re-fresh and bless
Your cho-sen pil-grim flock
With man-na in the wil-der-ness,
With wa-ter from the rock.

2. We would not live by bread a-lone,
But by your word of grace,
In strength of which we trav-el on
To our a-bid-ing place.

3. Be known to us in break-ing bread,
But do not then de-part;
Sav-ior, a-bide with us, and spread
Your ta-ble in our heart.

4. Lord, sup with us in love di-vine;
Your Bod-y and your Blood,
That liv-ing bread, that heav'n-ly wine,
Be our im-mor-tal food.

Text: James Montgomery, 1771-1854, alt.
Tune: ST. AGNES, CM; John B. Dykes, 1823-1876; harm. by Richard Proulx, b.1937, © 1986, GIA Publications, Inc.

819 In Remembrance of You

Verses
Cantor or choir:
1. Je - sus, hope for all, teach us to be - lieve. Reach us, hope for all, in wa - ter, wine, and wheat.
2. Je - sus, Son of God, you are liv - ing Word. Teach us, Son of God, to share what we have heard.
3. Je - sus, Lamb of God, bear - er of our sin, Free us, Lamb of God; come heal us from with - in.
Refrain
+Assembly:
Gath - ered at ta - ble, gath - ered in love,
Gath-ered at ta - ble, gath-ered in

food for the jour-ney sent from a-bove.
love, food that is sent from a-bove.
Strength - en and feed us in all that we do,
Feed us in all we do,
gath - ered at ta - ble in re - mem - brance of
gath - ered at ta - ble in re - mem - brance of
To verses
Final ending
you.
you.

Text: Paul A. Tate, b.1968
Tune: Paul A. Tate, b.1968

820 Come and Eat This Living Bread

Refrain

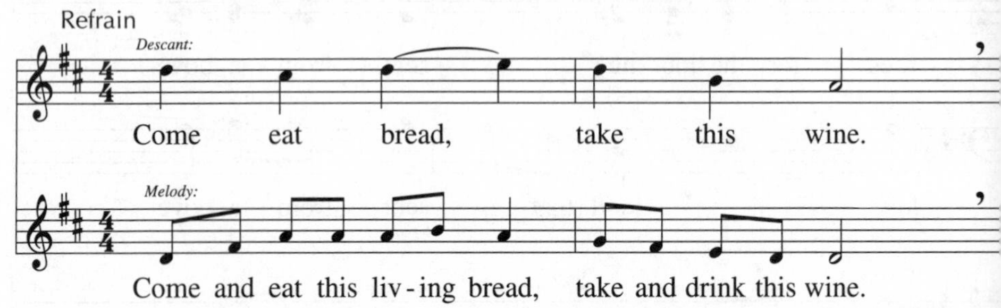
Descant:
Come eat bread, take this wine.
Melody:
Come and eat this liv-ing bread, take and drink this wine.

Come be healed in God's sign.
Come be nour-ished, healed and fed, shaped in-to God's sign.

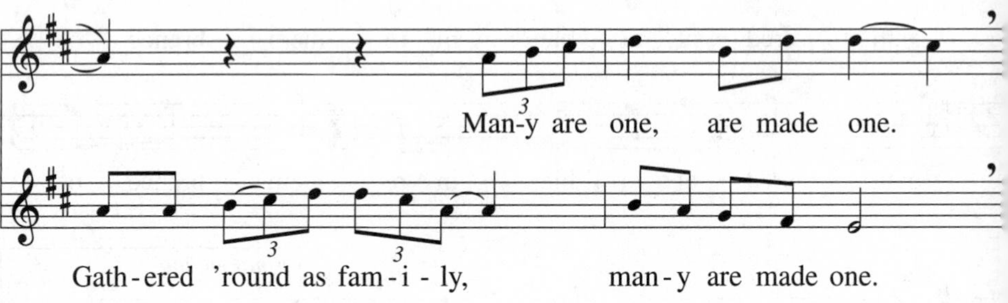
Man-y are one, are made one.
Gath-ered 'round as fam-i-ly, man-y are made one.

Form-ing u-ni-ty, one now be-come.
Form-ing love's com-mu-ni-ty, one we now be-come.

Verses
Cantor:
1. Saint and sin - ner wel - come in
2. May we see the Christ re - vealed
3. See the Christ in sad - dened sighs,
4. Bless us, Lord, and these your gifts,
5. Death and life in wa - ter meet,
6. Wit - ness - ing to love and peace,
to this meal of har - mo - ny.
in the break - ing of the bread.
blood poured out in ev - 'ry land.
fruit of vine and hu - man hands.
drench - ing us in floods of light.
hands of bless - ing we re - main.
Lone - ly peo - ple, next of kin
Liv - ing sto - ries, ho - ly meals,
Wound - ed peo - ple, wail - ing cries
With our hearts and minds we lift
Mark - ing us with oil so sweet,
Help - ing fear and hate to cease,
jour - ney t'ward the glo - ry tree.
we be - come what we are fed.
lie up - on our out - stretched hands.
all the good - ness of these lands.
cloth - ing us in glo - rious white.
we bring forth God's won - drous reign.
Gath - ered stran - gers, scat - tered sheep,
Bro - ken shat - tered, fra - gile life,
Je - sus is the way through death;
Praise and thanks we shout and sing,
Priest and proph - et, spir - it led,
Strength and pow - er here we find,

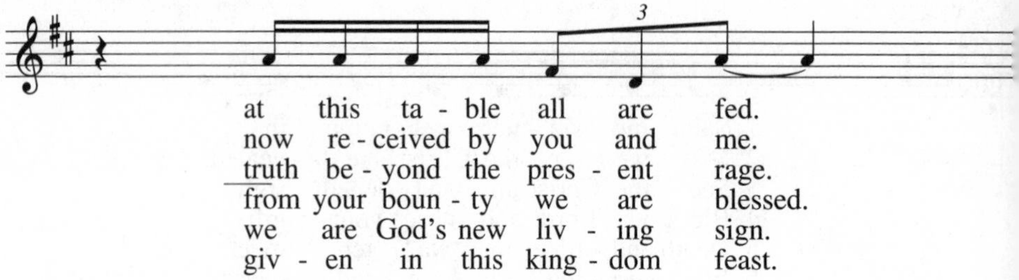

at this ta - ble all are fed.
now re - ceived by you and me.
truth be - yond the pres - ent rage.
from your boun - ty we are blessed.
we are God's new liv - ing sign.
giv - en in this king - dom feast.

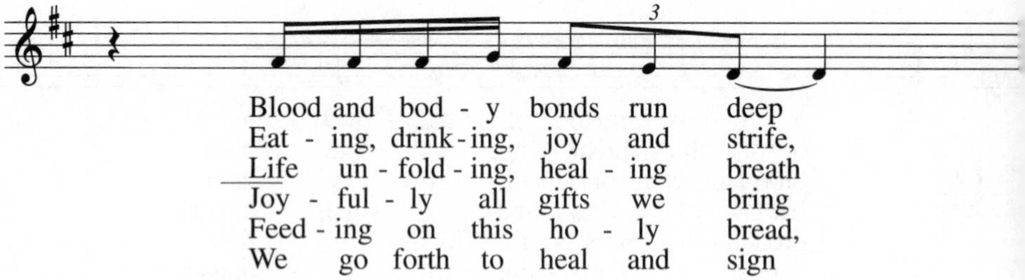

Blood and bod - y bonds run deep
Eat - ing, drink - ing, joy and strife,
Life un - fold - ing, heal - ing breath
Joy - ful - ly all gifts we bring
Feed - ing on this ho - ly bread,
We go forth to heal and sign

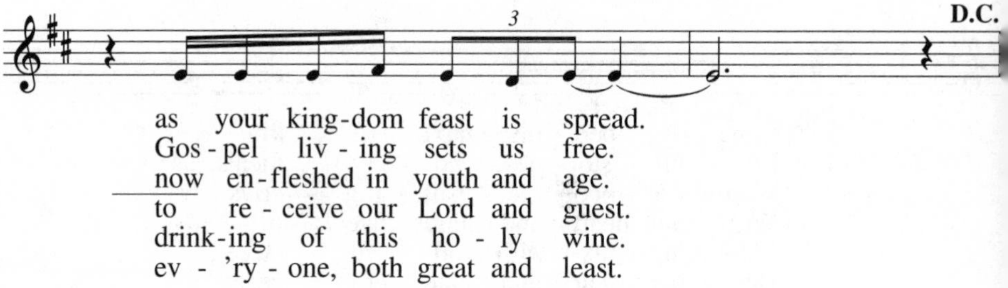

D.C.

as your king - dom feast is spread.
Gos - pel liv - ing sets us free.
now en - fleshed in youth and age.
to re - ceive our Lord and guest.
drink - ing of this ho - ly wine.
ev - 'ry - one, both great and least.

Text: Rob Glover, b.1950
Tune: ADORO TE DEVOTE, 12 12 12 12; verses and arr. Rob Glover, b.1950

821 Life-giving Bread, Saving Cup

Refrain

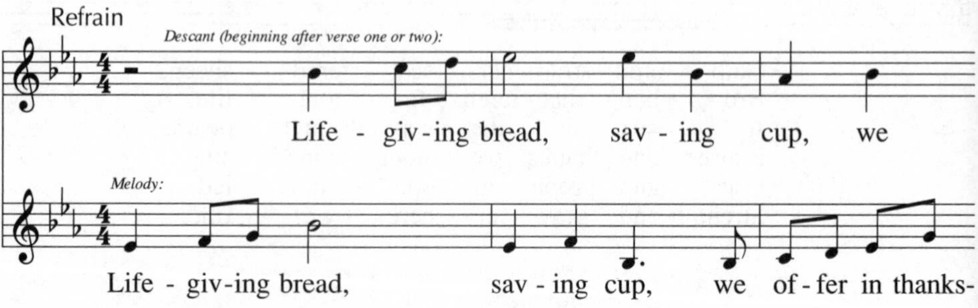
Descant (beginning after verse one or two):
Life - giv - ing bread, sav - ing cup, we
Melody:
Life - giv - ing bread, sav - ing cup, we of - fer in thanks-

of - fer you. Life - giv-ing bread, life -
giv-ing, O God. Life - giv-ing bread,
sav - ing cup, as a sign of love.
sav - ing cup, we of - fer as a sign of our love.
Verses
1. For bread that is bro - ken, we give thanks. For wine that is poured, we give praise. For life and for knowl-edge of the King-dom, all praise to you un - til the end of time!
2. We thank you, O Fa - ther, for your name which you give to dwell in our hearts. You bring us to - geth - er as one fam - 'ly: all praise to you un - til the end of time!
3. Cre - a - tor of all, we of - fer thanks. You give us a share in your life. You strength - en our bod - y and our spir - it: all praise to you un - til the end of time!
4. Re - mem - ber your Church which sings your praise. Per - fect it in truth and in love. And gath - er your peo - ple all to - geth - er to praise you un - til the end of time!
D.C.

Text: Adapted from the *Didache*, 2nd C.; James J. Chepponis, b.1956
Tune: James J. Chepponis, b.1956

822 I Am the Bread of Life / Yo Soy el Pan de Vida

Verses

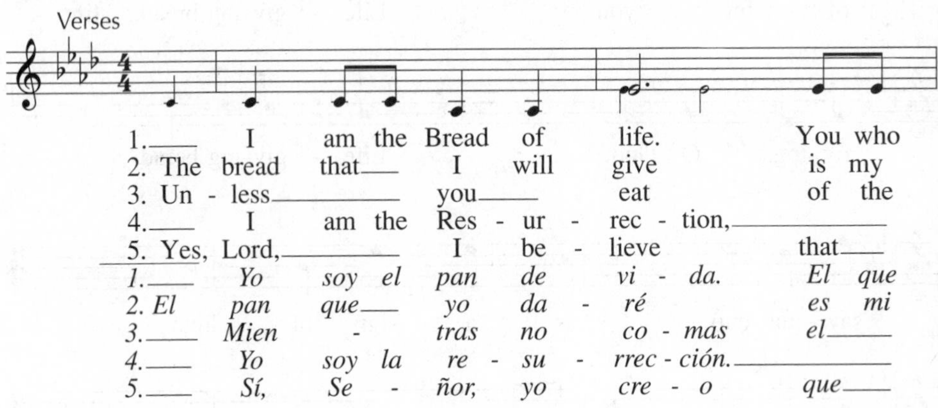
1.___ I am the Bread of life. You who
2. The bread that___ I will give is my
3. Un - less___ you___ eat of the
4.___ I am the Res - ur - rec - tion,___
5. Yes, Lord,___ I be - lieve that___
1.___ Yo soy el pan de vi - da. El que
2. El pan que___ yo da - ré es mi
3.___ Mien - tras no co - mas el___
4.___ Yo soy la re - su - rrec - ción.___
5.___ Sí, Se - ñor, yo cre - o que___

come to me shall not hun - ger;___ and who be -
flesh for the life of the world,___ and if you
flesh of the Son of Man___ and___
I___ am the life.___ If you be -
you___ are the Christ,___ the___
vie - ne a mí no ten - drá ham - bre.___ El que
cuer - po___ vi - da del mun - do,___ y el que
cuer - po del hi - jo del hom - bre,___ y___
Yo___ soy la vi - da.___ El que
tú e - res el Cris - to,___ El___

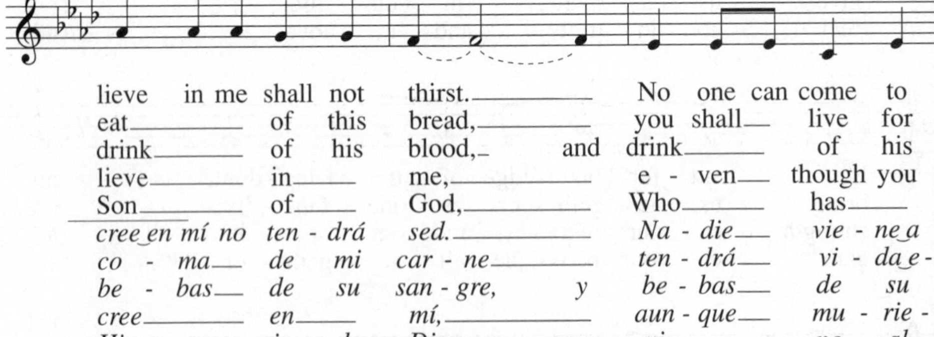
lieve in me shall not thirst.___ No one can come to
eat___ of this bread,___ you shall___ live for
drink___ of his blood,___ and drink___ of his
lieve___ in___ me,___ e - ven___ though you
Son___ of___ God,___ Who___ has___
cree en mí no ten - drá sed.___ Na - die___ vie - ne a
co - ma de mi car - ne___ ten - drá___ vi - da e -
be - bas___ de su san - gre, y be - bas___ de su
cree___ en___ mí,___ aun - que___ mu - rie -
Hi - jo de Dios,___ que vi - no al

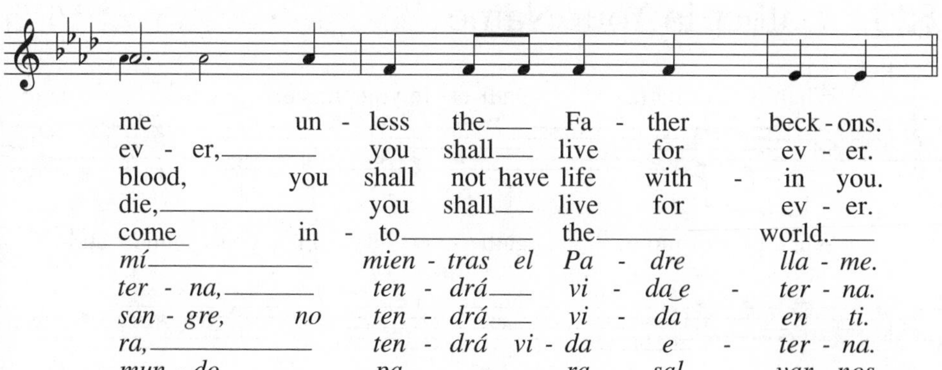
me un - less the Fa - ther beck - ons.
ev - er, you shall live for ev - er.
blood, you shall not have life with - in you.
die, you shall live for ev - er.
come in - to the world.
mí mien - tras el Pa - dre lla - me.
ter - na, ten - drá vi - da e - ter - na.
san - gre, no ten - drá vi - da en ti.
ra, ten - drá vi - da e - ter - na.
mun - do pa - ra sal - var - nos.

Refrain

And I will raise you up, and I will
Yo le re - su - ci - ta - ré, Yo le re -

raise you up, and I will raise you
su - ci - ta - ré, Yo le re - su - ci - ta -

up on the last day.
ré el di - a de El.

Text: John 6; Suzanne Toolan, SM, b.1927
Tune: BREAD OF LIFE, Irregular with refrain; Suzanne Toolan, SM, b.1927

823 Gather in Your Name

Refrain
When two or more gath-er in your name, and
When two or more gath - er in your name, and
see your pres - ence in each face, we
see you in each face,
treas-ure the gift of this sa - cred meal, blessed and
treas-ure the gift, sa - cred meal, blessed and
poured out for all in this place.
Last time
poured out for all in this place.
Last time
Last time

Verses
Cantor:
1. Bread, the gift of your bod - y.
2. Bread, our light and our life.
3. Bread, your man - na from heav - en.
4. Bread, your mys - t'ry be - fore us.
5. Bread, the path for our jour - ney.
6. Bread, the food for our long - ing.
7. Bread for those who seek jus - tice.
Wine, your life blood out poured.
Wine, our truth and our way.
Wine, the fruit of your heart.
Wine, the hope of our dreams.
Wine, of wis - dom and grace.
Wine, the sweet taste of love.
Wine for the hum - ble of heart.
All:
Come, join the feast! Take and be - lieve! Be -
come what you re - ceive!
D.C.

Text: Lori True, b.1961
Tune: Lori True, b.1961

824 Behold the Lamb

Verses
Descant:
Melody:
1. Those who were in the dark are thank - ful for the sun - light;
2. Peace - ful now, those whose hearts are blessed with un - der - stand - ing
3. Gen - tle one, Child of God, join with us at this ta - ble.
4. Lord of all, give us light. De - liv - er us from e - vil.
We who live, we who die are grate - ful for this
Of the wheat, of the wine u - nit - ed with God's
Bless our lives; nour - ish all who hun - ger for this
Make us one; be our shield. Make still the winds that

gift, thank-ful for God's love.
word and the love we share.
feast; shel-ter them with peace.
blow; cra-dle us with love.
gift, thank-ful for God's love.
word and the love we share.
feast; shel-ter them with peace.
blow; cra-dle us with love.
Refrain
Melody:
Be-hold, be-hold the Lamb of God. All who eat,
Harmony:
Be-hold, be-hold the Lamb of God. All who eat,
all who drink shall live; and all,
all who drink shall live; shall live; and all,
all who dwell in God, shall come to know
all who dwell in God, in God, shall come to know
1.-3.
4.
God's glo-ry! glo-ry!
God's glo - ry! glo - ry!

Text: Martin Willett, b.1960
Tune: Martin Willett, b.1960; acc. by Craig S. Kingsbury, b.1952

825 Now in This Banquet

Refrain
1.*
2.
Now in this ban - quet, Christ is our bread;
Advent: God of our jour - neys, day - break to night;
Lent: Lord, you can o - pen hearts that are stone;
Here shall all hun - gers be fed.
Lead us to jus - tice and light.
Live in our flesh and our bone;
Bread that is bro - ken, wine that is poured,
Grant us com - pas - sion, strength for the day,
Lead us to won - der, mys - t'ry and grace,
To verses
Love is the sign of our Lord.
Wis - dom to walk in your way.
One in your lov - ing em - brace.
Last time
Lord.
way.
brace.
Verses 1, 2
1. You who have touched us and graced us with
2. Let our hearts burn with the fire of your
love, make us your peo - ple of
love; o - pen our eyes to the

*May be sung in canon.

D.C.
good - ness and light.
glo - ry of God.
Verse 3
3. God who makes the blind to see, God who makes the
lame to walk, bring us danc - ing in - to day,
D.C.
lead your peo - ple in your way.
Verse 4
4. Hope for the hope-less, light for the blind,
rit.
D.C.
"Strong" is your name, Lord, "Gen - tle" and "Kind."
Verse 5
5. Call us to be your light, call us to be your love,
D.C.
make us your peo - ple a - gain.
Verse 6
6. Come, O Spir - it! re - new our hearts!
rit.
D.C.
We shall a - rise to be chil - dren of light.

Text: Marty Haugen, b.1950
Tune: Marty Haugen, b.1950

826 Alleluia! Sing to Jesus

1. Al - le - lu - ia! sing to Je - sus!
2. Al - le - lu - ia! not as or - phans
3. Al - le - lu - ia! Bread of An - gels,
4. Al - le - lu - ia! King e - ter - nal,
His the scep - ter, his the throne;
Are we left in sor - row now;
Here on earth our food, our stay!
You the Lord of lords we own;
Al - le - lu - ia! his the tri - umph,
Al - le - lu - ia! he is near us,
Al - le - lu - ia! here the sin - ful
Al - le - lu - ia! born of Mar - y,
His the vic - to - ry a - lone;
Faith be - lieves, nor ques - tions how:
Flee to you from day to day:
Earth your foot - stool, heav'n your throne:

Hark! the songs of peace - ful Zi - on
Though the cloud from sight re - ceived him,
In - ter - ces - sor, friend of sin - ners,
You, with - in the veil, have en - tered,
Thun - der like a might - y flood;
When the for - ty days were o'er,
Earth's re - deem - er, plead for me,
Robed in flesh, our great high priest;
Je - sus out of ev - 'ry na - tion
Shall our hearts for - get his prom - ise,
Where the songs of all the sin - less
Here on earth both priest and vic - tim
Has re - deemed us by his blood.
"I am with you ev - er - more?"
Sweep a - cross the crys - tal sea.
In the eu - cha - ris - tic feast.

Text: Revelation 5:9; William C. Dix, 1837-1898
Tune: HYFRYDOL, 8 7 8 7 D; Rowland H. Prichard, 1811-1887

827 Taste and See

Refrain
Taste and see, taste and see the
good - ness of the Lord. O
taste and see, taste and see the
good - ness of the Lord, of the

To verses

Lord.

Last time

Lord.

Verses

1. I will bless the Lord at all times.
2. Glo - ri - fy the Lord with me. To-
3. Wor - ship the Lord, all you peo - ple.

Praise shall al - ways be on my lips; my
geth - er let us all praise God's name. I
You'll want for noth - ing if you ask.

soul shall glo - ry in the Lord for
called the Lord who an - swered me; from
Taste and see that the Lord is good; in

D.C.
3
God has been so good to me.
all my trou - bles I was set free.
God we need put all our trust.

Text: Psalm 34; James E. Moore, Jr., b.1951
Tune: James E. Moore, Jr., b.1951

828 The Hand of God

Refrain

The hand of God feeds us,

heals us, the hand of God!

Last time

Last time

Last time

Verses

Cantor:

1. All your works praise you, your faith - ful ones

2. All eyes look to you, you feed us in due

3. You are just in all things, lov - ing and

Choir:

Oo
Oo

bless you! Let all pro - claim your glo - ry, your
sea - son. You come with o - pen hands to
ho - ly. You are near to all who call your name, who
div.
Oo
D.C.
pow - er, your king - dom!
D.C.
feed your cre - a - tion!
D.C.
cry out in love and truth!
D.C.
Oo

Text: Psalm 145; adapt. by David Haas, b.1957
Tune: David Haas, b.1957

829 Draw Near

Refrain
Draw near, draw near! Take the bod - y
of your Lord. Draw near, draw near!
Drink the blood for you out - poured.
To verses
Final ending
Verses
1. Draw near and take the bod - y of your Lord,
2. Christ our re - deem - er, God's e - ter - nal Son,
3. Let us ap - proach with faith - ful hearts sin - cere,
4. With heav'n - ly bread makes those who hun - ger whole,

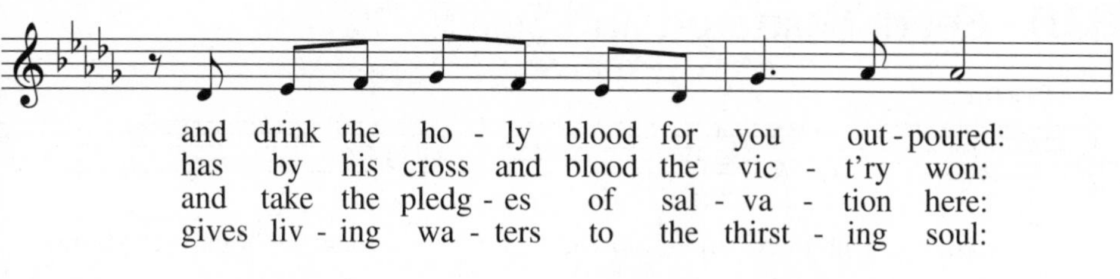
and drink the ho - ly blood for you out - poured:
has by his cross and blood the vic - t'ry won:
and take the pledg - es of sal - va - tion here:
gives liv - ing wa - ters to the thirst - ing soul:

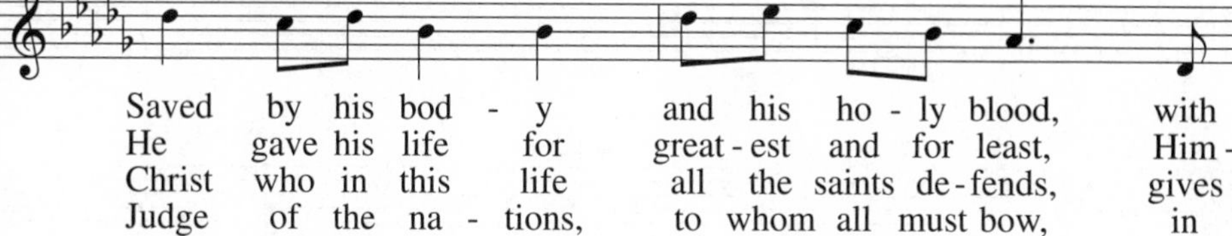
Saved by his bod - y and his ho - ly blood, with
He gave his life for great - est and for least, Him -
Christ who in this life all the saints de - fends, gives
Judge of the na - tions, to whom all must bow, in

D.C.
souls re - freshed we give our thanks to God.
self the of - 'fring and Him - self the Priest.
all be - liev - ers life that nev - er ends.
this great feast of love is with us now.

Text: *Sancti, venite, Christi corpus sumite*, 7th C.; tr. John M. Neale, 1818-1866, alt.
Tune: Steven R. Janco, b.1961,

830 Seed, Scattered and Sown

Refrain
Seed, scat-tered and sown, wheat, gath-ered and grown, bread, bro-ken and shared as one, the Liv-ing Bread of God.
Vine, fruit of the land, wine, work of our hands, one cup that is shared by all; the Liv-ing Cup, the

Alto:
Last time
Sop:
Liv - ing Bread of God.
Verses
1. Is not the bread we break a
2. The seed which falls on rock will
3. As wheat up - on the hills was
shar - ing in our Lord? Is not the
with - er and will die. The seed with -
gath - ered and was grown, So may the
D.C.
cup we bless the blood of Christ out - poured?
in good ground will flow - er and have life.
church of God be gath - ered in - to one.

Text: *Didache* 9, 1 Corinthians 10:16-17, Mark 4:3-6; Dan Feiten, b.1953
Tune: Dan Feiten, b.1953; keyboard arr. by Eric Gunnison, R.J. Miller

831 Come and Eat This Bread

Refrain
Melody:
Come and eat this bread, come and drink this cup,
Harmony:
Come and share this bread and sav - ing cup,
come and share the feast our God has spread.
come and share the feast our God has spread.
You have prom - ised us, you are here with us
You have prom - ised, you are here with us
To verses
Last time
in the break - ing of the bread.
To verses
Last time
now in the break - ing of the bread.
Verses
unis.
1. This is the bread of life, for all to share, bread of
2. This is the cup of Christ's own sac - ri - fice, blood of
3. Just as the scat - tered grains be - come one bread, make us
4. And as we share one cup of cov - e - nant make us
5. Each time we eat this bread and drink this cup, we re -
unis.

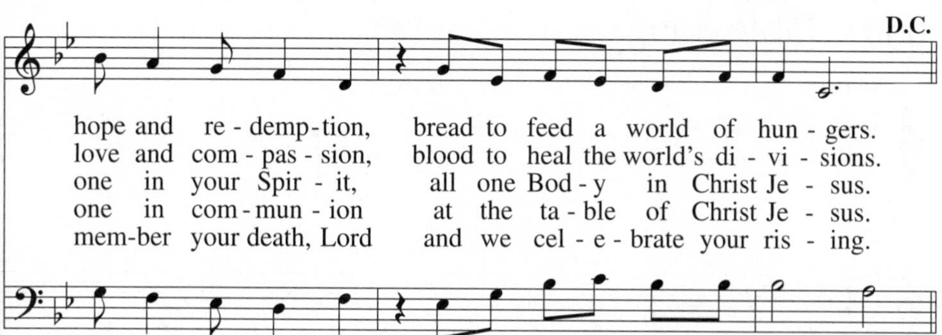
D.C.
hope and re - demp-tion, bread to feed a world of hun - gers.
love and com - pas - sion, blood to heal the world's di - vi - sions.
one in your Spir - it, all one Bod - y in Christ Je - sus.
one in com - mun - ion at the ta - ble of Christ Je - sus.
mem-ber your death, Lord and we cel - e - brate your ris - ing.

Text: Marty Haugen, b.1950
Tune: Marty Haugen, b.1950

Let Us Break Bread Together 832

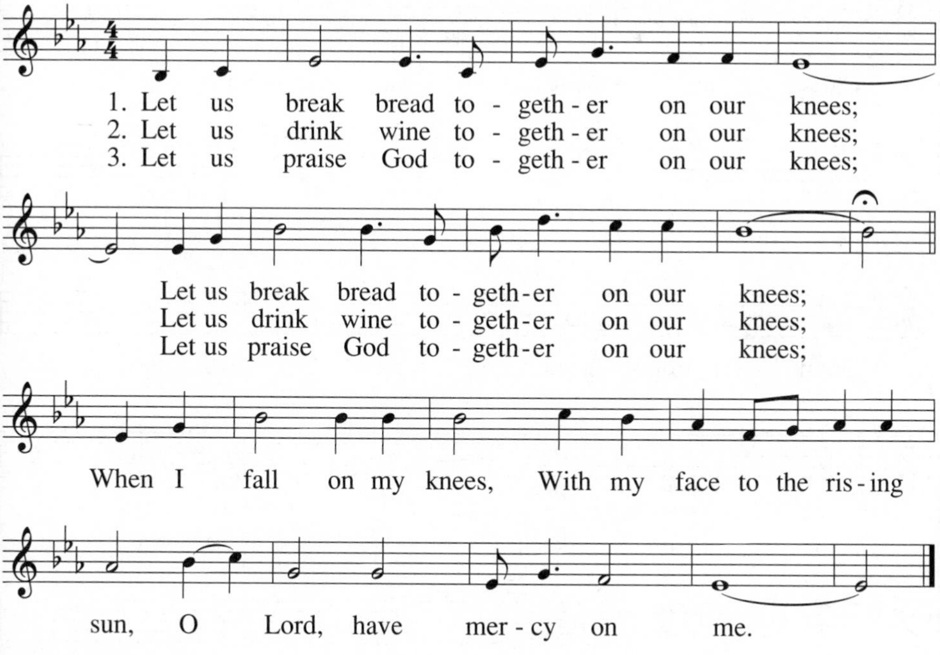

1. Let us break bread to - geth - er on our knees;
2. Let us drink wine to - geth - er on our knees;
3. Let us praise God to - geth - er on our knees;

Let us break bread to - geth - er on our knees;
Let us drink wine to - geth - er on our knees;
Let us praise God to - geth - er on our knees;

When I fall on my knees, With my face to the ris - ing

sun, O Lord, have mer - cy on me.

Text: American folk hymn
Tune: LET US BREAK BREAD, 10 10 6 8 7; American folk hymn; harm. by David Hurd, b.1950, © 1968, GIA Publications, Inc.

833 Table Song

Refrain
Descant:
We are the bod - y of Christ.
Bro - ken and poured out,
prom - ise from death, for we are the
We are the bod - y of Christ, the bod - y of
Christ, Bro - ken and poured out, prom - ise of
life from death, we are the
and poured out, prom - ise

To verses
Last time
bod - y of Christ.
To verses
Last time
bod - y of Christ.
Verses
1. Is not the bread of life we break a
2. How shall we make a re - turn to God, for
3. Un - less a grain of wheat shall fall up -
4. Come taste and see the good - ness, the
shar - ing in the life of God? Is not the cup of
good - ness un - sur - pass - ing? This sav - ing cup we
on the earth, it shall re - main a sin - gle grain; but
won - ders of the ris - en one! Come bless our God, in
D.C.
peace out - poured the blood of Christ?
shall hold high, and call out God's name!
if it dies, it will come to life!
all things, let praise be our song!

Text: David Haas, b. 1957
Tune: David Haas, b. 1957

834 For Living, for Dying

Verses 1, 2
1. For liv - ing, for dy-ing, Lord, for
2. Com - mun - ion, com - mun - i - ty, is
Harmony (Vs. 2):
2. Com-mun-ion, com-mun-i - ty,
ris - ing from the dead, we
what we claim this day. Your
is what we claim this day.
praise you with ev - 'ry breath we take.
bod - y, your Spir - it is our grace.
Your bod - y, your
We come to you, re -
With ev - 'ry heart, with
Spir - it is our grace.
with ev - 'ry heart,

mem - ber you in the break - ing of this
ev - 'ry hand, with ev - 'ry word we
with ev - 'ry hand, with ev - 'ry word
bread, we drink the cup, the
say, of rich and poor, we
we say, of rich and poor,
prom - ise that you made.
wel - come, we em - brace.
we wel - come, we em - brace.
Refrain
Nour - ish us well. Teach us to be all that you long

for us to be. Al-ways to live, nev-er to thirst,

hun - ger. *To verses 2, 3, 4*

nev-er to hun - ger. oo

hun - ger.

Last time

Al-ways to live,

oo al-ways to live.

Verses 3, 4
3. For lov-ing us, for - giv-ing us, for
4. So here we are, a part of you, a
Harmony:
3. For lov-ing us, for-giv-ing us,
4. So here we are, a part of you,

shar-ing in our tears, for laugh-ter, the
part of ev - 'ry one; a riv - er that
for shar-ing in our tears, for laugh-ter,
a part of ev - 'ry - one; a riv - er
ten - der - ness you bring. You
flows in - to the sea. From
the ten - der - ness you bring.
that flows in - to the sea.
call to us, we fol - low. You
east to west, from near and far, from
You call to us, we fol - low.
From east to west, from near and far,

guard us from our fears. Be-side you our
ev - 'ry time and place, a-round the world we
You guard us from our fears, Be-side you
from ev-'ry time and place, a-round the world,
D.S.
hearts will al - ways sing.
all join in your feast.
D.S.
oo our hearts will al - ways sing.
oo we all join in your feast.

Text: Donna Peña, b.1955
Tune: Donna Peña, b.1955; acc. by Paul Gerike

I Myself Am the Bread of Life 835

Refrain
I my-self am the bread of life.
You and I are the bread of life,
tak - en and blessed, bro - ken and shared by Christ
that the world might live.
Verses
1. This bread is spir - it, gift of the Mak - er's
2. Here is God's king - dom giv - en to us as
3. Lives bro - ken o - pen, sto - ries shared a -
love, and we who share it know that we can be
food. This is our bod - y, this is our
loud, be - come a ban - quet, a shel - ter for the
one:
blood: a liv-ing sign of God in Christ.
world:
D.C.

Text: Rory Cooney, b.1952
Tune: Rory Cooney, b.1952

836 We Remember, We Believe

Refrain
Melody:
We re - mem - ber in the break-ing of the bread. We re -
Harmony:
mem-ber in the cup that we re-ceive. As our thirst is quenched and our
hun - ger fed we re-mem - ber and we be-lieve.
Last time
hun - ger fed we be - lieve.
Last time
Verses
Melody:
1. More than ear can hear
2. Stran-gers, lov - ers, friends,
3. Ev - 'ry aisle a path,
4. As we take and eat,
Harmony:
2. Stran-gers, lov - ers
4. So we learn to

more than eye can see,
neigh-bors, fam - i - ly,
ev - 'ry step a sign
so we learn to give.
friends.
give
neigh-bors, fam - i -
as we take and
more pro-found than our minds can un - der -
in the bod - y our one - ness is dis -
of the jour - ney we walk to - geth - er
Like the bread, we must break; like wine, be
ly,
eat.
now our one - ness is dis -
We must break, like wine, be
D.C.
stand, more than mys - ter - y.
played in di - ver - si - ty.
to the end of time.
poured so that all may live.
played in di - ver - si - ty.
poured so that all may live.

Text: Thomas J. Porter, b.1958
Tune: Thomas J. Porter, b.1958

837 Look Beyond

Refrain
Look be-yond the bread you eat;
See your Sav-ior and your Lord.
Look be-yond the cup you drink;
Last time to coda
See his love poured out as blood.
Verses
1. Give us a sign that we might be-lieve in you. Mos - es had man - na from the sky.
2. I am the bread which from the heav-ens came; Those who eat this bread will nev - er die.
3. The bread I give you will be my ver - y flesh; My blood will tru - ly be your drink.
4. This man speaks harsh-ly; who can lis - ten to his word? We shall no long - er fol - low him.
5. You, my dis - ci - ples, will you al - so leave? Lord to whom can we go?
D.C.
Coda
See his life poured out as blood.

Text: Darryl Ducote, b.1945
Tune: Darryl Ducote, b.1945

Present among Us 838

Refrain

Je - sus, Je - sus Christ, pres - ent a -

Here in this place, bread and wine of
mong us. In this place, bread, wine of

grace: Je - sus
To verses
To repeat and last time
Christ.
Last time
grace: Je - sus Christ.
grace: Je - sus Christ.
Last time

Verses *a little faster*
1. In the tak - ing, in the bless - ing, in the break - ing,
2. In our sing - ing, in our heal - ing, in our giv - ing,
3. In our lis - t'ning, in our seek - ing, in our ques - tions,
4. In our search - ing, in our ach - ing, in our long - ing,
5. In our hop - ing, in our reach - ing, in our need - ing,
6. In the ask - ing, in the hear - ing, in our grop - ing,
7. In our birth - ing, in our liv - ing, in our suf - f'ring,
Christ.
Christ.
Christ.
in the shar - ing,
in our lov - ing,
in our si - lence,
in our griev - ing,
in our weep - ing,
in our cling - ing,
in our dy - ing,
here be-fore you at this ta - ble,
a tempo
D.C.
now we dine with you.

Text: David Haas, b.1957
Tune: David Haas, b.1957

Take and Eat This Bread 839

Refrain
Melody:
Harmony:
Take and eat this bread. Take and drink this cup. This is my bod-y and my blood. When you eat this bread, when you drink this cup, you live in me and I in you.
Last time
Last time
Verses
1. This is the bread come down from heav-en; this is the cup of our sal-va-tion.
2. Gath-ered as one a-round one ta-ble, sent forth to wit-ness to sal-va-tion.
3. With-in our hands we hold the mys-t'ry, dy-ing and ris-ing to sal-va-tion.
4. Come all who thirst for life e-ter-nal, come to the ta-ble of sal-va-tion.
D.C.

Text: Francis Patrick O'Brien, b.1958
Tune: Francis Patrick O'Brien, b.1958

840 At That First Eucharist

1. At that first Eu - cha - rist be - fore you died,
2. For all your church, O Lord, we in - ter - cede;
3. We pray for those who wan - der from the fold;
O Lord, you prayed that all be one in you;
O make our lack of char - i - ty to cease;
O bring them back, Good Shep-herd of the sheep,
At this our Eu - cha - rist a - gain pre - side,
Draw us the near - er each to each we plead,
Back to the faith which saints be - lieved of old,
And in our hearts your law of love re - new.
By draw - ing all to you, O Prince of Peace.
Back to the Church which still that faith does keep.

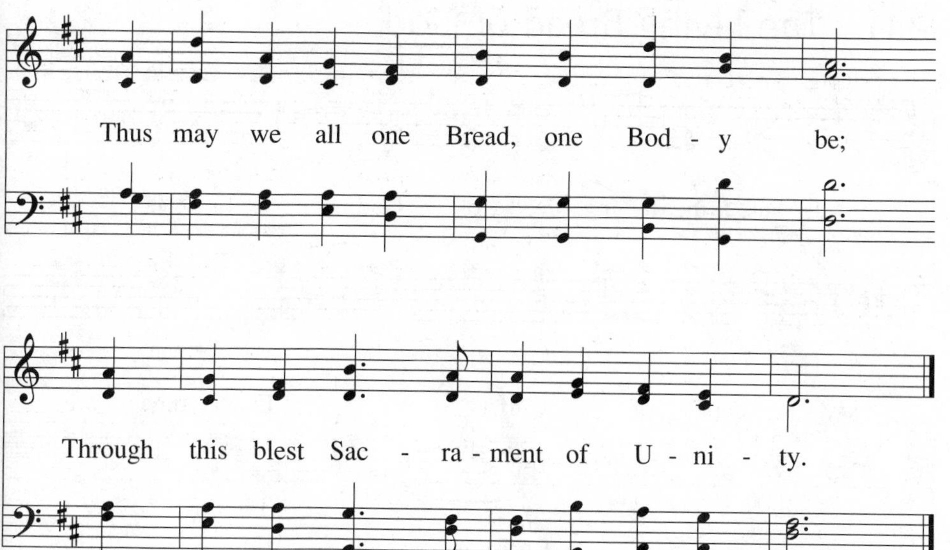
Thus may we all one Bread, one Bod - y be;
Through this blest Sac - ra - ment of U - ni - ty.

Text: William H. Turton, 1859-1938, alt.
Tune: UNDE ET MEMORES, 10 10 10 10 with refrain; William H. Monk, 1823-1889, alt.

841 The Living Bread of God

Refrain
Je-sus, the
Je-sus, the liv-ing Bread of God, Je - sus,
sav-ing cup of Christ. Ev-'ry time we
sav - ing Christ. Ev - 'ry
eat this bread, ev-'ry time we drink this cup, we pro-claim your
time we eat, we drink, we pro-claim your
1.- 4. To verses
5.
glo - ry un - til you come a - gain. gain.

Verses
Cantor:
1. You are the bread of life. If we
2. You are the life of the world. If we
3. You are the liv - ing bread, our
4. You are the liv - ing Christ. If we
come to you, we will nev - er be in need.
come to you, we will nev - er know death.
bread from heav - en, our food from a - bove.
fol - low you, we will see the face of God.
If we be - lieve in you, we will nev - er thirst, and
If we eat of this bread, we will be re - newed, and
If we eat and drink, we will be like you, and
If we die with you, we will rise a - gain, and
we will live for ev - er.
D.C.

Text: 1 Corinthians 11:26; David Haas, b.1957
Tune: Kate Cuddy, b.1953

842 Without Seeing You

Refrain
With-out see-ing you, we love you; with-out
we

touch-ing you, we em-brace; with-out

see-ing you,
know-ing you, we fol-low; with-out see-ing
we fol-low; see-ing

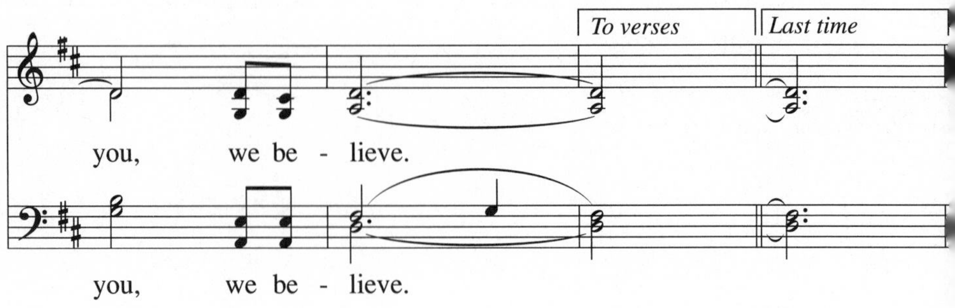
To verses
Last time
you, we be-lieve.
you, we be-lieve.

Verses
1. We re - turn to you deep with - in, leave the
2. The spar - row will find a home, near to
3. For - ev - er we sing to you of your
4. For you are our shep - herd, there is
past to the dust; turn to you with tears and
you, O God; how hap - py, we who
good - ness, O God; pro - claim - ing to
noth - ing that we need; in green pas - tures we will

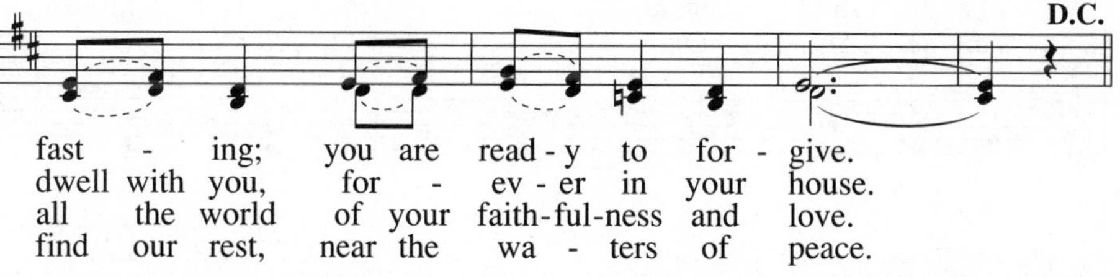
D.C.
fast - ing; you are read - y to for - give.
dwell with you, for - ev - er in your house.
all the world of your faith-ful-ness and love.
find our rest, near the wa - ters of peace.

Text: Inspired by 1 Peter 1:8; David Haas, b. 1957
Tune: David Haas, b. 1957

843 In the Breaking of the Bread / Cuando Partimos el Pan del Señor

Refrain

Melody:
Harmony:
In the break - ing
Cuan-do par - ti - mos el
of the bread We have known
pan del Se - ñor, lo co - no - ce -
him; we have been fed.
mos, nos da de co - mer. Je -
Je - sus the stran - ger,
sús des - co - no - ci - do, Je -

Je - sus the Lord,
sús, Se - ñor,
Be our com - pan - ion,
nues - tro com-pa - ñe - ro y
be our hope.
fuen - te de fe.
Verses
1. Bread for the jour - ney,
1. Pan pa - ra el via - je,
2. Bread of the prom - ise,
2. Pan del pro - me - sa,
strength for our years,
Pan de la vi - da,
peo - ple of hope,
Pan de es - pe - ran - za,
Man - na of a -
Pan de los si -
Wine of com - pas -
Vi - no de vi -

ges, of strug - gle and tears.
glos de lu - cha y do - lor,
sion, life for the world
da, de su com - pa - sión,
Cup of sal - va - tion,
y es - te vi - no, fru -
Gath - ered at ta - ble,
En es - ta me - sa
fruit of the land,
to de la tie - rra ben -
joined as his bod - y,
un so - lo cuer - po
Bless and re - ceive now, the
dí - ce - lo, Pa - dre, es
Sealed in the Spir - it,
en un es - pí - ri - tu, con
D.C.
work of our hands.
tu - yo, mi Dios.
sent by the Word.
u - na mi - sión.

Original Verses:

1. Once I was helpless, sad and confused; darkness surrounded me, courage removed. And then I saw him by my side. Carry my burden, open my eyes.

2. There is no sorrow, pain or woe; there is no suffering he did not know. He did not waver; he did not bend. He is the victor. He is my friend.

He Healed the Darkness of My Mind 844

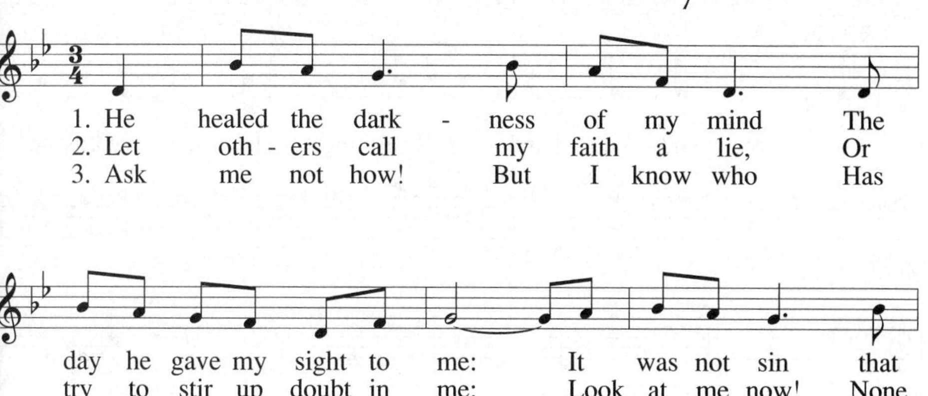
1. He healed the dark - ness of my mind The
2. Let oth - ers call my faith a lie, Or
3. Ask me not how! But I know who Has

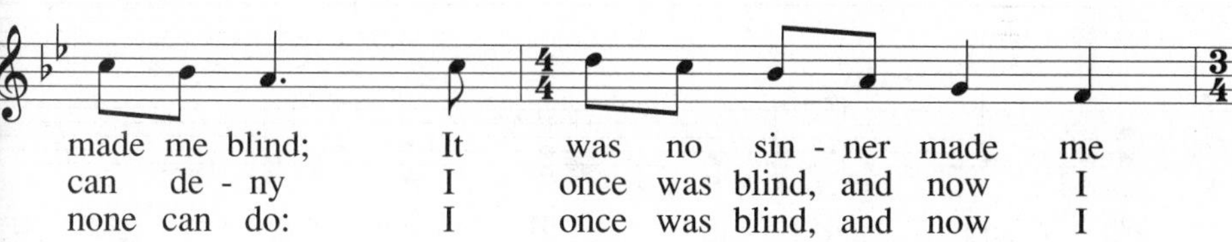
day he gave my sight to me: It was not sin that
try to stir up doubt in me: Look at me now! None
o - pened up new worlds to me: This Je - sus does what

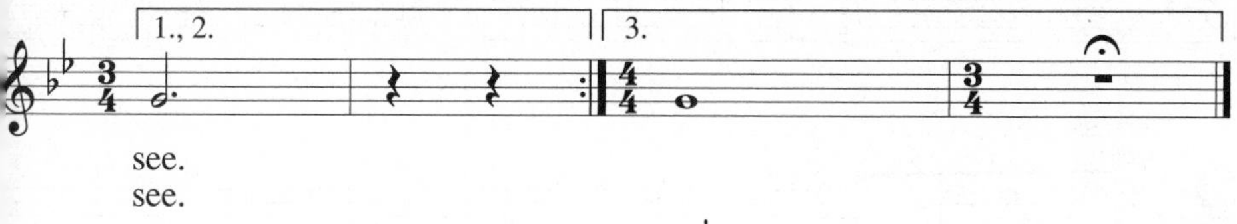
made me blind; It was no sin - ner made me
can de - ny I once was blind, and now I
none can do: I once was blind, and now I

1., 2. 3.

see.
see.
see!

845 Hands of Healing

Refrain*
div.
Let our hands be hands of heal - ing, let our words be
clear and true, In our work, God's love re - veal - ing,
just and gen - tle in all we do.
Verses
Cantor:
All:
1. Safe - ly lead the young ones:
2. Free the ones in bond - age:
3. Touch the ones who sor - row:
4. Com - fort for the dy - ing:
5. May we al - ways be your
hands of heal - ing,
Hm
hands of heal - ing,

*May be sung in canon (see overleaf).

Cantor:
All:
bring your joy and laugh - ter:
bring the reign of new hope:
hope be - yond all griev - ing: clear and true;
vi - sion of a new life:
make us in your im - age:
Hm
clear and true;
Cantor:
All:
sing the God of chil - dren:
sing the God of free - dom:
sing the God of mer - cy: love re - veal - ing,
sing the res - ur - rec - tion:
give us voice to praise you:
Hm
love re - veal - ing,
All:
D.C.
just and gen - tle in all we do.

Canon
1.
2.
Let our hands be hands of heal - ing, let our words be
3.
clear and true, In our work, God's love re - veal - ing,
Repeat as needed
Final ending
just and gen-tle in all we do.

Text: Marty Haugen, b.1950
Tune: Marty Haugen, b.1950

846 Jesus, Heal Us

Refrain
Je - sus.
Je - sus, heal us; Je - sus.
Je - sus.
Je - sus.
To verses
Last time
Je - sus, hear us now.

Verse 1
1. All who fear the Lord: Wait for God's mer - cy.
D.C.
All who love the Lord: Come, he will fill you.
Verse 2
2. All who fear the Lord: Fol - low the way.
D.C.
All who love the Lord: Hope in God's good - ness.
Verse 3
3. All who fear the Lord: Keep your hearts pre - pared.
D.C.
All who love the Lord: Be hum - bled in God's pres - ence.
Verse 4
4. All who trust the Lord: God will up -
hold you. Let us cling to our God; let us
D.C.
fall in the arms of the Lord!

Text: David Haas, b.1957
Tune: David Haas, b.1957

847 Precious Lord, Take My Hand

1. Pre - cious Lord, take my hand, Lead me on, let me stand, I am tired, I am weak, I am worn. (I am worn.) Through the storm, through the night, Lead me on to the light, Take my
2. When my way grows drear, Pre - cious Lord, lin - ger near, When my life is al - most gone, (al - most gone,) Hear my cry, hear my call, Hold my hand lest I fall. Take my
3. When the dark - ness ap - pears And the night draws near, And the day is past and gone, (past and gone,) At the riv - er I stand, Guide my feet, hold my hand. Take my

hand, pre - cious Lord, lead me home. (Lead me home.)
hand, pre - cious Lord, lead me home. (Lead me home.)
hand, pre - cious Lord, lead me home. (Lead me home.)

Text: Thomas A. Dorsey, 1899-1993
Tune: PRECIOUS LORD 66 9 D; George N. Allen, 1812-1877; arr. by Kelly Dobbs Mickus, b.1966

Forgive Our Sins 848

1. "For - give our sins as we for - give," You taught us, Lord, to pray, But you a - lone can grant us grace To live the words we say.

2. How can your par - don reach and bless The un - for - giv - ing heart That broods on wrongs and will not let Old bit - ter - ness de - part?

3. In blaz - ing light your Cross re - veals The truth we dim - ly knew: What triv - ial debts are owed to us, How great our debt to you!

4. Lord, cleanse the depths with - in our souls And bid re - sent - ment cease. Then, bound to all in bonds of love, Our lives will spread your peace.

Text: Rosamond E. Herklots, 1905-1987, © Oxford University Press
Tune: DETROIT, CM; Supplement to *Kentucky Harmony,* 1820; harm. by Gerald H. Knight, 1908-1979, © The Royal School of Church Music

849 Our Father, We Have Wandered

1. Our Fa - ther, we have wan - dered And
2. And now at length dis - cern - ing The
3. O Lord of all the liv - ing, Both
hid - den from your face; In fool - ish - ness have
e - vil that we do, Be - hold us, Lord, re -
ban - ished and re - stored, Com - pas - sion - ate, for -
squan - dered Your leg - a - cy of grace. But
turn - ing With hope and trust to you. In
giv - ing And ev - er car - ing Lord, Grant
now, in ex - ile dwell - ing, We
haste you come to meet us And
now that our trans - gress - ing, Our

rise with fear and shame, As dis - tant but com - pell - ing, We hear you call our name.
home re - joic - ing bring, In glad - ness there to greet us With calf and robe and ring.
faith - less - ness may cease. Stretch out your hand in bless - ing, In par - don and in peace.

Text: Kevin Nichols, b.1929, © 1980, ICEL
Tune: PASSION CHORALE, 7 6 7 6 D; Hans Leo Hassler, 1564-1612; harm. by J.S. Bach, 1685-1750

850 Softly and Tenderly Jesus Is Calling

1. Soft - ly and ten - der - ly Je - sus is call - ing,
2. Why should we tar - ry when Je - sus is plead - ing,
3. Time is now fleet - ing, the mo - ments are pass - ing,
4. O for the won - der - ful love He has prom - ised,
Call - ing for you and for me; See, on the
Plead - ing for you and for me? Why should we
Pass - ing from you and from me; Shad - ows are
Prom - ised for you and for me; Though we have
por - tals He's wait - ing and watch - ing,
lin - ger and heed not His mer - cies,
gath - er - ing, death - beds are com - ing,
sinned He has mer - cy and par - don,
Watch - ing for you and for me.
Mer - cies for you and for me?
Com - ing for you and for me.
Par - don for you and for me.

Come home, come home,
come home,
Come home, come home,
come home,
Ye who are wea-ry, come home;
Ear - nest-ly, ten - der - ly, Je - sus is call - ing—
Call - ing, "O sin - ner, come home!"

Text: Will L. Thompson, 1847-1909
Tune: Will L. Thompson, 1847-1909

851 Remember Your Love

Refrain
Descant:
Re - mem-ber your love and your faith - ful - ness, O Lord. Re -
Melody:
Re - mem-ber your love and your faith - ful - ness, O Lord. Re -
To verses
Last time
mem-ber your peo - ple and have mer - cy on us, Lord. Lord.
mem-ber your peo - ple and have mer - cy on us, Lord. Lord.
Verses
1. The Lord is my light and my sal - va - tion, whom should I fear? The Lord is my life and my ref - uge, when I call God hears.
2. If you dwelt, O Lord, up - on our sin-ful-ness, then who could stand? But with you there is mer - cy and for - give - ness and a guid - ing hand.
3. O Lord, hear the sound of my call and an - swer me. My heart cries out for your pres - ence; it is you I seek.
4. As watch - man who waits up - on the day - light, wait for the Lord. I trust in your kind-ness and re - demp - tion; and your faith - ful word.
5. Be - fore all the moun - tains were be - got - ten and earth took shape, e - ven then, O Lord, you were our ref - uge through - out ev - 'ry age.
D.C.

Text: Psalm 27; Mike Balhoff, b.1946
Tune: Darryl Ducote, b.1945, and Gary Daigle, b.1957

Ashes 852

1. We rise a - gain from ash - es, from the
2. We of - fer you our fail - ures, we
3. Then rise a - gain from ash - es, let
4. Thanks be to the Fa - ther, who

good we've failed to do. We rise a - gain from
of - fer you at - tempts, The gifts not ful - ly
heal - ing come to pain, Though spring has turned to
made us like him - self. Thanks be to the

ash - es, to cre - ate our - selves a - new. If
giv - en, the dreams not ful - ly dreamt. Give our
win - ter, and sun - shine turned to rain. The
Son, who saved us by his death.

all our world is ash - es, then
stum - bl - ings di - rec - tion, give our
rain we'll use for grow - ing, and cre -
Thanks be to the Spir - it, who cre -

must our lives be true, An of - fer - ing of
vi - sions wid - er view, An of - fer - ing of
ate the world a - new From an of - fer - ing of
ates the world a - new From an of - fer - ing of

1.- 3. 4.

ash - es, an of - fer - ing to you.
ash - es, an of - fer - ing to you.
ash - es, an of - fer - ing to you.
ash - es, an of - fer - ing to you.

Text: Tom Conry, b.1951
Tune: Tom Conry, b.1951; acc. by Michael Joncas, b.1951

853 The Master Came to Bring Good News

1. The Mas - ter came to bring good news, The
2. The Law's ful - filled through Je - sus Christ, The
3. To seek the sin - ners Je - sus came, To
4. For - give us, Lord, as we for - give And
news of love and free - dom, To heal the sick and
man who lived for oth - ers, The law of Christ is:
live a - mong the friend - less, To show them love that
seek to help each oth - er. For - give us, Lord, and
seek the poor, To build the peace - ful king - dom.
Serve in love Our sis - ters and our broth - ers.
they might share The king - dom that is end - less.
we shall live To pray and work to - geth - er.

Fa - ther, for - give us! Through Je - sus hear us!

As we for - give one an - oth - er!

Text: Ralph Finn, b.1941, © 1965, GIA Publications, Inc.
Tune: ICH GLAUB AN GOTT, 8 7 8 7 with refrain; *Mainz Gesangbuch*, 1870; harm. by Richard Proulx, b.1937, © 1986, GIA Publications, Inc.

854 Healer of Our Every Ill

Refrain
Descant:
Heal - er of our ev - 'ry ill, light of each to - mor - row, give us
Melody:
Heal - er of our ev - 'ry ill, light of each to - mor - row, give us
Last time
peace be - yond our fear, and hope be - yond our sor - row.
Last time
peace be - yond our fear, and hope be - yond our sor - row.
Verses
1. You who know our fears and sad - ness,
2. In the pain and joy be - hold - ing,
3. Give us strength to love each oth - er,
4. You who know each thought and feel - ing,
Grace us with your peace and glad - ness, Spir - it of all
How your grace is still un - fold - ing, Give us all your
Ev - 'ry sis - ter, ev - 'ry broth - er, Spir - it of all
Teach us all your way of heal - ing, Spir - it of com -
D.C.
com - fort: fill our hearts.
vi - sion: God of love.
kind - ness: be our guide.
pas - sion: fill each heart.

Text: Marty Haugen, b.1950
Tune: Marty Haugen, b.1950

Love Is the Sunlight 855

1. Love is the sun - light Shaped of your splen - dor,
2. Love is the spa - cious Qui - et of shad - ows,
3. May we in glad - ness Grow in your sun - shine,
Love is the star bright Born of your hand,
Love is the gra - cious Shade of re - lease,
May we in sad - ness Rest in your shade,
Bless - ing of heav - en Gra - cious - ly giv - en,
Mist of the morn - ing, Mid - day a - dorn - ing,
Giv - ing and gain - ing, Ev - er re - main - ing,
Ra - diant with glo - ry From your com - mand.
Cool with the twi - light Breath of your peace.
One in the mar - riage Your love has made.
Final ending

Text: Borghild Jacobson, © 1981, Concordia Publishing House
Tune: SHADE, 5 5 5 4 D; David Haas, b.1957, © 1993, GIA Publications, Inc.

856 When Love Is Found

1. When love is found and hope comes home, Sing and be glad that two are one. When love ex - plodes and fills the sky, Praise God and share our Mak - er's joy.
2. When love has flowered in trust and care, Build both each day that love may dare To reach be - yond home's warmth and light, To serve and strive for truth and right.
3. When love is tried as loved - ones change, Hold still to hope though all seems strange, Till ease re - turns and love grows wise Through lis - t'ning ears and o - pened eyes.
4. When love is torn and trust be - trayed, Pray strength to love till tor - ments fade, Till lov - ers keep no score of wrong But hear through pain love's Eas - ter song.
5. Praise God for love, praise God for life, In age or youth, in calm or strife. Lift up your hearts let love be fed Through death and life in bro - ken bread.

Text: Brian Wren, b.1936
Tune: O WALY WALY, LM; English; harm. by Martin West, b.1929

Wherever You Go 857

Verse 1
1. Wher-ev - er you go I shall go.
Wher-ev - er you live so shall I live.
Your peo - ple will be my peo - ple, and
your God will be my God too.
Verse 2
2. Wher-ev - er you die I shall die
and there shall I be bur - ied be - side you.
We will be to - geth-er for ev - er, and
our love will be the gift of our life.
Last time
3

Text: Ruth 1:16, 17; Weston Priory, Gregory Norbet, OSB, b.1940
Tune: Gregory Norbet, OSB, b.1940; arr. by Mary David Callahan, b.1923

858 God, in the Planning

1. God, in the plan - ning and pur - pose of life,
2. Je - sus was found, at a sim - i - lar feast,
3. There - fore we pray that his spir - it pre - side
4. Praise then the Mak - er, the Spir - it, the Son,
Hal - lowed the un - ion of hus - band and wife:
Tak - ing the roles of both wait - er and priest,
O - ver the wed - ding of bride - groom and bride,
Source of the love through which two are made one.
This we em - bod - y where love is dis - played,
Turn - ing the world - ly to - wards the di - vine,
Ful - fill - ing all that they've hoped will come true,
God's is the glo - ry, the good - ness, and grace
Rings are pre - sent - ed and prom - is - es made.
Tears in - to laugh - ter and wa - ter to wine.
Light - ing with love all they dream of and do.
Seen in this mar - riage and known in this place.

A Nuptial Blessing 859

Refrain

May God bless you, hold and keep you;
may God's mer - cy shine on you,
guide your work and guard your rest - ing,
keep your love for ev - er new.

Verses
Melody:
1. May God sat - is - fy your long - ing,
2. May God join your hope - ful spir - its,
3. May God make your home a ref - uge
Harmony:
be re - fresh - ment at your ta - ble,
fill your hearts with truth and cour - age,
where you warm - ly wel - come stran - gers
and pro - vide your dai - ly bread,
trust to share both joy and tears,
and the low - ly find a place;
and pro - vide your dai - ly bread,
trust to share both joy and tears,
and the low - ly find a place;
guard your go - ing and your com - ing,
teach love to your chil - dren's chil - dren;
make you car - ing, kind com - pan - ions,

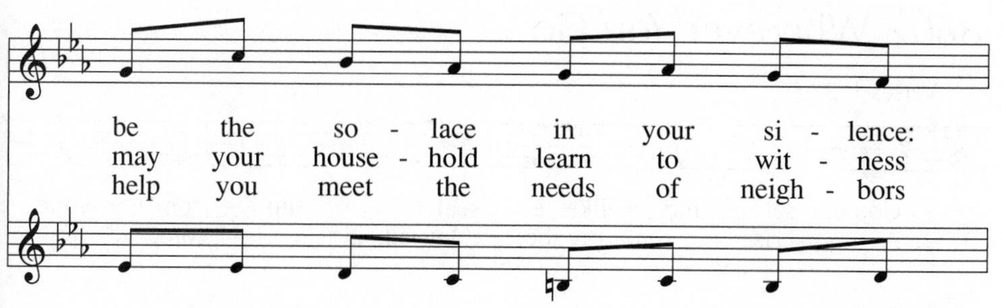
be the so - lace in your si - lence:
may your house - hold learn to wit - ness
help you meet the needs of neigh - bors

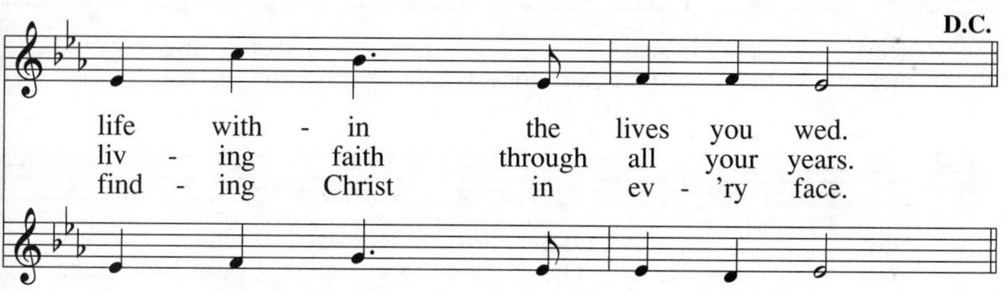
D.C.
life with - in the lives you wed.
liv - ing faith through all your years.
find - ing Christ in ev - 'ry face.

Text: Vicki Klima, b.1952; adapt. by Michael Joncas, b.1951, and George Szews, b.1951
Tune: Michael Joncas, b.1951

860 Wherever You Go

Verses 1, 2
1. Come, set me like a seal up - on your heart; a seal pro - tect - ing your arm. Deep wa - ters can - not quench this love; the o - cean will not sweep it a - way.
2. A - rise my be - lov-ed, come to me; the rains are gone, the win - ter is past. The flow - ers ap - pear, the vines are pruned, and the dove's song is heard in our land.
Refrain
Wher - ev - er you go, I will go; wher - ev - er you live, I'll be with you. Wher -

ev - er you lie, I'll be there be - side you. Wher-
ev - er you go, I'll be
there.
To verses
Verse 3
3. Wher - ev - er you stay, I will stay; your
peo - ple will be my peo - ple. Wher -
ev - er you die, so will I die
with you in the arms of God!
D.S.

Text: Ruth 1:16-17; Song of Songs 2:10-12, 7:6-7; David Haas, b.1957
Tune: David Haas, b.1957

861 May the Angels Lead You into Paradise

Gently
Cantor or choir: p
May the an-gels lead you in-to par-a-dise;
mf
may the mar-tyrs come to wel-come you and take you to the ho-ly cit-y, the new and e-ter-nal Je-ru-sa-lem.
All:
May the an-gels lead you in-to par-a-dise; may the mar-tyrs come to wel-come you and take you to the ho-ly cit-y, the new and e-ter-nal Je-ru-sa-lem.
Cantor or choir:
May the choir of an-gels wel-come you Where Laz-a-rus is poor no long-er,
p
may you have e-ter-nal rest,
rall.
may you have e-ter-nal rest.

The Hand of God Shall Hold You 862
Refrain
The hand of God shall hold you, the peace of God en - fold you, the love that dreamed and formed you still sur - rounds you here to - day; The light of God be - side you, a - bove, be - neath, in - side you, the light that shines to guide you home to the lov - ing hand of God.
To verses
Last time
Verse 1
Cantor 1:
1. May God's light shine ev - er up - on you,
Cantor 2:
may you rest in the arms of God;
Cantors:
may you dwell for ev - er - more in com - mun - ion with all the bless - ed.
D.C.
Verse 2
Cantor 1:
2. May the an - gels lead you in - to par - a - dise;
Cantor 2:
may the mar - tyrs come to wel - come you and
Cantors:
take you to the ho - ly cit - y, the new and e - ter - nal Je - ru - sa - lem.
D.C.

863 I Know That My Redeemer Lives

Refrain
I know that my re - deem - er lives:
on the last day I shall rise a -
gain, and in my flesh I shall see God.
On the last day I shall rise a - gain!
1., 2.
To verses
3.
gain!

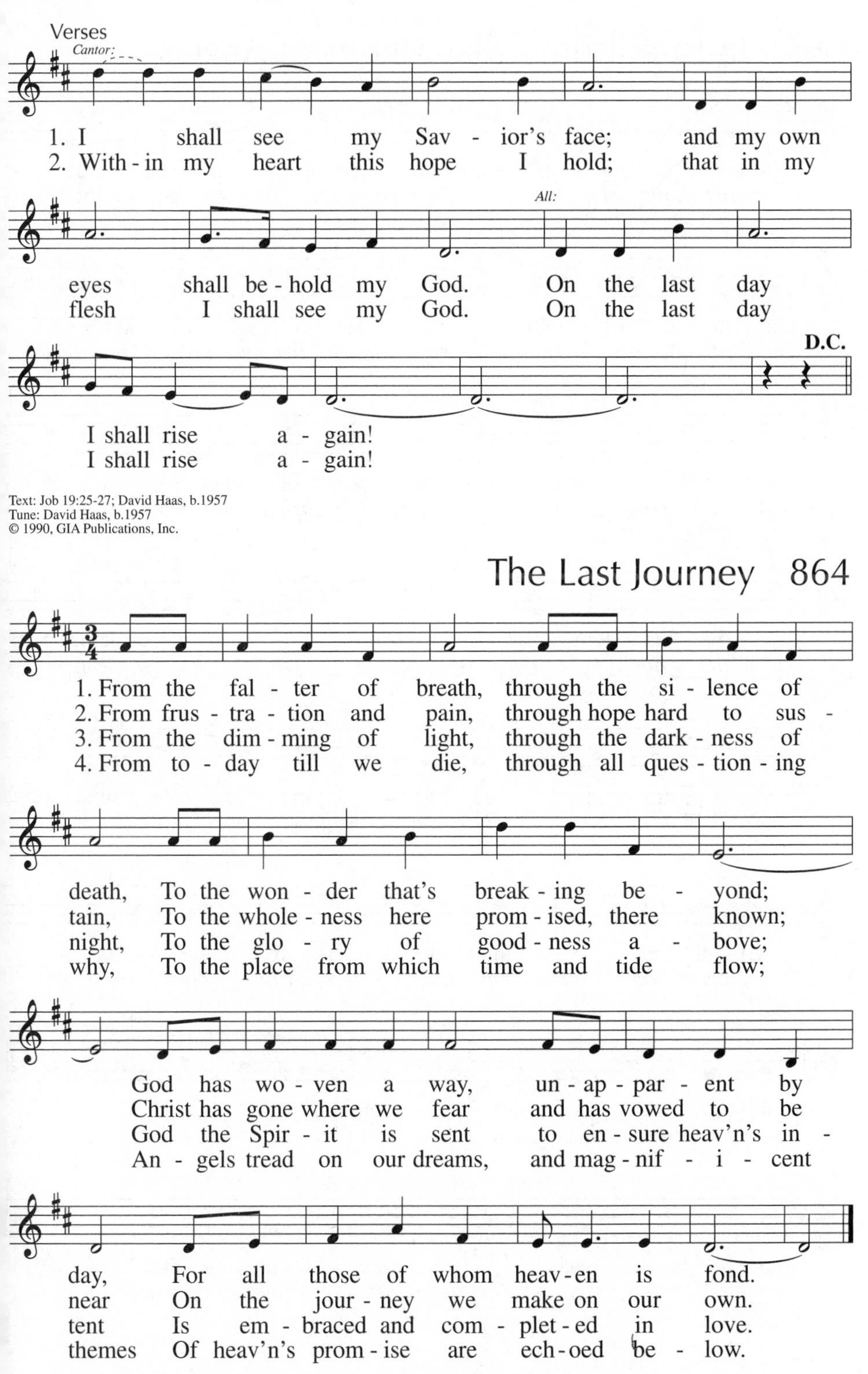
Verses
Cantor:
1. I shall see my Sav - ior's face; and my own
2. With - in my heart this hope I hold; that in my
All:
eyes shall be - hold my God. On the last day
flesh I shall see my God. On the last day
D.C.
I shall rise a - gain!
I shall rise a - gain!
Text: Job 19:25-27; David Haas, b.1957
Tune: David Haas, b.1957
© 1990, GIA Publications, Inc.
The Last Journey 864
1. From the fal - ter of breath, through the si - lence of
2. From frus - tra - tion and pain, through hope hard to sus -
3. From the dim - ming of light, through the dark - ness of
4. From to - day till we die, through all ques - tion - ing
death, To the won - der that's break - ing be - yond;
tain, To the whole - ness here prom - ised, there known;
night, To the glo - ry of good - ness a - bove;
why, To the place from which time and tide flow;
God has wo - ven a way, un - ap - par - ent by
Christ has gone where we fear and has vowed to be
God the Spir - it is sent to en - sure heav'n's in -
An - gels tread on our dreams, and mag - nif - i - cent
day, For all those of whom heav - en is fond.
near On the jour - ney we make on our own.
tent Is em - braced and com - plet - ed in love.
themes Of heav'n's prom - ise are ech - oed be - low.

Text: John L. Bell, b.1949, © 1989, 1996, The Iona Community, GIA Publications, Inc., agent
Tune: IONA BOAT SONG, 12 9 12 9; Scottish traditional, arr. by John L. Bell, b.1949, © 1989, 1996, The Iona Community, GIA Publications, Inc., agent

865 In Paradisum / May Choirs of Angels

In pa - ra - dí - sum de - dú - cant te án - ge - li:
May choirs of an - gels es - cort you in - to par - a - dise:
in tu - o ad - vén - tu su - scí - pi - ant te
and at your ar - ri - val may the mar - tyrs re - ceive
már - ty - res, et per - dú - cant te in
and wel - come you; may they bring you home in -
ci - vi - tá - tem san - ctam Je - rú - sa - lem.
to the ho - ly cit - y, Je - ru - sa - lem.
Cho - rus an - ge - ló - rum te su -
May the ho - ly an - gels wel -
scí - pi - at, et cum Lá - za - ro quon - dam
come you, and with Laz - a - rus, who lived in
páu - pe - re ae - tér - nam
pov - er - ty, may you have
há - be - as ré - qui - em.
ev - er - last - ing rest.

Text: *In Paradisum,* tr. © 1986, GIA Publications, Inc.
Tune: Mode VII; acc. by Richard Proulx, b.1937, © 1986, GIA Publications, Inc.

I Know That My Redeemer Lives 866

Gently
rall.
a tempo
Cantor (with simplicity and confidence): mf
I know that my Re - deem - er lives,
and on the last day I shall rise a-gain; in my
rall. All: a tempo
bod-y I shall look on God, my Sav-ior, in my bod-y I shall
mf
Cantor:
look on God, my Sav - ior. I my-self shall see him;
more intensely
rall.
my own eyes will gaze on him, my own eyes will gaze on him;
a tempo
rall.
a tempo
All:
in my bod-y I shall look on God, my Sav - ior, in my
rall.
bod - y I shall look on God, my Sav - ior.

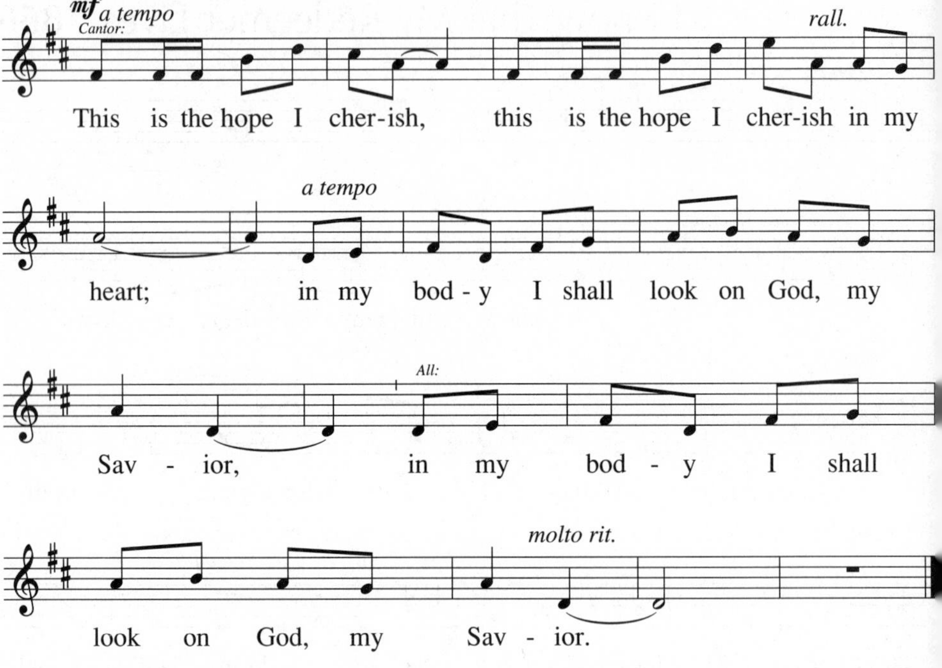
mf a tempo
Cantor:
rall.
This is the hope I cher-ish, this is the hope I cher-ish in my
a tempo
heart; in my bod - y I shall look on God, my
All:
Sav - ior, in my bod - y I shall
molto rit.
look on God, my Sav - ior.

Text: *Rite of Funerals*, © 1970, ICEL
Tune: *Music for Rite of Funerals and Rite of Baptism for Children*, Howard Hughes, SM, b.1930, © 1977, ICEL

Song of Farewell 867

Refrain

Dy - ing you de - stroyed our death! Ris - ing you re - stored our life!

div.

Lord Je - sus, Lord Je - sus,

div.

Lord Je - sus, Lord Je - sus,

come in glo - ry!

Verse 1

1. May Christ who died for you lead you in - to his king - dom;

may Christ who died for you lead you this day in - to par-a - dise.

D.C.

Verse 2
2. May Christ, the Good Shep - herd,
lead you home to - day and give you a
3
place with - in his flock.
D.C.
Alternate children's verse:
2. May Christ, the Good Shep-herd, take you on his
shoul-ders and bring you home,
bring you home to - day.
D.C.
Verse 3
3. May the an - gels lead you in - to par - a-dise;
may the mar - tyrs come to wel - come you and
take you to the Ho - ly Cit - y, the
new and e - ter - nal Je - ru - sa - lem.
D.C.

Verse 4
4. May the choirs of an - gels come to meet you,
may the choirs of an - gels come to meet you; where
Laz - a - rus is poor no long - er,
D.C.
may you have e - ter - nal life in Christ.
Alternate children's verse:
4. May the choirs of an - gels come to meet you,
may the choirs of an - gels come to meet you;
and with all God's chil - dren
D.C.
may you have e - ter - nal life in Christ.

Text: Memorial Acclamation, © 1973, ICEL; *In paradisum;* Michael Marchal, © 1988, GIA Publications, Inc.
Tune: Michael Joncas, b.1951, © 1988, GIA Publications, Inc.

868 Go, Silent Friend

1. Go, si-lent friend, your life has found its end - ing;
2. Go, si-lent friend, for - give us if we grieved you;
To dust re - turns your wea - ry mor - tal frame.
Safe now in heav - en, kind - ly say our name.
God, who be - fore birth called you in - to be - ing,
Your life has touched us, that is why we mourn you;
Now calls you hence, his ac - cent still the same.
Our lives with - out you can - not be the same.
Go, si - lent friend, your life in Christ is bur - ied;
Go, si - lent friend, we do not grudge you glo - ry;
For you he lived and died and rose a - gain.
Sing, sing with joy deep prais - es to your Lord.
Close by his side your prom - ised place is
You, who be - lieved that Christ would come back

wait - ing Where, ful - ly known, you shall with
for you, Now cel - e - brate that Je - sus
1.
2.
God re - main.
keeps his word.

Text: John L. Bell, b.1949, © 1996, The Iona Community, GIA Publications, Inc., agent
Tune: LONDONDERRY AIR, 11 10 11 10 D; arr. by John L. Bell, b.1949, © 1996, The Iona Community, GIA Publications, Inc., agent

869 There Is a Place

Verses
1. There's a time for re - mem - b'ring, a
2. There is gold that is gleam - ing, in a
3. There's a prom - ise of God that is
4. In the quiet of the eve - ning at the
time to re - call, the trials and the
past we once knew, in our tears and our
writ - ten in the stars, for all who may
close of the day, we will rest on our
tri - umphs, the fears and the falls.
laugh - ter 'twas love brought us through.
trav - el, no mat - ter how far.
jour - ney to the Lord we will pray.
There's a time to be grate - ful for
There's a road we have trav - eled where
God will be your com - pan - ion each
May we thank God for bless - ings, for the
mo - ments so blessed, the jewels of our
sun - light has kissed, that car - ries us
jour - ney you make, in the shad - ow of
mo - ments we shared, as we seek for to -
mem - 'ry where love is our guest.
on - wards when loved ones are
loved ones to light - en your
mor - row, our God will be
1.
D.C.

2.-4.
Refrain
missed.
way.
there.
There is treas - ure in our fields, there is
treas - ure in our skies, there is treas - ure in our
dream - ing from the soul to the eye,
for wher - ev - er we gath - er in the light of God's
grace, and for all whom we re - mem - ber,
there will ev - er be a place.
To verses
D.C.
Final ending

Text: Liam Lawton, b.1959
Tune: Liam Lawton, b.1959; choral arr. by Gary Daigle, b.1957; acc. by Kelly Dobbs Mickus, b.1966

870 God of Adam, God of Joseph

Refrain
Descant:
God of A - dam, God of Jo - seph,
Melody:
God of A - dam, God of Jo - seph,
God of sow - ing,
God of sow - ing, soil and seed,
Thank you for your world of prom - ise:
Thank you for your world of prom - ise:
Milk and hon - ey, wine and bread.
Milk and hon - ey, wine and bread.
Verses
1. God, you make us your com - pan - ions,
2. May your pas - sion for cre - a - tion
3. Thank you for all men en - trust - ed
4. Ab - ba (Fa - ther), God of Jo - seph,

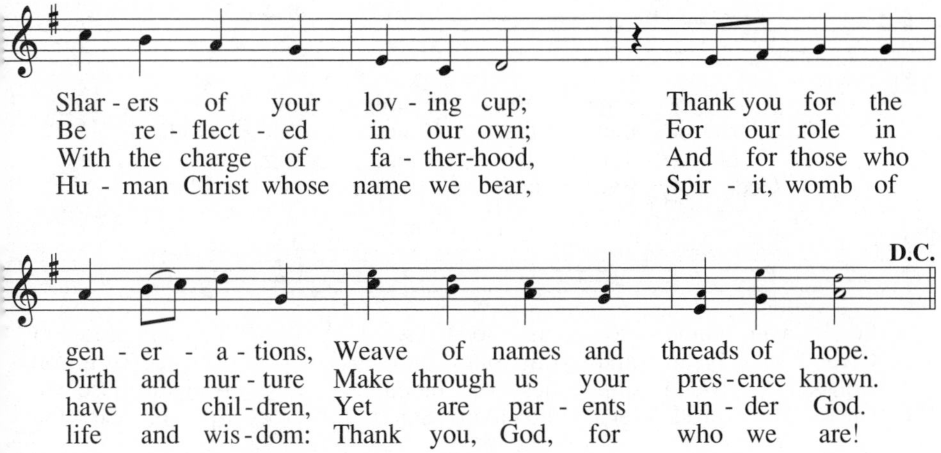

Shar - ers of your lov - ing cup; Thank you for the
Be re - flect - ed in our own; For our role in
With the charge of fa - ther-hood, And for those who
Hu - man Christ whose name we bear, Spir - it, womb of

D.C.

gen - er - a - tions, Weave of names and threads of hope.
birth and nur - ture Make through us your pres - ence known.
have no chil - dren, Yet are par - ents un - der God.
life and wis - dom: Thank you, God, for who we are!

Text: Fred Kaan, b.1929, © 1989, Hope Publishing Co.
Tune: FARRELL, 8 7 8 7 with refrain, Thomas J. Porter, b.1958, © 1994, GIA Publications, Inc.

God of Eve and God of Mary 871

Refrain

Descant:

God of Eve, God of Mar - y, God of

Melody:

God of Eve and God of Mar - y, God of love and

moth - er earth, Thank you for the ones who with us

moth - er earth, Thank you for the ones who with us

Shared their life and gave us birth.

Shared their life and gave us birth.

Verses

1. As you came to earth in Je - sus, So you come to us to - day; You are pres - ent in the car - ing That pre - pares us for life's way.
2. Thank you, that the Church, our Moth - er, Gives us bread and fills our cup, And the com - fort of the Spir - it Warms our hearts and lifts us up.
3. Thank you for be - long - ing, shel - ter, Bonds of friend - ship, ties of blood, And for those who have no chil - dren, Yet are par - ents un - der God.
4. God of Eve and God of Mar - y, Christ our broth - er, hu - man Son. Spir - it, car - ing like a moth - er, Take our love and make us one.

D.C.

Text: Fred Kaan, b.1929, © 1989, Hope Publishing Co.
Tune: FARRELL, 8 7 8 7 with refrain, Thomas J. Porter, b.1958, © 1994, GIA Publications, Inc.

872 America the Beautiful

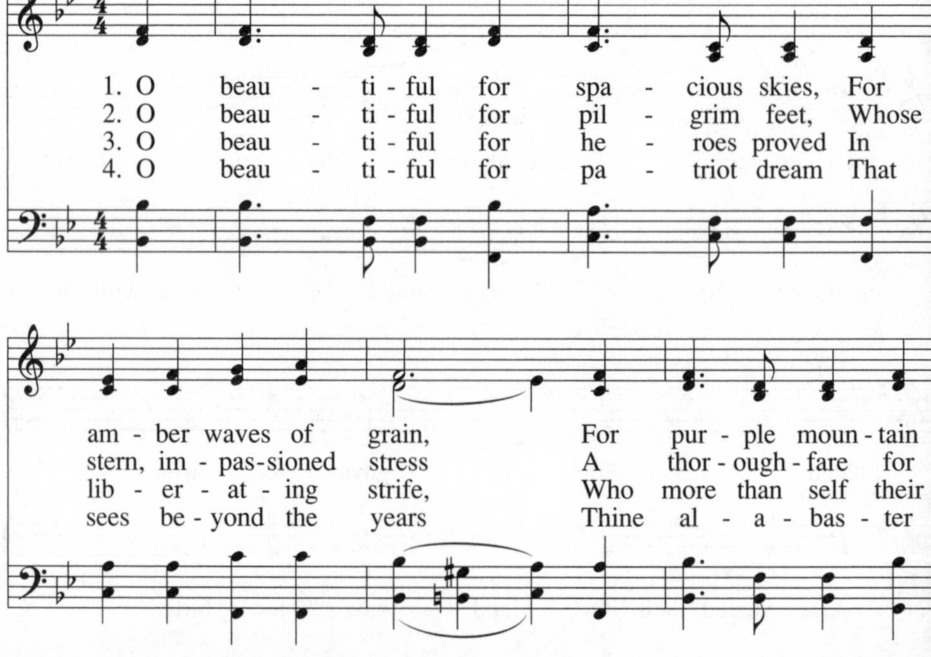
1. O beau - ti - ful for spa - cious skies, For am - ber waves of grain, For pur - ple moun - tain
2. O beau - ti - ful for pil - grim feet, Whose stern, im - pas-sioned stress A thor - ough - fare for
3. O beau - ti - ful for he - roes proved In lib - er - at - ing strife, Who more than self their
4. O beau - ti - ful for pa - triot dream That sees be - yond the years Thine al - a - bas - ter

maj - es - ties A - bove the fruit - ed plain! A -
free - dom beat A - cross the wil - der - ness! A -
coun - try loved, And mer - cy more than life! A -
cit - ies gleam, Un - dimmed by hu - man tears! A -
mer - i - ca! A - mer - i - ca! God
mer - i - ca! A - mer - i - ca! God
mer - i - ca! A - mer - i - ca! May
mer - i - ca! A - mer - i - ca! God
shed his grace on thee, And crown thy good with
mend thine ev - 'ry flaw, Con - firm thy soul in
God thy gold re - fine, Till all suc - cess be
shed his grace on thee, And crown thy good with
broth - er - hood From sea to shin - ing sea.
self - con - trol, Thy lib - er - ty in law.
no - ble - ness, And ev - 'ry gain di - vine.
broth - er - hood From sea to shin - ing sea.

Text: Katherine L. Bates, 1859-1929
Tune: MATERNA, CMD; Samuel A. Ward, 1848-1903

873 Star-Spangled Banner

1. O say can you see by the dawn's ear - ly
2. On the shore, dim - ly seen thro' the mists of the
3. O thus be it ev - er when free - men shall
light, What so proud - ly we hailed at the
deep, Where the foe's haugh - ty host in dead
stand Be - tween their loved homes and the
twi - light's last gleam - ing, Whose broad stripes and bright
si - lence re - pos - es, What is that which the
war's des - o - la - tion! Blest with vic - t'ry and
stars, through the per - il - ous fight, O'er the ram - parts we
breeze, o'er the tow - er - ing steep, As it fit - ful - ly
peace, may the heav'n-res-cued land Praise the Pow'r that hath

watched, were so gal - lant - ly stream - ing? And the
blows half con - ceals, half dis - clos - es? Now it
made and pre - served us a na - tion! Then
rock - ets' red glare, the bombs burst - ing in
catch - es the gleam of the morn - ing's first
con - quer we must, when our cause it is
air, Gave proof through the night that our
beam, In full glo - ry re - flect - ed now
just, And this be our mot - to, "In
flag was still there. O say does that
shined on the stream, 'Tis the Star - Span - gled
God is our trust." And the Star - Span - gled

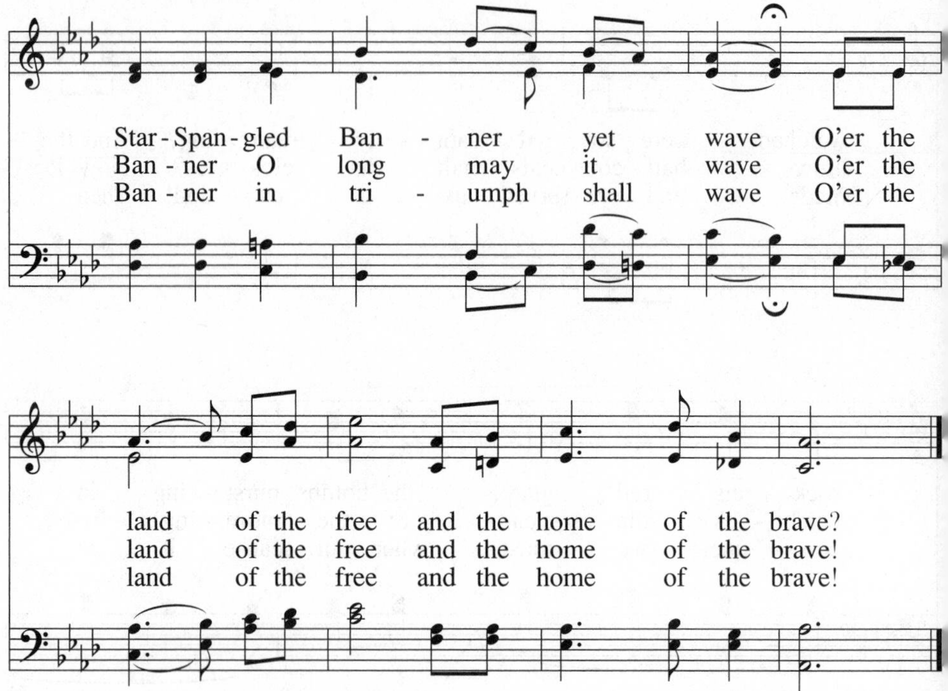
Star - Span - gled Ban - ner yet wave O'er the
Ban - ner O long may it wave O'er the
Ban - ner in tri - umph shall wave O'er the
land of the free and the home of the brave?
land of the free and the home of the brave!
land of the free and the home of the brave!

Text: Francis S. Key, 1779-1843
Tune: STAR SPANGLED BANNER; Irregular, John S. Smith, 1750-1836

My Country, 'Tis of Thee 874

1. My coun - try, 'tis of thee, Sweet land of
2. My na - tive coun - try, thee, Land of the
3. Let mu - sic swell the breeze, And ring from
4. Our fa - thers' God, to thee, Au - thor of
lib - er - ty, Of thee I sing; Land where my
no - ble, free; Thy name I love; I love thy
all the trees Sweet free - dom's song; Let mor - tal
lib - er - ty, To thee we sing; Long may our
fa - thers died, Land of the pil - grim's pride,
rocks and rills, Thy woods and tem - pled hills;
tongues a - wake; Let all that breathe par - take;
land be bright With free - dom's ho - ly light;
From ev - 'ry moun - tain - side Let free - dom ring!
My heart with rap - ture thrills, Like that a - bove.
Let rocks their si - lence break, The sound pro - long.
Pro - tect us by thy might, Great God, our King.

Text: Samuel F. Smith, 1808-1895
Tune: AMERICA, 66 4 666 4; *Thesaurus Musicus*, 1744

875 This Is My Song

1. This is my song, O God of all the na - tions,
2. My coun-try's skies are blu - er than the o - cean,
3. This is my prayer, O God of all earth's king - doms,
A song of peace for lands a - far and mine.
And sun - light beams on clo - ver - leaf and pine.
Your king - dom come; on earth your will be done.
This is my home, the coun - try where my heart is;
But oth - er lands have sun - light too, and clo - ver,
Let Christ be lift - ed up till all shall serve him,
Here are my hopes, my dreams, my ho - ly shrine;
And skies are ev - 'ry - where as blue as mine.
And hearts u - nit - ed learn to live as one.

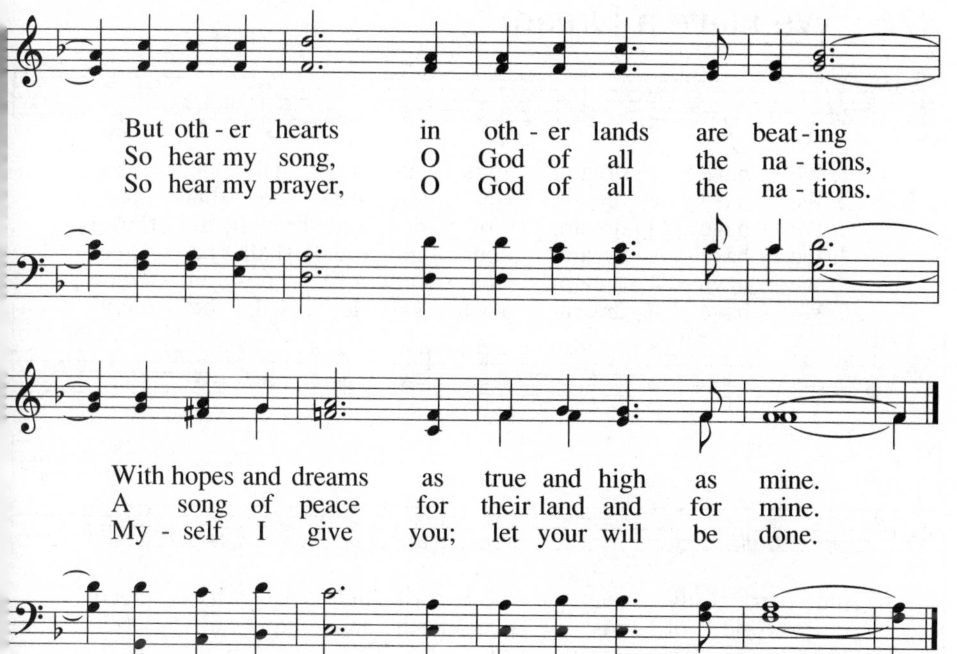
But oth - er hearts in oth - er lands are beat - ing
So hear my song, O God of all the na - tions,
So hear my prayer, O God of all the na - tions.
With hopes and dreams as true and high as mine.
A song of peace for their land and for mine.
My - self I give you; let your will be done.

Text: St. 1-2, Lloyd Stone, 1912-1993, © 1934, 1962, Lorenz Publishing Co., st. 3, Georgia Harkness, 1891-1974, © 1964, Lorenz Publishing Co.
Tune: FINLANDIA, 11 10 11 10 11 10; Jean Sibelius, 1865-1957

876 We Have a Dream

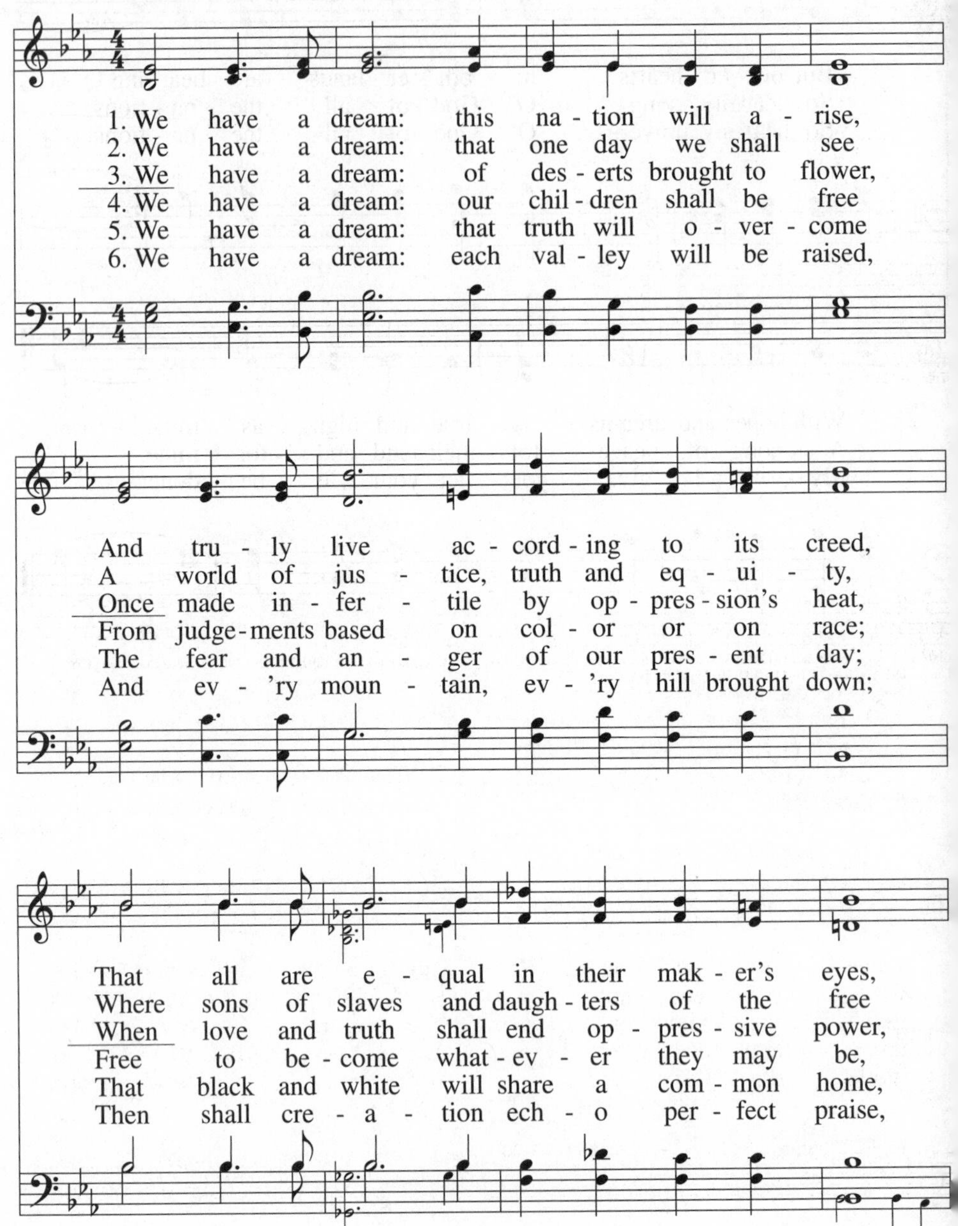
1. We have a dream: this na - tion will a - rise,
2. We have a dream: that one day we shall see
3. We have a dream: of des - erts brought to flower,
4. We have a dream: our chil - dren shall be free
5. We have a dream: that truth will o - ver - come
6. We have a dream: each val - ley will be raised,
And tru - ly live ac - cord - ing to its creed,
A world of jus - tice, truth and eq - ui - ty,
Once made in - fer - tile by op - pres - sion's heat,
From judge - ments based on col - or or on race;
The fear and an - ger of our pres - ent day;
And ev - 'ry moun - tain, ev - 'ry hill brought down;
That all are e - qual in their mak - er's eyes,
Where sons of slaves and daugh - ters of the free
When love and truth shall end op - pres - sive power,
Free to be - come what - ev - er they may be,
That black and white will share a com - mon home,
Then shall cre - a - tion ech - o per - fect praise,

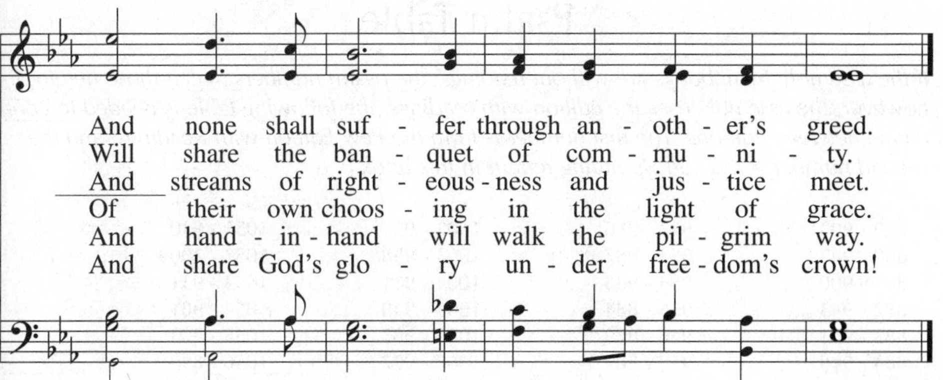
And none shall suf - fer through an - oth - er's greed.
Will share the ban - quet of com - mu - ni - ty.
And streams of right - eous - ness and jus - tice meet.
Of their own choos - ing in the light of grace.
And hand - in - hand will walk the pil - grim way.
And share God's glo - ry un - der free - dom's crown!
8

Text: Michael Forster, b.1946, © 1997, Kevin Mayhew, Ltd.
Tune: NATIONAL HYMN, 10 10 10 10; George W. Warren, 1828-1902

The God of All Eternity 877

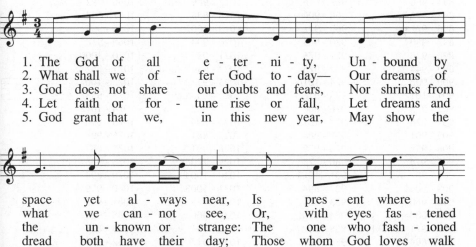

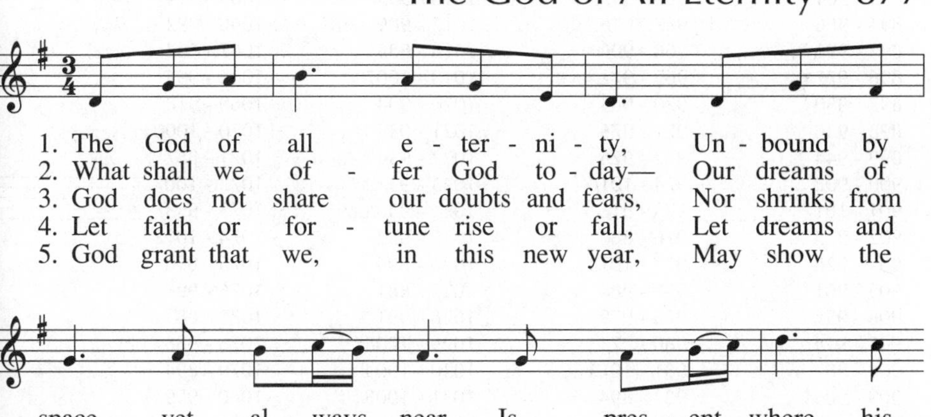
3
4
1. The God of all e - ter - ni - ty, Un - bound by
2. What shall we of - fer God to - day— Our dreams of
3. God does not share our doubts and fears, Nor shrinks from
4. Let faith or for - tune rise or fall, Let dreams and
5. God grant that we, in this new year, May show the
space yet al - ways near, Is pres - ent where his
what we can - not see, Or, with eyes fas - tened
the un - known or strange: The one who fash - ioned
dread both have their day; Those whom God loves walk
world the King - dom's face, And let our work and

peo - ple meet To cel - e - brate the com - ing year.
to the past, Our dread of what is yet to be?
heav'n and earth Makes all things new and ush - ers change.
un - a - fraid With Christ their guide and Christ their way.
wor - ship thrive As signs of hope and means of grace.

Text: John L. Bell, b.1949, © 1989, Iona Community, GIA Publications, Inc., agent
Tune: O WALY WALY, 8 8 8 8; English traditional; arr. by John L. Bell, b.1949, © 1989, Iona Community, GIA Publications, Inc., agent

Psalm Table

If the assembly hymnbooks are without readings, the psalm numbers match those herein. If however, the assembly uses the edition with readings, the following table is needed to coordinate between editions. The first number is from the Pew Edition with Readings, and the second number is the corresponding refrain in this book.

879 - 993
880 - 947
881 - 900
882 - 943
883 - 951
884 - 995
885 - 1010
886 - 1019
887 - 1016
888 - 897
889 - 953
890 - 947
891 - 953
892 - 961
893 - 964
894 - 966
895 - 996
896 - 977
897 - 950
898 - 936
899 - 944
900 - 908
901 - 1017
902 - 975
904 - 928
905 - 901
906 - 957
907 - 914
908 - 982
909 - 905
910 - 960
911 - 888
912 - 971
913 - 894
914 - 1002
915 - 917
916 - 999
917 - 929
918 - 995
923 - 892
928 - 983
931 - 910
936 - 976/915
937 - 885
938 - 1015
939 - 909
940 - 1017
941 - 888
942 - 923
943 - 986
953 - 987
954 - 988
955 - 884
956 - 879
957 - 909
958 - 894
959 - 989
960 - 970
961 - 914
962 - 893
963 - 1007
964 - 935
965 - 967
966 - 937
967 - 926
968 - 906
969 - 972
970 - 965
971 - 976
972 - 976
974 - 1018
975 - 916
976 - 880
977 - 1013
978 - 984
979 - 979
980 - 973
981 - 1017
982 - 894
983 - 920
984 - 920
985 - 962
986 - 905
987 - 902
988 - 889
989 - 1011
990 - 960
991 - 941
992 - 980
993 - 1014
994 - 1003
995 - 990
996 - 912
997 - 878
998 - 971
999 - 922
1000 - 971
1001 - 932
1002 - 971
1003 - 958
1004 - 911
1005 - 949
1006 - 985
1007 - 927
1008 - 999
1009 - 909
1010 - 970
1011 - 958
1012 - 913
1013 - 939
1014 - 978
1015 - 933
1016 - 953
1017 - 909
1018 - 885
1019 - 1007
1020 - 994
1021 - 935
1022 - 934
1023 - 951
1024 - 940/889
1025 - 952
1026 - 894
1027 - 881
1028 - 991
1029 - 1008
1030 - 1004
1031 - 1008
1032 - 945
1033 - 960
1034 - 951
1035 - 917
1036 - 916
1037 - 937
1038 - 917
1039 - 921
1040 - 1005
1041 - 917
1042 - 985
1043 - 933
1044 - 882
1045 - 938
1046 - 960
1047 - 1012
1048 - 955
1049 - 974
1050 - 982
1051 - 930
1052 - 1009
1053 - 931
1054 - 981
1055 - 903
1056 - 890
1057 - 1012
1058 - 948
1059 - 997
1060 - 960
1061 - 896
1062 - 956
1063 - 967
1064 - 963
1065 - 914
1066 - 992
1067 - 887
1068 - 995
1069 - 918
1070 - 1000
1071 - 887
1072 - 1007
1073 - 933
1074 - 1012
1075 - 886
1076 - 998
1077 - 883
1078 - 968
1079 - 894
1080 - 959
1081 - 993
1088 - 928
1138 - 898
1142 - 954
1144 - 920
1148 - 942
1149 - 1006
1151 - 891
1152 - 919
1158 - 965
1160 - 1001
1161 - 924
1165 - 946
1168 - 899
1169 - 894/895/900/904 905/906
1171 - 925
1175 - 969

Psalm Refrains from the Lectionary for Mass

Psalm 1
878
Bless-ed are they, bless-ed are they who hope in the Lord.
Psalm 4
879
Lord, let your face shine on us.
Psalm 8
880
Descant:
O Lord, our God, how won-der-ful in all the earth!
Melody:
O Lord, our God, how won-der-ful your name in all the earth!
Psalm 15
881
He who does jus-tice will live in the pres-ence of the Lord.
Psalm 15
882
One who does jus-tice will live in the pres-ence of the Lord.
Psalm 16
883
You are my in - her - i - tance, O Lord.

884 Psalm 16
Lord, you will show us the path of life.
885 Psalm 16
You are my in - her - i - tance, O Lord.
886 Psalm 17
Lord, when your glo-ry ap-pears, my joy will be full.
887 Psalm 18
I love you, Lord, my strength, my strength.
888 Psalm 19
3
Lord, you have the words of ev - er-last - ing life.
889 Psalm 19
Your words, O Lord, are Spir-it and life.
890 Psalm 19
The pre-cepts of the Lord give joy to the heart.
891 Psalm 19
Their mes - sage goes out through all the earth.

Psalm 22
892
My God, my God, why have you a - ban - doned me?
Psalm 22
893
I will praise you, Lord, in the as - sem - bly of your peo - ple.
Psalm 23
894
The Lord is my shep - herd; there is noth - ing I shall want.
Psalm 23
895
Though I walk in the val - ley of dark - ness, I fear no
e - vil, for you are with me.
Psalm 23
896
I shall live in the house of the Lord all the days of my life.
Psalm 24
897
Let the Lord en - ter; he is king of glo - ry.
Psalm 24
898
Who is this king of glo - ry? It is the Lord!
Psalm 24
899
Lord, this is the peo - ple that longs to see your face.

900 Psalm 25
To you, O Lord, I lift my soul, to you I lift my soul.
901 Psalm 25
Your ways, O Lord, are love and truth to those who keep your cov - e - nant.
902 Psalm 25
Teach me your ways, O Lord, teach me your ways.
903 Psalm 25
Re - mem - ber your mer - cies, O Lord.
904 Psalm 25
No one who waits for you, O Lord, will ev - er be put to shame.
905 Psalm 27
The Lord is my light and my sal - va - tion.
906 Psalm 27
I be - lieve that I shall see the good things of the Lord in the land of the liv - ing.

Psalm 27
907
I be - lieve that I shall see the good things of the
Lord in the land of the liv - ing.
Psalm 29
908
The Lord will bless his peo - ple with his peace.
Psalm 30
909
I will praise you, Lord, for you have res - cued me.
Psalm 31
910
Fa - ther, in - to your hands I com - mend my spir - it.
Psalm 31
911
Lord, be my rock of safe - ty.
Psalm 32
912
I turn to you, O Lord, in time of
trou - ble, and you fill me with the joy of sal - va - tion.
Psalm 32
913
Lord, for - give the wrong I have done.

914 Psalm 33
Lord, let your mer-cy be on us, as we place our trust in you.
915 Psalm 33
The earth is full of the good-ness of the Lord, the good-ness of the Lord.
916 Psalm 33
Bless - ed the peo-ple the Lord has cho - sen to be his own.
917 Psalm 34
Taste and see the good - ness of the Lord.
918 Psalm 34
The Lord hears the cry of the poor.
919 Psalm 34
The an-gel of the Lord will res-cue those who fear him.
920 Psalm 40
Here am I, Lord; here am I, Lord; I come to do your will.
921 Psalm 40
Lord, come to my aid, Lord, come to my aid!
922 Psalm 41
Lord, heal my soul, for I have sinned a - gainst you.

Psalm 42 923

Psalm 45 924

Psalm 46 925

Psalm 47 926

Psalm 50 927

Psalm 51 928

Like a deer that longs for run - ning streams, my
soul longs for you, my God; my soul longs for you, my God.
The queen stands at your right hand, ar - rayed in gold.
The wa - ters of the riv - er glad - den the cit - y of God, the
ho - ly dwell - ing of the Most High.
God mounts his throne to shouts of joy: a blare of
trum - pets for the Lord.
To the up - right I will show the sav - ing pow'r of God.
Be mer - ci - ful, O Lord, for we have sinned.

929 Psalm 51
Cre - ate in me, cre - ate in me a clean heart, O God.
930 Psalm 51
I will rise and go to my fa - ther.
931 Psalm 54
The Lord up-holds my life.
932 Psalm 62
Rest in God a-lone, rest in God a-lone, my soul.
933 Psalm 63
My soul is thirst-ing for you, O Lord, thirst-ing for you my God.
934 Psalm 65
The seed that falls on good ground will yield a fruit - ful har-vest.
935 Psalm 66
Let all the earth cry out to God with joy.
936 Psalm 67
May God bless us in his mer - cy,
may God bless us in his mer - cy.

Psalm 67
937
O God, O God, let all the na-tions praise you!
Psalm 68
938
God, in your good-ness, you have made a home for the poor.
Psalm 69
939
Lord, in your great love, an-swer me.
Psalm 69
940
Turn to the Lord in your need, and you will live.
Psalm 71
941
I will sing of your sal - va - tion.
Psalm 71
942
Since my moth-er's womb, you have been my strength.
Psalm 72
943
Jus - tice shall flour - ish in his time, and
full - ness of peace for ev - er.

944 Psalm 72

945 Psalm 78

946 Psalm 78

947 Psalm 80

948 Psalm 80

949 Psalm 81

950 Psalm 84

Descant:
Lord, ev-'ry na - tion will a - dore you.
Melody:
Lord, ev-'ry na-tion on earth will a - dore you.
The Lord gave them bread from heav - en.
Do not for - get the works of the Lord!
Lord, make us turn to you; let us see your face and we shall be saved.
The vine-yard of the Lord is the house of Is - ra - el.
Sing with joy to God! Sing to God our help!
Bless-ed are they who dwell in your house, O Lord.

Psalm 85
951
Lord, let us see your kind - ness, and grant us your sal - va - tion.
Psalm 86
952
Lord, you are good and for - giv - ing.
Psalm 89
953
For ev - er I will sing the good - ness of the Lord.
Psalm 89
954
The son of Da - vid will live for ev - er.
Psalm 90
955
In ev-'ry age, O Lord, you have been our ref - uge.
Psalm 90
956
Fill us with your love, O Lord, and we will sing for joy!
Psalm 91
957
Be with me, Lord, when I am in trou - ble.
Psalm 92
958
Lord, it is good to give thanks to you.

959 Psalm 93

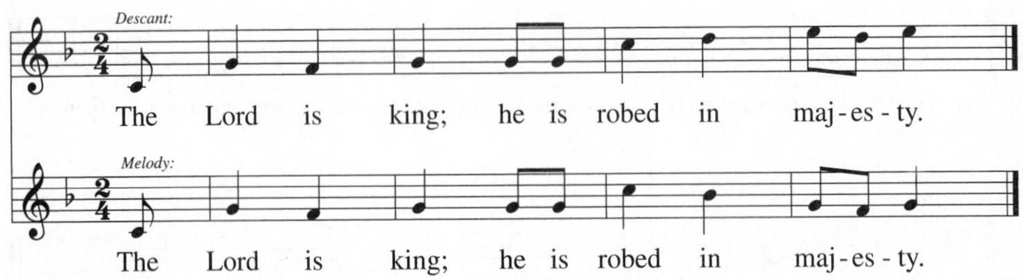
Descant:
The Lord is king; he is robed in maj-es-ty.
Melody:
The Lord is king; he is robed in maj-es-ty.

960 Psalm 95

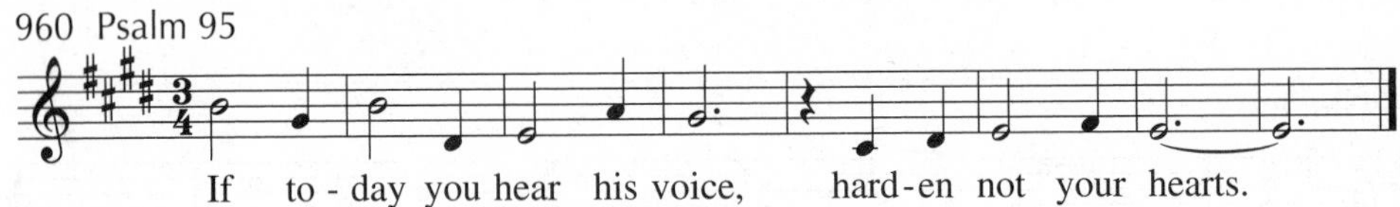
If to-day you hear his voice, hard-en not your hearts.

961 Psalm 96

Descant:
To-day, to-day, to-day is born our Sav-ior, Christ the Lord.
Melody:
To-day, to-day, to-day is born our Sav-ior, Christ the Lord.

962 Psalm 96

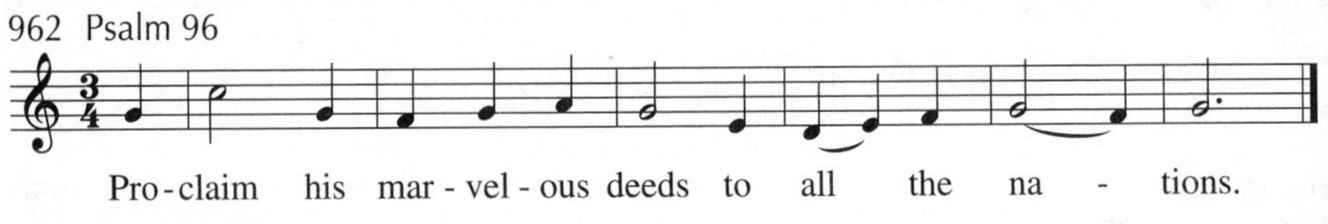
Pro-claim his mar-vel-ous deeds to all the na - tions.

963 Psalm 96

Give the Lord glo-ry and hon - or.

964 Psalm 97

A light will shine on us this day: the Lord is born for us.

965 Psalm 97

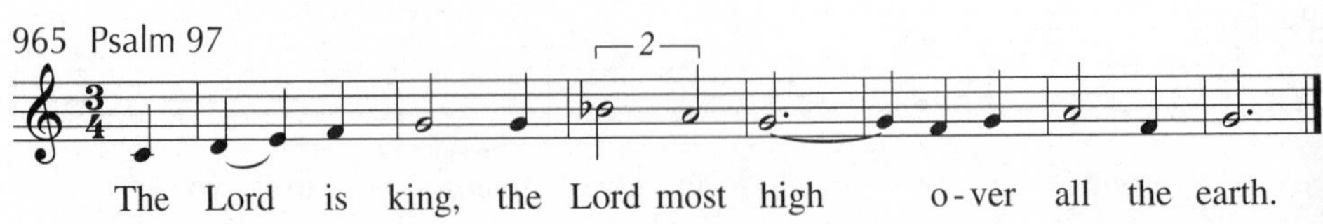
2
The Lord is king, the Lord most high o-ver all the earth.

Psalm 98
Descant:
All the ends of the earth have seen
God.
Melody:
All the ends of the earth have seen the sav -
of God.
Psalm 98
967
The Lord has re-vealed to the na - tions his sav - ing pow'r, his
sav - ing pow'r.
Psalm 98
968
The Lord comes to rule the earth with jus - tice.
Psalm 98
969
Sing to the Lord a new song, for he has done mar-vel-ous deeds.
Psalm 100
970
We are his peo-ple, the sheep of his flock.
Psalm 103
971
The Lord is kind and mer-ci-ful; the Lord is kind and mer-ci-ful.
Psalm 103
972
The Lord has set his throne in heav - en.

973 Psalm 103
The Lord's kin
is ev-er-last-ing to those who fear him.
974 Psalm 103
Lord is kind and mer-ci-ful, slow to an-ger, and
rich n com-pas - sion.
975 Psalm 104
O bless the Lord, my soul, O bless the Lord.
976 Psalm 104
Descant:
Lord, send out your Spir - it, and re-new the face of the earth.
Melody:
Lord, send out your Spir - it, and re-new the face of the earth.
977 Psalm 105
The Lord re - mem-bers his cov - e - nant for ev - er.
978 Psalm 107
Give thanks to the Lord, his love is ev-er-last - ing.
979 Psalm 110
You are a priest for ev-er, in the line of Mel - chi - ze - dek.

Psalm 112

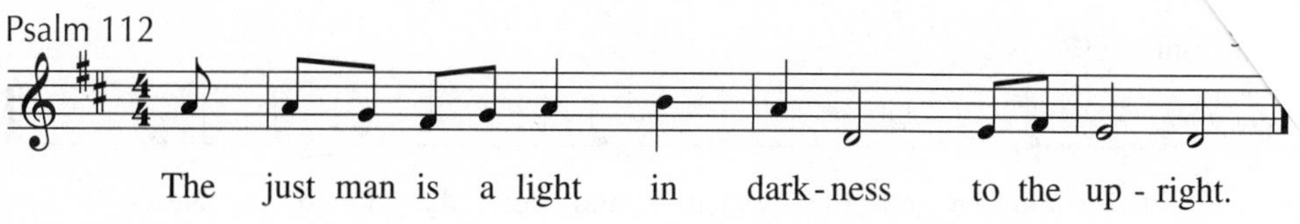
The just man is a light in dark-ness to the up-right.

Psalm 113 981

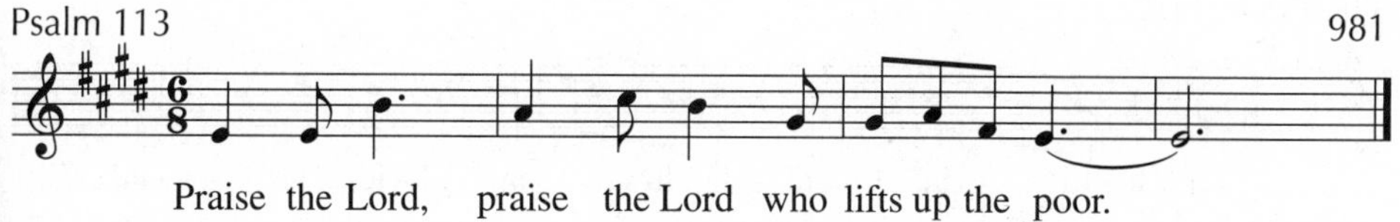
Praise the Lord, praise the Lord who lifts up the poor.

Psalm 116 982

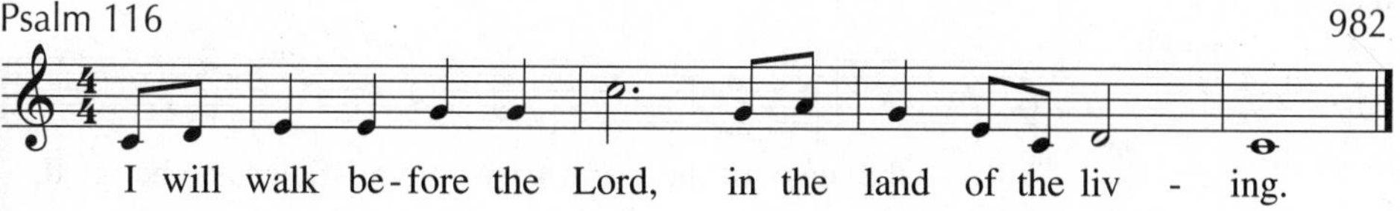
I will walk be-fore the Lord, in the land of the liv - ing.

Psalm 116 983

Descant:
Our bless-ing cup
Melody:
Our bless - ing - cup is a com -

is a com-mun-ion with the Blood of Christ.
mun - ion with the Blood of Christ.

Psalm 116 984

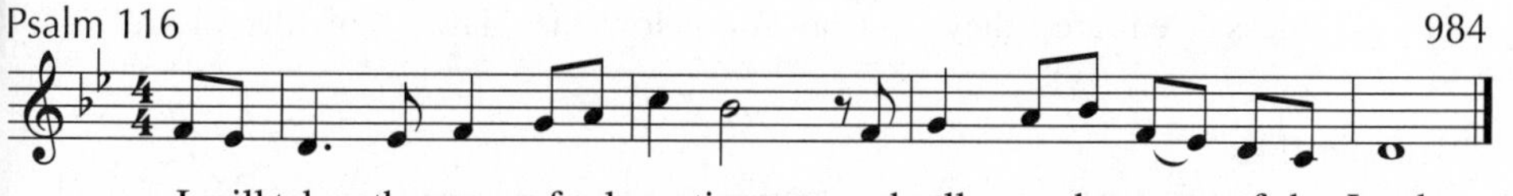
I will take the cup of sal-va-tion, and call on the name of the Lord.

985 Psalm 117

Go out to all the world and tell the Good News.

986 Psalm 118

Al - le - lu - ia, al - le - lu - ia, al - le - lu - ia!

987 Psalm 118

Descant:

This is the day of the Lord; let us re - joice and be glad.

Melody:

This is the day the Lord has made; let us re-joice and be glad.

988 Psalm 118

Give thanks to the Lord, for he is good, his love is ev - er - last - ing.

989 Psalm 118

The stone re-ject-ed by the build-ers has be-come the cor-ner-stone.

990 Psalm 119

Bless - ed are they who fol - low the law of the Lord!

991 Psalm 119

Lord, I love your com - mands.

Psalm 121
992
Our help is from the Lord, who made heav-en and earth.
Psalm 122
993
Let us go re-joic-ing to the house of the Lord.
Psalm 123
994
Our eyes are fixed on the Lord, plead-ing for his mer-cy.
Psalm 126
995
The Lord has done great things for us; we are
filled with joy.
Psalm 128
996
Bless-ed are those who fear the Lord and walk in his ways.
Psalm 128
997
May the Lord bless and pro-tect us all the days of our lives.
Psalm 128
998
Bless-ed are those who fear the Lord.

999 Psalm 130

1000 Psalm 131

1001 Psalm 132

1002 Psalm 137

1003 Psalm 138

1004 Psalm 138

1005 Psalm 138

1006 Psalm 139

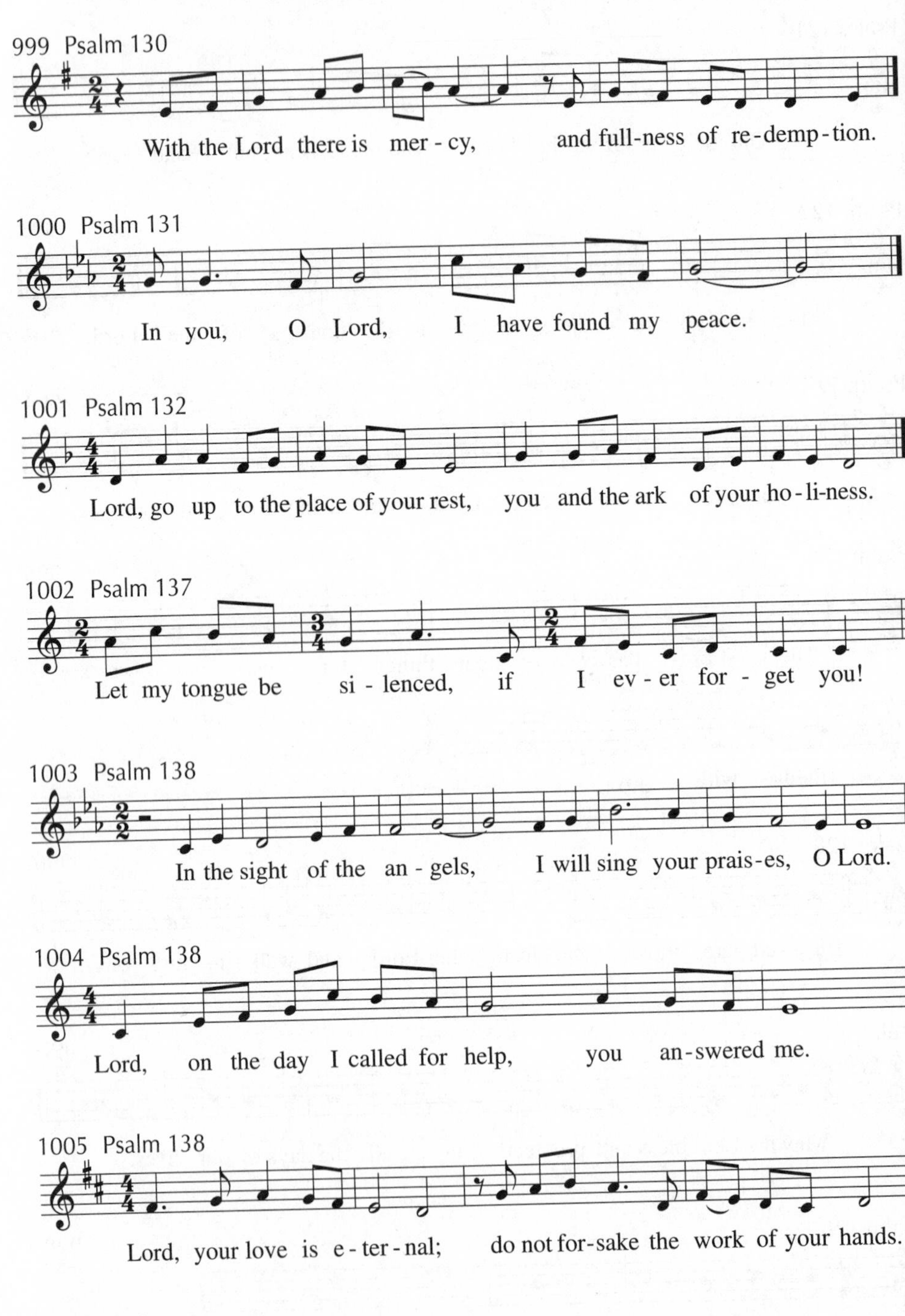
With the Lord there is mer - cy, and full-ness of re-demp-tion.
In you, O Lord, I have found my peace.
Lord, go up to the place of your rest, you and the ark of your ho-li-ness.
Let my tongue be si - lenced, if I ev - er for - get you!
In the sight of the an - gels, I will sing your prais-es, O Lord.
Lord, on the day I called for help, you an-swered me.
Lord, your love is e - ter - nal; do not for-sake the work of your hands.
I praise you, O Lord, for I am won-der-ful-ly made.

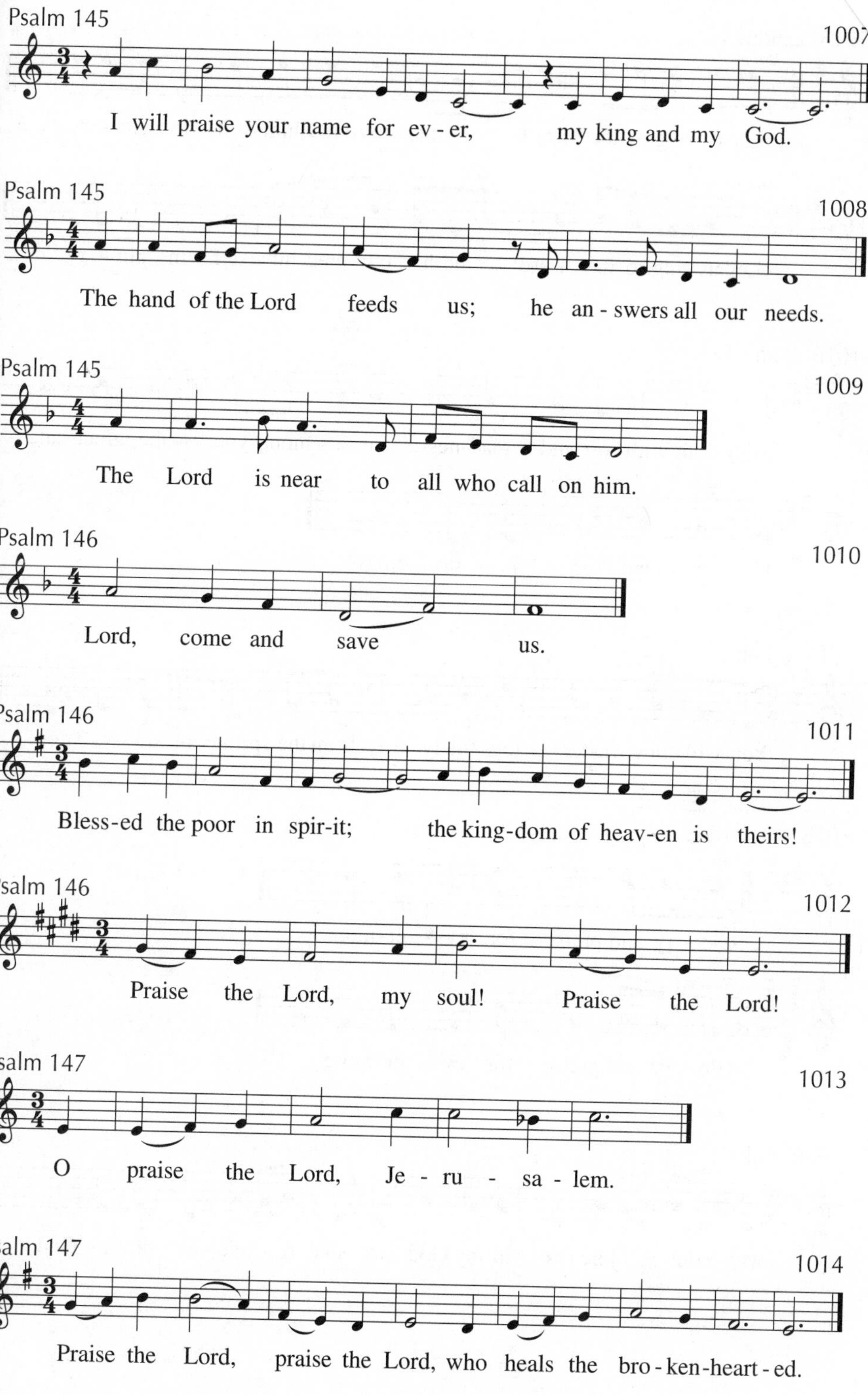
Psalm 145
1007
I will praise your name for ev - er, my king and my God.
Psalm 145
1008
The hand of the Lord feeds us; he an - swers all our needs.
Psalm 145
1009
The Lord is near to all who call on him.
Psalm 146
1010
Lord, come and save us.
Psalm 146
1011
Bless-ed the poor in spir-it; the king-dom of heav-en is theirs!
Psalm 146
1012
Praise the Lord, my soul! Praise the Lord!
Psalm 147
1013
O praise the Lord, Je - ru - sa - lem.
Psalm 147
1014
Praise the Lord, praise the Lord, who heals the bro - ken-heart - ed.

1015 Exodus 15

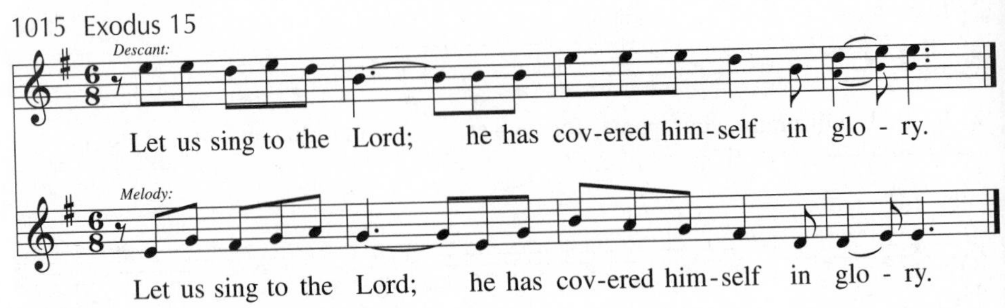
Descant:
Let us sing to the Lord; he has cov-ered him-self in glo - ry.
Melody:
Let us sing to the Lord; he has cov-ered him-self in glo - ry.

1016 Isaiah 12

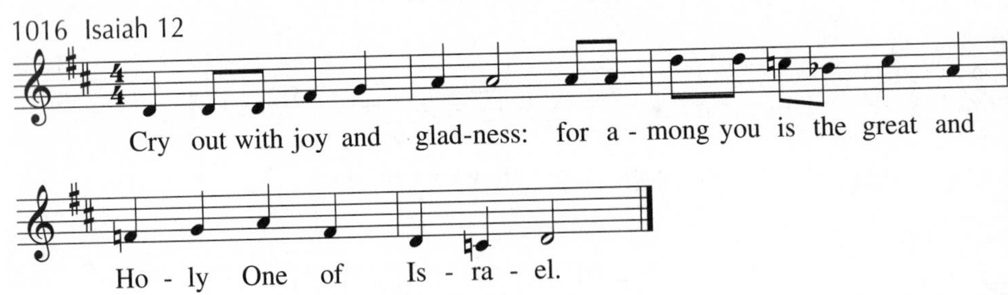
Cry out with joy and glad-ness: for a - mong you is the great and

Ho - ly One of Is - ra - el.

1017 Isaiah 12

You will draw wa-ter joy-ful-ly from the springs of sal - va - tion.

1018 Daniel 3

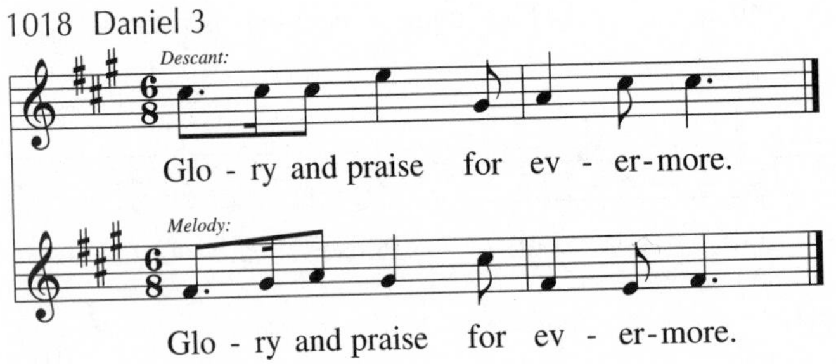
Descant:
Glo - ry and praise for ev - er-more.
Melody:
Glo - ry and praise for ev - er-more.

1019 Luke 1

My soul re - joic - es in my God, my soul re - joic - es in my God.

The following items are only found in the pew edition with Sunday readings.

OPENING ANTIPHON [920]

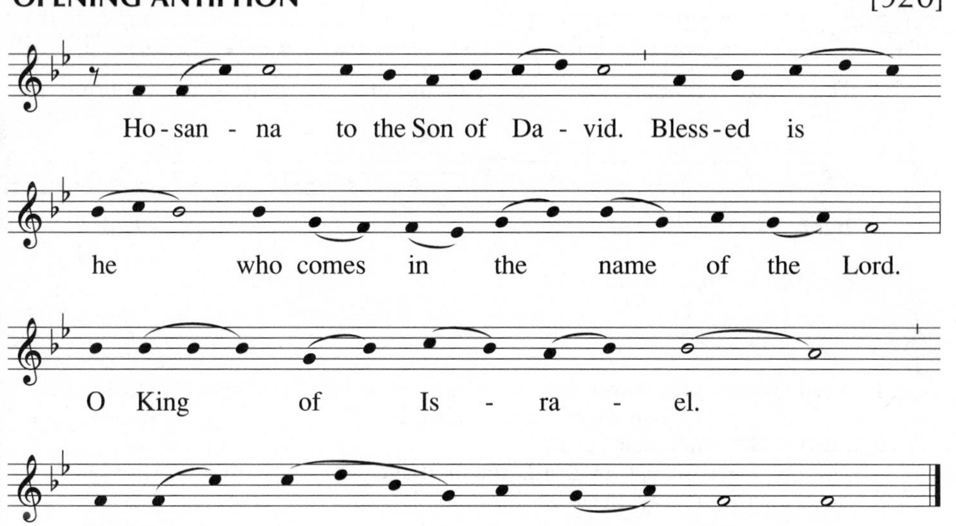
Ho - san - na to the Son of Da - vid. Bless - ed is
he who comes in the name of the Lord.
O King of Is - ra - el.
Ho - san - na in the high - est.

Music: Chant Mode VII; adapt. and acc. by Richard Proulx, © 1985, GIA Publications, Inc.

No. 945, *Blessing of Water,* may be found at no. 155.
No. 947, *You Have Put on Christ,* may be found at no. 107.

[1138] FEB. 2: PRESENTATION OF THE LORD—BLESSING OF CANDLES

Antiphon
The Lord will come to us with might - y pow - er, bring-ing
light to eyes of those who serve him well.
Psalm (118)119:105-108, 111-112
1. Your word is a lamp for my steps
I have sworn and made up my mind
2. Lord, I am deeply af - flict - ed;
Accept O Lord, the homage of my lips,
3. Your will is my heritage for ev - er,
I set myself to carry out your will
1. and a light for my path.
to o - bey your de - crees. ℟.
2. by your word give me life.
and teach me your de - crees. ℟.
3. the joy of my heart.
in full - ness for ev - er. ℟.

PROCESSION [1139]

Antiphon

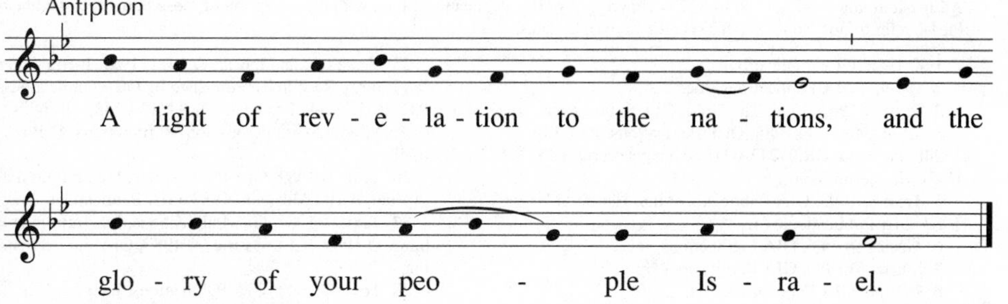
A light of rev - e - la - tion to the na - tions, and the
glo - ry of your peo - ple Is - ra - el.

Canticle, Luke 2:29-32

D.C.
1. Lord, now you have set your ser-vant free to go in peace as you have prom-ised.

D.C.
2. With my own eyes I have
seen the sal-va-tion, which you have
prepared for all the world to see.

Music: Mode VIII-g; setting by Richard Proulx, © 1985, GIA Publications, Inc.

1020 Acknowledgments

SERVICE MUSIC

All music found from nos. 86 to 322 is copyright by GIA Publications, Inc., with the exception of those items specified below. Please refer to nos. 86 to 322 for specific copyright dates.

1 © 1986, GIA Publications, Inc.
2 © 1987, GIA Publications, Inc.
3 Text: © 1963, 1986, The Grail, GIA Publications, Inc., agent. Music: © 1985, OCP Publcations. P.O. Box 13248, Portland, OR 97213-0248. All rights reserved. Used with permission.
5 Text: © 1992, GIA Publications, Inc. Harm.: © 1987, GIA Publications, Inc.
6 Music: © 1986, GIA Publications, Inc.
7 Music: © 1986, GIA Publications, Inc.
8 © 1986, GIA Publications, Inc.
10 Text: © William G. Storey. Acc.: © 1975, GIA Publications, Inc.
11 © 1979, GIA Publications, Inc.
13 Text: © 2004, GIA Publications, Inc. Music: © 1979, 1988, GIA Publications, Inc.
14 Harm.: © 1986, GIA Publications, Inc.
15 Music: © 1980, 1993, World Library Publications, a division of J.S. Paluch Company, Inc. Schiller Park, IL 60176. All rights reserved. Used by permission.
16 © 1986, GIA Publications, Inc.
17 Text: © 1989, GIA Publications, Inc., refrain trans. © 1969, ICEL. Music: © 1989, GIA Publications, Inc.
18 Text: © 1993, GIA Publications, Inc.; refrain trans., © 1969, ICEL. Music: © 1993, GIA Publications, Inc.
19 Text: © 1988, GIA Publications, Inc.; refrain III trans. © 1969, ICEL. Music: © 1988, 1994, GIA Publications, Inc.
20 Text: © 1983, GIA Publications, Inc.; refrain trans. © 1969, ICEL. © 1983, GIA Publications, Inc.
21 Text: © 2003, GIA Publications, Inc. English refrain trans. © 1969, ICEL; Spanish refrain trans., © admin. by Obra Nacional de la Buena Prensa. Music: © 2003, GIA Publications, Inc.
22 Text: © 1983, GIA Publications, Inc.; refrain trans. © 1969, ICEL. Music: © 1983, GIA Publications, Inc.
23 © 1986, GIA Publications, Inc.
24 Antiphons: © 1963, The Grail, GIA Publications, Inc., agent. Psalm tone: © 1975, GIA Publications, Inc. Gelineau Tone: © 1963, 1993, The Grail, GIA Publications, Inc., agent
25 Text: © 1993, GIA Publications, Inc.; refrain I trans. © 1969, ICEL. Music: © 1993, GIA Publications, Inc.
26 Text: © 1982, GIA Publications, Inc.; refrain trans. © 1969, ICEL. Music: © 1982, GIA Publications, Inc.
27 Text: © 1985, GIA Publications, Inc.; refrain trans. © 1969, ICEL. Music: © 1985, GIA Publications, Inc.
28 Text: © 2000, GIA Publications, Inc.; refrain trans. © 1969, ICEL. Music: © 2000, GIA Publications, Inc.
29 © 1983, GIA Publications, Inc.
30 Text: Verses, © 1963, 1993, The Grail, GIA Publications, Inc., agent; refrain, © 1985, Paul Inwood. Music: © 1985, Paul Inwood. Published by OCP Publicaitons. P.O. Box 13248, Portland, OR 97213-0248. All rights reserved. Used with permission.
31 © 1993, GIA Publications, Inc.
32 Text: © 1987, 1994, GIA Publications, Inc.; refrain trans. © 1969, ICEL. Music: © 1987, 1994, GIA Publications, Inc.
33 © 1978, 1991, John B. Foley, SJ, and OCP Publications. P.O. Box 13248, Portland, OR 97213-0248. All rights reserved. Used with permission.
34 Text: © 1980, GIA Publications, Inc.; refrain trans. © 1969, ICEL. Music: © 1980, GIA Publications, Inc.
35 Verse text and music: © 1971, 1991, North American Liturgy Resources. Published by OCP Publications. P.O. Box 13248, Portland, OR 97213-0248. All rights reserved. Used with permission. Refrain trans. © 1969, ICEL.
36 Text: © 1983, GIA Publications, Inc.; refrain trans. © 1969, ICEL. Music: © 1983, GIA Publications, Inc.
37 Text: © 1987, GIA Publications, Inc.; refrain I trans. © 1969, ICEL. Music: © 1987, GIA Publications, Inc.
38 Text: © 2003, GIA Publications, Inc.; English refrain trans. © 1969, ICEL; Spanish refrain trans. © 1970, Conferencia Episcopal Española. Music: © 2003, GIA Publications, Inc.
39 Text: © 1963, 1993, The Grail, GIA Publications, Inc., agent; refrain trans. © 1969, ICEL. Music: © 1998, GIA Publications, Inc.
40 © 1963, 1993, The Grail, GIA Publications, Inc., agent. Psalm tone: © Gethsemani Abbey
41 Text: © 1983, GIA Publications, Inc.; refrain trans. © 1969, ICEL. Music: © 1983, GIA Publications, Inc.
42 © 1982, GIA Publications, Inc.
43 Text: Verse adapt., © 1970, Confraternity of Christian Doctrine, Washington, DC. Refrain text and music: © 1987, GIA Publications, Inc.
44 Antiphon I text: © 1969, 1981, ICEL. Antiphon I music: © 1975, GIA Publications, Inc. Antiphon II: © 1979, GIA Publications, Inc. Psalm tone: © 1986, GIA Publications, Inc. Gelineau tone and psalm text: © 1963, The Grail, GIA Publications, Inc., agent
45 © 1982, GIA Publications, Inc.
46 © 1987, 1994, GIA Publications, Inc.
47 © 1982, GIA Publications, Inc.
48 Text: © 1983, GIA Publications, Inc.; refrain trans © 1969, ICEL. Music: © 1983, GIA Publications, Inc.
49 Verse text: © 1963, 1993, The Grail, GIA Publications, Inc., agent. Alt. text: © 1988, 1993, GIA Publications, Inc., refrain trans. © 1969, ICEL. Music: © 1988, 1994, GIA Publications, Inc.
50 © 1980, GIA Publications, Inc.
51 © 1983, 1994, GIA Publications, Inc.
52 Verse tr.: © 1970, Confraternity of Christian Doctrine, Washington, DC.; refrain tr. © 1969, ICEL. Music: © 1976, GIA Publications, Inc.
53 © 1998, GIA Publications, Inc.
54 Text: © 1989, GIA Publications, Inc., refrain trans. © 1969, ICEL. Music: © 1989, 1994, GIA Publications, Inc.
55 © 1983, 1994, GIA Publications, Inc.
56 © 1983, GIA Publications, Inc.
57 Text and Gelineau tone: © 1963, 1993, The Grail, GIA Publications, Inc., agent. Music: © 1986, GIA Publications, Inc.
58 © 1993, GIA Publications, Inc.
59 Text: © 1983, GIA Publications, Inc.; refrain trans. © 1969, ICEL. Music: © 1983, GIA Publications, Inc.
60 Text: © 1985, GIA Publications, Inc.; refrain trans. © 1969, ICEL. Music: © 1985, GIA Publications, Inc.
61 Text: © 2003, GIA Publications, Inc.; Spanish refrain trans. © 1970, Conferencia Episcopal Española. Music: © 2003, GIA Publications, Inc.
62 Text: © 1987, GIA Publications, Inc.; refrain II trans. © 1969, ICEL. Music: © 1987, GIA Publications, Inc.
63 © 1983, GIA Publications, Inc.

Acknowledgments/*continued*

64 Text: © Confraternity of Christian Doctrine, Wash-
ıgton DC. Refrain trans. © 1969, ICEL. Music: Pub-
shed by Cooperative Ministries, Inc., Exclusive agent:
CP Publications. P.O. Box 13248, Portland, OR 97213-
248. All rights reserved. Used with permission.
65 Text: © 1983, GIA Publications, Inc.; refrain trans.
) 1969, ICEL. Music: © 1983, GIA Publications, Inc.
66 Text: © 1963, 1993, The Grail, GIA Publications,
ıc., agent. Refrain text: © 1979, GIA Publications, Inc.
lusic: © 1979, GIA Publications, Inc.
67 © 2001, GIA Publications, Inc.
68 Text: © 1987, GIA Publications, Inc.; refrain trans.
) 1969, ICEL. Music: © 1987, GIA Publications, Inc.
69 © 1988, GIA Publications, Inc.
70 © 1987, 1993, GIA Publications, Inc.
71 Text: © 1983, GIA Publications, Inc.; refrain trans.
) 1969, ICEL. Music: © 1983, GIA Publications, Inc.
72 Text: © 1985, GIA Publications, Inc.; refrain trans.
) 1969, ICEL. Music: © 1985, GIA Publications, Inc.
73 © 1987, GIA Publications, Inc.
74 © 1989, GIA Publications, Inc.
75 © 1990, GIA Publications, Inc.
76 © 1983, GIA Publications, Inc.
77 © 1987, GIA Publications, Inc.
78 © 1964, World Library Publications, a division of
S. Paluch Company, Inc. Schiller Park, IL 60176. All
ghts reserved. Used by permission.
79 © 1997, GIA Publications, Inc.
80 © 1992, GIA Publications, Inc.
81 © 1988, 1994, GIA Publications, Inc.
82 Text: © 1970, Confraternity of Christian Doctrine,
Vashington, DC. Music: © 2002, World Library Publica-
ons, a division of J.S. Paluch Company, Inc. Schiller
ark, IL 60176. All rights reserved. Used by permission.
83 © 1989, GIA Publications, Inc.
84 © 1980, GIA Publications, Inc.
85 Text: © 1995, GIA Publications, Inc. Music: ©
003, GIA Publications, Inc.
95 Text: © 1985, ICEL. Music: © 1991, Morning Star
lusic Publishers, St. Louis, MO
100 Text: © 1969, ICEL
101 Verse text: © 1963, The Grail, GIA Publications,
ıc., agent. Music: © The Antilles Episcopal Conference.
efrain music: © 1984, Anthony E. Jackson
112 Verse text: © 1963, The Grail, GIA Publications,
ıc., agent
132 Text tr.: © 1969, James Quinn, SJ. Used by per-
ission of Selah Publishing Co., Inc., Pittsburgh, PA
5227. North American agent. www.selahpub.com. All
ghts reserved.
161 Music: © 1970, World Library Publications, a
ivision of J.S. Paluch Company, Inc. Schiller Park, IL
0176. All rights reserved. Used by permission.
162 Music: © 1970, World Library Publications, a
ivision of J.S. Paluch Company, Inc. Schiller Park, IL
0176. All rights reserved. Used by permission.
175 Text: © 1982, Jubilate Hymns, Ltd. (Admin. by
lope Publishing Co., Carol Stream, IL 60188). All rights
served. Used by permission.
252 Music: © 1978, John B. Foley and OCP Publica-
ons. P.O. Box 13248, Portland, OR 97213-0248. All
ghts reserved. Used with permission.
253 Music: © 1979, 1988, Les Presses de Taizé, GIA
ublications, Inc., agent
261 Arr.: © 1990, Iona Community, GIA Publications,
ıc., agent
263 Music: © 1984, Les Presses de Taizé, GIA Publi-
ıtions, Inc., agent
264 Music: © 1998, Les Presses de Taizé, GIA Publi-
ıtions, Inc., agent

265 Music: © 1998, Les Presses de Taizé, GIA Publications, Inc., agent
266 © 1985, Fintan O'Carroll and Christopher Walker. Published by OCP Publications. P.O. Box 13248, Portland, OR 97213-0248. All rights reserved. Used with permission.
267 Tone for verses: © 1978, *Lutheran Book of Worship.* Administered by Augsburg Fortress. Used by permission.
273 Music: © 1995, Veritas Publications/Liam Lawton, GIA Publications, Inc., agent
278 Music: © 1980, Les Presses de Taizé, GIA Publications, Inc., agent
279 Music: © 1998, Les Presses de Taizé, GIA Publications, Inc., agent
280 Music: © 1998, Les Presses de Taizé, GIA Publications, Inc., agent
283A-D Text: © 2004, Gabe Huck. Music: © 2004, GIA Publications, Inc.
285 © 1994, World Library Publications, a division of J.S. Paluch Company, Inc. Schiller Park, IL 60176. All rights reserved. Used by permission.
293 Music adapt.: ©1980, Church Pension Fund. Used by permission of Church Publishing Incorporated, New York.
313 Music: © 1973, Robert J. Duffortd, SJ and Daniel L. Schutte. Administered by OCP Publications. P.O. Box 13248, Portland, OR 97213-0248. All rights reserved. Used with permission.
314 Music: © 1973, Robert J. Dufford, SJ and Daniel L. Schutte. Administered by OCP Publications. P.O. Box 13248, Portland, OR 97213-0248. All rights reserved. Used with permission.
315 Music: © 1973, Robert J. Duffortd, SJ and Daniel L. Schutte. Administered by OCP Publications. P.O. Box 13248, Portland, OR 97213-0248. All rights reserved. Used with permission.
323 Acc.: © 1975, GIA Publications, Inc.
324 © 1999, GIA Publications, Inc.
325 © 1990, GIA Publications, Inc.
326 © 2001, GIA Publications, Inc.
327 Text: © 1982, Jubilate Hymns, Ltd. (Administered by Hope Publishing Co., Carol Stream, IL 60188). All rights reserved. Used by permission.
328 © 1990, Paul Inwood. Published and distributed by World Library Publications, a division of J.S. Paluch Company, Inc. Schiller Park, IL 60176. All rights reserved. Used by permission.
329 Text: © 1969, 1981, ICEL. © 1988, GIA Publications, Inc.
330 © 1984, Les Presses de Taizé, GIA Publications, Inc., agent
332 © 1976, Robert J. Dufford, SJ, and OCP Publications. P.O. Box 13248, Portland, OR 97213-0248. All rights reserved. Used with permission.
333 Harm: © 1958, Basilian Fathers, assigned to Ralph Jusko Publications, Inc.
334 Text: Verse tr. © 1985, The Church Pension Fund. Used by permission of Church Publishing Incorporated, New York. Refrain: © 2003, GIA Publications, Inc.
335 © 1996, GIA Publications, Inc.
336 © 1982, GIA Publications, Inc.
337 Text: © David Higham Assoc. Ltd. Harm.: from *The Oxford Book of Carols,* © Oxford University Press
338 © 1995, GIA Publications, Inc.
339 Text: © 1992, GIA Publications, Inc. Tune: © 2000, GIA Publications, Inc.
340 © 1984, Les Presses de Taizé, GIA Publications, Inc., agent
341 Text adapt. and tune: © 2001, Iona Communtiy, GIA Publications, Inc., agent

Acknowledgments/*continued*

342 © 1993, Tom Booth. Published by OCP Publications. P.O. Box 13248, Portland, OR 97213-0248. All rights reserved. Used with permission.

343 © 1981, 1982, Jan Michael Joncas Trust. Published by OCP Publications, exclusive agent. P.O. Box 13248, Portland, OR 97213-0248. All rights reserved. Used with permission.

346 © 1983, GIA Publications, Inc.

347 Arr.: © 1994, GIA Publications, Inc.

349 © 1988, GIA Publications, Inc.

350 Text and tune: © 1971, The United Church Press. Reprinted from *A New Song 3.* Used by permission. Acc.: © 1987, GIA Publications, Inc.

351 © 1983, GIA Publications, Inc.

352 © 2000, GIA Publications, Inc.

354 © 1987, GIA Publications, Inc.

355 Text: © 1994, 1997, Hope Publishing Co., Carol Stream, IL 60188. All rights reserved. Used by permission. Tune: © 2003, GIA Publications, Inc.

358 © 2002, GIA Publications, Inc.

360 © 1992, GIA Publications, Inc.

362 © 1996, GIA Publications, Inc.

363 Text: By permission of Mrs. John W. Work III. Harm: © 1995, GIA Publications, Inc.

364 Tune tr. and arr.: © 1990, Iona Community, GIA Publications, Inc., agent

365 Harm.: © 1994, GIA Publications, Inc.

368 © 1991, GIA Publications, Inc.

370 Text: © 1980, Hope Publishing Co., Carol Stream, IL 60188. All rights reserved. Used by permission. Tune: © 1985, GIA Publications, Inc.

372 © 1984, GIA Publications, Inc.

374 Acc.: © 1985, GIA Publications, Inc.

376 Text: © 1995, GIA Publications, Inc. Tune: © 2003, GIA Publications, Inc.

377 Harm.: © Bristol Churches Housing Assoc. Ltd.

378 Text and tune: © 1945, Boosey and Co., Ltd.; Copyright Renewed. Reprinted by permission of Boosey & Hawkes, Inc. Acc.: © 1993, GIA Publications, Inc.

380 Harm.: © 1957, Novello and Co. Ltd

381 © 1987, Iona Community, GIA Publications Inc., agent

385 © 1978, Damean Music. Distributed by GIA Publications, Inc.

386 Text: © 2002, GIA Publications, Inc. Harm.: © 1978, *Lutheran Book of Worship.* Administered by Augsburg Fortress. Used by permission.

388 Harm.: © 1961, Oxford University Press

390 Text: © 1984, Hope Publishing Co., Carol Stream, IL 60188. All rights reserved. Used by permission.

391 Verse text and tune: © 2003, GIA Publications, Inc. Refrain text: © 1973, ICEL

392 Text: © 1989, Hope Publishing Co., Carol Stream, IL 60188. All rights reserved. Used by permission. Tune: © 1991, GIA Publications, Inc.

393 © 1991, Les Presses de Taizé, GIA Publications, Inc., agent

394 Harm.: © 1986, GIA Publications, Inc.

395 © 1975, 1996, Robert F. O'Connor, SJ, and OCP Publications. P.O. Box 13248, Portland, OR 97213-0248. All rights reserved. Used with permission.

396 © 1996, GIA Publications, Inc.

398 © 1993, GIA Publications, Inc.

399 © 1990, GIA Publications, Inc.

400 Tune: © 1984, GIA Publications, Inc.

401 © 1984, GIA Publications, Inc.

402 Text: © 1994, World Library Publications, a division of J.S. Paluch Company, Inc. Schiller Park, IL 60176. All rights reserved. Used by permission.

403 © 1981, 1994, Robert F. O'Connor, and OCP Publications. P.O. Box 13248, Portland, OR 97213-0248 All rights reserved. Used with permission.

404 Text: © 1993, Oxford University Press. Tune: © 1995, GIA Publications, Inc.

405 © 1972, 1980, The Benedictine Foundation of th State of Vermont, Inc.

406 Harm.: © 1975, GIA Publications, Inc.

407 Text tr.: © Peter J. Scagnelli

408 © 2003, GIA Publications, Inc.

409 © 2003, GIA Publications, Inc.

410 © 1990, 1991, GIA Publications, Inc.

412 Text: © 1963, The Grail, GIA Publications, Inc., agent. Acc.: © 1986, GIA Publications, Inc.

413 Text tr.: © 1971, Faber Music, Ltd. Harm.: © 1986, GIA Publications, Inc.

414 © 1984, North American Liturgy Resources. Published by OCP Publications. P.O. Box 13248, Portland, O 97213-0248. All rights reserved. Used with permission.

415 © 2003, GIA Publications, Inc.

417 © 2001, GIA Publications, Inc.

418 © 2001, GIA Publications, Inc.

419 © 1987, GIA Publications, Inc.

420 Tune: © 1999, GIA Publications, Inc.

422 © 1981, Les Presses de Taizé, GIA Publications, Inc., agent

423 © 1997, GIA Publications, Inc.

424 Text: Verses 3-9, © 1991, GIA Publications, Inc. Harm.: © 1987, GIA Publications, Inc.

425 © 2001, GIA Publications, Inc.

426 Text tr.: © 1969, James Quinn, SJ. Used by permission of Selah Publishing, Inc., Pittsburgh, PA 15227, North American agent. www.selahpub.com. All rights reserved. Acc.: © 1964, GIA Publications, Inc.

427 © 2001, GIA Publications, Inc.

428 Text: © 2000, GIA Publications, Inc.

429 © 1969, and arr. © 1982, Hope Publishing Co., Carol Stream, IL 60188. All rights reserved. Used by pe mission.

430 © 1979, Les Presses de Taizé, GIA Publications, Inc., agent

431 © 1998, GIA Publications, Inc.

432 © 1997, GIA Publications, Inc.

433 © 1984, Les Presses de Taizé, GIA Publications, Inc., agent

434 © 1988, GIA Publications, Inc.

436 © 1997, GIA Publications, Inc.

437 © 1976, Daniel L. Schutte and OCP Publications P.O. Box 13248, Portland, OR 97213-0248. All rights reserved. Used with permission.

438 Harm.: © 1987, GIA Publications, Inc.

440 Harm.: © 1975, Romda Ltd.

441 © 1996, GIA Publications, Inc.

443 © 1972, Ediciones Musical PAX, U.S. agent: OCP Publications; trans. © 1988, OCP Publications. P.C Box 13248, Portland, OR 97213-0248. All rights reserved. Used with permission.

444 Text tr.: © 1983, Peter J. Scagnelli. Acc.: © 197 GIA Publications, Inc.

445 © 1995, GIA Publications, Inc.

446 Acc.: © 1975, GIA Publications, Inc.

447 © 1986, GIA Publications, Inc.

449 Text: © 1986, Hope Publishing Co., Carol Strea IL 60188. All rights reserved. Used by permission. Tune © 1991, GIA Publications, Inc.

450 © 1993, GIA Publications, Inc.

451 Text: From AN AFRICAN PRAYER BOOK selected by Desmond Tutu, © 1995, Desmond Tutu. Us by permission of Doubleday, a division of Random House, Inc. Tune: © 1996, Iona Community, GIA Publications, Inc., agent

452 © 1975, 1979, Robert J. Dufford, SJ and OCP ublications. P.O. Box 13248, Portland, OR 97213-0248. ll rights reserved. Used with permission.

453 Text: © 1975, 1995, Hope Publishing Co., Carol tream, IL 60188. All rights reserved. Used by permis-ion. Tune: © 2003, GIA Publications, Inc.

455 © 1984, Les Presses de Taizé, GIA Publications, ıc., agent

456 Text: from *Oxford Book of Carols,* © Oxford Uni-ersity Press. Acc.: © 1987, GIA Publications, Inc.

458 Text: © 1978, *Lutheran Book of Worship.* Admin-istered by Augsburg Fortress. Used by permission. Tune:) 1975, 1988, Richard Hillert

462 Text and tune: © 1973, Word of God Music. Administered by THE COPYRIGHT COMPANY IASHVILLE, TN) All rights reserved. International opyright Secured. Used by permission. Descant harm.:) 1979, CELEBRATION c/o THE COPYRIGHT COM-ANY, NASHVILLE, TN) All rights reserved. Interna-onal Copyright Secured. Used by permission.

464 Text: © 1991, 2003, GIA Publications, Inc. Tune:) 2003, GIA Publications, Inc.

465 © 1988, Iona Community, GIA Publications, Inc., gent

466 Text: © 1978, Hope Publishing Co. Tune: © 942, 1970, Hope Publishing Co., Carol Stream, IL 0188. All rights reserved. Used by permission.

467 Text tr.: © 1978, *Lutheran Book of Worship.* dministered by Augsburg Fortress. Used by permission. arm.: from *The English Hymnal,* © Oxford University ress

469 Text: © 1991, GIA Publications, Inc. Tune: from *he English Hymnal,* © Oxford University Press

470 Text tr.: © 1983, Peter J. Scagnelli. Acc.: © terkerkelijke Stichting voor het Kerklied Den Haag

471 Tune: from *The English Hymnal,* © Oxford Uni-rsity Press

472 Harm.: © 1986, GIA Publications, Inc.

473 © 1997, GIA Publications, Inc.

474 Acc.: © 1975, GIA Publications, Inc.

475 Text tr.: © 1971, John W. Grant. Acc.: © 1975, IA Publications, Inc.

476 © 1981, 1982, 1987, GIA Publications, Inc.

477 © 1989, GIA Publications, Inc.

478 © 1979, Les Presses de Taizé, GIA Publications, c. agent

479 © 1998, Les Presses de Taizé, GIA Publications, c., agent.

480 © 2002, GIA Publications, Inc.

481 © 1987, GIA Publications, Inc.

482 Text: © Timothy Wright. Arr.: © 2000, GIA Pub-ations, Inc.

484 © 2002, 2003, GIA Publications, Inc.

485 Text tr.: © 1959, The Liturgical Press. Harm.: © 58, Ralph Jusko Publications, Inc.

487 Text: © 1986, Hope Publishing Co., Carol Stream, 60188. All rights reserved. Used by permission. Tune: 1993, GIA Publications, Inc.

488 Text: © 1989, Hope Publishing Co., Carol Stream, 60188. All rights reserved. Used by permission. Arr.: 1991, GIA Publications, Inc.

490 Harm.: © 1975, GIA Publications, Inc.

491 Text: from *Enlarged Songs of Praise,* © Oxford iiversity Press

492 Text: © 1941, Irene C. Mueller. Harm.: © 1986, A Publications, Inc.

494 Text: © 1966, 1982, Willard F. Jabusch. Adminis-ed by OCP Publications. P.O. Box 13248, Portland, 97213-0248. All rights reserved. Used with permis-n.

495 © 1980, GIA Publications, Inc.

496 © 1953, Stuart K. Hine. Assigned to Manna Music, Inc., 35255 Brooten Road, Pacific City, OR 97135. Renewed 1981. All Rights Reserved. Used by Per-mission. (ASCAP)

497 © 1985, GIA Publications, Inc.

498 © 1989, GIA Publications, Inc.

499 © 1991, GIA Publications, Inc.

500 © 1993, World Library Publications, a division of J.S. Paluch Company, Inc. Schiller Park, IL 60176. All rights reserved. Used by permission.

501 Arr.: © 1997, Iona Community, GIA Publications, Inc., agent.

502 © 1978, John B. Foley, SJ, and OCP Publications. P.O. Box 13248, Portland, OR 97213-0248. All rights reserved. Used with permission.

503 © 2002, GIA Publications, Inc.

504 © 1979, OCP Publications. P.O. Box 13248, Port-land, OR 97213-0248. All rights reserved. Used with per-mission.

505 © 1991, 1992, Jaime Cortez. Published by OCP Publications. P.O. Box 13248, Portland, OR 97213-0248. All rights reserved. Used with permission.

506 © 2002, 2003, GIA Publications, Inc.

507 Text: © 1996, Hope Publishing Co., Carol Stream, IL 60188. All rights reserved. Used by permission. Tune: © 2001, GIA Publications, Inc.

508 © 1992, GIA Publications, Inc.

509 © 1992, Bernadette Farrell. Published by OCP Publications. P.O. Box 13248, Portland, OR 97213-0248. All rights reserved. Used with permission.

510 © 1998, Les Presses de Taizé, GIA Publications, Inc., agent

511 © 1985, GIA Publications, Inc.

512 © 1993, 2000, Bernadette Farrell. Published by OCP Publications. P.O. Box 13248, Portland, OR 97213-0248. All rights reserved. Used with permission.

513 Text and Tune: © 1970, 1975, CELEBRATION (Administered by THE COPYRIGHT COMPANY, NASHVILLE, TN) All Rights Reserved. International Copyright Secured. Used By Permission. Acc.: © 1987, GIA Publications, Inc.

514 Harm.: © 1992, Horace Clarence Boyer

515 © 1966, Vernacular Hymns Publishing Co.

516 © 1984, Utryck, Walton Music Corp.

517 © 1986, Bernadette Farrell. Published by OCP Publications. P.O. Box 13248, Portland, OR 97213-0248. All rights reserved. Used with permission.

518 Text: © 1966, The Hymn Society. (Admin. by Hope Publishing Co., Carol Stream, IL 60188). All rights reserved. Used by permission.

521 © 2002, GIA Publications, Inc.

522 © 1979, Les Presses de Taizé, GIA Publications, Inc., agent

523 Music: from *The English Hymnal,* © Oxford Uni-versity Press.

524 © 1999, GIA Publications, Inc.

525 Text: © 1991, GIA Publications, Inc. Harm.: © 1986, GIA Publications, Inc.

526 © 1981, Robert J. Dufford, SJ, and OCP Publica-tions. P.O. Box 13248, Portland, OR 97213-0248. All rights reserved. Used with permission.

527 © 1990, GIA Publications, Inc.

528 © 1980, Les Presses de Taizé, GIA Publications, Inc., agent

529 © 1984, Utryck, Walton Music Corp., agent

530 © 1998, Les Presses de Taizé, GIA Publications, Inc., agent

532 Text and tune: © 1981, Ernest Sands. Acc.: © 1986, Paul Inwood. Published by OCP Publications. P.O. Box 13248, Portland, OR 97213-0248. All rights reserved. Used with permission.

Acknowledgments/*continued*

533 © 1998, Les Presses de Taizé, GIA Publications, Inc., agent
534 © 2002, GIA Publications, Inc.
535 © 1979, Les Presses de Taizé, GIA Publications, Inc., agent
536 Descant: © 1953, Novello and Co. Ltd.
537 © 1976, Daniel L. Schutte and OCP Publications. P.O. Box 13248, Portland, OR 97213-0248. All rights reserved. Used with permission.
538 © 1983, 1987, GIA Publications, Inc.
539 Text: © 1972, Hope Publishing Co., Carol Stream, IL 60188. All rights reserved. Used by permission.
540 © 1978, Damean Music. Distributed by GIA Publications, Inc.
541 Text: © 1973, Hope Publishing Co. Tune: © 1973, Jubilate Hymns, Ltd. (Admin. by Hope Publishing Co., Carol Stream, IL 60188). All rights reserved. Used by permission.
542 Harm.: © 1986, GIA Publications, Inc.
543 © 1981, 1993, Roc O'Connor, SJ, and OCP Publications. P.O. Box 13248, Portland, OR 97213-0248. All rights reserved. Used with permission.
544 © 1972, Daniel L. Schutte. Published by OCP Publications. P.O. Box 13248, Portland, OR 97213-0248. All rights reserved. Used with permission.
546 © 1986, 1991, Les Presses de Taizé, GIA Publications, Inc., agent
547 Text: © 1940, The Church Pension Fund. Used by permission of Church Publishing Incorporated, New York.
550 © 1982, 1991, Les Presses de Taizé, GIA Publications, Inc., agent
551 Text: © 1939, 1966, E. C. Schirmer Music Co., Boston, MA. Harm.: © The Royal School of Church Music
552 Harm.: © 1986, GIA Publications, Inc.
553 © 1998, GIA Publications, Inc.
554 © 1995, Veritas Publications/Liam Lawton, GIA Publications, Inc., agent
555 © 1953, Doris M. Akers. All rights administered by Unichappell Music, Inc. International Copyright Secured. All rights reserved.
556 © 2000, GIA Publications, Inc.
557 © 2003, GIA Publications, Inc.
558 © 1989, Iona Community, GIA Publications, Inc., agent
559 © 1987, GIA Publications, Inc.
560 Text: from *Enlarged Songs of Praise,* by permission of Oxford University Press. Harm.: © 1975, Hope Publishing Co., Carol Stream, IL 60188. All rights reserved. Used by permission.
561 © 2002, GIA Publications, Inc.
562 © 2003, GIA Publications, Inc.
563 Text: © 1987, Oxford University Press. Tune: © 2003, GIA Publications, Inc.
564 © 1964 (renewed), Appleseed Music, Inc.
565 © 1997, GIA Publications, Inc.
566 © 1982, Les Presses de Taizé, GIA Publications, Inc., agent
567 Arr.: © 2003, GIA Publications, Inc.
568 Verse text and tune: © 1998, GIA Publications, Inc.
569 © 1988, 1999, Jesse Manibusan. Published by OCP Publications. P.O. Box 13248, Portland, OR 97213-0248. All rights reserved. Used with permission.
570 Text and harm.: © 2003, GIA Publications, Inc.
571 Text: © 2002, GIA Publications, Inc. Tune: © 2003, GIA Publications, Inc.
572 Text: © 1993, Hope Publishing Co., Carol Stream, IL 60188. All rights reserved. Used by permission. Tune: © 2003, GIA Publications, Inc.
573 © 1996, World Library Publications, a division o J.S. Paluch Company, Inc. Schiller Park, IL 60176. All rights reserved. Used by permission.
574 Text: © 1996, Oxford University Press. Tune: © 1998, GIA Publications, Inc
575 Text: © 1992, GIA Publications, Inc. Tune: © 2003, GIA Publications, Inc.
576 © 1998, Les Presses de Taizé, GIA Publications, Inc., agent
577 Text and tune adapt.: © 1997, GIA Publications, Inc.
578 © 1980, GIA Publications, Inc.
580 Text: Verses, © 1963, 1993, The Grail, GIA Publications, Inc., agent; refrain, © 1985, Paul Inwood. Tun © 1985, Paul Inwood. Published by OCP Publications. P.O. Box 13248, Portland, OR 97213-0248. All rights reserved. Used with permission.
581 © 1989, GIA Publications, Inc.
582 © 1976 by John B. Foley, SJ, and OCP Publications. P.O. Box 13248, Portland, OR 97213-0248. All rights reserved. Used with permission.
583 Tune: © 1984, GIA Publications, Inc.
584 © 1993, World Library Publications, a division c J.S. Paluch Company, Inc. Schiller Park, IL 60176. All rights reserved. Used by permission.
585 © 1976, 1979, Daniel L. Schutte and OCP Publications. P.O. Box 13248, Portland, OR 97213-0248. All rights reserved. Used with permission.
586 Acc.: © 1993, GIA Publications, Inc.
587 Harm.: © 1975, GIA Publications, Inc.
589 © 1994, GIA Publications, Inc.
590 © 1971, Daniel L. Schutte. Published by OCP Publications. P.O. Box 13248, Portland, OR 97213-024 All rights reserved. Used with permission.
591 © 1976, John B. Foley, SJ and OCP Publication P.O. Box 13248, Portland, OR 97213-0248. All rights reserved. Used with permission.
592 © 1980, Savgos Music, Inc. Administered by Malaco Music Group. P.O. Box 9287, Jackson, MS 39206
593 © 1979, OCP Publications. P.O. Box 13248, Por land, OR 97213-0248. All rights reserved. Used with pe mission.
594 Text tr.: © 1978, *Lutheran Book of Worship.* Administered by Augsburg Fortress. Used by permissio
595 © 1975, Daniel L. Schutte and OCP Publication P.O. Box 13248, Portland, OR 97213-0248. All rights reserved. Used with permission.
596 © 1975, 1978, Robert J. Dufford, SJ, and OCP Publications. P.O. Box 13248, Portland, OR 97213-024 All rights reserved. Used with permission.
597 © 1969, 1979, Damean Music. Distributed by GIA Publications, Inc.
598 Harm.: © 1988, GIA Publications, Inc.
599 © 1979, OCP Publications. P.O. Box 13248, Po land, OR 97213-0248. All rights reserved. Used with pe mission.
600 © 1972, Maranatha! Music and CCCM Music (Administered by THE COPYRIGHT COMPANY, NASHVILLE, TN) All rights reserved. International Copyright Secured. Used By Permission.
601 Text tr.: © 1975, 1986, GIA Publications, Inc. Acc.: © 1986, GIA Publications, Inc.
602 © 1969, Concordia Publishing House. Acc.: © 1975, GIA Publications, Inc.
604 Text: © 1992, GIA Publications, Inc.
605 © 2001, GIA Publications, Inc.
606 © Schaff Music Publishing
607 © 1988, GIA Publications, Inc.
608 © 1987, GIA Publications, Inc.

Acknowledgments/*continued*

609 © 2001, GIA Publications, Inc.
610 © 1960, World Library Publications, a division of .S. Paluch Company, Inc. Schiller Park, IL 60176. All ights reserved. Used by permission.
611 © 1992, 1994, World Library Publications, a divi- ion of J.S. Paluch Company, Inc. Schiller Park, IL 0176. All rights reserved. Used by permission.
612 Text: © 1985, Hope Publishing Co., Carol Stream, L 60188. All rights reserved. Used by permission. Tune:) 1988, GIA Publications, Inc.
614 Harm.: from *Cantate Domino,* © 1980, World 'ouncil of Churches
615 © 1995, GIA Publications, Inc.
616 © 1982, GIA Publications, Inc.
617 Acc.: © 2003, GIA Publications, Inc.
618 Text and acc.: © 2003, GIA Publications, Inc.
619 © 1997, GIA Publications, Inc.
620 © 1993, GIA Publications, Inc.
621 © 2000, GIA Publications, Inc.
622 Harm.: from *The English Hymnal,* © Oxford Uni- ersity Press
623 © 1998, GIA Publications, Inc.
624 © 1992, GIA Publications, Inc.
625 © 2003, GIA Publications, Inc.
626 © 1986, 1991, Les Presses de Taizé, GIA Publica- ions, Inc., agent
627 © 1991, GIA Publications, Inc.
628 © 1992, GIA Publications, Inc.
629 © 2000, GIA Publications, Inc.
630 Text: © 1991, GIA Publications, Inc. Tune: © 993, GIA Publications, Inc.
631 Harm.: © The Trustees of Downside Abbey, Bath A3 4RH, UK
633 © 1989, GIA Publications, Inc.
634 Text and tune: © 1984, Bob Hurd. Harm.: © 984, OCP Publications. Published by OCP Publications. .O. Box 13248, Portland, OR 97213-0248. All rights eserved. Used with permission.
635 Text tr.: © 2002, The Iona Community, GIA Pub- cations, Inc., agent
636 © 1985, GIA Publications, Inc.
637 © 2001, Les Presses de Taizé, GIA Publications, nc., agent
638 © 1999, GIA Publications, Inc.
639 Text: © Mrs. Olwen Scott
640 © 1986, GIA Publications, Inc.
641 Text: © 1995, 2003, GIA Publications, Inc.
643 Text: © 1992, GIA Publications, Inc. Harm.: © 985, GIA Publications, Inc.
644 Text: © 1991, Sisters of St. Benedict. Published y OCP Publications. P.O. Box 13248, Portland, OR 7213-0248. All rights reserved. Used with permission.
645 © 1994, Jaime Cortez. Published by OCP Publica- ions. P.O. Box 13248, Portland, OR 97213-0248. All ights reserved. Used with permission.
646 Text: © Christian Conference of Asia
647 © 2000, GIA Publications, Inc.
648 © 2003, Les Presses de Taizé, GIA Publications, nc., agent
649 © 1996, GIA Publications, Inc.
650 Text: Vss. 2-4, © 1983, Abingdon Press. English r.: © 2004, Abingdon Press (Administered by THE 'OPYRIGHT COMPANY, Nashville, TN) All Rights eserved. International Copyright Secured. Used By Per- nission. Arr.: © 2004, GIA Publications, Inc.
651 © 2002, Mairi Munro and Philip Jakob
652 © 1986, North American Liturgy Resources. Pub- shed by OCP Publications. P.O. Box 13248, Portland, R 97213-0248. All rights reserved. Used with permis- ion.
653 © 1998, 1999, World Library Publications, a divi- sion of J.S. Paluch Company, Inc. Schiller Park, IL 60176. All rights reserved. Used by permission.
654 © 1986, 1988, Bernadette Farrell. Published by OCP Publications. P.O. Box 13248, Portland, OR 97213-0248. All rights reserved. Used with permission.
655 © 1989, The Iona Community, GIA Publications, agent
656 © 1966, 1982, Willard F. Jabusch. Administered by OCP Publications. P.O. Box 13248, Portland, OR 97213-0248. All rights reserved. Used with permission.
657 Acc.: © 1984, Margaret Mealy
658 © 1965, World Library Publications, a division of J.S. Paluch Company, Inc. Schiller Park, IL 60176. All rights reserved. Used by permission.
660 Text: © 1997, GIA Publications, Inc. Harm.: © 1938, J. Fisher and Bro.
661 © 1977, Scripture in Song, division of Integrity Music. (Administered by MARANATHA! MUSIC c/o THE COPYRIGHT COMPANY, NASHVILLE, TN). All rights reserved. International Copyright Secured. Used By Permission.
662 © 1981, Damean Music. Distributed by GIA Publications, Inc.
663 © 1981, Daniel L. Schutte and OCP Publications. P.O. Box 13248, Portland, OR 97213-0248. All rights reserved. Used with permission.
664 © 1997, 1998, Steve Agrisano and Thomas N. Tomaszek. Published by OCP Publications. P.O. Box 13248, Portland, OR 97213-0248. All rights reserved. Used with permission.
665 Text: © 1971, Hope Publishing Co., Carol Stream, IL 60188. All rights reserved. Used by permission. Arr.: © 1989, The Iona Community, GIA Publications, Inc., agent
666 Text: © 1964, Abingdon Press. (Administered by THE COPYRIGHT COMPANY, Nashville, TN) All Rights Reserved. International Copyright Secured. Used By Permission.
667 © 2003, GIA Publications, Inc.
668 Text: from *The English Hymnal,* © Oxford University Press
669 © 1990, Bernadette Farrell. Published by OCP Publications. P.O. Box 13248, Portland, OR 97213-0248. All rights reserved. Used with permission.
670 © 2003, GIA Publications, Inc.
671 © 1981, OCP Publications. P.O. Box 13248, Portland, OR 97213-0248. All rights reserved. Used with permission.
672 © 1993, Howard S. Olson
673 Arr.: © 1998, The Iona Community, GIA Publications, Inc., agent.
674 © 1984, Utryck, Walton Music Corp., agent
675 Text: © 1992, GIA Publications, Inc. Tune: © 2002, GIA Publications, Inc.
676 © 1993, GIA Publications, Inc.
677 © 1997, GIA Publications, Inc.
678 Text and tune: © 1979, Cesáreo Gabaráin y Ediciones Paulinas. All rights reserved. Sole U.S. Agent: OCP Publications. English text: © 1982, Willard Francis Jabusch. Administered by OCP Publications, P.O. Box 13248, Portland, OR 97213-0248. All rights reserved. Used with permission.
679 Text: © 1991, GIA Publications, Inc.
680 © 1988, GIA Publications, Inc.
681 © 1978, OCP Publications. P.O. Box 13248, Portland, OR 97213-0248. All rights reserved. Used with permission.
682 © 2003, GIA Publications, Inc.

Acknowledgments/*continued*

683 © 1997, Tom Booth. Published by OCP Publications. P.O. Box 13248, Portland, OR 97213-0248. All rights reserved. Used with permission.
684 Acc.: © 1994, GIA Publications, Inc.
685 © 1986, GIA Publications, Inc.
686 Text: © Herbert O'Driscoll. Tune: © 1998, GIA Publications, Inc.
687 Text and arr.: © 1987, Iona Community, GIA Publications, Inc., agent
688 © 2001, GIA Publications, Inc.
689 Text and harm.: © Stainer & Bell, Ltd., London, England. All rights reserved. (Admin. by Hope Publishing Co., Carol Stream, IL 60188). All rights reserved. Used by permission.
690 Harm.: © 1983, Hope Publishing Co., Carol Stream, IL 60188. All rights reserved. Used by permission.
691 © 2003, GIA Publications, Inc.
692 © 1945, The Iona Community, GIA Publications, Inc., agent
693 Text: © 1986, GIA Publications, Inc. Tune: © 1970, GIA Publications, Inc.
694 © 1983, GIA Publications, Inc.
695 © 1998, GIA Publications, Inc.
696 © 1983, GIA Publications, Inc.
697 © 1987, The Iona Community, GIA Publications, Inc., agent
698 © 1997, GIA Publications, Inc.
699 © 1983, Bernadette Farrell. Published by OCP Publications. P.O. Box 13248, Portland, OR 97213-0248. All rights reserved. Used with permission.
700 Text: © 1991, GIA Publications, Inc. Tune: © 2003, GIA Publications, Inc.
701 © 1981, Daniel L. Schutte and OCP Publications. P.O. Box 13248, Portland, OR 97213-0248. All rights reserved. Used with permission.
702 © 1990, GIA Publications, Inc.
703 Text: © 1992, GIA Publications, Inc. Tune: © 1994, GIA Publications, Inc.
704 Text: "Baptism By Fire" from *Incendiary Fellowship,* © 1967, David Elton Trueblood. Reprinted by permission of Harper & Row Publishers, Inc.
705 Text: © 1998, Hope Publishing Co., Carol Stream, IL 60188. All rights reserved. Used by permission. Tune: © 2001, GIA Publications, Inc.
706 Text: © 1994, GIA Publications, Inc. Harm.: from *The English Hymnal,* © Oxford University Press
707 © 1984, Utryck, Walton Music Corp., agent
708 Arr.: © 1991, Iona Community, GIA Publications, agent
709 © 1991, GIA Publications, Inc.
710 © 1988, GIA Publications, Inc.
711 Text and tune: TRO © 1960 (Renewed) 1963 (Renewed) Ludlow Music, Inc., New York, New York. International Copyright Secured. Made in U.S.A. All Rights Reserved Including Public Performance for Profit. Royalties derived from this composition are being contributed to the We Shall Overcome Fund and The Freedom Movement under the Trusteeship of the writers. Inspired by African American Gospel Singing, members of the Food and Tobacco Workers Union, Charleston, SC, and the southern Civil Rights Movement. Used by permission. Harm.: © 1981 by Abingdon Press.
712 Text: © 1968, Hope Publishing Co., Carol Stream, IL 60188. All rights reserved. Used by permission.
713 Text: © 1983 and music 1995, Hope Publishing Co., Carol Stream, IL 60188. All rights reserved. Used by permission.
714 © 2001, GIA Publications, Inc.
715 © 1992, 1994, GIA Publications, Inc.
716 © 1985, GIA Publications, Inc.
717 © 1958, 1986, The Hymn Society (Admin. by Hope Publishing Co., Carol Stream, IL 60188). All rights reserved. Used by permission.
718 Verse text and tune: © 1985, GIA Publications, Inc.
719 © 2002, GIA Publications, Inc.
720 © 1987, GIA Publications, Inc.
721 © 1967, OCP Publications. P.O. Box 13248, Portland, OR 97213-0248. All rights reserved. Used with permission.
722 © 2001, GIA Publications, Inc.
723 Text and tune: © 1955, 1983, Jan-Lee Music. Used with permission. Acc.: © 1993, GIA Publications, Inc.
724 Acc.: © 1994, GIA Publications, Inc.
725 Acc.: © 1993, GIA Publications, Inc.
727 © 1980, 1986, GIA Publications, Inc.
728 © 1966, F.E.L. Publications, assigned to The Lorenz Corp., 1991. All rights reserved. Reproduced by permission of The Lorenz Corp., Dayton, OH.
729 Text: © 1992, GIA Publications, Inc.
730 © 1988, 2004, GIA Publications, Inc.
731 © 2002, GIA Publications, Inc.
732 Text: © 1994, Selah Publishing Co., Inc., Pittsburgh, PA 15227, North American agent. www.selahpub.com. All rights reserved.
733 © 1991, Ken Canedo and Bob Hurd. Published by OCP Publications. P.O. Box 13248, Portland, OR 97213-0248. All rights reserved. Used with permission.
734 © 1994, 1995, Bob Hurd and Pia Moriarty. Published by OCP Publications. P.O. Box 13248, Portland, OR 97213-0248. All rights reserved. Used with permission.
735 © 1999, 2001, GIA Publications, Inc.
736 © 1967, Gooi en Sticht, bv., Baarn, The Netherlands. Exclusive English language agent: OCP Publications. P.O. Box 13248, Portland, OR 97213-0248. All rights reserved. Used with permission. Acc.: © 1987, GIA Publications, Inc.
737 Text: © 1979, Hope Publishing Co. Tune: © 1942, 1970, Hope Publishing Co., Carol Stream, IL 60188. All rights reserved. Used by permission.
738 Text: © 1989, Hope Publishing Co., Carol Stream IL 60188. All rights reserved. Used by permission.
739 © 2001, World Library Publications, a division of J.S. Paluch Company, Inc. Schiller Park, IL 60176. All rights reserved. Used by permission.
740 © 1986, North American Liturgy Resources. Published by OCP Publications. P.O. Box 13248, Portland, OR 97213-0248. All rights reserved. Used with permission.
741 © 1994, GIA Publications, Inc.
742 © 1991, Bob Hurd. Published by OCP Publications. P.O. Box 13248, Portland, OR 97213-0248. All rights reserved. Used with permission.
743 © 1982, GIA Publications, Inc.
744 Arr.: © 1994, The Iona Community, GIA Publications, Inc., agent
745 © 1997, World Library Publications, a division of J.S. Paluch Company, Inc. Schiller Park, IL 60176. All rights reserved. Used by permission.
747 Text and arr.: © 1989, Iona Community, GIA Publications, Inc., agent
748 Text: © David Higham Assoc. Ltd. Acc: © 1997, GIA Publications, Inc.
749 Text: © 1969, James Quinn, SJ. Used by permission of Selah Publishing, Inc., Pittsburgh, PA 15227, North American agent. www.selahpub.com. All rights reserved. Tune: © 1993, GIA Publications, Inc.

750 Text: © 1985, 1994, GIA Publications, Inc. Harm.: © 1985, GIA Publications, Inc.
751 Text: © 1969, James Quinn, SJ. Used by permission of Selah Publishing, Inc., Pittsburgh, PA 15227, North American agent. www.selahpub.com. All rights reserved.
752 Text: © 1974, Hope Publishing Co., Carol Stream, IL 60188. All rights reserved. Used by permission. Tune: © 1985, GIA Publications, Inc.
753 © 2003, GIA Publications, Inc.
754 Text: © 1988, Oxford University Press. Harm.: © 1999, GIA Publications, Inc.
755 Text and arr.: © 1998, GIA Publications, Inc.
756 © 1997, GIA Publications, Inc.
757 Text: © Harper and Row. Harm: ©1940, The Church Pension Fund. Used by permission of Church Publishing Incorporated, New York.
758 © 1976, Bud John Songs, Inc./Crouch Music. Administered by EMI Christian Music Publishing. All rights reserved. Reprinted by permission.
760 © 2001, GIA Publications, Inc.
762 © 1987, GIA Publications, Inc.
763 © 1998, GIA Publications, Inc.
764 Harm.: © 1975, GIA Publications, Inc.
765 © 1995, GIA Publications, Inc.
767 Text: © 1992, GIA Publications, Inc. Acc.: © 1986, GIA Publications, Inc.
768 © 1992, Iona Community, GIA Publications, Inc., agent
770 Text: © 1993, GIA Publications, Inc. Harm.: © 1986, GIA Publications, Inc.
771 Text: © Esme. D. E. Bird
772 © 1993, GIA Publications, Inc.
773 © 1990, GIA Publications, Inc.
774 Acc.: © 1986, GIA Publications, Inc.
776 Text: from *English Praise,* by permission of Oxford University Press
777 Text: © 1987, GIA Publications, Inc. Harm.: © 1987, GIA Publications, Inc.
778 Text: Vss. 1, 2, 4, © Estate of Roland F. Palmer. Vs. 3 © 1984, World Library Publications, a division of J.S. Paluch Company, Inc. Schiller Park, IL 60176. All rights reserved. Used by permission. Harm.: © 1986, GIA Publications, Inc.
779 © 1975, 1978, Carey Landry and North American Liturgy Resources. Published by OCP Publications. P.O. Box 13248, Portland, OR 97213-0248. All rights reserved. Used with permission.
780 Text tr.: © 1954, GIA Publications, Inc. Acc.: © 1986, GIA Publications, Inc.
781 Text and arr.: © 1993, 2001, World Library Publications, a division of J.S. Paluch Company, Inc. Schiller Park, IL 60176. All rights reserved. Used by permission.
782 © 2001, GIA Publications, Inc.
783 Text: © 1971, Faber Music Ltd.
784 Harm.: © Willis Music Co.
785 © 1974, Hope Publishing Co., Carol Stream, IL 60188. All rights reserved. Used by permission.
786 Text: © 1996, The Iona Community, GIA Publications, Inc., agent. Arr.: © 1989, The Iona Community, GIA Publications, Inc., agent.
788 Text: © 1972, ICEL. Tune: © 1987, John D. Becker. Published by OCP Publications. P.O. Box 13248, Portland, OR 97213-0248. All rights reserved. Used with permission.
789 Text: © 1991, GIA Publications, Inc. Tune: © 1998, GIA Publications, Inc.
790 Text and harm.: from *The English Hymnal,* © Oxford University Press
791 Tune: from *The English Hymnal,* © Oxford University Press
792 © 1993, GIA Publications, Inc.
793 Harm.: © 1994, GIA Publications, Inc.
794 © 1988, GIA Publications, Inc.
795 © 1988, GIA Publications, Inc.
796 © 1984, Les Presses de Taizé, GIA Publications, Inc., agent
797 Text: © 1982, Jubilate Hymns, Ltd. (Admin. by Hope Publishing Co., Carol Stream, IL 60188). All rights reserved. Used by permission. Acc.: © 1987, GIA Publications, Inc.
798 © 1993, GIA Publications, Inc.
799 Text: © 1971, 1995, Hope Publishing Co., Carol Stream, IL 60188. All rights reserved. Used by permission. Harm.: © 1938, 1966, J. Fisher and Bro.
800 Harm.: © The Trustees of Downside Abbey, Bath BA3 4RH, UK
801 © 2002, GIA Publications, Inc.
802 © 1999, GIA Publications, Inc.
803 © 2001, GIA Publications, Inc.
804 © 1985, GIA Publications, Inc.
805 © 2001, GIA Publications, Inc.
806 © 1984, Les Presses de Taizé, GIA Publications, Inc., agent
807 © 1989, GIA Publications, Inc.
808 © 1990, GIA Publications, Inc.
809 Verse 2: © 1994, World Library Publications, a division of J.S. Paluch Company, Inc. Schiller Park, IL 60176. All rights reserved. Used by permission. Harm.: © 1986, GIA Publications, Inc.
810 Refrain text and tune: © 2000, GIA Publications, Inc.
811 © 1988, Bob Hurd and Pia Moriarty. Published by OCP Publications. P.O. Box 13248, Portland, OR 97213-0248. All rights reserved. Used with permission.
812 Verse text: © 1969, James Quinn, SJ. Used by permission of Selah Publishing, Inc., Pittsburgh, PA 15227, North American agent. www.selahpub.com. All rights reserved. Tune: © 1989, GIA Publications, Inc.
813 © 1978, John B. Foley, SJ, and OCP Publications. P.O. Box 13248, Portland, OR 97213-0248. All rights reserved. Used with permission.
814 © 1994, GIA Publications, Inc.
815 Text: © 2004, Gabe Huck. Tune: © 2004, GIA Publications, Inc.
816 © 1977, Archdiocese of Philadelphia
817 Text: © 1991, GIA Publications, Inc. Tune: © 1993, GIA Publications, Inc.
818 Harm.: © 1986, GIA Publications, Inc.
819 © 1997, World Library Publications, a division of J.S. Paluch Company, Inc. Schiller Park, IL 60176. All rights reserved. Used by permission.
820 © 1997, GIA Publications, Inc.
821 © 1987, GIA Publications, Inc.
822 © 1966, 1970, 1986, 1993, GIA Publications, Inc.
823 © 2003, GIA Publications, Inc.
824 © 1984, OCP Publications. P.O. Box 13248, Portland, OR 97213-0248. All rights reserved. Used with permission.
825 © 1986, GIA Publications, Inc.
827 © 1983, GIA Publications, Inc.
828 © 2001, GIA Publications, Inc.
829 Tune: © 1992, World Library Publications, a division of J.S. Paluch Company, Inc. Schiller Park, IL 60176. All rights reserved. Used by permission.
830 © 1987, Ekklesia Music, Inc.
831 © 1997, GIA Publications, Inc.
832 Harm.: © 1968, GIA Publications, Inc.
833 © 1991, GIA Publications, Inc.
834 © 1999, GIA Publications, Inc

Acknowledgments/*continued*

835 © 1987, North American Liturgy Resources. Published by OCP Publications. P.O. Box 13248, Portland, OR 97213-0248. All rights reserved. Used with permission.

836 © 1997, GIA Publications, Inc.

837 © 1969, 1979, Damean Music. Distributed by GIA Publications, Inc.

838 © 2003, GIA Publications, Inc.

839 © 1992, GIA Publications, Inc.

841 © 1992, GIA Publications, Inc.

842 © 1993, GIA Publications, Inc.

843 English text and tune: © 1984, Bob Hurd. Revised English text: © 1987, Bob Hurd and Michael Downey. Spanish text: © 1989, OCP Publications. Acc.: © 1984, OCP Publications. All rights reserved. Published and distributed by OCP Publications, P.O. Box 13248, Portland, OR 97213-0248. All rights reserved. Used with permission.

844 Text: © 1982, Hope Publishing Co., Carol Stream, IL 60188. All rights reserved. Used by permission. Tune: © 1988, GIA Publications, Inc.

845 © 1999, GIA Publications, Inc.

846 © 1988, GIA Publications, Inc.

847 © 1938, Unichappell Music, Inc. Copyright Renewed. International Copyright Secured. All Rights Reserved.

848 Text: Used by permission of Oxford University Press. Harm.: © The Royal School of Church Music

849 Text: © 1980, ICEL

851 © 1978, Damean Music. Distributed by GIA Publications, Inc.

852 © 1978, OCP Publications. P.O. Box 13248, Portland, OR 97213-0248. All rights reserved. Used with permission.

853 Text: © 1965, GIA Publications, Inc. Harm.: © 1986, GIA Publications, Inc.

854 © 1987, GIA Publications, Inc.

855 Text: © 1981, Concordia Publishing House. Tune: © 1993, GIA Publications, Inc.

856 © 1983, Hope Publishing Co., Carol Stream, IL 60188. All rights reserved. Used by permission.

857 © 1972, 1981, The Benedictine Foundation of the State of Vermont, Inc.

858 Text: © 1989, The Iona Community, GIA Publications, Inc., agent. Harm.: © 1975, Hope Publishing Co. Carol Stream, IL 60188. All rights reserved. Used by permission.

859 © 1989, GIA Publications, Inc.

860 © 1993, GIA Publications, Inc.

861 Text: © 1970, ICEL. Tune: © 1977, ICEL

862 Text and tune: © 1994, GIA Publications, Inc. Vs. 2: © 1970, ICEL

863 © 1990, GIA Publications, Inc.

864 Text and arr.: © 1989, 1996, Iona Community, GIA Publications, Inc., agent

865 Text tr. and acc.: © 1986, GIA Publications, Inc.

866 Text: © 1970, ICEL. Tune: © 1977, ICEL

867 Refrain text: © 1973, ICEL. Verse text and tune: © 1988, GIA Publications, Inc.

868 Text and arr.: © 1996, The Iona Community, GIA Publications, Inc., agent

869 © 2002, GIA Publications, Inc.

870 Text: © 1989, Hope Publishing Co., Carol Stream IL 60188. All rights reserved. Used by permission. Tune: © 1994, GIA Publications, Inc.

871 Text: © 1989, Hope Publishing Co., Carol Stream IL 60188. All rights reserved. Used by permission. Tune: © 1994, GIA Publications, Inc.

875 Text: Vss. 1, 2, © 1934, 1962, Lorenz Publishing Co. Vs. 3, © 1964, Lorenz Publishing Co.

876 Text: © 1997, Kevin Mayhew, Buxhall, Stowmarket, Suffolk IP14 3BW England, www.kevinmayhewltd.com

877 Text and arr.: © 1989, The Iona Community, GIA Publications, Inc., agent

Please refer to the pew or keyboard accompaniment editions of *Gather Comprehensive* for indexes 1021 through 1026.

Index of Tunes/*continued*

Psalm Refrains Set to Music 1028

Psalm Refrains Set to Music/*continued*

Psalm Refrains Set to Music/*continued*

1029 Index of Service Music

Index of First Lines and Common Titles 1030

Index of First Lines and Common Titles/*continued*

Index of First Lines and Common Titles/*continued*

Index of First Lines and Common Titles/*continued*

Index of First Lines and Common Titles/*continued*

Index of First Lines and Common Titles/*continued*

Index of First Lines and Common Titles/*continued*

Index of First Lines and Common Titles/*continued*

Index of First Lines and Common Titles/*continued*

Index of First Lines and Common Titles/*continued*